The
Actor's
Life

THE
ACTOR'S
LIFE

Journals 1956-1976

CHARLTON

HESTON

edited by Hollis Alpert

A Henry Robbins Book **HR** E. P. DUTTON · NEW YORK

For information contact:
E.P. Dutton, 2 Park Avenue,
New York, N.Y. 10016

Library of Congress Cataloging in
Publication Data
Heston, Charlton.
    The actor's life.
    1. Heston, Charlton.
    2. Moving-picture actors and
actresses—United States—
Biography.
I. Alpert, Hollis, 1916-
II. Title.
PN2287.H47A32   791.43'028'0924
[B] 78-14910

ISBN: 0-525-05030-2
Published simultaneously in Canada
by Clarke, Irwin & Company
Limited, Toronto and Vancouver

Designed by The Etheredges

10 9 8 7 6 5 4 3

This is for Lydia,
for Fraser, and for Holly
. . . of course

Contents

Acknowledgments

Hollis Alpert persuaded me there was a book in my work journals and helped me find it; Henry Robbins agreed to publish it. Both bore the megrims of a fledgling writer with constructive fortitude. Carol Lanning got it all down on paper, working tirelessly with patient and supportive good humor. Without any one of them there would be no book, and I am more grateful to them all than I can say.

At the Beginning

Early in 1956, I started keeping a work journal. Why just then, I have no idea. It would have made more sense in 1946, when I went to New York, or when I got my first Broadway part the next year, or my first leading role the year after that, or when live TV started to heat up for me, or when I came West to do my first film, in 1950. But why 1956? Perhaps because THE TEN COMMANDMENTS was finished, or my son had just had his first birthday. More likely it was because my wife had given me an appointment book for Christmas with room at the bottom of each page for a hundred words or so, and my Scot's soul rebelled at the waste of all that space.

It may even have been the first flickers of maturity. Unlike the days at Northwestern, when I knew absolutely everything about acting, by the mid-fifties I was discovering more and more about which I knew less and less. Acting is a very subjective craft (or art, or trade, or whatever it is), and almost nothing about it is absolutely, or even usually, true. I was beginning to find this out, but it seemed reasonable to write the questions down, even if the answers weren't as clear as they'd seemed at seventeen.

So I did. And here we are, twenty years later. I still don't have many answers, but I've got better questions. The journals have taught me a lot, mainly about myself, but also about makeup, and scripts, and shooting schedules, and leading ladies, and studio heads. But the main thing I've learned is this: *It's not always the way you remember it was.*

We all tend to sort things out in our memories according to the way they finally turned out. The lost girl, the failed job, the missed chance survive in fading recollection, but changed and colored by our need to think well of ourselves, and to have been right all along.

When I finish a day's shooting convinced I did well with it, and then find myself disappointed with the rushes I see the next day, I want to be sure what I thought when I did the scene. And what I think three months later when I see that same scene edited into rough cut, and six months later when it plays to an audience. The same is true of a day's rehearsal in a play, or a script I turn down. Does my rejection still make sense a year later if someone else makes it into a hit?

Anyway, that's what the journals were for, though they became a lot of other things as well: a record of tennis scores, books I should read, and times for the two-mile run. Also a collection of notes to myself to do this better, or quit doing the other entirely, plus some to God for not ordering the world to suit me. I've cut most of this out, for fear of losing you before we get out of the fifties.

What this *isn't*, just so you know where you are, is an autobiography. I'm not up to it, for one thing. Besides, I don't *remember* the story of my life. At least I don't remember whether that's the way it really was, because I wasn't writing it down as I went along, until I started these journals. In fact, in the course of editing all this into shape, and seeing what tricks memory plays, I've come to the point where I don't put much trust in autobiographies anymore.

"But you can't just start off in 1956," they said. "They'll need to know how it all started, how you got there." Well. I suppose so. "All right," I said. "Where do I start?" "Where do you *start?*" they said. "Why, at the *beginning*. Tell about when you were a boy. Tell about school, and New York, and so on." All right. When I was a boy, and so on.

I was born of poor but honest parents who lived in a hut in the very center of the deep, black forest. Well, you see, there you are. They weren't poor, though they were honest. They weren't *rich*, you understand. This was the depression; nobody was rich. And there wasn't any deep, black forest left in Michigan by then. The Paul Bunyan days were over, but where we lived was where it had all happened, and it was a fine place to be a boy in.

There were woods, all right. Thick, second growth pine-birch forest, grown back after the lumbering finished. Our house was in the middle of it, set back off a trail road, drifted thick with snow in the winter, and I had a big, cross-breed shepherd that pulled me on a sled and was later shot by an angry neighbor.

The town was called St. Helen. I went to an old-fashioned one-room school. Thirteen pupils in eight grades, and three of them were my cousins. I was the only kid in my grade. It's no wonder I got a part in the Christmas play. I was Santa Claus, which turned out to be a one-line bit. I spent the evening crouching in a cardboard fireplace, so I could come out at the end and say "Merry Christmas!"

No, I don't think that was the spark that kindled the creative flame. I spent most of my time by myself in the woods, running a trapline with no success, and fishing and hunting, with some. Or pretending to, sometimes. At ten years old, when you've been following rabbit tracks through the snow for two hours without seeing one rabbit, and your nose is running and your feet are numb in your boots (mail order every fall from Sears, Roebuck, laced to the knees, with a pocket on the side for a jack-knife) and your right hand is even colder, because you have to keep your mitten off in case you *do* see a rabbit, it's just as much fun to switch from being a kid hunting rabbits with a twenty-two to Kit Carson with a Kentucky long rifle hunting for elk to feed the starving settlers stranded in a blizzard in Donner Pass, and is that a Blackfoot behind that tree? Half the time, it was more fun, for me.

All kids play pretend games, but I did it more than most. Even when we moved to Chicago, I was more or less a loner. We lived in a North Shore suburb, where I was a skinny hick from the woods, and all the other kids seemed to be rich and know about girls. I'd never seen a football up in Michigan, but I went out for the team. All I got out of it was a broken nose, which has been a great asset to me ever since. I did make the rifle team, but that makes for a fairly limited social life. Discontented with who I was, I spent a lot of time pretending to be other people. In Chicago, there were movies to go to, so I could be Gary Cooper and Errol Flynn, which was fine with me.

There were plays, too. I saw a few, downtown, and then I found they did them at the high school I went to, New Trier High School, which was supposed to be the best public high school in the country at the time. Maybe it was. It certainly was for me. I suddenly realized make-believe wasn't just something you did by yourself if you had no friends. You could do it *with* people, on a stage, and even take classes in it. That was it; that's when it hooked me.

So I did. Took classes and did plays, in school and in the suburban little theaters. From one of them, the Winnetka Drama Club, I won a scholarship to Northwestern, which was another lucky break for me, because I couldn't afford to go away to college, and I could *walk* to Northwestern. It also had one of the best theater schools in the country, in which I buried myself. My freshman year, I did seven plays. I also met a girl.

Lydia Clarke wasn't going to be an actress, she was going to be a lawyer. She wasn't going to get married, either, but I wore her down on both counts. Before I finally talked her around, I was in the army and practically on my way overseas. We got married, Lydia was thrown out of her dormitory, and I went to the Aleutians. I'm told the first year of marriage is supposed to be the hardest. If so, this was the answer. I never laid eyes on her again for a year and a half, during which time she succeeded in getting her degree and I succeeded in not getting shot. When the atom bomb suddenly ended the war in the summer of 1945, it meant that instead of spending 1946 assaulting the main islands of Japan, I was able to assault New York, in civilian clothes.

I guess Dickens had it right. "It was the best of times, it was the worst of times." The war was over and we were finally where we wanted to be. We weren't acting, though. The thing you have to remember about acting is that you can't *practice* it. Van Gogh never sold a painting in his lifetime, but he painted masterpieces while being supported by his brother. You can write a great novel nights while you're pumping gas daytimes. Even the starving pianist can feed his soul playing sonatas in his garret. But the actor can only act if someone hands him a part and says, "There's the stage. Go fill it." This not only creates a basic problem for the out-of-work actor in learning to be better, but it can become an ultimate, consuming frustration.

Nevertheless, to be in New York at twenty-two, even with no parts and no money, but actually, honest-to-God making rounds in the actual honest-to-God professional *theater* was a shining time. (Don't trust this ... remember what I said about the altering power of memory.) I remember it that way, though. We weren't crazy about the cockroaches, and our cold-water walk-up had its shortcomings, but our friends had no money and no parts and roaches, too. And you knew you were going to *get* the parts. I don't know . . . maybe at forty-two, you'd begin to wonder, but at twenty-two, you *knew*.

We were lucky, of course. Any actor who works is lucky. Lydia got a part first (never underestimate the value of a working wife), while I was serving the Muse by posing for life classes at the Art Students League. I worked in a neat little gray velour jockstrap Lydia made. I got a dollar and a half an hour, with free tea every two hours. And cookies. (Never underestimate the value of free cookies.)

Then I got a part with Katharine Cornell. A very small part, in very remote support of Miss Cornell, in ANTONY AND CLEOPATRA. It was exactly the right first part. For one thing, it was a hit: It ran on Broadway longer than that play's ever run anywhere. For another, it's a great play. It can be very boring to play in a long run, but not if it's Shakespeare. Finally, working in Miss Cornell's company was an ideal apprenticeship. She was a consummate professional, so was her husband, Guthrie McClintic, who directed her. And you had to be a professional to work for them, or you didn't work long.

I think I got the part because of my size. Miss Cornell was very tall and she liked big men in her companies. It wasn't the last part I got for that reason, but it made a problem for me, too. One night, well into the New York run, I got to the theater a half hour before curtain. The stage manager told me, "Miss Cornell wants to see you in her dressing room, Heston."

"I'm fired," I thought, walking sweating down the hall to her suite instead of climbing the four flights to my cubicle. "No, it can't be that. McClintic'd have Gert Macy do that." Then vanity took over. "What if she wants to go to bed with me?" By this time I was at her dressing room door. "If she's wearing her robe," I thought, "and she sees me in the inside room, that's it."

"Go on inside," her dresser said. "Miss Cornell's anxious to see you."

There she was, in a red silk robe, looking fabulous. "Oh, Chuck," she said, sounding fabulous. "I want to show you something." She *parted the robe*. My mouth went dry. There, on her thigh (also pretty fabulous) was a bruise the size of my hand. "When you capture me in the monument scene, you bend me back over your hip, and your sword hits me every night. Do you suppose you could leave it off for that scene?" she said. Well, at least I didn't get fired.

So ANTONY closed, and Lydia and I both got other parts. The next season I ended up playing the lead in a play for which I'd been hired as the understudy. It only ran three performances on Broadway, but I learned from it. Mainly that when the playwright comes up to you in Boston and says, "Could you go on in this part tomorrow night?" the only possible answer is "You bet."

Then there was television. No, no, not like now. LIVE television, now eulogized as the Golden Age, though I recall at the time Newton Minow described it as a vast wasteland. It may have been, but it was also a superb opportunity for a whole generation of actors, writers, and directors. Half of them are household names now, but what they were then was out of work. And itching. Movie people weren't allowed to do television, and theater people of any reputation wouldn't do it because it didn't pay anything. The rest of us were untrammeled by these petty considerations, and for quite a while, we had the whole, brand-new medium to ourselves. Jack Lemmon and Anne Bancroft. Walter Matthau and Joanne Woodward. Directors like Frank Schaffner and Arthur Penn, George Roy Hill and John Frankenheimer. Mel Brooks, Rod Serling, Paddy Chayefsky, Neil Simon.

The thing was, no one had figured TV *out* then. The networks and the sponsors hadn't realized yet that the whole point was really the commercials. They didn't have the comic strip series, and the cost-per-thousand, and the reruns, and the laugh tracks then. All they had was this new audience, and some shows to do for them, and they let us do them. There hasn't been a chance like that since sound first came to movies.

I got my chance when they decided to do JULIUS CAESAR, and use only actors who'd played Shakespeare on Broadway (in retrospect, this seems an arbitrary criterion, but there it was, and there I was, fresh out of ANTONY). I only got a small part, but there I was again, when the actor playing Brutus was sent home from rehearsal one day to rest his bad throat. "Can one of you guys read Brutus so we can work on the funeral oration scene for the rest of the day?" Well, I *mean*. So I read the part, which any actor is going to sound good reading, in those circumstances. I didn't play it, of course, but over the next sixteen months I played a few others, just as good. JANE EYRE, MACBETH, OF HUMAN BONDAGE, TAMING OF THE SHREW, WUTHERING HEIGHTS. Some Henry James, some Turgenev. The actor doesn't draw breath who wouldn't look bloody good in at least one of those parts.

I did some plays, too, but not as good, and it's probably just as well Hal Wallis didn't see them. He did see me on television, though . . . I forget in what. JANE EYRE, I think, and a 16mm film of JULIUS CAESAR. (I played Antony in that.) I wasn't really all that keen to do movies. I was getting good parts on Broadway and marvelous parts on live TV, and we all more or less assumed film acting was kind of low-class, anyway. I mean, *serious* actors worked in New York, not in the *movies*. Besides, the only film offers I'd had so far were standard studio contracts, and I didn't want any of that. The studio contract system was really ending by then, but the studios didn't know it. Hal Wallis did, though. Already established as an independent producer, he saw that the future of film lay with the independent film makers. He offered me a contract with the independence I needed to do plays, and films for other producers. I grabbed it. Lydia was running in a leading role on Broadway, so I came out alone for the first film. I lived in a furnished apartment up behind Grauman's Chinese. Merv Griffin lived just down the hall, but a high proportion of the other tenants seemed to be hookers.

I don't remember finding it very hard to adjust to films, but I suppose it must've been. It *should've* been. When you're a kid, things seem easy because you don't know they're hard. I finished the film, and spent a good part of the summer doing a publicity tour as the latest of God's gifts to the American cinema (nineteen cities in twenty-six days, as I recall), and went back to New York, where Lydia was still ticking along in her play, to resume my life as God's gift to the American stage.

The first film didn't set the town on fire, but the second one, THE GREATEST SHOW ON EARTH, won the Academy Award for Best Picture, which comes to the same thing. Of course the fact that it was made by Cecil B. de Mille and starred Jimmy Stewart, Betty Hutton, Cornel Wilde and the complete Ringling Brothers, Barnum and Bailey Circus had a good deal to do with this, but my role as the circus manager set me off and running. I also got the best compliment I've ever received on my work from a lady who wrote a letter to Mr. de Mille. She thought the picture had captured the feeling of the circus wonderfully, and that Hutton and Wilde, and particularly Jimmy Stewart, had been fine in their roles. "I also was amazed at how well the circus manager fitted in with the real actors," she said.

Lydia came out for that film, and we commuted between both coasts for quite a while, doing plays in New York and films out here. I was lucky with some of the early films, and had more and more chances at character parts, and period parts, and learned a little. Then, just about the same time, Lydia got pregnant and I got cast as Moses. Both were events of some significance in my life. If you can't make a career out of two de Mille pictures, you'd better turn in your suit. And the experience of fatherhood changes your life. Acting is a very uncertain trade, but it was beginning to look like permanent employment for me. Our son, Fraser, was born while we were shooting TEN COMMANDMENTS. (He played the infant Moses at the age of three months and immediately retired, displaying an acute judgment of the acting profession.)

It *is* a hard trade, you know. Most actors don't get to act at all, most of the time, and they have to act in whatever they can get all of the time, and act it to fill out someone else's vision, not their own. By 1956, I was able to choose, a little. In my work, and in my life. I think that really may be why I started these journals: to teach myself to choose better. Anyway, that's more or less what they're about. Making choices.

—CHARLTON HESTON

*"Everywhere Man blames Nature and Fate,
yet his fate is mostly but the echo
of his character and passions,
his mistakes and weaknesses."*

DEMOCRITUS

1956

Filming *Three Violent People* . . .

summer stock . . .

New York's City Center with *Mr. Roberts* . . .

The Ten Commandments premieres.

On stage as Mr. Roberts
ALIX JEFFRY

February 12, Los Angeles. Fraser's birthday. My boy's a year old. Already it's hard for me to remember what my life was like before he was in it. He's become such a person. Now I know what I learned one year ago: why the race endures.

February 16. Accepted the Torah Award for de Mille from the League of United Synagogues today with the best speech I've managed so far, I think. I may learn to do this yet. We're slowly arriving at the right wardrobe for MAVERICK [*released as* THREE VIOLENT PEOPLE], but we're still fighting the casting of Cinch, but it looks like Tom Tryon, which worries me.

This was about the time when I began to have some voice in casting. Actors should have sound instincts in this area, but I don't think I was any good at it for a long time. Maybe the sheer power of it scared me. Obviously, I was nervous about Tom Tryon playing my brother in this film. Actually, though he later undertook an even more successful career as a novelist, he was very good in the part. We were lucky to have him.

February 25. Seven sets of tennis today . . . and very little else. I played fairly lousy. I've *got* to learn this damn game.

March 12. This morning I rerecorded one last line for what *has* to be my final contribution to THE TEN COMMANDMENTS. I also found, a little to my surprise, that de Mille agrees with me that it would be inappropriate to read the commandments to fireworks on the Fourth, so I can turn *that* down with a clear conscience.

March 14. Worked all day with Frank Cordell on the roping. We've progressed to a point where I feel we need real cows . . . new heights. Onward and upward!

Obviously, by this time I'd learned another basic truth: Anything you need to know how to do in a film, you have to learn before you start shooting. After that, there's no time to learn anything.

March 17. This was one of the happiest anniversaries Lydia and I have ever spent, I think, though its only formal celebration was dinner at Perino's with Joe and Maggie [*Field, among our oldest friends*]. They also took us to the Vigeveno Galleries in Westwood, where I bought my second Lautrec—a lovely sketch of a horse. God, he could draw a little bit.

March 19. I roped a real live cow for the first time today; the cow obviously knew more about it than I did. I can learn this, though, before I *have* to know it. The rehearsal was as dull as most of them are.

Rehearsing is a stage tradition. To rehearse before the start of production on a film is something not many directors do at all, and even fewer constructively.

March 26. Paramount back lot: Shooting starts on THREE VIOLENT PEOPLE. Well, I'm making a living again . . . as a prop in every shot, while I lie unconscious. But at least the picture is begun, and I expect to have a voice in the proceedings tomorrow. It's good to be back at it.

March 27. I spent the day dangling Anne Baxter's double by her heels, which seems a curious way to make a living.

March 28. I put on the Moses Golden Calf makeup and posed four hours for Karsh. A curious, but creative man. His manner tells me the first, his results the second. ALEXANDER THE GREAT was creative too . . . but not very. I thought it overlong. March was excellent . . . but Burton lacks the dimension of heroism.

There were in fact eleven different makeups for Moses, ten of them with beards, ranging from a stubble I grew myself to the long snowy beard of the last scene.

March 30. Fray took his first halting steps tonight . . . from his mother to me, as I walked in the door from work. Only two feet . . . but a brave journey! Again today the scene seemed to go well. A love scene . . . the only one we have in the picture, really . . . and I think I played it better than I did with Anne [*Baxter*] in TEN COMMANDMENTS. Or maybe *she's* better?

April 30. We began shooting the last scene today . . . and Tom's playing it better than I thought he would. Maybe this is a result of the rehearsal. It gives us a chance to bring the end of the picture up where it belongs.

May 3. They hit the panic button and forced us into a five-page, two-set day. I skipped lunch to give us some extra rehearsal time, and I think we have a good scene for the meeting with Cinch. (Tryon's key scene.) The dailies of my angles on the tag scene seemed as good as any I've ever seen. Camera *great!*

This embarrassingly exuberant estimate proved a little excessive. I've learned since to use harsher standards for judging daily film than anyone else is likely to do. Willy Wyler said to me once, "Did you ever notice how often the dailies are great and how seldom the pictures are?"

May 8. I took another crack at the voice of God this morning. Better, I think. I'm glad de Mille decided to use my voice for this.

May 9. Did the scene where I throw Anne Baxter off the ranch. I thought it went pretty well. I'm letting my hostility toward her well up now; this is the emotion I can use in all our remaining scenes. I'd say she's making this easy.

This was a very snotty-young-actor thing to say. Anne is a good lady and a pro, which is all anyone has a right to ask. It is useful to take advantage of accidental personal chemistries that fit the requirements of a scene. Some directors encourage this with fictions more inventive than any in the script.

May 16. The shooting is finished; now let's see how it cuts. I saw two batches of dailies today, both pretty good. I liked what I did in the last scene with Anne. I gave John Frankenheimer back his fight script for *Playhouse 90* with a tentative acceptance.

This turned out to be REQUIEM FOR A HEAVYWEIGHT. I can't remember now, and my journal offers no clue, why I finally turned it down, but it's a good thing I did. Jack Palance was far better in the part than I would've been, and the play was one of the ornaments of the Golden Age of Television.

May 21. As usual, out of work, I begin to itch. More than a week without something definite ahead and I'll start to sweat. I called Edie Van Cleve [*my MCA theatrical agent in New York*] about setting up a stock tour for Lydia and me in DETECTIVE STORY. She's played it before and I've always wanted to. I'm not constituted for a life of leisure, I guess. I'd rather drop dead in a dressing room.

May 22, Stills were the usual ordeal, the same poses and the same expressions they always ask for. I acted as a dress extra at lunch to watch de Mille receive something called the Order of the White Elephant. I don't mind; I'm learning speechmaking. He's fantastic at it. [*He was, too.*]

May 28. The film situation still being what it is, we locked up the dates on DETECTIVE STORY for the summer. This will be a good play to do and I'll finally get the part off my chest.

May 29. My day was largely stills . . . from checking portrait proofs to an hour spent holding a stock girl by her ankle for ad art. This is work? The TRAPEZE premiere was lavish, the film good, and the party enlivened by the Fields and the Seltzers.

When I came to Hollywood to do my first film for Hal Wallis, Walter Seltzer was Hal's chief of publicity. He met me at the plane, armed with a photo so he'd greet the right guy. We went to Romanoff's, where I saw Spencer Tracy eating strawberries. I never met Tracy, but Walter and Mickey Seltzer are our oldest friends here.

June 2, On the SUPER CHIEF. Well, we got off for Chicago after much panic over the packing (my panic is about being involved in it at all). I must say Lydia left me very little to do. The Fields and the Baurs [*Geri and Frank*] came over with a station wagon for the luggage and brought champagne for us, to help kill the two hours till train time. This last we lost by leaving two of Fray's bags behind, but Frank raced back for them and made it aboard in plenty of time for a share of the champagne in the club car. Fray was delighted with everything. He's getting good at saying good-bye.

June 4, Chicago. I managed to get the fan club journal letter finished in the club car this morning and got off the train with the gratifying sense of a man who hasn't loafed his time away. [*There was more of this then. I kept it up as long as I could, but to do it badly is a cheat, and to do it well becomes impossible.*] Chicago wasn't as hot as last August, but it was still midwestern heat, like a bear's breath in your face. Mother was delighted with her grandchild, of course, and the first day of homecoming was smooth and pleasant.

June 5. I got a call from Herman [*Citron*] this morning, saying he'd turned down the WHITE LINEN deal. His asking money *is* damned high, but I wish he'd arrive at *something* for me.

Herman Citron has represented me the whole time I've been in films. I'm no expert on agents, since I've only had one, but I don't see how I could've been handled any better. Herman is a man of immense acumen and superb negotiating skills. (I only found out recently that his nickname in the industry is the Iceman.) We have a comfortable working agreement: I choose the scripts and he makes the deals. So far, his record is better than mine.

My new freedom is welcome, but it makes the period between jobs a little harder to take with equanimity. Jimmy Grant, the screenwriter, wired me about a new script he has, but the main thing I want from Jimmy is a script on THE WASTREL, if I can ever get my hands on the property.

One of Herman's achievements was making me, in 1950, one of the first actors in films not tied exclusively to one studio. I didn't know it at the time, but I was part of a trend toward independent film-making that marked the end of the studio system. Herman had made a deal with Hal Wallis, himself one of the giant independents, for several pictures. Three Violent People, for which Hal sold me to Paramount, was the last of these.

June 12, New York Central TWILIGHT LIMITED *for Detroit.* The departure for Detroit [*to show my father, Russ, his grandson*] went amazingly smoothly. I even got in a last set of tennis and a quick haircut at the Ambassador while Mother and Lydia went on to the station to look helpless while the baggage men performed with the luggage. I must remember this strategy. Good luck and the connections Paramount has with the railroads got us the only drawing room on the whole train. Very nice trip . . . and very nice to see Russ waiting in the station when we got in. If I just didn't have to race off to New York tomorrow, now . . .

June 15. The meeting with the lawyers was satisfactory: worth driving through a downpour to accomplish. The stage is now set for Russell Lake Corporation to dip any kind of finger in the production pie it chooses.

> *This was the production company I set up before I learned that actors, if they can get it, are better off with a percentage of the gross than with any part, including all, of an independent production company.*

Now the only catch is to find a suitable property. Jimmy Grant sent another script . . . not bad, but not terribly demanding in acting terms, and rather close in story situation to *The Wastrel*, which makes me shy away a little bit. I begin to see why really good films are such a rarity. To get anything at *all* shot seems so difficult.

June 19, St. Helen, Michigan. Each time I come back here, there are a few more neat little cabins newly cut into the trees, and the blackwoods that were the landscape of my boyhood are thinner. Now there are streetlights on M76, between the Highland Road and the tracks; even if Fray walks that way on a winter afternoon, the white snow will not thicken smoothly into dusk the way I remember it. Thank God the government feels as I do about the state forest around my lake. Keep it. Keep it.

June 20. I went over to the old sawmill today and found some ten-foot oak logs, abandoned six years on the drying racks, that'll make ideal posts for a log fence at the gate of the property, increasing the actual security of the entry, and satisfying my castle-complex. Now I have to persuade my cousin Jack to bring over the boom truck and help me load them and truck them out there; the damn things must weigh six hundred pounds apiece.

June 21. I got my logs moved out this morning and took Fray over to Tippedy Beach, swimming. Lydia recorded it amply on film, since this was the place where I paddled my first puppy-stroke, a surprising number of years ago. I watched him sitting happily splashing in the gradual shallows with the heron tracks on the bottom, and tried to remember splashing at the same sand, long ago. I can remember blue wool bottoms, white wool tops, and a canvas belt with a nickeled buckle . . .

June 28. This was a fine day for being with little boys. We drove down to the lake and I ran him around in the wind tearing in off the North shore. We investigated the boats swamped in the shallows, motors awash, and exclaimed over the foam of dragon-spit that lined the sand. After much experimentation, we hit on the proper way to imitate the sound of the wind. I watched his tiny figure, staggering as the west wind caught him, and remembered how happy I am.

July 2. My last day up here. I walked over behind the old Highland Road house where I was raised, in search of shadows, but the tree Gene Stralow ran his sled into twenty-five winters ago is grown bigger now, and the blood he shed on it has long since dried. I know you can't go home again, but I wonder why you can't help trying? Russell Lake never looked better than walking my son through it in the late afternoon sun.

July 5, New York. The drive to New York [*to plan the stock tour in* DETECTIVE STORY] was one of the nicest solo trips I've ever taken, I think. It rained from Pittsburgh on . . . a thin mist smoking across the Pennsylvania Turnpike . . . but it only accentuated the dry quiet pocket I sat in. I got in at five and, on impulse, swung north from the Lincoln Tunnel and once more past the old weathered storefront on Forty-fifth, in Hell's Kitchen, where we used to live. The blue paint seemed no dirtier, and I suppose if I found myself living there again, it'd seem like home very quickly.

July 10, Newport, Rhode Island. The first rehearsal [*for* DETECTIVE STORY] went very well, I think. We got it blocked, and the package actors seem uniformly fine. Our juvenile and ingenue are weak, but everyone else seems so unusually strong, especially for a stock package, that I anticipate no problems. After two years in the part [*of Mary McLeod*], Lydia obviously knows where she is with it. Tonight we took Mother for a birthday dinner, with champagne.

July 13. The size of the task I've tackled in McLeod is beginning to be brought home to me. That part must run ninety damn sides, which is something of a job to learn in a week. The grays in the man will be far harder to reach than the lines; I won't get those in a week, maybe not even during the Newport run.

July 16. Opening night, DETECTIVE STORY. The opening was something of a triumph, if the word can apply to summer stock. The girl and boy aren't good, and the proscenium is a little narrow, but the show itself seems high, wide, and handsome. At the director's party afterward the surge of good words seemed stronger than the usual opening night magoo. I think I did well, and Lydia was wonderful. Odd to think that if Sidney Kingsley had waited till this year to write the play, I might have had a chance to play it in New York.

July 22, Fayetteville, New York. We slept three hours and left at six-thirty for Fayetteville. The AAA's map got us on the New York Thruway, and we rolled up to the theater, only slightly groggy, by four P.M. Large, comfortable, *and* air-conditioned, if in a high school. It looks like a good place to work. We're living half an hour from the theater, in a house belonging to Lydia's cousins, happily away at the seashore.

July 23. We had a good dress and a fair opening, I think. This company is superior to Newport's in several respects, particularly the ingenue and juvenile, who seem like a welcome breeze in August after last week. I miss Joe Silver, who's not doing Dakis this week, but most of the other roles are better than Newport. Everyone seems to feel we'll sell out most of the week, which makes me happy, of course.

We toured DETECTIVE STORY through four engagements that summer, in the format that was well-established by 1956 and still persists: a star or stars touring from theater to theater with two or three actors in other key roles. The remainder of the parts are cast locally and rehearsed ahead of the arrival of the company on Sunday, allowing an opening Monday with one day's work.

August 3, Chicago. Cut the tennis short this morning, so I could hurry downtown for a lunch interview with Irv Kupcinet. The meal was interrupted by calls from Citron and De Mille, both with the same reports on the first audience reactions to TEN COMMANDMENTS. I've never heard Herman so high. He said, "Now, I'm sure we're right..." De Mille was full of quotes from people like Rabbi Magnin and Cardinal McIntyre. It made for a happy afternoon.

August 5. I took Littleboy to his first polo match today, an event we both enjoyed enormously. The Oakbrook Club is the finest I've ever seen, and the whole afternoon kindled again my intermittent itch for that sport. Fray loved it all, clapping wildly as the horses rattled by, and swinging away at a polo ball with the miniature mallet they gave him. We had drinks on the veranda afterward, then played the show happily and well.

August 19, Newport, Rhode Island. The trip, starting later than I'd hoped, was fairly smooth, with Littleboy requiring little attention. One thing this summer has taught him is a special precocity in car travel and trouping. He discovered the moon tonight and rode along the seacoast from Providence listening to his mother sing "I see the moon, and the moon sees me . . ." his eyes shining. We arrived after dark, just in time to fit in a read-through. Seems like a good cast . . . and I *know* it's a good play.

We'd given the Casino Theater in Newport its biggest success of the season in DETECTIVE STORY, *and they were anxious to have us back in something else at the end of the summer. I chose* MISTER ROBERTS, *even though there was no part for Lydia, because I wanted to try the part again. I still know it's a good play: probably the best of that genre since World War II.*

August 23. MISTER ROBERTS is progressing, though we're not at the stage where it's any fun yet. The pressure of putting it all together so fast takes some of the pleasure out of it, coupled with the worry of giving them a successful show to close their season. During our lunch break, I went to Touro Synagogue and read George Washington's letter to the congregation. I felt flattered to be part of the ceremony in that old and beautiful building.

August 27. Dress rehearsal went a little way toward pulling order out of the chaos a show like this inevitably arrives at in only one week of rehearsal . . . but I still had many moments of fearing we'd bitten off a bite that could choke us. The show went all right, I thought, though not quite as smoothly as DETECTIVE STORY's opening. As for me, I was better than the last time I played it, which is all I ask.

September 2, New York. The drive down confirmed my faith in early starts on a motor trip. We got away at six-thirty A.M., just barely catching the first ferry to the mainland by virtue of loading the car at a literal run. Tonight THE MATCHMAKER, where Ruth Gordon showed me there's an aim in acting beyond the ultimately real, the ultimately convincing. You can also reach for a kind of superreal vitality and magnetism.

September 7. Today's lunch interview found the well-worn groove most of them fall into, after which I dropped into the Paramount office. *My* first publicity work for TEN COMMANDMENTS will be here, around the last of October. So far the only concrete advantage the film has gotten me was a pass into the Criterion tonight to see MOBY DICK. We found it quite a picture. They say Peck is not what Walter Huston would've been. Maybe not, but he by God *did* the part! That's what matters. You have to try the man-killers.

I still think that. In the long perspective, the only thing that
counts is how you did on the big parts. Not the ones for this year,
or last year, but the ones they play every century.

September 9. The day was crammed with cast-party preparations [*at an
apartment we kept in Tudor City*]. My prime contribution was
getting the upper terrace clean, with the fire hose and a bucket of
detergent. Against the house rules, but very effective. The clean tile,
decorated with tubs of greens to supplement our hedges, made a good
place for a party. Everyone came, everyone had a good time, and
everyone liked the script binders I'd had made up for them. Fray
received with complete aplomb, and Lydia served a wonderful meal.
Maybe the best party we've ever given.

September 14. My well-established phobia about packing allowed me to
simply keep out of the way today, except for getting our five-foot
lockers and four bags to the station to check through. I had a couple
of interviews to do anyway, thus putting me morally even with
Paramount for providing the limousine that makes catching trains
almost a luxury. This was a damn close call, though. After fighting
for the through-car space for a week, MCA damn near didn't get the
tickets to me in time. We caught the train, barely, after a frantic
sweep through Grand Central.

September 17, Los Angeles. We got off at Pasadena, stepping into a
September heat wave, but this was considerably mitigated by one of
Paramount's air-conditioned limousines. The studio even took care of
picking up the baggage, leaving me free to check on things. The city
has managed to withstand our absence.

September 18. De Mille invited me to a lunch for Annie Bauchens [*his
editor for fifty-odd years, making her surely the first woman in an
important behind-the-camera job in films*], then he ran TEN
COMMANDMENTS. I'm pretty sure it's my best film work so far, but
the whole picture is so much more than the sum of its parts that I
feel only the smallest responsibility for what's on the screen.
Everyone at the lunch, from Grover Whalen through Louis B. Mayer,
seemed impressed with it. I guess I'll stand or fall on this one.

September 20. My cup brimmeth, if not runneth over yet; the word from
Jerry Pickman [*Paris publicity chief*] is that THREE VIOLENT PEOPLE
is a hell of a picture. I have to see it myself to believe it, but it was
ego-massaging to hear him estimate it would do more money than
NAKED JUNGLE. [*It didn't.*]

September 21. The happy news that the City Center wants me to do MR.
ROBERTS enlivened the rehearsal of a *Playhouse 90* I was doing for

CBS. This is somehow beginning to come alive. I'm not overwhelmed with my own contribution yet, but the rest of the cast makes it look very promising. Actually I have a scene or two with Diana Lynn that has some substance to it.

September 26. Our first run-through of FORBIDDEN AREA was really quite good, though we'll have to cut six minutes. Maybe I can make something of this character, using Hemingway's thesis of the "walking wounded" man. It's not the acting challenge you hope for, but it may work.

September 29. Rehearsal was smooth today, with none of the nonsense yesterday's visit by the sponsor's men called forth. Civilians in rehearsal . . . Christ! PAL JOEY in a tiny little hatbox on La Cienega seemed damn good, largely because of Gene Nelson, Fred Clark, and his wife, Benay Venuta. We had drinks with them afterward and found Fred would like to play Doc with me at City Center when I do MR. ROBERTS. Good idea.

October 1. During lunch break, the president of Dot Records was flattering about the possibilities of recording some albums of readings from the Old Testament for them. I'll certainly do at least one, though I'm reluctant to hurry it out by Christmas. [*I eventually did these for Vanguard.*]

October 4, Playhouse 90: Telecast of FORBIDDEN AREA. The show took more of my attention today than did my birthday, which came and went with its usual inexorability. The show was something else again, less than I'd hoped, especially since I'd practically given in to an out-of-sequence cold [*I get colds before and after working, not while*] by performance time. We finished the live show and then went over to a large party the sponsors threw. The one Vincent Price gave later was better.

October 5. I slept late and had few appointments, the most important being to take Fray pony riding. It gave me time to weigh the show, though, which got a lousy notice from *Daily Variety.* On the other hand, the trade notices on TEN COMMANDMENTS came out today, too, and were really fabulous. *Really.*

October 8. Rudy Mate told a most intriguing story at lunch today, but the script he was talking about didn't read one third as well as he talked it. A story can sound so good over lunch; it's so tough to get it to come out of the typewriter the same way. A really good script is about the rarest item in town, I guess.

It still is. Writers will tell you this is because they have so little control over what they write. It's more complicated than that. Unlike the stage, which is a medium of words, film is a medium of images. Even though the actor is one of the most important of these, the words he speaks can fade before the power of another image. A butterfly, a broken window, a bloody hand, can sometimes speak for the camera more vividly. True, writers create some of these images, too, but you can only discover the final truths about a film script on your feet in front of the cameras, not sitting at a typewriter.

October 16. The day was filled with those maddening details that consume so much more time than the result seems worth. I turned down WAYWARD BUS at Fox . . . the first offer I've had in some weeks from a major other than Universal.

October 20. I didn't get the work done on my sermon for tomorrow [*in the church where Fray had been baptized*]. Indeed, my only constructive activity for the day was a little painting. The party tonight was a glimpse into that part of Hollywood which deepens my conviction that this is a town *not* to be broke in.

October 21. I got up early . . . though not quite early enough . . . and worked on the sermon. This method of putting off work on a speech until the morning it's to be given is all very well, but you can cut it too close, and I did that today. I got away with it again this time. Maybe even a success. A pulpit is a curious place for an actor to find himself, though.

October 23. We had a party here after the THREE VIOLENT PEOPLE screening. I liked the picture fairly well. It doesn't sag and is generally done well, I think. My reservation stems from a conviction that it's cut *too* tightly, almost. You don't have time to absorb the people, only their situations. I thought Anne and I were OK. Tom Tryon is very good; I was wrong about him last winter. Gil Roland registers with his usual impact. We'll see.

October 24. Had a hell of a problem today. City Center had gone ahead and set Johnny Forsythe for director on MR. ROBERTS, ignoring not only my request for Mike Howard but my director-approval clause as well. After about twenty dollars worth of long-distance calls to Josh Logan in New York, fifteen minutes with Herman convinced me I could only come out like a jerk if I either pulled out or threw too much weight about Forsythe. Never mind. It might work out for the best.

October 30, New York. After the day full of interviews, some of them good, I managed to get over to the theater to watch while Forsythe auditioned actors for the small parts. Really, I just wanted to walk into a dark New York theater again and listen to actors reading lines I'm going to do there. It's strange to sit out in the darkness I once faced so fearfully from the stark-lit stage and see the brave parade come by.

November 1. The session with Josh Logan was wonderfully fruitful. I'm impressed beyond measure at the complete recall he has on that play. He went through the whole second act scene by scene and managed in the space of an hour to correct two serious flaws in my concept of Roberts. I'd be very glad of a chance to work on a whole play with him.

November 5. Things went well today, including a lunch with Forsythe in which we established what can be a productive working relationship. Still not quite what I had in mind, maybe, but it'll work, and I can learn. The Ward Morehouse interview was fine, even managed to meet Jean Dalrymple [*producing this* MR. ROBERTS] at the same time. All's well there, except she wants Marilyn Monroe to play the nurse!

November 10. George Sydney flew in from the Coast, he claims, solely to persuade me to play opposite Kim Novak in THE JEANNE EAGELS STORY. I'm not attracted. Lydia and Fray came up to White Plains to watch me working with the jumping horses.

It's a damn lucky thing for me I've always liked to ride. Considering the amount of time I've spent in the saddle in front of a camera, my whole film career might have foundered if I hadn't known how to do it.

November 12, Boston. A busy day in Boston promoting TEN COMMANDMENTS. The turnout at the press lunch was large; much flattering attention as I went on about Moses . . . and on, and on. We fitted in a last TV interview and I caught an early plane back to New York, where I spent a pleasant hour or two before racing off again for the airports I seem to spend so much time in. Luxury aloft in a berth going home tonight.

I've always regretted the quick demise of the sleeper plane. They only had berths in the last generation of piston aircraft, and it was a marvelous way to fly.

November 14, Los Angeles. TEN COMMANDMENTS *premiere, Stanley Warner Theater.* The premiere tonight was a large success, with the audience far more glittering, and far more attentive, than in New York. All my guests were kind, even Bill Blowitz (than whom I know no more honest critic), waxing extravagant at our party afterward.

November 19, New York. MR. ROBERTS rehearsal at the City Center this morning. God, what a pleasure to be rehearsing a play again in New York City. I think back to the first New York rehearsal for ANTONY AND CLEOPATRA in the fall of '47, when I was so impressed with Kent Smith's French cuffs, and the whole idea of being a working actor . . . and today I felt the same. Orson Bean and Fred Clark and I were the only ones called today, to block the cabin scenes before I take off again.

November 21. After five viewings of the film, four in the last week, I'm pretty sure what I think of it. Unique and inimitable it certainly is, and often magnificent, as well. I'm afraid it's also shot through with flaws, but maybe the man who could've avoided the flaws wouldn't have captured the magnificence. As for my own work, it could be better. Right now, I could do it better. If I didn't know this, there might be cause for worry. It's been quite a picture. All the Michigan clan like it, of course. Why not? That counts, too.

November 26. The problems I anticipated with Johnny Forsythe because he'd played the role himself don't seem to be materializing, largely because I don't want them to. It's hard for me to tell yet whether his firm ideas about the end results of the performance are good for me or not, but it looks as though I can select from what he gives me and still use what I have, or can find. Bill Harrigan will be fine, and so will Orson Bean. Fred Clark will be excellent in his own terms.

November 29. The *Home Show* with Arlene Francis was the most elaborately produced TV interview I've ever been a part of. We ran short of time, but there was a lot of good material in it, including a very provocative segment with Arthur Penn. Rehearsal moved well enough today, and tonight we had a wonderful experience, seeing Durante open at the Copa. He was very kind backstage afterwards.

December 3. Today was filled with the unbelievable scurry of moving a show like MR. ROBERTS on stage, trying to run a dress rehearsal (which we never did, since the show wasn't hung until five), and giving a public performance on a stage where we'd never set foot before. I felt very low about it. Johnny and I are approaching a clash about projection in that great damn barn. Art Penn came tonight and felt there was a great deal in my performance, with more to come, but I remain unconsoled.

December 4. We had a grueling work-through this afternoon, overcoming some of the rough spots, and then another performance for an audience tonight. I have come to something like an agreement with Johnny about projection . . . he claims to mean more a projection of vitality than voice, and he may have a point at that . . . but I'd still be happier in a theater with some fewer than thirty-four hundred seats.

December 6. The notices were really remarkable, as good for me as I could've wished, considering the enormous impact Fonda made eight years ago. Kerr, Atkinson, and the *Daily News* were the best; their praise for me was probably in the right degree. The performance tonight was a little better. Before we close, I hope to get it where it should've been on the opening, had we had the usual four weeks on the road.

December 12. A rainy day to enjoy New York, which I find increasingly hard to do around Christmas anyway. The millions of folk you have to share this lovely city with are turning me into a Scrooge for sure. A satisfying number of them came to the show tonight, though, including Rod Serling, who gave me a number of convincing reasons for doing his film script DAWN MINUS ONE.

December 23, St. Helen, Michigan. Getting two cars loaded with luggage and Christmas packages consumed a crowded morning. The late start meant that the snow caught us south of West Branch, and the effort of getting up the long hills north of there turned the whole expedition into a real adventure. Fray was delighted by his daddy tramping off into the white swirling night looking for the road. We arrived safely and happy as bird dogs to be back in the woods.

December 26. The snow continued, although wetter today than yesterday, but the special indolence of the day after Christmas still colored it all with the taste of milk chocolate and the smell of pine needles falling. The whole day was rich with just-opened gifts . . . and gifts opened twenty-five years ago, when I spent such an afternoon in the window seat behind the tree, with the needles falling on the pages of TWO LITTLE SAVAGES.

December 27, New York. Another long and snowful day, which I had to spend largely indoors cutting the opening chapters of Genesis into a whole I can read on the "CBS Holiday Special" Saturday. I think I got a good version, running about four minutes plus. Then I packed my Bible into my briefcase and climbed into the wagon for a long, lonely drive to Tri-City to catch my plane for New York.

December 28. In typical TV fashion, the masterminds running the show changed their masterminds while I was in the air; I am now to read an introduction to a choral presentation of the Ten Commandments by Fred Waring and his Pennsylvanians. Sounds like a middling to lousy idea, but they're paying me for it, so I'll do what I can.

I can't remember who wrote it, but it's the best definition I ever heard: "A professional is someone who does his best even when he doesn't feel like it."

December 29, St. Helen. The New England storm cleared and gave New York beautiful weather for my morning there, but it still covered Michigan as I drove north. I didn't get in until ten-forty-five, when a bowl of Russ's oyster stew tasted fairly wonderful. All in all, it was a busy three days for only five minutes on the air. It worked out to nearly a thousand dollars a minute, though, or three hundred per Bible verse, figuring it another way.

I'm embarrassed by my preoccupation with my salary in those days. I hadn't gotten over my amazement at actually making a living as an actor, with that cold-water flat in Hell's Kitchen still vivid in my memory.

December 31. I'd say it's been a good year. It's possible TEN COMMANDMENTS didn't pay off personally in quite as overwhelming a way as we thought it might; but on the other hand, I'm certainly in a far better position than I was fifty-two weeks back. Further, the world is at peace for my son to grow another year in, and my happiness in our life with him is more than I've ever known.

1957

Touch of Evil
(Orson Welles) . . .

The Big Country
(William Wyler) . . .

live television . . .

The Buccaneer . . .

a ridge site
for a home.

Directed by, acting with,
Orson Welles: *Touch of Evil*
THE MUSEUM OF MODERN ART/FILM
STILL ARCHIVE

As Andrew Jackson in
The Buccaneer
PARAMOUNT PICTURES CORPORATION

January 1, St. Helen. The new year came in as the old one went out . . . muffled in snow and solitude. More of the latter today, in fact; Russ and the others drove off in a swirl of snow around ten, leaving us alone and sloshing through an inch of water in the entry hall, where the overflow from a jammed sewer left us without the usual conveniences. Not quite the weather to rely on nature's vast sewage disposal system, either. Anyway, it's pleasant to have some space and time to read scripts in. So far the Universal thing [TOUCH OF EVIL] seems the best, but who directs?

When I called Universal and asked them this cogent question, they said, "Well, that's not set yet, but we have Orson Welles to play the heavy." I made the obvious comment, "Why not have him direct, too. He's pretty good." It genuinely seemed to strike them as a radical suggestion, as though I'd asked to have my mother direct the picture. "We'll get back to you," they said.

January 2. My various loafing projects had to be put aside while I helped dig up the sewer line, searching for one of my son's diapers, which Lydia fears is causing the trouble. Since the ground is frozen more than a foot down, this is no idle task. We didn't find the diaper, but I did manage to resurrect from the bat guano in the attic up at the lodge an ancient but intact chamber pot, which works the way they always did. The movie prospect is still uncertain. I don't like LABYRINTH or JANE EYRE enough to do them. No word from Universal about Welles directing as well as acting in their piece.

January 3. Repeated efforts with plumber's snakes of various dimensions finally dug the diaper out of the sewer, and service will be shortly restored. This required two trips to West Branch and didn't leave me much time for anything else, but I read, and turned down, a Robert Montgomery TV show for January that would have netted me a lot of dough; this gave my sense of ethics and integrity enough food to allow me to phone Citron and urge him to push Universal on the picture with Welles. It's only a police-suspense story, like the ones they've been doing for thirty-some years, but I think with him it might have a chance to be something.

January 4. Citron says Universal agrees with my suggestion, has offered the directing job to Welles. If he accepts, I'll do the film for seven and a half percent of the gross. This seems fine to me, though I'd be glad of a little cash in the meantime. Now we have to see if Orson wants to get back in the swim again. I hope he does . . . he seems to me one of film's few authentic geniuses, and I'd like to work with him. The ritual clan poker session went well, especially from my point of view. I broke even, and boy did I need it . . .

January 8. Citron called to tell me Universal had accepted our gross deal and closed with Welles. I'm really pleased about this. I think we have a chance at a better picture than almost any I could make now. I'm bound to learn a great deal from Welles, in any case. I think he has what I need now.

January 10, New York. Over lunch Charles Laughton broached the possibility of doing some Shakespeare with him and Buzz Meredith. One thing is clear: An American actor has to take drastic steps to work in the classics because no one will help him do it. If you don't work in the great roles, you're just sluffing. An actor's career is meaningless without them. Now let's see how well, if at all, we can implement this laudable resolve.

January 14, Los Angeles. I arrived on time, but the day, as usual, wasn't nearly long enough for all the stuff I had to do in it. The main stuff, of course, was meeting Welles. He seems to be all he's said to be, which is a good deal. In five days on the picture he's rewritten the script. Almost all of it's different, and almost all of it's better. There's a lot to do, still, but he might bring it off.

January 21. I woke a little late and reread Orson's rewrite of TOUCH OF EVIL. It now lacks only good dialogue to make it a really meritable script. The makeup test was a great success. Bud Westmore made me look so acceptably Mexican they're cutting the covering lines about my *not* being. Orson thinks a moustache is in order; if I start today I can just make it. We also had a Mexican tailor begin work on a suit, which will help.

This is what's called taking pains. A good Mexican tailor makes suits differently from a good Beverly Hills tailor, who makes them differently from a good London tailor. A lot of things you do in films can't be measured, often can't be noticed, except by you. That's who you do them for. Studios sometimes aren't too keen about this.

As for the moustache, I've been dealing with this problem since I put on a white beard to play Santa Claus in a school play when I was seven. I've undoubtedly worn more beards, moustaches, sideburns, and long hair, both my own and the makeup department's, than any other living actor. When I was studying at Northwestern I thought the smell of spirit gum (the stuff you use to paste it all on with) was the most exciting aroma in the world. Now it turns my stomach, especially at five in the morning on top of a mountain in Afghanistan or somewhere. If there's time, I'd rather grow them myself. The trouble is, I'm a slow grower: three weeks for good sideburns, four for a moustache, six for a beard.

January 22. I had a busy morning with the accountant, signing away my dwindling cash reserve on current bills. He and Citron both seem to feel, however, that the returns on THE PRIVATE WAR OF MAJOR BENSON will continue to be high enough to feed the family.

There I go, worrying about money again. Actually, BENSON was a very important picture for me. I fell in love with the script at Paramount. When they sold it to Universal while I was off leading the Israelites out of Egypt for de Mille, I told Herman he had to get it for me. He did, for zero salary, just a percentage of the profits. Now, there almost never is any percentage of the profits, but there was on BENSON. Also, as it happens, it was a good picture.

I picked up the finished script, Orson's second draft, on TOUCH OF EVIL and found it a great improvement over what we began with.

January 26. I spent the greater part of the day at Universal, sitting in while Orson cut twenty-five pages out of his script. Al Zugsmith's [*producer of the film*] party for Welles tonight was interesting. We drove Orson, who proved a superb talker. We got into a provocative argument over viewing rushes, which bodes well, I think . . . I like to work with directors I can argue with.

February 4. Today was spent in plumbing Orson, trying to find out where we are, exactly. I didn't. Janet Leigh, it turns out, has a broken arm, but they're unwilling, or unable, to recast the part, so she will play. Joseph Calleia will do the part of Miller; offbeat casting, but not bad.

February 8. There is a stirring of unrest out at Universal about the way Orson's going about the film. They seem to fear what I hope: that he'll make an offbeat film out of what they'd planned as a predictable little programmer. They're bitching about budget and schedule and a dozen other things, but Orson is holding firm.

The studios still used to make "predictable little programmers" for theatrical release then. Now they call them "Movies of the Week" and put them on television.

February 10. Rehearsal again at Orson's house. I still don't have a clear idea of the hole I should cut in the air with this man, but the scenes themselves are rounding out. I'm shying away from a specifically Latin characterization: I know that I have to go further than I am now with it. Fortunately, I think we can bully them out of some more rehearsal time, perhaps till Friday.

February 13. We dyed my moustache black; it's better and so is the script. Orson's ability to improve on a routine piece of screenwriting is amazing. As I suspected in the beginning, I'm likely to learn a good deal here. Another party at that fantastic house of Hal Hayes's tonight. Bill Wellman was there; he seems to have something in mind.

Every year or so it seems some guy with a taste for that kind of thing moves to Hollywood to see how big a hole he can cut in the social scene. The house was fantastic, all right. It had whiskey, wine, beer, and champagne coming out of faucets; retracting rugs, revolving beds, and an indoor pool with a window on the bottom from which you could see the Sunset Strip, such as it was. I suppose somebody has to be a big spender. Mr. Hayes is gone now, but I believe his work is still carried on by occasional rock producers and skin magazine publishers.

February 15. Orson and rehearsals were under way again today, both shaky but undaunted. [*He'd been ill on the fourteenth, but we were still rehearsing at Orson's house, unofficially.*] It's difficult to get beyond a certain point without sets, but he's resourceful at providing actors with problems to solve. I still don't feel I've done anything at all toward making this cop Mexican, but I will. I tend to work shallowly at this stage, too often.

February 18. Well, we began shooting with a drama I've no doubt Orson planned. We rehearsed all day, lining up a dolly shot covering the entire first scene in Sanchez's apartment. We never turned a camera all morning or all afternoon, the studio brass gathering in the shadows in anxious little knots. By the time we began filming at a quarter to six, I know they'd written off the whole day. At seven-forty, Orson said, "OK, print. That's a wrap on this set. We're two days ahead of schedule." Twelve pages in one take, including inserts, two-shots, over-shoulders; the whole scene in one, moving through three rooms, with seven speaking parts.

February 20. We didn't perform quite as spectacularly today, out in the back lot, but the shots were interesting all the same. We shot in moving cars all day, using an 18mm lens Orson claims has been perfected for two years, but avoided almost universally. It certainly saves you from those deadly process scenes in mock-up cars.

February 27. I had the morning free while they finished murdering Akim Tamiroff, allowing me to get in a little tennis (welcome) and paper work (necessary). After lunch I persuaded Dennis Weaver to play the motel night clerk and saw the stuff we did yesterday, while I waited to shoot. I swear, some of [*cameraman*] Russ Metty's shots look like Cartier-Bresson stills.

Russ Metty is unquestionably one of the great cameramen. He is nearly the only one of them who is also fast. Most of the time you hear things like "Do you want it fast, or do you want it good?"

With Russ you got both. TOUCH OF EVIL *must've been one of the last films he shot in black and white.*

March 7. I didn't work again till the very end of the day, but I saw two or three reels of rough-cut footage. Even misedited (Orson fired his cutter today) it looked special. We also acquired another classy bit player: Marlene Dietrich. I really think this one's going to go; it all looks better and better . . . and it started with a bright idea up in the snow in St. Helen.

March 10. Herman called to say he closed the deal with Warner's on DARBY'S RANGERS for five percent of the gross.

I mentioned how lucky I was to actually make money on the only piece-of-the-net deal I ever made. I was even luckier to get into the piece-of-the-gross club. The mathematics are simpler, and you're less likely to get bookkeepered (bookkept?) out of your share. There are about eight or nine actors and one actress in the club.

The script's not as good as two other war scripts I've turned down, and the part is not flashy . . . but Wellman did direct OXBOW INCIDENT. Besides, I finally turned down THE VIKINGS, foreign location and all. Let's go with Wellman.

March 12. The shooting tonight with Dietrich was quite a thing, even though Orson greedily refused to write me into any of the bits he made with her. She looked fantastic. A gypsy makeup, with a cast-off black wig of Taylor's from MGM, in which Elizabeth never looked so good, and oddments of costume from every studio in town. The only sexy grandmother I know. I only did one scene with Janet at five of an icy morning, but it was worth it to be around.

March 13. The lunch with Wellman was interesting . . . it reassured me on my choice in doing DARBY'S RANGERS. The film is so much the kind of thing that ballsy son of a bitch can do well. He also managed to make the part sound better than I read it. Then out to Universal for dailies . . . the burning car stuff . . . excellent; and Marlene's stuff, silent. Tonight in a scene with Janet, Orson got me to use a kind of adolescent diffidence. Sort of the manner Cooper has in scenes with women. I think he's right; if I *got* it right.

March 14. Slept late and satisfied and woke to play a little tennis, but no dailies. The main setup tonight was the damndest shot I've ever seen, and that includes our first day's work. After Joe Cotten had finished his cameo scene, we started working on the opening shot of the film: a complicated setup with the Chapman boom moving three blocks, angling down over buildings to inserts, through two pages of dialogue to a car blowing up as I kiss Janet. The sun came up at six and wrapped our night, but I think we got it. To bed at seven, feeling *great*.

March 18. It poured all night long, but didn't affect us. We moved inside the hotel down in Venice, covering a scene scheduled for a set at the studio, in the DA's office. Orson never liked that set and when the rain washed out our night exteriors, he grabbed the chance to shoot this moving through the hotel lobby, into the elevator, up two floors, and along the hall, with dialogue all the way. That's a first, for sure. It would be remarkable as a planned and prepared shot; as a rain-cover pickup, it's really something else.

March 19. We finished up the scenes in the hotel room and the lobby. They tell me you have to come early to get seats at the studio runnings of our dailies now. If we can just get the title changed now . . . I'm inclining increasingly toward BORDERLINE.

March 25. The dailies were brief, good shots of me clambering around those derricks. We shot, with immense effort, a scene with Joe Calleia and me checking the bugging equipment. Very proppy and difficult to shoot. At three in the morning, outside his house in the car, Orson and I killed a bottle of brandy and more or less agreed on partnership, which seems a very exciting prospect to me.

March 27. The shooting went swimmingly tonight, and the adjective is thoughtfully chosen. Thank God it was the warmest night we've had because I spent a lot of it treading water across that damn antique travesty of a Venetian canal. Orson also was very excited about a novel he's found to make.

March 28. We cleared up quite a night's work . . . finished off Janet in the picture, and got some good cuts in the water and under the bridge for the last scene. The company is tiring a little now, after fifteen straight nights, but they still work well and cheerfully, full of the hope of a good film. Russ Metty cooked up a mess of spaghetti in the trailer, which saved us from that dreary catered stuff.

March 30. I came in after dawn this morning, too full of the exhilaration of work and watching the sun come up to go to sleep. My son took his first steps one year ago today, and I almost feel I'm only beginning to do the same on this film. Orson is certainly the most exciting director I've ever worked with. God . . . maybe it will all really begin to happen now.

March 31. A lazy, late-sleeping, tennisy Sunday morning, filled with sun and Fray's laughter and hot cakes after four sets. After lunch and the nap this night shooting schedule seems to require, even on a day off, I drove over to Orson's to pick up EARTH ABIDES, the science fiction novel he thinks might do for a film.

April 2. We finished work with a final dawn shot, of Orson's death, in an overturned chair on a dump heap, and then had a celebrant drink or two in the trailer. Orson and I took along the last magnum of champagne and found a place still open to give us bacon and eggs to go with it. A hell of a picture to work on . . . I can't believe it won't be fine. It was wonderful to loaf tonight, all the same. We had steak and saw Orson's LADY FROM SHANGHAI on TV. It's good, but not as good as ours, I think.

April 3. After my wardrobe fitting for Wellman, I had a dubious conference on the sales campaign Universal plans for TOUCH OF EVIL. After driving Orson home, I gave him a copy of WASTREL. I read it again and I still think it's damn good.

April 4. Herman seemed enthusiastic about the Welles partnership: Orson was enthusiastic about WASTREL. I wasn't enthusiastic about WRITTEN ON THE WIND tonight. I was right to turn it down.

April 9. Lunch with Herman and Orson, who now feels WASTREL will take too careful a scripting job to have ready by summer, so he wants to go ahead on either the science fiction thing or something else first. I'm disappointed, but willing to play it his way. I still think this road is right for me.

April 12. A complicated day today . . . all the way from arranging a loan for a friend to reading enough of the Communist Manifesto to discuss it intelligently at the Great Books group tonight. I'm glad we finally got around to that group . . . if we keep it up, I may not become an utterly one-sided man. At lunch, Orson expounded the reasons why he feels WASTREL ought *not* to be the first project.

April 14. Fray sang "Happy Birthday" very charmingly when we took Lydia's gifts in to her early this morning. The whole day was wonderful and devoted only to us. Orson sent over LORD JIM and THE SINGER NOT THE SONG, but I didn't crack either one. Joe Field and the Baurs came over to a birthday dinner at Perino's and a visit to the Fine Arts to catch THE BACHELOR PARTY. Del Mann's direction of the actors is better than the film itself.

April 15. I had what I hope will be the last wardrobe conference for DARBY'S RANGERS and also met some of his comrades-in-arms. This is the first time I've ever played a historical character whose contemporaries are still alive. They gave me a good deal of reference material and a line on looking up some more in Washington Thursday.

Orson thinks we might be well advised to find something to do at Universal, to fill the gap till we can get a script on WASTREL.

April 22. At this point Jack Warner discovered that by "percentage of the gross," we actually *meant* just that. He promptly fired me. Spent a very busy morning going over the details of the suit we'll bring against Warner's. Maurice Meyer will handle it, on a contingency basis. He seems not only very able, but very confident as well. At least now I don't have to worry about whether DARBY'S RANGERS is right for me.

April 23. After a ritual dance with the press, we formally filed today against Warner's for two hundred fifty thousand dollars. Written out like that it seems like a tremendous amount of money. It is.

April 25, San Diego. The trip to San Diego was a great success. My award acceptance was routine, but Fray received his first one with remarkable aplomb and a very effective, if brief, address, to wit: "Tank you, ladies, fa dis awahd." (Applause.) "It was fun t'be da BABY MOSES!" Of course, he only killed 'em, standing on the banquet table, clutching confidently at the edges of the lectern.

At two Fray was already in the twilight of the celebrity that accrued as a result of his memorable performance floating down the Nile in that basket. He was superbly equipped to play the infant Moses (for which de Mille cast him on the morning he was born), he performed with assurance, and promptly retired, his salary invested in Paramount stock. An ideal acting career.

April 29. There's some stirring from the Warner camp that may indicate an early attempt at settlement. Herman has many misgivings about the Welles partnership, but I still think he's wrong. I'm fully aware of Orson's chameleon nature, but I'm more aware of his talents, and anxious to use them.

May 28. I spent the morning in the lawyer's office, discussing the deposition I'm to give Friday for the suit against Warner's.

I remember after I'd given the deposition, the first time I'd ever testified under oath, I asked my lawyers how I had done. "Not bad, Chuck," they said. "But, you know, it's OK to answer some questions with a simple yes or no." Never mind. When Jack Warner gave his deposition, he answered one question by saying, "Ah, those goddamn actors deserve anything lousy that happens to 'em anyway," effectively losing his case.

June 5. Another sweltering day, good for tennis and sweating off weight, which is all I did. The Italian producers are still pressing for an answer on the De Sica property, but we are still wary. I did get an interesting script from CBS on the Andersonville court-martial. I like it very much.

June 6. I decided to do the Andersonville court-martial thing; scripts like that don't come along often enough to ignore. Orson's off to New York to do the *Steve Allen Show,* so he can hardly have anything started before I'm finished with this. I'm back at work again, or soon will be.

June 17. The day started at dawn taking Mother to the airport. She seemed to've had a happy time here. I very nearly finished my dubbing on TOUCH OF EVIL with a long session today. Orson continues to amaze me with the ideas he has. He created a climax for me in the bar scene that wasn't in the printed footage, simply having me dub one speech in four little pieces. Whatever happens, I am in his debt.

June 19. A long, dragging day rehearsing and fighting with McCann-Erickson. They want to make a few cuts in the script in deference to the Confederacy, and I'm unwilling to do so, both for the sake of the script and out of principle.

June 25. We started working in the bit parts today, but the level of the show didn't drop as much as I thought it would. I think we're near performance level; we should have a very good show for our pains. This one might make a play, at that. In any case, it's one of the best parts I've had, in a while.

June 27. Well, it went wonderfully, with the exception of a slight and I hope undetectable mishap with the moustache in my closing speech. [*This one was pasted on . . . posing certain risks.*] I think it may be my best TV work in some years. People at the party seemed inclined to agree. Ralph Nelson told me he has an option on it for the stage and wants me to do it. I don't know about that, but it's nice to have the offer.

Live television was a glorious era, but a very short one. By this time, they were already beginning to film the strip series, and in another year or so, live TV drama was dead. In another twenty years or so no one will remember how we did it. Live, for one thing. When the red light went on, you took it from the top, and if you blew a line or the director blew a shot, forty million people saw it. We went on the air at five-thirty P.M. for the East and the Midwest. The West Coast saw what they called a "hot kine," taped off the live performance, two hours later.

June 28. My work at Universal consisted merely of a few offscreen lines for Joe Cotten's benefit, but it was nice to be in on the windup of shooting. At lunch Orson advanced still another idea . . . a tele-film of DON QUIXOTE, with me as the eccentric don. What, if anything, will come of this, I can't imagine. Orson's argument is original and telling however. "All great actors," he says, "are really character actors." Also, Willy Wyler wants me to do a heavy in THE BIG COUNTRY with Gregory Peck.

June 29. A general unwinding, avoiding-packing-and-script-reading day. My main problem now is deciding which job to take. The Wyler film, the Italian project, or the ANDERSONVILLE stage version, which last Orson has more or less convinced me would be a mistake.

June 30. I spent an inconclusive and not too effective half hour explaining to Wyler and Peck why I didn't think the part in THE BIG COUNTRY was good enough. It's a hell of an opportunity to pass up, though. I finally had to leave to catch my plane.

July 4, St. Helen. A cloudy Fourth, threatening rain, like last year, but this time I had no speech to make and no eastern trip to begin . . . at least till tomorrow. I spent the day in pleasant vegetation, as well as worrying over whether to accept either, and if so which, of the two offers that are still waiting. Both Wyler and De Sica offer much, but neither is a part I'm in love with, and both require an ego-bruising drop in billing.

My ego was too tender. All actors get preoccupied with billing order, but I've learned it doesn't matter a damn as long as your name's in the same size type. No one remembers whose name comes first, or cares. (On the other hand, I still like what Olivier said when he resisted Larry Harvey's urging that he play the Chorus in the ROMEO AND JULIET film then in preparation. "But why not?" said Harvey. "Because," said Olivier, "I'm too fucking grand." No other actor can make that statement.)

July 16, New York. I knew it! Just as soon as I committed to Wyler's film Orson called in great excitement. I must come down to Mexico, *immediately,* to star in a tele-film of the second part of DON QUIXOTE, for God's sake! We are to make it in six shooting days and I'm somehow to get out to the Coast in time to do my fittings for both projects before the end of this week. It's too tough to bring off; yet I can't turn it down.

July 17. I spent the day trying various plans on for size, trying to get us to Detroit and me on to the Coast. Citron thinks the whole thing is madness, and so do I, really. But Orson is impossible to resist, especially with a part like this. I can manage it, driving all the way to

Detroit tomorrow and cramming in all my meetings with Wyler on Friday and Saturday. What a ridiculous way to make a living!

July 19, Los Angeles. Today was crammed with too many things to do for too many different people. The Wyler film may turn out to be more rewarding than I thought. The cast is excellent and the director has a certain talent, you could say. Orson hasn't left for Mexico yet, and I was able to get him on the phone, but not able to get much out of him about DON QUIXOTE. The only reason to do it is for fun, anyway.

July 22, St. Helen. Today flung the fat in the fire for fair, as far as DON QUIXOTE is concerned. After all the frantic gut-busting we've gone through, the elaborate device Orson had worked out whereby we'd enter on tourist permits and then pay a fine to make the film, kicked back in our faces. The bureaucratic machinery wouldn't have gotten me my passport back in time to leave Mexico Monday for the BIG COUNTRY location. I felt bad about it, but Orson doubtless felt worse. I was able to get a late plane back to St. Helen. At least I finished my fittings for Wyler, so I can stay back in the woods with my family longer.

July 30, Stockton, California. The flight from Chicago wasn't bad, but the drive to Stockton for the BIG COUNTRY location was pretty dreary. I went out on the set after lunch and got my wardrobe squared away, with much grumbling from Willy about how it should be, which was not the way it started out. I also changed horses, though not in midstream. I'll use a beautiful pinto stud, one of the best-looking horses I've ever seen. Handles well, too, for a stud; a little hard-mouthed. I didn't shoot today, but the way it all looks, I'm glad I came on board this one.

August 1. Well, I began today; just a brief exchange with Peck. Contrary to legend, Willy knows exactly what he wants, and tells you precisely how to give it to him. It's good to have that.

I've had the luck to work for some very gifted directors, but no one gets better performances from his actors than Willy. On the other hand, he doesn't empathize with them very well. Early in BIG COUNTRY I thought he'd given up on a shot because he just walked away to another setup, after some dozen takes. "Let's not quit, Willy," I said. "We've been on it an hour . . . I'll get it." "Look, Chuck," he said, "if I don't say anything after a take, that means it's OK."

August 3. I worked all day today. On one shot I never did get what Willy wanted. We left it at lunch; he's relying on yesterday's coverage of the same stuff. Maybe it was the arcs in my eyes that stumped me.

No, it wasn't the arcs, it was Willy. I hadn't yet learned that he never quit on a shot till he was positive no one involved in it, including himself, could do anything any better.

Also, his direction is very pragmatic. It's *right*, but it's hard for me to work this way. Still, it'll be a learning experience.

August 9. The work was, as always, exacting and damn detailed. That stubborn little Alsatian is awful tough to please. At least I've gotten Franz Planer [*the cameraman*] to give me a break on those bloody arcs, so we don't have such a problem with my eyes. Chuck Connors arrived today, another large actor. Chuck Robeson and I took him out to the Reef for steak. That made about six hundred and fifty pounds of just Chucks sitting at the table, if you want to look at it that way.

August 12. We began shooting the stampede today, elaborately covered by Globe Photo, *Life*, and the TV trailer crew, not to mention three cameras of our own and God knows how many belonging to the civilian contingent. As usual, Willy pottered around endlessly, kicking little clods of dirt off into the stream and chewing on a stick, and then gave Franz a setup that should show as much as you could hope to see of a stampede. A damn tiring day, but a good one.

August 17. They were still working in the corral with that bucking horse, so I had only one cut to shoot. Lydia and Fray joined me for lunch, Fray making a good impression on the company. After they went back in, I did that horse-swimming layout for Globe. Unfortunately, the paint stud went a little lame again. Tonight, after dinner, Lydia and I found ourselves in a four-hour song session with Burl Ives. That's not hard to listen to.

August 20. This was a day when I damn well earned my pay. Greg and I wore our asses off on that fight till nearly six. I missed a mark and got thrown on my back on a rock, but that's cheap enough. We skipped the last two close-ups so Jean Simmons could get her back-to-Los Angeles shot in, but it was a day's work, all the same. It was nice to look back on it driving to the hotel, exhausted, drinking beer in the back of the limo.

August 30. Willy's cut my favorite scene, in the opening, but I'm still sure now the part will end up better than I thought when I first read it. He's probably right about this opening scene, too. Losing it gets you into the story quicker. We seem to be moving well now. Yvonne De Carlo came up today, so Lydia had someone to lunch with, and we had someone to dine with tonight.

September 2. Most of the day, Willy was touching up sequences we've already done, but we did move in on the scene with McKay at the cottage. Unfortunately, I lost them some time when, after six or seven takes on the scene, I was no longer able to control that hard-mouthed stud well enough to do a clean running mount and ride-out. Just the kind of thing that shames me, of course, and brings out all my worst vanities. There are good ride-outs in the outtakes, but I still feel badly about it. I hate to come up *empty* on anything.

September 7, Los Angeles. I caught the charter plane home, after working through two different crews to finish the location. I slept on the set for two hours between the night work and the day shooting. Not too tough, actually. I had time for a drink with Chuck Connors before I took off; he told me about a project to be made in Spain that sounds promising. We'll see. It was marvelous to get back in the collective arms of my family again, and the big wide bed I've missed so much.

September 9. Good to be back in town. I had a busy morning catching up on everyone, squaring everything away. (Like a dog going around his yard, pissing on all the fence posts.) I went to Paramount to meet with Tony Quinn on THE BUCCANEER. He has some good ideas about Andrew Jackson, primarily that it should be played completely as a character role, which delights me. I'm very glad I'm doing it.

Tony is a very gifted man, and I learned a lot from him. Any director who can tell you something about a part you've played before is no slouch. (I'd played Jackson in a film for Fox in the summer of 1952. I reprised it for de Mille in what started out to be a cameo role, because I passionately admire Jackson, and also because it represented the very last contractual commitment I had to any studio.) THE BUCCANEER was the first film Tony had directed. He was hampered, and possibly a little daunted, by the fact that it was a very large project for Paramount and had been originally made very successfully for the studio in the thirties by his father-in-law, C. B. de Mille, who now chose for the first time in his career to stay on the sidelines and leave one of his films in other hands.

September 10. Spent the day racing around, except for a pleasant morning playing with Fray and taking a tennis lesson. Citron seems to feel my financial future is secure, that I should take Warner's offer of a settlement, and that we can go ahead on a house, if we like.

September 12. I spent half the day on the Jackson wardrobe and makeup, which is OK now. Even excellent. Quinn is an exciting man. If his skill equals his creative fervor, we have an interesting time ahead of us. I also had a provocative talk with Dore Schary, before reading his play on FDR, SUNRISE AT CAMPOBELLO. It's not bad, maybe very good. I'm not certain whether it's up to the subject, though. Or am I just running scared? Someday soon, I'll have to do a play again. It's been too long.

September 13. Didn't accomplish a great deal today. The company's still shut down to accommodate Willy's bad throat, and I could do nothing on BUCCANEER either. My decision on the FDR play is complicated by the news that MGM wants me to do Messala in BEN-HUR. Wrong part, mmm?? Anyway, I'll read it before deciding.

September 16. I spent a difficult day under pressure from different people to do different things I didn't want to do in the first place. First, Citron's trying to persuade me into BEN-HUR, whether Wyler does it or not. Then, at lunch, Phil Dunne finally talking me into the presidency of the Anne Frank Library Foundation. Finally Willy, telling me what a great part Messala is. I wish I could be sure of *some* of them.

September 17. A very frustrating day. I couldn't get in touch with Orson, I hadn't lost any weight, and I decided the bookshelf we were going to have built cost too much. I did manage to order a sport coat or two, and got a call for work tomorrow. (This being what's really wrong with me, of course.)

September 19. They got to me today for the BIG COUNTRY interiors, although my contribution to the scene was minor. I was unable to contact Orson, before the wrap, when I had to go over to Paramount to run the old-time Western stars' thing. I was glad to do it for the usual reasons, and because I got to meet both Ken Maynard and Hoot Gibson, my own two boyhood idols.

September 20. Still plugging away at the party scene, but it was a full day otherwise. Willy gave me a long lunch hour to talk things over with Orson, who is as full of nineteen enthusiasms as ever.

September 26. We finally wound up the party sequence. I think even Willy had enough of it. I got some good footage out of it, and I look forward to the scene tomorrow with Carroll Baker. It's one of the best I've had yet; a sexy sort of fight scene. Tonight we shot till past seven-thirty and were very late for the Arthritis banquet, which started late anyway. Lydia subbed for me till I got there.

September 27. I began taking my lunch in a bag today, heartily sick of fighting my way into one of those beaneries every noon. A damn good thing, because I was just too tired to do it today after Willy finally printed a master on the fight scene with Carroll. I think we got a good scene, though it didn't go as well after lunch. Carroll was exhausted by then, for one thing, and I'd hurt her wrists in the struggling as well. Willy deliberately kept urging her to break loose, while insisting I mustn't let her go.

September 29. We planned to house-hunt again today, but the realtor was unavailable. Instead, after tennis, we drove in a desultory fashion through Hancock Park, and then out Benedict Canyon with the Fields to look at a possible house. Extremely modern, but not what I would build, if I built.

September 30. THE BUCCANEER started today, although they'll have to wait about five weeks for me. The opening festivities were marked by a sip of some 1813 Madeira, De Mille sitting quietly on a stool, seeming older than I've ever seen him, while Quinn launched off into the filming. We looked at three houses this afternoon, none entirely right, or even very right. I don't know; maybe we should look for land, and just buy that for now. You can hardly lose on it, out here.

October 1. Well, we found it! Thanks to Russ's expert guidance, the same day we determined to look for land, we found what I'm sure is the best piece left in town, at a fantastic price. Just under three acres in Coldwater Canyon looking over the most compelling view I've *ever* seen out here, bar none. You'd think you were in the Cascades, it seems so wild and remote from the metropolis it's so close to. We're all delighted.

October 10. I finished my interiors for BIG COUNTRY today, unless Willy rewrites it all (which he'd be quite capable of doing if it weren't for my imminent departure into THE BUCCANEER). I wish we weren't faced with that quite so soon, in fact . . . I don't like to have Wyler rushed on this, and I think he is, a little.

October 11. A very busy sort of rushing-around day . . . the last before leaving is always like this, I guess. I got some dubbing done in the morning trying to resolve everyone's uncertainty as to just how much accent I should, or even have been, using for BIG COUNTRY. That's the kind of thing I tend to forget in moments of stress, I'm afraid. *I must watch this with Jackson.*

October 15, Red Rock Canyon, California. I damn near got thrown on my skull today, riding that iron-jawed mare they found to double the tender-tendoned Domino. She's a good camera double and very surefooted in the rocks we're working in now, but she tried to run away with me in one chase shot leaving the ranch; it scared the ass off me. Willy says I'm doing well in the part still, which is rare, and a blessing.

October 20, Los Angeles. Today was as big a day as a father could ask for: I took my son to the circus for the first time. Thanks to the circus film I made before he was born, I was able to take him back to touch all the wonders, too. He sat on an elephant and patted a tiger and shook hands with a clown . . . even rode in the parade during the show.

October 21. I was able to catch up on much of the paper work I've let slide. I called Russ and worked out a lot of the details still pending on the Coldwater property. I turned down NAKED AND THE DEAD at Warner's . . . what the hell do I want to play another general for after Jackson?

October 22. I got sort of caught up on Los Angeles activities today, marred only by Fray's flu. Not serious, apparently, but you note his small bravery: "It hurts a *liddow* bit . . ." At Paramount I discovered my weight is down to two hundred eight again, and that they don't expect to use me on BUCCANEER until the middle of November, which will be good news for Willy. Talked to Orson; he says he's turned down the Mexican film MGM wanted us to do. I'm relieved, frankly.

October 25. The publicity calls are getting almost as tough as the acting calls. I had to start at six this morning, having breakfast with a lady writer for *Esquire,* giving her my most considered and unique opinions on the hows and wherefores of the movie business. I did little else today, except a few sketches. By the time I drove down to Los Angeles my flu had turned into a cold. At least I have my cold at home.

November 2, Mojave. Today, to my staggered surprise, Willy wound me up on the film. After more than three months of shooting and exposure to at least as much talent as I've ever worked with, I finished. He concentrated on me in the tag scene today, pressed no doubt by the staggering proportions of my overtime paycheck. It was quite an experience, I must say. I drove home to Los Angeles through a driving rain, thinking about it.

November 3. Waking for the first time in three months without the pressure of BIG COUNTRY scenes ahead of me, I relaxed into a leisured, nondiet breakfast. Chuck Stine and I established a big lead in our doubles tournament match, and then got rained out, but I don't doubt we will win. Tonight with the Fields, we saw an excellent production of NANA featuring Boyer's superior acting, and Martine Carol's superior breasts. All three delighted me.

Today this sounds faintly male chauvinistic. In 1957 Mlle. Martine's breasts were the only ones being photographed.

November 4. Ran two related films today: PATHS OF GLORY, which I turned down partly to do the other: TOUCH OF EVIL. I think Kubrick's film is smoother and has many fine things, including Kirk's acting. TOUCH OF EVIL, on the other hand, has flaws. Unscored, undubbed, it seemed uneven in tempo and unclear in the opening sequences. Universal feels a day or so of additional shooting is necessary to clarify some ambiguities. Maybe so. There are truly *marvelous* things in the film. Orson's enormous talent is evident throughout.

November 5. I spent the day in an unsuccessful attempt to get together with Orson about the added scenes they want to do on TOUCH OF EVIL at Universal. He was shooting, and unavailable . . . or more unavailable than usual. I don't quite know what to do with this situation. I feel I have a moral obligation to Orson, but a smaller one to Universal as well. I don't want to shoot the stuff without him, but what the hell . . . something has to be done. You can't just sulk in your tent, like Achilles.

November 7. I spent a very tough morning letting Wally Westmore put rubber pieces all over my face. It's a good makeup, but a tough change from my freedom from all that paint and crap on BIG COUNTRY. I finally got together with Orson; he claims he's eager to do any retakes they want, and do them free as well. This settles it for me. If he doesn't do it, I don't.

November 8, Mojave. I went back to the desert to do "a few retakes" for Wyler. It was one of the toughest shooting days I've ever had in my life; certainly the *longest* one. It ran just under seventeen hours, portal to portal! I did the last scene with Bickford again. Willy felt we'd gotten a little too subtle with it before. I think it's maybe better now . . . it's certainly *longer:* two new speeches written in. Then I went over to second unit and did some extra close-ups from the tag scene, and also a close-up, on imported grass, from the fight with Greg. Home again long after dark, a worn, tired boy . . .

November 11, Los Angeles. This problem of the Universal retakes is getting more and more complicated. It becomes obvious now that they really don't *want* Orson to do the work, for whatever reason. Partly, I think, because of the overage on the budget, and partly because they don't like the way he made the film, I suppose.

November 12. Had a long do with Herman about the Welles retakes this morning. My ethical position still bothers me terribly, in the face of what is now Universal's apparently implacable determination that Orson will *not* direct them. It turns out that, legally, I *have* to do them in any case. That may get me out of a horny dilemma, but it doesn't satisfy me.

November 16 (Saturday). I played tennis this morning and reluctantly told MCA I'd answer the Universal call for their retakes Monday. But the big event of the day was Fraser's accident in the car. They were going to a party and some idiot ran into Lydia from behind, flinging Fray against the dash and raising a frightening lump. It's not a concussion, but it made us both feel we couldn't go to the Royal Ballet, so we gave the tickets to the Stines and stayed home.

November 17 (Sunday). Today, very tardily, I reached an important, expensive, but basically correct decision, I think. After a long phone talk with Herman, I agreed, despite a deep moral ache, to go ahead tomorrow, after again failing to reach Orson by phone. At that point, a messenger brought a letter from him outlining his position so eloquently it prompted me to further soul-searching. In the end, I called Citron again and canceled the call for tomorrow. I told him to tell the studio I'd reimburse them for all costs they couldn't cancel, due to my late pullout. Tomorrow I see a lawyer, Orson, and the studio brass.

November 18. A damn difficult day, on the whole. Meyer told me I had no legal ground to refuse to do the retakes, which is exactly what Citron had said, but I had to be sure. I told Orson this, and that I would make a final appeal to Ed Muhl [*Universal production chief*], which I did (and should have last week). He was pleasant, but adamant. They do not *want* Orson to do the retakes, though they seem to have only limited criticism of the film itself. So I *do* them tomorrow. The cost to me of the day's delay will be high, about eight thousand dollars in uncancelable crew calls, mostly . . . but not as high as the moral cost of finking out.

I didn't handle this too well. My reluctance to do the retakes without Orson was reasonable; postponing my decision not to do them until Sunday evening was not. In the end, the extra footage shot was not very significant, consisting of a dozen or so orienting shots. (Orson's film was very innovative for 1957, in terms of not always making clear to the audience just where you were. This was long before LAST YEAR AT MARIENBAD, where you never knew where you were.) Contrary to legend, there is no "lost Welles version" of TOUCH OF EVIL. The picture is very close, in my opinion, to what it would have been if the studio had let Orson stay on it till the final dub, as of course they should have. I think they would have if he had been a little less . . . elusive.

November 19. I have done worse work in the movies than this day of retakes, but I don't remember feeling worse. Harry Keller, who directed, was pleasant enough, but in a hell of a tough position. I was able to talk them out of one change I felt would be a mistake. I can't honestly say the other additions will seriously harm the quality of the film. What it will be, without Orson's cutting, I don't know. What it would've been had he been allowed to cut on it till the end, I won't know either.

November 21. I got up early for breakfast with Jolly West, whom I see too infrequently. Tonight, I heard him talk at a medical meeting. We had dinner afterward at the Trader's, but he can't come to the Springs with us over the weekend, sadly.

> *Jolly's one of my oldest and closest friends. We met when he was a resident in psychiatry at Payne Whitney and I was a struggling young actor in Hell's Kitchen. We used to play chess together when he was on night duty and Lydia was playing in* DETECTIVE STORY. *Now he's a scientist of formidable reputation.*

December 1. A very quiet tennisy and painting-at-home sort of day. But tonight Lydia and I went to the Directors Guild and saw BRIDGE ON THE RIVER KWAI. With the possible exceptions of HENRY V and CITIZEN KANE, it's the finest film I think I've ever seen. Guinness has my Academy vote already. The film is almost entirely flawless, the only one I can recall that reaches the dimension of tragedy at the end. A shattering, utterly memorable experience.

December 3. I had a very satisfactory match at the club, and a less satisfying meeting with Universal on the publicity situation on TOUCH OF EVIL. I get the feeling they're not as high on the film as they should be. I had an offer today to do a TV version of BEAUTY AND THE BEAST in January, if I can get a stop date from Paramount. I think I'd enjoy it. I hope it works. Tomorrow I start on BUCCANEER at last . . . seems as if I've been out of work six months, somehow.

December 4. I finally got started on BUCCANEER today. A late morning shooting call, which is just as well, because Wally Westmore needed plenty of time to get the makeup on. Quite a change, after spending a fast three minutes a day on BIG COUNTRY getting my eyebrows darkened, to have to sit for over two hours having Andrew Jackson constructed on top of me again. The shooting itself went well. I like Tony's approach, so far.

December 5. The first full day on the picture, and a damn long one, considering the time I have to spend in the gym doing my workout before I even go to makeup. But I think the part will be fun, and I think I'll be good in it. Tony continues to work with the vocabulary I haven't heard since my acting classes with Art Penn. It's pleasant not to have to think up your own actions and whatnot, but have the director define them for you.

December 7. I spent the morning playing tennis and the afternoon buying Christmas presents. Of the two activities, the latter left me much more tired. Herman called to say he'd closed a deal for me to do BEAUTY AND THE BEAST on TV in January. It'll be an interesting project. Claire Bloom will be the Beauty, and I will have another elaborate makeup to hide behind.

December 9. This was really a long damn day. I was on my feet the whole time, smoldering with anger at the rebellious Creoles for take after take . . . sixteen on one long setup, I recall. I think it worked out well, though it just occurred to me tonight that I should really have had the makeup a little younger, since Andrew Jackson was only forty-six at the time. However, we're committed now, and it's going well the way it is.

This was stupidly careless of me. By then I had learned the importance of research on a part. How I could've missed Jackson's age at the Battle of New Orleans I don't know. The makeup we used was based on paintings of Jackson at sixty. No excuse.

December 13. The battle stuff began well. Shooting in heavy fog, with the figures looming darkly out of it. Jackson huddled in a greatcloak, slumped in his saddle. We thought up some new bits with the young soldier that I like, too.

December 16. The Battle of New Orleans is going to take a lot more time to win on Stage 15 than it did by the old Chalmette Road in 1815. I'm sure I'm going to be good in this now. In the dailies tonight, I saw the close-ups on the Laffite-Jackson scene; they were better, *simpler* than the master shot.

I wasn't bad, though Jackson was such a spiny eccentric, it's an easy part to make an impression with. The picture was not good. It was probably one of the last films that attempted a big exterior (the Battle of New Orleans) on a sound stage, and it didn't really work, though some of the effects were fine. I think the film suffered from being made under de Mille's eye, without the stamp his hand would've put on it.

December 18. The dubbing session went very quickly, just to clean up a few odd loops left over on TOUCH OF EVIL. I then saw Orson for lunch. Seems he has managed to make a lot of his points on the editing of the film; also they plan to follow his advice rescoring. He is going to Europe, however, so we'll have to wait. I didn't shoot today, but saw some more good footage in dailies on the battle. FAREWELL TO ARMS tonight was disappointing. Falsely sentimental, which Hemingway *never* is.

December 27. Tony finished the battle under a little pressure from the production office and a cloud of pouts from Yul, who objected strenuously to having the Scottish drummer boy die in my arms (rather than his, I strongly suspect). I had a difficult lunch, weighing MCA's offer for CIMARRON, the TV series they insist would net me at least a million in keeping money. I don't know. Do I *want* a million? To do a TV *series?* Not a bad script, but how good can such a project *be?* What am I after?

This was before an important personal perception had hardened into dogma: If you can do film, don't do television. Since I had gained my first success in live television, the importance of not doing film TV can't have been clear to me. I was lucky to have chosen correctly.

December 28. I got up before tennis to give the most completely thoughtout answer I could on the TV series offer. It was no, and there are regrets. How can you pass up money in seven digits and not regret it? But I might have regretted more what I'd pass up to take it. I went in and looked at Fray asleep and thought of what I'd just done him out of . . . but he might not have been happier for that much money, if I got it for him. The BEAUTY AND THE BEAST rehearsal, on the other hand, was predictably promising. And tonight was blissfully quiet.

December 29. The day was devoted to BEAUTY AND THE BEAST rehearsals, which progressed, I think. Only Claire and I worked today, on the scenes between the two of us. I think she'll be excellent in this, better than in BUCCANEER. The dinner at the Herb Leonards' tonight gave me a very clear picture of what you do with the millions you can make off tele-film: You buy a huge house with it. They *did* have marvelous storage space, with lots of bookshelves and closets. That I would like.

December 31. The day was good, allowing a little loose time to go over BEAUTY AND THE BEAST scenes. I also played an excellent scene with Boyer, who demonstrates every time I watch him work what a fine actor he is. We saw the old year out with a good vintage champagne I couldn't have afforded a few years ago and some good friends we didn't have then either. I think, on the whole, things are looking up still. I made three films this year whose final value I can't determine yet . . . but I think they're all good. My son and my marriage are thriving, and I can still make a living doing something I'd do free. How can I complain? If the next year is only the same, I'll be happy.

1958

The title role
in *Ben-Hur* . . .

much chariot
racing . . .

residence
in Rome.

A conversational moment
with director William Wyler
TIMOTHY GREENFIELD-SANDERS

Team playing for *Ben-Hur*
AMERICAN FILM INSTITUTE

January 2, Los Angeles. For a glorious once, I woke with no place I had to run to. I called Universal, but TOUCH OF EVIL is in the lab and unavailable. No call on BUCCANEER, where they're doing Claire's and E. G. Marshall's scenes. Without them, I couldn't work on BEAUTY AND THE BEAST either. I did fittings in my Beast costumes, at least: very grand, very sexy, but they're OK. My family still ails a little, but all's well.

January 5. My tennis and my cold were both a bit better today. I spent the afternoon working on BEAUTY AND THE BEAST, of course. It's improving. Tonight, still fluey, I took time to go to an arty little theater and see the Cocteau version. Very, very fine.

January 12. Quite a day. Run-through at ten, dress at two, live performance for the East at five. I liked it when I did it, and I liked it when I saw the kine at home. Lydia saw it live at NBC, but then we skipped the party and went home so Fray could see it with us. It was the first performance of mine he's ever seen. He was a little uncertain, but warmed as the show went on.

January 13. BUCCANEER's going fairly well, but we're doing a lot of changes on the set, under the gun. They're good, I think, except that you lose time and it's a little unsettling.

The final handcrafting on a scene can take a lot of time, but there's no avoiding it. A lot of the crucial work on a script can't be done at a typewriter, only on a set.

As for BEAUTY AND THE BEAST last night, I seem finally to have hit the jackpot with a TV show. We had a huge rating, and all the notices I've heard anything about were excellent. It seems as though everyone I've talked to all day felt the same.

January 15. I had no shooting today, which gave me a rest I badly need. I improved the shining hours by a very glamorous doubles. Vic Seixas, fresh from the Davis Cup tour, didn't seem to care terribly that I got a few serves by him. [*I know more about tennis now; if he'd cared, I wouldn't have.*] As for BEN-HUR, there is nothing approaching a final word on it. Willy is proving the champion decision-avoider of the industry. Very damaging to the ego.

January 17. The retakes today didn't seem to me necessary, but they were done on direct orders from de Mille . . . the most active hand he's taken in the making of the film to date.

BUCCANEER was the last film made by de Mille's company, yet he neither directed nor produced it. This was the closest he came to involving himself in the shooting.

Their only function was to make Laffite's contribution to the battle clearer, which seems to me not enormously important, but then I'm prejudiced. A *Playhouse 90* offer, also MGM is anxious to make a deal for COMPANY OF COWARDS and *either* part in BEN-HUR.

MGM was by this time apparently anxious to get me committed to the picture, while waiting for Willy to make up his mind which part he wanted me to play.

January 21. The shooting went slowly today. I had trouble simplifying as much as Tony had in mind, but I think I got it. At lunch today, after much back and forth, I decided to do POINT OF NO RETURN on *Playhouse 90*, even though I have no word on BEN-HUR yet. Then, on picking up Herman tonight, I found Willy had finally decided I should play Ben-Hur. Ben Thau [*a top MGM executive*] was gracious at the meeting, where I tried to contain my exaltation, which flowed through the evening Lydia and I spent with a bottle of champagne and happy thoughts of eight months in Italy.

January 22. The scene today went fairly well, finally, after a really painful rewrite period. For one thing, it had to be short enough to shoot in one day. Besides, I had to carry my big news around all day in silence. According to agreement, I gave it to Hedda Hopper this morning, but no one else had it till tonight, when we told the people at the party.

By 1958, the huge circulation formerly enjoyed by Hedda Hopper and Louella Parsons had dwindled to a few dozen papers each. There were actually several press outlets more important than their columns, but the tradition of deference to the power they'd once wielded still prevailed. Any big announcement was automatically given as an exclusive to one or the other. The rule was to alternate between them. This was apparently Hedda's turn.

Edd Henry [*of MCA*] closed the deal today . . . two hundred fifty thousand dollars for thirty weeks and prorated after that. Plus travel and expenses for all. Not bad compared to the sixty-five dollars a week I got from Cornell ten years ago.

January 23. MGM is unquestionably the studio to go if you want to be treated like a big fat star. The era is past, but this is the place where it was created. Lunch in the executive dining room was in the imperial tradition, court jesters and all. The picture itself, in Willy's hand, looks pretty staggering. I hesitate to go on record about another mammoth undertaking, after TEN COMMANDMENTS failed to throw me to the top, but this surely won't hurt me.

January 29. I had a conference this morning with another architect, who served to convince me that my first instinct was the right one. After feeling Lydia out on this and discovering that she felt the same, I called Bill Beckett and told him I wanted him to design our house for us. He seemed genuinely delighted and came over this evening to go into details of what and how it should be . . . a fascinating time.

January 31. We sneaked TOUCH OF EVIL in Pacific Palisades tonight. I'm afraid it's simply not a good picture. It has the brilliance that made each day's rushes look so exciting, of course. Indeed, there's hardly a dull shot in the film. But it doesn't hold together as a story. My only consolation is that I was not wrong about any of the elements as we shot them and looked at them each day . . . just about the results.

I'm a little at a loss to explain this gloomy estimate. Maybe seeing it for the first time with a paying audience altered my perception. Certainly it was a little experimental for the fifties. Since then, it's become a small classic; audiences seem to have no trouble following it. In a sense, the whole process of watching film is a learning experience. The more films people see, the less you have to show them, or tell them, to make your point.

February 3. The day worked out pretty well, even with the rain still pelting down. I didn't get the BEN-HUR script back from Chuck Connors but had a pleasant lunch anyway.

There was nearly as much competition for the part of Messala as there had been for Ben-Hur (and no wonder, it's a hell of a part). I'd loaned Chuck my copy of the script, one of only two or three floating around, to give him what edge it might provide.

Tony Quinn and I more or less agreed on terms under which to purchase Niven Busch's THE ACTOR, but Herman has doubts about it as a fit project, following BEN-HUR. This puts me in an awkward position.

February 4. The first reading on POINT OF NO RETURN went well enough. This will be a difficult piece to bring off, but it may be worth the work it'll take. Nice to be back with Frank Schaffner again. How long ago was MACBETH?

Frank Schaffner was one of the half-dozen directors, just as I was one of the actors, whose careers were launched in the rich, heady decade of live television. He'd directed me in JANE EYRE and two or three other things besides MACBETH, and we both enjoyed the medium as it evolved to the West Coast and Playhouse 90. We've worked together successfully on a couple of films since, but I think we both wish somewhere, somehow, there was still live television.

Took Mother and all to the property to tramp happily around in the mud and then had a conference with Citron, in which he talked me out of doing THE ACTOR.

February 5. The show's blocking well. We didn't quite get it finished, but Frank's an old *Studio One* hand. He'll manage. I'm certainly *in* a lot of it. Every damn page, in fact. The session with the architect was as exciting as a first date with a girl. I think it'll be the kind of house I've always hoped to build . . . stone, and glass, and lots of it.

February 12. Three years ago today I was driving to Anaheim to shoot on MAJOR BENSON, my head whirling with the smoky pride of fatherhood. When I tucked Fray in bed last night and told him he'd be three in the morning, he said, "When will I be two-and-a-half again, Daddy?" I'm sorry rehearsal for POINT OF NO RETURN kept me from his birthday party, but it seems to have been a happy one, though a lot of work for Lydia.

February 19. I finally saw Tony Quinn this morning at Paramount after my workout. He seems to hold no grudge over my bowing out of THE ACTOR. Rehearsal wasn't much today, but we did run it through, which is more than we've done for several days.

February 20, 10:00 A.M.—CBS-TV—rehearse. 3:30 P.M.—Dress rehearsal. 6:30 P.M.—Live telecast—POINT OF NO RETURN, Playhouse 90. I think the show came off well. I managed the twenty to forty age span and learned something, playing a man whose situation let me use my own experiences . . . something I rarely do with a part.

February 21. We shove off tomorrow. I checked off the Paramount lot this morning, out of the dressing room that seemed (as indeed it still does) so magnificent when they moved me into it seven years ago for THE GREATEST SHOW ON EARTH. A wet, boisterous farewell party this evening at the Fields'.

BUCCANEER was the last of the commitments I'd originally made to Hal Wallis, the only contract I ever had. In a sense, Paramount had been my home lot. Oddly, I've only made one picture there since (out of the same dressing room). The next day, we began a leisurely peregrination east for New York from whence we sailed to start BEN-HUR. We went by train, stopping to visit several batches of friends and relatives. There really are few better ways to travel than locked up in a double bedroom on a good train with your shoes off, someone you love, no phones, and plenty to read. I'm sorry you can't do it anymore.

March 11, New York. 12:00 P.M.—Sailing, S.S. United States *to*

Southampton. It was a mad and wonderful departure. The usual scramble of late packing, tumbling into the car and off down the street. By the time we got to the ship, looming unbelievable and red-black at the foot of the street where I started all this, half our friends were ahead of us. The sailing of a liner is all anyone ever said it was. I'll never forget it . . . from the warmish vintage champagne to the paper streamers hanging wet in the spray as we passed Ambrose Light.

March 16, London, England. We woke to the gray and drizzly skies of Le Havre, where we stayed only long enough for breakfast. The trip across the Channel was short and full of packing and reporters. They began arriving on the tender and continued in a steady stream all the way up from Southampton and into the suite at the Dorchester. England is all I remember it: the Arthur Rackham hedgerows, the red buses, the sweep of Hyde Park. So, six years to the day from our first arrival, here we are again for our anniversary tomorrow; older, richer, wiser, and I think happier.

March 30, Dublin, Ireland. The flight to Dublin was routine enough, but the arrival made Ireland all it should be. We slanted down over the moist, unbelievably green fields you read about, bright with the sun you *don't* read about, and stepped out of our bright green aircraft into the largest, shoutingest mob of fans I've ever had waiting. Quite genuine and warm, like the little Scots girls in Glasgow in 1952.

MGM was pressing a bit, it seems to me, mounting a full schedule of interviews on BEN-HUR *a year and a half before it could be in the theaters. That chariot race kicked up a lot of dust, even in advance.*

April 6, Paris, France. The flight was smooth, and the arrival at Le Bourget a happy one. Paris seemed somehow closer to what it's supposed to be than I ever remember it being before. Even in the rather chill Easter sun, le Tour Eiffel was faintly misty, as befits the structure of a dream. Everyone else was enchanted with the place. As Lydia said when she saw the trick mirror in the bath, "Ahh . . . now *this* is a woman's town!"

April 8, Paris/London. After a morning spent juggling air schedules, I finally found a plane that got me back to London earlier than I needed to be there. I got a lot done, even more of the stack of mail that waited at the Dorchester for me. The city, along with the entire Continent, was cold and rainy.

April 9, London/Paris. Today was one of the most frustrating days I've ever had on a movie set. The makeup man was late, so I did my own hour late shooting the wardrobe tests. The same strike made us break for lunch when an hour's more work would've wrapped up the day, and start an hour late coming back. I finally managed to finish the tests in time to catch the plane to Paris.

In those days, the British technical unions were incredibly strict about shooting regulations. Often more attention was paid to the work rules than the work. In recent years, as production has declined, things have gotten much mellower. (The "small strike" was not *precipitated by my doing my own makeup.)*

April 12, Train en route to Rome. A long day, beginning with one of those interviews where you go on at greater length than usual. ("In-depth pieces," they're called.) Lunch gave me my first look at the French countryside, which is impressive, and the evening my first experience of French trains, which are not. We're reasonably comfortable, but the roadbed is rough and the food, while good, is very expensive, even by American dining car standards.

April 13, Rome. The trip ended at Rome's Stazione Terminale in a welter of journalists; a real mob scene. Then a train of Cadillacs out to the villa they've rented for us. It's really staggering: a sprawl of earthy terra-cotta, put up in the last century by a lady archaeologist, near the Baths of Caracalla. We have one whole wing, with a graveled patio and a fountain for Fray's boats, formal gardens, marble floors, arched and frescoed ceilings in the four large bedrooms, statues in the entrance hall. All in all, a hell of a layout. Lydia and I went out to dinner tonight at a little restaurant our driver found. Very nice to be out of hotels after so long.

April 14. I went in this morning to Cinecittà to see the layout where I'll be spending the rest of the year. I met the famous Yakima Canutt who'll be handling the race and teaching me to drive the chariot. The studio itself is elaborately decorated, passably equipped. Lydia's birthday dinner tonight at Alfredo's was very pleasant, echoing 1952, same day, same restaurant.

April 15. Surprisingly after yesterday's welcome sun, the day dawned gray and spattered with rain-gusts. I managed to get in a half hour in a chariot with Yak Canutt, relieved to discover that the four-horse team gave me less trouble than I remember in Egypt with two. Maybe it's like a lot of other things: The first two are the hardest.

April 17. Gray skies still this morning, but it cleared enough this afternoon to work with the chariots. A damn muddy track, but it gave us a good excuse not to let the teams full-out anyway, which is fine with me. *Newsweek* shot a few things (portrait of the actor as a very scared man). I finished full of good fatigue, had a brief cocktail date with the local MGM brass, and then home to the first dinner by our new cook. Damn good.

April 19. The sun finally struggled into view again, stiff and uncertain from long inactivity, but it made the world brighter. I'm working better with the chariots now, though still a long way from any skill, of course. I've got more than a month left before we shoot the race; Yak should be able to get me ready for it by then. I'm not very happy with the wardrobe footage I ran later. Some errors in cut and fit. (My general irritation with that whole day is certainly clear in the tests.)

April 22. Not a lot accomplished today. The javelin lesson ended abruptly when we broke both javelins . . . mere props . . . in the first five minutes. I'm going to have to have a talk with the brass about what I expect on this location.

I was quite willing to give MGM a couple of free months so I could learn to drive the chariot and all that. I expected them to have the equipment available.

When I got home, I was able to clear the grass out of an old sandbox for Fray, perhaps my most important accomplishment.

April 23. It dawned gray and raining again, just when I at last was sure the Roman spring had descended permanently. After the usual morning activities, I met Willy at the airport, as well as Sam Zimbalist and Gore Vidal, to a great accompanying fanfare of press and so forth.

Sam Zimbalist was the producer of BEN-HUR. *I believe it was he who persuaded Willy to employ Gore Vidal briefly for some work on the script.*

I had a drink with Willy in his suite, and we began to delve a little into the intricacies of the part, and I felt promising twinges of excitement.

April 26. Fray appeared at the commissary today in a Roman centurion's armor and inquired brightly, "Need any extras?" But the high spot of the day was my solo in the chariot. Willy seemed pleased to hear he'll be able to shoot most of my stuff without doubling.

I was able to do what I did only because of the skill and patience of Yak Canutt. He soloed me unaware, simply stepping out of the back of the chariot while I was frantically concentrating on the running team.

April 27 (Sunday). The day was not quite so fine today, but the sun shone, and my little boy played in the gardens while I breakfasted there. The luncheon at the Zimbalists' turned out to be a fairly fancy do, for all the brass we could collect at this early date. The only other performer present was Haya Harareet, the Israeli actress Willy's picked for Esther. An interesting-looking, earthy type.

April 29. Over lunch today we tried to arrive at the chariot costume, without much success. I can't work out the personal equations involved on the executive echelon yet. Zimbalist remains an enigma to me, whether he's just very quiet or just what else, I don't know. Dinner tonight was interesting, but not a howling success. Vidal is clever, cold, not happy, I'd say.

April 30. Yak is moving me up through some of the tougher teams with the chariots, and I'm gradually gaining a little ease with the reins. Steven Boyd came in today and struck me as a decent kind of guy, which is just as well, considering how long I'll be working with him.

May 2. Usual morning activity today, with an extra run of visitors after lunch, when Fletcher Martin and Harold Von Schmidt [*American painters*] came out to watch the chariots again. Before I left this afternoon, I had a talk with Willy, who seems to be getting the script under control. I was a little worried that even he might be outnumbered on this one, but he seems to feel confident, with Christopher Fry here now.

Christopher Fry, Willy's choice as writer, had arrived and from this point on was on the set every day through the end of shooting, to the profit of the picture and the eventual chagrin of Vidal.

May 5. Boyd is proving companionable, both on the track and off. We could've done a lot worse in that part, a whole lot worse. I caught a ride into town with Lydia after practice, to do my fitting for the third version of the race costume. This one I think is better; it'll probably be the one we use. It has to be; we start in two weeks. Dinner tonight was fun, with a few other couples, and a little more vino than I should have coped with. Or was it brandy?

May 8. Lydia had an interpreter out today to help straighten out our domestic staff problems . . . apparently some progress was made, according to her.

It was at about this point that Lydia realized you can't run a house without the language. From then on, she studied the language in whatever country we were shooting. I wish I'd had time to do the same.

Meantime, I had lunch with Christopher Fry on the script. I gather from Gore Vidal that Willy is not having it all his own way with the rewrites. Sam is all for shooting it the way it is.

Gore was a little out of touch by then. Willy always has it his own way, on rewrites and everything else.

May 9. I worked with a white team today and got a commitment from Willy to rehearse next week on some of the Messala-Ben Hur scenes. Sam is against this. I think the idea of the script being changed at all upsets him.

May 10. On the track today, I tried out the latest chariot costume and my skill as a charioteer. You wouldn't call it an all-out race, by any means, but at least there were several teams all running hell-for-Wyler. I managed to stay out in front with no difficulty.

And no wonder. Yak would've had a few sharp words to say to any of the stunt men who finished ahead of me. When I worried about learning to handle the team in time to shoot the sequence, he said, "Never you mind, Chuck. You just drive the chariot. I guarantee you'll win the damn race."

May 12. Yak's taking the heat off the horses for a few days, so there was no workout today. I did manage to take a free fall off a horse, barebacking (why didn't the Romans, along with all their other ingenuities, invent the saddle?), and get in a conference with Willy. His ideas on making Ben-Hur more than a lay figure in a costume piece are coming clearer and clearer to me. The main area for work here seems to lie in the beginning, when we must make him an untried, uncommitted man, thus allowing room for change, both in the galleys and on Calvary.

May 14. The toughest part of the day was lunch with one of those acid-eared London journalists, who seem to take an actual delight in being loathed by everyone they write about. I think I was able to skirt his more obvious pitfalls, but I wouldn't call it a pleasant lunch.

I have since learned to do a flawless defensive interview. They can't lay a glove on me.

May 15. Today we rehearsed Vidal's rewrite of the crucial scene with Messala. Indeed, the crucial scene of the whole first half of the story, since it contains the seed of so much that follows. This version is much better than the script scene, and Willy brought its virtues out in his usual manner as we worked: picking, carping, cutting, finding a reading here and a gesture there till you're smothered by his concept, which then proves to be excellent.

We never shot this scene of Gore's, nor indeed any of the attempts he made on other sequences. I stress the point because Vidal has gone extravagantly and disdainfully (qualities, I fear, he cannot avoid) on record about his authorship of the BEN-HUR screenplay as well as writer-director relationships in general. As I said, he's a clever man, but not about these things.

May 16. Steve Boyd and I read both versions of the scene through again, to convince Sam, I imagine, that the second one was better. After lunch, I spent the afternoon trying to get the trick of launching a javelin along a wire with reasonable reality and dosing the sore throat I acquired yesterday.

May 17. A gingerly talk with Willy this morning convinced me he's not satisfied with the rewrites on the script. The latest version [*Fry had taken over*] is better, certainly not typical MGM epic writing. It still looks like a Tuesday start, though a freak wind last night blew a wall down on our starting set. My throat, thank God, appears *not* to be developing into the usual psychosomatic cold.

May 19. The rehearsal didn't get away as planned; for one thing, they're still repairing the set from where it blew down the other night. They'll be lucky to be finished in time to shoot tomorrow, let alone today. After lunch we went over still another version of the Ben-Hur-Messala quarrel. I spoke too freely and annoyed Willy, but not seriously, I think. So anyway, tomorrow we begin.

May 20. The first day is behind me. It lifted off my chest like a weight that had been growing there imperceptibly, I suppose, since the day I knew most of this year would be spent Ben-Hurring with Willy. In keeping with his methods, we actually shot only a little. Some remarkable tracking shots of the harnessing action, with the Sheik [*Hugh Griffith*] and me going along the gallery from the drivers' rooms. I would say, on the basis of one day, Willy is no more awed by a ten-million-plus production than he is by a three-million-dollar one. So far, so good.

May 22. Today was a long day of shooting what should be the very spectacular (there's that word creeping in . . .) shots of the chariots lining up to enter the arena. Rather tricky driving, but not much acting. We did get into a shot with Messala and the Sheik and me that Willy added a lot to, but when he was finally happy the light was too yellow to print any of what we'd shot on it, so we'll begin there again tomorrow. This year, I'm surer than last how to use Willy's method in terms of playing a scene.

May 30. We shot the first Ben-Hur-Messala meeting to the point where we fling the javelins, and foundered there. Rigging the wires for the javelins takes so long, and there are so damn many things that can go wrong. On the last take, around seven-thirty this evening, the assistant cameraman forgot to shift the focus after the slate, and the whole shot was lost. The only time I've ever seen Willy give up on a shot.

May 31. This was the first day Willy really was faced with the full physical implications of this picture. They had two thousand people in that circus, and things were really in a turmoil.

June 2. Since today was another of the innumerable Italian holidays, we couldn't shoot, but rehearsed instead. I'd say it went fairly well. The final quarrel with Messala in the garden, which is the first time Judah really admits they're at odds, shaped up. I sense Willy doesn't entirely agree with me on all this. We talked after rehearsal, and he thinks I'm too flat through the opening scenes we've been working on. So tonight I worked on a long Selznick-type memo outlining my ideas about this section.

This was an absolutely terrible idea, one of the worst mistakes I ever made. Some directors love to have their actors write long themes about the character's back story and motivations. Willy doesn't. It took me a long time to get back in his good graces after this blunder. It may have something to do with the rough time he gave me during shooting. I don't really think so, though; he just read me right. I do best when I'm pressed.

June 5. Today was one of the toughest days I've ever had professionally. Willy really opened up on me; it was not an ego-boosting experience. He's dissatisfied, not so much with what I've done so far on the part, but how far I am from my potential with it. That's putting it rougher than he did, but that's about it. He held out high hope and much promise. Quoting him again, this could be the most important day of my career. It ain't gonna be fun for a while, though.

June 6. I worked my ass off this morning, getting my close-ups in the castle scene with Messala. Sixteen takes for me to say "I'm a Jew!" Maybe because I'm not, I damn near decided I never would say it right.

June 10. It went a little better today. I had very few lines in the scene, but that's when Willy's tough. He's harder to please when you're listening than when you're talking. What's the old saw about acting consisting of reacting? I came home exhausted with some sort of chill, complete with fever, and I fell into bed.

June 12. My close-up went like butter today. Either I've actually improved, which is a happy thought, or Willy's given up, which is contrary to nature. A lot of it's just going at it his way. I've learned he doesn't really like to discuss character in broad terms, or even in terms of a given scene. He doesn't work the answers *out* even, until he's explored the scene and the actor's possibilities, as well as his own.

This works if you have Willy's talent as well as his record. His record earned him the time it takes to shoot that way and disciplined the actors to submit to it. As for his talent, the record speaks for that, too.

June 13. We worked slowly today, as usual, but I managed to steer clear of any reefs with Willy. I think I'm doing better work, too, and there's little question his goading approach has a lot to do with it. I came home late, again; we shot till nearly seven-thirty. But I still had energy enough to accept a sudden invitation to drop in on some impromptu party Pili was at, given in a Borghese apartment by some international-set types. Not a very prepossessing bunch, I'd say, but the liquor was free and the view marvelous.

I'd resist this now. I was still a little dazzled then, I suppose. Acting and staying up late don't go together (unless you're doing a play . . . then you're staying up late in order to act).

June 14. Again today the scene went long and late, but well. I'm regaining my confidence, I think, without losing any of the salutary effects of the dose of cold water Willy threw. The daily footage I caught today looked fine to me. Willy's the only director I've ever known who doesn't rave about how great the dailies look, but these really *do*. The scene greeting Messala was as good as I could've hoped for. The party at the Zimbalists' tonight was very pleasant. Christopher Fry is a lovely man.˘

June 17. We had a very bad break today: After getting all the subsidiary shots possible in the quarrel scene (the gift of the horse, the exit, etc.), we set up an intricate three-minute shot embodying the heart of the scene. We got it all rehearsed and were standing "like greyhounds in the slip" when it became evident that Steve couldn't stand the contact lenses long enough for the shot. They're giving him a hell of a time. Never for me. If they don't want me blue-eyed, they have to get a new boy.

June 18. This was about as profitless a day creatively as I can imagine; I spent all of it acting with camels, confirming my strong view that they're the most ill-endowed creatures God ever made. Willy seemed to have a fine time setting up shots of me walking past them, though.

In a sense he was killing time, I suppose, since Steve's eyes are still too bad to tolerate the lenses so we could finish the quarrel scene.

June 19. Today was the toughest one yet, I think. We did the same close-up, the long scene of questioning Esther, with two or three camera lenses, till my eyes literally got tired focusing on the same spot. The problem's clear: I have to play with enough conviction in the early takes before he fences me in with so many instructions to that conviction that I can't reach it anymore. Willy's the toughest director I've ever worked for, but I still think he's the best.

June 21. Today was peculiar; I have an idea Willy's muse didn't strike him for once. We really didn't touch the scene at all. After rehearsing it once in his cubicle, and making two minor changes in the dialogue, he said, "This is too early in the day to play a love scene," and we all laughed. But in fact we did only one shot, the entrance.

June 23. We continued to circle around that damn love scene like wolves closing in on a fallen elk, but we never actually got to it. We did everything you can possibly do with the entrances and exits, and we did the little bit with Simonides [*Sam Jaffe*] afterward, but Willy is apparently not sure what he really wants to do with the scene itself. Tonight, the rain having stopped, Lydia and I drove in to look at the sidewalk art show. It became a public appearance, somehow. That's a thing I'm no longer able to do, I guess.

June 25. We finally did the love scene today . . . the only real love scene in the script. I'd say it went well. We worked with the intense concentration Willy demands, but each take seemed to progress, and there was none of that dead-end feeling of nowhere you sometimes get. Mr. de Mille is in the hospital, I discovered, but not critical.

June 26. Today we did the fight with the guards in the prison cell: thirty takes of the master shot. It took more than a dozen before Willy decided that Judah's escape should only be an attempt that fails. We finally got it, but I left a lot of sweat and a little blood on the floor of that damn cell.

After watching twelve full takes of a very complicated, very trickily choreographed master take on this scene, Willy said, "It's all those old Errol Flynn movies. No matter how well you do it, they know you're going to get away. We have to cross them up." He was right, but it can be a tough way to work.

June 27. The work was long and exhausting; still being chased up and down stone corridors. But the high point of the day wasn't the work, but the dinner with the Frys, Guthrie McClintic, and Katharine

Cornell. What a thing, with Hell's Kitchen only ten years behind us, to have her to dinner. She still has that otherearthly aura of some great fairy and a kind of wise quiet humor. It was a marvelous evening for us and I think fun for them.

June 28. Lydia and Fray came in this morning to watch my daring escape from the jailors. Willy, surprisingly, asked me for any ideas I might have as to how to manage the thing and seemed pleased with the way it all worked out. The last shot I did, jumping down twelve stone steps with my hands tied, scared me more than a little, but it worked out. The statued heads of ancient Rome in the Campodoglio tonight seemed to me to reveal all the virtues and later decay of the Empire, as Gibbon wrote it.

July 2. I won the race today. Thundering past those screaming extras over the finish line was as thrilling as anything I've done in pictures. I got word to Lydia so she could bring Fray and the Creedys [*old friends staying with us at the villa*] out to watch, along with, apparently, almost everyone in Rome. The drive to Tivoli was fine . . . except that the fountains were closed. We had a fine dinner, though, and I slept in the car coming home, a habit I've fallen into and everyone understands.

July 3. We shot late, then rushed through dinner to make it to Rome in time for THE BIG COUNTRY screening. After my wrong guess on TOUCH OF EVIL, it's a pleasure to see a film that lives up to its dailies. THE BIG COUNTRY is a superior film. [*THE BIG COUNTRY is superior, but I'm still puzzled by my sudden loss of enthusiasm for TOUCH OF EVIL.*] My character is far from central, and both Burl Ives and Chuck Connors come off better in shorter roles, but I'm content to be good in a good film. Everyone seemed pleased with it and had appropriate things to say about my performance, which I like myself, as it happens.

July 4. Willy's either getting softer or I'm getting better. When the crew applauded my final effort on the scene where Judah pleads for his family in the prison, he actually joined in. I did it well, as a matter of fact. We couldn't get Steve's close angles because of his eyes, but we have the scene, I know that. Tonight at the opera, I slept the sleep of the just.

I really don't always sleep through the opera, but I've always maintained that the central talent necessary for a successful career as an actor is the ability to go to sleep anywhere, anytime. I had a natural gift for this, which I have since trained to world-class levels.

July 5. In contrast to yesterday, I had an easy acting day, if a little taxing physically. I had to run up those stadium stairs exactly twenty times (plus how many rehearsals?) before Willy was satisfied with the one speech Hugh Griffith had to say to me at the top. Then there were similar complexities to Pilate's speech congratulating me on the race. It went well, as did our Fourth of July dinner party tonight for twenty-five. I'm afraid to think what it cost, but it went wonderfully. Lydia looked marvelous, too.

July 7. Again I had not a word to say all day, but spent most of it roaring past Steve's bloody, twitching form on the sand and then turning to go back for my victory wreath while he's carried limply off. This will play much better in Fry's vastly improved script, which I read yesterday, weeping at his ending, after Calvary.

July 19. A really long, gut-buster of a day, with the heat still beating down. It's difficult to shoot in that courtyard with Willy's methods because the shadows shift so rapidly, you lose the light on shots before he can get to them. At least I'm getting a lot of experience being arrested by Roman soldiers. The most arresting of all, indeed, was waiting in my dressing room when I finished my shower—my son, rigid in a Roman salute and a marvelously complete suit of Roman armor.

July 22, Fiuggi. The location for Nazareth is pictorially perfect, but I can't say I'd like a long session up here. The work day is too long and too tough. The routine we've settled into back at the studio is tough too, but easier than these hours. You drag back into the hotel too tired for anything but dinner and bed. We didn't get a whole lot done today: the train of slaves moving into the village, and a couple of oddments surrounding it. We have a good two days to go, I'd say.

July 23. Today we repeated the first shot from yesterday, partly because they'd failed to send up a bit player Willy wanted from Rome, which meant we waited till they did.

By the time the actor got up from Rome in the studio's fastest car, the wait had cost MGM some fifteen thousand dollars. There was a great deal of grumbling about Willy's arrogance, but the actor in question provided one of the most effective single moments in the film. He was the beefy, red-faced Centurion who said, "No water for him." I'd say it was worth the wait. As far as I know, he never achieved any remarkable film success after that, but he did open a very successful restaurant in Trastevere.

Another actor who seems effective to me is Claude Heater, who plays Christ. Part of it . . . perhaps all of it . . . is the resemblance he has to the traditional Jesus.

I can't really remember now whether Willy had already made his decision never to show the face of Jesus. In any event, the actor who played the part, a German opera singer, was very good.

July 29. Another long and demanding day, replacing the last of the footage shot with Marie Ney before Martha Scott came into the part. Martha is markedly better in the role, no question.

I think one of the reasons Willy replaced Marie Ney was that he'd by then decided there would be some value in having all the Jews in the story played by American actors and all the Romans played by British performers. Marie was the only exception to this, and her replacement by Martha Scott, aside from giving us a very good performance, conformed to Willy's casting theory.

Doing again a scene we'd done before, I was able to note what I'd felt for some time: a marked improvement in Willy's attitude toward me. I still can't quite figure out that early, tough, period . . . but I think it was for the best. The party tonight had a lot of pleasant folk, including Jack Hawkins, who arrived at last for his role.

August 8. Another day on the plunging chariots, still without Steve, retired behind dark glasses for at least another day. If I come out of this picture with nothing else, I'll at least be able to drive a wagon in and out of the shot in the next Western I do. Charioteering is a hard-won and largely useless skill, but I can't help taking pride in it. The party tonight was at the apartment of some Hungarian artist. Bohemian, kind of fun, but we ate too damn late for working people.

August 9. Today, barring whatever Willy may decide he wants to shoot later, again, or instead of what we've got now, we finally finished the race; I guess I've driven my last chariot. I'm really sorry about that. It's been quite an experience . . . and it should be quite a race! When I get back to the first unit next week, my hours will change again. Shooting with the horses, you have to rest when they get tired and quit when you lose the light.

August 25. A whole new set, whole new sequence, new costumes, and with Jack Hawkins beginning work, even a new character. It's almost like starting a new picture. It went very slowly today, but looked very impressive. Lydia, Fraser, and the Fields stopped by for a look and lunch. We worked late into the afternoon and finally did a shot of me waiting by the chariot that made Bob Surtees turn sullen, certain his reputation would be ruined by the light it was shot in.

August 28. My impressive Roman toga made its only appearance. I felt as if I were back in ANTONY AND CLEOPATRA again. We only got one shot done, and I doubt a final print on that, even. It wasn't a demanding day, but a strangely tiring one. Perhaps it's the social life we've been leading lately. In any event, I wouldn't have missed Tivoli tonight. The sight of those fountains in the moonlight is one of the most lovely I've ever seen.

August 30. Today Jack and I worked hard doing the angles over our backs to the togaed and perfumed crowd listening to the speech where he adopts me. I found Jack very moving in it and consequently did well myself, though the proof of that pudding will come when we move around to the reverse angles on us next week. Wandering through the garden, I caught sight of Leo Genn's costume from *Quo Vadis* on the back of an elderly extra. I wonder what future epic will find a place in the background for the fancy gold and green getup I'm wearing?

August 31. Today we rose in time to tool down to the antiseptic and awesome, but really quite beautiful, Stazione Termini to put the Fields on the train. Can it really be so long since we pulled up there and stepped into Ivo's black Cadillac? The whole summer's passed and still the cans of unseen (by Willy) dailies pile up in the cutting room. I'm beginning to feel like a tourist fixture in Rome. And I still don't know the geography or the language.

September 1. Today, for a change, was easy. I worked in only two shots, though they of course required several takes: one maintaining an attitude of amused detachment while stroked by several Roman beauties, the other watching with rapt attention while the African dancing girls cavorted half-naked in the fountains, but it was fun to watch. I can't conceive of it being in the finished film. [*It wasn't, of course, though the sequence wouldn't raise an eyebrow today.*]

September 6. Willy restaged Arrius's party so it took place at the other end of the garden, eliminating some clever business with a bas-relief in favor of some other clever business with a fountain. We didn't get all the scene. Since Lydia, Fray, and the Fields stayed in Florence an extra day so I could join them there, I'd planned to skip Willy's party for the Boyds tonight, but his distress was so evident that I stopped by for an hour on my way to the train. A good thing, too, since Jack Hawkins was almost the only other featured actor in the company there. It made a nice party, what I could see of it before I caught my train for a troubled three hours sleep in a compartment diabolically designed to prevent it. A *very* happy reunion at three A.M.

September 7, Florence. Florence is a city worth any words you can think of, except that it deserves better ones than you can think of. We spent the whole day wandering in a happy turista sort of daze, absorbing the sight and color and marvelous sauterne light of this true thumbprint of the Renaissance. Fray sucked it all in avidly, delighted with the Michelangelo *David*, as, God knows, was I. I don't know whether it's better than the *Moses* or not, but it's better than anybody else did, and a staggering testament to the divinity that was in that man's hands. In short, we drank, and ate and made love all day in a happy limbo of beauty, aware of it.

September 8, Rome. 7:30 A.M.—Start on galley sequence. A long, laborious day in which I came home too tired to be lonely, though the empty villa echoed with my son's footsteps, my wife's voice. On the phone from Venice they sounded busy and happy, though, and I was able to give them a good report on the work. We got very little done, to be expected the first day on a new sequence, especially shooting in such a tight space as that damned galley . . . surely the hottest set I've ever worked in. But the short beard's acceptable, and what we shot is good, I think.

September 9. Another long and draining day at the oars, in the course of which we didn't quite finish the scene with Arrius. I was dashed to discover that Willy has given in to the production pressure to the point of allowing Dick Thorpe [*brought in to direct the second unit on the galley*] to shoot my close-up on the scene, when we get to it. It may be the heat in the set made him determined to spend as little time there as possible. Lydia sounded happy as a Venetian lark (surely they must have them there, along with the pigeons?) on the phone tonight.

September 11. It's six months ago today that we sailed from New York, and sixteen-and-a-half weeks ago that we started shooting; as well as sixteen-and-a-half weeks until the end of the year, when I'm still convinced we'll be finished. We worked long and usefully on the last scene Steve has left in the film, one of his most important. I've always liked it in the script, and it went together very well, too. A few minor adjustments to the lines . . . very few blocks in the staging. We laid out a master shot including the whole scene, something Willy seldom does. By the time we got five or six takes on it, Steve's eyes were spoiling his performance a little, so we didn't print anything, but tomorrow should give us a good . . . a damn good . . . scene, with far less blood than usual.

September 21, Nettuno. Another day spent almost entirely on camels, and getting on and *off* camels at that. If MACBETH had camels in it, I swear I'd never play the part again. Finally finished with them and got to the well, before we lost the light. Nettuno is not the most intriguing location I've ever shot in. The hotel is clean, but colorless . . . like sleeping in an empty swimming pool.

September 22. Spent most of the day lying under a palm tree, pouring water over my face . . . but not in a way that satisfied Willy. We finally got the pastoral quality he wanted. The location is by no means proceeding at a breakneck pace, I'd say at least a week more. The weather's pleasant, and there's the sea to swim in . . . if only I weren't in every damn shot.

I remember sitting in the bleak, bus-station lobby of the hotel that night, wet with sweat and sand from the work still in my boots and Arab trousers. Willy came in, just as tired and dirty, and took me into the bar. It was closed, for some obscure Italian reason, but he mixed us both a martini. "You know," he said, "I'd really like to be a nice guy on the set. It's much easier, but you can't make a good picture that way."

September 23, Rome. Another long morning fighting lights and shadows under the palm trees. Lydia brought Fray and Mother down from Rome; I had a pleasant break by the sea for lunch, then only one long, difficult shot watching the Sheik, then they turned me loose and I came home with my family. I think I'd do a lot better driving back and forth to Rome each day; we'll still be shooting at Nettuno most of next week. Dinner tonight was pleasant, though for the first time it was too cold to eat outdoors. Now we've passed one whole season here; summer's gone.

September 26, Folliano. A new wardrobe and a horse today, instead of those bloody camels. On a horse, I don't *mind* sliding down sand dunes. The scene with the Sheik still confuses me a little. Why does Judah come back to the oasis? Shouldn't he kill Messala immediately, when he imagines his mother and sister dead? I'll sound Willy out on this.

September 30, Rome (second unit). In terms of pure physical effort, today was probably as hard as I've ever worked in any part. I spent the morning rowing, including the change of speeds Arrius tests Judah with. A real bone-breaker. The first unit's still shut down, while Willy fixes script and looks at film.

October 1. This was an all but wasted day; a series of diabolically timed accidents kept us from turning a camera until five minutes to six, when we got one high shot of Ben-Hur rowing in the battle. First the generator went out, then a wind blew down the canvas light screen, then a cloudburst flooded the area we were shooting in. The dailies were excellent, including some late light shots of Ben-Hur training the team, that should make a lovely short sequence.

October 4. Glenn Randall's efforts through the months with the horses paid off handsomely today . . . they worked very well.

Glenn was brought over solely to train one of the white teams to work loose, to hand cues. Horses are not bright animals; this is as hard as anything you can teach them.

We got the scene by lunchtime. Afterward we picked up the close-ups and, for a wonder, quit work by five-thirty . . . Willy's birthday present for me. So here I am thirty-five . . . Lydia put together a very handsome party for me tonight, celebrating the fact. I guess I could hardly hope to have come farther, halfway through my three score and ten.

October 7. Today was spent largely in getting Balthasar's long comment on the futility of violence. Finlay Currie did damn well with it; I only hope I'm that secure when I'm eighty. I still have misgivings about the scene itself . . . there is no clear reason for Ben-Hur's later decision to drive in the race. We don't need to *see* the decision, but we need to understand it when it comes. Willy may come up with something.

October 8. We didn't finish today, but we improved the scene. The insertion, in the Sheik's last speech, of the line, referring to Messala, ". . . defeat and humiliation . . . at the hands of a Jew!" seems to me to solve my problem with the scene. We shot so late tonight, trying to insert a light touch into the opening of the sequence, that I had only energy for a quick dinner and bed, after phoning Lydia, happy in Paris. The pope's apparently terminal illness canceled a cocktail thing.

October 9. I talked only to horses in the scenes today, but I've played with many actors who didn't do as well. What read to me like a very sticky sort of scene felt fine in the playing, thanks to the life they lent to it. We didn't finish with the Sheik, leaving tag ends on both tent interiors to do later, but we'll go out to the Valley of the Lepers tomorrow anyway. Unless we do those added chariot shots, I've seen the last of those white horses . . . till the premiere.

October 10. The location for the leper scenes is excellent . . . caves cut by the Romans, quarrying rock, extending now in deep receding blocks of dark and dimming light. That's the problem of course: We lose the light awfully fast in any given spot there. We got maybe three shots of Ben-Hur coming to the cave, what with light problems and a touch of cloudishness in the afternoon.

October 29. We finally wrapped up the last of the location shooting for the film, by the handy expedient of cutting the sequence with my mother and sister. I got the close-ups this morning with some difficulty. Apparently there's something about the way I drink water that fails to enchant Willy . . . every scene we've had with water in it, we've had trouble with.

October 31. I spent the day dashing around naked and wet in the late October air, performing horrifying deeds of cinematic derring-do with flaming torches and flung javelins in the battle on the deck. Later, we retreated indoors and I rowed awhile.

It was about then I said to Willy, "Look, I want to get back home, but I'm dammed if I thought I'd have to row all the way."

November 4. After struggling all day on the last scene with the Sheik, I was shocked to find, not an hour after I'd spoken with him on the set, that Sam Zimbalist had dropped dead in his driveway. Dear God.

There are many parallels between a film and a military operation, and the reaction to death is one of them. The pressure, and the stakes, are so great that somehow, the choice is always to keep shooting.

November 5. Before shooting began this morning, Willy said some simple things about Sam that were true, and brief. I'd settle for that myself, I think . . . to have men I'd worked with stop the cameras for a moment and think about me, while the work waited.

November 12. My primary contribution today was knife-throwing, not acting. There was a scene, and I did it well enough, but the peak of it was Ben-Hur's dagger, flung into the carpet next to the Sheik's sword. It worked every take with a luck that surprised me. It's fall now, our summer guests have all gone.

November 13. After laying on enough makeup to hide the beard I was saving for the return scene this afternoon, we finished off Hugh Griffith this morning, almost six months after he began and in the same sequence he began *with.* I'll miss him . . . the wild Welsh goat! Though Willy was most understanding about it, I just couldn't integrate the reaction thing with Esther into the homecoming this afternoon. There really is no *place* for the love story here.

Christopher Fry put it well one day at lunch. "If I were writing an original screenplay instead of adapting a semiclassic novel," he said, "I wouldn't have the girl's role in the story at all. The significant emotional relationship is the love/hate between Messala and Ben-Hur. The audience knows this, and they're not interested in the Ben-Hur/Esther story."

November 16. Ty Power's shocking death on the set in Spain yesterday made me aware of my mortality all day. A good time for it; we were shooting through Sunday again, to take advantage of the continuing fine weather. Thinking of Ty, I carried the ninety-pound stand-in for Tirzah most of the time, instead of Cathy O'Donnell. We lost the light a little early, so I can't claim it was a *long* day . . . I was home by four. But it *was* Sunday.

November 24. That beard gets pretty boring after a day or two straight. So does the rowing. I think I pulled my last oar today, though. Everything else we have left in that sequence is after the galley is rammed. That water's getting damn cold to splash around in this time of year.

November 28. I didn't work very hard today, at least not in very many shots. Willy seemed enthusiastic about smashing the mezuzah instead of just tearing out the parchment (a niggling gesture). We then explored three possible ways of doing it and one version where I didn't do it. I can't tell now whether we'll finish in time to catch the boat home or not.

December 11. After a grinding session beating the scene out on the couch in Willy's trailer, with Christopher Fry perched on the desk, the last scene with Esther finally came back closer to a love scene. I was dubious about this, but it seemed to play. A face from the past appeared in the endless train of VIPs on the set . . . Susan Hayward, very impressive and very well-off as a transplanted Georgian. She seemed happy, but tense.

December 25. The day was all of ours, instead of just Fray's, because it went so well for him. After dinner, when he went down for his nap, he smiled and said happily, "I remember when I saw da tree first . . . I was so ex-*cited!*" I was, too. The Roman Christmas was snowless, and the tree was tiny on a tabletop, but the day was the same . . . a shouting, glittering morning, aimless and sleepy after lunch.

December 31. I suppose this is a pivotal year, half my three score and ten. In it I made the picture that may or may not be the best I'll ever make, but it'll certainly either finally press me into the thin, airless reaches where the supernovas drift or demonstrate conclusively that my orbit is a different one. Eaten though I am by the drive to that further space, I'm not sure I'd be unhappy with either end. That's probably because so much more happiness stems for me now from my family. My son grows finer and my wife more serene each month, this year more than before. Whether the film I made turns out to be memorable or not, I know the year we spent making it will be . . . and Rome will mark us all forever.

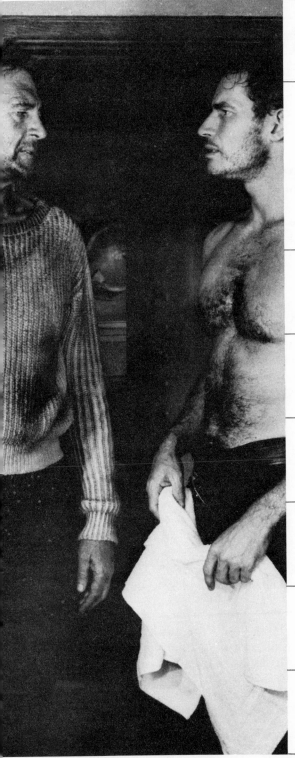

1959

The Wreck of the Mary Deare (with Gary Cooper) . . .

summer stock with Lydia . . .

building a house . . .

a lunch with Olivier.

With Gary Cooper in
The Wreck of the Mary Deare
METRO-GOLDWYN-MAYER

January 3, Rome. Today we explored further alternatives for the last scene with Esther. Lord knows we have to make it work, but I'm not high on the scene as written and this, coupled with the dripping atmosphere in which it must be played, threw me into a sniffling, surly mood all day. I'm getting old for sure. The startling sight of a thin, wet snow falling tonight rejuvenated me.

January 4. Tuesday's a holiday, so we worked today, but it's the last Sunday we'll shoot here; the last Sunday we'll do anything here. Eddie Carfagno's done a job recreating Golgotha with cement and plasterboard; I hope we can do as well with the event that marked it. The terrible mechanics of crucifixtion root you sickened in your tracks. Willy is using his talent well so far in the scene. The last one...

January 5. After an impassioned and eloquent justification to Willy for the absence of tears in the Crucifixion scene, I crossed myself up by weeping copiously at the sound of Christ's voice from the cross. It should work well one way or another. We didn't finish, but we'll certainly wrap Wednesday.

January 7, Rome/London. The last setup finally came, but it was through in such a flurry of grab-shots there was hardly time to mark it. For the record, it was a close-up of me watching the descent from the cross. After the wrap, we had to hurry to catch the plane for London for THE BIG COUNTRY premiere; as we got in the car, Willy stopped to shake my hand, grinning. "Well, thanks, Chuck," he said. "I hope I can give you a better part next time!" Fray sent me his toy rifle and cowboy hat to take with me, since I was going to a cowboy movie.

Willy and I were in the air, bound for London, just two hours after we wrapped the last shot on BEN-HUR. We arrived before midnight, did a full publicity schedule and a premiere the next day, and were back in Rome forty hours after we left.

January 9, Rome. The trip back to Rome was no effort save a slight pang at leaving a city I never seem to be in as long as I'd like. When I got back the afternoon was crowded: checking out of Cinecittà at last, getting my first haircut in a year, and then picking up the portrait of Fray, which I like.

January 10, Naples. There wasn't time for a final walk in our garden, any more than there'd been time to walk a lap around the Circus when I left Cinecittà last night. From the first sip of coffee at seven till we finally crunched around that fountain for the last time, we were frantically pressing to fill case after case after trunk after crate with the residue of ten months here. By the time we were rolling south to Naples, everyone was happy though. The bay and the city were worth waiting for.

January 12, Genoa. The *Independence* is a much more homey sort of vessel than the *United States* last year; people stopping to chat in corridors and whatnot. I know that's the whole idea of a cruise ship, but it's not suited to my private misanthropy (growing with the years, I guess). We were given a fine time in Genoa by a friendly, scrubbed American executive of the line, who put in a damn good day's work.

January 14, Barcelona. Relieved to find my weight's only up to two hundred one and a half. A boat's a poor place to watch your weight, but I've got to try. Barcelona didn't help; a marvelous Catalan restaurant, good Spanish beer. The whole look of the town is startlingly beautiful; the Gothic feeling I've always imagined as the stamp of Spain is clear in the architecture. It may be clear in the people, too, which is how Hemingway read them, but I had no time to check this.

January 18, Madeira. This is all a port-of-call should be. The cliffs shoulder sheer out of the Atlantic swell where we anchor, and the bum-boats dance and sway in the chop, waiting for wind. The men stand, dark and white-eyed, lean as lions, to dive, or hold their sons overhead like spears to fling after the silver. The people are proud and courteous, with the same eyes that watched Nelson chasing Napoleon's frigates off these headlands.

January 21, At sea. Cecil B. de Mille died today. I was sunning between the stacks on the foredeck, turning over the things the sea brings to the top of your mind, when Lydia brought me the report. The death of a man of seventy-seven can hardly be surprising . . . but it shook me. Still, if ever a man died at his moment, he did. He'd achieved all he wanted or could've hoped for. I radioed and was sorry to get a reply that the funeral will be Friday, before we land.

January 24, New York. We came through the Narrows before dawn, and the sight of the moon setting over the shoulder of the big lady with the torch was one I've been aching for longer than I knew. Considering the amount of luggage we had, we disembarked with a minimum of friction, into a cold, cold day. The apartment looked . . . like home, of course, and our old friends did, too.

February 8, On the train to Detroit. Considering it was another leaving day, it was fairly relaxed. I got in a last session fighting the waistline at the New York Athletic Club, then stood by while Lydia closed up the last of the bags. I'm getting awfully tired of trouping around the world followed by twenty-nine pieces of luggage. The train was nice, especially considered as dying transport. The passenger service is cut down already; only one train a day to Detroit.

February 9, Flint, Michigan. The Detroit arrival was marred only by the time we had to spend waiting for Russ to fight his way downtown to pick us up over a glare of ice. By the time we left to pick up my new Corvette however, driving conditions had eased. The new Ford wagon looks fine and handled well going north, but it doesn't match my new blue bug. The ice was too bad to drive it back tonight, though.

February 10, Detroit. Once we got the ice melted off the two new cars, the drive back from Flint wasn't particularly dangerous at the speeds you have to hold, just long and boring. I spent the afternoon chipping ice off the drive; tonight we did a party the Ford Motor people set up, showing off the lions.

February 12. My son was four today. His babyhood behind him, he stands tall and slender on the edge of boyhood. The back of his neck still smells irresistibly wonderful, but his voice already has a prepubescent frog in it somewhere. I'm not done with his baby years, but he is. I can remember them perfectly, from that first dawn when I drove back to work, awestruck with the wonder of fatherhood, to the last time he clung in baby fear when the noon whistle on the stack of the *Independence* blasted at us.

February 15, Chicago. The drive to Chicago was simple, the cars behaving well on a route so elaborately engineered they practically drove themselves. Lydia, ahead in her T-bird, set a pace a hair slower than I'd have chosen, maybe because the late start activated my time neurosis and made me a little testy. Mother and Lilla [*my sister*] were waiting patiently when we rolled in, shortly after dark.

February 26, St. Claire, Missouri. After the usual delay, we whipped off westward, a handsome caravan driving through the wet snow the city provided for a farewell. The route to St. Louis is easy now, but we got trapped in the plant traffic at five there. The Mississippi looked marvelous, though, even viewed from a traffic jam.

February 27, Oklahoma City, Oklahoma. The second day's drive was not oppressive. The cars performed well and the weather was adequate, till we ran into rain squalls on the Turner Turnpike. The Wests were waiting warmly at the end. I looked forward to this drive during those dawn walks in our Italian garden; now I'm doing it.

March 3, Needles, California. Today was more tiring than it's been. The roads west of Albuquerque aren't as good. We lunched in the Painted

Desert, to give Fray a glimpse of it. He was delighted to be back in "da *weal* West . . ." and did well for a little fella on a big trip.

March 4, Los Angeles. Thanks to an early rising and an improvement in the California roads since we last drove through, we got home in good time. It was wonderful to be back, too. I haven't been away this long since we first came out nine years ago. The new house looks as though it'll be everything I'd hoped for.

March 5, Los Angeles. I spent the morning at Paramount, part of it in de Mille's office, dark and carton-crammed. There was a box full of memo pads with his name imprinted that will never hold anything else.

March 6. Falling back into the routine of this town was painless. I must be turning into an orange . . . it's too easy to enjoy California. MGM seems corporately glad to see me, all sorts of executive brass with extravagant opinions about the BEN-HUR footage. Let's see what Willy says when he's through cutting.

March 8. This afternoon we entertained for the first time in Coldwater, with a picnic lunch: wieners cooked over a fire I built in my own hearth. The walls aren't up and there's no roof, but the kites flew, soaring in the light breeze lifting over the ridge, and the sun was warm.

March 9. A busy day checking things out on both lots, but mostly weighing THE WRECK OF THE MARY DEARE at MGM. We finally more or less closed them out; it would have many advantages, but I couldn't do MACBETH at the Ann Arbor Festival in May. A second part to an actor like Cooper isn't a bad idea, though.

March 17. I went to the meeting with Citron and the accountant to find out what has to be done to help me keep any money. THE WRECK OF THE MARY DEARE looks more and more tempting. They're now trying to postpone the start date so I can fit in MACBETH. If they do, I'll take it. Our fifteenth anniversary finds us a long way from the shiny kids that ran through the rain to get married . . . but happy. Very happy.

March 20. I got up very early for my physical, which still consists of my saying no to almost every question the doctor asks. Give me another ten years and the yeses will start cropping up, I imagine. Tonight at the Wylers' I had the enormous pleasure of dining with Olivier. Now if I can meet Hemingway, I'll have it made.

March 25. Had a pleasant lunch with Chuck Connors and an unavoidable drink with a rather pitiful man trying to persuade me to undertake another biblical film ". . . we can shoot it for less than a million!" Orson's OTHELLO tonight must have been shot for not much more than that and was claw-marked throughout with his animal talent. Better than the MACBETH, I think, since it's better acted.

March 26. Well, after walking out of the negotiations in high dudgeon, Herman pulled it off again at MGM. I was doing another interview this afternoon when he called to say they'd finally come around on THE WRECK OF THE MARY DEARE deal . . . including a piece of the gross. More important, they're allowing me time for MACBETH, too.

March 27. Dr. Hoytt says I'm in excellent shape. The house is, too, though for the first time, with walls going up, the rooms looked a little small. I had a pleasant sort of ritual lunch at MGM with Julian Blaustein, Mike Anderson, and Eric Ambler on WRECK OF THE MARY DEARE. This is always part of beginning a new picture. It has almost nothing to do with the film, but it establishes the sunny mood of mutual congratulation. This suits me now; I always feel better, looking to work.

April 2. Lunched at Romanoff's today with Gary Cooper, whom I've admired fervently clear back to when I could do it for ten cents. The lunch was another celebrant offering on the part of the executive echelons. Hedda's dinner tonight paid off the rash bet she made in Rome when she was convinced we'd shoot till spring. Very much high Hollywood but a pleasant evening, especially since it was on her.

April 4. Aside from getting my Corvette tuned properly, I suppose the important event of the day was meeting Aldous Huxley. He has a lean, distinguished-author sort of face and seemed much concerned with concealing his near-total blindness. He spoke very little, though his wife talked a great deal. They both were much interested in Jolly West's comment on various chemicals. Huxley discussed that with enthusiasm. He's much hurt by the failure of his play, I think.

The chemicals discussed were hallucinogens. This was before much was known about them and a good many responsible people were playing with mushrooms and so forth. Jolly did some of the early research that established their dangers.

April 5. With some misgiving, Lydia laid low with some bug, I drove alone to Palm Springs for a tennis tournament. I liked the simple drive down in the foggy morning air, the scent of orange blossoms lacing through the wet chill. It reminded me of mowing lawns in the early mornings in Winnetka, earning money while we were shooting PEER GYNT.

This was a 16mm version I did for David Bradley while I was in high school. At the time David was one of the few underground film makers in the country, and I may be the only member of my acting generation to have done both a silent film and an underground movie. PEER GYNT wasn't too bad, actually, though I played the part totally unaware of the fact that Ibsen had written a satire.

April 8. My last day before MARY DEARE begins was crowded. A great hassle about the ceiling in the living room of the house . . . should it be wood as Bill Beckett specified or acoustic plaster, which seems best now? I hoped to get to work on the MACBETH cutting tonight, but the Stines dropped by, and the evening melted. John O'Shaughnessy wrote regarding his reaction to the cutting Burgess Meredith and I used in Bermuda.

My last previous assault on MACBETH had been in Bermuda, in the summer of 1952, under the highly imaginative direction of Burgess Meredith. The only way to learn to play those man-killer parts is to start when you're twenty and keep coming back till you get too old for them.

April 15. All my practice rope-climbing in the Paramount gym didn't mean a damn thing when I had to do the shot today, climbing from the deck of the tug in the big tank at MGM, up to the deck of the MARY DEARE. What with the wind, spray, wet rope, and the rolling ship, it was a hell of a lot different from the gym. I popped a ligament or something on the first take and barely made it the last ten feet up and over the rail. As I lay moaning on the deck plates, Mickey yelled up on the bullhorn, "Could we have one more please, Chuck?" "Better print, Michael," I said. "That's all there is." A great scurrying of nurses, heat treatment, and whatnot, but I was able to work before the day was over. No more rope shots for a while, though.

I had prepared for this, but obviously not well enough. The injury wasn't very serious (not a torn ligament) and I didn't miss any shooting days, but I never was able to provide them with another take climbing that damn wet rope.

April 21. Finally got into words today, after another solo sequence this morning. I have a small problem trying to find the correct accent for John Sands. He can't be British, but he mustn't be American. Midatlantic diction is best for it, but will it be accepted? Not universally, I guess, but what is? Russ brought over some excellent broadswords for MACBETH tonight.

April 27. Back in the MARY DEARE, with some misgivings today. We made useful changes in the scene today, but I wonder how well I can possibly come off in this. It's more and more clear this is Cooper's film.

Well, of course it was Cooper's film. After having borne witness all my moviegoing life to the enormous presence he brought to the screen, I should've been able to figure that out. I was lucky to be in it. The experience of working with him and the friendship it created is one of the most valuable I've had in film. He was a lovely gentleman (that sadly outmoded word) and a total professional. There aren't many like him.

May 1. Tough day. Dangling half-drowned over the side of that ship in the roughest gale the special effects men can whip up is not my idea of a swell day. Mickey seemed very happy with the result, however, and we did all the cuts needed in the shipboard sequences, so they won't need to double me while I'm off Macbething.

I have no idea how Herman Citron managed to bully MGM into giving me time off in the middle of shooting to do MACBETH. I'm amazed MGM felt they needed me enough to compromise their schedule to this extent. It wasn't really wise, even from my point of view. MACBETH isn't the kind of part you can rehearse for a week, play for a week, and get anything out of, even if you have done it before. I'd have been far wiser to concentrate on the play or the film and not try to do both. I don't think I slighted MGM, but I didn't help MACBETH.

May 2, Ann Arbor, Michigan. Arrived unexhausted, though the flight wasn't long enough for good sleep. I was met and deposited efficiently in the hotel, then went at once to check sets and costumes. I'm delighted with both. They will greatly help the overall success of the production, also the overall success of me. Rehearsal went well enough. We got the play blocked through the murder scene, except Duncan. Jacqueline Brooks may be a good Lady. She looks good, plays well in the scenes, though yet no great power in the solo bits. There's time for that to come.

May 5. We got the entire show blocked, by which time most scenes had been explored a little as well. I gave in gracefully to O'Shaughnessy's reluctance to use the small high balcony in the theater for some of the short scenes, which seemed to put him in a good humor. We had a lot of trouble assembling the necessary equipment for the combat; I must get a set of all those things and keep them so I don't have to go through this all the time. I had an hour alone on the stage late tonight, working on the soliloquies.

May 11. It went well. A hell of a day, naturally, unable to meet anybody because of the run-through, which I purposely paced lower in energy than I've ever done in a run-through of any performance in rehearsal. But I needed all the calories I had for the opening. I was content, on the whole. I believe I reached something fresh on "Life's but a walking shadow . . ."

May 15. I spent the whole day resting except for a fruitful lunch with G. B. Harrison [*one of the country's outstanding Shakespearean scholars*]. He was generous in his opinion of my cutting of MACBETH. It played well tonight, as well as we've done. Lydia was properly impressed. I feel I'm finding more soft places in the part . . . the right places.

May 16. The week went by too fast. I wasn't nearly through with the part when it was over. With the matinee, I had nearly twelve hours on it today, but I still felt cheated. As for the result, I'm better in it this time than last time, but I'm not done with it, yet, by God. I must cut down almost to nothing the savage shouting I've relied on so much. Next time . . .

May 18, Los Angeles. I was swept back into the film with no ceremony this morning. My now quite respectable beard was cut back to a grubby stubble, and I was scuba-suited and tumbled into a tank to help Coop subdue the heavies. They seem to've managed very well without me.

May 23 (Sunday). After the usual morning of tennis, we ran up to the house, where the electrical conduits are in. The reality of that place grows on me all the time. I find myself daydreaming how it will be to live there. The party, or parties, tonight were very nice. Much smaller do at the Coopers' than last time; David Selznick's was large and appropriately Hollywoodish.

May 26. Today, after a long discussion with Mickey Anderson, we made some crucial cuts in the scene in the corridor with Patch. I'm coming to the conclusion that Eric Ambler does not write speaking dialogue.

Very few writers do, oddly enough. Dialogue that reads perfectly well on the page quite often doesn't sound at all the way people talk. The two writers with the best ears for spoken English, Ernest Hemingway and John O'Hara, wrote almost nothing for performance, though the novels of both have been frequently dramatized by less skillful hands.

Serling's dialogue is very good on the other hand (in a pilot they asked me to run after shooting), but it's in tele-film. Much as I'm tempted by his script, I think I must stick to my resolution to avoid that medium again. It's impossible to do superior work in TV. [*It's not impossible, just very hard. And very rare.*]

June 1. Today I was back with Willy Wyler again for a BEN-HUR retake, plunged into the draining strain of a day he devoted to digging as deeply as he could into everyone's resources and endurance. Two close-ups of me at the end of the quarrel with Messala and after breaking the mezuzah went well, but the shots with Esther in the quarrel on the steps were very difficult, the results only fairly good.

June 5, New York, en route to London. I arrived at the apartment, jet-early, but dog-tired, with time to catch up on the sleep the short flight had prevented my getting earlier. Some routine interviews, then a meeting with Maynard Solomon of Vanguard Records. We decided to do four LP sides. I'm relieved at having a decision on this; I can now proceed with the Moses cutting when I get back to London. BOAC's departure was slightly delayed, but their routinely opulent champagne supper, somewhere over the Grand Banks, was satisfying, in a decadent, Fall-of-Rome kind of way.

This album was redacted from the books of Moses (the first five books of the Old Testament). Later on I did another four-side album on the life and passion of Christ, redacting the four gospels. Those albums used some superb renditions of spirituals, arranged by Bob de Cormier and sung by his chorus. The albums were only moderately successful commercially, but I think it's some of the best work I've done.

June 6, London. Nice day, considering that my flight against the sun hacked out the middle of it. The Savoy is certainly not up to the Dorchester. After dinner I went over with Coop to the Dorchester so the manager could show us the Oliver Messel suites we couldn't move into. It's still fine to be back in London. A lovely town.

June 8, Elstree Studios. My total contribution consisted of sitting with my back turned in one long shot and glancing meaningfully in profile at one of Coop's answers. I hardly feel I earned my salary, but I'm persuaded the life of an extra is horrible.

June 17. Spent a large part of the morning shopping; also posing by Big Ben for far longer than I found interesting. I was carelessly frank at lunch with Tom Wiseman, one of the Terrible Triplets of the English press. I'll probably be sorry. Got a great slug of work done on the Moses cutting. Dinner with Coop was fine, but Onassis's vast party for Callas was excruciatingly dull. I guess owning all the ships in Greece is no guarantee of a good party.

I've never been very good at these big parties where public personalities are assembled for display like a dog show. I enjoyed much more the dinners I often had with Coop during this location, usually in a little restaurant called The Guinea in Bruton Place, which served (and still does) the best steak in London.

June 18. Shut up in the suite the entire damn day, dragging the final section of the Moses story out of the last four books of the Pentateuch. It's like untangling the backlash on a fishing reel. I do feel the narrative that's finally emerging is the best of all those I've worked on so far. It better be, it's the climax of the album. I boarded the sleeper plane with some regret at leaving London, but relieved to be homebound.

July 1, Los Angeles. I spent the entire day on MGM's Stage 9, eating pounds of roast lamb, grapes, and rice while listening to Hugh Griffith expound the glories of the horse, albeit somewhat haltingly. Hugh is not the most secure actor on lines I ever worked with. I raced home, changed to a proper blue suit, and was off to church to give a completely unprepared speech which I'm sorry to say sounded that way.

July 6. Willy's extra coverage on the Crucifixion gave me another chance on that scene, which I felt I'd done well in January. Maybe I did it better this time. Then we went back to the tent and flailed away with Hugh. Several film offers are pending now: SUNRISE AT CAMPOBELLO looms large; also a firm offer for THE ALAMO from John Wayne; some script from Sophia Loren; plus a navy story. Bill Darrid called tonight with details of the progress of the stage version of the Andersonville piece. That sounds possible.

July 8. Plunged, literally, back into THE WRECK OF THE MARY DEARE today . . . a little too deep, too soon. The bottom of that big tank brings the blood out of my ears. Working under pressure for sure, but it'll make a good sequence. I finished early enough to come home, ears full of water, and work back to sweaty earth with a tennis racket. We wrapped up the deal to do STATE OF THE UNION in Santa Barbara with Lydia. We've come a long way since doing that play in North Carolina in '47.

July 9. Still sucking on a scuba all day, but as the temperature climbed into the high nineties, underwater was an ideal place to be. I managed to read the script on ALAMO (no) and most of the script with Loren (no). We had a session on landscaping the grounds at Coldwater.

July 23, Chicago. THE WRECK OF THE MARY DEARE finished, we got away in fine style, especially for this family. Fray was fascinated by his first flight in a jet, determined to take his toy dog along. It's good to be back in the settling, midwestern frame house, reeking with reminiscence. That wide, summer-green veranda is still the essence of adolescence for me, as the dusty St. Helen trail roads are the essence of my boyhood. A nice interlude for us before taking on STATE OF THE UNION.

August 2, Santa Barbara, California. For the first time in stock, I'm seized with the strong feeling that a week is not enough time to put together a show like this. At least not with this cast. I find myself intruding into the blocking, trying to bring some order to the early chaos. This is not good actor's ethics, but I don't know what else to do.

August 6. The opening of STATE OF THE UNION. Well, as Godfrey Tearle used to say in ANTONY AND CLEOPATRA, "Whatever goes wrong, I've found about eleven o'clock, the curtain invariably comes down." The evening was close to disaster, though Lydia looked marvelous and did damn well. I was pressing too hard to be any good.

August 10. We wrapped up STATE OF THE UNION tonight, to a fairly good house. The show was just beginning to be adequate. Barely. Still I don't regret it. I learned something from the part and about my profession. There are people who spend a lifetime trying to do this work who are in fact terrified by it. That's very sad.

August 11, Los Angeles. I played a little tennis while the packing was done behind my back, then we took off for home, Fray talking happily to his toy dog in the back. We arrived before sunset and stopped at Coldwater, luxuriating in the growing feeling of home about the place. (The doors even lock now; I had to break into my own home, through the delivery hatch in the kitchen.) A lovely evening with Lydia, searching out the house where I first stayed in Hollywood, when I came out alone for DARK CITY. It's gone now.

This was the house where I stayed for several days in early 1950, when I came out to discuss my contract with Hal Wallis. It belonged to the Deane sisters, who had been silent stars of some magnitude, by then long retired. They were very kind to me, I remember.

August 19. The voice lesson at MGM with Gertrude Fogler is still largely lecture, though I said two words today. I still think it's possible to use some of what she says in recording this week; I hope I'll really have soaked some of it in by the time I next do Shakespeare. We went to the Adoption Institute tonight for the first step in adopting a daughter. We were both a little anxious, but all was well when Lydia drove me to the plane for New York.

August 22, New York. The work on this recording project is so stimulating and the experience of working with chorus so exciting that a long session like today's leaves me unexhausted and eager for more. We finished with the singers, tomorrow there's only my solo work . . . really the bulk of the album. I'm able to apply a surprising amount of the voice theory gleaned from my work with Fogler.

August 24, Los Angeles. Things are going more slowly on the house than we hoped. Tile setting is delayed by nondelivery of the damn tiles, now not expected for ten days. I didn't sleep as well as I usually do on planes, and the day was unsatisfying, except for being home. Citron's not too high on the concert idea; he's anxious for me to consider INHERIT THE WIND, for Stanley Kramer.

August 25. I gave MGM a free half hour of dubbing, completing all the work on WRECK OF THE MARY DEARE, which Julian Blaustein tells me now will be held for spring release . . . much better in view of the fall release of BEN-HUR and the impossibility of getting THE WRECK OF THE MARY DEARE ready for November. The lunch with Stanley Kramer was very persuasive, but the part he wants me for in INHERIT THE WIND is not good, though the script is. March and Tracy will be excellent . . . without me.

They were, too. The part Kramer offered me wasn't much, but I've always regretted never having worked with the two men I think were the best American actors.

August 29. My day was brightened by an early call from Ed Henry, dawning off for San Francisco, anxious to relay his reaction to BEN-HUR, which he saw last night at a running for Joe Vogel. Most, *most* extravagant. I can't remember if the comments run differently from the way they did when TEN COMMANDMENTS was first screened, but the thought gives me pause. A telling point by Ed: "Of all the people there, not one came out saying, 'What a great race!' " If this one won't do it, it can't be done, I guess.

September 14. Fray's first day at nursery school. He walked off with Lydia, proud and shiny-faced (both of them, for that matter), his new tin "Gunsmoke" lunch pail swinging, babyhood behind him. Still nothing much going on in town, except more progress on the house and less on the money to pay for it. I turned down (fits right in) still another TV spectacular . . . this one a gigantic Christmas show written by Paul Gallico. I'm afraid it wasn't much. I spent part of the evening slowly getting to work on notes for the record album. God, how I hate to write! Thank heaven it's not my livelihood.

September 15. A little more work on the piece for the record jacket today, though it's very hard in that rarest of California weather . . . a day with a faint ghost of autumn in it. The sort of day when actors' hearts are high and confident on Forty-fifth Street, whether you're on the way to the rehearsal of a sure hit or the office of a scabby agent who probably won't see you. The gold September weather, when we should all be in New York. Here, I still have no job I want.

September 16. Accepted a *Sid Caesar Show* for October. It'll mean going to New York for a week, but this is not an impossible end. Willy Wyler contemplates still one more, *final* close-up for BEN-HUR, maybe next week. I finished the album notes for Vanguard with a great sigh of relief. The money situation is increasingly complicated. There is even a possibility of shutting down the house.

September 18. Party tonight out in Bel Air given by a prince whose name I've forgotten. He wants me to fly to Iran preliminary to do a film on Darius the Great. One of the guests was Ann Blyth, who is against the idea of the Khrushchev lunch tomorrow at Fox. That's an odd opinion. I'd assumed we have no choice.

September 19. Lunch at Fox was very interesting: I've never seen such a large turnout of capitalistic movie luminaries as for Khrushchev, chief of the Soviet proletariat. His smile is indeed cheery, but his eyes are hooded and hard with concentration. Skouras made an ass of himself trying to fence politically with him . . . like heckling Milton Berle at Ciro's.

This luncheon was Hollywood's political event of the year. I was not an admirer of Premier Khrushchev, but I was convulsed by Spiro Skouras's attempt to engage him in debate. Skouras stood up after the toasts were exchanged and launched into a speech describing how his life demonstrated the virtues of the capitalist system. "I was poor boy from Greece," he said. "I came to America with nothing. Now I am head of Twentieth Century Fox." Khrushchev listened to the translation, stood up, and replied. "I was poor boy from Caucasus. I came to Moscow with nothing. Now I am Premier of Soviet Socialist Republic."

September 20. Full-scale debate today over how to proceed with the house when I run out of money. We finally decided it's best to shut down, at least for the time being. This was a crushing decision for me to accept, but I see no way out of it. I don't dare, for any consideration, get into hock too deeply.

September 21. More finance talk today. The thought now is merely to slow down on the house, till I have a little more dough so the cement contractor can proceed with the terracing. In the meantime, the terrazzo will be finished (one wing is now polished and looks great) and the cabinet work will go on. Citron is still very confident the riches of the world will fall on me this autumn.

September 23. A long, long session this afternoon with the Adoption Institute counselor weighing our potential as adoptive parents. Personally, I'm convinced we'd be great. This is important to us and to Fraser as well. We all look forward to the idea with great anticipation. It also looks now as though the house can be completed with no further slowdowns. A good omen.

September 25. We seem to be emerging from the most immediate of our financial troubles: The loan was successfully negotiated on the house (the first mortgage it's had, actually). At the meeting to get the best advice possible, Paul Ziffren gave us pause on the wisdom of the WRECK OF THE MARY DEARE loan-out. This may have to be torn down and reconstructed in some way. Somehow I feel the whole thing will be on a sounder basis now.

It was about this time that the stewardship of my legal affairs, previously untended, was taken over by Paul Ziffren, his brothers Leo and Lester, and more recently his son, Ken. I couldn't be in better hands.

October 5. I'm still idling in a backwater of no-part-to-play, but the fall looks more exciting. MGM now wants us to go to London for the premiere there in December. It appears we won't be here much of the last two months of the year; I won't, at least, so the slowdown in Coldwater isn't so depressing. Lydia is impressed by the Vanguard tapes, which still seem superior to me. On second hearing, I found more things I'd do differently, but the whole is still damned good, I think.

October 8, MGM: Screen BEN-HUR. I don't see how I could be surer, seeing a film I'd made, that it's good work. BEN-HUR certainly seemed good at the MGM screening tonight. My best frame of reference is my initial enthusiasm for TEN COMMANDMENTS and this seems better. It's surely worth all the aching effort and painful months. This one should do it; this one should surely do it.

October 9. Most of the day was colored by the savor of last night's screening, like the aftertaste of fine brandy. I visited Coldwater this afternoon and was delighted to find the upper pool terrace poured and Fray's bath tiled. If we had nothing to take us away this fall and unlimited resources, I think we'd be in by December. As it is, it's hard to tell. But it'll be a fine autumn for us, anyway. The ball tonight was the usual duty chore, enlivened by Peggy Lee being locked in her dressing room backstage. I broke her out.

October 13. The interview with Joe Hyams was successful, but it's still hard for me to strike the right note with him. My prime fault in interviews is a tendency to go *on* too long, and too seriously.

October 19. Major event of the day was a conference re the eternal tax problems. It now seems we'll end up with three corporations. I trust all will be well, but it's staggering to contemplate the commercial complexity of my career, suddenly. Lydia finally turned down the film offered her.

Actually, she did accept the picture, but was fretting when she found the location would prevent her from attending the royal premiere of BEN-HUR *in London. "Look, honey," her agent said, "you've got to decide whether you want to act or go to Chuck's premieres." "All right, then," my girl replied, "I'll go to Chuck's premieres." I realize this is an unfashionable story now, but I've always felt complimented by it.*

October 21. Sol Siegel reiterated MGM's powerless position in getting Fry screen credit for BEN-HUR, but Willy was most warm at lunch, said I couldn't miss an Oscar nomination. Jack Warner's now ready to settle the DARBY'S RANGERS suit, after all this time.

October 22. Finally ran THE WRECK OF THE MARY DEARE, which will be released in November, right under the guns of BEN-HUR. We had a screening for twenty-odd, ranging from young Joe Field through Willy Wyler. He had many reservations, but seemed to like what I'd done. Almost everyone else was very high, which surprised me a little, because I felt the film drags a bit. Technically it's very well made; the camera, etc., is excellent. I like myself, I like Coop, but I don't think it's a fine film.

October 23. A crowded day, tying up loose ends. I was surprised to find myself honorary mayor of Hollywood. I question the function of this office, but I'll operate on Jefferson's principle: "The best government is the least government."

October 26, New York. The damn jet arrived at dawn, of course, depriving me of most of the airborne sleep I usually get. Oh, for the days of piston planes. It was a very full day rehearsing two sketches for Sid Caesar's TV show. One on the Japanese movie should be very good, the other, a satire on a courtroom TV show, is less so. Caesar is still fantastic to work with.

November 2. The day was thick with rehearsal, show, and departure (someday I must do a show and *not* leave the same night). I think the show went well, though I must look to be sure. The courtroom sketch, which seemed weak in first reading, improved greatly through drastic revision, turned out OK. It got good laughs throughout. The Japanese movie skit went better; I feel that may be the hit of the show.

Caesar's ninety-minute program, done live every week and in large part improvised, may have been one of the funniest programs ever aired. Small wonder: his writers included Mel Brooks, Neil Simon, and Carl Reiner.

November 3, Boston. Damn plane cancellations and whipping across New York in the middle of the night delayed my Boston arrival till dawn. The sky was reddening over the Common as I drew the blinds and went to bed. I canceled the morning interviews to get even on my sleep. The day wasn't bad, though curtailed and crowded. No time to prepare my lecture at Boston University; I faked it adequately. The show tonight was not much; I thought the little off-Broadway thing I saw Sunday was far better.

That shows how much I knew. The show was THE SOUND OF MUSIC. What the "little off-Broadway thing" was I can't remember.

November 7, St. Helen, Michigan. Thomas Wolfe wasn't entirely right. You can go home again. North of Sterling, the pines still turn black against the winter sky in a way I've seen only in St. Helen. Standing on the shores of Russell Lake, I find a welcome, somehow, in the bleak water, leaden under the scatter of snow. I can remember the way my son felt in my arms, when he was two, and snow fell on his face beside the same lake. I can remember snow falling on my face, not much older.

November 10, Philadelphia. Philadelphia is a town full of memories and promises for any actor. I long for Lydia, now en route to Detroit. I can't remember an absence so hard, or are they always this way? I'm counting the days till a lusty bedding Friday, anyway. Bobby Fryer's show, SARATOGA, tonight was sumptuous physically, with two or three low spots, but probably it will pick up in time for New York City. He still wants me to do ADVISE AND CONSENT on Broadway.

Though he'd given me most of my early parts in live television in New York, I never did a play for Bobby on Broadway. Since he's become managing director at the Ahmanson, in Los Angeles' Music Center, I've done three. The decentralization of the American theater in the last twenty years is one of the most important developments since sound came to movies. Now you can do a play in this country, and have it count, without having to do it on Broadway.

November 12, New York. A leisurely breakfast interview, then off to Temple University to explain to the drama students why they shouldn't take up the trade.

I always take this gloomy position when speaking to drama classes, though my wife insists it makes me sound condescending. The plain fact is, acting is a terribly hard way to make a living.

November 16. The day wasn't really hard. With Willy in town, some of the public relations pressure's off me. I've covered the waterfront pretty well, anyway. My interview with the sports press on charioteering was interrupted by the distinguished critic for the *Herald Tribune*, hungry for liquor. Petronius, the arbiter of taste.

November 18, 8:00 P.M.—BEN-HUR premier. BEN-HUR opened in a beautifully refurbished State Theater, and seemed as good on second viewing as it had at first. I liked Lydia's comment: "With his film I don't care what the others think." Actually, they think very well. Crowther wrote a great notice, others ranging down to fair, but most are raves. For the record, I still think this is my best film work.

November 23. The end of a complicated, though not very constructive day left me bushed. I had offers in two media with the same director: Olivier. He's slated to direct a film on Charlemagne and, on Broadway, THE TUMBLER, the Benn Levy play Alfred De Liagre wants me for.

November 24, Los Angeles. The Los Angeles premiere of BEN-HUR was a benefit for the University of Southern California, but it still played very well. Everyone had fine things to say, though I got only one great personal notice here.

These were the days when major films played first-run engagements on a reserved seat basis, starting with lavish premieres. The premieres were often undertaken as benefits for major charities, who resold the tickets at inflated prices to their patrons. There is nothing more formidable than a benefit audience. A man who's paid a hundred and fifty dollars to see a movie to support his wife's favorite charity can be very surly about it.

November 30. Before I left for Dallas, I had to decide whether to accept Olivier's offer to do THE TUMBLER or the Monroe film at Fox. I don't know if a verse play can run, but I have to go with Olivier. I hate to think of not moving into that beautiful house to live with my beautiful family, but I can't let this chance pass.

Eventually Yves Montand did the Monroe film. I never saw it, but it could hardly have been a greater failure than THE TUMBLER Nevertheless, I'd make the same choice again.

December 1, Dallas. The day was too heavily scheduled, but I worked my way through it without dropping many interviews. De Liagre phoned from New York, willing to limit my TUMBLER engagement to four months, if he can get the theater deal. Tonight I saw the most beautiful theater that ever cradled an actor's dream [*Paul Baker's Theater, designed by Frank Lloyd Wright*]. I can hardly believe the theater I came down to raise funds for actually stands there, a monument to Wright and the American stage. I'd love to play there, but I hardly have the time to play New York.

December 4, Miami. Got an offer I can't accept to do a film [THE GRASS IS GREENER] with Cary Grant in London. Flattering, but frustrating, like finding a naked girl hiding in your room.

I never got to work with Grant either, to my sorrow. Not only because I admire him immensely, but because he always did those films where you stand around in beautiful clothes, saying beautiful things to beautiful women. It's always seemed like a fine way to make a living. Of course, the trick is being able to do it the way Grant did.

December 9, London. The delayed departure from New York gave me time to get some checks signed and sent off, and Fray time to wake up in Chicago so we could call him before Lydia and I took off. The flight was sybaritic, a surfeit of champagne, plus an Ian Fleming novel (right for a transatlantic flight?). Claridge's isn't the Dorchester; the suite's like early Noel Coward. It makes me feel as though I'm in DESIGN FOR LIVING . . . but we're in London.

December 10. A little tough starting a full public relations schedule at breakfast when you're still on New York time. I got through it, set up lunch with Olivier, then launched a TV schedule that took the whole afternoon. As always, there is endless overpreparation for the really brief interviews I've found typical of British TV. I managed to pick up my shoes from Maxwell's, filling me with good feeling. (The main value of custom shoes?)

December 12. Lunch at the Garrick Club, where I last went with Godfrey Tearle, on our first trip here, in '52. Still the same warm mélange of stage tradition we lack utterly, and thus maybe value more than they do here. Benn Levy is a delightful, bearded man, perfectly cast as a poet-playwright. We agreed his play is good. Lydia and I felt the same tonight of IRMA LA DOUCE . . . except that Clyde Revell sings worse than I do. [*No, he doesn't. Nobody sings worse than I do.*]

December 14. Today I lunched with Larry, which I've not yet been able to call him, of course (like Bob Mulligan, directing him: "Do I *have* to call you Larry?"). He had much to say about the play and its problems, which are several. I'm still convinced I'll learn from this, however it turns out. Over a long dinner with Willy tonight, he expressed the same confidence.

December 16, Premiere BEN-HUR, Empire Theatre. The London opening, as well as the London reviews, surpassed anything in New York or Los Angeles. The reviews were not only raves, from the *Times* through the *Mirror*, but included really extravagant personal notices for me. The premiere tonight was very gala indeed, with an appropriate sprinkling of royals. Willy gave a champagne party afterward; we were all floating on a high tide.

December 17. A leaving-London day; one last tape interview, order shirts from Sulka, shopping, much dictating of letters and sorting of clippings while Lydia packed for home. It seems the Bel Air brush fire didn't damage our house much; it won't delay moving. We caught the plane in good order; Art Buchwald very thoughtfully delivered the blue bunny he'd promised Fray as we went out the door. The trip was smooth, the food not up to snuff, but the chance traveling company of Leo Genn made up for it.

December 20, Chicago. Got a call from some wild man on the Coast who wants me to *direct* a film on Christ. Must check Willy, to see if he wants to play the lead. I'll at least read it. When anyone talks, even through his hat, in seven digits, it bears reading.

December 25. It seems to come around oftener than when I was ten, but it's still a day to remember. Too many gifts, too much food, too little Christmas observance, and too little hope in a menaced world, but there are few moments in anyone's year to compare with watching the light in your child's eye when he first sees *the tree*. It's my first Christmas in this house since I went overseas in the war.

December 29, Los Angeles. All morning I felt dazed with our luck that the fire missed our house almost entirely while burning down half of Bel Air. This afternoon I got a little unlucky. Hedda doesn't love me anymore. I spent the evening talking to more newsmen than should care about it. I'll survive without too many bruises, though certainly low on Hedda's list for life.

This seems even more trivial now than when I wrote about it. The formidable power wielded by gossip columnists in the thirties and forties had really evaporated by this time, but a lot of them didn't realize this. Hedda's chagrin at my refusal to do a TV show with her exploded into what she obviously felt was a major vendetta, Ed Sullivan on my side, Hedda on hers. A decade earlier, it would've rocked the newspapers for as long as they wanted to go on writing about it. As it was, it was a two-day wonder and not worth that.

December 30. L'affaire Hopper is growing into a major item, but Bill Blowitz thinks it's all really working out OK. I spent some time on a letter to her. Really, it's a silly thing to waste time over.

December 31. This year may have done it. BEN-HUR turned out to be all we hoped for and my work in it nearly that. I think I'm a better actor now; I know I'm a happier man. The house is all but finished; I know we'll thrive there. As for the play, I can't tell. It might make me the more-than-good actor I need to be. We'll find out.

1960

The Tumbler on Broadway (directed by Olivier) is a bust . . .

the Oscar for *Ben-Hur* . . .

an Oriental junket . . .

to Spain for *El Cid.*

As the Cid
SAMUEL BRONSTON PRODUCTIONS

January 2, Los Angeles. Usual morning tennis, then up to the house, which now looks more like home than the apartment does.This is not just an emotional shift of allegiance, either . . . the apartment's a shambles of boxes and naked parquet; it looks obscene. The house won't be ready, but we'll have to move in now, before I leave for New York to do THE TUMBLER. At this point I'm regretting the whole play project, a mood that had better pass before rehearsals begin.

January 4. Well, we made it at last. Tonight we slept under our own roof on the ridge where I stood dreaming over two years ago. The move was incredibly difficult, complicated by lack of experience and lack of time. The vans didn't arrive at the house to unload our furniture till well past dark, and the move-in was complicated by the unfinished repair of the fire damage . . . carpet not all down, etc. The Fields, Baurs, and Stines brought champagne and bread, though, and we kindled our hearth appropriately.

January 6. I hardly got to see Fray all day, and when I did, he was unconscious. His tonsil operation went well. I feel very guilty though, that I missed being there before supper, the only time he was awake and calling for me. What am I doing, going off to do a play when my house and my son, not to mention my wife, need me here? I doubt if I can be both a family man and a totally dedicated artist. I'd rather be the former.

January 7, Los Angeles/New York. I somehow managed to get my son home, wan, heartbreakingly subdued, but doing well. ("I'm so weak . . . you might as well throw me out . . . I wouldn't care.") I got him installed in his just-carpeted bedroom, an interim TV set up, had a breakneck series of meetings, packed, showered in my just-finished shower, and planed for New York City. Olivier came over to the apartment and we read four fifths of the play. He says I must be straighter. "Don't try for color . . . don't try to be liked." We had a late steak at Danny's, and I wired some flowers to Fray.

January 8. We began with a reading in Olivier's suite at the Algonquin. It's remarkable how right a part seems for you when you first read a script and how hard it becomes when a good director sets a mark you must hit. Larry's not yet opened with Levy the delicate question of necessary cuts. They'll help, but the acting problem is still a huge one. I must not worry about making Kell likable, because *he* doesn't worry about this: the disinvolved alienated man. I stepped on the stage of the Helen Hayes Theater today with a lovely feeling of self-realization, to *be* there again.

January 9. This wasn't much of a working day, though Levy did prove amenable on some cuts. I tried to curb my eager tongue, in deference to Olivier, but I feel the part still needs deep cutting. Kell mustn't run *on* so! The trick is to strike the thin line between poetry and rhetoric . . . with a character like Kell, it's particularly important because of the laconic nature of the man. Slowly does it.

January 11. Long steadily slogging day of work today; to my surprise it was the pleasantest blocking session I can recall. Olivier uses a model of the set, moving little dolls while he reads the text with the actors watching. It goes much faster than standing around for hours bumping into each other. We even got to run the act through twice. Olivier's main comment today: "Don't read for poetry . . . keep it clean and unadorned." I'm beginning to understand the importance of this.

January 13. The last act was blocked by lunch and we managed a stumbling sort of run-through for Benn in the afternoon. This play is really hard to bring off; I have no idea if it'll satisfy anything except my urge to be directed by Olivier.

January 14. Plunged with both feet into the first act today. Very hard for me to achieve the edge note of arrogant "fuck you" quality Olivier says is central to Kell. He's right, but it's tough not to blur it. I'm learning something about playing humor. Olivier insists, "Kell never tries to make anyone else see the joke, indeed, he's better pleased if they don't; then he has *two* jokes."

January 16. Short work day today. Olivier feels little can be done till the actors have the lines solidly. I agree, since I have mine. We had a pleasant lunch, talking mostly about Shakespeare. I even broached, with warm response, the idea of supporting him in something, somewhere, sometime. Let's solve this one first, though. I somehow can't believe this will work commercially, but I could be wrong.

January 20. A good long session in Act Three today. I feel more at home in this one than the other acts, though the suicide is still an enigma to me. I still don't feel the surge of confidence you need for any part. Olivier's helping immensely, but he hasn't yet dug into my guts, where the performance I hope for has to be. At Arnold Weissberger's party after rehearsal, I met Igor Stravinsky, who said he admired me vastly in BEN-HUR, to my pleasure.

January 21. Run-through this morning revealed the immense distance still to be traveled for Act One. I must somehow get at Olivier, or get him to get at me. He must *not* be satisfied with competence. If I'm ever to reach anything special creatively, it surely must happen with this part, this director.

*That was asking a great deal, even of Olivier. THE TUMBLER was a
very difficult piece in blank verse about an embittered English
farmer with a harridan wife, who is first enchanted and then
driven to suicide by a wandering girl, who was beautifully played
by Rosemary Harris. Whether anyone could have made the farmer
interesting, I don't know. Conceivably Olivier himself might have,
ten years earlier.*

January 22. Work on the two acts was crammed with detail, but lacking
in inspiration from my quarter. Everything Olivier says adds a touch,
and he's unfailingly good-humored and light about it, but the sad fact
is I'm not measuring up to my standard, thus can hardly be reaching
his. I'm rapidly reaching the conclusion this part requires a great
performance.

*They all don't, you know. There are parts so good they will of
themselves sustain almost any performance. Hamlet is probably
the outstanding example of this. The role is so fascinating, I've
seen schoolboys carry it very well.*

January 31. As Olivier predicted, the run-through with the small audience
of a dozen or so people sitting out there set us back several steps. I
tensed and swaggered with my voice back in my throat. I'm glad to
have this behind us before we leave town, though. The first audience
you play to, no matter how small, shifts your focus to the wrong side
of the proscenium. Lydia was supportive, both of the play and me.

February 1, Boston. MCA called today with an offer I probably won't
accept . . . I can't direct films . . . but still, the fee offered was two
million dollars. That's surely one for the bloody books. Boston is truly
the town for tryouts; the trains going up, full of actors, are among
the few places where the glamour and fabled fun of theater ring true.
How many actors have sat before me in this same bedroom, looking
out on the Common, weighing the chances of how many shows? The
Shubert's even shabbier than I remember, but Roger [*Furse's*] barn
set is excellent. I certainly didn't play with any particular grace, but
we ran both acts twice, including the technical bits.

February 2. I managed a good interview with Elliot Norton, my old
nemesis. I'm in favor of meeting critics face-to-face . . . they're
convinced actors are idiot children, so it's easy to rise in their
estimate by talking in complete sentences. Later I went to the
theater and finally learned to make a proper hangman's noose. I'll
chance the throw over the beam tonight, though it'll be a difficult ad
lib if I miss.

*I've acquired all kinds of highly specialized skills in the pursuit of
my profession; tying a hangman's noose is one I hope I never have*

to use again. (I didn't have to actually use it in THE TUMBLER, *just tie it and throw it over a beam before the curtain fell.)*

February 4, Boston opening: THE TUMBLER. It went fairly well, not marvelously. I was effective often, good now and then, very good once or twice, great never. I was also tense, fighting the play and the whim-whams. All this by my standards; public reaction on the whole was good. Lydia was lovely in a new silk suit, all happy at the party afterward. The critics split: Norton very good, Hughes bad, but we could've done worse for Boston, God knows.

February 5. Rehearsal didn't amount to much . . . for one thing, we can't use the stage for rehearsals without a full crew (!). Olivier gave few notes, apparently not anxious to start tearing things down before we get settled a little. He helped that greatly with vast quantities of champagne and lobster after rehearsal. I steamed all this out at the Town Club, then back to a lonely sleep (Lydia's off for New York), a light supper, and a much better performance tonight. By much better, I mean much *surer.*

February 7. The morning featured a long talk on acting, mainly mine, with Olivier. It's hard to pin down any truth about so intangible an art, but I remember one thing he said: "Star acting is really a question of hypnosis: of yourself and the audience." I'm now the age he was when he played Oedipus. I doubt if I can quite catch up, but I'm running. So is the play, if we can get the new opening Benn wrote into it, after cutting the rest more deeply than he will like.

February 8. We rehearsed the new opening, tightened other things. I never played Act One worse, nor Act Two better. This part's terribly hard to get hold of, somehow. I fight it all the time, trying to get in the saddle. I've never felt such an overwhelming sense of the *difficulty* of acting. Maybe this is always true, past a certain point. Who said it was supposed to be easy?

February 10. Houses are running on the small side, but very attentive. The matinee today consisted largely of movie fans, of course, but they listened. Tonight Olivier broached the startling news that De Liagre is anxious to replace Hermione Baddeley with Jo Van Fleet. Olivier's against this, dubious about the whole idea of replacement. God knows it would be difficult. She's not right as my shrewish wife, it's true. Her comic image colors all she does in the part.

February 12. Fray's birthday morning was interrupted by a distress call from Olivier's suite, where I spent the next four hours in an anguished effort to recast Nina. Prime choices are Judith Evelyn and Martha Scott, who seems best, but it turns out she's pregnant. After much soul-searching, Olivier decided she's *still* best, pregnant or not. She came up from New York tonight to see the show. A long, long conference afterward thrashing around about the whole thing. There's no other choice, really.

February 13. Not to bed till four in the morning, discussing the problems of replacing Hermione. For me, the main one is that Olivier has to concentrate totally now on Martha and leave me to my own resources. I guess this is where I carry the can. Martha will be better, much more plausible as my wife than sweet, funny Hermione. Thank God, Olivier had to tell her, I only had to tell Rosemary on stage, after the curtain call. Even that was sticky.

February 16. Toti's still playing till Martha's ready, which is brave of her. Martha felt uneasy rehearsing with the principals before she had the lines, so I found myself, shockingly, with the afternoon off. I played some terrible tennis, tense and angry, finally straining my damn back again.

February 17. Twinge in my back still stabbed a bit, pulling both performances off. Still, at two in the morning and slightly Scotched, but firm and clear, Laurence Olivier said, "I'm sure you can be a great actor . . . the only one in America in my time." Well.

February 18. A long, grueling session running Martha through her part four times today. She went in tonight with many misgivings, but better prepared for it than she knew, I think. The play picks up from her new chemistry in the role. There's no question the change was wise. I wish it could've been made sooner; now we're under the gun.

February 20. This morning we took out the new ending to Act Two (manufactured to make a curtain) and replaced part of a new opening we dropped four days ago. Now I have part of the long speech back; it seems to help me get off the ground with the scene. Tonight was the best performance the play's ever had. Elliot Norton came back and agreed with this estimate. I caught the midnight train south with Olivier and sat drinking late and convivially. He reiterated his estimate of my potential: "The theater hasn't had a heroic actor in America in my lifetime . . ."

February 22, New York. With great problems getting the sets on the Hayes stage, no full rehearsal was possible. Besides, Rosie has a cold, so we only ran Act Two on the set, late at night, with the understudy. Bill Blowitz phoned the news I was Oscar-nominated for BEN-HUR. That's damn nice, but it's hard to believe I could actually win it. At least Fray let me win the race to the elevator tonight. Surely that's prize enough. But fame is a food you're always hungry for, isn't it?

February 24. My first opening on the Street in ten years, the play hanging now from my shoulders "like a cloak" in Olivier's compendious phrase. I felt it played well, considering the pressure. I've never yet made the opening fly, though. This play's like an overloaded bomber, straining down the runway. I can't lift it.

February 25. The first word came at Sardi's, while the party was still in full swing. Atkinson thought it was awful. The other notices were kept out, though the party dampened visibly anyway, as the knowledge of failure seeped like ink through the throng of happy drinkers. I spent the rest of the day lounging around the apartment, reading the notices . . . all but two bad. I was treated OK personally, but the play wasn't. De Liagre put up the closing notice tonight; we all bore up, as actors do. I got the only profit from it: what I learned from Larry.

February 27. The day was colored flat gray, for failure. Even when a show hits, it closes sadly. For a flop, you creep out of the theater like thieves. We played the last one well, I thought, at least nearly as well as this play will go. I still didn't get the first scene right. We had a good wake here at the apartment afterward.

Again, I don't know if THE TUMBLER could've been made to work. Certainly Olivier made an enormous effort with it. He was heavily burdened at the time with the disintegrating fragments of his marriage to Vivien Leigh, and the necessity of recasting Hermione Baddeley's role in Boston put an added burden on us. A play is always a gamble. Maybe the dice were loaded a little against us in this one.

March 7. The Screen Actors Guild began the first strike in its history against all major studios today, which may mean no films will be shot for some time. Arnold Weissberger raised an interesting proposition tonight at dinner: do ANDERSONVILLE on stage in Los Angeles. If the strike runs on, this may prove a good idea.

March 9. Fairly full day of interviews, plans for trips to Washington and Japan, but the high point was five sets of doubles with Don Budge. It was an odd feeling standing across the net from a tennis legend. He was generous about it all and I played as well as I could, most of the time.

March 17, Los Angeles. Not the first wedding anniversary we've spent traveling, nor even the first in a plane, but in some respects the least festive. That's no doubt because we're trying hard to save money. We got the best present we could've had, though: the look of our house, after two months of weary, demanding wanderings. So I'm home, damn near broke, but richer than I left.

March 18. God, it was blissful, just to wake up here and savor the sound
and look of this place. I accomplished nothing all day long, just
wandered around my ridge. Jim Bacon made an easy and friendly
listener when he dropped in for the twenty-five-cent tour and
interview. He claims he's picked me for the Oscar. I don't know
whether this is a good or bad omen, but it's good for the ego.

March 21. Spent the morning sunning and experimenting with my steam
room (very difficult art, owning a steam room); also brooding over the
paucity of scripts (not surprising, in view of the continuing strike).
That seems stalled, as my first meeting as a member of the SAG
Board tonight revealed. Meantime, I can only plan still more foreign
openings of BEN-HUR and luxuriate in our lovely, unpaid-for house. We
decided to leave Fray behind when we go to Japan this Friday. As he
said, "I'm so *eager* to get back to my school!"

March 25, Los Angeles/Olympia, Washington. Our departure was flawed
only by Fray's stricken reaction at not riding to the airport with us.
Unable to bear his grief-strong arms around my neck, I gave in,
whereupon the tears shut off like a faucet, and he rode out, happy as
a clam. We damn near missed the plane fighting the rush-hour traffic
and a stubborn driver clinging to the wrong route out, but we made
it, to the public relations man's palefaced relief. We arrived in Seattle
in time for the usual press reception, then comfortably enough to bed
in Olympia. A far cry from my last visit here, overseas-bound, in
World War II.

March 26, En route to Japan. En route east, we were soothed and
swaddled by kimonoed hostesses who make an entrance from a
DC7C galley with a tray of hot towels and look like the beginning of
a Kabuki drama. Anchorage airport is not the one mapped in my
memory, but to be in Alaska again still shrouded me in the
melancholy of a twenty-year-old at war and far from home. The city
looks very modern; I have the feeling I'm beginning to look less so.

March 28, Tokyo. We arrived in Tokyo to find Sunday had disappeared
over the Pacific. We're supposed to get it back at the end of the
week, going home, but what good will it be to me then? The doors are
too low in the Imperial, but Wright's thirty-five-year-old hotel still is
an incredible piece of work. One of the few architectural values I've
seen so far, in fact. The city is largely a crowded jumble of small
drab buildings, enlivened by myriad signs in beautiful black and red
characters. (Who was it who said the neon signs in Times Square
would make a wonderland of beauty for a man who couldn't read?)
The restaurants are fabulous, however, the people wonderfully
friendly.

March 30, Tokyo. 6:30 P.M.—opening BEN-HUR at Tokyo Theater,
attended by the Emperor. 8:30 P.M.—Audience with emperor
during intermission. Day began shockingly with Russ's voice, reedy
and twittering on the transpacific phone. Lydia's mother has had a
heart attack. Lydia took it well, even slept, and the day went off as
planned, once arrangements had been made for her to fly home
tonight. She came to the premiere, which was properly imperial,
except for three film breaks, due to the overwrought projectionists
quivering at the physical presence of the God-emperor in the theater.
I got Lydia airborne safely by midnight, standing on the night-
breezed observation platform, watching her into the belly of the 707.

April 1. The trip to Osaka was bumpy and very late, putting me into a
fairly foul mood, but the crippled children's cheery welcome utterly
washed this away. I accomplished little else. Japanese newspapermen
are reluctant to ask any but the most routine questions, making it
very difficult to do interviews, especially bilingually, but the trip was
worth it just to hear the kids. Back in Tokyo, I went to a full-drill
geisha dinner hosted by Toshiro Mifune. My God, what a presence. If
he could act in English, he'd conquer the world.

April 2, Over the Pacific. The last day in Japan was crammed with all I'd
missed so far, as well as everything I've *not* missed so far. I've never
seen so many photographers fighting for shots, nor so many fans
asking for autographs. The Kabuki Theater was fine; one of the highs
of the whole trip. I finished my chores and was sent off loaded with
gifts of all sorts, for all sorts of people. I was happy to fall into my
berth on the JAL flight for home, though. I get another April 2
tomorrow.

April 2, Los Angeles. The house was chaotic and full of relatives, all
relieved that Lydia's mother seems past her crisis. She looked not bad
at the hospital this evening. We also had a small fire in the steam
room and a drift in the Academy odds slightly in my favor. This kind
of thing can get ridiculous.

April 4, Academy Awards. I made it. Looking across the orchestra, just
before Susan [*Hayward*] read it off, something popped in my head.
"I'm going to get it." And I did. I kissed Lydia and walked to the
stage dripping wet, except for a pepper-dry mouth: classic stage
fright. I'll never forget the moment, or the night, for that matter.
Backstage, posing beside Willy with his third Oscar, I said, "I guess
this is old hat to you." "Chuck," he said, "it never gets old hat!"

April 5. Celebrating an Academy win is an all-night job. We went to the
hospital, to show the Oscar to Lydia's mother, then did the ball at the
Hilton. We stopped by the Fields', where the Baurs and Blowitzes

were assembled. It got very wet there, then on to the Seltzers, where we saw the night out. Still cold sober, daisy-fresh, I came home to sit on our patio steps with Lydia reading the victory headlines in the paper by the light of the rising sun. The day was a fabulous round of phone calls and wires pouring in. It gets kind of frantic, but I wouldn't miss it; I wouldn't miss a minute of it. Oscar looks smug, imperturbable on my desk.

April 7. A hell of a day. Just when I finally had the details of the house mortgage squared away, I had a call from the SAG asking me to join the negotiating committee to wind up the strike. Flattered to be asked, interested to think I could help, I canceled my TV rehearsal and went over. We sat there all day, arguing, caucusing, confronting grimly across long tables. I think we may be close to a deal, at that.

April 8. I shoehorned a Christmas seal film appeal (the only filming in town not struck) into a schedule of TV rehearsals and strike negotiations that already provided ample occupation for an April day. By three in the afternoon, we reached agreement with the studios, ending the strike. The contract's good, and fair; I'm proud to've helped get it.

April 13. I turned Oscar back to the Academy for engraving on the way out to Republic Studios to pick up a toy *Rifleman* gun from Chuck Connors for Fray. Another negotiating session all afternoon, still fighting over pension-plan clauses in the SAG contract. I was struck again with the dichotomy of my feelings, dealing with the men I usually work for. The familiar relationship is actor-to-businessman. This is very strange.

April 15. Most of the day was spent polishing my reply to a ridiculous letter from the Writers Guild because I thanked Christopher Fry in my Academy acceptance speech. I did fit in a lunch interview at the Brown Derby on the SAG contract. Hedda, at the next table, delivered a masterfully freezing "hello" to my greeting. I sent off the letter, plus copies to several newspaper friends, then fought my way through the bulk of Oscar thank-you letters, leaving only maybe a hundred to do.

April 19. Our first sit-down dinner party in the house tonight went off well. Willy was delighted at the press reaction to the Writers Guild letter to me, plus my reply. This is rapidly becoming an entertaining controversy.

The Writers Guild really wasn't angry at me just for saying "Thank you, Christopher Fry" in the course of my Academy thank you. They were annoyed that the membership perceived their refusal to give Fry screen credit on BEN-HUR *as unfair and registered their rebuke to the Writers Guild in their vote.* BEN-HUR *won eleven awards out of twelve nominations, a record unlikely to be broken. The only award it did not win was for Best Screenplay. The nominated writer was Karl Tunberg.*

April 21. I was finally installed as honorary mayor of Hollywood at a large lunch; much ceremony, and a weighty chain of office. Once again, I faked a better-than-so-so speech, ad-libbed during dessert. This is a very tempting method of handling speaking engagements, but as dangerous as Russian roulette. Someday I'll fall right on my ass.

April 24. It was clear and windy up here on the ridge today, though the smog still lay like dirty laundry down in Hollywood. I hate to contemplate the weeks I'll be gone from here, but after Australia, it looks more and more as though Orson's film of JULIUS CAESAR will work out, in England. God knows Brutus is a part I should play, but I hate to leave here for so long.

April 30, New York. Lydia never phones me during work except in crisis. When her call came during the Ed Sullivan TV rehearsal, I knew what it must be: Her mother died this morning. It's hard to accept, with her gradual improvement through the past weeks. Lydia seems to be taking it with some composure, though it was hard to tell on the phone. Now they won't fly with me to Australia Monday, though I hope I can persuade them to join me there later. They'll have to come to London if we do JULIUS CAESAR, since Lydia's to play Portia.

May 2, Los Angeles. I borrowed an MGM secretary and got out an awesome number of letters and whatnot this morning; taped down details of our stay in London, for one thing. They're still trying to get us a hotel suite. I couldn't talk to Lydia today; she's en route east on the train for her mother's funeral, but I sent flowers to meet her in Chicago. I must have flown over her as I started west on the long flight Down Under.

May 3, En route to Australia. This seems to be a day I'll go to my grave without. I lost it crossing the International Date Line; continuing west as we are, I'll never get it back. I have no great feeling for Tuesday, May 3, but I hate to give it up without a struggle.

May 8, Sydney, Australia. The biggest significance of Mother's Day for me was the welcome arrival of my family, a bit bedraggled, but here at last. Both of them spent the day sleeping, though I managed to get Littleboy wakened long enough to take him to Taronga Zoo, where he fed a gorilla, petted kangaroos, held a koala, and played with a lion cub, by and large making all available animal contacts.

May 11, Melbourne. The predictable (I suppose) Wellesian chaos exploded today. Orson phoned from London to announce CBS had somehow screwed up and failed to reserve the necessary studio space (they claim); thus it's impossible to do JULIUS CAESAR now. A later cable from Orson said a new deal's being made elsewhere, but I can't see how this will work.

> *Aside from the traumas of the JULIUS CAESAR crisis, what this reminds me of most clearly is the peculiarity of Orson's telephone phobia. If you're in the same town, you can't get him to answer the phone if your house is on fire. Should a continent separate you, he may very well call. If you're ten thousand miles apart, he's in your ear day and night.*

May 12, Sydney. It's a pleasure to be back out of the dank drafts of Melbourne to the autumn crispness of Sydney. The day was peppered with cables from all quarters; Orson is increasingly impassioned in his insistence I come at once to London, which is now impossible, since there's no plane space. Citron's increasingly suspicious of the whole thing. I'm in the dark on the facts, since I'm dealing by cable and transoceanic phone. It doesn't make for a full briefing. I think we'd better go to Honolulu tomorrow.

May 16, Honolulu. The day was punctuated by cables from Orson, Citron, etc., outlining the increasing brouhaha bubbling up around JULIUS CAESAR. Orson inevitably works in an atmosphere of mystery, improvisation, and contradiction that's very hard on everyone but (apparently) him. It begins to look unlikely that we'll make JULIUS CAESAR at all.

May 18, Los Angeles. We're home on our ridge. The breeze is cool, the pool and steam room warm, the sun bright, though the valley below is wreathed in smog. So is the JULIUS CAESAR situation. CBS is paying off; there's a possibility we'll do it later. Meantime, several movie scripts to read, almost every one son-of-Hur. Tsk . . .

May 23. Other than sun and fun in the new house, the days still revolve around the hassle in London on whether or not JULIUS CAESAR will go. Orson sends off daily cables of anguish, each implying that I have somehow left him flat. Citron meantime is complying with my instructions to try and make a deal with him. All very cloudy and Byzantine. I *still* would like to play the bloody *part!* Also, the writers are now on strike, here.

June 1, En route, Honolulu. The usual chaos of leaving; a mad dash to
Paramount en route to the airport to pick up what will probably be
the last honor given to anyone for TEN COMMANDMENTS. I'd certainly
love to have a small piece of that and BEN-HUR.

*That was remarkably greedy of me. I'd already gotten something
more valuable from those pictures than money: the roles
themselves.*

June 3, Tokyo. The landing at Wake broke my sleep, but it was worth the
loss. The flat coral beach, with a corroded Grumman propeller still
bent and lonely above the tidemark, moved me inexpressibly. Our
bloody, noble past. Tokyo seems familiar now, but I had somehow
missed a Japanese bath before. Sturdy girls scrub, soak, shampoo,
and rub, all unaware of male nakedness. Toho Films gave me a
reception in honor of the Oscar.

June 4, Manila. The flight to Manila was no joke. That last lap from
Okinawa is a damn long one. We landed at last in a fine warm mist of
jungle rain, completely not affecting a larger mass of fans than I ever
recall waiting for me before. The usual assortment of local brass was
waiting to escort me to Hotel Manila, where a decent suite (the
biggest is being remodeled for Ike next week) waited, complete with
welcome Scotch, idle jokes for a half hour before an even more
welcome bed. A long way from home, Lydia, and Fray.

June 9. This was a valuable day. The navy took me to Corregidor. The
stubborn, dumb barrels of the heavy guns still rust in the jungle,
pocked with small arms fire as the defenders fell in the last bitter
days. The blind, shattered walls of the stone barracks sink, like the
memory of war, into the swallowing jungle. You can't look at these
artifacts of old bravery and not feel your heart quicken. Could we do
it still?

June 12, St. Helen. I continued on across the continent, completing the
thirteen-thousand-mile trip from Manila. No one, surely, ever went so
far to a party before. I damn near missed the plane in Chicago where
Lydia joined me, but we were there for my father's silver wedding
anniversary. Everyone seemed astounded to see us, imagining we
were still in the South Pacific. Kay [*my half-sister*], who gave the
party, was delighted. I've no idea what time it was on my inner clock
when we finally hit the sack, but I was ready for it.

June 14, Two Rivers, Wisconsin. We got into Chicago early after a
surprisingly sleepless night on the train. (This is unlike me; I guess
my entire interior time system is still somewhere out in the Pacific.)
We changed trains with time left for a workout at the Athletic Club,

only to find this was Ladies' Day in the pool. For once, I could take advantage of this: Lydia got the swim, I got a workout and steam before catching the train to Wisconsin. It's greatly changed since I rode up to meet Lydia's parents for the first time. Her family is sadly smaller now.

June 15. We had the picnic we've planned ever since I first came up here, even though rain was falling as we drove north through the Wisconsin woods. We built our fire in a fine drizzle, but it cleared to a brilliant afternoon of tumbled cumulus and sunshine as we finished eating. Fray and I explored the rock cliffs bordering the lake, busy being lost scouts and Indians in turn; God, I'd love to have him in the deep woods for a summer. Citron was on the phone with more complications in the deal with Orson. It gets harder and harder to figure this out.

June 16. I spent the day trying to put JULIUS CAESAR back together for Orson. It seems the dates for Lydia and me are now different, as well as our locations. I work in Rome, she in London. (I'm to play Antony again, not Brutus.) It may work if I can fit in a trip to the Berlin Festival to pay for the extra transportation. I'm beginning to feel a vast disenchantment for the whole project, but the parts are very tempting, for both of us. *Why* can't Orson proceed like other people?

June 17, Wilmette, Illinois. We got back to Wilmette, lush with midwestern green, in good order. Citron called with the not surprising news that Orson has disappeared for the weekend, thus making my trip east unwise in the extreme. This, coming just as I'd gotten the reservation for New York Sunday, was very irritating. I'll go back to Los Angeles Monday and stand by there for a Polar flight if the damn deal at long last works out . . . as God knows it yet may!

June 20, Los Angeles. I was delighted to sit in the audience and sweat out Olivier's Emmy, which I accepted for him. None of the pressure, almost all the pleasure. I said *almost* all. He wired me afterward: DEAR BOY HAVE JUST READ YOUR VERY BEAUTIFUL SPEECH FOR ME THANK YOU FROM MY HEART FOR YOUR GREAT KINDNESS AND GENEROSITY ALWAYS YOUR GRATEFUL FRIEND—LARRY.—

June 22. Just as I'd managed to set up my flight to London on Friday, Berlin on Saturday, and alerted the Berlin Festival, Orson cabled that he definitely can't meet his start date. I'm damned if I'm going to fly off across the Atlantic in the hope he'll have the money raised when I get there.

June 27. The Welles's Wonderful Dog and Pony Act is definitely sidelined. I'm damn glad we didn't kite off across the Atlantic from Wisconsin. I moved the plane reservation to Thursday, the last day I can profitably leave for Berlin and London. I'm still inclined slightly to go, but I hate to leave home and family now (never before realized the pleasures that cliché contained!!). Everything else professional is still drifting. This is a damn difficult spring . . . only it's summer already!

Just how firm Orson's arrangements with CBS to do JULIUS CAESAR were, I've never been able to determine. I'm sorry it didn't work out, even though I got another chance to play the part later on. Orson would've been a far more exciting director than the one I had.

June 29. I lunched with Chuck Connors, let Steve McQueen give me a ride in his new D-Jag, watched Rosewall beat Hoad, and then canceled out the Berlin trip. I decided it's bloody nonsense. I have to just sit here and sweat out the scripts until one comes along that makes sense. It's not easy to pick the right one to do after the Oscar.

July 5. A morning meeting with Citron; we decided only that it would've been wise to take the Monroe film last year. For now there seems only EL CID and O, MISTRESS MINE looming large. I don't know how either one will turn out, but I have many misgivings about both, especially the former.

I think it was Herman who decided I would've been wise to do the Marilyn Monroe film. I knew I'd been right to grab the chance to work with Olivier on THE TUMBLER. O, MISTRESS MINE was one of the Lunt's successes that probably should've been filmed. It never was. Of EL CID, more later.

July 13. I have a better excuse for my lack of productive labors this week, at least. The Democratic convention looms large here in Los Angeles. Everyone's sweet-talking the actors to come out for Kennedy or (mostly) Stevenson. I found the convention, the first I've attended, appallingly frivolous. Who was it said, "Such a spectacle must offend the thoughtful and shock the fastidious"? It was like a giant premiere party. In the end, Kennedy won on the first ballot.

July 14. Today we had a final interview qualifying us to adopt a baby girl to complete our family. It seemed simple enough to me, but Lydia was anxious.

That's just because I have a bigger ego than Lydia's. Adopting our daughter was terribly important to us both. I was positive they'd see what marvelous parents we'd be.

I met later with Joe Shaftel on his project on the assassination of Trotsky [*done ten years later with Dick Burton*]. I'm not vastly excited, but it's very close to being the only game in town just now, so I see no reason not to go through talks on it. The part is good, and Shaftel impresses me as an energetic and creative man.

July 19. The only things that went well today were my tennis and the Gary Coopers' party, where I got far more loaded than I can understand. It may have been my reaction to the still blistering heat, or the EL CID first draft. I'm bitterly disappointed; it's appallingly bad writing. I don't see how they can seriously undertake such a script, nor how I could, without whoring. I called Herman later and turned it down.

July 21. I accepted EL CID, conditional on a full new script, after turning down BY LOVE POSSESSED, which is a worse script than the current EL CID version, as is FROM THE TERRACE . . . they're going with those as they stand. Still, I have accepted a film I'm sure can't be superior, instead of sitting tight and waiting longer. I can't afford to wait longer, of course (the fruits of homesteading so elaborately). A piece of the world gross should bail me out of that problem. So I may be started down the road to whoredom . . . we'll see what comes of it. At least I go in open-eyed.

I'd forgotten how deep my misgivings were when I accepted EL CID. It's true that the first script was very stiff and clumsy. It's also true that producers are reluctant to undertake the final draft on a script until the central actor/director elements are set. I don't know the solution to this. Older and wiser now, I don't think I'm a whore. I'm just aware of the vulnerability of my virtue.

July 28. My research on EL CID is going slowly, but usefully. There's a hell of a lot more in the man than there is in the script, more than the bloodless ideal of medieval chivalry that the legend leaves us with. He seems, as I read the rather meager material the Paramount research department turned up, to have been nearly as often a bad man as a good one. Always, though, he refused to take for himself the crown he had won back for Alfonso. I wonder why? I wish I could find more material on him. For one of the outstanding men of the twelfth century, there's damn little contemporary comment.

August 7, Madrid. After a solid sleep in the largest berth I ever found on an aircraft, I awoke to find Portugal had sprung out of the sea below me, unawares. Almost at once, Spain was there, too, a broad, brown table of land tumbled with mountains older than ours. The climate, just now, is very hospitable. So are Sam Bronston and Anthony Mann.

August 8. I spent the day settling into Madrid (superficially like Rome, with less traffic) and finding out something about the people on this project. Mann is intelligent, emphatic, confident, perhaps a bit offhand.

Bronston is small, pale, pleasant-voiced, apparently very anxious for me to be happy (as they all are, for that matter). The costume sketches are excellent, and all agree the present script is not shootable. Then why *send* it?

They send the scripts because they have to get the project launched, as I've long since discovered. The conflict between art and commerce in films is unavoidable and can only rarely be solved in perfect balance. What really screws you up is to pretend it doesn't exist.

August 11, Paris. I've never gone so far for a writer. Phil Yordan's chosen an unlikely place for inspiration (or perhaps he likes the challenge to his discipline). In any case, here he is, with a remarkably good concept of the Cid. He sees him as a Job character, enduring all, finding in each fruit of victory the seed of personal defeat. Now let's see if he can write this.

This was before I knew Phil's well-earned reputation as the best storyteller in movies. Phil told a marvelous script; the trick is getting it on paper.

August 12, En route to New York. Still raining, but there was no time for any exploration of Paris anyway. The weather's been bad like this all year here . . . possibly de Gaulle repealed the sun along with the Fourth Republic? I said farewell to Mann and Yordan, leaving them to what I hope will be a productive development of the new script, and boarded the plane for New York, only just barely having finished cutting the Passion of Christ. A damn long flight, what with head winds, but it was worth waiting for . . . to get home again.

The next two and a half weeks were supposed to produce the rewrite on the EL CID script. This was an unreasonable timetable of course, but they'll promise you anything. By the time we left Los Angeles, on our way to Spain, I'd received about thirty pages of the new script . . . enough to send me on my way.

August 29, Los Angeles. The trunks were closed and tagged just as the truck rolled up to take them away. Lydia was justifiably proud of accomplishing it all, a lot more than I managed today. Joe Shaftel chatted with me for a desultory cocktail, bound by his promise not to discuss directors for the Trotsky film. What I'd really like to see is the rest of the new EL CID script. I'm beginning to have misgivings again.

September 5, New York. I slept late, but got a lot done today. I feel fine about the music for the New Testament album. I have doubts only about the closing on the first record: "What I say unto you I say unto all . . . watch!" I finally delivered Olivier's Emmy to him, only to discover they'd misspelled his name on it. I threw it back in the box in annoyance, breaking off the wing, but he insisted on keeping it. (I kept the wing.) Larry seems now a somewhat sad man; with all his triumphs, some things have gone wrong for him . . .

September 10, At sea. A remarkably smooth departure, considering last night's events.

> *Bronston's empire, a formidable factor in the film world for several years, depended on highly intricate and delicately timed financing. Herman Citron, well aware of this, bypassed these uncertainties by insisting that the whole of my salary be deposited in an American bank before we sailed from New York. When this had not happened by the time the banks closed the day before we were to embark, Herman instructed me not to sail, though most of our luggage and several cases of champagne for our bon voyage party were already on board. We had a busy evening disinviting all our friends, and then phoning them again when the money suddenly materialized as contracted.*

You can't get a good *look* at a great liner in dock, but aboard, the *Leonardo da Vinci* seems lovely. The suite is handsome, with plenty of room for us all, plus our suitcases. It was wonderfully crowded, of course, for the hour before departure, full of the sound of friends and champagne corks.

September 16, Torremolinos, Spain. I can hardly believe it's nearly two years since we sailed past Gibraltar en route home from BEN-HUR, and here we are again. The landing was delayed while a stowaway was ferreted out of the tender, while the passengers sat rocking in the swell, but the trip up the Spanish coast was worth waiting for. Mischa Waszynski and Jaime Prades [*production executives for Bronston*] made a fine welcoming committee, and the Andalusian campaña is wonderfully photogenic. We stopped for the night at a surprisingly modern, if faintly chilly, hotel.

September 17, Granada. Fray and I got in a short ocean dip before entraining our two-car troupe for Malaga, first diverting the luggage direct to Madrid by truck. The drive to Granada was a breathtaking experience of the Sierra Nevadas. We arrived just in time to see an overwhelming sunset from our balcony, not to mention Orson Welles, equally overwhelming in the lobby. After absorbing the former, we dined with the latter, his usual fascinating self, then on to the gypsy caves for a mild display of the famous gypsy abandon. Granada also had something for Fray: a chance to see again the early love of his life, Orson's daughter, Beatrice.

September 23, Florence/Rome. I must've had a lot of sleep coming to me; I caught up in Florence last night. I felt better for it, able to endure the peculiar torture of fitting fifteen eleventh-century costumes [*these were being made in Florence*], plus armor. I wish I was as confident about every aspect of the film as I am of the design. The script is still not complete, nor the casting. We came down to Rome tonight to interview an actress for Uracca. No.

The costumes for EL CID *were made most beautifully, in Florence, partly to help qualify the picture as an Italian coproduction, a tax advantage of which I was completely unaware.*

September 24, Rome/Madrid. A very full, largely fruitless day trying to fill the gaps in our casting. Sophia Loren is still an open question, so we're searching for alternatives. I saw none today. I did see a little of the Rome I remember so well. Strange; that experience was so vivid a part of my life, now bits of it will be threaded through this year. It seems we're shooting interiors here at the end of the film, at Cinecittà.

October 4, Madrid. I don't really recall being thirty-seven, but here I am. Who said that middle aged is always someone fifteen years older than you are? Seems reasonable. I can't complain about a year in which I won the Oscar, but I'd like to have worked more. I must learn to deal with this problem, I suppose . . . how to work often enough to satisfy my appetite for acting and still do worthwhile things. Let's hope EL CID is that.

October 13. We have Sophia Loren—a competent actress, and a star. She may not be a box-office guarantee, but who is? Not me, certainly. We should have a certain chemistry together, too. I'm content with this. It'll screw up my schedule, though, since we have to shoot her stuff first, in twelve weeks. It looks like most of the winter in Spain for Charlie.

We actually had Sophia for only ten weeks, which complicated an already difficult problem.

October 19. The usual workout—crammed morning. We still have no suitable candidate for Babieca. You wouldn't think a horse would be harder to cast than a leading lady, but so it seems. Horses aren't asking very much salary these days either.

Casting the Cid's horse, Babieca, was Yakima Canutt's problem. He solved it by finding two magnificent white studs in Yugoslavia. (Principal horses are usually double cast, to ease the work load on them. This might be a good idea with actors, too.) Our Babiecas were identical in appearance (magnificent) and temperament (terrible).

October 23 (Sunday). This could only happen in Europe. They got the elaborate clearances they needed to extract the genuine sword of the genuine Cid from its case in the genuine Museo de las Armas, to photograph me with it. I dragged out of bed this morning and got over to the museum. We went through all the brouhaha with the officials, all hands producing passes, letters, etc. . . . only to find at last that the case where the sword rests is sealed. It can't physically *be* opened!

November 1. Another one of Spain's innumerable holidays, eliminating any chance of work, with either horses or broadswords. I went over to talk to Phil Yordan about the script, but he was full of preparations for departure to Rome (again) to soothe Sophia. I don't know what this can accomplish, but it's not my place to bitch about it.

It was my place to bitch about it, of course, but it wasn't going to help anything. All this puts Sophia in an unfairly bad light. She must have been as insecure about the script as I was, and anxious that her part might melt away in the rewrite in a mélange of male heroics. As a matter of fact, Chimene is one of the most remarkable women's roles in medieval literature.

November 3. While broadswording at the stables this morning on the white stud (he still hates that blade swinging past his head), a frantic message came that we have lost Sophia (then again, we may *not* have). This created considerable consternation on high executive levels. (I think they're more worried about the loss of their Italian production license than their leading lady.) I wish to God I were in Rome, so I could figure out what the hell has happened. I'm uncertain to what degree she's bluffing, is ill-advised, or has been conned. If there's no progress tomorrow, I may go to Rome.

November 6. A long back and forth meeting with the executive echelon on the Loren casting. Everyone finally more or less conceded it would be better to go without her. Probably the best replacement would be Jeanne Moreau. She is certainly a superb actress.

November 7. Mother got in today, an hour early, but happy to be here, and eager as always to tag along and watch. Tony phoned from Rome: Sophia's back in the picture. I'm nonplussed to hear this, but Tony's the one who has to make the choice.

November 8. The usual sort of working day: swords and horses, horses and swords. There's no final word on Sophia, not much to my surprise. The rest of the cast is now largely assembled and looks promising, but we *do* need to set our leading lady. I met with Nick Ray about THE TRIBE THAT LOST ITS HEAD; nothing conclusive except a degree of mutual interest in the property. I may need a modern piece badly after EL CID. Dinner at Sam Bronston's was pleasant, but I just couldn't stay the full time. They always *start* so late!

Spanish social habits have changed a little since we shot EL CID, but in 1960 you were invited for dinner with cocktails at nine P.M. If you actually got there then, you were the first guests. Dinner usually was served about midnight, with entertainment to follow. This is too late a schedule for a working actor.

November 10. I put my mother on a plane to Rome, had a brandy in the VIP lounge, and met Tony Mann coming back from that Holy City. He convinced me the script changes he contemplates (which I must approve finally anyway) are improvements. It certainly tells a tighter story. I feel better about it now than at any time since I got involved with this opus.

Of course these changes were made in response to Sophia's feelings about the script. They did *improve it. This kind of grinding interface can be painful, but the results can be valuable, too.*

November 12. Well, we finally have our actress in hand. She certainly comes up to specifications. Hank Werbsha's expert public relations and Sophia's charisma stirred up a small tempest at Barajas Airport on her arrival. I got her into the limo slightly askew, but unmarred. She really seems a very nice lady. All may yet be well.

November 14. We finally got the show on the road; we'll shoot French hours [*noon to eight P.M. with no break*] for the interiors. We all gathered with some formality, much good humor, champagne, and shaking of hands, including all actors not shooting and all possible members of the production staff. Sophia was breathtaking, all warmth and bonhomie, but she can't be photographed today, anyway. Her costume, like my horse, is still en route. Bob Krasker accommodatingly worked out a very difficult single of me to light for the first setup. We did well to get to that, with all the celebrant carryings-on.

Obviously, the first day of shooting was largely a social ritual. Bob Krasker, our British cameraman, whose photography is one of the outstanding qualities of EL CID, is not fast even when pressed. Under the circumstances, he was delighted to design a setup that took some five hours to light. I must admit it's a beautiful shot.

November 16. Today I got back to my trade. I spoke my first line as an actor since we closed TUMBLER ten months ago. (The silent shot yesterday doesn't count.) Actually, I think I did well in the scene. It's the first in the script with Sophia and has to be right. She did well, too, though the language barrier keeps her a little insecure. You have to wait for the dailies to be sure, but I feel I'm reaching some degree of flexibility and simplicity. (That means cutting down the crap.)

November 25. Sophia Loren is proving easier to work with than some I've labored opposite. She seems concerned with her nose, which she feels is unphotogenic. I think it's a fine nose, but it's for her to say. (She *is* one of the great beauties of the world, for God's sake.) We may do well here.

November 30. My night-dark, grave-cold rising was worthwhile not only for the beauty of the dawn shot we used to begin the Cid's exile; you also get a feeling of personal virtue, simply being up before the sun. I came closer than I have yet to inhabiting this man, who rode off on his war-horse leaving behind his life and his home, with "open doors and the perches empty where his hawks stood." The Cid as exile. This is the key.

December 13. I'm falling into a grinding schedule with this duel scene. I damn nearly had my head cut off today; no doubt would've, but for Enzo's skill and steadiness. I came home a touch shaken, hoping to avoid the meeting set on the Bardot film (PRIVATE LIVES) and one other, a swashbuckler in Italy. The Bardot film is appealing, but impossible to undertake, since she wants to shoot it in French. I don't want another swash to buckle now, either.

Sword fights are tough to stage and a little dangerous no matter how carefully they're planned. Because of the weight of the blade, broadsword duels are tougher than rapier fights. (That's one reason MACBETH is harder to bring off than HAMLET.) We'd shot on this duel all day; by seven in the evening, tired and careless, I rolled left when I should've rolled right. Enzo Musemici Greco, the Italian fencing master who staged the duel and was doubling the British actor who was supposed to be fighting with me, fortunately had a wrist like iron, just strong enough to stop the blade of his broadsword short of the side of my neck.

December 15. I had a mean argument with Tony today. It began over my wardrobe for the dawn scene, while dressing in the stable. How long a speech do I need to put on a chain-mail shirt? What can Sophia say, buckling it up the back? Of course, the problem is really my growing conviction that Sophia's Italian writer is no use to us. As we finally cut it down, the scene's not bad, but the overall problem is still there.

Sophia felt understandably uncertain at judging the quality of a script in English, especially English that was supposed to suggest the eleventh century, and had asked to have an Italian writer put on the picture. He translated her script into Italian and the changes he felt appropriate back into English. Neither version was very successful, I'm afraid.

December 25. Christmas morning was a great success, even though we all would've like it even more in Coldwater, I think. Lydia and Fray were properly overwhelmed by the sable stole and the Cid costume, respectively. I doubt if Fray will take his off except for bed. Lydia maybe not even then (not a bad idea). I had a long talk with Phil Yordan tonight, at Bronston's party. He was all too eager to assure me I have no need to worry about the script, or the picture. I am not persuaded.

December 28. The coldest day on location yet, and we were working with Sophia and an eight-year-old girl. All did their best, I presume, though Tony was in a fearful temper over something. The scene itself was the first I can recall, in this or any film, that I'm positive will not work in the finished picture. Cut down still more and with the little girl's voice dubbed in, we can stand a bit of it, but it really didn't come off. It was largely a lost day, and we can't afford those.

December 29. Another day of supplying an offstage voice for Sophia's close-up reactions watching the tournament. She sometimes tends to carry her remarkable beauty through a scene as though it were a soufflé . . . very, very gently, lest it break.

December 31. Well, this turned out to be a year full of a great many things for us; perhaps that's why it seemed to go by so fast. Is this something that happens as the middle years draw nearer? Anyway, 1960 was the year that carried me to several corners of the world, a new house, and the peak of my profession. (This last, measured by a rather limited standard.) The last three and a half months of it I poured into a picture I have only guarded hopes for (which is the way I began the year, come to think of it, with THE TUMBLER). I also realized I can no longer be the eager boy player on the way up. Maybe the most important milestone was that this is the year my son lost his first tooth, most of his baby talk, and learned to swim.

1961

Playing opposite
Sophia Loren in
El Cid . . .

Rome again for
*The Pigeon That
Took Rome* . . .

a new family
arrival,
Holly Ann.

The Cid at home with
wife (Sophia Loren) and kids
ANTONIO LUENGO

January 4, Madrid. Today was positively the coldest day I've ever spent on a location. Poor Sophia nearly couldn't make it. She stood huddled in my arms between takes, her teeth literally chattering. I persuaded Tony to do the reverses on our dialogue in the studio later. It'll be tricky to match the light, but a helluva sight better than acting in the teeth of that icy wind off the Guadarramas. We did get what should be an excellent dawn shot with the mounted men. In this weather, it's really a miserable experience to settle into a cold saddle in chain mail.

January 9. The location was weathered out again. It gave me a chance to try and deal with the problem scenes we're coming to now in the script. I had a long, inconclusive talk with Ben Barzman [*the new writer on the film*] about them. I hope something was accomplished. I really hate to upset people I like by telling them I don't like the work they've done.

January 11, Manzanares. The second unit went swimmingly today . . . there's a wonderful feeling of freedom working with those guys. Someday I'd love to make a film with nothing *but* a second unit. No dialogue, no star egos . . . just horse falls and sword fights, out in the boondocks.

I know, this sounds very idle. It's just that you don't have any responsibility on the second unit. You just do the shots they tell you you're able to do. Everyone on a second unit—the stunt men, the second unit directors, and the special effects men—are marvelously good at what they do. This is the fun of movie-making. The other stuff, fixing the script and making the scenes work, that's what you do for your life, and it's not fun.

January 12. We got in a helluva fat day on location: clear, cold, not a shred of cloud, though the wind was a bit too much for Sophia. Tony's really knocking on it now, desperately trying to finish her up within her guarantee. This means leaving some of my close-ups till after she's gone, which is reasonable. My main problem is still the reunion scene, which comes too early in part two and is not right yet, anyway. To make matters worse, Ben Barzman's gone off to London for the weekend, having turned in thirty good new pages, none of them with this scene on it.

January 13. Finally got into the older, battered Cid. The makeup is really very effective . . . my concept of the scar cleaving through the face contributes considerably to the total. Even in heroes a feeling of vulnerability is helpful. It also fits the Job concept of the Cid as a man who endures. Sophia's megrims kept us off the crucial reunion scene for one more day. I'm slowly bringing Tony around to the idea of change. With Ben gone, I don't know what the hell we can do, but we can try.

I wish we could've persuaded Sophia to accept an aging makeup in the second half of the film. Certainly her incredible beauty was one of the visual assets of the picture, but the story covered more than twenty years, after all. It did look odd for me to appear in the second half as the graying, scarred veteran of the Cid's weary campaigns, while Sophia was still unchanged as the beautiful Chimene. On the other hand, she did look absolutely marvelous.

January 15 (Sunday), Near Toledo. I hunted wild boar for the first time in my life, the guest of the duke of Arion. The country is fairly rough to move over, the cover dense and nervous-making (when you consider the size and agility of the Spanish boars). It made me nervous, anyway; I shot badly (with a borrowed ducal Mannlicher). I'm sure I was wide with the only open shot I had. The boar went down, but I think the duke shot after me, out of courtesy. He's a nice man, and a *very* nice shot. I had a fine day anyway, feeling the sun on my back, a rifle in my hand, and the look of the boar moving through the olive scrub. It's also the only time I've ever hunted where lunch was served twenty miles into the bush from tables trucked in by Land Rover, the wine cooling properly in buckets and the napkins folded.

January 16, Madrid. We shot, very easily, the Cid's meeting with his daughters, using a pair of tiny twins impersonating the daughters (it's much easier now for me to call up memories involving fatherhood). Then we turned to our big problem scene, where the Cid talks to Chimene about his disappointment, etc. We finally worked out a version that seemed to work, but the master shot was very hard to light . . . and at last Sophia decided to go home, with the scene unshot. This is the first time this has happened on any picture I've ever worked on. I was shocked.

It still shocks me, but I understand it a little better now. It was very late in the day by then and Sophia probably didn't want to be photographed at all, certainly not in an important scene.

January 17. Another damn full day spent chewing away at Sophia's remaining scenes. Tony's crucial choices on one of them made me damn mad; the first time I've ever openly questioned a director's coverage of a scene. This either means he was badly wrong or I'm getting tougher to work with.

I sound very bad-tempered through here. I was worried about the film, and it was very frustrating to shoot Sophia's remaining scenes as her tight schedule demanded: getting only the master angle and her close-ups, leaving everything else till later.

January 18. I finally launched the sequence that first attracted me to this project: the death of the Cid. The first time I've ever died in bed. The makeup department contributed an excellent arrow in my breast, and I gave an excellent performance of being carried in unconscious, which is as far as we got. George Marshall, over here to do a film with Rex Harrison and Rita Hayworth, was very sprightly at dinner tonight . . . full of reminiscences of W. C. Fields.

January 20. For some reason we seem to be flowing through this scene like silk. That's a good way to gauge the writing on a scene: how easily it blocks out. I think I'm playing the Cid's death very well, though I haven't actually expired quite yet. Dying in bed has much to recommend over getting your head hacked off, or being gunned down in a swamp, or most of the violent ends I've met professionally. I look forward to character roles for this reason, among others.

January 25. This is bloody nonsense; we waited again for Sophia's by now predictably late arrival. I'm not good at this kind of crap, I admit; I hate it so. I refused to speak to or look at her. (Big deal. I'm supposed to be dead anyway . . . or there might have been a certain lack of communication in the scene.)

January 27. We wrapped up Sophia at last, today; all in all the most trying work time with an actress I can ever recall. Mind you, she is not a bitch. She's a warm lady, truly; she's just more star than pro. She behaved very decently today, to work on time, even. Babieca was the heavy today (if not the leading lady, it has to be the horse, I guess). He'd been in a fight in the truck on the way to location and began the day determined to kill any horse he got near. Short of that, he was willing to settle for bucking me off. I lucked out, with both the lady and the horse.

January 28. Whatever else this film may be, it's certainly shot with luck. Four hours after finishing her last shot yesterday, Sophia fell downstairs and broke her shoulder. I took her flowers and regrets before she left for Rome, but I couldn't help a private thanksgiving that her misfortune didn't happen a month ago.

February 2. The first day since the start of shooting when I had no call. Of course, I had workout calls for both horse and sword, but these left me plenty of leisure. I worked over the script a bit with Ben, who's going back to London (but will return when needed, he assures me). A horrifying social experience tonight watching a ravaged ex-Love Goddess wrangling with her husband like an unhappy fishwife, which she now seems.

February 5, Peñiscola. The drive down from the still chilling sweep of the Spanish meseta to the balmy Mediterranean coast above Valencia was long, but seductive with the promise it holds of pleasanter weather to shoot in. After those dreary winter dawns in the Guadarramas, I can use a little Mediterranean sun.

February 7. Another lovely morning spent basking in the unaccustomed sun. It was a pleasure to get back on a tennis court again . . . even an ill-marked one, with no fences. We don't start shooting till tomorrow, which is typical of our production planning, but I'm so overwhelmed by this set, I can overlook a great deal. Let's see if we can get some overwhelming footage out of it, now.

We shot the siege of Valencia in Peñiscola, one of the last cities in Europe still walled as in medieval times. Modern Valencia is a big city with TV, traffic, and smog. Peñiscola, as we photographed it for EL CID, looked very much as Valencia must have in the eleventh century.

February 12, Sagunto. I can hardly believe it was six years ago I drove back to location down in Anaheim with my head in a whirl over the look of that tiny male body Lydia made from my seed. Now he's a gangly, bony boy, sprouting out in all directions toward life. The Roman ruin where we celebrated his birthday has seen a lot of it. I stood at sunset watching my son run up the cruel slope where Hannibal sent his legions plunging, two hundred years before Christ.

February 13, Peñiscola. No shooting for me today; the weather turned overcast, and they didn't finish the opening scene of the film with Beni Youssef (not Orson Welles, after all, for reasons I don't entirely trust, but a good actor in any event: Herbert Lom). I had a good work session with Babieca number two. We're trying to teach him some show paces for me to show at the local bullring Sunday. It's either that or fight a bull, and I'm nowhere near that stupid.

February 15. Today was as gray as yesterday, and I had the runs as well. Thank God I didn't have to be belted into that chain mail; it could've been disastrous. Tony and Mischa are both very gloomy (about the weather, I hope, not my nagging on the script). I got a call from New York: Olivier wants me to alternate roles with him, the last month he plays BECKETT. Damn! I'd love the chance . . . but I have to be ready to rehearse by the end of March. I'll never make it.

February 18. Today we shot the assault on the walls of Valencia. The switch of hurling groceries instead of stones from the siege engines looked rather comic to me, though it may read well enough in the script. It was really hilarious to see it shot though: One basket lit right on the camera, trucking along, and a man-at-arms neatly impaled a cabbage on the point of his helmet.

February 19 (Sunday), Castellón de la Plana. We went to the bullring in Castellón to show Babieca number two's high school steps just before the corrida. It was an exercise in public relations, of course, but more fun than most. I can't say I exactly performed magnificently in the ring, but the horse got us through, to the wild applause of the crowd. Fray looked very fine parading with his *traje de campo* with the matadors and was delighted when I swept him into my saddle and ran out of the ring. He accepted the killing of the bulls, or at least I think he did. Lydia disagrees.

February 25. Somehow the twenty-week schedule didn't look this long from the other end, last July. It'll certainly be six or seven weeks more, too. I'd be more sanguine about it if I weren't increasingly convinced of the basic weaknesses of our setup here. Tony still seems bent on shooting the battle himself. I can't understand this. If Wyler was willing to trust Yak with his chariot race, can't Tony trust him to take Valencia?

February 27. A really exhausting day today, jamming both Babiecas again and again into a tight-packed mass of horses with highly unreliable soldiers on their backs. I literally came back to the start mark after each take panting with effort. My God, to really fight all day like that in armor you'd have to be some kind of a man. Seems to me Tony, enamored of the mass of armed and mounted men at his disposal, is trying to get them all into each take. Only de Mille could bring that kind of shot off.

March 1. More battle shots. Tony's still not planning them right. You have to use a group of men in each one small enough so they can be directed into convincing individual action. Otherwise it's just a mob shot. I've never seen quite this problem come up before.

I have since. Wyler, George Stevens, de Mille were secure enough to delegate the shooting of action sequences to second unit directors, confident in the unique abilities of these specialists. Young directors now are often anxious, lest their own authority be compromised somehow if they surrender the camera to another man. I understand their feelings, but I think they're wrong.

Fray spent the afternoon fishing. To my astonishment, he actually caught a three-inch fish, which he ensconced in Lydia's bidet. It promptly died, to his horrified grief.

March 2. The special effects crews almost never goof, but they blew one today. They rigged some burning tents that got out of hand and ruined a take. Since I was running Babieca number two through the shot, it could've ruined me, too, but fortunately, whatever his shortcomings, he's remarkably phlegmatic about fire: He never flinched as we disappeared in a cloud of black smoke.

March 11. I convinced the company that I should stay over tomorrow and work with Yak and the second unit. I'm positive the shots he plans will prove vital to the battle in the final cut.

They were, too, but the shots Yak was able to make in one day weren't enough to make the battle for Valencia the sequence it could've been. For most of the four weeks we shot there, we had two thousand trained Spanish troops, plus a thousand cavalrymen. Tony insisted on playing with these, when he should've been shooting the scenes, *leaving the battle to Yak.*

March 15, Madrid. This morning I finished off my close-ups from the throne room without particular distinction and then ran what must have been a week or more of location work. It included some good footage, particularly of the Cid claiming Valencia, which ought to make a *very* good scene. We still have about twenty-five reels to run . . . a rather staggering prospect. Sam Bronston gave a nice dinner tonight for a number of international types, including Zan Carver [*a friend from New York*] over with a script on William the Conqueror.

March 20. It rained today on location for the first time on this film, which is damn lucky. At that, we really weren't rained out today; we got the vital cuts left in the scene and lost only some gravy shots Tony wanted. This means we're off to Valladolid tomorrow, ahead of schedule, though; bad weather is likely here for the rest of the week. I don't like the WILLIAM THE CONQUEROR script, so Zan's off for New York, too. When the rain wrapped us, I had time to talk to Bob Lawrence [*the film editor*] on the advisability of my doing my dubbing here, after we finish the film, rather than at London.

Dubbing is the crucial postproduction process of adding the music track to the edited film, as well as enhancing or replacing any sound that's not satisfactory. (On many European pictures, all sound is added at this point and nothing whatever is recorded during shooting.) The actor's share of this work is called "looping," for reasons too boring to bother with here. Since any dialogue that is technically or creatively unsatisfactory must be rerecorded in sync with the picture, this is a highly pressured and difficult chore. It was Orson Welles who taught me it can also be a creative time.

March 23, Valladolid. I've finally arrived at where Rodrigo started, though I can't tell how our version of Bivar [his birthplace] compares with the real one. The Castle of Torrelobatón is quite large, a perfectly restored example of a thirteenth-century feudal stronghold, now maintained by the state as a combination monument and grain silo. (No kidding.) It suits our purposes perfectly: Shooting from a bridge over a small stream gives you exactly the classic view of a castle in Spain. It's going well, but slowly, so I had Lydia and Fray come up by train from Madrid.

March 24. I still insist this is not a medium for sluggards; I put in seventeen hours portal-to-portal today. I must say Tony had some real insights on the quarrel with Ordonez over hanging the emirs. This scene has hung over me from the beginning; he helped me with it enormously today. Locked inside that sour, unhappy man there seems to be an artist, screaming to be let out.

My general entries during the shooting of EL CID don't treat Tony Mann very generously. He was a gifted man and made some good films, but in retrospect, I don't think he was the right director for EL CID. It was an extremely difficult project, putting enormous pressures on the director in terms of script and casting. The most relentless and painstaking kind of creative control was needed to bring it off. It also had enormous potential. The story and the characters are far more complex and subtle than in BEN-HUR. I've come to feel that if Willy Wyler and Tony had traded assignments on the two pictures, BEN-HUR would have been not much less than it is and EL CID might have been the greatest epic film ever made.

March 26. Citron phoned, pressing me to accept the Fox offer of a three-picture deal, including COMANCHEROS, with an unknown director. I was very leery of this and put him off.

March 27, Manzanares. Manzanares' unseasonably springlike March seems a lot more than three months away from the same location in December. When I remember how we froze up here shooting the knights' sequence, I can hardly believe it's the same *country*, even. I had very little to do all day . . . riding at a gentle trot through a flower-strewn mountain meadow, allowing a stunt man to jump at me from a rock, but miss. A piece of cake.

March 28. The same lovely location, doing the sort of work people think actors do all the time, though today was somewhat more strenuous. I chopped as many Moors as ever I did at Peñíscola, and certainly as many as the Cid ever did in a day anywhere. I also damn near made Babieca number one step on a fallen stunt man's face.

March 30, Madrid/New York. By really well-advised elimination of all dialogue from the river crossing scene, I was suddenly finished with the location in time to catch the jet for New York. One minute I was up to my knees in water doing the close-ups, two hours later I was halfway to Lisbon. The scene will turn out fairly well, I think. (I finally got that damn convent bedroom scene cut out, too.) New York didn't look as though it had missed me; I expect it hadn't.

The long Easter weekend, and some very nimble work this last day in the river, made it possible to fly to New York and read some of my cutting of the Passion for a television special. (I said it was possible; it seems a hell of a way to fly, in retrospect.)

April 1, New York. Tennis was rained out, which indicates the care of Providence, because the day turned into a gut-buster. Eight CBS engineers went on strike at midnight, so we had to tape the television show before then. This resulted in something less than a perfect performance, you could say. Before flying back to Spain, I had time to run films of two directors Fox submitted for COMANCHEROS. They seemed routine to me.

April 3, Madrid. I spent most of the day in a desperate effort to get back in sync with Spanish time after a draining weekend in New York. It's fine to be home, even while Lydia is packing it into crates and trunks. She's in wonderfully high spirits: Fray was in bed with the tail end of a fever, but delightfully appealing in a yellow sweater. He *talks* to you now, man to man. The baby is there only when he's sleeping.

April 10, Belmonte Castle. We finally began the last sequence I'll shoot in the film: the tournament. Tony is carefully staying away from actual tourney shots, since Yak finally served an ultimatum: Let him do the fight he was hired to shoot. Babieca number two behaved marvelously all day, making me look very good indeed, and the set is remarkably right, with the castle on a hill, the village below. (A real village, mind you, and a real castle.)

April 11. Another good day shooting, though we still haven't broken a lance. (Yak's still waiting, as he agreed, while Tony shoots the dialogue and the prefight shots.) After lunch Lydia went back to Madrid to wrap up our packing (and make sure of our space on the *Queen Mary*), while Fray stayed down with me. It's the first time in his short life he's been overnight without female supervision. He was very manly while we ate in our room, resolutely conversing in very adult fashion. God, he grows so fast . . . so fast.

April 15. They finally got the last shot they needed of me, after finishing off the fight and Don Martin in spectacular fashion. I headed back for Madrid feeling a weight lifting off my neck at last. I finished it. I'm still somewhat dubious about the creative potential of the film, though much of it should be excellent. Commercially it seems a good bet. Everyone tonight at Sam's party was excited, of course. Sam was enthusiastic about all I'd done to "make the film work" and seems determined to buy me a Jaguar XKE, which staggered me a bit. [*He did, too.*]

April 18. They finally came out with it, on the phone from Rome: They want me there not for fun, not for publicity, but because they *need* me for the Italian nationality. This isn't entirely clear, but it convinced me. Sooo, I fly to Rome tomorrow and we leave a day later. I spent my last day in Madrid savoring the city; it seems even more attractive now that I'm about to leave it. I had a marvelous lunch with Lydia in the garden of the Ritz, then this evening the Foreign Press Club gave me a dinner at Botin, in the old Moorish cellars that still exist far below the streets.

April 19, Rome. There's nothing like flying across the Mediterranean for a cocktail party to make you feel things are a little out of proportion. God knows Sam's people were desperate to persuade me it was *necessary*, and Rome was breathlessly beautiful in April . . . but it still seemed a wasteful gesture. Oh well, it made the distribution executives in Rome my friends for life, to hear them tell it.

This curious episode had to do with the fact that EL CID was ostensibly made as a coproduction with DEAR Films, an Italian company. We used several Italian performers in the picture, in addition to Sophia, and the costumes were made in Italy. They also actually planned to shoot one scene in Rome, all this qualifying them for certain advantages when the picture was distributed in Italy. When it developed that I was not in the scene scheduled for Rome, consternation erupted. Of course I had to be in Rome, even if only for a day . . . I must come to Rome . . . a great party would be set up to draw as much attention as possible to my presence there, and so on. None of this was discussed with me, of course. Instead, through the last days of my work on the picture (in Spain), I got a series of increasingly seductive phone calls, first suggesting perhaps my family and I would like a week's vacation in Italy. When I pointed out that what I really wanted was to get on the boat back to the States, the calls became desperately importunate. Finally, they confessed they needed me to come to Rome. Of course I went, then. Film is a curious profession.

April 20, Rome/Madrid/Burgos. I left Rome after lunch at Nick Ray's house on the Appia Antica. He wants me to act in one film for him, then coproduce, codirect another one, on the Children's Crusade. I must look into this. I reached Madrid to find Lydia with bags and son ready to get in the car, overloading it somewhat. The drive to Burgos was no great problem, but we found a mob waiting outside the hotel, so we went to another, where a quiet night was possible.

April 21, Périgueux, France. We left Spain at San Sebastian and crossed the border into France in (of course) a driving rain, which persisted all day. Biarritz had the dank, forlorn aspect expected of seaside resorts in the off-season. We drove a little later than we should, but were rewarded with reasonable lodging in a small hotel in Périgueux. The book Nick Ray wants me to do, ROAD OF THE SNAIL, is amusing, but it's not a part for me.

April 24, Loire. I finally undertook the tour of the Loire châteaux that Lydia's been looking forward to for so long. Even the weather abandoned its Gallic perversity for the day, at least. Weather intermittently cloudy, but not one drop of rain. Chenonceaux is the most memorable, in the sense of being livable, of any great house I can recall seeing. Blois was chiefly interesting as the site of the murder of the duc de Guise, a particularly bloody incident in medieval history. Fray was spellbound by the story and of course recounted it later with perfect accuracy.

April 25, Chartres. We arrived in Chartres in a rising wind, boiling with black clouds, but Gothic architecture is not diminished by weather. After Salisbury, this is the most moving cathedral I've seen, the least cluttered by errors of later taste. Rain started again shortly after we took the road to Alençon, confirming the reputation of French weather. The Gare is a simple, clean hotel, but my taste for haute cuisine is about satisfied. God, for a steak *without* Béarnaise sauce!

April 26. It was still raining, but it should be when you see the D-day beaches. First we stopped at Bayeux and saw the tapestry celebrating the Norman Conquest. It's overwhelming, especially on the day you walk Omaha Beach. The mailed men-at-arms Duke William loaded into boats for England on those beaches seemed still vivid and near in time, to me and to the GI's Bradley dumped in the shallows here sixteen years ago. They *are* close to each other, surely . . . maybe they're the same men.

April 27, Cherbourg. The sailing preparations were Gallicly chaotic. The sailing itself was even delayed, but we finally saw Europe fade behind us and relaxed into the sybaritic joys of the *Queen Mary* . . . the biggest goddamn floating hotel I can imagine.

April 28, Aboard the Queen Mary. I cabled good luck to Coop [*I'd heard he was very ill*] with chill foreboding. An extra workout failed to wash away my uneasy awareness of mortality or justify the gluttonous eating habits I inevitably fall into at sea. I also have to decide whether to accept one of the fat offers bobbing up or wait in the hope of something better.

May 2, New York. It's much more satisfactory to come through the Narrows and up New York Harbor by daylight. It was all as I remembered when we came home from Rome . . . but much *warmer.* The city seemed in a welcoming mood, somehow, as the tugs nudged us in between the *United States* and the *Mauretania.* After a delayed disembarkation, avoiding much red tape, who should be waiting patiently but Forrest [*Wood, another old friend*], Joe, and Maggie. Our energies revitalized by our friends' affection, we celebrated with a dip into Gotham night life.

May 8, New York. We went to see BECKETT, where Larry Olivier has switched roles. It's hard to judge without having seen him as Beckett, but it's clear why he wanted to play the king instead: It's the best part. Afterward, in the dressing room, he said, "I cannot describe to you the black depression that descended on me about the third day of rehearsal when I realized I had *chosen the wrong role!*" Ah well, there's been a movie sale . . . perhaps we can both do it.

Of course, we didn't; Dick Burton and Peter O'Toole were cast and did some of their best work in the film. I still feel one of the missed chances of my career was not being able to alternate with Olivier in those two parts. Aside from the learning experience it would have involved, we would have revived a fine tradition from the nineteenth-century theater, when actors often used to alternate two roles in the same play. As it was, Olivier decided simply to switch to the role of the king and play only that till they closed. Arthur Kennedy played Beckett.

May 9. I had a ghastly lunch press conference at "21." I was introduced as "Charles, Chuck Heston," and it went downhill from there. I screwed myself up with an awkward sort of unprepared speech, in a situation completely inappropriate for it. I hate to really blow one like that; it put me in a foul temper for the rest of the day, though my outlook on life in New York was improved by viewing it from a spectacular restaurant on top of the new Time-Life Building, at dinner with Lydia tonight.

May 11. I was really horrified to turn down a TV offer to work with Olivier, in Graham Greene's THE POWER AND THE GLORY. Citron and his men were against it because of giving up pay TV control and the plan to release it theatrically in Europe. I was more concerned with the part, which is not much. Still, I feel a slight pang of guilt.

May 13. Coop died today . . . safe in the bosom of his church and his family; surely the way he wanted it. I'm moved at his death; I'm proud to have known him and worked with him. He's a good man gone, and I sense a sleeve-tug of mortality in it.

May 15, St. Helen. The trip over the lake was smooth. Russ was waiting, offhandedly cordial as usual, with Lydia's new T-bird. We drove north to the woods through a rainstorm that kicked the hell out of the new polish job on the car, but didn't diminish my pleasure in looking at my lake a bit. The pin cherries are out, the maples and oaks young and lime-green along their branches. I wonder how long I'd have to spend here to get really tired of it?

May 19, Two Rivers, Wisconsin. The trip north from Wilmette began badly when we couldn't get on the tollway; we crossed it twice before finding the entry. When we got to South Milwaukee for lunch, Fray's feverish indisposition showed clear signs of becoming measles. We smuggled him north, where the doctor who'd tended Lydia as a child diagnosed him as definitely measly. He is spotted and subdued, but in good spirits, on the whole. We had a pleasant kind of clan reunion evening and ended up bedding down all over the house, eleven-strong. Tomorrow, with Bob and Carol [*Lydia's brother and his wife*] it will be thirteen.

May 20. Bob and Carol arrived, though not as early as Dr. Zlatnik, who turned up while relatives were still spread in sleeping bags over the living room floor. We were still in bed too, for that matter, but delighted to hear that Fray apparently has only German measles, which means we probably can stick to our schedule traveling west. Fray is very frail, all measly in the middle of a big bed. ("Daddy . . . I don't have a *heart* attack, do I?")

May 25, The way west. Got another late start . . . we *used* to get going early. We also promptly lost the proper tollroad again, finding ourselves en route for Iowa in a blinding bloody downpour. We still made it beyond St. Louis by dark and slept where we spent the night westbound from our BEN-HUR sojourn, three years ago.

May 26, Oklahoma City. New roads are really amazing: We had a latish start again, but reached Oklahoma City well ahead of our ETA nonetheless, and found the usual warm Westish welcome waiting. Jolly West wants me to join him tomorrow picketing for desegregation of the restaurants here. I guess it's time I did something about this kind of thing besides deploring it at cocktail parties. I can think of no one I'd rather do it with than Jolly.

May 27. The picketing was valuable, though it didn't create the confrontation I guess we were braced for. We encountered almost no hostility. Except for the sandwich boards we wore (mine carried a quote from Jefferson, surely a safe authority). The whole thing was more like a triumphal procession than a protest demonstration. The warm gratitude of the Negroes we met, who have more at stake than I do here, seems more than we deserve.

May 28. It's futile to consider leaving tomorrow; now there are interviews to be done on all this. Bill Blowitz phoned from Los Angeles to say the picketing story was carried by all wire services. I'm comfortable with the moral value of the action, but uncomfortable to think I'll profit from it in publicity terms.

May 31, Needles, California. Again, though we started later than I'd hoped we could, we got into Needles earlier than last trip, less tired and surely more eager to get back home. When we crossed the Colorado River, Fray urged us all into a rousing chorus of "California Here I Come!" which carried us into Needles. Meanwhile, Trujillo was assassinated and Kennedy was a wild success in Paris . . . or was it Jackie?

June 1, Beverly Hills. Homecoming was never so rich. The house looked absolutely marvelous, with green coming back on the hill after the '59 fire. I spent the rest of the day unwinding, hoisting a ceremonial glass or two during the evening. That was a long damn nine months to put in one picture. I can't tell yet whether the investment was worthwhile creatively. In commercial terms, I'm confident.

June 2, Los Angeles. Citron has a number of promising projects . . . one that appeals to me, without reading the script, is Preminger's offer to do ADVISE AND CONSENT. For one thing, it'll be done in Hollywood. We opened the new court with formal ceremonies, amply recorded by Lydia's Leica. Sam served the first ball, I returned same, and we went on from there. More tennis, champagne, ending at last at an Italian restaurant. A good day.

June 5. I slipped back into the routine of physical conditioning this house makes easier and read ADVISE AND CONSENT. Preminger wants me to play Brig Anderson. I'm not put off by the homosexual angle, but the part isn't very interesting. Anderson is acted upon rather than acting . . . essentially a static character. The role of old Senator Cooley, now, would be a plum . . . I'll try to buck for that.

June 6. Herman made a pitch to Preminger for Cooley, but he wants Tracy (who can blame him?), so we walked away. [*In the end, he settled for Charles Laughton, who was very good in one of his last roles. It was the part to play.*] My boy now has a dog: a seven-week-old shepherd with better bloodlines than mine, to whom the whole family immediately took, even Lydia, unused to dogs and a little nervous of a male. He passed a somewhat restive evening, but seems intent on settling in with a minimum of fuss. We gave him a name with proper medieval echoes: Arthur Pendragon.

June 11. Much tennis again, including a lesson. The day was pleasant and sunny, filled with loafing. An early, easy dinner at the Wylers', Willy a little gloomy because he's shooting.

Willy was always gloomy when he was working. I think he cultivated an interior climate of dour skepticism as the only fit context in which he could judge harshly enough what he and everyone else were doing.

He seems to feel it would've been very unwise to do Cooley in ADVISE AND CONSENT even if it had been offered me.

I did think he was wrong about this. He felt, as a leading man, I might damage my basic commodity by doing character parts. I've always felt one of the luckiest things that happened in my career was the early opportunity I had to wear gray beards and warts and play foreigners who wear skirts with feathers and other odd things. By now, audiences seem willing to let me take a shot at anything.

June 17. Again, much, much tennis . . . really lousy for the most part, I'm sorry to say. A long drive down to Newport Beach for a Bourbonish kind of party. (They always have one guest who says "nigger.") I've about finally made up my mind to go to Berlin, for at least part of the time. I don't *have* to, I suppose, but there it is. Where?

I don't know where. Wherever it is they keep asking you to go, I guess. This was the Berlin Festival, and the State Department wanted me to be the official delegate. The trouble is, the more of these things they ask you to do, the more they ask you to do. And the more you do, the better you get at it, more or less.

June 22. Today, with some reluctance, I decided to do a filmed TV. I know they never turn out, but I want to practice my trade. Besides, it's rather interesting, about a one-eyed Irish carnival man. A curious combination of sentimental love story and suspense thriller (which probably prevents it from coming off in terms of either one of them). Also, the part is far enough away from me to make it possible to learn a little. They insist this can be a worthwhile show.

June 26, En route to New York/Rome. The great part of my energy today was devoted to falling asleep. One thing they overlooked in welcoming the jet age was what we'd do with all the extra time. What we do is not have enough sleep. I managed to be courteous to various State Department types who were briefing me during the New York stop on things I really know already. The reel or so I saw of the U.S. official entry, TWO LOVES, looked second rate to me.

June 27, Rome/Berlin. I flew to Berlin via Rome today solely for a fitting on a tailcoat for the Berlin Festival Ball. Cifonelli was waiting at the airport, the fitting went well, and I had time to check into a hotel at Ostia for a shower and sunbath before enplaning for Germany. Frankfurt looked exactly as you'd imagine . . . black fir trees to the edge of the runway. Berlin is shaggy with green foliage filling the unbuilt bomb sites, but the result pleases the eye. I think I'll enjoy my stay here.

June 28, Berlin. I slept late, but had time to chat with Mischa Wazsynski (he insists EL CID is *great*) before going off on a long round of official functions. I feel more responsibility here not to slight anyone than I do on usual tours; the main point they made in Washington was to give every attention to minor delegations (God, there are certainly a *lot* of them). The French party offered some amusement, but the French film is very self-conscious, I thought. I've still seen little of Berlin, but that's not what I came for.

June 30. The skies brightened with Lydia's arrival. She sensibly slept most of the day, only emerging bright and bushy for Mischa's party. The festival continues under full steam: The press of the world is full of comment on the Berlin crisis, but here in the eye of the hurricane all is calm and full of optimism.

July 1. The peak of the festival was supposed to be the ball, which was indeed a very impressive gala, Lydia resplendent in yellow, me in my new tailcoat, both holding our own against the background of international beauty. But our tour of the Eastern sector was far more memorable than anything else I've seen here. The window this city provides to the East gives a clear picture of Communist society, even though it's softened by the necessity of appeasing their citizenry, who can escape to the West.

Not much longer. This was only days before the Communists stopped the flow of refugees with the Berlin Wall. Touring East Berlin that day on a diplomatic passport, with instructions to ignore any efforts to restrict our movements on the part of the East Berlin guards, I must be one of the last American civilians to move freely there. The contrast to West Berlin was horrifying.

July 5, Berlin/Chicago. The oversolicitous waiters didn't waken us when they brought in breakfast, so we damn near slept through our plane.

Somehow we cleared the hotel in forty minutes flat from waking, a new record for Lydia. From Frankfurt, Pan Am gave us absolutely the best flight across I've ever known. We reached Mother's house in midsummer dusk while Fray was still up, like a white bear cub in a terrycloth robe, angular little-boy arms reaching up for a rough little-boy hug.

July 10, Los Angeles. We're still not finally set on the actress for the TV opus, though the studio turned down my suggestion: Glynis Johns. They couldn't afford us both, they said. The director seems sincere and enthusiastic, but I can't seem to work up the proper enthusiasm myself. This may pass. It better, if we're going to do anything good.

July 11. We finally settled on a girl for the part . . . Jennifer Raines, whom I don't know. She's not a bad actress, though understandably nervous (convinced she was going to be fired, it turned out). I felt a little more creative today, but we didn't achieve nearly as much as the director felt we did, though I guess talking Universal into a day of rehearsal on a film TV show is achieving a hell of a lot. I worry about the prevalence of enthusiasm in this profession. A little honest skepticism in the arts is a healthy thing.

July 13. Well, we got off to a reasonable start on my first filmed TV. We failed to complete the scheduled day's shooting; a good sign we're taking more pains than they usually do in TV. I felt I did well enough in the stuff in the cave with the little boy. I was interested in the meeting tonight on improving the U.S. posture at film festivals. I think there's really a chance to do something here, even if only getting someone useful to go to them.

I've changed my mind. Film festivals serve as a useful marketplace for independent film makers trying to get some sort of distribution, but this is their only valuable function. In terms of relating to film as an art form, they're nonsense.

July 15. The party tonight at the Manulises' to meet Tad Mosel was unusually good. One of those rare evenings where you don't feel frivolous for spending your time partying. These people seemed to have something to say . . . or at least they were willing to listen to me, which seems like the same thing, of course.

July 23. Poor Fray's ear is no worse, but hardly better. He chafed under house confinement all day and bore it with better spirits than I would. Lunch with Mel Shavelson to confer on EASTER DINNER revealed a promising personality. I think I could work well with him. My main problem is their determination to make the film in Italy. I don't want to do that; not just after EL CID. The location maybe, but not the whole damn film.

July 24. Herman made a deal for me to do EASTER DINNER at Paramount. So I'm a working actor again, though with some misgivings. Why black and white, for one thing? At least I got my wish . . . I'm doing a modern comedy. It should be a pleasant change from nobility.

July 27, New York en route to Rome. I cut it a little close leaving for the airport this morning, but I left my family in one piece, with Fray not very disturbed at my departure. I reread EASTER DINNER on the plane. (I hate that title. I think AMERICANS GO HOME is much better.)

Everybody hated that title. Especially with me in the picture, it seemed to suggest a film about the Last Supper. The picture was released as THE PIGEON THAT TOOK ROME.

I got a few calls made, looked in on the calm summer serenity of our empty apartment, then had a relaxed dinner with Bill and Nina before catching the Italian jet. Why do Italian flight crews wear those lumpy caps? It makes them look very *incompetent*, somehow, set square on their heads like that.

July 28, Rome/Taormina. The hardest part of the trip was the last hour and a half, driving over the mountains from the airport to Taormina. The back of a Fiat 2000 is exhausting over that distance, even compared to the eight thousand miles in the DC8 . . . more dangerous, too. Our driver insisted on glueing himself to the tail of the car ahead, come hell, high water, or ten-ton trucks. We got here at last, and I opted out of the visit (maybe with the same driver?) to Messina. They were chagrined, but I felt justified in a solo dinner and early bed.

This was a multipurpose trip, which is the best way to set up those overocean shots. I had to go to London for several days to do my looping on EL CID and I set it up so I could go by way of Sicily and attend the Taormina Film Festival, where I was awarded the David di Donatello, the Italian version of the Academy Award. (This prize is distinguished by the fact that it's one of the very few award statues I've ever seen that has any artistic merit in itself. Most of them, as sculpture, are about on a par with bowling trophies. The Italian award is a twenty-inch replica of Donatello's statue of David. It may not be quite as good as Michelangelo's version, but it's not bad.)

July 30, Catania/Rome/London. I was up at an ungodly hour, bounding around in the back of that same damn Fiat (different driver though), back across the Sicilian mountains to Catania. Flying out, Mt. Etna sprawled below in stiffened folds of black icing, like the mountains of the moon, the crest boiling coils of volcanic smoke and drifting gases. Jimmy Stewart and his family were beside me on the jet from Rome, just back from safari in Africa. Jimmy was unshaven, slightly bleary, and bubbling with enthusiasm. It'd be marvelous to go there sometime when Fray is a little older. God help him grow older and happier than the world seems just now.

July 31, London. I finally launched off on the dubbing of EL CID, at Beaconsfield. I was horrified when Mischa Waszynski told me offhandedly that over seventy percent of the sound track must be redone . . . something to do with inconsistent Spanish current. This may have a shattering effect on the end quality of the film. (Orson, of course, would be delighted; he'd see it as a chance to do all the sound over.) I must say Tony doesn't seem terribly perturbed about it, but I have misgivings.

August 2. Heroic effort by all hands brought the dubbing in well under the wire. I think some scenes were actually improved by what we did and I don't believe we hurt anything, but I'm still a little shaken by the enormity of the task. I had dinner and a long session at the Savoy with the Bronstonites on THE FALL OF THE ROMAN EMPIRE, which they're most anxious to get my reaction. I'd prefer to wait till I read a full script (they have only half now) and see EL CID finished. We agreed to postpone the decision a month at least.

August 3, London/New York. A busy departure day, what with fitting in the usual meetings, etc., as well as gift shopping for my family. We tried to arrive at some idea for casting on Mel Shavelson's comedy, but only looked through a few stills. It probably would be best to use new Italian actresses and trust to me for the marquee weight. The trip was damn long; weathered out of New York, we had to refuel at Philadelphia. I read all the books in my bag, plus a hundred pages of script on THE FALL OF THE ROMAN EMPIRE (I found it only fair) before we finally got on the ground at Idlewild, near midnight.

August 4, New York/Los Angeles. A dead-run kind of day in New York, but I touched all the bases. It's clear Allied Artists wants me to tour as much as possible for EL CID in December, earlier if I can . . . which I doubt. The plane was delayed in takeoff, further by a storm in the Midwest, but I finally got back to my ridge.

August 10. I finished dubbing the TV film, looping with that annoying sound-track-only method they use for TV. Still, I finished in less than an hour. I went to see a Greek film, NEVER ON SUNDAY, tonight to look at Mercouri for our film. She's very good indeed, but seems remarkably un-Roman to me. I suppose it could work, but I have some misgivings about the casting. (Don't I always?)

August 11. An inconclusive meeting with Mel Shavelson on casting. He's now toying with the idea of switching the locale to Paris, then casting Chevalier or Boyer as the father. I thought this a good idea at first, but Lydia disagrees . . . she may be right.

August 15. Well, the tennis court may not be painted yet, but at last we have our family. The Adoption Institute called today: They have a baby girl for us. We'll have her Thursday. She sounds like exactly what we hoped for.

August 16. There were various career oddments today, but we're really thinking of little but the baby girl we're getting tomorrow. It'll be strange and wonderful to have an infant in our house again; I can hardly believe it. All of us are happy.

August 17. We brought Holly Ann home today. She seems tinier than I remembered babies could be, certainly smaller than Fray ever was. A small, pretty face, with an open bud of a mouth. We all took to one another at once. Joe Field came over to help me put up the tennis court backing, stayed for a look at our daughter, then we had our first evening alone with our whole family.

September 1. I'm quite pleased at the idea of doing FDR's voice in a series on his career, using newsreel clips. It'll be a fairish amount of work, though there will be no photography. Afterward, Herman discussed the whole problem of film roles. It's probably unwise, he feels, to turn entirely away from the hand that has fed me so often in the past. Perhaps THE FALL OF THE ROMAN EMPIRE will turn out to be doable. The main thing, of course, is to wait and see what EL CID looks like.

September 14. I did some research on the period of Marcus Aurelius, satisfying myself that the Bronston script is largely without solid historical basis. This still doesn't mean I shouldn't do it, but it makes it less attractive.

September 19. I lunched at the Derby with Walter Seltzer. He seems to feel VIEW FROM THE FORTIETH FLOOR would make a good film. I must say, my enthusiasm was rekindled for it. I caught SPARTACUS tonight with Lydia and was impressed. Kirk's made a good film, in which Kubrick's hand is evident. An advantage it has over both BEN-HUR and EL CID is some humor and the women's acting. Why am I so anxious to *compare?* This is not a track meet.

September 20. There's still a great deal of pro and conning as to when and why I'm to go to Rome. They're most anxious to have me there September 29 for "tests." What kind of tests they could have in mind or why I must be there a week ahead of shooting to make them is something I don't know.

September 21. Citron submitted to me today an idea for a remake of BEAU GESTE, with me as Sergeant Markov, Dean Martin and Tony Curtis in the other roles. I turned this down indignantly, but was persuaded to run Coop's version. Surprisingly, he's right; Markov *is* the best part. Of course, Coop dominates as he would in any role, and Donlevy makes less than the best of Markov. This could be a very interesting project. Ernie Kovacs's dinner was a lot of fun. Where but Hollywood can you go to a dinner where the host has a wine cellar with plastic cobwebs?

September 27, New York. I checked into the apartment and slept late, before going off for a lunch interview. New York looks fine with fall in the air. Everyone should spend all of October, one week of November, and the last of September in New York. It makes me think of walking up Sixth Avenue to rehearse at the old Center Theater for ANTONY AND CLEOPATRA, all that time ago. Fall is the time when a kid actor in his first Broadway part feels like God.

September 28, Tape ABC Thanksgiving Show. A steadily demanding, but not exhausting day taping my Thanksgiving poetry. Both Browning and Whitman worked; the O. Henry bit was cut down, but I ended up quite happy, on the whole. I was disappointed in what I saw both off and on Broadway tonight. CAMELOT is ridiculous.

That's *ridiculous! I expect I was probably feeling grumpy because I hadn't done as well with the Browning and Whitman as I thought I should have.*

September 30, Los Angeles. Back in Los Angeles, I'm surprised how much I miss the autumn I just got a taste of in New York. Coming back, California seems dry and bland. Not my house and family, though. I've honestly never felt more a part of them nor they of me. This is a *good* year, by God.

October 2. We're beginning to swing into high gear at Paramount, though Shavelson's absence all these weeks makes it still seem unreal to me. Certainly THE PIGEON THAT TOOK ROME is a much better title than EASTER DINNER. As for my little experiment in tele-film, it was disappointing to me. My acting's OK, as is the film, but the cutting and the whole thing seem *loose* in spots. I'm afraid it's nothing to scream about. I guess that proves it: You can't do much there. *I* can't, anyway.

God knows I'm no authority on film TV. I only did two or three of them . . . this was the last. Certainly some very good work has been done, certainly the medium imposes sharp limitations. I applaud anyone who does well in it.

October 5, New York/en route to Rome. A mightily compressed trip, the jet cramming a continent, half an ocean, and the whole day into about seven hours. I sat there lapped in luxury, but plagued by one of those curvy damn 707 seats that allow you to do nothing but sit in an attractive attitude suitable for ad photos. I read Mel's current rewrite of the script, which I find very good. There are many funny bits added; I have no quarrel with what he's done. I tried to watch THE PLEASURE OF HIS COMPANY in flight, courtesy of TWA and some inventive fellows who've figured out a way to run movies on airplanes, but I fell asleep.

The in-flight movies are presented better now than they were then, but I still dislike them. Even though I profit from it, I hate having my films shown on the jets. The sound is terrible, the image is weak, and you're playing to an audience who may have no interest whatever in seeing your film. It's even worse than showing them on network television, with commercials every seven minutes.

October 6, Rome. I spent the day catching up and rearranging my sleep schedule, also exploring with Alan Brown [*one of Sam Bronston's top executives*] the reluctance I have for their FALL OF THE ROMAN EMPIRE script. I said I was willing to think about it a little. (*Why can't I say no?*) The evening ended predictably and late, but we're not shooting yet. This town has certainly turned into Hollywood-on-Tiber. You wonder if there's anyone left home to make ripples in the swimming pools.

October 9. Wardrobe, for me, was a lot of standing around waiting. None of the civilian clothes seemed right, really. We even toyed with the idea of having me masquerade most of the time as a German officer, simply to give me some good-looking wardrobe. This was discarded, for a variety of good reasons. [*I should hope so!*] Reading Elsa Martinelli's scenes with her, I doubt she's read the script more than once. Much, *much* work will be required with a dialogue coach, and there are five actors that need this attention. I think we need more coaches.

October 11. At the bottom of the Janiculum Hill, we shot my first scene in PIGEON THAT TOOK ROME, spending an unconscionable time getting what should've been a very simple dolly shot. It was complicated by a bad boom crew and poor Arthur Shields, who had some insecurity on his lines. Zanuck's man called from Paris; they have a new role for me in THE LONGEST DAY.

October 12. The first scene with Elsa began better than I had expected; she knew all her lines and spoke with a minimal accent. The problems of shooting around Roman traffic are compounded by the early loss of the sun on the Bernini fountain, so we shot as late as possible, then had lunch and broke for the day. Relaxed a bit tonight with eight or ten miscellaneous folks, including Art Buchwald.

I don't mean Art Buchwald is miscellaneous . . . he's a very gifted and special man (though he has absolutely no *backhand).*

October 14. Though frustrated by the late arrival of our Italian ingenue (and it's only her second film, too . . . what will she be on her tenth?), we got fairly along on the scene with the radio. I find Mel is a probing kind of director, he often seems to give me things I can use. I must guard against the initial impulse to reject direction out of a need to defend my identity as a star and serious actor. I should be past that by now. Big black-tie do tonight, got very late, rather tight, but Liz Taylor had sequins on her eyelids. You don't get to see that every day.

This was a birthday party for Joe Mankiewicz, the director of CLEOPATRA, *then languishing in its second year of shooting. You could say Joe was in a gloomy mood when I stopped at his table and said lightly "Hey, Joe . . . got any work for chariot drivers?" He gave me a look of black despair and replied, "Only for losers, Chuck . . . only for losers."*

October 23. I haven't acted with sheep since TEN COMMANDMENTS, and I don't care if I never do again. They're almost as bad as camels, I swear. I feel I probably did my best performance of the day at lunch with Sheilah Graham, but I put in a busy time wrestling Elsa through the crowd of extras and aforementioned sheep. (They stink, too.) [*The sheep, not the extras.*] A letter from Lydia advances the possibility of her not coming, since we may finish early. This distresses me; I'm getting mighty restive alone here.

October 31. This was a marvelously happy day. Lydia's arrival was delayed by her missing her flight out of London, but she showed up at last, without baggage but looking fresh as dew and beautiful as spring. After one more long last setup, we finished all of the wedding scene coverage they need me for (they may come back later after I'm gone) and we finally got back to the hotel for dinner and an ecstatic reunion.

November 2. We got quite a lot done, but it was a fiddling around sort of day. There's still hope of finishing here by Saturday, but it's dimming rapidly. We had a terrible time with a bit player who was totally unable to remember the lines for a half-page scene. We got through at last, and I had a drink with Orson at the hotel. He's looking trimmer, but is in as full cry as ever. I'd *still* like to do JULIUS CAESAR with him, but I turned down Warwick's CROMWELL script.

November 5. Sunday shooting was well worth doing, since it finished us up here. We just beat out the winter weather, too, I'd say. A knife-edge tremontana swept down off the mountains this morning, making me glad I wasn't shooting in that slave galley again. Lydia packed us for an early departure tomorrow. Paramount is not exactly happy with me leaving ahead of the negative OK, but rank has its privileges, as the army used to put it.

The lab sends word each day that the negative for the previous day has been safely developed. Maybe once every hundred times, something goes wrong here. If the actors have left the location, this makes problems.

November 6, Rome/New York via Paris. Italy never looked more beautiful than driving out along the road to Ostia under a classic blue sky, poplars dropping leaves in yellow scraps to swirl behind the car. Paris, of course, was gray, but the long flight back home, chasing the twilight, was very easy. The crowded customs bustle, then a sharp-edged black boat of a limousine to sweep back over the Triborough to Tudor City at last. We're both a little worn out, but not too much to catch some theater after a soup and sandwich supper.

November 8, New York/Detroit. I did stills this morning in the RCA Building, suddenly struck with the memory of the day I walked through that lobby to call Lydia, the bit part McClintic gave me in ANTONY AND CLEOPATRA firmly in hand. Now Guthrie's dead, I'm where I am . . . but the marble in the lobby floor's not worn down a millimeter, I'm sure. I was struck again with echoes of time past, checking into the Cadillac in Detroit after visiting Russ and Velda tonight. We first slept there together when I was at Selfridge Field, just before going overseas.

November 12, Los Angeles. Having been spared any damage to our home in the brush fires that ravaged Bel Air last week, we had our own independent production today. The damn steam room is inadequately vented still and set a fire in the roof. The firemen did well to save as much of the wall and roof there as they did. It could've been much worse. The Nehru dinner at the Beverly Hilton tonight was a very posh affair, not as crowded as these things are apt to be. My cold was not enhanced by the afternoon on the roof with a garden hose, though.

November 13. Shooting at Paramount went not more than fairly well today. Elsa's difficulty with lines (in English only?) plus the corrosive effects of ten years on top of this trade made me violate my own commandment about staying the hell out of another actor's work. I found myself in anxious conferences with Mel all day. SAG elected me third vice-president tonight, then we listened to a lot of nonsense re overseas production.

November 16. I ran EL CID and was very disappointed, though I'm still sure it will make a lot of money. The plus values are an impeccably tasteful physical presentation, as well as some very good performances. The whole last third of the film is extremely good. The flaws are excessive length, one minute too much footage in each fight scene, and ten feet too much in each silent close-up of Sophia (who is very good). I'm very good in the last, a bit stiff in the opening, patchy in the middle till I get into the beard scenes.

November 20. I all but turned down THE FALL OF THE ROMAN EMPIRE, though I'm giving Herman one last inning on the subject, which he'll take tomorrow, I think. I'm still convinced there is no good reason for me to make the film, since it can do nothing but make me a lot of money.

November 22. I finally finished in that apartment set, which was getting a little tired anyway. I'm not working as hard as I should in this; it's an easy part to drift through. I may regret it. I went over what my congressional testimony for SAG will be at lunch, though I have other things pressing ahead of that, God knows. (I *must not* take on so damn many things!)

November 30. The rest of the beach stuff went well. I did a good running fall (if you can't get a laugh with a pratfall, you might as well quit). Yesterday's footage looked good, too. We'll have a scene here. Nick Ray, now that FALL OF THE ROMAN EMPIRE is out of the way, stepped into line with a treatment of a story on the Boxer Rebellion, 55 DAYS AT PEKING, also for Sam. I haven't read it, of course, but it might be an interesting period for a film. I'd like to work for Nick, too. I feel myself getting reservations already, though. Why can't an actor be content to take jobs and *do* them? Must every film be the best one ever made?

I had no idea how determined Sam was to have me follow EL CID with another film for him. No sooner had I turned down THE FALL OF THE ROMAN EMPIRE than they shoved it back a year on their schedule and began work on 55 DAYS AT PEKING, converting the enormous and already half-built set representing Rome into an equally enormous and even more beautiful set representing Peking.

December 1, Los Angeles/Washington, D.C. Mel invented many happy bits for the bath scene today. It should be funny. The shaving scene is OK too, I think. I know the fall is; I saw it in the dailies. Cora delivered the mimeo copies of my SAG statement just in time to catch the late plane for the East.

December 2, Washington, D.C. A hellishly tiring day, but interesting, successful and possibly even useful from my point of view. (I doubt very much whether any action whatever will be taken by Congress as a result.) At least I got my views on overseas production on the record.

December 4. I really worked only two hours . . . damn little to fly the extra six thousand miles for. [*I'd had to double back to Los Angeles from Washington, instead of going on to London.*] I was glad, in fact, to have a little time to expand in. I got to pick my son up at school and read *two* chapters of TREASURE ISLAND to him (this is our third trip to that durable archipelago!). Nick Ray and Alan Brown undertook a big sell on the Boxer story, but I'm not so sure about it nor about doing MEASURE FOR MEASURE for John Houseman. I'll read it (one always says "reread" with Shakespeare, but I never *had* read this one.)

December 5. I got in an early visit to Dr. Peschelt, to replace the old amalgam filling (a mark of success: have your old filling replaced with gold . . . I'd be a real prize for a corpse-robber), then Alan Brown ran me out to the airport in plenty of time for a polar jet to London for the EL CID premiere. I'd never flown that route before, but you can't see Santa Claus, it seems. I did manage about six hours of sleep, pausing only to eat the usual gluttonous meal, and go on about 55 DAYS AT PEKING at some length with Nick Ray, who came along expressly to continue his selling job, I gather. He does seem serious . . . it may be a conceivable project.

December 6, London. London, even on a one-day trip, never seems to fail me. Fray's favorite statue, of St. George killing the dragon, is gone from the front of the Dorchester, but it is still all you could ask a hotel to be. The Fields are right next to us; it's delightful to have them aboard. I must say, surprisingly, the film seems much better on a second viewing, with an audience. Is this because I'm now considering 55 DAYS AT PEKING, with the same management? Or because I've adjusted to its flaws and can now examine its virtues? I still doubt it'll receive serious notices, but I'm convinced it will do well. Probably very well.

December 12. I got back home early to read some more offers. I'm attracted a bit by the opening pages of an offer from Columbia,

DIAMOND HEAD. A good part in an overwritten and melodramatic script. If it's treated with great care, it might work out all right. Maybe.

December 19. A long and exasperating day wrapping the picture with bits and pieces. Mel and I gave the company a tacky kind of wrap party, since we finished so late, but end-of-picture parties are always tinged with melancholy. We barely made THE CHILDREN'S HOUR premiere tonight (after making a pact with Willy to go to each other's openings, too). I was strangely disappointed in his film: It seems negligible, to come from him. A mountain laboring, birthing a mouse.

December 24, Los Angeles. I finished decorating the tree, except for a large hole left for the children to fill, in good time before the guests came. It went well, everyone listened patiently while I read A CHRISTMAS CAROL. Fray sang a carol for the group, disproving our fears that he had inherited my ear. He still harbors some sibling hostilities, but he caressed Holly in her crib, somewhat tentatively, and said, "You know, this is the first time I've had any mercy on her . . ."

December 25. Well, of course, it was marvelous. For our first Christmas in Coldwater, the weather was the way they keep saying it was in California thirty years ago. We burned the Baurs' Yule log in the fireplace, Fray made at least ten trips up and down the drive with his red two-wheeler, but the Union cavalry tunic I'd had made was a large success, too. The bracelet made Lydia's eyes glow, as I remember they did for a little green wool hood I bought for her our first Christmas in New York.

December 26, New York/en route to Madrid. Flying east over the Grand Canyon, I was amazed to see snow on the ground, white to the rim of the canyon. From twenty-five thousand feet, the pine trees showed through it like pepper scattered through a salt dish. New York, what I could see of it, crawled with holiday bustle. I must confess I felt very put down flying over the Atlantic for the thirteenth time this year, but it's worthwhile, I suppose.

December 27, Madrid. I wouldn't have thought it was eight months since I saw Madrid. It's still there, gray-green and pinched in the winter with the cloaked Guardia Civil stalking silently along the ridges against the sky as you drive along the long, straight roads. Franco, a shotgun having exploded in his hands yesterday, did not attend the EL CID opening, but the audience reaction was, of course, the best yet. (If the film won't play here, it won't play anywhere.) I had three meetings on the 55 DAYS AT PEKING project with Nick and Phil. I think I'll do it.

December 28, Madrid/London. The last talk in the limo with Nick before catching the plane for London and the DIAMOND HEAD meetings with Guy Green persuaded me he may do what Tony couldn't do last year: get an honest sort of script out of Phil. Guy Green, in our brief London lunch meeting, gave me a good feeling.

December 29, London/Los Angeles. I spent a very fulfilling morning going through the Turners at the Tate. He was a modern painter a century before anyone else; a fantastically original talent. He was able to fulfill all aims simultaneously; he makes the nonobjective painters look like nursery-schoolers. We were lucky to get out at all this afternoon; fog hung over Heathrow like a cold wet horse blanket waiting to drop. I sat for hours in the VIP lounge, discussing the script with Jerry Bresler [DIAMOND HEAD *producer*]. This continued as we finally got off, and over the Pole, all the way home, where Lydia, Fray, Holly, and Mother waited patiently.

December 31, Los Angeles. Sixty-one crept by me rather unaware . . . or would "swept" be more apt? I began it buried in the creative morass that marked the EL CID shooting and ended it committed to a rematch on the same court, though with new balls and different linesmen. EL CID put no stars in my crown, but maybe a ruby or two in my pocket. As for 55 DAYS AT PEKING, I feel uneasy. But I'm now convinced I must go basically on what confidence I have in a director's talent. My ridge is still an achingly lovely place to live, perhaps because I'm here so seldom. To live here, it begins to look like I have to work elsewhere. I left the last of my little boy somewhere in '61, looking for a too-big cowboy hat. He's lanking out now, gap-toothed and too big to carry in one arm anymore. Holly is just right for that, though, and Lydia fits beautifully in both.

1962

55 Days at Peking, in Spain . . .

John the Baptist in *The Greatest Story Ever Told* (George Stevens) . . .

developing a film from *The Lovers,* a play.

Losing one's head: to Ava Gardner in *55 Days at Peking*

As John the Baptist in *The Greatest Story Ever Told*

January 2, Los Angeles. I seem to be spinning my wheels getting running in 1962. I fiddled with a few odd jobs around the place, some good tennis, but little else till evening, when we gave a satisfactory dinner for visiting firemen from Europe. My desk is still two inches deep with unanswered mail . . . even some unopened Christmas cards. Herman closed gross deals for DIAMOND HEAD and 55 DAYS AT PEKING. We're trying to get Yvette Mimieux for DIAMOND HEAD.

January 4. The usual sort of preproduction social lunch today at Columbia. Jerry Bresler strikes me as an amiable man. The casting's still not set, except for George Chakiris. I did what amounted to an open question forum tonight for Arthur Knight's class in film at USC. It's really an easy chore, though I doubt if I talked anyone out of trying this odd line of work.

January 11. Mimieux is not available for DIAMOND HEAD, it develops, which is a bit of a blow. Guy Green's gone to Hawaii to scout locations, so I can't discuss it with him. I don't think Carroll Baker is right.

January 18. I dutifully went through the ancient tribal ritual at Grauman's, putting my foot in wet cement, attended by a full complement of photographers and fans. So now I'm immortalized, right on top of Marilyn Monroe and Jane Russell. (How many men can make that statement?) Guy's film tonight (LIGHT IN THE PIAZZA) was good, possibly not quite as effective as his other two, but demonstrating his ability with actors. Mimieux would be excellent, if we can get her.

January 23. My throat is still ominous, but I betook myself to a dimity little luncheon to receive an award for EL CID from eighteen ladies comprising the Film Council. Never mind . . . I'm grateful. We stopped by to see Edie Kovacs. She's in pretty good shape, I thought. Appropriately, we saw Ernie's last show tonight. TV will miss him as much as we will.

Ernie had been killed in an auto accident a few days earlier. I think TV needs him even more now than it did before.

January 24. My really ferocious throat scared me into bed for the day, where I tossed and fumed, thoroughly bored by midafternoon. I did get the happy news that we have Mimieux for DIAMOND HEAD. On the basis of what we saw in LIGHT IN THE PIAZZA she's ideal for the part. My main concern now is to see what kind of rewriting Guy can elicit from our scrivener.

January 26. It was an odd experience, trying on the BEN-HUR chariot costume for a gag appearance on Milton Berle's show Sunday. It's still the same as when I wore it those three tough months four years ago, but that summer's sweat has dried into the leather now. I had dinner with the DIAMOND HEAD people tonight. Guy Green, of our producer: "He seems a very intelligent fellow; but how could a man refer with pride to the fact that he'd made a film called GIDGET GOES HAWAIIAN?"

January 29. I finished reading a treatment of Fitzgerald's RICH BOY. I'm more interested in getting the writing on DIAMOND HEAD right. I was glad to hear from Ned Brown, though. He's come up with a price on THE LOVERS.

THE LOVERS was a play by Leslie Stevens that had been submitted to me for Broadway a few years earlier. I turned it down, primarily because the casting problem on the other roles proved insoluble, but the play fascinated me. By 1962, it had occurred to me that it could be adapted into a superb film script. Through Ned Brown, a literary agent for MCA, I was exploring what it would cost me to buy the film rights.

January 31. I looked at the DIAMOND HEAD wardrobe sketches. Why is it designers like to do *costumes*, instead of clothes? It's a grievous fault even in a period film, but there's no excuse in a modern story. I lunched with Walter Seltzer over the potential of THE LOVERS for film. First we need a script, which will be expensive, and must be, to be good. If we make it, it must not be a huge picture. We should advertise instead "A Cast of Dozens!!"

I've probably read more epic film scripts than any other living actor. Aside from the basic problem of rendering another period and another way of talking and thinking about the world so it will be comprehensible to a modern audience (something whole generations of talented film makers are unequipped to do), the main problem with such scripts is that they almost always deal with a major historical event. This event not only has to be made clear to the audience, but the historic figures involved in it also have to be presented, each in his turn. By the time all of this is done, you've used up most of your movie. You're usually reduced to a kind of cinematic shorthand. THE LOVERS was unusual in that it involved a small number of characters in a very remote part of eleventh-century Flanders. Their story in no way changed the course of history and touched only themselves. It seemed to me it could touch an audience too.

February 2. I finally did that damn interview I've been putting off, in my old Paramount dressing room. It's musty and unused now (apt illustration of the atrophied state of local production). I had a late, long meeting with Herman over the LOVERS buy. We finally decided to offer three thousand for a three-year option, then haggle later on the purchase price. I have an idea Herman's not really mad for me to do this. Walter of course is eager to plunge ahead. I must balance this out. It's impossible to shoot sooner than a year anyway.

February 5, Washington, D.C. Today I met the president, the vice-president, the Speaker of the House, and some twenty or thirty assorted senators and congressmen. I was overawed, though I couldn't help wondering who was minding the store. Reasonably enough, JFK impressed me most, clearly a very high-powered character. His instant assessment of people and situations, coupled with a remarkable store of information on unlikely subjects, was formidable.

Happily, he also admired my work in EL CID, *which I think showed great taste on his part. A few months later, I was severely chastised by a Palm Beach socialite who told me she'd almost frozen to death, trapped by protocol in the garden at the Kennedy compound there one unseasonably chilly night while the president, warmly wrapped in blankets to protect his bad back, watched the film for the third time.*

February 12. So now he's seven. I turned my back and the baby who awed me the dawn he was born has disappeared entirely inside a gangling, gap-toothed boy with a grin. He enjoyed his birthday very much, I think, including screening THE BIG COUNTRY. I found the film still fine, but I was disappointed with my work in it. I'm stiff and contrived through much of the footage. When will I see an old film of mine I like?

February 19. Up and off to Columbia to test Chinese actresses. They have the same problem black performers do: There are so few good parts available, they have little chance to get the experience you need to be good. One of the two girls we tried today wasn't bad, but hardly five feet high, which is a problem, playing opposite me. I met Yvette Mimieux at last. She seemed an OK lady, though I've learned a certain wariness on this. James Darrin is set for the younger brother. The wardrobe is coming better. It's starting to look like *clothes*, now.

March 3. John Collier came to the house and met with Walter and me on THE LOVERS. I don't really know how to tell from a meeting whether a writer can do a script or not. [*Nobody knows, including the writer . . . or whether the actor can act it, for that matter.*] He seems interested, also knows something about the period. I'm sure we could do a lot worse.

March 5. The usual jammed day-before-leaving. I always seem to get a tremendous amount done then, which is an indication of how I usually use the time I have. The Golden Globe Awards dinner tonight was very ill-run. Too many speeches, and mine wasn't very good. Monroe was absolutely smashed, unable to utter a word. Probably just as well.

March 6, Hawaii, Island of Kauai. The flight out was uneventful, except that for the first time in my life (since that one night in the army in '43), I was sick enough to call a doctor. Not really sick, just a contemptible gut-cramping for no good reason. Of course, it passed away, but I'm disgusted with myself, all the same. This island will be a very quiet place to shoot, clearly. It's raining at the moment, but we have assurances from all sides that this is very unusual. It seems to me I've heard this comment in South Dakota, Peru, Texas, Florida, and a few other spots.

March 7. It rained hard all day, so we had a reading rehearsal of the whole script. It was awful. I suppose it gives a director something useful, but it always fills me with a gnawing conviction the whole project is doomed. The suite is comfortable, which is just as well; till the weather changes, I'll be spending a lot of time in it.

March 10. Well, we started it. Not stills, not publicity, not riding . . . but actually shooting film. It's a relief to be at it again. Guy Green works carefully and thoughtfully, but I don't feel I did very well. My main problem today was fighting light. Those brutes and reflectors loom larger in my mind than the scene. I must get into this with Guy. I make too many pictures on location to sluff this problem.

One of the banes of my career has been acting in exterior locations with arc lights and reflectors focused in my eyes, which are very light sensitive. (Dark-eyed actors have an unfair advantage, I've always felt.) Most people really have no idea of the dimensions of this problem. They always ask you how you can remember the lines . . . they should wonder instead how you can concentrate on the scene when your every nerve is straining simply to keep your eyes open. Happily, in recent years the film has become much faster, requiring less supplementary lighting in outdoor shots. Also, I've learned to negotiate my problem with the cameramen, who are always responsive.

March 15. We got the scene well-rehearsed and shot a take or two before the rain killed the day, but Lydia's arrival, looking bloody marvelous, made my weekend. We had a magnificent reunion with rain spattering down outside (it's raining violets . . .). The coming-togethers make the partings worthwhile. Suddenly Kauai seems a brighter place, even wet.

March 17. We started the nineteenth year off with a quart of champagne and pearls before breakfast for my girl, which strikes me as ideal. To have work to do, Lydia and champagne for breakfast is as much as I can ask. I actually did little today, though we shot while the weather held. We couldn't get the key coverage on the scene before the rains came. I ran dailies, then Lydia and I took off for the weekend. Hanalei is breathtaking. I've never seen a more beautiful resort hotel anywhere. We ended the evening most glamorously, sated with luxury.

March 18 (Sunday), Hanalei. Our day here was just about perfect, even though the rain we've come to expect came, inevitably, in the afternoon. By then we were en route back to Nawiliwili, our day of sun behind us. We could hardly have imagined a better place to spend an anniversary. Lydia's stay is too soon over, but it was marvelous. If we'd only get some weather, I could look forward to the end of this location, instead of her next visit.

March 20. I worked all day on the key breakfast scene with Yvette. We both can do better, though Guy hasn't really gotten around to her close angles, anyway. Still, I'm relieved to hear he plans to retake all we've done, tomorrow. I have to project Howland's need to be loved, though he conceals it. You can't *play* this, of course, but it has to be in the scene, in the whole film, if we're to bring it off. I had a good work talk tonight with Guy.

March 25 (Sunday). We started out marlin fishing, then turned back to drop one of the actors ashore when he decided he was too afraid of water to stay aboard. I confess myself a little taken aback by this; Fray was easily encouraged out of this attitude last summer, when he was six. The expedition started out again and turned out to be fishless, but enjoyable anyway. I had one marlin strike, which was as exciting as any fishing experience I've ever had. A lovely big blue, leaping like a king. For forty seconds, we were tied together, then he was gone.

March 26. We're inundated with foreign press. They're looming larger each year, of course; you can't overlook their importance. John Ford came on the set today and mentioned a film to me, sort of sideways, from under his eyepatch. What the hell, Duke Wayne can't be wearing out yet.

March 29. We finally got a full day of good shooting light and finished off the riding sequence in the woods. Not too well, really; we had a good deal of anxious horsebacking among the actors, which makes for anxious acting. I ran the dailies on the saddling scene, which is OK, and my scene in the tack room with Yvette, which is only so-so . . . no, that's not true; the shots are good, but we're not marvelous. We'll see . . . a few more weeks of work with a Movieola can do wonders.

You have to work in film quite a while before you understand the subtle and shifting responsibility shared by actor, director, and editor for the performance finally seen on the screen. (Critics, for example, write an awful lot of nonsense about this.) It depends in part on the talents and creative authority each of these has, as well as the complexity of the role. Some parts, Shakespeare's for example, absolutely require an initially good performance to work at all. Others, well directed and edited, require from the actor only a chemically effective image on the screen. In any case, you can never tell, watching on the floor during shooting or looking at the dailies, how it will turn out in its final form.

March 30. I did the confrontation scene with Yvette and George today. I don't think we were superior, but the staging and camera concept was. My personal contribution was complicated by the fact that the classy flying mount I'd planned for my exit didn't quite come off; that son-of-a-bitch big stud is harder to handle than I figured . . . he damn near ran me into a gatepost. Anyway, the day ended on a high note: Just after I finally managed the horse, my family arrived, filling my soul.

April 4, Honolulu. I was delighted to finally shake the dust of Kauai off my feet. It's a lovely island, but finishing there means a large part of the work is done. Before we left, we saw a Pacific version of the Grand Canyon [*Waimea Canyon, Kauai*], with attendant family pleasures. (Fray made the sandwiches.) Back in Honolulu, we checked into the Royal Hawaiian, still good, and still damned expensive. Fray stayed without a sitter tonight. "I'm not a *baby* . . . I don't need a baby-sitter!"

April 5. We had a fine time stick-and-balling at the Waikiki Polo Grounds this morning. I wish I'd explored this sport a little deeper, a little earlier. That would've been one advantage of being in films in the thirties . . . you could afford this pastime then. The Pearl Harbor tour is impressive. The weight of the bones of the eleven hundred men still locked in the *Arizona* hangs over the waters of the bay yet. Some of them were no older than I was the day they died, while I sat in my room in Wilmette, reading.

April 7. At dinner tonight with Guy, we discussed the function of the producer . . . any producer. Guy feels the more he's on the set, the less he's able to function as an objective eye, which should be his most useful area of creativity.

April 8 (Sunday). Lydia and Fray got off in good order on a beautiful day, ending one of the more delightful interludes in our chaotic family history. I sat at the end of the runway watching their jet hurtle thunderously over my head out over the bay east for home, and knew how much I loved them both.

April 12. We knocked off the location in one long desperate gulp . . . starting early (all hands on time, for a change) and almost running between setups, everyone performing manfully. It's curious how a company's efficiency lifts at the thought of the homebound planes . . . like a horse when he smells the barn. It's a helluva strain, but I don't think the scenes suffered. It was all geographical nonacting stuff today. My last scene alone on the volcano, fortunately, we'll do back in the studio.

April 13, Hawaii/Los Angeles. So much for Hawaii. I regretfully realize that exotic climes are losing almost all their appeal for me as a result of these junkets. It certainly was worth going there to get the footage we got, but there's an awful lot of work and damn little pleasure in getting it. My home is getting to be a treasured vacation spot, on the other hand.

April 14. Lydia's birthday was a good day for my first back home. She enjoyed her gifts, especially Fray's decoration of the wrapping on the Hawaiian watercolor he gave her (working studiously at his desk with crayons, blond head bent rapt). The SAG Board meeting tonight was fraught with concern with overseas production. The craft unions are raising funds to "fight foreign films." "O, brave new world . . . that hath such creatures in it."

April 19. France Nuyen proved surprisingly effective in the scene we did today. She has exactly the right quality for the part, and does it well in addition. I'm not entirely pleased with the daily, though Yvette has one very effective close-up at the door which looks better than it shot.

April 24. I more or less squared away the next move on THE LOVERS. We'll make a deal for a treatment with John Collier. I'd like to get this going for one year from now. Nick Ray called today; the 55 DAYS AT PEKING script's nearly done. I'm researching marine uniforms for the period so I can do proper sketches. I'm not sure I can count on Bronston's designers to handle this.

This was excessive zeal on my part. Sam's designers were very gifted, and perfectly capable of handling the job. I think I wanted to tackle it myself because of its relative simplicity (U.S. Marine uniforms, circa 1900).

May 1. I had dinner with John Collier, to discuss THE LOVERS. His ideas on reconstruction of the play seem most stimulating, basically sound. He feels Chrysagon must be given something to lose, or sympathy for him won't sustain. He'd make his holding awarded in war, rather than heredity . . . this makes his position less secure. I'm anxious to see his ideas on paper.

May 6. I did some more background reading on the marines in China for the 55 DAYS AT PEKING picture and little else today but savor the delights of my ridge, thinking of how soon I'll be taken off it again, trekking after another film. Citron told me George Stevens wants me to do John the Baptist in his film on Christ. At least it'll be shot here in California, so they think now. I'm very flattered by an offer from Stevens. Of course, I must talk to him.

May 7. A long day of steady work on two scenes, both of which went pretty well, I think. Citron's very high on the offer from George Stevens for me to play John the Baptist in GREATEST STORY EVER TOLD. Herman says this is the main role. That's not the way I remember the story. John Collier called, anxious to talk to me over the weekend on the LOVERS treatment, then Bronston, who wants me to fly to Spain for preproduction work.

May 12. George Stevens came to lunch at the house to talk about his film on Christ. I still feel that the role is basically unactable, but he doesn't want me for that, after all. I hadn't thought to make another biblical epic, but I don't see how I can turn down a chance to work with George Stevens.

May 14. No shooting call, so I proceeded on the uniform designs for 55 DAYS AT PEKING. Nick phoned from Spain with disturbing news: It seems they want to use Ava Gardner (Sonny *Tufts!*). I'd better get my ass over there next week and find out what the hell is happening.

May 15. A very full day, during which I lunched with Stevens again to tell him I wanted to do John the Baptist for him. It'll involve any number of scheduling problems, since the baptism scene must be shot this summer in Utah, when I'll be in Spain. The part's not really a long one, very close to being the cameo role I had in mind to begin with, and the chance to work with Stevens is impossible to pass up. Collier has progressed well on the opening thirty pages of the LOVERS treatment, I think.

May 16. I did my next-to-last shot for DIAMOND HEAD today . . . a trivial scene in which I had one word: "Brief!" Now I only have the water shot from the dream sequence left. A frantic flurry of transatlantic calls on the 55 DAYS AT PEKING casting: Nick from London, Sam from Spain, but I'm still convinced Gardner is wrong. I don't see how I got myself into this bind; I begin to wish I were out of it. We'll work it out, but I hate using muscle in setting up a picture.

May 18. To finish shooting DIAMOND HEAD I waited around through most of the day to do one piddling shot from the dream. No dialogue, just my face looming up out of the fog. That finished the film for me. It's hard to tell what I think now, except that I'm still high on Green. He may have made a film that rises above the melodramatic qualities of the script. He didn't push me as hard as I should be pushed, but he gave me a lot, all the same.

May 21, New York/en route for Madrid. During the course of a long, lonely day in the air, I read and was disappointed by a script on the Renaissance (or is it?) that Art Penn sent me. I also found very shallow bottom in CATCH 22, currently best selling. (I paid four dollars and fifty cents for it.) There was time between planes to run in for dinner with the boys in New York, which I'll probably bypass returning; Allied Artists is urging me to do the EL CID opening in Rio when I'm through in Madrid.

May 22, Madrid. I arrived at dawn, beat out, of course. Fell into bed at the hotel, and asleep reading the script, not pleased with what I got through. The love story is very arbitrary, I think; the dialogue primitive. Lunch with Nick and Phil filled me with vast apprehensions. The casting problem on the girl seems almost insoluble. Deborah Kerr won't work this summer, and they're not too excited about Mercouri or Moreau. It's hard to think of anybody else . . . possibly Joan Collins, or Dana Wynter? Hmmm.

May 23. A damn exhausting day fighting over who should play the lady in 55 DAYS AT PEKING. My eyes are actually tired from looking through stills in the casting books. Anne Bancroft looks interesting and can act, but I wonder how she would be as a stylish Russian lady? Don't we need a European? I'm still convinced Gardner would be wrong, in these terms . . . her whole color is totally American. In a bearish temper about all this, plus Collier's problems on LOVERS, I chewed at Herman for a while over a very bad overseas connection. I doubt much of it got through.

May 24. This casting problem is about to drive me up the walls. I can't believe there aren't a few women you can risk an expensive film on. All available European distribution opinion (Sam says) insists Gardner is still very big in foreign release. I can't believe this either. I gave up on it for a while and took the night off. Jolly West is in town to address some tony bunch of professors; we had a pleasant evening, catching up. It's too damn seldom we have a chance to do this anymore.

May 26, Rome. I was reluctant to come to Rome, and I was right. David Niven's on location so I couldn't see him. The print of PHAEDRA

(Mercouri's film) is not available, nor was the English version of Gardner's last effort. I saw several reels dubbed in Italian, but that didn't help me (or Ava) very much. Jolly came along from Madrid as a sort of detached scientific observer of all this brouhaha, so I blew the evening showing him Rome.

May 27 (Sunday), Rome/Los Angeles. A long, theatrical meeting (everybody vigorously acting but me . . . I just sat there) at the Grand with Nick and all the Bronston brass resulted in painful agreement: We will ignore the shouts of dismay from distributors and make a major effort to get a European star, first Mercouri (who may not even want to do the damn part, or may want the moon in return for doing it). Nick seemed somewhat less than delighted with this position, but agreed nonetheless. I hate to stand fast in the face of all this, but I can't see it otherwise. A long flight home, paradise waiting.

May 29, Los Angeles. Still no firm word on casting our Russian countess in 55 DAYS AT PEKING. Collier has come up with a bit more of his treatment for LOVERS, though, and it looks good. We had several friends to dinner, several more at the theater to run THE PIGEON THAT TOOK ROME. It looks pretty good. Mel claims it's better than the first sneak two months ago. I find most of it hard to understand, but this is a combination of the dialects used and a poor sound track. We may have to redo much of the dialogue track.

May 31. I got cables from Nick advising Niven's accepted his role, Mercouri wants "major rewrite" on hers. Don't they always? Still, I'm inclined strongly to use her, if we can get her without distorting the whole script. Harry Friedman [*a colleague of Citron's at MCA*] is flying back to London tomorrow to investigate. I did at least see a marvelous Chinese actor for Prince Tuan.

I can't remember who this was or who decided to cast Robert Helpmann instead. (Actually, he was good, and he taught me a court waltz for the ball scene.)

June 6. Today was the day they gave babies away . . . or at least gave us ours. Holly, who was mine from the moment I saw her, became legally so in the judge's chambers late this morning, with the whole family in attendance. Fray had to stay out of school for the event, so Lydia used the time downtown to get his passport renewed and get Holly her first. Poor baby girl, she'll use up a lot of those, with me for a father.

June 11. Collier's work on LOVERS continues to be most promising. No, more than promising . . . exciting is a fair word. Citron is unwilling to proceed with Bronston on it until he gets a public reading on a film with me without a huge budget (i.e., THE PIGEON THAT TOOK ROME). This makes sense. The SAG Executive Committee meeting was largely devoted to Dean Martin's problems at Fox. We may meet with him tomorrow. (As though I didn't have enough problems of my own this week.)

Dean had just started filming a picture with Marilyn Monroe, who was by this time really unable to work. Fox recognized this a few days into the schedule and fired her, intending to replace her with another actress. Dean, while taking no position on the Monroe firing, was not happy with any of the actresses suggested for her replacement. Since the possibility of Monroe's not finishing the film had not (oddly) been anticipated, he was not protected contractually on this point, and he turned to the Screen Actors Guild for help. After two or three meetings, Fox decided to abandon the film, which struck everyone as a wise move.

June 12. Another long session at SAG on Dino's problems over the Monroe film, then discussed with Henry Wilcoxon [*de Mille's longtime associate, both as actor and executive*] his idea for a TV special on de Mille. It seems to be a good idea, if written with some objectivity. I ripped easily through a trailer at Columbia, less easily through a few more loops (new sound crew). The evening at home was very relaxed, what I need, so close to leaving. I only fiddled a bit on makeup ideas for the Baptist, in advance of the Stevens meeting Thursday.

June 14. George Stevens stirred a few sparks again when he came up for lunch. We more or less arrived at how the Baptist should look, while feeding him leftover Mexican food from last night's brawl. My last night here, California gave us a wonderful sunset.

June 15, New York. I got very little sleep last night, up at six-thirty or some such, but we caught the plane in leisured grace, some style being lent by Drago, who manfully endured the shattering experience of jetting to New York City in a crate (dogfully endured?). We were too tired to do anything in the way of theater tonight, but the whole family settled content in the apartment (that suddenly seemed much cozier, with Holly part of us).

June 18. For once, departure day wasn't impossible, maybe because I didn't try to fit tennis into it. I ran the FDR show on the Land again. It's genuinely good. I'm sure of that on two viewings. I bought another drawing pen, for which I've always been a sucker. (I no doubt imagine one of them will someday come equipped with Lautrec's line.) We caught the plane easily; only Drago was reluctant.

June 19, Madrid. That damn transatlantic jet is really not feasible for sleep, unless you're alone. I got here, in consequence, quite washed out, slept most of the day away in Nick's house, which we decided to take after all. To my relief, Lydia seemed to find it more than adequate. We took Fray over to the Selmers' for an evening with his old friends before they go off for the summer. So here we are, ready for 55 DAYS AT PEKING, though it's far from ready for us.

June 20. Of course, the damn uniforms, due here on the tenth, haven't arrived, and of course the rewrites discussed at such great length haven't come through mimeo yet (just as, of course, the set, the new sound stage, dressing rooms, and offices aren't ready yet either). Fray had a better day than I did, racing around the gate of the Forbidden City (unfinished) with the Selmer boys, his old buddies from EL CID.

June 28. En route to choose my horse, I stopped to watch Fray start his formal, Spanish riding school lessons, trying desperately to sit straight, bouncing around in a flat trot. He took it, which is about all the first lesson amounts to. Cocktails at Ava Gardner's went surprisingly well. I'm glad to know her a little. She has a softer quality than you get on the screen . . . more accessible vulnerable. She may be able to use this in the part, somehow.

Sam Bronston had by this time persuaded me that Ava was the best possible casting for the role of the Countess in the film. I recall a painful luncheon at the Ritz where Sam literally wept over the issue. To me, it was important, but not worth crying about.

June 30. The Wests arrived, full of beans, to the delight of all. They came out to tour the set while I rehearsed some of the physical stuff on the walls, then relaxed before dinner . . . until Holly suddenly came down with a tearing fever. Lydia and Jolly dealt with it, and all was well in time for dinner. I wish I could say the same about the late session I had at Nick's with Ava on the script. After forty minutes, I slid out (coward!) of what looked like a macabre evening, when she launched a total attack on her entire part.

July 1. I walked over to Nick's house to go over Ava's problem. Oddly, her rejection of the script has the curious effect of throwing me into support of it, which is not good, since it does still need a lot of work. I took the Wests and Fray to the corrida later. The bulls were brave, but not the toreros. I've still never seen anything like a superior corrida, but this one was enhanced visually by the trappings of the Goya period, also by one fight mounted, in the Portuguese manner.

July 2, Las Matas. We began shooting 55 DAYS AT PEKING with the night work we'll be on for a week or so. I start this picture with more misgivings than I remember about a film since I've had any creative controls. The work itself was incidental tonight: all press and public, toasts in champagne, and so forth. I did one shot, over my shoulder, my primary responsibility being to hit very precise marks, avoiding the split-focus center line. *Ars gratia artis.*

July 8 (Sunday), Madrid. I met with Nick again, at length but to no great purpose. I can't put my finger on the lack of contact I feel there. He's intelligent, articulate, and committed, but I feel a barrier . . . a performance, somehow. Maybe it's my fault. I haven't worked up the basic enthusiasm you need for this, or any project, yet. The day I make a film without it, I'm a whore.

July 16. We finally got down to work on one of the interiors (I can't count the stuff on the wall as scenes). Nick didn't finish in the throne room on schedule, so he was late on the set, but not very. So was Ava, but not very. We had time to block through it, in a way that should play reasonably.

July 17. Up early to meet Mother's plane, since I had no shooting call. She's in good shape and happy, as always. Then I did a long, beery interview with an English journalist (like English actors, they often seem to be heavy drinkers . . . why is this?) The dailies are OK photographically; I showed too many teeth, as I'm prone to do in fight scenes, from nervousness. I watched Ava shoot . . . she seemed nervous too. Nick is handling her with the thinnest kid gloves.

July 18. The damnedest thing about shooting in Europe is the number of holidays they have, studding the calendar like balloons. Today we shut down for anniversary of the start of the Civil War. I stopped by Nick's to discuss the script. The new scene for after the ball is not bad, though the tag in the hotel is still wrong, I feel. I haven't been able to *read* the whole script, because I only have pieces of it.

July 19. The heat's an enormous problem on the stages. It may turn out to be more difficult there than on the blazing Castilian plain at Las Matas. They're so fearful of losing time to the problem (makeup, wardrobe, fatigue) that they decided to blow ten thousand dollars on air-conditioners for the stages, instead of just cooling the star dressing rooms, as heretofore.

July 23. The intense heat generated on that small, uncooled stage makes the shooting very rough. They're working desperately to get the air-conditioners installed, will no doubt do so by tomorrow, when we, of course, move over to Seville for several days. I read a remarkably filmable SAC novel, FAIL-SAFE. It would be tough to get USAF cooperation. Also, there are no acting parts.

August 3 (Sunday), Madrid. I didn't shoot today, which gave me time to see Lydia and Fray off for Sitges with Bea and her boys, and Mother off for Chicago, on various planes. Only my daughter and my dog were waiting when I got home tonight; both did their best to comfort me. I went back and rehearsed the first scene with David [*Niven*], then we dined at Botin to talk about it. He doesn't like it and he's right. It doesn't go anywhere; I can't tell where it *should* go. This film is going to be damned hard to make well.

Working with David Niven was one of the few undiluted pleasures of making 55 DAYS AT PEKING. He's a first-class actor and a lovely, funny man to boot. I remember sitting at one of the press parties we gave about this time, earnestly explaining the politics of the Boxer Rebellion at great length to some weary journalist. In one of the pauses, I overheard David at the next table talking to his journalist. "Of course, if we get involved in the politics, we're lost."

August 9. We finished what we could of today's scene and hammered away at the rewrite of what we could of tomorrow's. I really think Phil Yordan has failed us here. Most of the dialogue we've shot has come from either me or David. It seems reasonable to say, if the actors can make it up as well as it's written, then it isn't written well enough. I made this point at some length tonight; I think I've pushed them into bringing Ben Barzman down to work on it.

Any good actor should be able to invent dialogue that actually sounds like people talking. Most of them can. Any good writer should be able to do better than this. Surprisingly, some of them can't.

August 10. I fear our best efforts have failed to rescue this scene. It's now barely credible as human speech, but unbearably complicated plot material for an audience to follow. The main point of the scene—*why* David is sending me to Tientsin—still falls into the hole Phil left in what he wrote. Word now is that Ben Barzman is on his way down, but I'm uncertain how much he can add to a script this deep in production.

August 14. I rushed sweating in tennis clothes to the set to give them something to shoot when Ava no-showed (they insist she's honestly ill; I suppose she deserves the benefit of the doubt). They took a helluva time to get the shots they switched to: interior of an opium den or whatever it's supposed to be, but we worked. Fray returned, brown, lean, and happy from his ten days on the beach, loaded with gifts from the sea and a white-toothed grin, having flown his first trip alone. God, how will I manage this film after they all go back to the U.S.?

August 18. We managed once again to resurrect an ill-written scene into some semblance of life, sort of by mouth-to-mouth resuscitation. Curiously overwritten lines seem to keep popping into the script every day or so on new pages. I'm drawn inescapably to the conclusion that these are from the nimble typewriter of Nick's wife, Betty. This will not do . . . especially not in Ava's part, which is where they are now. She must find another hobby.

August 20. No shooting for me today, but I did put in the time constructively on our script problems. Mischa insists Betty Ray is now out of the picture entirely, though no one has yet made clear to me how she got in it in the first place. Phil has some new ideas on the scenes with Ava and me. Some seem good, some transparent tomfoolery. In one of the action sequences, he wanted to include her manning a Gatling gun.

August 25. This must have been the longest day, and one of the toughest, I've shot on the film yet. I'd rather have retaken Valencia, or rerun the chariot race, than whirl through the sixteen bars of the Victorian waltz the scene required.

By this time Bobby Helpmann was having a fine time playing the prime minister to the dowager empress of China. How his background as a ballet star equipped him to play an Oriental diplomat so effectively, I don't know. It was obviously no trick for him to teach Ava and me a formal court waltz. He made us both look marvelous.

About this time, we moved out to Las Matas, some thirty miles outside Madrid, where Sam's crews had finished building the most impressive set I've ever seen in a film. There on the Spanish plain they had reconstructed most of the essential features of Imperial Peking, including the Tartar Wall, the Gates of the Forbidden City, the foreign legations, and all manner of markets, canals, bridges, and houses, from palaces to hovels. What's more, Sam had peopled it with Chinese extras. At that time, there weren't more than a hundred Chinese in all of Spain. Sam filled that lack by stripping the Chinese restaurants and laundries of Europe. I'm told you couldn't get a decent Chinese meal in any European capital the rest of that summer . . . the cooks were all off fighting the Boxer Rebellion for Sam Bronston. Unhappily, we never turned a camera on two thirds of this incredible city. I begged Sam to give Orson Welles a hundred thousand dollars and turn him loose with a film crew and some actors. Orson would have ad-libbed a marvelous spy story, shooting in the parts of the set we never got to.

Our problems on 55 DAYS AT PEKING mounted as we floundered about this vast and beautiful set through the growing heat of August. It was very hard on everyone . . . hardest of all, finally, on Nickk..

September 1, Las Matas. Today marked the worst behavior I've yet seen from that curious breed I make my living opposite. Ava showed up for a late call, did one shot (with the usual incredible delay in coming to the set), and then walked off just before lunch when some Chinese extra took a still of her. She came back after a painful three-hour lunch break . . . only to walk off again, for the same reason (this time untrue; the Chinese extra did *not* take a still of her). Great day.

September 2 (Sunday), Madrid. A long morning meeting on ways and means did nothing to help the picture or my peace of mind; it just eliminated my Sunday tennis. Obviously, if Ava's turning difficult, we'll have to sweat it out as best we can. The drive through the Guadarramas put all this behind me, for the afternoon. Salamanca is probably the most beautiful Spanish city I've seen . . . a pool of golden sandstone, with a wonderfully pure eighteenth-century plaza as its center.

September 4, Las Matas/Madrid. I got home exhausted after the frustrating complications of a long night's work. I don't know the answer to all this, but I suppose it will require simplifying and cutting down Ava's shots. The dailies, all very simple shots, seemed OK. I was on standby for tonight, but was called abruptly to the set, where Nick had simplified, all right. He'd given most of Ava's lines to Paul Lukas. Not many scenes where this switch can be effected, but I'm all for it where possible.

September 5. Ava behaved most irrationally, possibly in part through chagrin at having to lie silent all night while her scene was played by Lukas. I've never before seen someone literally writhe in frustration and shame. Poor, sad lady. We finished at six in the morning, I slept, and still managed to get in one last still layout for Lydia . . . incredible that we still have not gotten into the battle stuff she wanted to shoot before she left.

September 6. It got pretty bad last night, I hear, though I was not on call and was thus spared a direct view. A cable from Citron said Stevens doesn't need me this month, so our problem is simplified a little.

Originally, my 55 DAYS AT PEKING contract had stipulated that I could go back for a week in September to shoot a sequence for Stevens in THE GREATEST STORY EVER TOLD. George had by this time postponed his schedule.

Not much though . . . if you can't shoot on the leading lady, you're in trouble. The only solution is in cutting down her scenes, I guess, cutting around her silent close-ups, laying mixed dialogue over, with long shots of the double.

September 7. Not too tough a day . . . a nice one to have for the last with my family all here. Spain will have a bleaker climate after tomorrow.

Ava was surprisingly good-spirited for the first scene tonight, which meant merely that she showed up more or less on time. After we broke to shift sets, though, her time in the dressing room put us in the soup again; she never came back. For once, Nick didn't wait; he killed the scene and went on to something else.

September 8 (Sunday). The family departed for home, after a day spent in a torrent of suitcases, spare boxes, Kleenex, and odd socks. I only observe this from afar, of course, rigidly (nay, hysterically) holding to my posture of nonintervention in packing (except for an occasional remark, quivering with ill-concealed tension. "Uhh; are any of these bags ready to close yet, Honey?"). Even Drago seemed faintly more accustomed to his crate, or at least resigned to it. I moved out of the villa and back to town at the Castellana, where I'll try to be resigned, too.

September 10, Las Matas. We waited a long time to get going today . . . not for Ava, but for the set. Of course, we didn't finish the scene. It needed a rewrite anyway. Ben's arrived, and feels he can't contribute much; I hope I convinced him he's wrong. He went to a conference with Nick, who's under too much pressure now, God knows, while I relaxed over dinner with David.

September 11. Nick finally caved in [with what proved to be a major coronary], collapsing on the set this morning as we waited for the first setup. They bundled him into a car, white-faced and sweating, and drove him in to the hospital while I told Ava. She reacted with guilty energy and worked well through the morning, which was all we needed her for. Bundy Marton [*second unit director*] took over the company efficiently enough. We'll proceed with exterior cuts for a few days till we can find out how ill Nick is, whether he can go ahead or not.

September 12. Nick's no better. He'll be out at least four weeks, which probably means we must get a replacement director for the acting scenes. I'll try to get Guy Green to come down and take over. Bundy can do the battle stuff.

September 13. No change in Nick's situation. There seems no chance of his shooting at all on the rest of the film. I'm content with the makeup I arrived at for the Baptist; at least I got a different effect from Moses, Ben-Hur, and El Cid.

We were shooting very little at this point, more or less marking time until the gravity of Nick's condition became clear. I took advantage of the slack time to design the makeup for John the Baptist, apply it one day with the help of a Spanish makeup man, and have the results photographed and sent back to George Stevens.

September 15. I got in to see Nick in the hospital. He looks . . . not bad, really, but *quelled,* somehow. Apparently he has accepted the fact that he dare not work again on 55 DAYS AT PEKING, though we didn't speak of it. I think Guy can do well on those two major scenes we have left. We're lucky to have him. As for the battle stuff, we can manage that as we're going now. A strange way for the dice to fall.

They fell very badly for Nick. He's not the first good man brought down by the pressures of directing a major production, but this was a blow from which he hasn't been able to recover. His health is good now, but he's not directed a film since PEKING.

September 18, Madrid. Guy got in, lean and cool. He seems relaxed at the prospect of taking over the delicate responsibility for getting us out of all this mess we've gotten ourselves into.

September 19, Las Matas. We ran into the first bad weather of the summer, which slowed us considerably in the afternoon. It was just as well; they didn't have a full day's work lined out anyway. Guy had some harsh things to say about the script as far as the Natalie-Lewis [*the roles Ava and I played*] relationship goes. He says there's no basis for what happens between them; it's all arbitrary. He feels he can't do the two big scenes left if the relationship isn't corrected from the beginning. This may augur well, for us, in the long run.

September 21, Madrid. Guy now feels some reshooting must be done on Ava's early scenes, to make Natalie a more plausible and interesting woman. He plans to cut her first scene with Kurt Kasznar; thus making her an unknown, enigmatic figure when Lewis first sees her. This makes some sense . . . if the audience knows no more about her than Lewis does, they may be interested in finding out a little. God, when I think of the sweat that's gone into this bloody script.

September 23 (Sunday). Orson called from Paris . . . *he* has a project on Cortes, too. What is possessing everyone to leap into this knotty and prodigious undertaking . . . surely not just that I'm right for the part?

Oddly enough, a very moving (though historically inaccurate) play about the conquistadores had been submitted to me only a week before. It was ROYAL HUNT OF THE SUN, since produced successfully in several countries. Orson never did get his film mounted, although I have an idea it might have been the more effective treatment of the Cortes/Montezuma story.

September 25. A major problem in Sam's company, I think, is the intense rivalry on the executive level. I'm amazed to discover—or to assess— over the years I've been able to observe it, the virulent hostility between almost all his executives. Sam has failed to delegate authority, maybe. You've got to make clear who is to do what, and why (not just to whom). Where Sam stands, to duck this decision is to sow dragon's teeth for yourself.

September 26. Cable from Stevens (re makeup stills sent last week): AM SO STRUCK WITH PICTURES AM WAITING TO COOL DOWN BEFORE EVALUATING NOTES. MAKEUP IS MAGNIFICENT. THERE'S A JOHN THE BAPTIST THEY WILL NEVER FORGET. AS I LOOK AT HIM HERE ON TABLE I FEEL SURGE OF EXCITEMENT THAT TELLS ME HE WILL TAKE PLACE BESIDE MOSES, BEN-HUR, EL CID, NO LESS IN ONE'S MEMORY THAN THESE.

The fall rains began, though I trust they'll clear by next week, when we'll have finished Ava and moved back outside to Las Matas. The change from blazing summer weather was abrupt. The drop in temperature and the perpetual gloom of a sound stage make you start with surprise when you walk outside at six in the evening and find it still daylight. How many more weeks do we have? This is a tough one . . . especially when you weigh the effort against the result.

September 27. Well, Guy began today. Ava was normally late, of course, but she seemed to respond to Guy's brand of quiet competence. He approached the patchwork assignment with his usual attitude; I think his ideas are good. The scene is now much shorter, more enigmatic; I think it'll play. He's solving the shooting problem in terms of short setups, she saying very little in any one of them. I had a pleasant evening when the work was done, for a change. We may not be doing great, but we're doing better.

September 29. Well, we finally wound up Ava, at eight-thirty tonight. It's been as difficult a working relationship as I've ever known, but you have to feel some sympathy for a sick and lonely person. I suppose she feels ill-equipped for the situation in which she finds herself, and reacts with suspicion and hostility because she has no capacity for richer response. I felt lonely myself, at Mischa's party later.

I'll never forget how she looked as I left the party very late that night. She was standing alone in the middle of the Avenida Generalissimo in a gleaming white satin evening gown, performing matadors' passes on the taxis going by with her red satin cape. She was incredibly beautiful.

We'd completed shooting Ava's role, but we were several weeks behind schedule and we had no director, since Guy Green had agreed to come down, accepting no screen credit, only to do the last few remaining scenes with Ava and me. We had to finish David's scenes, since he was scheduled to start another film in Italy, and I was now due to report to George Stevens in Arizona by November 4. Since there were at least six weeks of scheduled shooting remaining, both day and night work, this seemed a goal we were unlikely to meet. I proposed a solution for which I was much praised but didn't deserve. Like so many things we ostensibly do for others, it was only enlightened self-interest. We'd finished most of the acting scenes—we had only the siege of Peking to reenact— with both day and night shooting. My family'd gone home anyway, I had nothing else to do, and nothing I wanted more to do than finish the picture. "Lay on two different crews," I said, "with two different second unit directors. Shoot both day and night units, and I'll live in my dressing room out at Las Matas and work with them both." I know it sounds very noble, but I swear it wasn't, and not very hard, either. The day unit would start at eight with shots that didn't involve me. I'd waken like a gentleman of leisure at nine, with breakfast brought to me in my dressing room, nestling under the walls of Peking. I'd read the paper over breakfast, then put on my uniform and go defend the foreign legations until about three in the afternoon, when I'd knock off and nap until about eight in the evening, when they'd bring me a steak and a half bottle of Marques de Riscal. I'd shower, put the same uniform back on (the siege lasted fifty-five days, remember), and stroll back over to defend the same legations again, this time for the night crew. They'd schedule their work to require my services only until two in the morning or so, and I'd get a solid five hours or more of sleep before starting again with the day unit. It really worked like a charm, and we finished the six weeks' shooting in under three.

September 30 (Sunday), Madrid. I went to the hospital and saw Nick, who looks better and better, and now talks of coming back to the film next week. I can't believe this is a good idea . . . either for him or for us. It's a horrifying thing to say, but maybe the best contribution he made to our enterprise was falling ill when he did. I recall now Bill Blowitz's wry estimate, when I asked him about Nick last spring. "He's talented, Chuck, but I've played poker with him for years. He's a loser."

October 3. Another brute of a day, working with both units. David and I accomplished a small miracle of rewriting on today's scene, most of it with a secretary called out posthaste to type the dialogue we were only one setup away from shooting. Another long conference during dinner, at which the rest of the shooting was settled. Daylight looms ahead, showing the way out of the morass this film has become. Who knows, it might even turn out to be good.

October 4, Las Matas. At three minutes after midnight, while I was busy defending Peking, they ceased firing long enough to bring me a cake on top of the Tartar Wall. I seem to have reached that point in life where you neither feel nor (thank God for my livelihood) look as old as you are. I do begrudge having spent the last months of my thirty-seventh year slaving away at this unresponsive lump of material we still hope to end by calling a film, but that's the way of it. Lydia gave me a sword, delivered on the set by Bea. An effective symbol for the rest of this film, the rest of my life. Do what you have to do . . . and cut through the crap.

October 7. Today was as tough as ever, but we're moving well, with the two units shooting. This opened the possibility of going to New York for the weekend, where Lydia could meet me while I narrated a film on Kennedy for the Defense Department. She's delighted at the idea. God, I am, too; to be in bed with my wife again! The scene today was the oldest thing in movies: lighting powder trains. It never fails, either, though I nearly did. I didn't jump fast enough in one shot, and the powder flash burned half my eyebrows off. I didn't sleep at Las Matas between the day and night work this evening; I came into Madrid and let Orson Welles buy me a fancy dinner at Horcher's while he told me why I should play Cortes in his film.

October 8, Las Matas/Madrid. We shot till nearly dawn with the night unit, slept a few hours, and came back into Madrid to do another round with Orson on the Cortes film. It *is* a fantastic part, but not now. I said at last, "Orson, I feel like a lady who's just come back from an orgiastic month of screwing on Capri . . . I'm not in the mood to be seduced now." I went back out to Las Matas with the day unit, working out a respectable version of the tag scene with David, then hurried in to show the flag at the EL CID opening. They let me off night shooting tonight, so I slept in town at the hotel.

October 11. The day unit wasn't too tough, but the night shooting was a real bitch. I was up to my neck in that damn canal in every shot. In October, that water's *cold.* (Over the years, I've come to observe that crews are totally unable to conceal their broad smiles in any shots where actors are suffering physically.)

This is quite true and I bear them no malice for it. Actors get most of the glory, most of the girls, and most of the money. Contemplating this clear injustice, you can't blame a cameraman or electrician for smiling as he stands warmly wrapped in his down jacket, watching an actor shivering half-naked at two in the morning up to his neck in a filthy, ice-cold canal.

I feel all alone, turning into the homestretch on this. We're through with Ava, David is finished, Nick is out; I'm glad I'm off for home for the weekend at least.

October 12, New York. The weekend began perfectly . . . worth all the waiting and looking forward. Even Air France was almost on time. I managed to sleep a bit crossing the Atlantic, but had no need of anything but Lydia when I finally got in . . . and there she was.

October 14, New York/Madrid. Having finished my chore for the government, I didn't really do a damn thing all day long. It's incredible how perfectly this whole weekend has meshed . . . like a daydream you make up through a long, hard time. It couldn't have happened to a nicer fella. The New York autumn remained at its brilliant best while I put Lydia on her plane back home, and climbed on mine for the long ride back to work.

October 20, Las Matas/Madrid. We wrapped it at five this afternoon, on schedule, as I said we could. On schedule is one thing . . . you can get that with sweat. Good is something else, and there I'm dubious, though we may just barely luck out. Niven is very good, Guy Green made a key contribution. I'm photographed very well, and I suppose the chemistry they pay for is there, but my acting is only competent, from the dailies. Still, it may, in the classic phrase, cut together. What I have learned from this, I hope permanently, is *never start a film without a good finished script.*

Well, I hadn't learned it, permanently. I made the same mistake again within a year. As a maxim, it's perfectly sound, but it's terribly hard not to go on a project you like, simply because it hasn't all come out of the typewriter yet.

October 21 (Sunday), Paris/Los Angeles. Twenty-four hours after I stirred at the clerk's get-up call, I held Lydia in my arms outside customs in Los Angeles. A long, long day, for damn sure, though I was able to get some sleep in the VIP lounge in Paris between planes. Now I'm back home, and the long, possibly barren summer is gone. I'm afraid I made some wrong choices and that my ability to judge men is not what I thought, but I came out of it wiser than I went in, at least.

October 22, Los Angeles. I fell into life on my ridge with a happy sigh. Walter had thirty-odd pages of LOVERS ready for me. I like it better than he does, apparently. It's somewhat overwritten, but basically seems to me the sort of thing I hoped for from Collier. Then, at four this afternoon, we sat in a row on the sofa watching JFK on TV, announcing the naval blockade of Cuba. I felt scared, and proud. It's been a long time since we took any initiative in the world.

October 25. I climbed back into a beard again for the Baptist makeup tests for Stevens this morning. The hell with this . . . I'm going to grow one. I'll be ready for the January work.

I'd forgotten how annoying it is to spend an hour or so every dawn having a beard laid on. I decided to endure it for the week or so I was to shoot in Arizona, with my own beard growing underneath. By January, I'd have the homegrown article ready.

Von Sydow seems a very decent man. He has an effective makeup for Christ, and his face helps, too. We both almost got squashed by a falling set piece between shots . . . that would've presented George with a casting problem. DIAMOND HEAD looks very slick, smooth, not terribly real, and as though there might be some money in it. I have acted better. I must not *indicate*.

October 29, Page, Arizona. It's the first day of shooting THE GREATEST STORY EVER TOLD, only we didn't shoot, of course. George is kind of easing into this one, I gather. He seemed in no hurry to crack a can of film. I recorded a sound track of the apocalyptic speech, as well as the baptism scene. I wasn't prepared for this last, and didn't do it particularly well, though we finally arrived at something fairly creative. The work isn't final, of course, except possibly in terms of George's impression of my acting, in which case I have a lot to do.

October 31. We got a good day of shooting done, but when I got back to camp, there was a call from Lydia . . . from Fraser, really . . . to tell me he'd broken his arm. I can't accept it, somehow. It's not a bad break and will no doubt heal rapidly and easily, but the thought of that golden, lovely boy flawed and in pain is hard for me. He, on the other hand, seemed in good spirits.

November 3, Los Angeles. At four-forty I was baptizing Max von Sydow; ten minutes later I was lifting off in the chopper with the film for home. From waist-deep in the Colorado to my ridge in barely three hours. Fortunately for my plans, you lose the shooting light early in November.

Shooting on location near big cities, you can usually send the exposed film back each night on a scheduled flight and get your daily quota of raw stock back the same way. On remote locations like this, though, you have to charter small aircraft for the purpose.

Fray's in good shape, though a slightly pathetic figure in his cast. ("I wish I could still be perfect, that's all.")

November 4 (Sunday), Los Angeles/Page, Arizona. I had to leave by noon, so the film plane could be sure of getting in and back out of Page before dark, so it made a short weekend at home, but it was worth it just to breathe a little there, sleep in a bed with Lydia in it, kiss my daughter, and watch Fray grin when I signed his cast. On the spur of the moment, they all rode down with me, accepting the charter pilot's last-minute hospitality. It gave a delightful color to what would've been a dull and downbeat kind of trip. The Grand Canyon offered us a lovely afternoon light in which to look at it, and I got to walk up and down the airstrip with them for a bit before they took off for the trip home. So now we have another week.

November 5. We were supposed to shoot Jesus' return from the wilderness and the Baptist's defiance of the Sanhedrin, but the day fell into what is apparently a not uncommon pattern with Stevens. He spent most of the morning thinking (walking up and down the bank, unapproachable), then I sold him three cuts in the lines. I've been having some luck with this; I think we've made the dialogue a little more direct. George is a wonder in rehearsal . . . using ideas, improving on them all. I think this'll be a good scene; I'm anxious to get into it, but we lost the light without turning a camera.

November 7. Another long day, starting very early, in the course of which news filtered from the outside world to the effect that Brown had won in California, sealing Nixon's political fate. [*A misjudgment shared by sharper political observers than I.*] It's odd to remember there *are* events that have importance outside this film.

November 8. I did very little work today; George is intent on exploring in full all details of this scene before moving on to the next. I can't argue with that, but the breadth of his exploration runs pretty well back into extreme long shots and close-ups of extras and goats, to which I can't contribute. I applaud his absolute concentration on the scene at hand (the shot at hand, the film at hand), but it does make things go slowly. My original eight days here will certainly run into next week now.

George Stevens was surely one of the best directors who ever lived. Like Wyler, though, and a very few others I've worked for, his method included the infinite taking of pains. I think I've done my best work for directors like this. I have the energy and enthusiasm to respond to this method, in the hands of a man with the creative authority to employ it. One of the flaws in my own method, though, is an overwhelming urge to get on with it, an instinct I firmly conceal from directors like Stevens and Wyler. This was very difficult to do during the several days I spent standing waist-deep in the Colorado River baptizing Max von Sydow. The Colorado River that November was no place to linger . . . it got down in the forties every morning. At the end of one trying day, George noticed my discomfort and asked me how I felt. "I'm OK, George," I said. "But I'll tell you this: If the River Jordan had been as cold as the Colorado, Christianity would never have got off the ground."

November 13, Page/Los Angeles. Somewhat to my surprise, George finished me on location today. He had Henry Wills [*stunt coordinator on the film*] talk me out of taking the bulldog into the river myself. (I was not hard to persuade.)

This scene involved the Baptist's capture by Herod's soldiers, climaxed by one of them leaping from his horse and knocking me off a bluff into the river. Stunt men call this a bulldog, from rodeo usage.

I really had little to do, except for the close-ups. Thank God for that; the water temperature was down to forty-eight degrees. I used up most of my voice rerecording the apocalyptic sermon, then caught the film plane for home and happiness.

George wanted to have this recorded on location where the Baptist's exhortation could echo through the rocks of Glen Canyon (buried now, along with all our sets there, under several hundred feet of water backed up behind Glen Canyon Dam, then waiting to be closed while we finished our shooting. Oddly, I shot in the water of the great lake thus created several years later on PLANET OF THE APES. It was very strange to think of Stevens's sets, drowned below us.).

December 3. I did a mass luncheon at the Derby for the fan book trade. I loathe movie magazines. They have to be the nadir of journalism. [*It turns out I was wrong. Now all but one or two of them are gone, and we have* HUSTLER.]

December 6. A very long conference with Walter and John Collier on THE LOVERS progress. He's revised the first fifty-odd pages, gone ahead with the next fifty-odd. We're getting our money's worth. He's working very slowly, but is determined to give his best, which is not typical of all his colleagues in the Writers Guild.

December 7. Fray and Lydia are now going to Japan with me, which will make for a much more pleasant week. In consequence, though, the house is suddenly filling with the frantic pressure of our imminent family departure, plus the usual Christmas crush. I'm still convinced the tour will prove useful for the film.

By this time it had been noted, both by me and the various studios, that my films invariably did well in the Far East and throughout Southeast Asia. Films that flopped elsewhere did fairly well, those that were hits elsewhere did incredibly. The fact that this pattern has continued unchanged accounts in no small degree for my continued viability in films. Whenever I do a tour for one of my films, I try to include one or two stops in the Far East, as I did in 1962 for DIAMOND HEAD. I've never had any firm explanation for my continuing popularity with Eastern audiences, but I heard a very flattering one from a journalist in Taiwan not long ago. "Oh, that's very simple," he said. "Audiences in this part of the world go to your films because you represent the Confucian virtues: responsibility, justice, courage, and moderation."

December 11. Collier's new pages are really good. He's incredibly slow, but the material is worth waiting for, at least for as long as we *can* wait. We're rapidly using all our script time getting a first draft screenplay, which should be well behind us by now. I must have something I can submit when I go to London in January. The financial burden of developing this property personally is tough to carry.

December 15, Over the International Date Line. The usual flurry and tangle of getting away, with Drago hovering anxiously in the background to see whether he'll be left behind. Holly, of course, was oblivious to the dimension of the parting, a muzzy cherub in yellow Doctor Denton's, waving us off as though we were bound for Beverly Hills instead of the Orient. We had the usual easy departure, padded by VIP upholstery. Honolulu was heady with perfumed Pacific trade winds and plumeria leis all around. We flew into the date line with Fray happily exploring a cardboard carton of toys.

December 16, Japan. Most of the day was sucked up into a limbo of time change, whence I trust we can resurrect it on the return flight. We arrived on time, were met without great ceremony (though the usual boggle of press and public at the airport) and whisked through the sprawl of metropolitan Tokyo to a new hotel, the Okura, which strikes me as somewhat more amenable than the Imperial. (*Pace*, Frank Lloyd Wright!) We're entirely out of joint with the time, of course, so went to bed early.

December 18, Tokyo. A full day, beginning most pleasantly with a bath in the full tradition of an American in Japan. The girls are most skillful, entirely asexual . . . the thing to do is relax and forget it. I've decided to make a stage appearance here. Usually, it's not a good idea, but it has the value in Japan of making possible some sort of personal contact with a body of public I seldom see. The party tonight included some of the MUTINY ON THE BOUNTY group, here for their opening. Much polite exchange of felicitations.

December 19. We're getting gradually loaded down with the fruits of Japanese generosity . . . everything from cameras to china dolls. A family bath this morning (Fray's learning early the traditional joys of the Orient) began a TV-ish kind of day. The DIAMOND HEAD opening tonight went well, except that I was unable to learn my Japanese speech completely . . . I had to read it. It still went well. I must modify my rule: I *should* make stage appearances in countries where I can show off with a speech in the language, however ineptly.

December 21, Fukuoka/Tokyo. I got through to Lydia on the phone . . . she's safely back in Coldwater. [*Lydia had taken Fray home early to prepare for Christmas.*] Fukuoka is rather more interesting than Osaka, if only because it's much smaller, less visited by tourists, off the mainstream here a bit. I was presented with an incredibly beautiful samurai sword, over three hundred years old, which at one stroke gives my collection some importance. I caught the late jet for Tokyo, arrived in time for a pub crawl on the Ginza.

December 22, Los Angeles. The intricacies of the International Date Line made me arrive in Los Angeles before I left Tokyo, but the day began long, long before that, with one last interview. It went well, considering how tired I was. The trip was worthwhile, especially for a film that may need help. I hope it pays off.

December 23, St. Helen. Ten more Collier pages waiting last night when I got here, still good, still a little overdecorated in dialogue. The first brothers' argument must be redone entirely, I think . . . the first of John's scenes not to work. The date line gave me two morning departures, on opposite sides of the Pacific. It was tough getting up for another plane today, but marvelous to arrive in the woods again. The dream landscape of my boyhood always repeats like rushes run again. The black pines sharp against the snowbanks, the swirling snowflakes a tunnel for the headlights . . . driving North, always. The lodge at Russell Lake still waits unchanged, unchangeable in the woods, silent against the end of the world. There are still beds that no one sleeps in there, and the eagles still nest on the point across my frozen lake, somehow ominous through the snow. And yet desired . . .

December 25. Christmas hasn't passed for me so little marked since '48 when I was in Boston about to take over the lead in LEAF AND BOUGH, and sat alone on the bed in the rooming house, methodically opening my gifts early Christmas morning before going to rehearse. (Lydia sent me a belt, I remember.) No presents were opened here today; most of ours still wait back in Coldwater. But the north country gave us a wintry day saved from my boyhood, which was a very special kind of gift for me. Lydia and I walked the woods behind the old Highland Road house, where tracks showed that children still sled there. All the other geography of those memories seems smaller, revisited, but that hill still looks steep.

December 30 (Sunday), Los Angeles. Los Angeles has never looked so green as it did driving back home from the airport. After the frost-black branches and white drifts of Michigan, the fat green palm leaves in the Beverly Hills gardens dripped with jungle lushness. The air was as clear and soft, the house as warmly welcoming as ever. We opened the bulk of our gifts left behind, of which the hit for Fray was his electric toy raceway. (That went over pretty big with me, too.) Home again.

1963

Marching in
Washington . . .

several offers,
little filming . . .

in the offing:
Major Dundee with
Sam Peckinpah.

As Major Dundee
for Sam Peckinpah

January 2, Los Angeles. We saw LAWRENCE OF ARABIA at the Academy theater. It may be a more nearly flawless film than either KANE, HENRY V, or BRIDGE ON THE RIVER KWAI, but it's oddly uninvolving. In the end, you can't care as much about O'Toole's Lawrence as you do about Guinness's colonel, Larry's warrior king, or Orson's Charles Foster Kane. Lean's handling of the while thing is world class, of course. I'd love to make a pitch to him to direct LOVERS. Not that it's much of a chance or that it would be an entirely unmixed blessing if he did do it, but it would be a chance we couldn't afford to pass up.

January 7. Small excitement on the ridge when a car turned over on our drive and fell into Hidden Valley. The man escaped unhurt; I did not. Attempting a gallant rescue, I tore my palm open plunging down Fray's private path. The new LOVERS pages need more work, some of which we supplied ourselves. The first scene with the brother will finally have to be redone, beyond question. There's a lot that's right now, though. It begins to really look like a script.

January 10. Long full day of racing around (as always, going-away-time increases my efficiency). I presided over my first Screen Actors Guild meeting, chairing the negotiating committee for a new contract. A gavel does a lot for your sense of power.

January 14, London. I read through the current version of the LOVERS script before we landed, and found it pretty much right. Now if we can find the right man to direct it, we'll be in business. Unfortunately, it won't be Olivier. I saw him after his play, SEMI-DETACHED, tonight; he's undertaking both the Chichester Festival and the National Theatre. His play's not much, but he displays remarkable range in it.

January 17. I may cost a lot of money, but I was worth it today. I saved Sam Bronston a full day of dubbing studio costs by doing my loops in one day instead of two. Eighty-five separate loops and fifteen wild tracks in five hours. I went back to the Dorchester and got a nap I needed, then went to Scofield's LEAR with Orson. It disappointed me and contorted Orson with agony. He deliberately chooses a conversational Lear, and I doubt the part can be handled that way. Why do English producers slight *all* battle scenes? Shakespeare would spin in his Stratford grave to see the butter-knived dolts.

January 19, New York. PAA #121 for New York is one of my favorite flights. By daylight the whole time, chasing the sun, landing with time to rest, then catch a show at night. It turns out Ustinov is in Boston; it'll be difficult to approach him there, but he seems a logical choice for our next try at a director.

January 26, Los Angeles. I slept an hour late this morning, but still caught the plane to Los Angeles easily, since the departure was delayed. I even had time to get toys for Holly and Fray. It's curious how all these activities fall into a ritual pattern. Does one's whole life gradually assume this color? Anyway, I've learned two different ways to sleep on both Pan Am and American Airlines jets. Pan Am is the only line where you can take the armrests out of the seats in first class, so you can use them as a bed.

January 27 (Sunday). My tennis is gradually improving, but I'm far more delighted to discover that Fray's is, too. He now can actually hit the ball about half the time, sometimes twice in a row. If he stays with it, he'll learn to play as I never can. I saw DIVORCE ITALIAN STYLE with Lydia; it's a funny, bitter film. Could the U.S. film economy make a film as small as this? I really doubt it. Shot here, the world gross of this very good film wouldn't pay for its U.S. negative cost, I fear.

I'd finished my work in Arizona for George Stevens in November. The company had remained there through a very hard Christmas and was now back in Culver City, doing some interiors at Desilu Studios. They built a marvelous set for Herod's palace, where I was about to start my last scenes of the Baptist's imprisonment and execution.

January 29. I'm back in the saddle again, though I failed to get my feet wet today, to mix a metaphor. The set is quite impressive; I feel the scene needs much cutting, some work on the words. George Stevens was, as always, available to each suggestion. If I weren't totally sure of his relentless determination to get it right, I'd be worrying over his malleability on these things.

He wasn't so malleable . . . he just seemed that way. George got it the way he wanted.

January 30. The work day was tough again. Why is it I seem so often to get parts that require me to be tied up and hit at by burly extras? The wooden handcuffs they've devised may be biblical, but they're damned uncomfortable, too. I must remember to avoid them in the future.

February 6. Today we shot most of my coverage in the second scene with Herod. I did well with it, too, I think. After work I had a most interesting conversation with George on something I've become more and more sure of: A performance is somehow diluted by film. No matter what you've done in front of the camera, or watched another actor do, it's simply *not* as vital, ever, in the screening room as when you shot it. George said, "There's no blood there . . . it's only shadows up on the screen, after all. That's what you do in the cutting room . . . try and get the blood back into it."

I've worked for three directors whose reputations allowed them to work just about any way they chose: George Stevens, Willy Wyler, and C. B. de Mille. They all worked on very long schedules, but each spent his time very differently. de Mille did a great deal of preparation on his scripts, having models made of the sets and sketches of many of the setups he planned. The major setup at the beginning of each day was chosen the night before and largely prepared by the beginning of the day's work. Nevertheless, his reexamination of it was so detailed that he seldom turned a camera before ten in the morning. His coverage, on the other hand, was not extensive. He did neither a great number of setups nor a great many takes in each one. Wyler would seem to improvise his way into a scene, choosing the first setup on the set and proceeding from there as the rehearsals indicated. He wouldn't do a great many different setups, but probably did more takes per setup than any director I've worked for, though not as many as legend has it. I'd say he averaged about eight takes a setup. Stevens would only do two or three, but he would devise more different angles from which to cover the scene than you'd think possible. You'd finish a day's work on a scene confident that there was no other possible coverage, yet find yourself there a day or two longer while George explored further ideas.

February 10, (Sunday.) It poured all day, which was bad for the tennis, good for LOVERS. We worked all day, fitted in a good piece of one scene from the play, which I knew would work most in adapting this piece to the screen. Walter suggested a good title: THE WAR LORD.

February 13. The scene went extremely well today. I work at my best with Stevens, partly because of his startling awareness (especially in a film director) of actor's ego. He finally reduced this last scene in level, but not in intensity. It makes for a very simple approach, but reveals a great deal. The SAG meeting tonight included the board members from the New York branch. I gave my report on the negotiating committee, which prompted the most circular debate I've ever heard. Round and round the same old ground on pay TV . . . to no new purpose whatever.

Even in 1963, subscription television was recognized as the wave of the future. Some of the actors involved in the negotiations perceived this as a source of immediate riches. This was inconceivable then, and indeed has not happened yet. It was important to get the concept of subscription television into the union contracts.

February 14. I had little to do for Stevens, since most of my remaining angles were shot yesterday. I'm suddenly coming to the end of this part and find myself sorry to finish it. George is quite a man to work for. Citron reports Columbia doesn't want to back WAR LORD up to four million unless they can put in a coproducer. There's only one answer to that, of course. If we make this film, I don't want a studio second-guessing it.

This was naïve of me. If the studio pays for a picture, of course they're going to second-guess it. Film makers chafe at this basic reality of the economics of film, but it's perfectly reasonable. As they've been saying since the Middle Ages, the man who pays the piper calls the tune.

February 16. I worked most of the afternoon on LOVERS (which will *not* be WAR LORD, it appears, since too many people imagine it to be a story of China in the twenties, apparently). [*Not so many, apparently; WAR LORD was the final title.*] Walter's worked out a story line for the ending which avoids the Norman invasion, the perfidy of the absent duke, and other devices which require much talk to little purpose. I think he's right. Now let's see if Ustinov is interested.

February 17 (Sunday), New York. I was leaving for New York, so of course the weather in Los Angeles was perfect. My tennis was tense, shot through with anxious phone calls from John Collier, working hard on the last few pages of the scenes I was to take with me. They were waiting at the American Airlines desk as I ran by, cutting my departure a little close for comfort. I thought they were OK, though he wrote them before he knew we're cutting the Norman conquest, etc., from the end.

February 18. What started out on paper as a deceptively sparse schedule of interviews for the DIAMOND HEAD opening here thickened up considerably as soon as we got under way, in the time-honored fashion of flack tours. The picture's opened extremely well in other parts of the country, however, and Columbia is anxious to make a major effort for it here. At lunch at Sardi's, Peter Ustinov was charming and noncommittal, just as I would be. I'm not used to being on the other end of this kind of professional seduction, but I played it as coolly as I could.

February 21, Los Angeles. I went back to do my last shooting for GREATEST STORY EVER TOLD today . . . some added shots in the water with the stunt men for the Baptist's capture. I was astounded when George (who obviously had better things to do) told me to direct it. "But what do you want me to do with it, George?" I said. "Whatever you want, Chuck," he replied. So I did. I must say it made for an interesting day. Citron's anxious to have Walter budget WAR LORD high enough when he goes to London for the budget meetings with Columbia. So we're back on the big-dollar picture again. Hmmm. Elisofon's GREATEST STORY EVER TOLD color stills impressed us all tonight, as did Lydia's dinner.

February 24 (Sunday). This was the kind of day that makes me want never to move off this ridge. Indeed, I spent a large part of it mulling over the possibility of constructing a combination projection room-office at the end of the tennis court, which would really set us up here. Now that the RLC deal is all but finalized, there will be a little extra capital which might be spent usefully, especially on a professional building. Anyway, it'd be fun to plan. I remember when I designed a white apartment for Lydia, when we were in school. We never thought we'd have anything like that, either.

In the early sixties, as did a dozen or so other actors, I had formed a corporation. Its dubious value to me was clear by this time and I was exploring various means of selling it. RLC stood for Russell Lake Corporation: the name of the lake where I was raised in Michigan, surrounded by fourteen hundred acres of the timberland I bought with the first money I made in films.

February 26. During our script conference, I tried to deal forthrightly with Collier's fury that any changes are sketched in without his participation, but he's very hard to reach, accusing us of all sorts of moral depravity. This shakes and angers me, but doesn't alter my conviction that I acted honorably, as well as for the good of the script.

March 5. John's back in the saddle again, apparently all ready to plunge into work, unmindful of his distress (not to mention mine) of last week. Well, this may yet do . . . we'll see. He's incredibly picayune on words and commas, going very slowly, but at least his feathers are smooth again. The Golden Globes, with me presenting instead of accepting this year, was as mishmashed as ever, but I did OK.

March 12. Got a call from Walter Seltzer in London . . . Columbia is not quivering visibly at the budget of $3,538,000 (above and below the line), but wants no part of Ustinov; they insist on a director of greater experience. (Walter is talking with Carol Reed.) Since Ustinov has still given us no firm expression of interest and we have made no offer, our position is OK, though rather awkward if Ustinov calls to announce he wants to do the film. Reed might be better, anyway. His name and reputation are surely more formidable.

I include this episode confident that Peter Ustinov's reputation can withstand Columbia's low opinion of his directorial experience.

Besides, the whole process of putting WAR LORD *together is worth noting. The excruciating process of getting a script and finding a director whose availability, price, and interest fitted into our schedule, budget, and estimate of his talents is repeated, of course, with the principal casting, and even then you haven't turned a camera. You've still got lots of chances to screw up. Making films can maybe be best described by Samuel Johnson's comment about the dog who danced on his hind legs: "The wonder is not that he doesn't do it well . . . but that he does it at all!"*

March 17. It doesn't seem like nineteen years since I married her . . . sometimes it doesn't seem like a week. Lydia seemed enormously happy with the earrings I bought to complement her bracelet. Rain and sleet marred the day, but didn't spoil it for us. Tonight we threw a nice loose bash for twenty or so, plus kids. They stayed upstairs painting and whatnot, the rest of us partied in only slightly more adult tones downstairs. I've got a good girl . . . I'm lucky to have kept her.

March 21. Tonight we ran TARAS BULBA as an example of how not to make a period film. It certainly proved a prime one. Collier proved a prime example as well . . . of how to behave with childish irresponsibility. He stamped out of the screening in a petulant rage some twenty minutes after it started, for reasons not at all clear to me, probably not to him either.

March 29. I had a long conference on the line John's taking in the weeks left on his contract. We skirted discussion of pages he's turned in recently . . . we are editing same without reference to his further comment. He's a gifted man, but most intractable, still reluctant to alter his position on anything.

March 31 (Sunday,) London. I hit my departure time for LAX right on the nose, fitting in a flurry of paper work plus a set and a half of tennis first. (I quit at three-all to run from the court, to shower, to limo.) I flew the high thin polar air in a boozy semifuddle, due in equal parts to rich food, rich whiskey, and a remarkably bad action script I read en route. I'm not getting too many of those now, thank God. AMBUSH BAY: definitely negative, negative, double negative.

April 2. I began the day rather ridiculously, posing with a glass of milk while trying to stem the blood flowing steadily and stubbornly from a shaving cut. This can't have been quite what the Milk Board had in mind [*which was to get an elegant photo of an elegant fellow drinking milk in the elegant Dorchester, thus promoting lots of elegant milk-drinking in Britain*].

April 3. Not a tough day; before the plane, I managed too long lunch interview for the GUARDIAN and an equally long TV interview. The English TV people do these well, but there is such elaborate huffing and puffing in preparation, they somehow make it seem harder than it is. On the other hand, at home, you run into interviewers who think it's easier than it is. Paris as always . . . raining. Why does this town bring my hackles up?

April 4, Paris. It's raining still, of course, and the Musée de l'Armé did *not* have the example of reconstructed Norman link armor they were supposed to have. I dropped in on the Louvre and renewed a few old acquaintances, though. The Davids and Delacroixs are in fine shape, and the *Mona Lisa*'s back home, no longer pampered with air conditioning as she was on her visit to the U.S. I saw a broken skylight dripping rain thirty feet away from her. We both smiled.

April 5, New York. I escaped the Paris weather a few hours early, having done all I could and more than I expected. We got good space, all things considered. The French press is curiously hostile, but they seem to soften a bit if you answer questions in complete sentences. (I can't think why . . . everyone knows actors have no brains.) A long polar Pan Am flight with average sleep, but I enjoyed New York, and God knows I enjoyed a good steak. ENTER LAUGHING is very funny. Alan Arkin is much more than that, though some of the rest of the cast are surprisingly miscast. Broadway doesn't usually miss that way.

April 7 (Sunday), Montego Bay. The plane to Jamaica was late, and longer (now you can't fly over Cuba), but the flight over the turquoise tangle of islands is beautiful, and worth prolonging. Montego Bay is all it's cracked up to be, too. The Tennis Club's very grand, very small, very secluded, and with both grass and concrete courts.

I had a few free days ahead, coming back from Europe, and I seized the opportunity to have my family join me for a holiday in Jamaica.

April 11. Another day with the leisured classes, which I gather David O. Selznick has joined. Jennifer's maybe more relaxed than when we made RUBY GENTRY, though she looks no older. David's more relaxed, too . . . though he does look older. This kind of day, with echoes of Noel Coward and all that, is a little uneasy-making for a country boy from Michigan, but they gave us a fine lunch. Tonight was a pleasant taste of traditional calypso routine . . . it seems better on a beach under stars and a Jamaica moon.

April 14, Los Angeles. Columbia has pulled out of WAR LORD, which is where they were in February. We've wasted two months while they worked their way back to this position. Now the move seems to be to turn to the Mirisches. Citron will give the script to Walter, who's been waiting (anxiously, I hope) for some time. He (Citron) is still against going to Bronston. This is not all clear to me . . . I suspect I'm left a little in the dark here and there, still.

April 17. Danny Mann's enthusiasm for WAR LORD is gratifyingly high. There's a certain amount of performance in his manner, I guess, but a lot of valid energy, too. He feels Leslie Stevens might be a good source of whatever we might still need in the script. I had hopes for the vignette they want me to do in the Shirley MacLaine film, but it's a barren part. Sinatra has the only appealing role of all these male cameos. I'll pass; let Paul Newman play it. [*Oddly enough, as I remember, he did.*]

April 26. It looks like the Mirisches may take over on WAR LORD. They're very careful, in addition to which they have to sell United Artists on anything they want to do, but I feel much encouraged. Now, over the weekend, we must somehow get the script retyped, so we can submit a clean copy to United Artists in New York when I go through.

Don't laugh . . . this is more important than you think. All of us prefer to read neat, unscuffed scripts; each of us likes to protect his conviction that he's the very first one to see the script. In addition, some of us have strong prejudices about the proper color of the script cover. (I'm drawn to black myself, with red a close second.)

April 29, New York. I took Fray to school, a chore I always look forward to, but will do without for ten days now, and then back to finish packing. Walter brought up the script, out of mimeo at last; several copies for delivery en route and in London. The length is a shock: 212 pages. Even typed long, as Walter instructed them, that's far too much. It reads fat, though; it'll cut like butter. New York looks fine . . . I'm glad to sleep here with Lydia beside me.

May 1, London. A long, long flight over, spent rereading the script for typos (of which there are too many) . . . and fighting off the extra Scotch they keep pressing on you. This first-class jet travel can turn you into a sot. (If that isn't class discrimination I don't know what is.) We arrived late, but Lydia's travel method had its advantages, no doubt of that.

When I'm flying over the Pole alone, I take a flight that gets into London early in the morning. I check into the hotel, sleep for three hours, and schedule a luncheon meeting that absolutely requires my struggling up for. Then I try to find time for tennis or running to get my blood circulating, on the theory that I can fall into bed that night more or less adjusted to European time. Lydia, on the other hand, likes to get in in the evening, go to bed, and stay there till things settle down. This trip was for the 55 DAYS AT PEKING *premiere, though I always try to schedule any trip, especially overseas, to polish off as many different chores as I can . . . a practice Lydia deplores as excessively Puritan.*

May 5 (Sunday). I breakfasted with Phil Yordan in his suite, he busily promoting several projects, as he happily conceded. He's now cold on the slave-ship idea, but has another (which sounds much the same to me) about the Suez Canal. He also has a chance to buy BRAVE NEW WORLD for a hundred thousand dollars. Then I spent a more useful, if less entertaining, five hours working with Walter on cutting the frosting off the cake John Collier baked for us. For starters, we must get at least twenty pages out . . . more, really.

May 6. I took a break from my public relations chores and went by the British Museum, where I discovered (Aha!) a scrap of chain mail on display as part of the Sutton Hoo treasure, circa 650. So it *was* known in the eleventh century, no matter what the bloody scholars say.

This represents a small triumph. All the experts I'd consulted maintained that chain mail was unknown in the eleventh century (the period in which WAR LORD *was laid). I wanted to use chain mail because it's more comfortable, cheaper to reproduce, and looks better than plate armor. Thus my delight at finding out it was also historically accurate.*

As for the royal 55 DAYS AT PEKING premiere, it went well, with the Duke of Edinburgh doing the chore I usually do at openings. He did it damn well, too. The party the Rank people gave afterward was attended, along with HRH, by Walter Seltzer, Bea Sellmer, and the Creedys. It was late, wet, and a smashing success.

May 7, London/Paris. We took the afternoon plane for Paris, leaving me the morning to dictate letters and grab a session on a fairish clay court (tennis also fairish), and Lydia time to catch up on her sleep. She's holding up marvelously through this trip. These junkets are really woman-killers, but she seems to have it whipped. I've never seen Paris so beautiful . . . indeed, it's the first time in five trips I've seen it dry. Our terrace at the Crillon, overlooking the Place de la Concorde, was an ideal place to drink champagne at sunset with a pretty woman.

May 8, Paris. Paris weather returned to its normal rain, appropriate for hearing, via a phone call from Citron, that United Artists has blown cold on WAR LORD. Walter Mirisch liked it, I gather, but Arthur Krim, sweating no doubt under the costs of GREATEST STORY EVER TOLD, is nervous. In any event, I felt this was the time to open, at least tentatively, with Sam Bronston. I talked to him, as well as Phil Yordan and Paul Lazarus, after a successful 55 DAYS AT PEKING opening, at the party at Lasserre, while they were releasing baskets of white doves. I promised to make a script available to them.

May 9, Paris/Los Angeles. I phoned Walter out of bed at three in the morning to arrange a retype of the script, incorporating the cuts we've made in the last few days. He can then get a clean script to Paris for the Bronston people to read (after two turndowns, I'm anxious to make this script easy to read). Also, the retyping will tell us exactly how much we've cut. We should get a reaction from Bronston early next week. The trip over the Pole was *long*, but we got home to find all in order, both kids happy, as was Mother, who stood by for us here.

May 13, Pittsburgh. I spent an early-starting, long-running day in the saddle, jetting to Pittsburgh. It seems to me I got there sooner than I need have, since the only thing laid on was dinner with a grizzled old columnist of the Hecht-MacArthur school (which I rather enjoyed, actually). No word from Sam Bronston on his reaction to WAR LORD, but there hardly would've been yet. So, for a few days, I'm a salesman again, traveling in Chinese movies.

May 14, Pittsburgh/Washington, D.C. I woke early enough to see Major Cooper crawl into his capsule, while I breakfasted in the suite, but by the time they'd hauled him out again, I was off on my rounds, away from a TV set. It must have been a frustrating day for him . . . it was routine for me. He was to blaze a trail in space; I've traveled this one before, with the good, clever interviewers and the tired hacks. I fitted in tennis (better here than last year) and caught my plane for Washington and a good steak, then two more interviews before bed.

May 20, Los Angeles. I got into the studio this morning to do my thank-you letters from last week's junket, then to a meeting at the Ziffren office to go over details of the Columbia deal. It's more or less as we outlined it six months ago, but, Lord, what a mass of legal-sized paper has been spoiled since then. So it seems I can count on twenty years more of eating after all, broken back or whatever. I don't know that security is a healthy environment for an actor . . . but then, luxury is bad for us too.

May 28, New York. My flight to New York was routine enough, but the day undid me a little, somehow. Maybe my energy was low; my spirits certainly were when I got in. That's not like me, and I don't approve of it. At the [55 DAYS AT PEKING] opening tonight, the film played only fairly well, I thought, though the party we gave at the apartment afterward was filled with well-wishers and yeasayers. Bill Blowitz, a confirmed naysayer, said his nay, but the rest was positive, and probably fulsome. Well, how can you tell, anyway?

May 30. I left New York with split notices on 55 DAYS AT PEKING (but very good early box office) and a strong feeling of having accomplished little but fight with my wife.

Obviously, my low spirits and general surliness had nothing to do with Lydia. I was disappointed in the way 55 DAYS AT PEKING had turned out and felt I'd had at least some hand in screwing it up.

June 1, Los Angeles. Tennis was . . . thorough, I guess is the word for it. There's a marvelous kind of pleasure in totally spending yourself physically like that. You feel the same kind of satisfaction that sex gives you (well, maybe not quite the same). So far, nothing has turned up I want to act in. Fox sent me over MORITURI, an action script more or less like 55 DAYS AT PEKING, but smaller. This is always the way of it. They offer you what you've just done. [*Marlon Brando later did this one. He should've passed, too.*]

June 5. I spent most of my day vamping around, waiting for word from Citron, who had another round or two with Lazarus on WAR LORD. Herman read him a long lecture on the realities of how any deal with me must be set up. Paul has asked for a week to try and get a completion bond from Rank, since he's reluctant to go to Dupont, Bronston's normal source of this money. It seems ironic that this film, which to me seems special, should prove so hard to get made. [*The special ones are even harder to set up than the rest, as I've since learned.*]

June 13. On the strength of the unfinished MAJOR DUNDEE material Jerry Bresler submitted, I ran RIDE THE HIGH COUNTRY, directed by Sam Peckinpah, to see whether he might be the man for this. He's made a damn good Western, for almost nothing, though MGM blew it in release. I'd like to work for him and I phoned him from the screening room and told him so. Lunch with Bresler and the Columbia brass seemed to promise a chance to include in the film an honest statement about the Civil War, which has never been seriously treated in film. I think I'd like to do it.

June 17. A meeting with Peckinpah and the Columbia types on MAJOR DUNDEE was rather promising . . . but this stage of work on a film always is. The air rings with high protestations of creative integrity. Still, this seems like a good chance, using the conflict between the two major characters, both Southerners, one a loyal officer, the other Confederate, to explore the Civil War a little. Citron reports a call from Phil Yordan; more stirring on WAR LORD. I'm skeptical. From lunch till we broke off, stalemated, at four-thirty, I hacked away at the negotiations [*for a new contract between the Screen Actors Guild and the Motion Picture Producers Association*]; the last session I can attend till I get back from Europe.

June 18, Los Angeles/London. I tore down to city hall to testify against the high-rise building project for Mulholland Drive. I read a highly subjective statement, which may or may not have had any effect. It was an interesting experience. I found myself swept with emotion and a kind of unease I'd never use in acting a similar scene. How to trap this for use sometime? I limoed straight to LAX from the hearings and caught my familiar polar trolley. There's something indecent about lolling in liquored luxury seven miles above the ice men scrabbled over, dying for the glory of walking there.

June 19, London/Amsterdam. I had time between planes in London for a pleasant but not very sanguine breakfast with Walter Seltzer. He doubts Rank will put up the whole WAR LORD financing. I'll try to catch Rank's George Davis in Brussels for a talk, but it looks thin. Holland is small, indeed, but most interesting. From a canal boat, you get the feel of the seventeenth-century paintings of the same kind of houses. (Amsterdam was not bombed in the war, so many of them *are* the same houses.) I had a royal audience with Princess Beatrix, who was very kind and lives in the smallest palace I've ever seen . . . even the moat is miniature.

June 20, Amsterdam/Rotterdam. Investigated Holland's two principal glories today: Heineken's beer and paintings. Both lived fully up to expectations. The Rembrandts are really so good you can't believe it. THE NIGHT WATCH is up to the best of Velázquez as a masterful—old masterful—execution of a major group composition. (Why do the young masters never try a tough one like this?) The royal opening of 55 DAYS AT PEKING was a great success, I'm relieved to note.

June 22, Antwerp/Ostend. Driving through the Low Countries offered an interesting variant on jet commuting. Antwerp's a most handsome and interesting city, especially in view of the fact that I was awarded my second Till Eulenspiegel there today for EL CID, the first time an actor's gotten two. [*This was the Belgian version of the Academy Award, which I'd won also for* BEN-HUR.] I also saw Rubens's newly restored DESCENT FROM THE CROSS in the cathedral there . . . a remarkable blaze of color, with two centuries of grime scrubbed off. Ostend is a kind of Atlantic-City-on-the-North-Sea, but I had a chance to rest, before the exhibitors' banquet. Exhibitors and their wives are remarkably similar the world over, I find.

June 25, London/Los Angeles. I dozed and ate my way through one more lap on my commuters' route again, vastly tempted to stop off for a few hours in London to see some of the Wimbledon matches. The urge to see Lydia and the kids kept me airborne.

June 26, Los Angeles. I talked fruitfully with Peckinpah about what chance we have with the Civil War theme in MAJOR DUNDEE. We were both very taken with THIS SPORTING LIFE last night. Richard Harris, who was good in a small part in THE WRECK OF THE MARY DEARE, is very good indeed. He could be excellent in the other part in MAJOR DUNDEE. There were a lot of Irishmen in the Civil War. We must not compromise the casting on this one. It occurs to me that 55 DAYS AT PEKING, last year, was spoiled by compromise, and commercial slant. We have to do this one differently.

This was high-principled of me, but it shows an incomplete understanding of how film is arrived at. All art is compromised: the painter's by his control of his medium, the dancer's by his control of his body. No art depends more on compromise than film. It is the only art whose raw materials are so expensive the artist cannot buy them for himself, but must contract for them with an investor who expects a return on his money. Above all, film depends on the successful collaboration of various artists and craftsmen, whose different visions must be . . . yes, compromised. Making film, you compromise every day. If you do it wisely and frugally, you can still fulfill your vision. If you do it carelessly, you will fail. As Jack Warner put it when he barred an actor from Warner's, "I never want to see that son of a bitch on this lot again . . . unless we absolutely need him!"

July 9. CLEOPATRA is not a good film, not because of any shortcomings in Taylor's or Burton's performance, but because Mankiewicz felt his instincts were superior to Shakespeare's. He's reduced Antony from a hero to a drunk, leaving nothing for Cleopatra to have a high passion about. It's maddening to have a tragedy with no protagonist, and you can't make a protagonist out of Cleopatra. In trying to do so, he has destroyed Caesar, Antony, and the potential of his film.

No, I'm not going to contradict the entry above. The well-publicized faradiddles that crippled the CLEOPATRA schedule forced all sorts of compromises on Mankiewicz and marked his film, no doubt. But the choice he made to alter Shakespeare's (and history's) view of Antony's character was crucially his and had nothing to do with how long he had to wait for Miss Taylor to come to work.

July 13. My tennis is sicklied o'er a bit with the pale cast of thought, or some damn thing. The serve may be improving, but not very quickly. Never mind; we shall overcome . . . someday. I put in a ritual appearance at a cocktail thing for a new actress Paramount has in a film. God, I hate those parties. How much the same they all are; how much striving for the casual, happy note, and how much the tension shows. I did enjoy a barbecue at Glenn Ford's, at which Melvyn Douglas told Hedda she was full of shit. She was, too.

July 15. A fruitless meeting with Citron on both KHARTOUM and WAR LORD (no real action on either, except to avoid it on the former). I don't really want to tie down to another epic, even with as good a script as KHARTOUM has, just yet. For a change, we made real progress in the SAG negotiations today. I dictated most of the clause that may break the deadlock on pay TV. In effect, it postpones the issue till the next contract, but even this was incredibly difficult to arrive at.

July 17. Columbia rewarded me out of all proportion (and for what? I'd rather they'd finance WAR LORD) with a lovely suite of offices out of which to prepare MAJOR DUNDEE. Later, at Desilu, I was enormously impressed with two reels of footage from GREATEST STORY EVER TOLD. I think the scene, even rough-cut, of the raising of Lazarus is probably the best single scene I've ever seen in a film. Max is superb in it. I didn't like the few shots I saw of mine much, but all those scenes need editing to work at all.

July 26. I spent half the day burrowing through old files to demonstrate my honesty to the tax people. What a society we've evolved . . . so much time and energy are spent quarreling over taxes. Tonight I went to a meeting at Brando's house, down the road, to discuss the D.C. demonstration. I found myself chairman, when the dust cleared. I'm not sure I like that . . . or whether the rest of the group does either, if you get down to it.

This was a group (mostly film and theater people, with a sprinkling of painters and musicians) who eventually formed what was called The Arts Group and took part in the civil rights march in Washington that August. We were small in number, compared to the several major organizations that planned and took part in that remarkable event, but so many of us were public faces that we seemed far more important to the undertaking than in fact we were. I suppose I was elected chairman because of the time I'd put in with SAG . . . or maybe just because I'd gotten all those folks through the Red Sea.

July 31. I spent most of the day on the NAACP vs. MPPA [*Motion Picture Producers Association*] thing. I thought the meeting with the creative guilds was a waste of time, in the face of the intransigence of the technical unions on integration in the industry. Dinner with the Urban League tonight was interesting; my first exposure to a major segment of organized Negro opinion. There were some very impressive people, though I can't agree with those who feel there's some sort of racial indemnity due for "the failures of the past." I think it's going to be an eventful summer.

Though the actors, writers, and directors had been historically almost totally free of bias, the technical unions had up until that time been closed shop, and almost impossible for anyone, *no matter what color he was, to get into. As I said to the head of the NAACP delegation, "It isn't a question of their discriminating against blacks. They discriminate against everyone who isn't the son of a member." Oddly enough, pressure on the technical unions in the film industry from black groups also opened those unions to applicants of all races.*

August 5. I couldn't convince George Stevens to join us on the Washington thing. Indeed, he almost convinced me I was wrong to go. Instinctively I share his opposition to group action. I don't like to follow other men's drums; I like to walk by myself, but here I am, ass-deep in a complicated, emotionally charged group action, with ninety-seven people running off in forty-seven directions. The way to do this would be just to go to Washington by my damn self.

August 12. We had another long session here at the house on the D.C. march. I managed to get Jim Garner chosen as cochairman with Marlon for the short time I'll be in New York. A cooler head prevailing, I trust.

By this time, it had become clear that there were some of us who were primarily hooked on the drama of a civil rights demonstration, not on making it work. Our meetings were studded with rousing speeches about chaining ourselves to the Jefferson Monument and lying down on Pennsylvania Avenue. "No, we won't," I said. "Not if I go. We live in a country where we have the right to do this, and we're going to do it the way it says in the book." Most of us really agreed with this, but I had to go to New York for several days before we all met in Washington, and I wanted to be sure there were steady hands around. There were lots of them.

August 23, New York. I arrived in New York to find Marlon had taken Paul Newman and Tony Franciosa to Gadsden, Alabama, without checking with me, or anyone else, as far as I can tell. This is the hook you hang on with a group. You can answer for what you do yourself, but how can you answer for what all the others do?

As Marlon has demonstrated more than once, he regards undertakings of this kind primarily as acts of theater, rather than civil function. Like many people, he finds it hard to accept this basic truth about group actions, especially in the public arena: You are responsible for the group, as well as to it. Whatever they do, you do.

August 26. The TODAY SHOW was worth getting up for, though Lescoulie failed to ask me the question I wanted to answer with the Tom Paine quote I found. Maybe I can use it in Washington, in place of the James Baldwin statement I still haven't seen (and doubt more and more I'll want to use to express what I think). I don't know how the hell to solve this honorably. I suppose I should write something myself.

No, I shouldn't have, and I didn't have to. Unlike my problems with Marlon, which were a lot like kids arguing on a playground over who gets to pitch, this difference with James Baldwin proved readily solvable. Far more politically aware, as well as far more radical, than Marlon, he recognized readily that the statement he was committed to write for me to read at our press conference in Washington had to encompass not merely his own views, but the whole group's. He did it brilliantly.

August 28, Washington, D.C. It was a very stirring day. I'll never forget it, and I'm proud to have been part of it, even the small part we were. I went out early to the airport and met our group coming in by charter from Los Angeles. They were all there: Harry Belafonte, Burt Lancaster, Sidney Poitier, Marlon, Paul, and they all did wonderfully. We had our press conferences and made our statements, and then joined nearly a quarter of a million other Americans, moving quietly and happily up the Mall to the Lincoln Memorial. There were many individual voices raised eloquently through the day: Dr. King, Marian Anderson, many others. But the true voice heard was the people's. It spoke for Lydia, walking alone through the moving thousands, and for the old black man with broken shoes she walked beside for a while. Whatever else it meant for Americans, black or white, it shows the strength of this country when our constitutional right to peaceable assembly can be exercised in such thousands, with such dignity and happy determination. Jefferson, whose monument was the last thing I saw tonight on my way to the airport, would have approved. Indeed, he would've said "I told you so."

I still remain as moved by the memory of that day as I was then. I know of no other country in the world where so many thousands of citizens could've assembled in peaceful protest with such magnificent, quiet purpose. It moved the Congress, too. This day is credited with the passage of the Civil Rights Act five months later. It was the high-water mark of the civil rights movement in this country.

August 29, Los Angeles. Having finished functioning as a citizen for a while, I got back to making a living today with the first reading on THE PATRIOTS for Hallmark. The script still reads very sludgy to me, but we're making some cuts to loosen it a bit. The question is whether I can provide enough spark to bring Jefferson alive. Of course he was a great man, but he seems somehow passive in the script. George Schaefer is extremely intelligent, but I'm beginning to feel that only rarely does a director have the time, let alone the insight, to provide really meaningful help of this kind to an actor during rehearsals.

September 13, New York. I spent one last day among the gilt chairs and colored tapes marking the sets at Central Plaza. We got a good run-through, I think, the second time. We'll lose this, of course, down in the Brooklyn studios, but the seeds of it should be there when we finally get around to playing again. There can be a peak of performance in a live show that's not like anything you get on film. I hope we can get it with this!

Live television drama, born in New York, traditionally rehearsed most of the shows in those garishly sleazy rooms on the Lower East Side available for rent for wedding parties and banquets. The furnishings consisted of gilt chairs, walls of mirrors, and plaster cherubs and cornucopias on the pillars. They could really be depressing when rehearsals weren't going well.

September 15 (Sunday). Another weekend disappeared without a trace in a crammed limbo, blocking the show for the cameras. I'm only aware of the sudden harsh edge of autumn in the air while waiting for a taxi at the beginning and end of the day . . . the rest is the bright, neutral weather of the sound stage. I must *not worry* about camera responsibility, mike shadows, things like that. That's George's problem. Mine is Jefferson. Make him alive.

September 17. We taped THE PATRIOTS today, in seven hours. It's not quite like the old days of live TV, but it's close. There's a performance pressure, but there's still the option of a retake, which changes it. Still, on the whole, I'm pleased. I think we made what is basically a drama of ideas come off. Jefferson's stature stems not from the color of his character, but the quality of his thinking. This is very difficult to act. The limo was waiting, my bags in the trunk, when I got the makeup off. I caught the jet home in a walk.

September 25, Los Angeles. Universal is nibbling tentatively around the edges of WAR LORD, but they seem to want a different kind of film than I do. They're really just attracted by the idea of a movie with me in chain mail. I honest to God think it'd be easier to get this made with an unknown actor. The studios are so committed to the idea of a period film with me in it grossing forty million dollars that they can't imagine a more modest undertaking.

October 1. Columbia is breathing harder on WAR LORD. They want to meet Thursday and talk a deal. On the other hand, Universal is also stirring. In addition, Citron reports Fox is close to a firm offer on AGONY AND THE ECSTASY. For all this to work it'll mean a lot of shuffling. MAJOR DUNDEE should start in December, AGONY AND THE ECSTASY either immediately after or in the late summer, so as to get the Hollywood interiors scheduled back here during the school term.

October 4, Los Angeles/Dallas. A long conference with the Columbia production department on whether we can, and if so why we should, try filming WAR LORD here. There are lots of dunes, of course, and a few swamps up north, and some woods of the type we want. It might work out very well. We'll see what the location department (also the budget folks) come up with. Cutting it a little close, Lydia and I got off for the Planned Parenthood thing in Dallas, the land of the last big rich. Or do they just make it seem that way? Anyway, Clint Murchison's new house has fifteen thousand square feet of floor space.

October 5, Dallas. A long day with a lot of tennis and so forth, raising money to fight the population explosion. The Texans do these things with characteristic panache, such as grading out a special landing strip for Bob Cummings's plane, so he could give flying lessons to local civilians willing to part with a hundred dollars for the privilege.

October 8, Los Angeles. For the first time, I think, I received firm offers for three films on the same day. FATE IS THE HUNTER, AGONY AND THE ECSTASY for Fox, SATAN BUG from Mirisch. It's reassuring, if nothing else.

October 9. The Michelangelo script strikes me as possibly the best written that's ever been submitted to me. It would be a different part for me, and might be a helluva movie, though whether it can work commercially, I don't know. It seems too good a script for that, frankly. I read the Mirisch script tonight, too. It's not bad, but not like Michelangelo. Besides, three films in one year are enough.

October 10. I told Citron I'm anxious to do AGONY AND THE ECSTASY; he pointed out Fox had a two-picture deal in mind, including FATE IS THE HUNTER. They're also very gloomy about paying a percentage of the gross from the first dollar. I'll leave that to Herman; I just want this part.

October 11. Citron made the deal he wanted for the Michelangelo film with Fox without tying the other film to it. I'm very pleased. Now, who will play the pope, who will direct? I read THE GREAT RACE, which is a very funny script, but taking it would mean pushing back WAR LORD again. Besides, Lemmon really has the better part.

October 19. I've started working my way through my reading list on Michelangelo: the standard biographies, the collected letters, and of course Irving Stone's novel.

October 23. A very satisfactory meeting on AGONY AND THE ECSTASY today. They now want to shoot the whole thing in Italy (and try for an Italian coproduction deal). They're not going to be ready to go before June, which means my family can come over with me, but also that I'll have to pass on THE GREAT RACE. I'm relieved at the former, disappointed at the latter. They'll make an offer to Zinnemann for director, to either Olivier or Tracy for the part of the pope. They're certainly prepared to go first cabin on this one.

October 24. Columbia still has its corporate thumb up its ass on WAR LORD, so Citron is pressing ahead with Universal. He reports them impressed by the script, but anxious for a happy ending. I don't know what the hell to do about that. Certainly not change the ending.

I've been killed often, on film, the stage, and the television tube. Studios insist the audience doesn't like this. It's been my experience that it makes them unhappy, but that's not the same thing. In any event, they often attend those undertakings where I come to a violent end even more enthusiastically than they do those where I survive. There may be a message for me somewhere there.

October 26. The Wylers' party tonight was fine; we were glad to see Willy and Talli hit their twenty-fifth, and they had some nice people there. I talked to Rex Harrison, who is interested in playing Pope Julius in AGONY AND THE ECSTASY. He wants more money than they want to pay, but they're still talking. He'd be good.

November 1. The MAJOR DUNDEE script wasn't out of mimeo today, so I read some of the research material Fox sent over on Michelangelo. The Papino biography is good, but the other stuff is thin. The man isn't in there anyway, I suspect. Whatever I can bring to him is in the statues he made, not the books people wrote about him.

November 4. I finally got the MAJOR DUNDEE script today. There's a lot of good work in it, but I'm more than a little disappointed. The characters are there, and the bones of the story, but there's a lot of excess mishmash, as well as the kind of theatrically seriocomic violence you find in part of Ford's work (and not the best part, at that). But it's a hand you can draw to, I'll say that.

November 12. I was touched by my visit to Stan Laurel. He's living in a tiny apartment in Santa Monica with his wife and the flotsam left behind by the high tide of his career. I had the feeling he's more or less content, though his poor health must color his reactions to his life now. It contrasts sharply to the clipping he showed me of the triumphal reception they had in London in '32. He seems happy about the award, but I doubt he'll have the strength to accept it in person.

The Screen Actors Guild had chosen Stan Laurel as the first recipient of the Guild Award. We were hopeful he could accept it in person, and I'd volunteered to explore the question with him. In the end, he couldn't get to the meeting where we honored him. Danny Kaye accepted for him, most graciously.

November 13. Tony Quinn's unavailable for Tyreen, so they're now submitting MAJOR DUNDEE to Steve McQueen. This wouldn't be a bad choice, in some ways better than Tony. A lesser name, but fresher. Lee Marvin will be Potts, I think, and maybe Omar Sharif for Gomez. There is still no reaction from Zinnemann on AGONY AND THE ECSTASY. We may have to move on to the next name. I'd like very much to get him, still.

November 14. I reread the MAJOR DUNDEE script, taking notes. I'm convinced the woman's role is a major flaw. She's artificial and contrived. We'll have to rework all of this. At a later meeting on WAR LORD (where the woman works perfectly) we had to arrive at a list of writers who can give us a better ending. Not necessarily a happy one . . . just more satisfying.

Sometimes on a film, the people making it or the studio financing it feel that more work on the script is needed, and that the writer responsible up to that point has given his best shot. The problem then is to find another writer who can make a useful contribution. Writers hate the idea of being used and disposed of like Kleenex and I don't blame them. The method works for film, however.

November 19. Though Universal is willing to pay five thousand dollars for two weeks' work on a step sheet outlining other possible endings for WAR LORD, I'm not very sanguine about Millard Kaufman's ability to satisfy us, let alone Universal as well (though that may be the easier task for him). Anyway, he'll try. Meanwhile, we do not have Zinnemann for AGONY AND THE ECSTASY, but we *do* have Harrison.

They're moving toward Guy Green for director. Who the hell would be right? Who the hell can we get?

November 22. I was in Walter's office, on the phone, when one of his staff ran in, stammering, "I just heard Kennedy's been shot!" It's a blind, brutal, pointless act, and because of it we're much less than we were, or might have been. If you believe in our system, then you have to believe it won't fail because of this, but it will falter. Today, surely, we're all faltering.

November 23, New York. I was given a purpose to carry me through this dark weekend, which I seized on eagerly. ABC called me this morning to fly to New York and take part in a memorial service they're rushing to air tomorrow. I spent the flight poring fruitlessly through my Shakespeare concordance looking for meaningful lines. In a meeting with ABC at the apartment, we chose some Psalms, and tentatively, some Frost. Kennedy liked Frost.

November 24. I spent the morning redacting four Psalms . . . the nintieth, the ninety-first, the one hundred and twenty first, and the twenty-third . . . into one whole, which seemed apt. I also read "Stopping by Woods" and "Fire and Ice," from Frost. The poems seemed to me to say something. The program was . . . worth doing, I think. It's all we can do.

I was one of the lucky few in those first numb days. I had something specific to do that could be called a response to the shock we all felt.

November 25, New York/Los Angeles. I watched the caisson roll down Pennsylvania Avenue on TV while I dressed to go to the airport. Before we took off, there was a minute of silence there, and then we flew west, ahead of the sun, across the land he led, well or ill, but strongly, for less time than he deserved. Now we have to do, as all men must, the best we can.

November 26, Los Angeles. The world, or at least my experience of it, slowly began to return to normal, though the waste of that tough man's death still stabs as you pick up the threads you dropped on Friday. I read through the second version of MAJOR DUNDEE which is . . . not much better, I guess, and did, really, not much else. I played with my son a little. We're building a model of an archaeological dig. This seems very important.

November 28. A muted kind of Thanksgiving, with friends for dinner. We have things to be thankful for. Not only that the Republic has not fallen with the president, many more things than that. True, most of them are THINGS, of which we should no more be thankful than we should covet them. Lydia cooked our turkey alone today, which made it like old times, surely. Before dinner, I read the passage from OF TIME AND THE RIVER that I wish I'd read at the memorial for JFK.

November 29. We had a fine day, winding up through the rock-rough draws on horses, ducking under the golden branches of the sycamore, fall's only trademark in California. Fray sits taller in the saddle each time we go out, and his grin is a little toothier. I will hate badly being away from him and Holly, and my girl, for as long as this next location will be.

December 3. Sam convinced me he's willing to go with Dick Harris, as much from a desire to get things settled as anything else. He's not as right as Tony Quinn, not as tall, not as good a horseman, but he's a good actor; the best we can get, I think. He's also a rising and fashionable one, which means more than many people realize.

The preoccupation with things like horsemanship in this entry seems shallow, I know. In casting, though, you assume acting ability. The other technical requirements are then crucial, though secondary. Lydia always gets annoyed at me when I describe an actor as being "fashionable." She says it sounds frivolous. Of course actors do go in and out of fashion, as a result of some particularly effective performances or a string of ineffective ones. Dick was very hot just then, having just been marvelous in a very good picture: THIS SPORTING LIFE.

December 6, New York. The routine flight to New York was unusually tiring but gave me a chance to go over the latest MAJOR DUNDEE script. Sam and Jerry Bresler, meantime, are off to Rome to talk to Dick Harris. I had enough energy for an interview with Earl Wilson, and a drink with Jolly West.

December 7. I found myself back on the deck of the AK101 again, doing MISTER ROBERTS for the fourth time. Harrigan is the captain again, seemingly none the worse for wear, full of stories of his recovery from a broken hip last year (and I don't blame him for boasting!). Ray Middleton is a bit more at home in musical comedy, maybe, than as Doc, but perfectly sound. My word, the show's a damn delight to work on. The two scenes we're doing are only enough to make your mouth water for the rest.

The New York City Center Theatre was celebrating its twentieth anniversary with a benefit of scenes from various successful productions. I did a scene from MISTER ROBERTS, which I'd played there with Bill Harrigan several years earlier.

December 9. We did the show tonight with one run-through on stage, but it went well, if not quite loud enough for that echoing barn. It was filled, at least, at fifty bucks a head, so the time was well spent. The party afterward was a great ego sop, too.

December 11, Los Angeles. It's strange to be here without Lydia. [*She'd flown to Spain to see Bea Sellmer, who'd just lost her husband.*] My baby girl came in the room this morning, where I take up only slightly more than half of the huge bed, and said anxiously, "Wheah Mommy?" "Mommy's in Spain, honey." "In Spain?" "Yes, sweetheart. She'll come home soon." "Home soon?" This plaintive echo was inexpressibly touching. Fray was handsome at his dancing class, where he won a prize. I rehearsed the reading tonight for the memorial on JFK. It seemed a lot less than perfect to me . . . but then.

December 12. Making film deals is much harder, I begin to realize, than making films. Jerry Bresler is back from Rome with the news that Tony Quinn's available to us after all. Harris's agents are upping the price for him, so we may go back to our first choice.

December 13. A long morning of work at Universal gave us a good solution to their insistence that we find a less bleak ending for WAR LORD before they put up financing. We may be treading a whorish path here, but I'm finally persuaded they are our last hope to make the film at all. I did the JFK reading at the Friars' tonight. I was all right, but very radio-ready. With Everett Sloane, John Forsythe, et al., we sounded a bit like the grand old days on the Blue Network.

December 18. We finally signed Dick Harris for Tyreen, so now we can cast the rest of the film. (Not to mention rewriting it.) I'm in a rather surly mood, partly because of our problems on MAJOR DUNDEE and WAR LORD (which still has no firm reaction from Universal) and AGONY AND THE ECSTASY (for which Fox is now trying for Carol Reed) and partly because of the season. The flood of *stuff* pouring in this time of year always makes me feel beleaguered, and overprivileged. Besides, there are always too many premieres to go to this month.

December 19. George Stevens was a gracious and entertaining host at lunch, as always. He seems to be progressing firmly on GREATEST STORY EVER TOLD. He was most interesting on the subject of the rhythm of cuts on a film. THE CARDINAL tonight wasn't a good example of that, or of much else, I think. It tried to cover too much ground, thus seems diffuse and uninvolving. Tryon seemed unable, as were most of the rest of the cast, to convey the feeling of faith absolutely essential to a story of priests.

December 24. I spent most of the day delivering gifts, just under the wire. Then I took time out to have a meeting with Al Hart, of City National Bank, set up by Paul Ziffren, briefing me on the shopping center deal I'm going in on. It sounds promising; at least it's the only time I've talked to a banker who had a Brueghel over his desk. We put up our Michigan tree tonight . . . the tallest and finest we've ever had, I think. Fraser helped this year, with all of us aiming at Holly's delight tomorrow morning when she sees it.

When we moved into the house on Coldwater, we began a family tradition, which still persists. For Christmas, we have a tree cut on the Russell Lake timberland in St. Helen, Michigan, where I was raised. It seems to survive the journey to California and the holiday season in our living room better than anything you can buy on Sunset Boulevard. (Also cheaper.)

December 25. The day was deluged in gifts. Certainly too many for one family. Giving is fine, but this much getting verges on gluttony. With children, it's hard to resist. Fray seemed most delighted with his Daisy BB pistol, which charmed Dad a bit too. Holly had the first Christmas she really could understand; I heard her say softly, "Gorgeous . . . gorgeous . . . i'n' it *gorgeous???*"

December 27. We have a deal for WAR LORD at last. Walter called to say Universal had agreed on terms, as outlined by Citron. I don't know the details yet, but it requires us to deliver a negative not more than two hours in length; for the rest, we have complete artistic control. We celebrated with Mickey and Walter tonight at the Magic Castle. This was appropriate; it took some sort of magic act to get this thing committed to film.

December 28. The first day in which the flood tide of holiday cheer began to ebb enough to give a man time to draw breath. The presents are not all unwrapped, the parties are not all attended, and God knows the material cheer is not all dispensed. We're surrounded by food we'll never eat, books we'll never read, clothes we'll never wear. It makes my Scottish-reared, depression-conditioned sensibilities twitch . . . but we're all together, and we love each other. This, at least, is in the true spirit of Christmas.

December 31. Sam Peckinpah wants to make an offer to James Coburn for MAJOR DUNDEE. I don't really know his work, but I trust Sam. On AGONY AND THE ECSTASY, they want to make a firm offer to Carol Reed to direct. That's fine with me. On WAR LORD, Universal wants a finished screenplay before finalizing. It's annoying, but reasonable, I guess. Lydia had a sore throat, so we passed the old year out quietly, alone on our hilltop.

This was an odd year, professionally. I worked very little, really, but I think I grew. The only screen work I did was half of my performance as the Baptist; on television, I played Jefferson, and on the stage, the fragment of MISTER ROBERTS. All of these I did at least well with, I think; . . . the Baptist maybe more than that. And I worked in all three media.

I did grow, I'm sure, in what I've learned about how to deal with the disparate and disappointing fragments out of which films, and plays as well, are made. The long struggle to put WAR LORD together taught me almost as much about men as it did about writing, and a great deal about movies as well.

For a man in this time, which is not always easy for an actor to keep in focus, this was a bad year, with many days we'd wipe away if we could. Yet the dark, endless river rolls on, and we're carried with it. Each day you do the best there is to do that day. This is true for an American whose president has been shot, as well as for an actor with a script that won't jell, or a father, or a husband.

Father . . . husband. There, all's well. The children are treasures growing under my eyes, and Lydia is . . . Lydia, more mine than she was under the lilac tree. I don't know her yet, certainly, and probably never will. I can't tell if any woman is ever known, or knowable, but I know mine isn't. I know she's mine, though.

1964

To Mexico for
Major Dundee . . .

to Rome for
*The Agony and
the Ectsasy* . . .

finally, *The War Lord*
emerges from *The
Lovers.*

With chisel in
The Agony and the Ecstacy
LYDIA HESTON

With battle-axe in
The Warlord
UNIVERSAL PICTURES

January 4, Las Vegas.

By 1964, we'd established a tradition, more or less by accident (as I suspect many traditions begin), of spending an annual weekend in Las Vegas with eight or ten old friends, as the guests of Bill and Clori Isaac. I know how the guests of Diamond Jim Brady must have felt. We sample the shows, play a lot of tennis, and some of us gamble. Since the logic of this last obsession has always escaped me, my prime function during the gambling sessions is to shepherd the women in the party to whatever show attracts them. My title for this activity is Leader of the Squab Squad.

Even without gambling, it's very difficult to get to bed before three in this town. I didn't make it, but did get up in time for tennis. Outside in this air, you feel as though the inside of your skull has been polished, anyway. I performed my usual ringside role as dress extra at two shows tonight. Eddie Fisher, who seems to have survived his unhappy experience of cuckoldry with a measure of maturity, sang better, I think, than I've ever heard him.

January 8, Los Angeles. No word yet on MAJOR DUNDEE except a few minor changes from Sam. We still haven't isolated exactly what this picture's *about* . . . maybe because we can't agree, or just don't know . . . but we have to *decide*. It has to be about the Civil War, I'm convinced. The word from Fox is that we have Carol Reed for AGONY AND THE ECSTASY. This is good, I'm sure. We have a chance for a superior film with him; he confers class on the whole project.

January 14. A full morning meeting with Carol Reed on AGONY AND THE ECSTASY. These first meetings are always spent largely convincing each other you're both men of high artistic purpose. Nonetheless, I think he can do this film. He's intent on getting rehearsal time before shooting begins on the scenes between me and Rex Harrison. I'm for this. We have to find a way to keep them from being simply a series of quarrels. I made my point about avoiding the high-key lighting Fox loves (vide *Cleopatra*). So far, this one smells OK. At least we have a good script.

January 21. It now seems we won't leave for Mexico until the fifth; Dick Harris won't get here till that weekend. Antonioni [*for whom Harris was then working*] is still behind schedule on his film in Italy, wired for more time from Columbia, but was turned down. I wish they'd given him a couple of weeks; we could use it ourselves on the script. If we can't get it right after five and a half months in the typewriter, then we have to get it right in front of the cameras.

January 23. We got some good out of the thirty WAR LORD pages Millard Kaufman gave us. His dialogue's a little verbose, his medieval scholarship spurious compared to Collier's, but there's something there we can use, with a little more work. We've been on this for a year and a half now.

January 25. I took Fray out to Ralph McCutcheon's new ranch in Sand Canyon, anxious to try the horses again before they truck them off for Mexico.

The horses ridden by principal actors in a film requiring them are almost invariably rented from Los Angeles ranches specializing in stock for films. It's not easy to get green horses to work well near reflectors, cameras, and other bizarre pieces of equipment. It's even harder to get them to hit and hold the marks necessary for filming, especially when ridden by horsebackers of uncertain abilities, whose hands are likely to be too heavy or too light on the reins. These horses are moved by truck to the location, a process that takes some time when it's as far off as Mexico.

I also wanted to have an hour or so in the sun with my son on a horse. He did well, we had a happy day. There can't be many things that give a deeper, truer kind of joy than watching a boy you helped create trot along behind you over a ridge, growing easy in the saddle as he goes. He learned today that you can slide a horse down a steep grade.

January 28. We checked out the MAJOR DUNDEE cast in the saddle today. Only Jim Coburn can horseback. Dick Harris looks loose on a horse, which is a plus. The others will get by, I expect. I suddenly recognized the stable we rode from: the same one where I learned to rope for THREE VIOLENT PEOPLE eight years ago. I've been hacking away out here for a long time.

January 29. We pressed on with our rehearsals, till Dick was . . . stricken is the only word that leaps to mind. Certainly that's what Dick thought he was. I can understand it, I guess. He's been working damn hard with Antonioni and now must feel some pressure on this part because of the riding and the southern accent. He'll manage in the saddle, but Sam's now convinced he'll never reach the accent. I'll concede he makes an unlikely cracker. Sam says forget that and make him an honest Irishman. He may be right.

Dick Harris is a very good actor and by and large a charming man. Though he appears very strong, he does seem to be one of those people who enjoys ill health. In any event, on this picture, he was from time to time spectacularly taken with a seizure of one kind or another.

January 30. Rehearsals are more or less shot to hell without Dick, but we managed to get in a little work on the scene with Jim Hutton

(Lieutenant Graham). He'll be good, I think. At lunch we threw out Harris's southern accent and my beard. I hate to lose the beard, but Sam feels very strongly on the subject. Now he wants me to grow it during shooting, for the end of the film.

Feeling as I do about having beards pasted on, I'd spent six weeks growing a good cavalry beard, then Sam decided it was wrong for the role. It wasn't, of course. (In those days studios were still uneasy about beards on leading men.)

February 2 (Sunday). I spent some time today thinking about the rewrite Sam's done for us on *Major Dundee.* There are holes in it; serious holes, I think. That means either he knows a lot less about scripts than I do . . . or a lot more. I'm perfectly willing to accept the latter premise, but it's a bit spooky just now. The main thing wrong is the girl's part, which is very sloppily written. I wish I knew who the hell's going to play it.

February 5, Durango. All three of them rode out in the limo to see me off on the charter for Mexico. Holly, incredibly doll-like in her little blue coat, Fraser long and lean, with hair like wheat. Lydia was as always when I leave: her most beautiful. I felt unfairly deprived when I kissed them and climbed the steps of one more plane carrying me off on one more location. Durango is . . . not very much.

February 6. The usual confusion starting a film: the usual sifting of old grips coming up to say, "Hey . . . ain't seen you since the de Mille days!", the usual backing and circling horses full of anxious actors. Still, we got some good shots. I said only two words, not very well. I can ride, at least. We're getting into more significant stuff tomorrow.

February 12. We cracked open the girl's part today. Senta Berger looks very right: no lipstick, loose hair. She was a little nervous, flubbing her English a bit, but she'll work out fine, I'm sure. The scene's OK; I found a good bit with Tyreen's saber.

February 22. Lydia got in much delayed, her DC-3 from Mexico City rolling down the tattered runway with a little dog barking to meet it. We had time for a passionate reunion before I had to climb into my cavalry boots and rush off to the Civil War. We did some work in the fiesta scene, changing both the start and the finish. Sam gave me a better tag than the one I'd invented, and agreed to the other cuts and additions I'd found.

February 23 (Sunday). Waffles in bed with Lydia, then the dailies. The scenes on the wall were OK; the one with Graham may be better than that. I then went out and foolishly fell off the black stud, showing off for the girls, of course. I turned out to have stretched, or smashed, or some damn thing, a cartilage in my left elbow. It's damn painful. Ultrasonic treatment and X rays; the doctor says it'll be two weeks healing. Like hell it will. One week, and I'll work tomorrow. Goddamn it, I can't even type!

February 24. I managed to smuggle my bum arm on the set, concealed beneath the serape I'm wearing in the fiesta scene. I took only John Veitch [*the production manager*] into my confidence; he promised discretion. If Sam finds out, he'll start trying to shoot around me and I don't want that. Luckily, the shots today required little action. I managed to lift my left arm enough to dance.

February 25. Lydia buzzed off into the clear dawn, subduing her terror of tiny airplanes, and left me behind. It turned out someone had finked and told Sam about my arm, but he didn't suggest any modification of the shots. The only riding shot was at a trot, presenting no problems. (I couldn't mount alone; they had to shoot around that.)

March 1 (Sunday). A damn full day, for a Sunday. We waited an hour for Jim Hutton to show as best man for Rock Tarkington's wedding, which he finally did, in a visible miasma of guilt, after a late poker party. The corrida wasn't very good, marked by the bad goring of Trainero, just after he'd dedicated his first bull to me. He stood slumped against the barrera eight feet from me, blood leaking through his fingers clutching his groin. His eyes, looking at the sky, were just like the dying bull's. "No . . . not me, not today . . . surely not to me!"

March 2, Durango/Saltito. The new location is marvelous. There's no place to live, so we have to commute from Durango, but it's worth the long drive. We lose the light early and got shadowed out of two locations without a shot on either scene, but we did get the big master on the sequence of Hadley's desertion. I feel relaxed about what we have to do here, except for the scene with Senta, which we must shoot down south.

March 6, Saltito/Durango. Sam's cold nerve astounds me. With the production brass breathing down his neck, he continues to shoot every shot he feels he needs, including a shot of the sky for the death of Hadley. (Perhaps suggested by what I said about the goring of the bullfighter Sunday?)

Sam Peckinpah, as his subsequent career has aptly demonstrated, is a director of remarkable ability. He's also a little paranoid. On the other hand, as my wise friend Jolly West has pointed out, even paranoids have enemies. Sam has a spectacular gift for making enemies and he'd already succeeded in arousing a good deal of suspicion and hostility on the part of the producer and the high Columbia brass. They suspected, accurately enough, that he was likely to prove difficult to manage. Eventually, we got into a great deal of trouble as a result of all this.

March 7, Mexico City. Cantinflas sent his jet to help carry the company to Mexico City. We waited on the runway an hour for Senta, finally left her to take the charter. After four weeks in Durango, it's marvelous to be in a town with long beds and hot water.

March 11. In the middle of a fine shooting day, there was terrible news from New York. Bill Blowitz, walking on Fifth Avenue last night, was killed by a taxi as he crossed Fifty-seventh Street. It seems such a pointless, idle death. (Which one doesn't, of course? Why do we make these observations only when it's someone important to us?)

Bill Blowitz was a remarkable friend and a remarkable man. He handled my public relations for several years, as his partner, George Thomas, still does. I think everyone who knew Bill misses him still.

March 15. This was a very Spanish day. Sooner or later, any man who spends much time in this country, or in Spain, is going to find himself in the ring with one of those damn bull calves. Today was my day. I managed neither to get hurt nor make an ass of myself. Jim Coburn and I shared a quarter of an ear. Later, my family arrived. The baby burst into laughter when she saw me, Fray's taller, and Lydia more beautiful, I swear, on the eve of our twentieth anniversary.

March 16, Vista Mermosa. Sam and I bumped heads today over the scene where Dundee leaves his command to Lieutenant Graham. Sam wanted to play an exchange with Tyreen. I convinced him it should be between Graham and Tyreen, but failed to persuade him to do it without lines, just looks. We shot it his way.

People are always asking me what you do when you have a difference with the director about the scene. In my experience, it's seldom a difference you can't work out. This was an example to the contrary. When that happens, you're supposed to do it the way the director wants it.

March 30, Cuautla. Lydia decided to go see the Mayan ruins in the southern jungle. Holly, a bit off her feed, left for Los Angeles and pasteurized milk. Fray was desperately anxious to stay on the location. We got damn little shot today; essentially just the big setup with the French cavalry. This is not the kind of shot Sam, or any director, should waste time on. He would disagree, but I know Wyler or Stevens would turn it over to the second unit. I had a phone call from Citron. Columbia's decided to accept my offer of my DUNDEE salary. I didn't expect this, but I'm convinced it gives me an enormous moral advantage.

Like hell it did. It gave me no moral advantage whatever. In fact, the whole episode was pretty ridiculous. As DUNDEE progressed, more and more overbudget and overschedule, Sam's position as a relatively unknown director became more and more precarious, especially given his basic pugnacity with studio brass. When the overage passed a quarter of a million dollars, it became clear that the studio was on the point of replacing Sam with another, more tractable director. I thought this was an absolutely lousy idea. Aside from Sam's talent, the adage about horses in midstream applied. Contractually, I had no part in the decision. DUNDEE was made under an old commitment to Columbia, under which I did not have the creative controls I normally exercised by 1964. Nevertheless, the leading actor on a picture actually has almost as much muscle as he cares to use. Ethically, I totally disapprove of this kind of thing, but I was positive the picture's only chance lay in Sam's finishing it. I made this point with careful moderation; they got the message.

Overwhelmed with guilt at my flouting my own rules on professional behavior, I impulsively called the head of Columbia, then Mike Frankovich, and told him that in an effort to make up the extra costs I recognized they were incurring on the film, I would be happy to waive the six-figure salary they owed me for it under the old contract. "Oh, no!" Mike said. "We wouldn't dream of taking your salary, Chuck. It's a nice gesture, and we appreciate it, but we'll just go ahead as we are."

Flushed with success, I reported this to Herman Citron by phone. Herman, far wiser in the ways of the world than I, said, "You're out of your mind, Chuck. They'll take it."

"No, they won't," I said. "They were just very pleased with the gesture." Herman was right. They took the money back, and I did DUNDEE for nothing. A wire service reporter called me at the time and asked me, somewhat portentously, "Tell me, Mr. Heston, do you feel this action on your part will start a trend with other actors?" "Trend, hell," I retorted. "It won't even start a trend with me!"

March 31. We got a fair day, though the pressure on Sam is beginning to leak down. I don't think it shows in the work yet, but we're all edgy and a bit short-spirited. The WAR LORD script is finished. I think it's damn good, an improvement over Collier's version, though the love scenes aren't right yet. We'll submit this to Universal, though. Walter feels they'll go with it. So do I.

April 1. I sat all day today, waiting for Sam to work his way through the horses and let me do a shot. I finally did, of course, but I don't wait well. Kramer [*Columbia production head*] came for another go at Sam. I'll meet with them all myself tomorrow.

These next few days got very difficult. We'd shoot all morning, then during the lunch break the contingent of Columbia brass would come out over the desert to talk, picking their way through the rocks in their black suits and attaché cases. After lunch, they'd go back to the motel and wait while we shot all afternoon. When we got in, we'd meet them in the hotel bar for "a short session before dinner." Five hours later, still in wardrobe, still unshowered, still without dinner, you'd finally break off, with the next day's schedule looming at six in the morning.

April 2. After a brutal day's work, we had a brutal night. We fought it out from seven till eleven in the bar of the Hosteleria Vasco. They've given up on replacing Sam, but they're absolutely ready to pull the plug on the finish date. I waxed fairly eloquent, finally talking them out of cutting the Rostes Ranch. [*In the end, they shot it, then cut it.*]

April 8. We began work today in a village that was here before Cortes came. Did he realize when he rode down these streets in armor that he carried in his baggage a culture that put stories on film?

I'll never forget my first sight of this village, which is more than four hundred years old. It's a desolate little pueblo huddled in the desert as it has since the time of the conquistadores. They have no radio, no telephone, and certainly no experience of movie companies. We'd finished shooting a sequence two or three miles away and while they were wrapping the unit, Sam said, "Why don't you lead the troop over the ridge to the village, Chuck? It's only a couple of miles, and you all have horses." We found it readily enough, and rode down the one street, a dirty, ragged troop of cavalry coming out of the desert, as so many other troops had over the centuries. I saw the wide-eyed women and the somber, silent men watching from the shadowed doorways, and knew in my bones the ageless feeling of the mercenary riding into one more town. I knew, too, what those Mexican farmers felt. "Oh God, here's some more . . . here they come again."

April 10, Tlayacapan. The village is marvelous; I wallowed in it all day. I'm always stimulated by a set like this. Maybe I can really find the rest of DUNDEE here.

The village was worth the trouble it took to shoot there. It made the scenes believable to me in a way a set on a sound stage never could. I remember feeling the same thing in Spain, in the walled city of Peñíscola, standing on the ramparts while three thousand people shouted "Cid! Cid!" after we'd taken Valencia. I know what it is to take a city.

April 11. We didn't finish the fight in the bar. We did our damn best, but after waiting an hour for Sam's five-peso whore, we had no chance.

She wasn't Sam's whore in the possessive sense. She came with the village and Sam wanted to use her for a silent bit in a scene. She worked well enough, when she got to the set. Understandably, she was unaware of the conventions of this other profession, only slightly less ancient than hers.

April 14, Mescala. We made the move to the river, which is a hellhole. It's unbelievably hot; the brass buttons on my tunic literally burn to the touch. Somewhat to my surprise, I managed to persuade Sam to shoot Brock Peters's scene in the night camp as a studio interior instead of here on location, shooting day for night. There we can light it properly for night. Besides, that scene's too important to shoot in heat like this.

April 15, Rio Mescala. Christ knows how I picked up a cold in this heat. Son of a bitch! I *never* catch cold when I'm working. I had almost no voice. We'll have to loop what I shot. Otherwise, the stuff is coming, though it's bloody tough to shoot. I've given up on lunch since I found a piece of meat in my stew yesterday with the hide still on it. Now I spend my lunch break lying in the cool wet clay of the riverbank with my boots in the water.

April 17. We got into the final battle with the French today, not that we got to fight many Frenchmen. We got a good early start, and then Richard used the wrong rifle in two important shots, which we had to repeat after lunch, costing us an hour and a half of shooting light. He's something of a fuck-up, no question. For that matter, tempers shorten all around. The pressure of trying to get this film done in the time we have and maintain any of its quality is frightening.

I seem to have been unloading all my frustrations over the location on poor Dick Harris. In retrospect, I was unfair. It was a grueling location, and Dick wasn't used to working with either horses or guns. If he was a fuck-up, I was a hard-nosed son of a bitch.

April 21, Rio Mescala/Mexico City. I've never been so glad to finish a location. Mexico City looked like heaven, the Hotel Bamer seemed like the Dorchester. (It's not far below, at that, but any place with a bath and clean sheets would've done fine for me.) We worked at an incredible pace all day to finish the battle, just barely squeaking in under the wire. I pulled a horse over on top of me in the river, trying to do a Cossack drag for a shot, but Joe Canutt's rigging saved me from drowning. [*Joe is Yak's son.*] I think we got all the cuts we need. Now we're here, it turns out we can't start at the ranch tomorrow after all: The horses won't be here. This is better for me, maybe. These last weeks of location have been a bitch; I'd just as soon work indoors for a few days.

April 22, Mexico City/Estudios, Churabusco. A long, full day, but I didn't feel terribly beat; life on a sound stage is a piece of cake after the Rio Mescala. Besides, we got a very good scene with the Indian girl in the bedroom. The Mexican actress we used has no English, but the scene grew as we worked on it. I like this facet of Sam's method: keeping the structure of a scene loose enough to interject ad-libbed lines.

April 28, Marquesas. We worked high, ten thousand feet up in the pines all day, very right for this ranch scene. We were held up an hour because some slob screwed up the permits to move the horses, then we had bad luck with a dolly shot that somehow got more and more intricate the more you worked on it. There's no chance of my getting out before the late plane tomorrow. I'm content with that.

April 29, Marquesas/Los Angeles. Sam got all the shots he wanted with me, wrapping my part just in time for me to catch the plane for Los Angeles. As I've done once or twice before on a windup, I had my clothes on the set, leaped out of my wardrobe and into them before the dust from the last shot settled. Suddenly, unbelievably, I was in the arms of my family before I drew a full breath.

April 30, Los Angeles. I took pleasure in the simplest kind of routine today . . . running my son down the hill to school, checking the mail at the studio, having my hair cut (for the last time in six months, I'd guess), and having lunch with my wife. It's a pleasure beyond rubies to be back home, just going through the motions of living here. I'll find out tomorrow how long I can go on doing it before leaving for Rome.

May 4. I wandered over to Columbia and got a vivid postmortem on DUNDEE from Kramer. I get the feeling Bresler would almost be willing to have the film fail, if only to justify his misgivings about Sam. Sam, on the other hand, apparently failed to endear himself to the studio in that one day of shooting after I left.

May 5. Dr. Rubin confirms that my damn elbow is slowly improving. I know *that*. At the budget meeting at Universal for WAR LORD they agreed to add five shooting days to the overall schedule. This works out to a little more than two pages a day. There are some signs Columbia feels some guilt over their eagerness to take back the DUNDEE money. They may not take it, after all. [*They did, though.*]

May 7. I never thought they'd have to make *my* nose look even more broken than it is [*as Michelangelo's was*], but we did a good job with paint and a little rubber washer. We won't have to go to an exterior appliance, I think, which'll save endless time in makeup.

May 8. I spent the day dealing with reporters after releasing my statement on the Columbia salary rebate. It was really a delicious brouhaha. We opened our new screening room tonight with a party for thirty, and ran HENRY V. I figure if it's my room, I might as well run my favorite picture. The room works very well; the projectors and sound are first class. The film, of course, is as good as ever. It's hard to find a flaw in it, or in the evening.

May 14. I ran BILLY LIAR today, in which Julie Christie looked like she might be very good for the girl in WAR LORD. She has a natural quality, she's very striking, and she can act.

We tried very hard to get her, and could have, for thirty-five thousand dollars. Since she shortly became an international star of considerable importance, this would've been a bargain, but the studio balked at what they felt was an excessive price.

May 19. We took another shot at the Michelangelo makeup this morning. The bit of plastic tube up my nostril, accented by paint, creates a very effective beak. My beard's growing in well, trimmed according to Nye [*head of makeup at Fox*]. I learned something about beards today, and I thought I knew it all. We cut my hair in a Florentine bang; the result looks a great deal like the portraits of Michelangelo. I had my teeth cleaned, checked up on my guts, which have been running ever since Mexico, and came home and swam with my son.

May 20. Universal, *still* not finally locked into WAR LORD, had a session with Walter and me in an effort to wring a quarter million out of the budget (now three point eight million, with overhead). This seems a worthwhile goal, and we tried our best. You deal with such items as cutting down the height of the tower, the number of extras, the number of changes in my wardrobe (my idea, and a useful one). Also, the number of shooting days, which I shy away from, but Walter says we're all right. They want us to go up to Stockton next week and look for locations.

May 25. We finalized M/A's nose for AGONY. It seems right to me . . . not too much, yet it gives me something to hide in a little, and get away from my familiar public image. Does this bless or curse my work? Is there an answer to this? I doubt it; it's both. Anyway, I'm stuck with it.

May 30, New York en route to Rome. No, I didn't finish everything before I left. I must remember to pack the damn briefcase the night *before.* I saw two middling movies on the two planes . . . Brando in a part Jack Lemmon could've done better (BEDTIME STORY) and Sellers in a part where two kids had better ones (THE WORLD OF HENRY ORIENT). So here we go again. THE AGONY AND THE ECSTASY. Let's hope for less of the first, more of the last.

May 31, Rome. The day was telescoped, as always when you fly east. Rome looks the same as when I left it last (and before I ever saw it, or before anyone alive ever saw it). The villa is ridiculously luxurious; it makes me feel like Elizabeth Taylor; just the environment to corrode the soul. On the other hand, Carol Reed seems a creative and resourceful man, and the Tuscan steak at Nino's is as good as ever.

June 1. It's curious to walk around the lot where I put in so many months on BEN-HUR. The grass has grown entirely over the track where we ran the race, and the doors swing empty on the stables where the horses were. Now even the smell of them is gone. I remember it all, all the trials. This one can't possibly be that hard. I'm drawn to Carol. He's a very available man, easier to reach than Willy. I hope the film comes out as well.

June 2. I drove up with Carol to check the second location at Todi; it was really an excuse for a long talk in the car going up. I feel I'm learning a great deal from him this way. He's made changes that tighten and intensify the story as well as the character. The set at Todi [*of St. Peter's under construction*] will be good, if the glass shot works. Rex Harrison, on the other hand, will not be an easy man to work with. Perhaps he's insecure over who has the best part, which is understandable. The way we all carry on about these things . . .

June 3. We've set M/A's makeup, with a slightly wilder beard for the Carrara sequence. Carol Reed's a little dubious about the harsh lines of my beard, but a lot of that comes with my face. Besides, M/A was a harsh man. I'm beginning to feel a little closer to him. I spent the rest of the day reading his letters; solitary, useful time.

June 4. I've been nibbling aimlessly around the edges of this part for months. It finally hooked me in the guts when I went back to the

Sistine today, for the first time in many years. Thanks to the Vatican and Fox, I saw it not in a wash of twittering tourists, but high on a scaffold they rigged, alone with the incredible miracle that driven, angry man wrought there over the four years he was nailed to its ceiling. Surely no work of art was ever torn out of so much anguish, against such odds. The physical obstacles marshaled against painting anything there at all are overwhelming. To see what one man, driven by his tearing need to spend his talent, did here is a shattering rebuke to every one of us who calls himself an artist. We can't hope to have a teaspoon of his torrent of talent, but I'm seized by a sudden conviction that the glory of the ceiling sprang first from his *will* . . . and that's something all men share. His talent rejected it; his talent ached for marble, but his will drove him to make this work he loathed maybe the best painting a man ever made. Maybe, with smaller talent and a weaker will, I can at least make of this film, whose difficulty is that it's made in a country not my own, away from the home I love, something that's at least *my* best.

June 6. A lazy morning, ending with a good interview. I find M/A an easy man to be eloquent about. Now I'm really feeling the itch to act this part; without that you can't do anything. I spent the afternoon walking the neighborhoods he knew here, the street where he lived. Then I took another look at those of his marbles that are here, and replicas of the rest—everything he did, really, from plans for fortifications through St. Peter's itself, and the Campidoglio. My God, the sum of it all. You could say he had some talent. I'm glad we're starting at Carrara; he saw that before he saw Rome.

June 8, Carrara. We never got a shot. The mist rolled in from the sea just as we were about to roll, and hung all the rest of the day. But I got a chance to soak in the set, which helps me. You can still see the scarred white shelf where M/A cut the block from which he carved the Moses, nearly five hundred years ago. This is the place to start work on this giant.

June 9. I began today, easing gently into the role in a scene without dialogue. We made very few shots: cutting marble blocks, sitting thinking about the ceiling, hiding from the papal troops. Carol prints very quickly . . . maybe too quickly, though I don't see how such simple shots could have been done very differently. (Of course Wyler would've worried around the edges of it for a long time.) So far, Carol seems straightforward; he knows what he wants and is pleased with what I give him. Let him not be too easily pleased. Zanuck has an anxious bee in his bonnet over my general theatrical effect in the role. He has a point, but we're doing all we can to reach what he looked like. I am tall, I do photograph. We're scruffing down the wardrobe as much as we can.

This was Darryl Zanuck, who was exercising a loose function as executive producer on the film. "Jesus, you look like an actor in that outfit," he said. "You look like Othello or some damn thing in that turban!" The "turban" was the headcloth they wore in the Carrara quarries in the fourteenth century . . . and still do, for that matter. Actually, Darryl was wrong. I had a very simple wardrobe for the film, all copied from portraits of Michelangelo. The hair, the beard, the broken nose all added up to a startling resemblance, as close, I think, as any of the biographical roles I've done. It's true that I am six feet three, whereas the great sculptor was five feet eight. When an English journalist asked if I didn't think I was too tall to play Michelangelo, I said, "No, I think I'm too small."

June 10, Florence. We'd finished my scenes yesterday, so I didn't shoot. Instead I did some interviews and went through the motions of working for the benefit of our huge press junket. They seemed content to see me standing about in makeup. (They never can tell whether you're shooting or not, anyway.) When I finished the interviews I drove over to Florence for my own purposes: to eat a Tuscan steak and see the M/A David again, trying to look at it through the eyes of the man who made it. I slept in the city he grew up in.

June 11, Rome. I drove back to Rome at five in the morning and devoted the entire damn day to servicing over 140 journalists. I've learned to do this well by now, and I think it paid off today. I communicated to some of them, at least, something more of that ceiling than its dimensions and formidable reputation. I thus felt justified in accepting the publicity department's hospitality overnight at the Hilton, which is not a bad hotel. Good tennis court, good sauna . . . good food, and a night's rest, which I had coming.

June 15. Well, they finally arrived . . . the baby first down the steps happily burbling at me, then Fray, still tousled with sleep, Lydia, brilliant in a white turban. Drago, as usual, was frantic to get out of his crate, unable to contain his distress at having flown the ocean yet again. It took all day to get settled in the villa; the sea of crates and cases has not yet subsided, but it suddenly looks like a house instead of the dank museum I've been camping in.

June 17, Todi. It's a helluva commute up to the hill town we've found for the St. Peter's scenes, but it's worth it to come home at night. As for the city and the scene, both are fine. Carol gives a great deal in rehearsal; I agreed with all he said today. We cut a lot of literary crap out of the dialogue . . . writer's decoration that's just frosting on the scene . . . and Carol took a little actor's crap out of it too.

June 26. They didn't get to me today . . . either the set's still not ready or Leon Shamroy is taking an unconscionable time to light it . . . maybe both.

Both were true and both conditions, the unreadiness of the sets and the camera, continued to cause us enormous problems on this film.

The dailies looked OK. I'm beginning to realize it's seldom possible to say more than this. They're really just so much raw material. You can say they're bad, but this is rare. Usually, all you can is "They're OK . . . the scene's in there somewhere."

June 27, Bracciano. Shooting in Italy, I always have the feeling that the lunch break is a lot more than an hour . . . I must check this. What little we did went well . . . we got a chance to rehearse and improve the later scenes. Rex requires careful handling, but he'll be damn good in the part. So will I, I now believe.

Rex is a very gifted performer. He also has the temperament of a thoroughbred racehorse . . . highly strung, with a tendency to snort and rear and kick at the starting gate.

July 1, Monterano. The new location is tougher to get to than any we've had so far. This makes some of the drives to location in Mexico look like pleasure jaunts. We spent the last ten kilometers, over a dirt road, trying to find a spot to get our little Fiat past the buses full of extras. It's a pretty good location, but we might have found it closer to Rome. We didn't get much done today, but it's always that way, the first day on a new set. Tomorrow will be better. Rex was late today . . . I hope this isn't the shape of things to come.

July 4, Bracciano. We spent a long time on one setup in the courtyard today. A long time waiting, a damn short time shooting. Shamroy is a good cameraman . . . as was Krasker, as was Hildyard, but by God, they take a hell of a time to get ready. Maybe I'm just getting more hard-nosed as I get older, but I think Shamroy takes *too* long. On this picture, Carol and the actors are getting the set about fifteen percent of the time; Shamroy has it the rest of the day.

All these men were indeed magnificent cameramen. They were also all trained in the thirties and forties when shooting time was cheaper and the pace of production thus more leisured. I suspect a tradition grew up in this period that a good cameraman took his time. It's time that can't be afforded now. Even in the sixties, Russ

*Metty, the equal of any cameraman alive, was incredibly fast.
Since then, many of the best of the young cameramen seem to be
following his tradition. Certainly, the director and the actors
should have the set at least half the time.*

July 10. We finished the scene early today (it was a slop-over from
yesterday's schedule), but we couldn't move into anything else for
complicated scheduling reasons that sounded thin to me. Carol's not
happy over this or with what the second unit did on the siege. I think
he rides with too easy a hand for a director of his reputation. Now
there's some nonsense we have to go through in the tavern scene
with a girl Darryl wants tested.

July 15, Monterano. I spent a long half day with the second unit for two
shots in the plague-deserted village Carol found to shoot the ruined
villa in. This is the last of the location work on the film. I went to
Cinecittà and checked the set for M/A's studio. It's not right . . . they
have the Moses in it, almost finished, thirty years too early, as well as
other errors like this they should know better than to make. Still, at
something like the halfway point on the film, we're doing well, I
think.

July 18, Rome/Cinecittà. The scenes were tough today. The relationship
with the Contessina isn't easy to get, though Diane Cilento seems
very right for the part. These are delicate colors to play. Carol works
in terms of praising his actors, which I can't object to, but it makes
me a little uneasy. ("Why is he praising me? I must be screwing up.")

July 21, Rome. I saw our Sistine Chapel today. It's a remarkable
re-creation of the real one, in full scale, with a blue ceiling on it for
the first time since M/A started his purgatory scraping it off, more
than four centuries ago. It won't be as hard for me as it was for him.

*The full-scale replica of the interior of the Sistine Chapel that Fox
erected on the largest sound stage in Europe at Dino di Laurentis
Studios outside Rome was an incredible achievement, certainly one
of the most effective sets I've ever seen. Originally, the plan had
been to shoot in the real Sistine Chapel and negotiations with the
Vatican for the necessary permission were nearly completed. It
soon became clear, though, that it would be incredibly dangerous
to the great painting Michelangelo had put there to shoot anywhere
near its fragile plaster surface. Moreover, there were cracks wide
enough to put your thumb in evident at close range, and the colors
of the panels have darkened in four centuries from what
Michelangelo originally used. Even if these problems could be
solved, there would be no way to photograph the painting in
progress, or the bare blue ceiling that Michelangelo covered. This*

*left only one choice: to re-create the entire interior full scale.
Again, a first choice was to have Michelangelo's panels copied by
artists. Carol Reed insisted this was a mistake. He said the
millions of people in the world who would see the film, but never
the real Sistine, had a right to see the real painting. Therefore, the
panels were very carefully photographed, printed full scale, and
applied to the ceiling of the set, their colors chemically restored to
the original tones. (Since a movie is in itself a photograph, we then
indeed photographed the real ceiling.) All the panels were sealed,
thus making it possible to cover them with plaster and prepare
them in any stage of completion a given scene required. The whole
thing was really a staggering achievement, both technically and
creatively.*

July 23, di Laurentis Studios. We dropped a little more time today, but
still finished the scene with no particular problems, other than a slight
tendency on Rex's part to blow his lines. (I find this in some British
actors and I have no idea why . . . a problem of age? I doubt it, since
Harris suffered from it greatly, and he's younger than I.) Anyway, we
got a good scene. That chapel's a remarkable set. I hope it lifts us to
the heights it deserves.

July 26 (Sunday). We had a marvelous family day, drinking not-bad
champagne and eating boned chicken and cheese in the cool, piny
shade of the exquisite ruins Hadrian left of his villa (and his hopes?).
Tonight, as has become our custom, we walked through the rose
twilight down the side of the road in single file to dinner at the
restaurant on the other side of the Appia Antica, Fray heeling Drago
in the lead, Holly in the rear, discussing whether or not she should be
carried. By and large, she was.

August 1. Tonight, for perhaps the last time this summer, we had an
evening with no house guests. I took my wife in to Rome. It's a
beautiful city to be with a woman in . . . particularly if you love her.

August 6, di Laurentis Studios. By shooting late, we finished the Caraffa
sequence . . . leaving only my close-ups to do later, when we can have
the unfinished ceiling behind me. We did get an excellent shot of me
actually painting on the ceiling, the first we've done in the film. It was
quite an experience . . . to lift a brush to that enormous expanse, and
have paint drip down in your eyes and realize what it must have been
to do it all . . . alone.

August 7. We shot all day on that immense set, crowded with people
looking at the blazing wonder of the finished ceiling, but they never
got to me. At least I figured out where M/A should be . . . over in a
corner, nerving himself for the ordeal of watching all those people

look at his work . . . and what he would wear . . . not the elaborately beautiful outfit they prepared for me, the like of which M/A never put on his back.

August 11. Rex and I finished the scene without problems, although the sound security is very uncertain, as seems inevitable on continental sets. They're simply not used to recording direct sound here. Still, I like what we got very much. We're closing in on the end of the whole thing. It still looks very good. Word from Walter Seltzer: Frank Schaffner is available for WAR LORD. I did my first MACBETH with him . . . also JANE EYRE, a couple of others. I think he'd be fine for this.

August 14. We finished the Contessina's last scene today, but not as soon nor as well as we should have. They got Diane [*Cilento*] back on the set on time after lunch by practically hand-feeding her, or we would've been in trouble again. Once there, she was damn good.

August 19. I finished the last scene I have with Rex. I think he's fine as the pope, worth all the megrims. Frank Schaffner got in today; he seemed very high on the WAR LORD script and had some provocative ideas about it. We're really damn lucky to be clear of Danny Mann.

August 21. Twice today I came as close to quarreling with Carol as I ever could. (He was wrong both times, in fact: about how to block in a figure before painting and how the pulley would react to my fall.) Still, we did well. All the other principals are finished in the film now, there's nothing left but me and that awesome painting. Frank and Walter came out to look at some of THE BIBLE . . . the girl who plays Eve may be right for us. We got a lot done on the WAR LORD script. Frank knows what he's after; he doesn't care about demonstrating what a fine director he is, which was one of Danny Mann's problems. Dino [*di Laurentis*] offered me two scripts tonight, including, of course, a role in THE BIBLE.

August 27. The cuts today were a bit spooky. The cameras were far below on the floor, the scaffolding was unbraced, no one up there but me. It makes for good shots, but it's a little shaky. I even painted in chocolate pudding (which M/A never tried), to get a shot of him lying on his back, painting the ceiling with paint falling in his mouth.

The scaffolding Michelangelo designed to get him within painting distance of the ceiling, seventy feet off the floor, was exactly duplicated for the film; his original plans are still in the Vatican files. When we had a full crew, cameras, and lights on it, it was heavily reinforced. When we shot from the floor and the scaffolding was serving as a set, it remained as Michelangelo designed it. Frankly, it's the only one of his works I don't totally admire. It was a pretty rickety affair.

September 1, Fono Roma Sound Studio. We looped *Agony*, with one
hour of trouble, after which my fifty-two loops went very smoothly.
This looping system, with instant playback, works well, I must say. I
recall the slow, painstaking method de Mille used on the circus film.
It's maddening work, with any method. Now I only have the silent
shots left. My creative contribution to the film is finished.

*By this time, we'd wrapped the sound unit on the shooting
company and were shooting silent. Since there was no dialogue in
the shots we had remaining of Michelangelo painting, climbing
ladders, moving the scaffolding, and so forth, the company could
shoot more cheaply and more efficiently in this way, dubbing in
the sound effects later.*

September 7. We finally wound it up. After four days of mechanical
shots, my very last shot in the film called for something more. It
showed, appropriately, M/A's last stroke on the ceiling, the finish for
both of us. Four years for him to do it, four months for me to
pretend to. I don't think I've made a better one, or acted better,
either.

September 8, New York via Paris. A bloody long day getting home from
Rome. I can't say why I was so fed up with it this time, but I couldn't
wait to get on that jet. Rome was warm and full of friends as we left,
but as we drove in to Manhattan over the bridge, the paling lines of
buildings against the autumn haze across the river were incredibly
beautiful. Eighteen years and a couple of weeks ago, I came here for
the first time. Eighteen years . . .

September 11, New York/Los Angeles. I got in a long meeting on ways
and means of selling AGONY to a waiting world (which now will not
occur, it develops, until next fall . . . *not* Easter. That will be MAJOR
DUNDEE, about which I hear much distressing news). The Seltzers
were waiting at the plane, our house was waiting on its ridge. I had a
chance to rest a little, then, before dinner, discuss new locations for
WAR LORD. It'll be Marysville now, instead of Stockton. I'm not certain
this will all work as well as Walter imagines, but he seems certain.

September 14, Los Angeles. I checked into our new WAR LORD office at
Universal (with a sign on the door "Fraser Productions") and my new
dressing room on the roomy Universal lot. We got Universal around
to making a firm offer to Dick Boone for Bors, and closed a couple of
minor parts as well, but they balked at Stanley Baker for Draco. This
leaves us Gary Raymond, who seems to me almost a better idea, come
to think of it. We auditioned two girls, but neither seemed marvelous.
Let's find someone marvelous. Sam Peckinpah told me his troubles at
lunch. They seem formidable. I can't tell yet how DUNDEE turned out,
though.

September 16, Columbia: Run MAJOR DUNDEE. MAJOR DUNDEE, as is so often the case, is neither as bad as I feared (talking to Sam) nor as good as I hoped (working with Sam). The people are believable, the dialogue good, as are all the performances (yes, I think all). The opening, cutting the one we shot at such cost, doesn't work for me. Most of the rest of the film does, but the whole thing is somehow diffuse. The story is as it always was, too complicated. It may work though . . . you never know. Too often, bad films succeed and good films fail.

Sam, of course, felt that if he'd been given a totally free hand, DUNDEE would've been the film we all hoped for. Frankly, I doubt it. Looking back, I think we all wanted to make a different sort of film. Columbia wanted a cowboy and Indian story, I wanted a film that dealt with the basic issue of the Civil War, and Sam, as it happened, wanted the film he later got to make. Very few directors get two chances to make the same film. Sam did and the second time around, it turned out very well. It was called THE WILD BUNCH.

September 21. The work on the script goes with agonizing slowness. I never before realized quite how hard it is to hammer out a line of dialogue . . . even when all you're doing is inserting talk into an extant scene structure. We're getting it, though, bit by bit, and line by line.

September 22. More work on the script, more looking for the right girl for Bronwyn. We found Gary Raymond is doing a film, which they swore he wasn't. Still, the girl is the key. Diane Baker seems wrong. There are three new Universal contract actresses who may be possibilities. We'll probably test all three, certainly read them all. This is a hard part to cast, partly because it's so hard to judge their period potential, when they come swirling in for interviews in modern clothes.

September 29. Dean Stockwell in BONANZA shows he can control what he does. We'll go with him. I still wish we could do a little better for the girl. I'm not certain any of our three test candidates is marvelous. Somewhere in the world there must be the perfect young actress for this part. Whether we can find her is beginning to be a question. At least we're getting close on the script. I reworked another scene, in toto. [*A script in revision can be as compulsive as a dish of peanuts. Leave it* alone!]

September 30. We ran some film on the last-minute candidates for Bronwyn, but came up empty. Meantime, I'm getting pressure from every actor I ever knew for parts in the piece. I spent an hour on wardrobe. They talked me out of using metal chain mail, but the German stuff they used in EL CID, instead. The costumes are good, though the pants are the wrong material. The colors are all muted . . . reddish earth tones for Chrysagon, which seems right. Now, let's see if they can age them down from costumes to clothes.

If there's anything harder than auditioning for parts, it's listening to other actors auditioning. It's very painful to tell an actor you know and admire, "I'm sorry, you're not right for this."

October 2. We ran the test film on our three Bronwyns and decided to go with Rosemary Forsyth, who seems closest to the idea of the part. I went to Columbia and ran DUNDEE again. I still feel maybe something can be done to pull it out. Whether Sam and Bresler can agree as to what that is, I don't know. Sam's out of town, location hunting. When he gets back we'll run it again.

October 6. It can be a tough ordeal, seeing a train of small-part actors. You can't give them the proper time for an interview, so the whole thing seems phony, somehow. God, why do people want to follow this ridiculous profession . . . this degrading beggary for the favor of others? I got a part for Dal, failed with Johnny Crawford, Quinliven. Then I went to Columbia for the DUNDEE meeting. I kept Jerry and Sam from each other's throats, but that's about all.

October 7. We've got the casting just about locked up now. I'd say the eleventh century is as difficult to cast for as any period I've found. Faces now are too soft for it. Harry Wilcoxon will do the Frisian Prince. It felt odd sitting on the other side of the desk from him, after all those interviews in the de Mille wing. [*Harry was de Mille's associate producer during the two films I made for him.*]

October 12. Rosemary Forsyth came in to read through her scenes today. It's almost unreal to actually get down to it at last, after all these years. She already has a lot of what should be there when we shoot. She seems very direct, which is a prime color in the role. She's a little nervous about the nude scene; I can understand that.

October 13. A long day of wrangling with Universal executives, Frank, Walter, and Rosemary herself, as to just how she should do the nude scene in the film. She's concerned, uncertain whether it should be done, let alone how. This made for some tense moments.

October 17. I luxuriated in my last free day before taking the deep six into production. Three times in one year seems a bit much, come to think of it. But I'm staggered to think we're about to shoot WAR LORD at last . . . after however many years since I read the play in one afternoon lying on the couch at 5 Tudor City Place.

October 19, Marysville, California. I got up early one more time and climbed on one more charter. (When was the first time I drove out to Burbank to get on a plane just a little older than what the airlines were using on the scheduled runs, and flew off to some small airport like Marysville?) Once there, I did very little save settle into a plastic-wrapped, germ-free motel with, God save the mark, a good bed.

October 20. Well, we finally exposed film on it. I can hardly believe it. All the weeks and months and years . . . yes, *years* of effort have at last put actors in wardrobe, standing in front of a camera. Riding in chain mail through the marsh for the first shot, I had the weird feeling of reliving the experience. I've read that shot so many times, in so many different versions of the script. Today we really did it.

October 24. Lydia watched the shooting today, which went, again, very well. It's strange how the mailed, medieval figures fit into the marshes of northern California. Frank kindly arranged the last shots so I could catch the late plane for home and my Sunday off. Looking back on our first week, I think we're doing well. Frank has a grip on this; I think we can make it.

November 2. We had solid cloud cover all day long, but we shot in the grove anyway. Russ [*Metty, our cameraman*] has the nerve of a riverboat gambler. We lacked the shafts of light down through the trees, but we had the lowering quality we need there. I played a scene with Maurice Evans for the first time; it's odd to remember he starred in the first professional production I ever saw . . . with Helen Hayes in TWELFTH NIGHT, when I was in high school. The scenes went well and quickly. We even had time to rehearse with Rosemary for tomorrow. She was a little nervous, but had a firm honesty in the way she went at the scene.

November 3. While LBJ was sweeping the country with what was the greatest majority in the twentieth century, we were slaving away back in the eleventh. We had brilliant sun all day and managed twenty-one setups . . . damn good ones, too. We also found that whichever studio executive said our dailies were light-struck yesterday must've been sunstruck. They looked fine. Russ is getting incredible photographic quality. We rejoiced over this and the election returns with beans and beer in the motel tonight.

November 16, Los Angeles.

By this time, we'd finished the location and returned to the studio where they'd built a remarkable (and authentic, not MGM-medieval) Norman tower: the interiors on a sound stage, the exterior on Universal's huge back lot (not then given over to public tours).

We shot outside, in really un-Californian cold. If it'd been like this when De Mille got off the train with the script of the SQUAW MAN, he would've turned around and gone back to Flagstaff.

Where he'd planned to shoot his first feature. It was raining when his train pulled into Flagstaff, thus denying that city its chance to become the film capital of the world. Mr. de Mille, ever a forthright man, got right back on the train and took his company on west to Hollywood, where he shot the first film ever made here.

Nonetheless, we got what we needed, just barely. Russ's stuff in dailies is fan-bloody-tastic, especially the night interiors.

November 22 (Sunday). After the morning tennis I read some Frost and Wolfe at a memorial service for JFK. Fray came with me, to my pleasure and I think to his. Then I went on to the Wylers' dinner for Carol Reed at which we exchanged mutual congratulations on how well AGONY seems to have been received (by the Zanuck family, at least).

Carol was on his way to Tahiti to direct Marlon Brando in the remake of MUTINY ON THE BOUNTY. Apparently only Willy apprehended the disaster that awaited them all, from which Carol was to resign in horror some momths later. Very late this evening, he leaned over his bar and clutched Carol's arm. "Carol!" he said fiercely. "Don't go. Don't do it!"

November 24. I spent a long lunch with Herman and Dick Zanuck exploring a film they want me to do on Custer. Basically it doesn't seem like a very good idea to me. If I remember history, Custer just does not provide a protagonist. I don't see how you can make a serious film about a man who seems to have been not only egocentric, but muddleheaded. He was neither a very good soldier nor a very valuable man. [I *was right; Fox never did make the film.*]

December 12. The party tonight at Irving Stone's house was navel-deep in Ph.D.'s and Nobel winners, including A. L. Rowse, so saturated with scholarship it spills out whenever he speaks. It made a pleasant change from actors and directors, though.

I have great respect for novelists and professional academics. Oddly, in my experience, they seem to bear celebrity far less easily than performers do. Actors generally understand that, officially at least, the proper stance is humility. Writers, basically more private people, sometimes seem bemused by fame.

December 18. The day started out as an absolute bust, with my driver getting lost en route to location, so I was late on the set, and then the rain kept us from shooting, anyway. We had only a fragmentary day left when we finally got the company back inside the studio, when we discovered Dick Boone had gone off on an unauthorized departure to Hawaii yesterday without clearance, so we had to shoot around him. But the daily film on yesterday's scene is as beautiful as any shot I've ever seen. Rosemary will have to be looped, but the scene will still be fine. We gave a good party tonight for Carol, and ran his THIRD MAN. It's still a hell of a film.

December 20 (Sunday). Another day like yesterday; a good day to sit in the bedroom with a fire going and the rain misting over the valley, reading and listening to music with my family. Lydia's under the pressure of preparing for Christmas and it's giving her a bad week. I'm still postponing my decision on HAWAII. One part's not very interesting; the other I'm not right for. Citron will have trouble getting our gross deal from United Artists, anyway. One thoroughly constructive act today: I helped Fray build a model monster (monster model?).

December 21. I turned down HAWAII, with a few regrets. It has too much plot and not enough people for my taste.

I don't think Walter Mirisch, who produced the picture, was quite sure which part he really wanted me to play. In any case, he was better served by the actors he chose. Dick Harris gave one of his best performances as the roistering sea captain, and Max Von Sydow could hardly have been bettered as the driven missionary. It made a very successful film. I undertook the next portion of Michener's massive novel for Walter a few years later. Of that, more when we come to it . . .

December 25. The day began as it always does. A little earlier than you'd like, but not early enough for the kids. We got, for a wonder, everything opened and noted for thank-you letters before brunch. We had wild turkey this year and then made our annual call on the Seltzers. Then we came home to a fire in the steam room, which we caught before it grew into anything more than an unusual way to end Christmas.

1965

Mission to
Nigeria . . .

*A Man for All
Seasons* in
Chicago . . .

the stolen Jaguar . . .

to Cairo and
points beyond for
Khartoum.

In Chicago with Lydia for
A Man for All Seasons
GORDON DEAN

January 2, Los Angeles. We'd planned to go to the new Music Center, but somebody blew our seats. [*In my situation, you get careless about things like this; you assume the seats will* be there. *Once in a while, they aren't.*] We stayed home and looked at Lydia's slides instead. How long it's been since BEN-HUR, and Rome. How small Fray looked then, and how tall he is now.

January 4. We're still busily burning the door.

The difficulty of accurately scheduling the time required to shoot action scenes is one of the traditional imponderables of film production. The standard two to four pages of script a day (ten to twenty for tele-film, I believe) simply doesn't apply. In this case the script said simply, "Chrysagon and his men defend the door." It took us the better part of a week to shoot.

We ran the editor's rough assembly of what we have. It's not marvelous, but I'm convinced the film is in there. Rosemary is effective in what she does, less so in what she says. We may have her loop her dialogue. I'm good, so is Stockwell. Dick Boone's not as good as he would've been if he'd done it differently. But it will work.

January 5. More of the same today, including a brave shot where they set me on fire (a little bit). I survived that, as well as the minimal acting requirements of the scene, without great difficulty, then Frank shot around me for the last half hour of the day, allowing me to get home in time to host a brief publicity bash for the FDR series, screening one show I'd not seen, which looked fine. Citron, at lunch, seems unaccountably anxious for me to reconsider both HAWAII and Mel Shavelson's CAST A GIANT SHADOW.

January 15. Tonight at MGM we saw GREATEST STORY EVER TOLD. It knocked me out. It has the formless irresistible momentum of a river, and the same inevitability too. Von Sydow gives surely one of the best performances I've seen as Christ . . . and I do very well as the Baptist, too. I'm proud to be in it.

January 18. We started to bit and piece our way through the last of WAR LORD today, leaping around from stage to stage, set to set. There wasn't a lot to it in acting terms, though it's harder to concentrate in a series of short shots like that. I should have focused a little better on my reaction over the dead body of my brother, but I couldn't make it. In dailies, the Palos Verdes stuff looks marvelous. Russ shot on three different days, in different light, and still got an exquisite dawn effect throughout.

January 20. SIX P.M.: *Finish principal photography* WAR LORD. I found this morning that my finances are sounder than I thought. Indeed, there is a healthy surplus. For an actor to have security in an insecure world seems almost indecent, but I cherish it, all the same. We haven't decided yet whether or not to go ahead with the suit against LO SPECCHIO.

One of my most grievous drawbacks as a public personality is the paucity of really first-grade scandals in my life. Lo Specchio an Italian scandal sheet, provided me with one of the few acceptable examples I can muster. (It's not world class, I know, but it's the best I can do.) When we'd moved out of the villa we rented on the Appia Antica for the AGONY filming, the magazine staged a series of shots of the "wrecked" interior, with chandeliers dramatically askew and broken crockery and empty bottles strewn orgiastically about. They gave it four pages and the title "I Pulci di Michelangelo" The lice of Michelangelo). I considered suing them for a while, but decided it wasn't worth the effort. Besides, it did give me a public scandal.

We finished shooting, except for the extra second unit pickups. Today's shots were nothing very demanding, but it was nice to lift a glass with Frank and Walter afterward. I'm almost positive it'll be a good film.

January 25. Harold [*Willens*] finally got me to Santa Barbara for a meeting of the Center for the Study of Democratic Institutions. I was impressed; I'll contribute some money, maybe some time, too. The prime problem is the same one we have at SAG Board meetings and, no doubt, in the U.S. Senate as well: how to get any sense and function out of any group of more than four people discussing anything.

"The Center," which sufficed to identify it during its days of glory, was a significant factor in forming liberal positions on public matters (indeed, on a good many private ones as well) during this period. I was impressed during the several meetings I attended in their secluded retreat in the Santa Barbara hills. I gradually became disenchanted, however, with what I've come to feel is a flaw common to most professional intellectuals: They have absolutely no capacity to laugh at themselves. Every man must be sure to take himself less seriously than other people take him. A number of the Center people had advanced cases of galloping pompositis. That disease is so contagious, I was afraid of a fatal infection.

February 3. A long meeting at Universal reconciling the widely differing views on our added WAR LORD stuff. All agree it should be done (no doubt), and that we have it all in hand (probably). Somewhat to my surprise, I turned out to be a fairly effective negotiator. The main thing is to keep calm, concentrate on the areas of agreement, then move out from there. At last we won what Frank (and Walter and I) feel we need: We reopen Thursday, shoot a total of twelve days, including three unshot days of shots originally scheduled for the second unit.

February 5. I saw the release print of DUNDEE tonight. It seemed not quite good enough to be a success as a serious film, and probably has too many subtleties, too much footage devoted to character, to succeed as an action film. There are excellent things in it; I think I'm good, but we didn't make it with this one.

I guess this is almost exactly what I still think of MAJOR DUNDEE. I hate to look at theatrical movies on television, particularly my own. If they're lousy, I hate to see them exposed to the light of day. If they're good, I hate to see them mutilated to make room for commercials, and I cringe at the poor-quality 16mm prints they use. But when DUNDEE plays, as it often does, I sneak a look at two or three scenes, just to check. There's the smell of a great film in there somewhere, among the ruins.

February 8. I beat Efrem Zimbalist in singles, which made the day a good one. Tonight I dangled half-naked on the chain for a close-up for WAR LORD, to juice up the drawbridge fight, and spent the rest of the evening more conventionally clothed at SAG, listening to the usual large measure of tommyrot (with now and then a grain of sense, mind you).

February 12. My son was ten today. I can remember being ten very well. The earlier years are blurred into smallboyhood, but I remember ten. It was a sad, broken time for me. I hope it's not for him . . . I *know* it's not. He's a happy boy, growing well.

February 15, New York. Premiere: THE GREATEST STORY EVER TOLD . The film seemed to me to go well, but I've never so ill-estimated a critical reaction. Neither the *Times* nor the *Tribune* liked either the film or me. I'm less upset over their opinion than over my own inability to predict it. It puzzles me. Is it the theme, the sheer length? Was I really objective in my reaction? I think I was; I'm still convinced the film is remarkable.

The official critical position at the time was that Stevens had failed totally at what he had attempted: the definitive film on the life of Christ. I think they were mistaken. The film has enormous quality; certainly Max, in the most difficult of all possible roles, was overwhelming. But George was probably wrong to use so many American stars in bit parts, most of them uneasy in period costumes and incapable of handling New Testament syntax.

February 16, Los Angeles. I got up and flew back to the Coast, arriving in time to hit a few tennis balls with my son. I'm still weighing the generally adverse critical reaction to GSET. There's a strong bias against a large-scale film, especially on this story, perhaps. Also, our time is oriented to the loser, and while Christ is the greatest loser of all, he's also the greatest winner. This is not very fashionable these days.

February 17. The dailies on the added footage for WAR LORD looked good to me, but my confidence in my capacity to judge film is a little shaken at this point. At least I'm positive that what Frank shot is better than what the second unit had before.

February 21, Washington, D.C. A good day to work on my speech [*on brotherhood, in response to an award I was to be given by the National Conference of Christians and Jews*]: It rained all day, keeping me off the tennis courts. It was to little purpose, however. I checked all the references Lydia found for me in the Bible, found nothing useful in my Shakespeare concordance (that's odd . . . interested as he was in the paramount importance of order in society, brotherhood seemed less significant to him . . . not very Christian of him).

February 22. Today was the day for SAG. I made the rounds on the Hill, touching what bases I could to express the SAG position on the TV networks' monopoly of the air. Senators Kuchel, Murphy, Kennedy, Pell, and Attorney General Katzenbach all made sympathetic noises. We'll see if anything comes of it.

It was about this time I began taking on chores like this. Actors are usually welcome on Capitol Hill. Though they are loath to admit it, politicians are performers, too. Given a choice, they'd much rather give hearings on public issues to someone whose picture will get on the six o'clock news.

February 25, Los Angeles. A rueful experience has taught me that any speech more than ten minutes long absolutely has to be prepared, but once again, I barely left time enough to do that. I went to a luncheon for Martin Luther King; his speech ran over an hour, which put me behind schedule (on the other hand, you couldn't get a better lesson in public speaking). I just had time to get my effort on paper before leaving for the National Conference of Christians and Jews dinner. I was OK.

People assume actors should be automatically good at public speaking. Not so. Part of the reason for being an actor is that you have other characters in which to conceal yourself in public. The thought of appearing as myself before an audience appalled me in the beginning. Over the years, I've taught myself, very painfully, a minimal competence as a speaker, but I stand in awe of those who do it well. There aren't many these days. The best I know is Jack

*Valenti, formerly President Johnson's chief aide, currently
president of the Motion Picture Association. Oddly, there is
currently no one in politics very good at it. The last really great
politician-orator was Winston Churchill.*

March 2. Over breakfast, I listened to [*producer*] Julian Blaustein's pitch
on KHARTOUM . . . in the Polo Lounge at the Beverly Hills Hotel
where he first gave it to me two years ago.

*Tip for tourists: The place to go to see the film makers in
Hollywood is the Polo Lounge, at breakfast. I suspect half the film
deals in the world are discussed at some point over bacon and eggs
in that room. (My own taste runs to English muffins and peanut
butter.)*

Lydia read the script later in the day and feels I should do it. I
mulled it all afternoon while trying to get my shots for Africa, plus
other enterprises of great pith and moment. I have doubts about
undertaking yet another epic, but the script is too good to pass. The
problem of playing an Englishman and an older man is interesting,
too. I told Citron (who's in favor) to see if Carol Reed's available to
direct.

*Robert Ardrey has by and large given up dramatic writing since
his overwhelming success as a popular writer on anthropology
(African Genesis, etc.). His script for KHARTOUM, nevertheless, was
beautifully done. One of only two scripts I can recall out of more
than fifty that we shot largely without revision.*

March 3, To Frankfurt, Germany. The late-night trip to San Francisco
was worth it; I got a good night's sleep, girding myself for the long,
long flight across the Canadian snow fields that took up the short,
eastbound day. How many times have I dozed at thirty-seven
thousand feet over the incredible sweep of this continent? How many
times have I drunk a little too much free brandy, eaten a few too
many free hors d'oeuvres?

*This was the trip the State Department asked me to make to
Nigeria as a pitchman for American culture. These were the days
when we had high hopes for the emerging nations of Africa.
Nigeria, with its immense resources and British-trained
bureaucracy, seemed one of the most promising.*

March 4, Frankfurt. This is a familiar road, too. The early morning
arrival at the airport, the gaggle of reporters clustered at the foot of
the ramp, the flick of flashbulbs, and the chirr of the TV cameras.
Inside, in the VIP room, the floodlit TV interview and at last,
everyone satisfied, along the snow-clogged streets to the hotel. I slept
all day, then a good dinner and the plane for Nigeria.

March 5, Lagos. I spent a lot of the day trying to sleep my metabolism into sync with Nigerian time. Outside the air-conditioned oasis of the hotel, the heat is palpable, like the warm breath of a horse on the back of your neck. In the moist, fecund air, you feel if you hold your hand to the breeze from the jungle, green things will sprout in your palm.

March 6. An easy day, especially when considered as work. I did a press conference and some radio interviews this morning, then tennis. Tonight there was a Presidential command performance of BEN-HUR, which I hadn't seen in three years or more. It's still long, still lets down after the race, but it works. It's the first time it's been shown here. It was (says he modestly) a smash.

March 7 (Sunday), Enugu. I got up rather earlier than I would've liked for the ostentatious delights of a flight to Enugu in the Premier's private plane. The drive from the airstrip north to the university where I was doing my poetry reading gave me my first look at the Equatorial bush, complete with thatched huts, juju dancers along the road, cowherds in conical straw hats, and naked Nigerian madonnas. The Premier was most gracious at dinner, I did my Yankee best.

March 8, Lagos. My record in Nigeria is unbroken: up too early with too little sleep. Still, I got back to Lagos with time enough to sleep a bit before doing my chores at USIA. That done, I had an exhibition tennis match, where I found I had adjusted to the slow clay court here. I felt physically redeemed by all this, ready for Sir Mobilahi's large black-tie dinner tonight, though it went on too long. Interesting to see the white adjustment to the black power structure in Nigeria, as evidenced at a big social do like tonight.

March 9, Ibadan. Early (again) for Ibadan, where everything seems a bit screwed up. We scrubbed one meeting entirely, the other wasn't effective in terms of total students reached. [*This was in the North, which was the source of the split that wracked the country for so many years and destroyed its early promise.*] I was touched, however, by kids from several countries attending the International School. The statehouse and embassy farewells were very impressive. I think they feel I did a good job. My departure was dramatized by the disappearance of my passport, which precipitated some screaming and yelling, much to-and-froing on motorcycles. Finally, it took assurances by cable from the President (theirs, not ours) to clear me into London. Off into the 707 and airborne at last, a little breathless.

March 10, London. I missed my first connection to Frankfurt/London, but I never really thought I'd catch that one anyway. When I arrived, there were no problems in immigration, thanks to President Azikiwe's cable. It turns out they can't mail U.S. passports overseas. Having found mine in Lagos, in the desk of a minor official who'd absentmindedly locked it there, they burned it. I got a new one at the embassy here with minimum fuss. I relished the usual pleasure of the Dorchester, though my talk with Julian Blaustein over steak at the Guinea was only mildly productive. Carol Reed's not available for KHARTOUM.

March 11, Boston. I arrived on time, after a clear, sunny crossing (the Bay of Fundy sparkling in the morning sun) . . . no problem getting through customs with my virgin passport (though I miss the stylishly visa-jammed pages of the old one, now lost forever). I called Lydia on the Coast (there was delight in her laugh, after even a week away), then spent a long afternoon serving the Boston press. I didn't see the film tonight, but understand Stevens has cut twenty-eight minutes out of it. I'm inclined to think this is a good idea. I must see this version.

March 12, Los Angeles. We flew north, avoiding the winds, and over the Great Lakes. I could see the thumb of Michigan, blurred with snow from seven miles up, and even made out St. Helen as we passed. Oh . . . winter there, and lace-and-hook boots with a pocket on the side for a knife, and skating on the bumpy gray ice. Two Rivers was clear, too, below, and then I was home, marvelously home. Bed, and Lydia, and all was as it should be. Just as it should be.

March 14 (Sunday). The party for the premiere of GSET was a success, the film less than that. Walter had an interesting opinion: He found it beautifully made, but not involving. If true, that's the answer. You have to *care* about the people and what they're trying to do.

March 15. We ran a three-hour-and-twenty-minute paste-up of WAR LORD which persuaded me our story is not too complex for the film to be good. I guess this may be a distillation of what I've learned about film: Given the limitation of the form, you have to begin with a story simple enough so that the art lies in the *telling* of it.

March 16. We're still no further along with a director for KHARTOUM. Herman suggested Bernhard Wicki; I'll run footage on MORITURI tomorrow, though Ken Hughes still seems the best bet to me. Question: Why do I want to do this? Answer: It's a good part, presents the challenge of doing a mystic, as well as the English thing. Also, it's a helluva good script. I jumped the gun on our anniversary just before midnight and gave Lydia a Weisbuch [*a French painter*], along with a little twenty-year-old Scotch and a lot of love.

March 20, Palm Springs. I had some fair tennis this morning, in which Dick Zanuck showed a modest collection of strokes and the aggressiveness and determination that's brought him where he is in films. The view from the top of San Jacinto was spectacular, well worth giving up the afternoon for. Coming down the mountain, I found from Julian that Ken Hughes is double-talking (or his agent is).

Bitter experience has taught me that his agent was probably responsible. There's a great deal of stealthy shuffling about on the part of the less scrupulous agents, and the number of scrupulous ones, unhappily, is not large. Happily (on the other hand), Herman Citron and his colleagues are pillars of probity, which is one of the reasons I've never been represented by anyone else.

March 22, Los Angeles. Since I have to go to New York for a TV interview Lydia's going ahead tomorrow, to work on the apartment a little. I now may go to Montgomery, Alabama, for the last day of Dr. King's march there. I have to decide (A) is it meaningful (to me, to the movement) and (B) is it necessary? Yes, I think, on A and B. Now there's C: Can I fit it in?

March 23. I got Lydia off in fine shape, then ran Basil Dearden's SAPPHIRE. It's not bad, but I don't think the direction's the best part of it. Guy Green may now be available a bit earlier. I read the script again . . . it's really bloody good. We *must* be able to find someone good to direct. I had to drop the trip to Alabama. There's no way to get there, then to New York by Thursday.

March 24, New York. I got the kids to school, my suits fitted at the tailor, and myself on the plane for New York by ten in the morning. The trip was, as always, smooth, though there was a very bad Sinatra film on the airborne screen. This is becoming almost as much of a commuter trip for me as it is for the crews, I think. I got in to find Lydia deep in housecleaning. It wasn't hard to persuade her to come out to the theater. FIDDLER ON THE ROOF was a great success. Mostel is an example of Olivier's theory of the function of the star . . . an actor with more than ordinary candlepower, who is larger than the role.

March 26, Minneapolis. I ran another Basil Dearden film before we left for the airport and the sneak of AGONY. It's good, but dependent, like the other, on plot rather than character. KHARTOUM is character over plot, so this doesn't help. I called Carol Reed; he says he didn't know of our interest in him for KHARTOUM and is available this summer. Carol would be my first choice, if it can work. Meanwhile, AGONY played better in its first public showing than I would've believed possible. A great preview reaction, all cards fine.

I've been involved in some enormously successful films, but AGONY AND THE ECSTASY had far and away the best sneak preview response of any film I've ever been in. The audience stamped and screamed and gave us an ovation at the end, a response we never got quite as fully from even invited audiences of friends and colleagues. I have absolutely no explanation for this, especially since the film had only a modest commercial success.

March 27, Detroit. We woke to a city blanketed by a classic midwestern blizzard. While we waited to find if the planes were going to get out, I had time to explore KHARTOUM with Carol Reed. He insists he has nothing on for the summer, seemed most interested. I told Julian this on the phone; he swears Carol's agent says he's not available. It's a mystery, but the main thing is to get him a script. As the next best, I busily sold him on the history of Gordon on the plane to Detroit (which we providentially shared, though he went on to New York, while I stopped off to see Russ).

The problem here was Carol's diffidence, not his agent's duplicity. It's always very hard to turn down an offer from a friend. This is what tough agents are for.

March 28, New York. The apartment is still inundated in a high tide of belongings stretching back over our life in New York that Lydia's unearthed as candidates for discard in her monumental housecleaning. I worked through it all before going off to do the Jack Paar interview on AGONY. Since I'd filmed most of it in Rome last summer, it was a cinch.

March 29, Los Angeles. The most satisfying event of my day was watching Fray take a tennis lesson. It may have been the most constructive, too. Carol's left New York for London, presumably with script in hand, but there's no chance of an answer there for a day or so yet. I hope very much he decides to do it . . . I'd feel very relaxed with his driving. MGM submitted ICE STATION ZEBRA. It's a good script, but I don't like the part. Columbia offered a curious comedy called TWINKLE, TWINKLE, KILLER KANE, if you can believe it.

Actually, it was a fascinating script and a very good part, written by William Peter Blatty before the enormous success of his EXORCIST. It's a surrealistic kind of black comedy I still wish I could've done. We made several efforts over the next ten years to get it mounted . . . none successful, alas.

March 31. At lunch in the Derby with Jim Silke, I discussed the critical reaction to GSET. He has an interesting theory: The critical fraternity is basically antireligious, but unwilling to say so, thus can only attack the film in other terms than its offense as a statement of faith. It's possible. I read a terrible script Sam Peckinpah wrote for his current film and wrote him an impolite letter about it. Still nothing from Carol.

April 1. I finally heard from Carol, with information he really could've given me in Minneapolis: He feels tired, wants really most of all to rest, and can't undertake such a large project this summer. I sympathize with all this and can't really even quarrel with his tardy deliverance of this opinion, but it does put us almost a week behind where we were. Now we find Guy Hamilton's available. He has the script.

April 4. Guy Hamilton came over after Sunday tennis to talk about KHARTOUM. He seemed very interested, but can't commit, since he's still tied to VENETIAN AFFAIR for MGM. For a script as good as this, we're taking a hell of a long time to get a good director.

April 7. Sensing Acapulco will be all play, I was determined to get *some* work done before we left. I did. We set Basil Dearden to direct KHARTOUM. We could do much worse.

April 15, Acapulco. We spent the day with the Miguel Alemáns. They seem very decent, intelligent people. Fray won a victory over himself (the most valuable, and the hardest). He finally water-skied. This is our last day in Acapulco. It's been a golden, sun-dappled kind of time, and I treasure its memory. As Fray said in a card to his Grammajo: "It's truly heaven."

April 16, Los Angeles. I'm not used to taking vacations. This one was as happy as any I can remember. We all came back brown with sun, gilded with delights, and glad to be home. I'm only a little fat, and eager to get a look at WAR LORD. Everything's squared away on KHARTOUM; now I can begin to prepare MAN FOR ALL SEASONS.

I had just agreed to do a limited engagement of Robert Bolt's play in Chicago. I thought then, and still do, that it's the best play written in the past twenty years.

April 19. Lydia will play the wife in MAN FOR ALL SEASONS. It'll be her first performance in some years and I think she'll be damn good, though she's young for it. I hesitate, a little, to take on so much just ahead of KHARTOUM, but it's time I did a play again, and this part is marvelously right for me. I'm still hanging a little in the limbo you feel about a part (both Gordon and More, now) after you've accepted it, but before it's grabbed you. You commit your body before your soul, I guess.

April 20. I met Herman for a long lunch. He had a great deal to say about my doing small films. I think part of his concern, though he doesn't know it, or at least won't admit it, stems from his feeling that I shouldn't develop projects independently. He has a legitimate point;

he feels it jeopardizes the whole image, but this is a bit too standardizing for me to go along with. In fact, I think the identification with huge and/or hugely successful films has some drawbacks.

April 21. We ran WAR LORD at two hours, fifty-four minutes today. The film is in there, I have no question. The battles are much, much too long, complicated by the fact there are three of them back to back. Structurally you can't eliminate any one, so each must be pruned to the bone. I'm very good in the part; one of my best pieces of work, I feel sure. I'm also confident this will work with audiences. I'm learning more about how to read this kind of reaction, too. I'll go down the line on this opinion.

Wrong again! Though WAR LORD remains one of my favorite among my own films, it had only a modest box-office success. As I now realize, the studio was convinced from the beginning that they had the ingredients for a huge tits-and-armor piece. If we'd been allowed to shoot in the English marshes with an English cast, away from the studio's enthusiastic urgings that we spend more money on flaming siege towers, I think we'd have had the film we envisioned. Even as it was, I think Frank's first cut of the picture was chillingly close to this. I'm sorry audiences never saw it.

April 23. I'm still a little cool on the idea of Dearden to direct KHARTOUM, but we're committed on it. One thing I must learn better: Don't commit till you're sure. There are moral and creative considerations involved, but it's also a simple question of people's feelings.

April 24. I had a pleasant evening, ending with a slightly overrated film, TOPKAPI. It demonstrates the dangers of filming a woman you're in love with: You lose objectivity, as Ford did with Ireland [*the country, not the actor*] on QUIET MAN. Dassin is in love with Mercouri, so he keeps cutting to close-ups of her looking sexy, which isn't quite as sexy as he thinks it is. The film works, though, and Ustinov is marvelous.

April 27, London. I did what I came over the Pole for: I met with Dearden. He impresses me about as his films do: seriously but not overwhelmingly. I guess my prime enthusiasm on this one is for the script rather than the director. Now let's get the rest of the cast. We made no progress on that today, other than eliminating Nigel Patrick, who is a bit old to play an officer junior to me, especially when I'm playing a part older than I am.

April 29, London/Los Angeles. We spent a busy morning fiddling with
the Gordon makeup, a part of the work I always enjoy. We tried
three different versions, with progressively shorter moustache and
sideburns. The middle version's probably best . . . it avoids the
dashing cowboy look, yet misses the dreary Dickensian muttonchops
effect as well. Still stinking of spirit gum, I barely caught the Polar
Pan Am, and slept in my own bed and the loving arms waiting there.

May 2 (Sunday), Los Angeles. I read a Western script from the Mirisches
(not so good) and worked on my weight (pretty good). Then we went
to a party for Teddy Stauffer, given in Gary Cooper's old house, now
occupied by a lawyer, who is very preoccupied with redecorating it so
it doesn't look like Coop's. I can't blame him for that, but Coop's
shadow is still on the place for me. Really, it was one of those big
Hollywood parties I don't do well with.

May 6. I took another step toward Sir Thomas More, though this is the
easiest of them all, perhaps. The outside won't be so tough for me . . .
his inside may be another thing. As for Gordon, he's moving along.
The accent seems to be coming more quickly than I thought it would,
though I haven't had a chance to listen to it myself yet.

*The film tradition has always been that American actors played
non-American roles with their American accents intact. I've
probably played more such parts than any other American and
I've worked it out a little differently. For parts like Moses,
Michelangelo, the Cid, or Cardinal Richelieu, I use the neutral
English I was taught at Northwestern. English is the lingua franca
of international film anyway; its use in these parts merely
connotes the language they would actually have spoken. Gordon
was a different case, however. He was an Englishman and he didn't
speak English the way I do. I worked for several weeks with a very
good British voice coach, Helen Goss, who set out to teach me, not
just a British accent, but the accent used by Victorian army
officers.*

I thought of Chris Plummer for Colonel Stewart . . . but his price is
now two hundred twenty-five thousand dollars. That's out of line;
SOUND OF MUSIC is only one hit film.

May 11, Los Angeles. I spent some time on HILO with Sam Peckinpah and
Walter, in effect postponing any action on it till Sam decides what
he'll do with his project in Spain (which he really wants to make by
himself in his beloved Mexico, of course). But the main thing today
was running WAR LORD for our wives. Lydia didn't like it as well as
I'd hoped, but I can't tell (nor can she, I think) to what degree her
reaction is influenced by the unfinished state of the film. We still have

problems at the end. Frank's not finished trimming, but there's still too much battle there.

May 14. I'm happy to say that, again today, the best tennis in the world was played on my court. Laver, Emerson, Rosewall, and Ralston made a doubles match you couldn't equal in any tournament I know of. We all played a bit, of course, but the tennis to watch was when the big boys played together. Fray got to hit a few with Rod Laver, which should be something for his memory book. Quite a day, all in all.

I've cut most of the references to my passion for tennis out of these pages, fairly confident that no one but me is interested in my record of wins and losses over my friends and the progress of my forehand volley. I must record somewhere, though, the deep pleasure I've gotten from the game. Hooked like most American schoolboys on team sports, I started tennis far too late (any time after twelve is far too late) to learn to play it really well, but it's become a very satisfying part of my life. Not the least of these satisfactions is the chance it's given me to associate with the players. My basic tennis boast is that I've played tennis with more great players than any other lousy player in the world.

May 21. I'm nonplussed. No, I'm damn mad. Universal wants to take Frank off the film and turn the final recutting over to Ernie Nims [*a Universal executive*]. Ernie *Nims!*? The only pleasure I got out of the day came watching my son stand up to the recoil of a shotgun and break a few pop bottles out in the hills behind Newhall this afternoon after I finished at the studio. I should've gone into another line of work.

May 24. The fan got hit today, though very decorously. Herman handled negotiations for our side. Universal still insists they want to start working on the film without detailing to us what changes they have in mind. This seems very fishy to me. It may be a ploy against Frank, with whom they're involved in a contract fight, but it seems unlikely they'd jeopardize the film in this way. I hate like poison to relinquish control even for a week or so, but there seems no way out of it.

This is the classic conflict, of course. Film makers have had fights like this with studios all the way back to D. W. Griffith. In the end, you never win the ones they really don't want you to win. They paid for it, they own it, and sooner or later they take possession of their property.

May 25. Universal started cutting the film today, but there's nothing we can do. Our contract establishing creative control depends on a negative two hours long, costing three and a half million dollars, neither of which condition has been fulfilled. Still, Citron feels we can get the film back the way we want it if we bide our time.

May 28. I read the Gettysburg Address to a student convention before going to the studio, but a successful morning with Lincoln did little to reduce my outrage at the arbitrary, pointless changes Universal has made in WAR LORD. Their prime purpose seems to be to reduce the girl's nudity to a series of peep-show tease shots. For the rest, they've simply conventionalized the cutting to the standards of the forties. I don't see how we can win through all this crap, but we'll try.

June 1. The meeting with Universal to determine the final WAR LORD cut was not a bed of roses, but in three hours we won more points than we lost. The main technique, which I record for future reference, is to keep it civil. I managed to do this, and thus gained a great deal, I think. Julian called from London while we were screening to tell me Olivier might be available. I'm delighted, particularly since the casting was my suggestion.

June 4. Another long session on WAR LORD, at the end of which we had resolved everything except three reels of battle, which I've not seen yet, and how nude the girl should be on the top of the tower, and in the stream. Oddly enough, you reach the point where you get a little bored, fighting it out cut by cut. (Maybe this is a negotiating technique?) I think we ended up with something like the film we wanted, and a cut or two actually may be better their way. [*No, it wasn't. It was better the way Frank shot it, believe me.*]

June 5. A damn full day, what with two picture conferences, a TV interview, tennis, and two parties. The high point was Arthur Jacobs's pitch for the film he wants to make of the Boulle novel, PLANET OF THE APES. It sounds marvelous to me, and I haven't even read it yet. Julian had happy news: We've got Olivier for the Mahdi, though his scenes will have to be done in December.

June 7, Chicago. On the plane to Chicago, I finished Arthur Jacobs's script and the novel too. It seems like a marvelously good idea for a film. I'd like to play in it. The rest is up to Citron. As for the Mill Run [*the theater we were to play in*] it looks promising, but it's nowhere near completion. I don't see how it can be by the eighteenth. I told them so, but was reassured in fulsome terms. We'll settle it after rehearsal tomorrow.

June 8. The first rehearsal (which had to be shifted to another location, since the theater's ankle-deep in mud and crawling with workmen) went pretty well. The cast on the whole is very good . . . almost all of them have done the play before, which helps. I met with the management afterward, in a torrent of rain with tornadoes (no kidding) ripping through the suburbs. In this lurid setting, I made them bite on the bullet: They are out of their minds if they imagine that theater will be ready in time. They must postpone the opening. They agreed.

June 10, Los Angeles. I took the early plane back, got in a little tennis, though my jock itch gave me a little trouble. The situation at Universal gave me even more. Over some old Scotch, Walter and Frank and I felt sorry for ourselves, leading to the inevitable conclusion that we've been screwed. Now let's see what we can salvage. I still can't believe the basic quality of the film won't remain.

June 14, Washington, D.C. A long but fascinating day. Some four hundred artists came to Washington for the Arts Festival. I was proud to be one of them. We lunched at the National Gallery with Mrs. Johnson, then to the White House. There was a great deal to see and hear, though for me the most impressive art of the day was Wyeth's CHRISTINA'S WORLD. The film went off well [*an American Film Institute compilation of several scenes from great American films*]. I did the narration live, revising a little of Jim Silke's text. At dinner on the South Lawn, I had an exhilarating chance to fence with Dwight Macdonald, who was fussing around like a petulant bumblebee over Vietnam.

June 15, Chicago/Los Angeles. Feeling pretty good over the way everything went, I caught the plane with no waste motion. The stop in Chicago worked and was worth the pains to schedule it. We got almost through the whole play before I had to climb back on the plane again for the trip to California for my last WAR LORD chores. This will be my last trip back here for some time. MAN FOR ALL SEASONS seems a better and better play as I work on it. A part like this is a feast.

June 17, Los Angeles. I filmed two special trailers for WAR LORD today, and performed, if I say so, spectacularly, winging yards of dialogue without error. Poor Harry W. had a hard time. That seems to wait for all actors, down the road, but I can't believe, somehow, it'll ever be true for me. (I may live to read these words and weep.)

The whole question of forgetting lines seems to fascinate laymen more than any other aspect of acting. "I don't see how you can remember all those words!" Actually, like most things you spend your life doing, there's no particular trick to it. Of course, there are actors who have trouble with their lines, and not all of them drink too much, either. As nearly as I can figure out, it's a question of insecurity: You forget a line because you're afraid you're going to forget a line.

June 18, Los Angeles/Chicago. The last I'll see of Coldwater for a good many months. [*After* MAN FOR ALL SEASONS *we were going to England to start* KHARTOUM.] Of course it was as beautiful as possible, to reproach me. We got away in reasonable time, awash in the usual sea of luggage. Unlike Mr. Eliot's little man, my life is measured out in zippered suitcases, not coffee spoons. Also in unfinished theaters, at this point. There was a roof on, but damn little more since I last saw it. Mother's house on Maple Avenue was as always, though . . . and welcome.

June 19. Leaving the kids happily settled with their grandmother, Lydia and I launched off again into a play—the first for her since STATE OF THE UNION, in Santa Barbara, four or five years ago. It went damn well; the play's magnificent, the cast is excellent. This will be fine, I think.

July 1. We finished after dawn, rested during the day, and got to the theater to find it a ferment of finishers, but still a long way from ready. We couldn't run a real dress; we were lucky to complete a half-assed technical, which means we'll have to run through the light cues for the crews tomorrow. Also, many props are wrong. Still, the play is right. That's what counts.

July 2, Open MAN FOR ALL SEASONS. Well, we almost had the play ready before the theater was, which is not really the way you do it. When we got there at noon to run the technical cues for light and sound, we found the sound system out. By the time this was fixed the audience was filtering in, stepping gingerly on the still-tacky paint on the lobby floor. It's the first time I've ever opened a play without either a technical or a dress rehearsal. Reasonably enough, the performance was not marvelous, but not bad. The play itself carries a helluva lot alone. I could've been better, but under the circumstances, I'll settle for adequate.

So did the opening night audience; they loved it. I guess this was the most successful disaster (or disastrous success, if you like) I can remember.

July 7. We had our first regular matinee day today. We played to full and rapt houses at both performances. I'm amazed at how readily and richly this fairly wordy play reaches audiences. I can't put it all to my drawing power, either. I may get them in the house, but the play holds them there.

As it still does. I've done the play twice since (and hope to do it yet again). My opinion of it remains intact. This side of Shakespeare, it's the most rewarding experience I've ever had on the stage.

July 11. It was a fine closing day, from the brunch the cast gave me in the Pump Room, along with the pewter mug from the play, appropriately engraved, to the curtain call tonight when the audience stood and screamed for me . . . the first time I've ever experienced that particular ego-massage (and it is). I did the show . . . we all did the show . . . as well as we ever have. I was glad Fray came back to see it again with his grandmother. I was also glad to find we broke the all-time Chicago record for a nonmusical play—nearly fifty-two thousand dollars for the closing week.

July 15, New York. Another full day in the salt mines, doing interviews for Universal. I keep forgetting how much you have to do (or at least how much I *do* do) in return for the limos and theater tickets and extra whatnot this kind of life carries with it. It evens out, I guess. They give me things I wouldn't buy for myself, I give them services not many would, or could.

July 16, Los Angeles. The *United States* having canceled, I seized the opportunity to fly to Los Angeles for the sneak of WAR LORD. They invited a selected cross-section sort of audience, for whom the film played very well, I thought. Not a stir or a cough throughout, though the battles are clearly at least a minute long, each. The Universal brass were notably noncommittal afterward. Home overnight . . . Drago was delighted to see me.

July 21, The Queen Mary, *at sea.* Sailing a great liner can never get to be routine, but we've done it enough times for it to be familiar, however fine. The *Queen Mary* is all of that: rich with the luxury of the years just before the war. We have plenty of room, in a very 1930ish suite, and the sea is smooth. What else can you want? [*United Artists had somehow managed to get us space. How, I don't know.*]

July 24, West of Land's End. The last full day at sea, which continues smooth. I continue to wage a fierce battle with my appetite, to which I succumb at the table, then expiate pounding round and round the sun deck, and in the gym and steam room, sweating out the results.

July 27, London. The drive up through the green hedgerows from Southampton was lovely, the suite's exactly right . . . far better for us than a house here. The costumes are coming well and the latest version of the script is very good. Now that we're sure of Ralph Richardson, as well as Larry Olivier, I think we have a helluva good chance.

July 30. I picked up my new XKE and timorously piloted it through London traffic . . . afraid not so much of losing my way as forgetting to drive on the left. I got safely out to Pinewood, however, and did a test scene (with a good actor who may well prove to be our best bet as Zobeir). I found my way back with little more trouble, had a really good session of doubles on the wood, indoors at Queen's Club. It ended up being a lovely day, all round. A nice mix of work and play; XKEs and spirit gum, indoor courts and close-ups.

August 3. The high point . . . no, good Christ, the *low* point . . . of the day was having my XKE stolen from in front of the bloody hotel last night, delivered to the thief by a garage attendant, with the doorman looking on benignly. There seems damn little hope of getting it back. The hell with that. We celebrated Holly's birthday today, since the children for the party couldn't come yesterday. She looked enchanting and seemed to have had a marvelous time. What an adorable four-year-old she is. I don't *care* about the damn car.

I did. I loved that car, though it was only a thing. It smarted a lot to lose it.

August 6, Newcastle. A busy, long day, trying to get the right degree of gray in my hair for Gordon. As I was leaving the studio, Scotland Yard called with heartening news: They found my E-type under a plane tree down in Brighton, undamaged, with only 120 miles extra on the clock. It had been taken by two men who knocked off one of the gambling clubs in Curzon Street, around the corner, and wanted a car fast enough to get away from the police on the M1, southbound to the coast. We got away in good time for our long weekend in the Border Country in United Artists' chauffeured Rolls. No one's going to pinch that.

I don't usually share the admiration most people feel for the dashing bandit, but I had to admire the cool self-possession of the man who stole my car. He strolled into the Dorchester lobby in faultless evening clothes about ten in the evening, lifted the housephone, and said to the garage in impeccable Mayfair accent, "Would you please bring Mr. Heston's car 'round?" They did, of course, whereupon he said to the doorman, "Put my case in the boot, please," stepped in, and drove off. Even if it's your car, you have to applaud the performance. Especially because they caught him, later.

August 7, Carlisle. Hadrian's Wall is surely one of the most impressive Roman remains in the world, beyond question the most memorable in England. Just a year ago we picnicked at his villa in Rome, but the wall that marked the boundary of his ambition is surely a better measure of the man than the villa that housed his heart. All day long we walked on what is left of the wall from which the legions guarded the northern limits of Rome for nearly four centuries . . . twice the time of our little Republic. It was raining and cold . . . a fit climate for the lean ghosts of those brave men.

August 11. The shooting's well begun. The scene today is one of the keys in the piece. I'm not certain we did it justice. As sometimes happens, my first reading of it in the walk-through was the best I ever managed. Also, I note Basil doesn't shoot a lot of close-ups. I'm coming more and more to believe that the only moments in which a performance tells on the screen are in close-ups. Well . . . we're not done yet. My XKE, all checked out at Henley's, is back in service again for the run to Pinewood, though I have a helluva time prying it loose from the hotel garage now. (I only wish they'd been so vigilant last week.)

August 19. I spent the day being hacked to death by tribesmen's spears. How many violent deaths have I suffered, in one medium or another? This year alone I've been speared, beheaded, and sickled to death.

August 26. I sat all day in the glittering full-dress uniform of a British general, impassively watching a belly dancer. We had a scene, too, mind you, but I suspect the audience's eyes will not be on us. It's just as well . . . this is the only girl we've got in the film: We might as well wring all we can out of her.

This film was scheduled in somewhat unorthodox fashion, partly to take advantage of Olivier's availability in the late fall. Having completed most of the interiors in London, the company shut down for several weeks to prepare the Egyptian location. I went to Cairo early with my family. None of them had been there before and I wanted them to see something of that remarkable country before I plunged into the work.

August 31, Cairo. Egypt seems very different than it did on COMMANDMENTS, when I was here alone. It's better now. I didn't really *do* anything today, but laid on riding, tennis, one thing and another to fill the time till we shoot. We took Fray with us to dinner with Abbas, whom I remember from the de Mille days here. He seems happier now than when he was married to de Mille's granddaughter.

This was Major Abbas Boughdadli, whom I'd met when he was commanding the Egyptian cavalry unit we used to impersonate the pharaoh's soldiers pursuing the Israelites during TEN COMMANDMENTS. He was a darkly handsome and enormously engaging man, with whom de Mille's granddaughter promptly fell in love and married. Unhappily, the union did not last.

September 1. I know one reason Cairo seems so significant to me. Not since I went back to St. Helen in '44 have I returned to a place I've been away from so long. To come back here now with my family is a remarkable experience. Before we left for the Valley of the Kings, I checked with Joe Canutt. He's not happy with the horses they've bought for the second unit. The trains south to Luxor are modern, made in Hungary, and reasonably prompt over a very rough roadbed.

September 2. The whole Luxor experience was very special. The record of a civilization buried so deep in the centuries is curiously stirring. The best part of the trip, though, was sailing on a light wind at sunset on the Nile, under the same kind of sail the pharaohs knew, with the same simple human delight.

September 7, London. I worked with Ralph Richardson today. He does a lovely job (of course); an easy, delightful man to work with. We didn't finish the scene, but it runs more than four pages. I think we did it well, I was proud to be acting with him. I'm sorry to say I wasn't proud of WAR LORD tonight, in its final, truncated Universal version.

I had come back to London to do a key scene with Ralph Richardson that could neither be shot elsewhere nor postponed.

September 15, Cairo. Shooting here will not be easy. Our end of it seems organized up to normal professional standards, but there's appalling mismanagement from the Egyptians. Transport isn't showing up, no water for the second unit . . . that kind of thing. This is something of a puzzle to me, since de Mille shot here with none of these problems that I was aware of, callow youth that I was. [*Ah, "callow" is the key. I just didn't know enough about it to tell, on COMMANDMENTS.*]

September 17. Since I didn't shoot, I did what I should've done ten years ago and climbed the pyramid of Cheops with Lydia and Fray. Holly stayed below and rode a donkey; Mother came up a hundred feet and sat on a stone writing letters. It was very special, putting my feet in the troughs worn there by the millions of feet that've climbed before me in the five thousand years since it was built, polishing with the sweat of my palm the gleaming handholds men have worn in the time-carved stones. The view from the top was deeply stirring for us. Lydia shot busily with her Nikon, we climbed down fulfilled.

September 19 (Sunday). A very gloomy morning. The family was ready to leave at the appointed hour, but it seemed very hard to let them go. As I carried Holly up the steps and through the door of the Comet, she patted my cheek and said, "Poor Daddy . . . has to stay alone." Then I stood on the runway and watched the bouquet of hands waving from windows as the plane lumbered onto the strip and angled into the hot Egyptian sky, carrying all I love away from me. So now there are six weeks.

September 21, Mazghouna. Shooting conditions can hardly have been better than they were today . . . possibly never in my whole career. We worked in an intricate little Nile steamer [*formerly the property of King Farouk*], the height of thirties luxury, paddling up and down the river shooting not very difficult scenes and resting in puffy, plush-fitted staterooms betimes. Of course, we couldn't get decent sound with the generator tied alongside, and the arcs were something fierce to act into, and we had to wait so long to shoot we missed the helicopter shot . . . but aside from all this it was a lovely day's work.

September 24. We got out in good time today, only to find that, through some Egyptian oversight, the steamer was not there. It's the first time I've ever shown up for work and found the set missing. Actresses, wardrobe, cameras, yes . . . but not the *set*. It finally arrived, an hour and a half late, and we threw ourselves into the day. The scene went well, and we came within two shots of finishing it, even with the late start, which speaks well for the efficiency of the shooting company, if not the local logistic support.

September 26 (Sunday). Somehow, Egyptian sun feels quite different lolling by a pool, smeared with oil, from the way it does when you're toiling over the dunes under the same sun in pursuit of those twin bitches, art and money.

October 4, Mazghouna. We shot Gordon's arrival at Khartoum today. I suppose it's not everyone who can celebrate his birthday with a tumultuous reception by happy thousands greeting the savior of the Nile. Actually, it reminded me a bit of when I took Valencia, only this was a little smaller, and on foot. At this point, you don't really celebrate birthdays, anyway; you mark them, uneasily. I can't complain, mind you. I have no vantage point for retrospect at the moment, but I seem to be getting where I want to be. I have work, health, happiness, love. What else is there?

October 5. We're still slaving away re-creating Gordon's entry into the city he died in. We've made Khartoum, or at least its roadstead, in a dusty little mud village on the Nile. With the walls and buildings we're adding, it looks remarkably like the prints of Khartoum. As for the mobs of Sudanese shrieking their welcome to the man they thought could save them, the local types do very well. Between shots, tiny boys prance about imitating their elders, crying "Gor-doon! Gor-doon!" at me.

It's curious how many opportunities my career has afforded me to experience, if only secondhand, the sweet triumph of the savior, borne on the shouts of the adoring multitude. Gordon at Khartoum, the Cid at Valencia, Jackson at New Orleans, Moses at the Red Sea. It's a rare and deeply stirring feeling.

October 6. This being my last day on the set before the shot back to the U.S., a heady winding-things-up atmosphere prevailed, however spurious. (I *am* coming back, after all.) I hit a very good moment in one take of Gordon touching his hand to the soil of Khartoum, saying, "It's . . . good to be home." Of course, it'll have to be looped anyway, where I may lose it.

We couldn't get printable sound over the constant babble of crowd noise from our extras, who thought it was all real and had no thought of being quiet on cue.

October 7, New York. The premiere [*of* THE AGONY AND THE ECSTASY *with a party afterward, at the Metropolitan Museum*] went very well, considering the trouble it was to get here for it. It was a bloody tight day but it all worked out. I even managed to fit in a Sullivan TV interview after the premiere. With the newspaper strike on, we only got two notices: The *Tribune* hated it, the *Post* loved it. This is beginning to bug me a bit. I'm good in this film. If it doesn't register, there's something bloody wrong somewhere.

October 8, Los Angeles. If today were the only day I had back here, it would've been worth the long flight across the country . . . or around the world, for that matter, never mind the New York premiere. This ridge has a mystic capacity to revive me. I walk along it, and I'm healed. My children leaping in my arms to greet me, my wife's embrace, do that, even more fully.

October 10. Woke again early, on Egyptian time. Walter came over to discuss his plans for the BEAU GESTE remake. [*He'd offered me the role of the sadistic sergeant.*] I ran the Cooper film again, and Walter's right: With anyone but Coop in the title role, the sergeant *is* the best part. It would be a good switch for me to play a heavy, but I have misgivings about the director Walter's stuck with and a conviction the studio's going to force him to make it on the cheap. I'd love to work with Walter again, but I think I'll pass on this one.

I was right. The studio felt they had a property that couldn't miss. Any film can miss, if it's not made right. They've since tried it yet again, as a comedy. That wasn't made right either.

October 11, To London. I drove the kids to school, met Fray's teacher, and got a copy of *Innocents Abroad*, to use in the reading at the embassy next week. Then it was over the Pole again for the last lap of this location. I spent it not studying enough, eating too much, and sleeping just about right.

October 12, London/Cairo. I used the time during the plane change in London to work on the Twain cutting, in the Pan Am VIP lounge, then slept during most of the long leg east over the Mediterranean to Cairo. I arrived on time and ready to work, only to discover that they'd lost a day. I don't shoot tomorrow, which is what I bloody came *back* for, of course. After a stormy scene with the production people, I decided there was no point in stirring things up and did the only useful thing I could do: put in the time doing dinner with some foreign news types. It wasn't a wasted day, then, really.

October 14, Cairo. Got a fair amount done on the steamer today, though it goes damn slowly, swinging that lumbering old paddle-wheeler around in the river. The reading tonight at the U.S. Embassy, for a mixed audience of diplomats, artists, etc., went very well. I found bits of the Koran, pharaonic poetry, some Mark Twain, the Noah story from Genesis, and some Frost. The party after in the residence garden was obligatory, but pleasant. I had an odd heart-thumping moment of insecurity, waiting upstairs just before I began, but it all came right, I think.

October 22. Bad news: Some intricate internal dispute in the English film unions now dictates "work to rule" [*this means drag your feet*] from now on, thus no Saturday work, thus we can't finish tomorrow, thus I can't meet Lydia in Madrid. She was very good about this on the phone; I'm sulking. I hate having this kind of thing happen.

October 26, London. I took a last look at the Nile (for a while, at least) while the Qantas jet slanted up toward Alexandria in the early light. The trip was easy, but we held over London a helluva long time waiting for the fog to clear. Thus, I got in only at the end of the lunch for the critics (most of whom remained ominously noncommittal), then to the Dorchester for an hour of sleep, waking to find Lydia unpacking, after arriving from Madrid.

October 27. Royal premiere with HRH Prince Philip, party afterward. I spent a busy day touting AGONY, which the London critics are not taking to their bosoms. I feel more and more this is a problem of critical backlash centering on me, having to do with my last half-dozen films. On careful (agonizing?) reappraisal, I'm still convinced the film's bloody good, and I'm bloody good in it.

October 28, To Los Angeles via Chicago. A long, long flight across an ocean and a continent, but the two children bouncing and bubbling at the end of the journey made it a light and joyful one. The pleasure of coming home is the surest one I have now; my pleasure in my work is somewhat shaken by developments of the last week. I'm now less sure of my capacity to judge how I'm doing in KHARTOUM or, if it's good, what difference that'll make in how it's received. The work should suffice for itself, of course.

October 29, Los Angeles. Largely liked by critics and me: THE BIG COUNTRY, BEN-HUR, THE WRECK OF THE MARY DEARE, EL CID. Busts with me and critics: PIGEON THAT TOOK ROME, DIAMOND HEAD, 55 DAYS AT PEKING, THE BUCCANEER, MAJOR DUNDEE. Liked by me, not critics: THE GREATEST STORY EVER TOLD, THE AGONY AND THE ECSTASY. What's created the critical backlash, if it exists? My last ten pictures? See above; though almost all made money, there were not many I liked myself . . . let alone the critics.

Obviously, the AGONY notices smarted a bit. Actually, a lot of them were very good. Even some of the critics who didn't like the film had good things to say about Rex and me. I expected a great deal more than that, though. I think I've learned a little better since then the basic truth involved. You do the work for itself (and for a living, of course). If people don't come to see it, you don't get to do any more, but beyond that, you aim for your own standards, which should be tougher than anyone else cares about, or knows how to set.

November 2. I went over the whole thing with Citron, trying to get a fix on whether I've become too strongly identified with large, highly commercial films. He says no. Still, I'd like to try something different for the next one. Something small, something black and white. (How transparent, Mr. H . . . how transparent . . .)

November 3. THE PLANET OF THE APES project seems in limbo. Jacobs is now thinking of trying to sweat the budget down to two million, which seems ridiculous. He also wants to go with a mechanic-director from television. This seems a mistake, too. On the other hand, it'd be very good for me if this one came together. It's certainly the different kind of script I'm talking about.

November 4. I went over to SAG and investigated the dimensions of my new job as president. At least I have a very impressive office, probably no more to do than I'll have time for. Especially if I take my time picking a new script. The piece about the South African gold fields isn't the one. I saw DARLING tonight; a good example of what I'm looking for, though neither part is right for me, of course. It's largely a good film, though it thins out a bit toward the end. Christie is excellent.

November 8, Detroit. A busy morning, doing paper work, preparatory to leaving for the WAR LORD tour. The lunch for Princess Margaret was an interesting demonstration of Hollywood's flappability over royals. (Mind you, I flapped a bit, too.) I sat one place down from the lady at lunch. Her voice was quite gone from all her speeches on this tour, but she was doing her valiant best to live up to her social responsibilities. James Stewart passed on to me her remarks, which she whispered in his ear. I thus had the unique experience of conversing with Princess Margaret as played by Jimmy Stewart. Unusual casting.

November 9. A long, hard-sell kind of day. Not the way I'd lay on publicity for this, or any film, but they're determined this is the best way to do it. I would've liked to bring in people from the outlying cities . . . the ones I can't visit . . . and talk to them instead of to every disc jockey with a portable tape machine. [*This was somewhat quixotic of me.*] Russ doesn't seem too well, though not as bad as I feared he might be, with a second stroke to bear. He can't walk, of course, but this should be temporary.

November 12, Chicago. I indulged myself at lunch in the suite, lecturing the Chicago critics on the concept of the period film, pointing out very professorially just how it differs in difficulty from contemporary stories. The problems of dialogue, accent, costume, the exposition of complex historical backgrounds. These schoolteachering impulses ill become me, but you don't often have a captive audience of critics.

November 15, Los Angeles. The damn rain, bucketing down relentlessly all day again, ruled out any activity but reading. National General has a book, THE QUILLER MEMORANDUM, which interests me mainly because it's a modern story and a simple part. Pinter's doing the script, but I don't know how serious they are, let alone how serious I am.

November 19. Still drifting on choosing work for '66. It seems set for me to go to Vietnam in late January, but whether to do a film after that or take another crack at MAN FOR ALL SEASONS, I can't decide. If it's a film, should I do one of the period pieces waiting for me or find something modern?

November 21. Lydia's Egyptian slides tonight were incredible . . . really creative, effective work. I'm very proud of what she's doing. To learn to function in an art so technically complicated is not easy.

November 24. Leo [*Ziffren*] explained some complicated material re money, taxes, and insurance. Citron did likewise on THE WAY WEST and one or two other offers. I think more and more that after

Vietnam I should do MAN FOR ALL SEASONS out here. I got into a spy novel Watler Seltzer has . . . it's readable, might be actable. WAR LORD business is not holding up the way they expected, nor the way it opened. AGONY, on the other hand, is. There must be a lesson in there somewhere.

November 25, Thanksgiving. A quiet sort of holiday. I finished Walter's spy novel and talked a bit to Herman about various projects cooking on the back burners, but mainly marked time (the healer of all wounds, all jaundiced views . . .) while gnawing moodily on a turkey drumstick. I'm not really depressed, just adjusting to my situation, which apparently is not quite as rosy as I'd imagined.

November 29. Somewhat to my surprise, Dick Zanuck seemed more than casually interested in the pro football film idea. He wanted to read it, and call me tomorrow about putting a writer on it. This is a helluva long way from a film, but it's the first step, certainly. I held the gavel for my first regular meeting as SAG president. I did well enough, I suppose; I got through the agenda without open mutiny.

December 2, London. I didn't sleep as well on the plane as I usually can. TWA doesn't have seat dividers that come out. I got some rest, though, before plunging into my day. What I saw of KHARTOUM looked quite good, but I'm now very leery of high-rating footage ahead of time. The scenes seem to play, with some exceptions: The scenes on the camel with the little girl and with the Bible and Khaleel don't.

December 3. My usual rate of looping was not quite up to par today. I think I took slightly greater pains and also had an added factor to consider in each loop beyond the sync and the occasional change of reading: This was the maintenance (and occasional correction) of my Gordon accent. We got a good day's work, and I think I did well on what we finished, but I'm still not able to say how remarkable the film will be. Or *if* it will be remarkable.

December 7. Two dozen years ago I sat in a third-floor bedroom listening to the news of Pearl Harbor interrupting a symphony on the radio. Today, a long way and a long time from then, I did a rather dull day's work, though I had an interesting lunch with Olivier, in to test his makeup. He looks fine . . . perhaps a bit too dark at the moment, but another lovely putty nose, of course. [*Olivier's penchant for false noses is well known. Perhaps I'm jealous because my own is so large there's no room to add another on top.*]

December 9. A very dull shooting day once again, but the play tonight (TRELAWNEY OF THE WELLS) was fascinating for me because I played the lead in it at New Trier High School . . . more than twenty-five years ago. I found I could only recall the entrance and the last line. I discovered what I could never have known when we did it as midwestern American high school kids: just how delightful a record it is of how the Victorian theater *was* . . . how the actors behaved. Actors are like that still.

December 14. Today I began the memorable experience of acting with Olivier. He's quite marvelous in the part . . . complete African characterization, borrowed from his Othello, perhaps, but utterly valid for this. On top of it he has superimposed a careful Sudanese enunciation. The whole thing, down to painting the inside of his mouth, is an example of the total devotion to the role that is probably part of his success. Part of it. He also happens to be an incredibly gifted actor.

December 18. This was the day I could've flown home, but for Basil's party for me. That was one reason to stay. A better reason though was the chance I had to run out to the studio and improve one reading from yesterday's work. (*"You* whisper to *me,* Mohammed Ahmed . . .") So I wound up KHARTOUM. I've learned not to try and deduce from my own reactions what the public and/or critical response to a film will be. However, *I* like this one.

December 19. Spent the ocean-spanning hours contemplating the film I left behind. To work with Olivier was a great experience. I learned and accomplished something as well, though I don't know whether it'll be recognized. (This shouldn't matter, you idiot . . . but it does, damn it, it does.)

December 29. The rain gave me a good reason to spend most of the day on the problems of THE WAY WEST, which Citron's pressing me to accept. At his urging, I ran SHENANDOAH, to check the direction. I didn't like it much, or the film. It's predictable and pointlessly antihistorical in terms of the realities of the Civil War. Still, all this has somehow brought me to the point where I gave Herman a reluctant OK. I'll be playing Tadlock.

December 31. We saw out the year in high style, combining celebration with what has come to be our ritual weekend in Las Vegas. It was fun, of course, if a little more frantic than even that town usually is. We were with our friends, though, and it helped to sing the year out amicably, even a year that's been far from perfect for me. I learned a great deal, much of it not pleasant. I came to realize, for the first time, that I am not exactly the critics' darling. There are two explanations for this dubious phenomenon: that I am in fact not the actor I thought all along I was becoming, or (and this seems at least plausible) a performer who's been in as many popular pieces as I have is not likely to earn critical kudos at the same time. Now that I've taken steps (or taken steps toward taking steps), perhaps this will change.

Anyway, another year. For last year, the notices on AGONY AND THE ECSTASY and what happened to WAR LORD certainly amounted to two swift kicks in the balls. Never mind, Shakespeare said it, as usual: *"Time and the hour run through the roughest day."*

Charlton and Fraser Heston, Rome, 1964
LYDIA HESTON

A sail with Lydia and Fray to
Australia's Great Barrier Reef (1966)
With Holly and Fray at
the great sphinx, Gezah, Egypt (1965)
LYDIA HESTON

While in Rome...(1964)
A visit from Heston's mother;
Top right, Fray at Hadrian's
Villa; Holly learning to write
LYDIA HESTON

Time off from Khartom *in Egypt (1965);*
here with Lydia Heston
FRASER HESTON

Holly has her third birthday in Rome (1964)
LYDIA HESTON

Celebrating a Roman Christmas with Fray and Lydia (1958);
PIER LUIGI

With Lydia aboard
The Queen Mary (1961)
GEORGE V. BIGELOW

Her arrival in Italy (1964)
TWENTIETH CENTURY FOX

Lydia with camera,
York, England (1969)
F. SPENCER,
YORKSHIRE EVENING PRESS

With Fray while on location for El Cid in Spain (1960);
with Holly in a Cairo bazaar (1965)
LYDIA HESTON

Reading to Fraser, Rome, 1958
LYDIA HESTON

With Holly, Rome, 1964; that's Drago, lying on the floor
GENEVIEVE GERALD

ROMAN NEWSPAPERMAN
PIAZZA NAVONA JULY '64

*Heston with sketch pad
in Rome (1964)*
LYDIA HESTON

DE MILLE'S
SOUND MAN — SARASOTA, FLA.
cheston

With Fraser and Lydia (1976);
Holly at fourteen (1975)
SIDNEY TELEGRAPH

1966

Vietnam . . .

touring with
*A Man for
All Seasons* . . .

New Zealand
and Australia . . .

a conductor's role
in *Counterpoint*.

Conducting a symphony
orchestra in *Counterpoint*
THE MUSEUM OF MODERN ART/FILM
STILL ARCHIVE

January 7, Palm Springs. Fray didn't go to school today; he drove down to the desert with me and we rode all day long. I remember carrying him on the saddle in front of me when we first went to Smoketree Ranch. Now he rides a horse of his own, beside me up the rock slopes and skidding down the sides of dry washes.

January 9 (Sunday), Los Angeles. The last day was fine, with easy traffic driving home. I can't remember how many times we've done this La Quinta thing, but it's a tradition that mellows over the years. The sharp, clear air, the deep desert heat of the sun, and mainly, I suppose, the joy of the kids are what make it work so well for us.

January 12. We canceled the casting meeting on MAN FOR ALL SEASONS; neither the director nor the actors we wanted to see were free today. Of the Chicago cast, only Mike Egan is available for sure . . . perhaps Heffernan, if the Albee play closes, which it undoubtedly will. I hope we can cast the rest with actors who've at least done the piece before, if not with me. Tonight I helped Fray a bit on his title role in the class production of THE PIED PIPER OF HAMELIN. I've had a lot of practice in these Pied Piper parts . . .

January 13, En route to Vietnam via Hawaii. Most of the day, as usual, was given over to packing for departure. A little tricky this time, since I have to take a dinner jacket for Tokyo, along with field clothes for Vietnam. I did fairly well playing tennis, very badly arranging it . . . I failed to get Dick Zanuck on the winning side in even one set. So much for customer's tennis. He'll read the Mexican story anyway.

This trip was arranged by the USO and implemented by the services involved. Any number of entertainers were visiting Vietnam during this period, ranging from very large and elaborate shows like those Bob Hope mounted, complete with bands and pretty girls, to small units with a singer and a couple of musicians. Obviously, there was nothing I could do on this scale. It had become clear, however, that logistics required that the large entertainment units limit their appearances to the big bases, where more troops could be reached. Even very small units couldn't be sent very far into the field, particularly if they included women. Since I could travel both light and alone, I was able to go to fairly remote areas. Though I'm sure they'd rather have seen Bob Hope and the girl singers, at least I was able to let some of the men in the boondocks know they weren't forgotten . . . by me anyway.

January 15, Saigon. Saigon seems a much more French city than I'd expected. It's also more crowded . . . mostly with soldiers. Now I know what London was like in '44. I have a decent billet and they take elaborate care of me. (Getting the actors shot is a no-no, I expect.)

January 17, en route to Danang. We lost our flaps taking off from Saigon, but it didn't delay us (nothing dramatic, just a hydraulic leak). The flight had a little drama in the form of artillery fire north of Pleiku (no, no, not at us). The crowd and bustle of war is more apparent here in Danang. Every unit needs more space than they have. War is still waiting in line.

January 18, In the North. I spent my time with seabees and marines today, some of them in an advanced field hospital, badly shot up. I'll remember them . . . lying loose on the bloody stretchers, red dust on their boots, carried lurching along the muddy duckboards from the heli-pad to the surgical tent. I slept at a marine airstrip. The MAG F6s are huge, beautiful brutes like no plane I ever saw. There are some very sharp types flying them too, led by a lean little marine colonel from World War II.

January 21. I went with the Special Forces today. What they're trying to do, both in a civil and a military sense, is impressive. I also had a chance to mark the beauty of the country. It could be a rich and happy land, if it ever finds peace.

January 23 (Sunday). I got a little farther out into the boondocks today, again with the Special Forces. We hit several camps out away from Pleiku, going in a convoy of gunships, for all the world like a cavalry patrol out after Sioux. I think I talked the CO here into letting me go on a patrol tomorrow. I can't help wanting to try it . . . just once.

January 26, Saigon. Back to civilization, if the sandbagged streets of Saigon can be described as civilized. It was a pleasure (and, at the same time, a curious loss) to climb out of the tiger suit and into a sport shirt. The evening was spent tasting Saigon's bright lights. When the French were here, they used to call it the Paris of the East. I see why.

January 27. I had to get up too early for the meeting with Westmoreland, who probably shouldn't have taken the time to see me. I finally got out for Tokyo an hour late, feeling wiser than when I came. The most important commitment we have here is not merely military, though it may depend on it.

January 29, Tokyo/Los Angeles. This was about as long as a day can get, beginning with a breakfast interview in the Okura ("How do you define love, Mr. Heston?") at nine in the morning, and ending some thirty-odd hours later going over the whole experience with old friends on my ridge in Coldwater. It was a remarkable time for me, both as a citizen and as an individual.

January 31, Los Angeles. I'm readjusting somewhat slowly; my jet lag this time was a memorable one, coupled with the runs, which are only now beginning to ease off. (It was that damn cow's blood and rice wine initiation that did it.) It's a helluva bug; ruined my sex life and my tennis at the same time.

I'd spent a couple of days with a Special Forces unit in a remote part of the Montagnard country, out of Le Hai. The Montagnards are a primitive, fierce, and fascinating people, not Vietnamese. While I was there, I was initiated into the tribe, a relationship that still remains somewhat vague to me. The key to the ceremony was drinking a mixture of rice wine and blood from a bullock that had just been brained on the spot. This constituted a gastronomic test only equaled in my experience by the time I had to eat the eyeball of a sheep off the point of a Bedouin's dagger during the celebration in the desert while we were shooting TEN COMMANDMENTS. *The Special Forces major who was with me, noting my distress, said encouragingly, "The blood's not so bad, it's that goddamn rice wine they mix it with. It'll give ya the runs sure as hell." It sure as hell did.*

February 1. I spent most of the day on the phone, talking to the wives, fathers, mothers, and girls of some of the men I met in Vietnam. It didn't turn out to be as tough as I thought it would. I usually hate to talk to strangers, but these people seemed so overjoyed to have word from their men that the calls became a pleasure, not a chore.

I was glad to go to Vietnam, but once there, there wasn't an awful lot I could do, unequipped as I was to entertain the troops with songs, jokes, or pretty girls. Somewhat desperately, I hit on the idea of taking down the home phone numbers of men I talked to, promising to call when I got back. This worked out pretty well. Dick Zanuck let me use some of Fox's telephone facilities for several days, which made it possible to complete several hundred calls in that time.

February 2. I spent the whole day trying to cast the parts we can't get back from the Chicago production of MAN FOR ALL SEASONS, and very up-hill work it was, too. So far we haven't found more than one or two actors with any concept of what the play is about, or how to play anything but modern parts. Poor kids, that's all they get a chance at these days. It's hard to sit and watch them leave, discouraged, but it's discouraging to listen to them, too.

February 4. I spent most of the day working down the long list of Vietnam calls still outstanding, breaking only for lunch with Lydia on her last day of jury duty. I had time to explore the direction-Leslie Stevens is moving on the pro quarterback story. It seems right so far (we're still at the yellow-lined pad stage, so this isn't saying a helluva lot). For some reason, we went to two cocktail parties later, certainly not our usual pace, and a damn good thing, too.

February 10. We moved a little further along on PRO today; as far as a name for our quarterback: "Cat" Catlin, as well as some semblance of a story line. We've at least pinned down some characters and conflicts that should be valid . . . it remains to be seen if they will work out on paper so they'll appeal to Dick Zanuck (or someone else running a studio).

February 15. Had a good lunch interview with Cecil Smith [*L.A. Times critic*] about MAN FOR ALL SEASONS, then drinks to no purpose with some South Americans who want me to come to a film festival. (I hate film festivals. Everyone you meet has a script to press into your hot little hand . . .) Lean's film tonight, DOCTOR ZHIVAGO, has a curiously disinvolved central character to build a film around. It's beautifully made, all the same.

February 18. We started rehearsals on MAN FOR ALL SEASONS. We're working so far without our Cromwell or Common Man (both are still in New York). God knows we had enough to do today, blocking the rest of it, but I still wish we could've had the whole cast, as well as three more days of rehearsal. Everyone'll be good in the roles, if they have time to get them down.

February 23. The thing's beginning to come together. Chris Carey gave me some good direction. I'm trying to lighten the part now and find the easy points in the scenes. This'll put some sun through the piece, I think, and still keep it true to the man. More important, it'll keep me well away from self-pity, which remains the prime trap for every actor in almost every part. For this actor, anyway.

February 24. The play moves along. Now we may do a week in Miami, just after Easter. I'm drawn by the chance to work on this part in a proscenium stage, which'll give me the experience of it in all three possibilities (except a circus tent, I guess).

In Chicago, where I'd done the part first, we'd staged MAN FOR ALL SEASONS in a full arena theater, with the audience seated on all sides of a circular stage. This presents certain advantages in terms of intimacy, but I've always felt there should be part of the set that's actors' country, to which the place and time of the play can be anchored. We came closer to this in Los Angeles, playing in three-quarters round. I was anxious to do the play again in a traditional proscenium theater. Now I'd like to try it one more time, in a proscenium theater, with an extended apron for certain parts of the play.

March 1. Opening A MAN FOR ALL SEASONS, Valley Music Theater. I think it went bloody well. The pressure of opening prevented as full and focused a performance as I hope I can give (the distraction of mentally reviewing just-finalized details of blocking . . . will the props work as planned, will the dresser remember the details of the changes?). Still, given those reservations, it worked. The power of the last scenes to lift me remains, and the audience came with me.

March 2. Well, after a long dry spell with the critics, I struck gold again. All five notices were incontestable raves, including really enormous personal notices for me. Lydia got good mentions, too. Of course, the adjustment you make to survive the bad notices means you have to discount the good ones, too, but it's still a comfortable ego-massage. I only hope the flu subsides: We should sell out the engagement. [*There was something of an epidemic in Los Angeles at the time. My concern for public health is touching.*]

March 4. Approval of the show continues to mount in an unbroken chorus of praise, which of course delights my slightly battered (this year) ego. Both Wyler and Stevens came back with extravagant things to say to me. That really meant more than the notices. If only Zinnemann could see it, I might get a chance at the film. Herman is making overtures to London, but I doubt there'll be any give there. Scofield created the part, after all. It's too bad; I know I could do it better. Really, I do.

I still do. Although Paul Scofield is one of the finest actors alive and was widely admired for his interpretation of Thomas More, the dry asceticism of his nature isn't close to the real More. Scofield's performance is still a memorable achievement. Nevertheless, More's sanguine physical quality is something I was able to reach in striving for the quality of his greatness.

March 7. This afternoon I went over to Fox for an hour to rehearse the test for THE PLANET OF THE APES. I'm a little sorry I agreed to do it, on a film not even approved yet, but I did agree. (So shut up and do it.)

Some weeks previously, Dick Zanuck had said, "Look, this is all fine, but what if people laugh at the makeup?" The point was reasonable, so was his offer to finance the research on the ape makeups. "We'll spend whatever it takes to get them right, then do a test. If the test works, we'll go on the film." Frank Schaffner and I agreed to do the test, and Eddie Robinson played Zaius, the ape played in the film by Maurice Evans.

March 8. Not a very long, or very hard day, doing my part in what, inevitably, is a selling job for PLANET OF THE APES. Herman's right in saying it's not a good idea, but I think Dick Zanuck needs it. The ape makeup is very good; it remains to be seen what they look like on film. Herman says United Artists has submitted Mitchum and Widmark for the other parts in WEST, which is OK with me. I'm still not certain it's something I want to do, though I seem to be slowly circling in on it, like a stick in a storm drain.

My misgivings on this film hardened, and I withdrew a few days later. I was readily dispensable; they did fine without me.

March 15. The APES test looked good. If the question is whether or not the ape makeup is laughable, the answer is no, it's very plausible. Chris Carey went on as the Common Man tonight and was very good. Horgan as the king was much less than that . . . was rather bad, in fact, I thought.

The success of the Los Angeles run caused them to extend it for a week. Two of the actors weren't able to fulfill this longer engagement and had to be replaced. This is always a dicey arrangement. Actors have to be chosen under pressure and usually have to go on with inadequate rehearsal. We were lucky Chris Carey, who'd directed the play, was good casting for the key role of the Common Man. Also, unlike most directors, he could act a bit.

March 17. Twenty-two years ago, I ran through the rain to a blue-roofed church and walked Lydia up the aisle, her hand on my bandaged one. I could hardly have hoped to be so happy today, or have so much. Today, I had a bit more . . . a cherry tree she bought me (there was one outside the church that day) and her pleasure in the portrait of the children I'd commissioned.

Lydia and I were married while she was still in school and I was about to go overseas with the air force. My hand was bandaged because I'd put my fist through a window in circumstances I have no intention of repeating here. She took the bus from Northwestern down to Greensboro, North Carolina, I got a weekend pass, and we picked the prettiest church we could find (Grace Methodist). The minister kindly performed the ceremony on two hours' notice, and I persuaded two ladies who were arranging flowers in the church basement to act as our witnesses.

March 29. Arthur Jacobs's office is going on again about Fox's interest in APES, but I can't help but discount it, in view of Arthur's past history on the piece. Dick Zanuck reported to Herman that PRO is not their dish . . . "too special" . . . was how DFZ in New York is reported to have labeled it. Well, at least we got a treatment out of them. This is a better way to go about it than we did on WAR LORD.

> *Maybe you're beginning to get the idea of what a long, tortuous, and disheartening process it is to get a film mounted. Arthur Jacobs was a man of absolutely unquenchable enthusiasm. Though he'd taken PLANET OF THE APES to every one of the major studios at least twice and had been turned down, he remained dauntlessly optimistic, a state of mind that seemed laughably unrealistic to me. I was wrong, Arthur was right.*
>
> *We traveled a long road to get PRO made, too. (That film was eventually released as NUMBER ONE.) From WAR LORD, I'd learned actors should not put their own money into scripts. Dick Zanuck had agreed to finance a treatment on PRO. When the treatment was completed, Darryl F. Zanuck, then still active in the company's affairs, passed for the studio.*

April 4, Miami [*Where we'd come to do MAN FOR ALL SEASONS again*]. The first day in Florida was sunny, with a humid Gulf wind like a breath in your ear. The theater's nicely redone from its former status as a vaudeville house. It'll be nice to play for a change in a theater with solid plaster and steel tormentors, a banked mezzanine, and raked auditorium. We'll have no trouble switching the play to a proscenium staging.

April 12. We didn't have enough run-through, but the opening went smoothly. I didn't think the audience was a good one, though God knows it was big. They liked it, but not with the electric kind of response we had in California. The performance was good, but not marvelous. (The party was, however.)

April 17 (Sunday). We wrapped it up today. It may be the last time I'll ever play Sir Thomas, though I hope not. We broke the house record, and I thought I gave the best performance I've managed yet in the evening show. I like what I arrived at with this play. It's time to put it away for a while.

April 19, Los Angeles. We got back home, underslept (especially Lydia) but happy. The ridge was bursting with spring, lush as a woman. I had my usual love affair with my own homecoming, even losing at tennis with complete equanimity. When Walter [*Seltzer*] came up, I found that National General had passed on PRO, but Marty Ransohoff still has an interest. It remains to be seen how vital it is.

April 20. Nothing stirring on PRO; Citron's quite right to counsel patience, as he did this morning. He also thinks we shouldn't peddle the project. I see his point (that it tarnishes my image as an eminently-in-demand actor), but I still want to move on this, however circumspectly.

Herman's point was valid. After an actor reaches a certain point in his career, he's supposed to sit in isolated splendor, selecting from among the offers humbly left at his door. This doesn't work quite as it should if the actor is also going around leaving humble offerings at other people's doors. Still, if you want to make films based on your own projects, the two concepts have to be somehow reconciled.

April 22. I spent most of the morning, after catching up on back letters, trying to balance our somewhat limited finances with my projected trip to Australia. (The State Department won't pick up the tab for the family, of course.) We may work something out; it'd be fun if they all came.

April 28. It develops the State Department is reluctant to change the film used in last year's White House Festival at all for my trip to Australia. This is understandable from their point of view, but Willy Wyler's not happy with his segment. It'd be better in many ways to substitute a piece from BIG COUNTRY, but that costs money that's not in the budget for the trip.

This was another one of those cultural junkets the State Department kept laying on for me during this period, with appearances at universities and so forth. The White House Festival film was fine for this purpose, but Willy felt the scene we'd chosen from FRIENDLY PERSUASION didn't work, out of the context of the whole film.

April 30. More California heat, more tennis; a muscle-spending day. Tonight we went to a party that oppressed me. Standing in a crowd with no one I knew I felt as I did in the old days in school. I dislike meeting new people still. One of the problems of being a sanguine, unproblemed man is that no one ever believes your neuroses.

May 16. Julian B., back from cutting KHARTOUM, says it's ready for answer print. [*This means all the editing has been finished (on a black-and-white work print), the musical score and sound tracks have been dubbed together, so the negative can be cut, and balanced color prints run from it.*] He was full of heartening opinions from reliable and disinterested sources about the film. I don't question the honesty of the opinions, nor the accuracy with which he quotes them. I've learned, though, that none of it counts till the film gets in the theater and people go . . . or don't go. Everyone can be right; the film can be good, even great. But if nobody sees it, it doesn't count.

True enough. Never mind posterity. Nobody's yet rediscovered and enshrined a failed film. Mind you, this doesn't mean a successful film is necessarily a good one. A lot of them are lousy. Equally, many fine films are flops. And they still don't count.

May 18. That State Department trip's growing like a weed, choking up the whole garden. Now they want me to go to Rangoon and Bangkok as well. This excited Lydia wildly, of course; now she wants to come there with me. In that case, I won't go to Vietnam this trip, obviously. We could deposit our offspring in Australia somewhere . . . maybe with the Isaacs, until we get back to join them on the Barrier Reef. It looks like a complicated three weeks.

May 21. I spent most of the morning helping Lydia persuade my daughter in and out of a series of dresses for a magazine layout for Father's Day. She looked, I must say, enchanting. But I don't want her used that way again, however much it feeds my father's ego. This is the last layout like that for Holly.

I've always been reluctant to use my children as props for my public relations. Actually, they do interviews with cool aplomb, having understood all their lives that in air terminals and other public places they must respond courteously to interviewers' random questions. I no longer feel that home is the place for any kind of prepared publicity.

May 31. It seems now almost pointless to record my impressions of my own films (the main reason I started these damn journals), since I have been so spectacularly off recently. Nevertheless, for the record: KHARTOUM seemed to me to be a very, very good film. The script is literate, with some of the best writing of the year. All the performances are good, including mine.

June 6, London. We arrived in better than good time, I took my planned patches of sleep [in *the backs of limousines, the corners of TV studios. I'm very good at this.*] and did my chores. I met the critics after the press screening of KHARTOUM. They either liked the film, or the ones who didn't avoided me. I'm still skeptical of the good reactions I'm getting to this one.

June 9. The important thing, of course, was the royal premiere of KHARTOUM. I'm still as suspicious as a surly sow on ice of trusting my own or anyone else's early reactions, but it seems clear the British critical response will be good. We've gotten five notices, only one less than a rave, and several say this is my best work so far. The audience tonight was very enthusiastic (and I'm able now to separate the polite murmurs from the enthusiasm of people who liked what they saw). This audience liked what they saw.

June 10, London/Washington, D.C. The postpremiere party, for once, could fairly be called a celebration. It thus ran far into the morning hours, but we (Lydia) finished most of the packing before falling into bed for a minimal few hours of sleep. We made our separate planes (Lydia's off for the weekend with her family in Two Rivers) in good time. I caught up on a little more sleep and arrived in D.C. ready for what proved a very simple (dare I say unnecessary?) briefing at the State Department on the details of my Far East trip. It appears Burma's now out of the picture, Indonesia may be in.

June 11, Detroit. My duties posing in a Buick interior (in return for being given one) were not very onerous. [*I really hate having done this, but I did.*] The hardest part consisted of taping studs on my shirt, since I'd come back from England without a clean dress shirt for my dinner jacket. Russ seemed weak and older, but less so than I'd feared. His strength is very low, but he made a touching effort to be up for my visit. I've not seen him since last November, when he seemed worse than he is now. Maybe I can get him to come out this summer.

June 12 (Sunday), To Minneapolis. The day passed in an easy drift of hours, chatting with Russ, lying in the sunstruck shadowed haze of a midwestern backyard reading Sandburg for my tour poems. Kay went to the airport with me, and the bumpy flight over the lake and up to Minneapolis was wondrous.

June 15, Lincoln, Nebraska. I discovered to my horror that I was scheduled to address the Chamber of Commerce on foreign policy . . . well, on Vietnam, but that means foreign policy these days, as I pointed out. I faked through it somehow (not bad, actually), then off for Lincoln, where I rode in a parade, chatted with Ladybird, and dined with the governor (ahhh, the uses of power . . .). A long, western kind of day.

June 17, Denver/Los Angeles. I cut short the Denver schedule and jetted home [*God, I sound like* People *magazine*] for a last day with the family, and found Fray down with a rash of some kind which required taking him to a doctor instead of New Zealand. It's not serious, but Lydia decided to postpone her departure for a week and leave with me. I'll be glad to have them here with me a little longer, not to mention on the plane.

June 23, Los Angeles. Hollywood premiere, KHARTOUM. The opening, to the usual horrible audience of benefit people, seemed to go well. The

L.A. *Times* has already printed a rave and we can hope for the other two papers here, as well. We seem to've done very well so far. I really think we may have one of my best films here.

June 25, For New Zealand. The whole day sank without a trace in a morass of my gloom over still another trip. It's really too bad that all these voyages, the kind people save two years for, are for me just one link after another in an endless chain of the same-smelling air terminals, the same-smiling hostesses, the same bags to carry, and the same shirts to get laundered. Also, I have some misgivings about my programs there.

On this trip I was doing a series of readings similar to what I'd done in Egypt and Nigeria, combining significant American literature (if possible relating to the area I was visiting) with selections from the literature of the country I was visiting. In this case there were obvious choices from Australian and American literature. I think my misgivings had to do with the fact that I hadn't gotten around to cutting the selections I'd chosen.

June 27, Auckland, New Zealand. The plane was some six hours late into Auckland, but I managed to touch all the bases laid on, including a dinner given by the American consul here. Auckland is cold, rather like Manchester in January (it's winter here), but the welcome was both warm and diligent. I've finally assembled my reading program. Typically, I edited the last chapter of MOBY DICK on the plane.

I left Lydia, Fray, and Holly in New Zealand to explore more of that beautiful country than I had time for. I went on to do my State Department chores in Australia, where they were to join me later.

July 1, Sydney. Sydney is as I remember, with the big, roughly beautiful bridge spanning the harbor, but the city's larger than it was, with something of a traffic jam now. We had a small one of our own at the airport, trying to accomplish the usual interviews while the British foreign minister was trying to do the same thing. I finally did it all, as well as a full press schedule at the hotel, and finished off with a great plate of Sydney rock oysters and a Foster's beer.

We're all conditioned to resisting high-pressure advertising claims for the virtues of one soap or one brand of car over another. Sydney's rock oysters really are, hands down, the best in the world. I have them for breakfast in Australia.

July 3, Canberra. Canberra is a very impressive town . . . high in the hills inland from Sydney, bright, thin-aired, planned as Washington probably once looked when it was young. I stayed at our embassy, which looks very Williamsburgy, sleeping in a bed barely cool after Secretary Dean Rusk's stay for the SEATO conference. I had a full day, ending with an offhand sort of dinner hosted by our very folksy ambassador. I guess that's a mark of LBJ's group.

July 5, Melbourne. Melbourne in winter is still not my favorite town . . . a little dank and blowsy, I'd say . . . but I had very successful readings, both at the university, where we crowded nearly a thousand people into a theater built for 250, and in the evening for an older, much quieter crowd. I felt it went really well, for both audiences. This program is working better than I thought it would.

July 9, Brisbane. I fiddled through the morning with growing frustration as I realized how late the plane bringing my family to me would be. They finally arrived with winter dusk falling over the airport as we whisked them through customs and into the hotel, where they somehow changed in time to be lovely for Bill and Clori Isaac's party, where everyone shone. A happy time . . . Holly and Shauna singing for the guests, Fray lecturing on the New Zealand glaciers. It was fine.

July 14, Sailed for Great Barrier Reef with both families on cruiser Gypsy. At last we undertook the adventure we've been aiming this whole trip for and it's all we hoped. The reef, reached after a roughish crossing, is quite incredible. We anchored and explored while it was awash at low tide. The colors, the corals, the sponges are all part of an experience you couldn't duplicate anywhere else in the world. The company's special, too. I've never read MOBY DICK better than on deck after supper, anchored, the reef hidden at high tide.

July 16, Reef to Hayman Island. We made an easy crossing in, a porpoise swimming under our bow. Five miles out, a green sea snake passed us, coolly turning its head to watch, and then a full-rigged barkentine, outbound from Hayman. It could hardly have been a better trip. That reef was the highlight for us, I think . . . of this or almost any other vacation.

July 18, Hayman Island. We spent the day on that barkentine we saw coming in from the reef. It's the first time I've been under three masts full of canvas, with the sea hissing under the bowsprit. It's a marvelous feeling; you suddenly understand Conrad and all the sea writing you've ever read. I stood and held the wheel and felt it kick, and thought of the opening lines of the last chapter of MOBY DICK . . . "The morning of the third day dawned fresh and fair . . ."

July 19. An interesting morning in which I managed to get stranded with Fray on a small islet where we'd gone in a motor dory where I'd promised to let him lunch while Lydia packed. While we struggled to dig up a giant clamshell the size of a bloody washtub, the tide went out, leaving us stranded with the dory hard aground. We were picked up by a passing motor cruiser, which spotted us when I tied my red trunks to the end of our oar, a move that seemed to delight the girls on board. We got home just in time to catch the plane for Sydney and civilization.

July 21, Sydney/Los Angeles. In Mark Twain's theory, this made up for the day we lost going the other way. It certainly was a crowded one. I did interviews all morning so I'd have time to take Holly to the zoo, where she held a koala as I remember Fray doing in . . . '6o? Then the Hopkins took us to the plane for that jolly seventeen hours in the air, and we were home to find the Seltzers waving a champagne bottle and the sun just setting over Coldwater . . . all in one day.

July 22, Los Angeles. My first day back in harness, the problem of untangling the thread of my life here and getting it stitched into place was complicated by the back problem Lydia picked up slipping on the reef, contorting madly in midair to save her cameras from falling in the drink. Now she's laid up, poor baby. KHARTOUM is getting great notices all round, but not uniformly great business, sorry to say.

I don't know which is more frustrating: to have a film get marvelous notices and do no business, or do fabulous business and get poor notices. I've had it both ways. The only place where KHARTOUM *got both good notices and good business was in England, which pleased me.*

July 27. Lunch today with Herman confirmed my growing conviction that he's not enthusiastic about PRO. Walter's had a nibble from one of the team owners who thinks he wants to be a producer. This seems an unlikely avenue to me, but I'm willing to explore it. There is no other project that interests me more. We're still looking for directors on the Universal film.

August 5. I did that festival narration that's been hanging fire for so long. It was a little dicey, since I had to wing it all, but I snuck through on it one more time. (There'll come a day, I suppose, when I can't cut the mustard on that bit of professional legerdemain . . . but not yet, happily.)

"Winging" is actor's slang for memorizing material that you only have to use once. You kind of float it on the top of your mind. I can wing fifteen or twenty lines of dialogue in about five minutes and hold it long enough to do it.

August 10. I read the first forty pages of a damn good Western . . . if the rest is up to the beginning, it could really be something.

This was WILL PENNY. When I'd finished it, I told Walter Seltzer, "This is really fantastic. I think we can get Huston or Wyler or Stevens interested in this one." "Well, there's a catch, Chuck," Walter said. "The writer wants to direct it." "What's he done?" I said. "Just some TV," he replied. "Ohhhh, come on Walter," I demurred. "You must be kidding." "I may be kidding," said Walter, "but he's not. If he doesn't get to direct it, he won't sell it." The decision took me five seconds. "I just changed my mind," I said.

August 17. I spent the morning unburdening myself to the Stanford Research people of my thoughts, random and otherwise, on what the shape of the projected American Film Institute should be. I maybe made some sense, here and there. I *know* we must avoid beginning by erecting a large building.

August 24. A very busy morning, wearing various hats [*for SAG, the State Department, and myself*], ending at lunch where I met Tom Gries, who wrote WILL PENNY and is determined to direct it. The script's so good, there's really nothing else to do but give him a go at it.

August 25. We finally picked a director for BATTLE HORNS [*the title was changed to* COUNTERPOINT]. I looked at a reel or two of a very ordinary comedy, very ordinarily translated to film by another man, but this didn't tell me as much as I already knew about Ralph Nelson, who's made two excellent films and did well in the old live TV days, too.

August 30, Washington, D.C. I stepped on for another ride on what feels more and more like my personal Washington merry-go-round. I got there in good time for the White House limo, checked into the new Hilton, sweated an hour on the courts, then over to the Watergate to read some Jefferson as part of a concert for the kids who worked during the summer on the proliferating federal programs to aid poverty and education simultaneously.

August 31, Detroit. I caught the late jet for Detroit and stopped the night. Russ looks better than when I was here last, but still very feeble. He had an attack during the evening which set him back and shook us all. I still hope he can come out for Christmas. I feel . . . sad and desperate.

September 1, Los Angeles. My father died this afternoon, while I was flying over the mountains, coming home. I must have known he couldn't live long when I saw him sit with drooping head at his own table and shuffle with painful care from room to room. Still . . . to have him dead is hard and hurtful. Not for him. He was ready, I think, but I'm not. I remember him strong and taller than I.

September 2. I kept my appointments, watched my son take his tennis lesson, hit some balls myself, and fit into my life the fact that my father is dead. That's what happens . . . life goes on, like a stream flowing at the same speed, over the same bed as before, making only a ripple or two over the rock that's dropped into it.

September 3, Detroit. The Stines having come to stay at the house for a few days, we left for Detroit with no misgivings about leaving Holly and only a few about Lydia traveling so far so soon out of traction. She seemed all right through the difficult tribal rite at the funeral home and the tribal gathering at the house afterward. I hated to see my father with a painted wax face, lying like a doll in a velvet coffin.

September 4. There was a memorial service today. I didn't find it easy, but it wasn't designed for me. I know Velda got some comfort from it; surely it filled some of the hard hours she now fears to find empty. There were many people there . . . more than I would've thought, though I knew his capacity for making friends. They all wanted to be there, and then come and talk and drink a little.

September 5, St. Helen. We chartered a light plane north and buried my father in the woods. I felt better being there, in a clearing cut out of the forest my grandfather saw half a century ago. There was a light rain falling as we carried the leaden weight of the coffin, slipping on the leaves, with his old friends helping. Then I went to the house where I was a boy, and I drove with my son over the roads and trails my father drove over with me . . . and it was much better.

September 7, Los Angeles. Not a lot to do here, though things are heading into a busy time. We're waiting for United Artists' reaction to WILL PENNY. I'll go in tomorrow and work on COUNTERPOINT. Other than that, nothing but the healing sore of Russ's death. And it does heal. The sun goes down and the sun also rises.

September 8. Jimmy Lee is out to do a rewrite on COUNTERPOINT, which I think is strongly indicated. It's hard to say what he'll do, but his ideas on the restructuring seem good ones . . . eliminate the subplot, add some texture to the character of Evans. I was shocked to find the United Artists board turned down the WILL PENNY script three to two. I can't believe they don't recognize the value of this. I may open a candy store.

September 9. The only new development was a call from De Sica in Paris. He wants me to play a part in the Shirley MacLaine film he's shooting there. He described it as a good cameo, which is attractive from several points of view. I'd like to work with him, also with her, and it would be nice to have ten days or so in Europe, so I could attend the opening of my exhibit in London. Still, it might be wise to read the script first.

I draw a little bit. I have all my life. It's always seemed to me that the true pleasure of any art is the amateur's pleasure. The professional should set standards for his work too high for him ever to be pleased by what he's done. I'm told Andrew Wyeth and his family are devoted to amateur theatricals at holidays. I'm sure he gets more pleasure from acting than I do and, knowing what I do of how many of his own canvases he destroys, I imagine I get more pleasure out of drawing than he does. I was putting this pleasure at stake when I agreed to let an exhibit of some of my drawings be hung in a London gallery.

September 12. I began what's going to be one helluva daunting assignment: learning to pretend to conduct. Unlike, say, charioteering, jousting, and fresco painting, where I was at least familiar with the territory, this is a new line of country entirely. As always, though, work will do it. Poco a poco, as we musicians say.

This turned out to be the toughest thing I've ever learned for a part. (Oddly enough, one of the most physically exhausting, too. I used to come out of the sessions dripping with sweat. I don't see how Arthur Fiedler does it.) Leo Damiani, a California conductor, spent two months of almost daily sessions coaching me into a plausible semblance of a symphony conductor for COUNTERPOINT. *Since I can't read music, he even invented a simplified system of musical notation, so I could memorize the scores.*

September 13. I spent the day up to my neck in conducting. I'm trying to learn the Mozart MARRIAGE OF FIGARO overture, for God's sake. I read the script from De Sica. Unfortunately, it's nothing. I'm disappointed. Of course, you have to give some weight to De Sica as a factor, but it still doesn't seem worth doing.

September 16. Tonight I saw DARK CITY [*my first film*] for the first time in sixteen years. (Sixteen years!) It's not bad, other than the omnipresence of musical numbers for Liz Scott to sing in it, but it's really nothing more than the kind of movie they make now for television. I'm fat, callow, and trying too hard. The best I can say, I suppose, is what I can always say: I could do it better now.

September 19. Dick Zanuck turned down WILL PENNY at Fox. There's still much wheel-spinning about getting me to do the cameo for De Sica. I also worked away on my conducting and attended a dinner tonight for Governor Brown, extolling the virtues of his incumbency as opposed to "the monstrous threat from Reagan." It's hard to take this seriously, really.

September 23. There seem to be some stirrings from Fox on PLANET OF THE APES, which I thought had long since disappeared. (The success of FANTASTIC VOYAGE obviously is triggering this interest.) Meantime, WILL PENNY has gone to all the studios with no takers. I'm up to my ass four hours a day on the opening thirty bars of the Beethoven Fifth, which takes about all I've got.

Eventually, my limited repertoire included not only the Beethoven but the last half of the second movement of the Brahms Second Symphony, most of the Overture to TANNHÄUSER, and the Overture to Tchaikovsky's SWAN LAKE.

September 26. A very busy day for deals. It turns out Lew Wasserman at Universal decided he liked WILL PENNY (or me in some film) the same day Dick Zanuck decided to go on APES. We'll do the Western first, as soon as I finish COUNTERPOINT, then off to England in the spring for APES. This is a staggering amount of work, but at least it shows the commodity's still hot.

September 27. Universal still hasn't finalized on WILL PENNY (which we'll have to retitle . . . that won't do, no question). [*Wrong again.*] Meantime, Herman made the deal at Fox: the usual guarantee against a percentage of the gross. They want to pay a flat sum for expenses in London, which is all right, I suppose. [*Oddly enough, Universal didn't make WILL PENNY, and we didn't shoot APES in England, though I'm damned if I can remember why.*]

September 30. I sent off the sketches for the exhibit which will end my cherished status as an amateur drawer. It's probably a bad idea, but it appeals to my vanity, even though I know damn well they'll sell not because they're good drawings (only a dozen or so are that anyway) but because I'm an actor. That's a helluva reason to buy a sketch. Of course it's the same reason I figured in the party for Ted Kennedy at Jennings Lang's tonight. I think I've discovered something: Assembled in lots of more than half a dozen, Democrats tend to be a pain in the ass. I suppose Republicans do too, but I don't see so many of them.

Although I've never belonged to either party, I really think this is true, and I suppose I've cast eighty percent of my votes for Democratic candidates. Maybe it comes from being the majority party, but they tend to be a little loudmouthed, a little softheaded, and terribly sure of themselves.

October 6. Walter Seltzer called to say he's made a deal for WILL PENNY, at Paramount. It'll be my first time there since PIGEON. I'm pleased, though it'd be simpler, geographically, to make it at Universal. In theory, I now know the entire first movement of the Beethoven Fifth, but in practice I have only the most fragile kind of hold on it. I understand now how insecure actors blow lines: There's simply no way to hold something firmly in your head that you're not totally confident about.

October 25. We'd hoped to test some actresses for COUNTERPOINT today, but it jammed up somehow. Anne Heywood and Jessica Walter seem to be our prime candidates. Now we'll start November 17, I think. Lydia's almost convinced I'm right about getting Fray into Harvard [*a prep school in Los Angeles*] next year. On the other hand, Fray's a long way from being convinced, but he doesn't need to be. I can still tell him.

October 31. A long conducting session, fighting to get a grip on SWAN LAKE, but today was Halloween, always an important holiday in this family (probably because it involves performances). Fray made a fine martian, courtesy of the studio makeup department, and Holly was an enchanting fairy princess, though she flatly refused to alter one detail of her dime store costume. "It *won't* be like all the others! It'll have *me* in it!"

November 8. It was a rainy Election Day, but the people chose again . . . California went Republican by nearly a million votes. On Election Day, I always get asked if I'm a candidate. My current answer is "Yes, for pope." Ralph and I like Anne Heywood, Dick Berg liked Kathy Hays. (So, I think, did the boys in the big black tower.) Since I have no approval on this part, this is where we'll go, I would imagine. This is OK, really; she should be fine. Max Schell struck me as a most interesting but exhausted actor. [*He was just off a jet from Germany.*] He'll be rested, I hope, by the time we start.

November 20. I got up very early, having gotten in very late from the party for Norman Jewison, to attend a not very productive rehearsal with Max on the first scene we have tomorrow. My speech at the annual membership meeting of the SAG seemed a success, as was the whole meeting. We had a good turnout, largely to see Governor-elect Reagan present the SAG award to Barbara Stanwyck. The dinner tonight for George Jessel was damn stupid; a four-hour display of the humor of insult, a peculiarly American institution.

December 2. A bloody frustrating day. It began well with my first session facing the full orchestra. It wasn't full, actually, but there were a lot of them. Standing in front of a symphony orchestra gives you a great feeling of power, I must say. It's better than parting the Red Sea, since you feel God's less inclined to help.

December 21. I actually conducted the orchestra through SWAN LAKE, without benefit of the tape. Not a memorable performance . . . indeed, you could probably say it may have been one of the worst performances ever given of the work . . . but I did it myself. It was quite an exhilarating experience.

December 25. The day is less and less for me each year, and more and more for the kids, which is as it should be. My statue for Lydia was a big flop . . . she thought it was a gag, unfortunately, which put me in a pout. Otherwise, the day was as good as they always are . . . Fray swinging in his new hammock in the thin winter sun.

December 29. They've switched to night shooting again, but not with me, save for one shot, so I had a very easy day again. I didn't use it to particular advantage except to work on the Brahms, where I need it, God knows. I ran enough rough-cut film to decide, again, that you really can't tell from looking at rough-cut. All you can say is whether it's lousy. This isn't. Whether it makes a film, I can't tell. What *does* make a film, anyway? What combination of audience receptivity and originality of ingredients . . . story, casting, approach, coupled with what degree of actual artistry? (Surely this last is always in short supply, no matter what anyone says.) Antonioni's BLOW-UP tonight, for example, was very well made. Hardly great, but valuable, I guess, and certainly original.

December 30. A full day going round and round with Walter and Tom on who should be the girl in WILL PENNY. They're very high on Lee Remick, who's a good actress, but seems very contemporary to me. I don't know if she'd be much help at the box office, either. (I know: "Who is?") We went over all this endlessly, without coming to any conclusions. We'll "talk further." I really hate having to fight through this, especially since I don't really feel I *know.* Christ, who does?

December 31. We expected to see the old year out with the Isaacs in Vegas, but just as we were about to step into the car with the Matches for the drive to the airport, Lydia's back went out with a loud *poinng!* She's really in agony, poor kitten; otherwise I'd have been quite happy to spend the weekend here quietly with my children instead of noisily in Vegas with my friends. Fray and I saw the New Year in rather sleepily (I was, anyway) in front of the fire, looking at the televised hilarity from Times Square. We talked a bit. My last look at him as the year turned was of a boy older than I'm ready for, somehow. This happens to me all the time. Still, it's been a good year. I didn't get to film MAN FOR ALL SEASONS, and KHARTOUM didn't kill 'em, but I did good work in both and was well regarded by my peers.

1967

Will Penny . . .

sailing the
Greek Islands . . .

Planet of the Apes . . .

revisiting Vietnam . . .

working for the
Screen Actors Guild
and the National
Endowment for
the Arts.

In the far West as *Will Penny*
LYDIA HESTON

In the future (with Roddy
MacDowell and Kim Stanley) in
Planet of the Apes
TWENTIETH CENTURY FOX

January 3, Los Angeles. I spent most of the day and all the good sense I could scrape up trying to cast the woman's role in WILL PENNY. I still don't see Lee Remick, who is the studio's choice, in this part. I have approval, but I can't bring myself to veto her casting, let alone impose my own choice. I suppose I'm more interested in being a good guy than in having it go right.

January 4. After an agonizing reappraisal, I finally decided I'd rather say to them "I told you so!" six months from now than risk having them say it to me. I called Walter and told him to go ahead on Remick. After all, in the classic phrase, it's only a movie.

The woman's role in WILL was a marvelous part, but very hard to cast, perhaps partly because she was described in the script as a plain woman. Also, for reasons I've never understood, the opinions of those making the choices of who is right for a woman's part are always much more sharply divided and more firmly held than they are on the men's roles. Doubtless Gloria Steinem would detect a sinister reason for this, but I can't.

January 11. In the COUNTERPOINT scene tonight, I had an interesting problem: to handle the weapons, as Evans would, like a man who knew nothing about them. I think I seemed properly clumsy. I *was* clumsy, when I fell over a trailer hitch just before dawn: I thought I'd cracked my damn kneecap. That's one trouble with extended night shooting: You get tired and careless. It hurts like hell, though I'll no doubt survive. All the fuss over Remick was for nothing: She turned the part down. We'll now go with Jean Simmons, I gather. The woman should be plain, which Jean (God knows) is not, but she's a helluva good actress, no matter what Bob Evans says. We arrived at a pretty good idea of what Will should look like, I think, as well as most of the wardrobe. I haven't really begun to get inside the part yet, but the look is the beginning, then you dig for the center. [*I do anyway. Some actors go the other way, though I don't see how.*]

January 13. I had a brute of a day, shooting from nine till after seven on the Brahms. As I suspected, Ralph *did* need to cover me conducting all of it, and from several angles, too. It's a damn good thing I went ahead and learned it. Of course they can't possibly stay with the orchestra throughout the movement, with two other scenes to cover during the music. Also of course, there's no way to tell before editing *when* they will be cutting back. Therefore you cover it all. Elementary. At Walter's tonight, we found Jean Simmons won't be available in time for WILL. So now we go to Eva Marie Saint, I suppose. She's closer physically to our frontier woman, and a good actress to boot.

January 16. The shooting was a series of inconsequential, not very
   interesting shots . . . the kind of thing you run into toward the close
   of a schedule, when they're finishing off actors and sets. We found
   out Eva Marie Saint doesn't want to do WILL either. I guess the part
   doesn't seem good enough (or glamorous enough?) to attract a name,
   which surprises me; the quality of the script and the role seems so
   clear to me. They're wrong.

*They were, too. This was one of the best women's parts of that year.
   At* least *that year. In the end, it worked out for the best. Joan
   Hackett, who accepted the part soon after, couldn't have been
   bettered.*

January 19. I had time this morning to work with the orchestra until I
   had the Beethoven well in hand. There's honestly nothing quite like
   the feeling of power you get lifting a baton and seeing eighty
   musicians respond. We shot the Fifth all afternoon and did very well,
   except for the usual demonstration of general slobbery displayed by
   some of the extras. We got through far more than we'd figured on
   today, at least, so we're almost finished with them, thank God.

*There are of course some fine professionals in the Screen Extras
   Guild, but the work by and large doesn't warrant the extremely
   high daily wage negotiated by the union, all of whose members are
   desperately underemployed as a result. I've always felt extra work
   should be made available to the elderly, the handicapped, students,
   and other unemployed and needy groups.*

January 24. A long day, but we wrapped COUNTERPOINT. I think the last
   day's work was good. The scene (the same one we'd used to test all
   the girls in) went much better with Ralph's restaging. My feeling
   overall is that the film may be in the footage, all I hope to know at
   this point. We have certain weaknesses . . . not in the writing,
   exactly, but in the genre. It's a melodrama, after all. The music's a
   plus and may prove to be more than that if they notice the work I've
   put into it. (On the other hand, why the hell *should* they notice?)

January 25. It's odd to have the film behind me, though it's strange to be
   stepping into a new one so soon, with hardly a breathing space
   between. I wish passionately I didn't have to do this damn reading
   thing in Washington first, but there seems no escape from it.
   Meantime, I've read seventy pages of Michael Wilson's new script on
   APES, which seems to me immensely good, an improvement on the
   Rod Serling script. I must begin looking ahead to the next roles, not
   back on the last ones.

January 29 (Sunday). A quiet morning on the courts, in which I failed to
   play very well. I should've spent more of the day working; God knows

I've got enough on my plate. All I did was fiddle a little with the SUNRISE AT CAMPOBELLO reading. [*I was to read the play at a White House reception marking the presentation of a new portrait of FDR.*] I find myself getting into these things and then approaching them under some sort of a pall, wondering how it happened.

January 31, Washington, D.C. It was quite a day. I was quite keyed up. It's a helluva thing to play that part in that place in front of an audience composed entirely of FDR's blood relatives and close friends. They were all very complimentary. LBJ gave what I thought was a moving talk, accepting the painting ". . . this painting will hang where I can see it . . . where I *need* it."

February 1. A busy morning, trying to include all the things I had to do, and the main thing Lydia wanted to do. One of the problems of my life is that there's too little room for the quiet times together. I'm uneasy to note that any of the two or three public-sector jobs I've taken on now could be full time. You fall short of what you should contribute to each one, not to mention your career and your marriage. I'm glad Lydia was with me this trip. She held the Bible when I took the oath as a Councillor on the Arts, then we had a good, if compressed, tour through the Smithsonian.

Since appointments to the National Council on the Arts were by the president, you had to be sworn in formally. I can't remember what it was we swore to do. Not waste the public money, I hope.

February 2. I had a long, abstract, but useful lunch with Tom Gries, talking acting, directing, and such trivialities for two hours. Then I was presented with a problem I mishandled badly. Joe Canutt found that the horse we'd picked from Ralph McCutcheon's stable for me to ride in WILL was not sound, and hesitated to tell Ralph, to save his feelings. I went along with this; now I realize I have to go out and see Ralph and be frank with him. This will be embarrassing but, I suppose, good for the soul. No progress on the studio tour problem. They still want to bring tours on sets, for which they're charging the tourists.

I was involved in this because the Screen Actors Guild felt that its members shouldn't be required to perform for the commercial tours that were then planned at several studios. They still do the tours, but they don't visit the working sets.

February 7, Bishop, California (location for WILL PENNY). Today I plunged off into the wilderness again, as I have so many times before. At the end of the journey a comfortable apartment waited for me . . . a variation on the many I've lived in on all the other locations. The town could be Marysville, or Kanab . . . or even Durango in English.

London, Rome, or Madrid it couldn't be . . . there is that comfort to foreign location; the Dorchester has it all over the Ace Travel Lodge. Bishop will be a damn dreary place for five weeks . . . but I'll have the family up for most of it. I've learned to kind of run under banked fires on locations anyway; I sort of half–shut up shop.

February 9. It's curious how quickly the time passes on location. The days are long, hard, and soon over. Your energy lasts through dinner, a drink or two, then bed is all you want. We got another good day, though we didn't quite meet the schedule, I noted. Tom shoots a lot with multiple cameras . . . more than any director I've seen, in fact. We have four, for this week we're working with the cattle herd. Hard to tell what'll come of it till we see some daily, but we got a lot of film exposed, including some fair bucking footage.

February 10. The day seemed longer . . . and harder. I was in the saddle for every shot, but it was the wind that washed fatigue through all of us, all day. It picked up from first light and flung a plume of pale dust behind every rider, every steer that moved. It wears through you, on a long day like this, though it'll make the shots we got better. I thought today's stuff played well, and the dailies from Wednesday looked good. (If you feel careless, you can say they were marvelous.)

February 11. We started on the wrong foot today and had to shift the first setup because of light problems, but it worked out well as we went on. My problem with Will seems to be simply one of correctly balancing the laconic flatness the character and dialogue require, against the comment the scene often demands. It's no great trick to reach; you just need a few takes to get it right. I finished early and got a head start on the long drive home. It wasn't hard to take, stretched on a mattress in the back of a station wagon.

February 13. Fray's first day here. He rides better, sits taller in the saddle, and seemed to have a totally marvelous time racketing around the prairie on his own. He met some old friends, including some who helped float him down the Nile in that basket twelve years ago. He's growing; now there are sealed-off corridors in his mind that I no longer have the key to, as it should be. The shooting went OK, though we had trouble with the horse lie-down. [*I've forgotten why we wanted this, but it's not an easy cue to train into a horse.*]

February 18. The day was complicated by delays. I'm aware that my capacity for patient waiting is diminishing as I get older, but the first shot this morning really took too goddamn long to set up. I felt the scenes themselves, including our first work with Joan Hackett, went well. She's bloody good.

February 19 (Sunday), Los Angeles/Bishop. I spent two hours on PRO today with Herb Jaffe. He feels it's almost unfeasible for United Artists, but he'll at least investigate it with his New York folks, if I'm willing to undertake it for no guarantee. [*I was naïve. If he really felt it was unfeasible, he wouldn't have been discussing it. He was negotiating, and happy to be doing it with me instead of Citron.*] The drive up to Bishop with my family was long, but not wearisome, really. We arrived at the outskirts of town in time for a good meal, then we all tucked into bed in my not-quite-large-enough apartment.

February 24, Bishop. One helluva day. Lydia agreed to do a bit in the film, as a convenience for them. I don't think she enjoyed it, really, though she's obviously far better than anyone they could've gotten. We spent an inordinate time getting the wagon into town, then had to rush like hell to get the interior shot. Fortunately since it *was* an interior, we could shoot well after dark. We did.

February 28. We covered most of the fight today, and a long and miserable time it was. I can still manage scenes like that, but it makes you ready for bed at night. Tom's shooting this slowly, but we're getting the angles we need. Lots of close-ups, which many directors neglect in action footage. We're working at higher altitude now: The daily run is a little tougher. But we still chug away, inspired by the professional running reputation of Bruce Dern to egg us on. [*Bruce, who was just coming into prominence as an actor then, started me on running. I hate him for it.*]

March 5 (Sunday), Los Angeles. Today was a good day. Fray and I entered our first father-son tourney. It was about his tenth match in which they kept score, but we managed runner-up. Fray's delight was the richest prize I could've gotten. He played steadily, without much apparent tension, bore down on several points he needed, and generally comported himself well. His prize was the sense of value he can now put on that part of himself.

March 6, Los Angeles/Bishop. I got up in the chilly darkness to catch the light plane taking me back to work. The extra night in my own bed was worth the early rising. We're coming to the end now; we spent a long day doing unimportant pickup shots around the shack: carrying wood, milking cows (a task for which I find I have no aptitude). I found Fox is assigning Leon Shamroy as cameraman on APES, while Universal is taking Ralph Nelson off the editing of COUNTERPOINT. Both moves seem to be errors. I called Herman and made loud noises about it.

I was wrong about Leon. Though he'd been very slow on AGONY AND
THE ECSTASY, *taking much more than the camera's share of each
working day, he shot* APES *with great creativity and efficiency. I
was distressed at the studio's move to take Ralph off the final
editing of* COUNTERPOINT, *on the principle that a director should
always stay with a picture through its editing.*

March 10, Bishop. Another balmy day . . . our snow's melting a little
each day; we're covering the bare spots with detergent foam,
satisfactory enough in close angles, but we can't cover enough
ground for a long shot. It's also too slippery to work in for fight
scenes. (For sex scenes, it would be fine, but we don't *have* any sex
scenes.)

March 13. We arrived on the set today to find it covered in six inches of
new snow. This is exactly what we need, five days late. Now we have
to reshoot what we did last week, except for the close-ups. Tom
insisted on starting with the scene he wanted to do up here all along:
sitting on the log with the boy. This seemed a waste of our fragile
snowfall; we could shoot that scene easily on a sound stage. Still, I
felt reluctant to push to a showdown on this with Tom. He has to
choose.

March 15. Waiting for the first setup this morning, Tom began talking
extravagantly in terms of staying here through next Monday, which
is totally unrealistic. I called Walter out for a heart-to-heart, and this
concept vanished. "A misunderstanding." But it hadn't been. With our
lovely snow melting away beneath us, we *must* race to finish the
shots we need in it. We managed today's stuff, except for some of the
insert car [*a multipurpose camera vehicle*] shots. I did my shot
driving the wagon OK (it's a little easier than a chariot), but thank
God Joe Canutt vetoed Lee Majors driving it down. The camera car
ran off the road and we would've smashed into it sure as hell if
anyone but Joe Irigoyen, doubling Lee, had been driving. I talked
with Walter about United Artists' offer on PRO: me taking nothing
ahead, Walter and Frank Schaffner taking a small sum, with the three
of us splitting up seventy-five percent of the profits. [*Lest you
wonder, this is* not *a good deal. It's the kind you get offered when
you want to make a film more than the studio does.*]

March 17. We managed to piece out the remaining angles on the rain
sequence by shooting in the shadow of a building. [*Luckily, it had
rained the day before, just when we were doing a sequence, for
once, where rain was good. It was clear again this day.*] We have to
go back up to the line shack tomorrow for the last insert shots, but
we'll only be fractionally over schedule. The short day made it
possible to make the long drive for a very pleasant dinner to celebrate

our twenty-third. It's been a happy year. All of them have been happy years. I can't believe there've been twenty-three of them since that rainy afternoon in Greensboro, though.

March 18. Well, it isn't every picture . . . indeed, hardly any . . . that finishes a long location within half a day of schedule. We had incredible luck, with the weather and everything else. We got progressive snow on one set, and rain on another . . . everything we could've hoped for.

March 20. We moved indoors today, for the first time on the film. That's always a strange moment on a picture . . . after sweating, freezing, struggling with the elements on location, the ease and comfort of a sound stage, even one as old and drafty as Stage 1 at Paramount, seems sybaritic. Even the primitive interior of the Flatiron bunkhouse (very well done) looked quite palatial, somehow, in contrast to the High Sierra.

March 21. Tom solved the problem of getting Lee's and my reaction to the rotgut moonshine by surprising us with straight gin, rawing the edge with lemon juice. I damn near strangled. If Wyler'd been shooting it, we'd have been unconscious by the time he got a print. As it was, I was a little blurred around the edges. [*This was* not *a good idea. To play a good drunk scene, or anything else, you have to be cold sober.*]

April 4. I realize that I've arrived at a way of going at a film scene that works for me. Since what you're aiming for in a performance is the illusion of the first time, I like to start working on takes as early as possible. I don't forget lines, so I can nail down the necessary physical matches, then try to reach some truth in playing the scene.

April 10. Today I learned again how film acting works. The scene with Joan wasn't really valid as written; to talk so intimately within earshot of the Quints was unreal. We finally arrived at a concept of the scene where the Quints *allow* her to talk to Will (also a little unlikely), so they can overhear, and bait them. The scene may well work in these terms. We didn't finish—couldn't have, in any event, since I had to quit early to climb into white tie for the Academy Awards ceremony. I looked odd, in full dress and two-week beard, but I was very happy to present the little gold man to Yak Canutt, who received a Special Academy Award. He deserves it.

April 13. I *told* Tom we should begin with the acting scene and do the pickup shots with the sulfur down the chimney and so on later, but he wouldn't listen. I was right. After however the hell many films, it's time I knew a little bit about how it works. I saw Tom's point . . . he wanted to shoot in sequence. True, the special effects crew worked very slowly . . . but you *know* these things will happen. The last scene needed a little work on the dialogue (rare, with this script), but we managed to do this as well as the master and several angles in reasonable time. We went on till both Joan and I were scraping bottom, and still didn't finish. What we got was good, though.

April 14. A full day, starting late because we had to wait for Joan's hair (not her fault; SAG says they couldn't begin on her till twelve hours after quitting time last night). We finished the big scene easily. The first part, from yesterday, looked fine in daily. This scene is vital; if we hold them for this one, we have them. Now the film's finished. I think it may be very good. It's as well-written as anything I've played in recently. We had a fast birthday celebration for Lydia, crammed in between appointments. She's delighted with the Hasselblad; she literally leaped off the ground, opening it.

April 16, (Sunday). I'm in firm pursuit of those last few pounds of flab (now hovering around 202) and played tennis pounding around the court draped in Jim Brown's lead belts. (Maybe a masochist is not merely the man who gets pleasure from pain, but the man who can turn his pleasure into pain. Or is that a Puritan?) I also spent some time musing how to get a better script on APES. Arthur Jacobs is so difficult and slippery a character to deal with, I hardly know where to begin. The work must be done, though.

April 17. Now that's it's clear Frank Schaffner can't do PRO on spec, or at least that his agents don't want him to, we must turn elsewhere. Tommy Gries seems a good idea and he seemed interested. APES is now up in the air. Eddie Robinson feels very claustrophobic about the ape makeup . . . we may move to Maurice Evans. [*We did.*] Julie Harris is anxious about the same thing; probably Kim Hunter will do it. The casting problem's really Nova: who will do it, and how naked can she be. The tests I saw were not good. There's also a problem on how to clothe the astronauts after their capture, to make them blend in with the subhumans.

Logically, since the subhumans in the story were animals, they should have been naked. This was not a feasible option in 1967 and would be a distracting choice even now. We finally arrived at some bark loin cloths that did well enough.

April 28. Fox, in a panic over the projected cost of APES (brought on in part by their decision to shoot the film here instead of overseas), has now decided to bring the budget down a bit. On paper, at least. By cutting the shooting days from fifty-five to forty-five, they seem to save a great deal of money, but the film can't be *shot* in that time. I wanted Citron to do battle on this, but he counseled against it, as out of my province.

May 1. The meeting at Gar Kanin's was interesting. I knew of course they'd have some offer and feared it might be a play for New York. How hard to turn down a play with him, yet how hard to give up a season here at home. It was a film, to be made from a novel of Thornton Wilder's HEAVEN'S MY DESTINATION, adapted by Ruth Gordon, directed by Gar. I'll read it at once, of course. I'm flattered he asked me.

May 12, Tarrytown, New York. My first meeting of the National Council for the Arts. A circular green baize table, surrounded by prestigious names, Roger Stevens with a silver gavel, and a stenotypist turning in the center like a supplicant gladiator in the arena. All this set in the swelling green hills of the ex-Biddle estate, now devoted to an endless series of executive meetings, which is the color of the mid-twentieth century, I guess. At each place was a fat notebook of projects, totaling several millions of dollars. Mostly on poetry and art today . . . I kept my mouth shut and listened a lot.

May 13, New York. I felt a little surer of myself today, having learned one or two of the ropes yesterday. Also, the SAG Board has taught me a handhold or two in the intricacies of parliamentary procedure. It helped when we got to Lincoln Center. They've lost (not spent, *lost*) $750,000 in the past year on productions alone. I don't want to reward this kind of profligacy with the public's money; not in the spotlight that shines on Lincoln Center. So I shot their grant down. I hope the lesson is not lost on others seeking grants. [*Lost? It wasn't even noticed. I was a child to imagine anyone in government is going to spend less.*]

May 14 (Sunday), New York/Los Angeles. The morning session was an interesting one, sparked by fireworks when I hatcheted another grant application. (I seem to be rapidly acquiring a certain identity as a hit-man there.) This was only ten thousand dollars, for a cultural center in the Haight-Ashbury, in San Francisco. On the surface, it seems a plausible idea, but I read a letter from within the community that indicted the whole thing . . . a cry for help, really. I read it aloud, complete with scatological syntax, and pointed out my conviction that the problem was a medical one, to be solved by juvenile aid, not culture-encouragement.

May 16. I think Frank's new ending on APES is very good . . . Taylor doesn't die, now; he finds the Statue of Liberty, and knows where he is. Fade-out. I ran Fray by the rock shop to contemplate a rock-saw he had his heart set on. He plans on going into business, turning out cuff links. I think he might even pull it off. [*He did, but never quite got into profit. I think he still owes me some of the capital I advanced him to buy the saw.*]

May 17. I had a long conference on the Thornton Wilder novel with the Kanins. They seem convinced it can work, and that Wilder will be involved. I don't know how it'll turn out, but it seems irresistible.

Unhappily, this never materialized. I'd like very much to have worked with that remarkable, talented pair.

May 21, Page, Arizona: Begin PLANET OF THE APES. I've never understood why the first day of shooting on a film, no matter how good the crew is nor how well-organized the schedule, *never* goes well. We were more than half an hour late starting this morning because the beards weren't sent up for the other astronauts, who of course haven't had time to grow their own. They weren't well applied when they did come; our makeup man could be stronger, also quicker. The heat is bad here. One of the other two actors playing astronauts passed out from the heat.

May 28 (Sunday), Los Angeles/Page. A lovely day at home. Actually, it was overcast all day, but just to be there was lovely. To waken beside my wife, to see my daughter come in the bedroom in her little silk nightgown, a rumpled angel with tangled gold hair; to sit beside my son at the pro tennis matches and point out the strokes to him . . . all this was worth twice the trip I made to get home. So now I'm back at work, with another week ahead of me. It's a short location, but it seems long just now.

May 31. We had a fantastic day's work, in consistently good light, catching up what we missed yesterday, finishing off the apes on the location, which is a blessing. The makeups are only just bearable for them, and the more days off they can get the better they'll be. I'm impressed at how well Roddy McDowall and Kim Hunter act in the makeup; you can actually read emotion through those animal faces.

June 6, Los Angeles. United Artists will make PRO. Tommy Gries will direct, and I'm damned if we know yet who'll write the script. No one very expensive, I guess. Meantime, WILL PENNY. We ran it tonight; I think it's just about as good as I hoped it might be. Even without a score or proper sound, it came off. I'm good in it, Joan Hackett's fine, so's the boy. The photography's excellent, too. We won't have to cut much, either; we're a little under two hours. We may have something very worthwhile on our hands.

June 7. The usual problems attendant on moving back on stage from a location. The prop truck isn't back yet, the crew has to shake down. In addition, the makeups are so rough for the apes, their calls are so bloody early, that we've decided to start at ten in the morning and finish at seven in the evening. Personally, I'm not delighted with this plan, but it makes sense overall. I was unconscious through most of the scene today and thus had little to contribute, but Frank shot it well.

June 13. Today was really a horrible day. I'd caught a cold, something I almost never do while working. I felt lousy when I came to work, and worse every time that damn fire hose hit me, topped off when I had to scream the last speech of the sequence, dripping and hose-battered. The hoarse rasp I was able to produce is really ideal; this is the first scene where we hear Taylor speak after his throat wound. Frank's staging was very telling. The cage stuff looks good in dailies, the ragged blanket's appropriately ratty and unheroic.

June 14. We had a very physical scene today, cleaning up the escape, followed by Maurice Evans's first appearance as Zaius. His orangutan makeup is excellent, and he is learning how to use it.

June 15. We moved faster today than we have been . . . perhaps because we're finished in the cages, which made an extremely difficult set to shoot. I had a meeting with Dick Zanuck and Frank on whether or not to make a script point of the fact that the apes speak English. To me, it's patently obvious we should ignore this. English is the lingua franca of film, which is reason enough to use it, but it seemed to require a meeting to arrive at this conclusion. This film begins to shape up well. It may not be great; I don't see how it can avoid being successful. I seldom say this . . . let's see if I'm right.

June 16. The main thing we have going for us in this film is that the damn thing's *interesting*. On top of this, I like Frank's ideas about the scenes; I think Maurice, Roddy, and Kim are excellent. Linda H. has problems, but Frank's keeping her nearly immobile in her scenes, which works.

June 19. We began the trial scene today. If this comes off, we'll have something special. I said to Frank, "I thought from the beginning we'd have a hit, but we may have a helluva picture, too." Frank's thought of several telling touches to underline the dehumanizing of Taylor: stripping him in court, for one. It's the first time I've ever done a nude scene, even photographed from the rear.

June 20. What with shooting all day, negotiating all night (we quit at midnight, still a good way apart on respective proposals) I'm beginning to bend a little.

I led the SAG negotiating team working out a new contract with the producers. Labor negotiations frequently seem to involve marathon sessions into the morning hours, with people napping on couches and nodding at the conference table over cups of black coffee. It seems the wrong way to go about it, though very dramatic.

The pressure of the scene, the problems of makeup calls for the other actors all combine for a helluva workday for me, too. We have, thank God, some first-class people with us. Jim Whitmore, Jim Daly, and of course Maurice, are well worth much more than their salaries. Whitmore, particularly, makes a frightening orangutan. (I don't know how complimentary he would consider that observation.)

June 21. The first day of summer was a bitch for me. The trial scene involves, as so many of my parts seem to, another manhandling (or ape-handling, in this case). It hurts after ten takes. They're trying to think of a different way of tying me up from those used in TEN COMMANDMENTS, BEN-HUR, etc., etc., etc.

June 29, Fox Ranch. I spent the entire day pattering barefoot (bare*foot!?*, bare *ass*, for God's sake!) through the undergrowth, picking up more than a touch, I fear, of poison oak; it was luxuriating on every hand. A chase sequence is always easy to act, no matter how complicated it may be to shoot. The fugitive syndrome must lie very near the surface in all of us, ready to burst into the open, panic-stricken.

July 6. A helluva long day, in the course of which I was finally brought to earth as Taylor. Having evaded clubs, whips, horsemen, crowds, they tripped me ass over tea kettle into a thrown net and hoisted me high. It should make a damn good sequence; shooting it took about all the stamina I was relieved to discover I can still muster. It's surprising the perspective an experience like this gives you. Upside down in a net, a man isn't worth much.

July 8, San Diego. I spent the day in the New Orleans Saints training camp in San Diego investigating pro footballers in their natural habitat. It was a useful day: Everywhere you turned you found stuff that belongs in the film, which I believe more and more will be made, and can be good. I stood five yards behind the quarterback during scrimmage: giving me a vivid picture of his problems. They seem to consist mainly of about a thousand pounds of linemen coming at you on every play.

July 17. Our best effort failed to finish the hunt sequence today, though I was successfully shot through the throat before the day was done. We have less than a day's work left out there, but we'll have to leave it and go into the studio Tuesday. I was late to a special meeting of the Arts Council tonight. I'm not sure why they had it . . . the major items on the agenda were more money for Bill Ball's ACT theater and setting up a residential co-op for painters in a New York warehouse. To vote approval, I missed the Royal Ballet, Fonteyn, and Nureyev. It goes with the territory, I guess.

July 18. We're back on the sound stages again. After the Fox ranch, this is luxury. Included in the cast today (as the long-dead Stewart) was an eighty-year-old woman who played what must surely be the only role in the history of the drama as an octogenarian lady astronaut. The dialogue between the casting director and the agents on this one must have been marvelous.

July 19. Another long day sloshing around inside that space capsule, gargling my lines through torrents of water spraying in from off camera. It occurs to me that there's hardly been a scene in this bloody film in which I've not been dragged, choked, netted, chased, doused, whipped, poked, shot, gagged, stoned, leaped on, or generally mistreated. As Joe Canutt said, setting up one of the fight shots, "You know, Chuck, I can remember when we used to win these things."

July 23 (Sunday). A nice day for me, less so for Lydia, who's feeling the pressure of preparing for the Greek trip, which will entail three separate departures for our family alone. I wish it didn't have to be quite so complicated, but she likes to plan in great detail . . . just the reverse of my impulse.

We'd chartered a sailing yacht to tour the Greek Islands, along with our old friends the Isaacs and the Seltzers, including all the children. Joining us were Bea Sellmer and my mother. The itinerary by which we all met in Athens was extremely complex.

August 3. The fog didn't creep in on little cat feet; it squatted sullenly on the sand all morning. Not a camera turned till after lunch. Frank still got most of what he planned, though. Mort Abrahams [*executive producer for Jacobs*] drove out for an inconclusive discussion on what I should say in the final speech, looking at the ruined Statue of Liberty. Fox wants to shoot three versions, giving them all possible choices. I obviously prefer to shoot only the speech I wrote, since this is my only chance to put muscle behind that choice. Besides, it's the best. I can't believe the Code still forbids the use of "God damn you!" It's surely acceptable in the context of this speech; Taylor is literally calling on God to damn the destroyers of civilization.

It did make a good scene, and the line was right. We only shot one version.

August 6. Fray got off for Europe easily, along with his friend Jeff
Match. Mother will join them in New York and they'll be with Lydia
and Holly in Athens by tomorrow. The house is lonely now . . . but I
had a good steak alone by the pool, watching the sun go down. David
Moessinger's story line on PRO seems viable; he'll go ahead with it,
hopes to be through with a draft when I get back.

August 10. The last day of shooting on PLANET OF THE APES. An ideal kind
of scene for any actor . . . everybody else lay mute and motionless
while I had all the words. More than three minutes of them, for that
matter, and they were pretty well worked out, too, after the usual
intense effort with a red pencil. We did two different masters on it,
then the usual coverage. I think it's good. I think the picture will be,
too. It'll certainly be different. If the social comment comes off as well
as the wild adventure, we may get some attention.

August 11. For the first time in a year, I have the lovely release of
waking in the morning without a shooting schedule staring at me, no
camera crouching in waiting . . . and I savor it.

August 12. My latish departure left me time for three sets of tennis
before Bill Isaac drove me out to the airport, overburdened with
luggage, as usual (even to a tape recorder for the boat, this time). I
read LION IN WINTER as the evening came quickly toward me at jet
speed over the summer land.

August 13 (Sunday), Athens/Delphi. As I always do in aircraft, I slept
enough to arrive in reasonable shape. God knows they pamper me in
airports . . . I'll have a helluva time adjusting to non-VIP travel.
When my career's over, I think I'll just stay home. Greece is as I
imagined it: olive trees, pines, and cicadas clicking in the heat. Gray
rock and old stones carved by dead men. Tonight in Delphi, I sat
under the waning moon, watching actors trace the patterns of my
trade in a theater twenty centuries old.

August 14, Delphi. The glory of Greece is a true glory, worth coming so
far to see. The ruined marble and the tumbled columns speak
eloquently of what is gone. (The Python priestess to the emissary of
Julian the Apostate, seeking to refound Apollo's faith: "The glorious
house is fallen, tell the king. Apollo has no shelter here; the watered
spring is quenched.") Part of the glory is in the fall. I had that today,
from the past, and the pleasure of running through a grove of olive
tress, from the present.

August 15, Delphi/Athens. Our cultural exposure was minimal today, but
we covered a lot of ground, most of it between Delphi and Athens in
a large bus . . . well, a *small* bus, but large for eleven people. We

saw some memorable things in the little museum in Delphi, and then left on what proved to be a longish trip back to Athens with breaks for a lunch of cheese and wine and fruit, and for me to get out and run two or three miles behind the bus through the Greek hills. I felt like the messenger from Marathon.

August 17, Athens. I slept in a bit this morning; Walter arrived during breakfast (milky coffee, croissants, and Attic honey). He reports a fine reaction to WILL PENNY in New York from the Paramount people (save Bluhdorn, who hated it), also the finalization of our arrangements with the NFL to use the New Orleans Saints as our team in PRO. We had an early look at the *Alexandra Lisa* today, the sailing yacht we chartered . . . an ocean racer, 110 feet. She's lean and fast-looking, yet luxurious enough to please the most sybaritic taste. We sail tomorrow.

August 18, Serifos. There are some experiences in life that fulfill your expectations; sailing for the Greek Islands is one of them. Even our flurried departure from the hotel, our luggage almost crowding us out of our bus, didn't deter us. Nor did the wait while our food stores found their laggard way dockside. The Greek sea is as Homer said it was . . . wine-dark and memorable. We anchored after dark, eager for the days ahead.

August 20, Santorini. The island of Santorini seems right for the site of lost Atlantis . . . the black cliffs looming over the gaping lagoon left when the volcano that drowned Crete blew up. We mule-backed (I ran) up eight hundred feet to the town, and then in the afternoon we went over in the launch to the Burnt Island, still smoking from its birth pangs sixty years ago, and swam in the hundred-degree water, stroking among the floating bits of pumice. I lost my gold Fraser ring in the depths . . . a fit offering to Poseidon for this trip, I guess.

August 28, Kos and Patmos. Another night of sailing brought us by morning to an island we decided we didn't want to see, or at any rate had no time for. Our voyage is coming to an end: We must begin to plan our time. So we abandoned the birthplace of Hippocrates to voyage to the island where John wrote Revelation. We had a somewhat stormy crossing, and tied up next to a French charter . . . a motor yacht of Danish registry, with laundry drying on the foredeck. We had drinks ashore, in an eddy of polite Greeks.

August 31, Vouliagmeni. So our argosy's over. My son pressed me, before we sailed, to swim ashore and back to the boat. I did, just. More and more, his challenges bring me to the raw edge of my strength. Sailing back, when it was too rough for Lydia to go out in the launch to shoot the *Lisa* under full sail, I did my best to do it for her. I got, I hope, some usable shots of the boat, to mark what's surely been our most memorable vacation.

September 2, Athens/Ismir. A fairly frantic day, beginning with a dawn visit to the Parthenon. It was as remarkable as our first view at sunset. Our packing schedule was thrown into chaos by a move-up in our flight time, unannounced by the airline. We made the plane anyhow and arrived in Turkey somewhat precipitously, lunched lavishly, and managed to see something of the ruins of St. John's as the light left us.

September 6, Istanbul/airborne, eastbound. Woke in the fake Byzantine splendors of an ornate Presidential Suite (to become Royal tomorrow when King Hussein follows us here) and went on to inspect the genuine Byzantine splendors, as well as the even more lavish sultanate ones the city has to offer. So the vacation's over, as abruptly as a jet engine cutting off. It was a rich time. My only misgiving is leaving Fray and Lydia to manage his first week or so at a new school without me. [*I had promised to do another Vietnam tour, and flew on east alone from Istanbul to Saigon.*]

September 7, Karachi/Bangkok/Saigon. A long, long day of flying. The hours tick by, you read, and eat, and drink, and open one eye as the plane sits in Karachi, and get out to stretch in Bangkok, and walk the steamy heat of the runway, and then you're there, slanting down over the rice paddies. Saigon is at least as crowded as before, though much of the U.S. Army has been moved out since '66. At dinner, there was much talk of the degree of commitment on the part of our people here.

September 9, Saigon. Longer and tougher day than I thought it would be. Hospitals are hard to do . . . the lines and lines of beds, with the young faces lying there. There was a boy who'd been hurt very badly by a mine, his body stitched like quilting, red and seamed. He thanked *me* for coming. I spent a valuable evening at the Italian Embassy learning more than I expected to about the war from both the professional and the Vietnamese views.

September 10 (Sunday). I was up early, and into the stiff new field boots and the starched combat fatigues, then out to the airfield for the not long flight to Pleiku, which has expanded enormously in twenty months. I remember one strip and a scatter of buildings; now there's an enormous complex, which I spent the day touring. I spent the night in an old C47 (two wars beyond its time, like me), circling over a nameless target below the DMZ, tumbling flares out the door to light the incredible weight of firepower poured down.

September 11, Pleiku. I was with the First Cavalry today, their horses changed now, not to the tanks of WWII, but to choppers. This was in the An Khe Valley, where twenty months ago the Special Forces had cut a perilous foothold. Now there's a whole division, whose choppers fly almost without hindrance. You can't be here, having been here before, and not feel things are going better. Even in a forward company, on a patrol sweep in VC territory, it seemed easy and confident.

September 13, Luach. This was supposed to be my rest day, but I couldn't see sitting on my ass over here. They laid on a light schedule, but that left me room for some letters and a nap. I'm glad they put me in here now; I enjoy being around fliers. They're like actors in many ways: an out group with its own standards, similar feeling of informality, professionalism, and concern with talent. I feel at home with them.

September 15, Tan An. A crammed, jammed day with the Ninth Division. They've been in the country as a unit only six months, located in the rubber jungle east of Saigon and in the Delta South, clear to the Cambodian border. As nearly as I can tell, they're doing well. I know some of the correspondents take a very dim view of the field claims, and it may be I take too much at face value.

I know, I know. Everyone, especially if he never saw it, has the proper line on Vietnam: "It was an immoral, stupid war, we never should have been there in the first place, and we couldn't have won it." Certainly most wars are fairly immoral and stupid, as we may have been by going there in the first place. But our greatest stupidity was in not winning it, once there, as we could have done in about a tenth the time we spent not winning, thereby killing fewer people and making fewer enemies, at home and abroad.

September 16, Long Bin. Today was lightly scheduled, which was lucky for me. I've picked up a small bug somewhere, so I was glad to have an hour between hospital visits to lie in a sweaty daze. It helped. Hospital touring gets no easier. I talked to several men who'd been hit in the action in the Delta with the Ninth yesterday. It's very difficult to be cheerful with a man who's had his fingers blown off.

September 18, Saigon. After a good night's sleep in the borrowed bed of two nurses who gave me their quarters so I could have all the amenities (save themselves) my last night in the field, I flew north for a last half-day of work. I ran into some Special Forces men I'd known my last trip out, got back to Saigon very tired, but in time for the obligatory interview with the commanding general. Dinner with some correspondents tonight wasn't bad. I'm glad I'm through here, though.

September 19, Leave for Manila. A frustrating day. I wanted to give a
   day to the hospitals in Manila, but it looks like lengthening my trip by
   at least three days, which seems to be a penalizing virtue. I hung
   around all morning in the hotel, then half the afternoon at the airport,
   finally caught a ride to Manila where I had a drink or two and fell
   into bed. So much . . . this year . . . for Vietnam. Will I have to go
   again next year?

September 22, Los Angeles. I began to ease back into it, though you still
   wake from any sleep as though you were lying under a dead horse.
   My tennis game has gone to hell, of course, but everything else, even
   my waistline, is not bad. This includes the first forty pages of
   Moessinger's first draft on PRO, which I read today. It's not
   startlingly insightful, but it's a workmanlike effort. The character is
   there. At Lew Wasserman's party tonight, I had a chance to outline
   to Jack Valenti my feelings on Vietnam, the second time around.

September 26. I got to work calling the families of the men who asked
   me to while I was in Vietnam. Not quite so many as last time. (I
   think the long-distance facilities they have in Saigon now make it less
   of a thing for them.) It's still a tricky chore, but one I wouldn't pass.
   This is a good week for it: Monday, the National Association of
   Christians and Jews is giving me the Brotherhood Award. I can't have
   them changing their minds.

October 4. At lunch with Frank S. today, I found he's all but finished with
   his cut of APES. He takes it to New York next week to show Jacobs,
   then I'll look at it. I arranged a special SAG Board session to allow
   George Stevens, Jr., and Greg Peck to brief us on the progress of the
   American Film Institute. It seems to be going well, if so cumbersome
   and difficult a project can be detected in movement at all the first
   year. Tonight I had a birthday. (I had it all day, in fact, though
   they're now occasions I try to ignore as long as possible.)

October 5. I finally found time [*and high time, I'd say*] for a meeting
   with George Schaefer on ELIZABETH AND ESSEX. We actually didn't
   have a helluva lot to talk about, creatively. As I recall when I worked
   for him in THE PATRIOTS, George is a director/technician, rather than
   a director/artist. Television demands something like this sort of
   creative orientation, I think. If you can't get it together on time,
   nothing else counts. George can surely do that. Let's see what else
   we can do. I think I understand Essex, instinctively, at least. The
   historical references are very contradictory, but the man comes
   through. I don't like him, or don't like much of him, but I see him.

October 9. The whole day was buried in the play. That's what it feels like,
   too, at this stage. We'll be struggling to get free now till everybody

learns the lines and blocking. Meantime, it's miserable, sludgy work. It's surely the hardest part of acting, when nothing flies.

October 13. I think Essex is progressing a little. He's a lighter man than I am, but there's a certain sanguinity of character that I can relate to. I find Anderson easy to work with (that's Dame Judith . . . the playwright Maxwell's not such a cinch, confused as he was as to whether he might not in fact be William Shakespeare), and the rest of the cast is good. We have more than a week yet; I think we're in good shape.

October 23. I don't know if any of us could actually do it anymore. Maybe we made up the whole "Golden Age of Television." Did Frank Schaffner and I ever really throw MACBETH together in ten days, sort it all out in one camera day and hurl it live through the tube at an audience? Of course, at twenty-three, none of us knew it was tough. Certainly the method they've arrived at now for tape is a little less desperate, even preserving some of the virtues of the old, pure live TV (the sense of *playing*, of performance you never can have in film). With the new editing capability of tape, which didn't exist even when last I did Hallmark, you have some capacity to control what you get on the screen in the end. We blocked and fiddled with the changes and sets and cameras and sound all day, to some purpose.

This was the last acting I did for television, to date. The show won an Emmy. I was fairly good, and Judith Anderson was marvelous. Even with the improved technical capacities of video tape, I've never found anything I wanted to do since.

October 28. I'm still winding down a little from Essex; it was nice to have an easy day, spent mostly on the PRO script. I don't feel David's succeeded in dramatizing the most difficult (and the most important) element in the story . . . *why* Catlin feels as he does. I read some of it to Lydia. I don't think it comes through to her either. If women can't relate to the story, then it's just a picture about a football player and we're in trouble.

October 31. We saw APES today, with no score, no looped dialogue, and an unbalanced print. I liked it enormously. I think it may find a bigger audience than anything I've done since BEN-HUR (well, since EL CID, anyway). I also think we may get notices reflecting the comment in the film. Lydia concurs, displaying her taste and acumen.

November 3, Washington, D.C. A damn full day, working through a National Council on the Arts agenda, which leaves no time for full discussion. You're skewered neatly between your responsibilities to the council and the necessity of getting through the damn agenda. I questioned here and there, more than most did, not as much as I'd have liked to, trying to understand what the hell we're doing. Of course we didn't finish. At the White House dinner tonight, I talked briefly with LBJ and gave him some of my impressions of Vietnam. [*Ah, what a heady feeling, to have the ears of the mighty, even if they're not listening.*]

November 6. I spent a long morning at SAG trying to make intelligent staff decisions; an area I'm not equipped for. How do I know which of thirty-odd secretaries deserve a raise, and how much it should be? I guess given the responsibility, you just deal with it as well as you can. At least it gave me a good excuse not to buckle down to work on my SAG state-of-the-union speech. I seized this, of course, and finally only chatted with my two gagmen about it. Whoever would've thought I'd have two gagmen working for me?

Conscious that my annual address to the membership tended to solemnity, I'd turned for help to an old friend, Leonard Stern, one of television's more gifted producers. He lent me two of his writers to insert some humor in my speech. I was grateful for their help, but I learned a thing or two in the process. For one thing, gag writers seem to come in twos, and are always referred to as "the boys." For another, I found that I can't write with anyone. Len's boys came up with some funny lines, but I really have to do it myself. As Red Smith said, "Writing is easy. You just sit at the typewriter till drops of blood come out of your forehead."

November 15. I got some more PRO pages from David Moessinger today. There's some improvement, but there's still no "wow!" in the story. I think Tom's going to have to write on this to get it to a shootable stage. Within the next week we must have something to show United Artists, so they can decide whether to go forward or not. I just heard Universal has decided to release COUNTERPOINT at Easter, simultaneously with APES and WILL. Why do they *do* this?

November 28. If it isn't the rain falling, it's the damn Santa Ana blowing. Washed out, or blown away, we lost the tennis again. I was cheered to discover Herb Jaffe likes the PRO script as it stands. He wants to go. He's not the final hurdle, of course . . . it must still go before their eastern echelons. If they don't grab this deal, they're out of their minds, which they must think we are, to stand still for it. Never mind. I want to make this film.

December 16, Two Rivers. A rather frantic departure from L.A. finally saw us into Two Rivers, where we settled in across the street from the narrow little green house where I first came, twenty-five years ago, and saw Lydia shoveling snow on her driveway in a red knitted cap. All in all, it's been a magnificent quarter of a century.

December 17 (Sunday). The weather's most unseasonable for Christmas in the Midwest . . . warm and rainy. If it continues like this, the kids will never forgive me for taking them away from the Coast. I read and played Monopoly with the kids—Fray's Christmas present from his grandfather.

We spent another day with Lydia's family in Wisconsin, visited my mother in Wilmette, and then headed for the woods.

December 22, St. Helen. We got away in good order, flying across the lake for Christmas in the woods. A trace of snow was whirling down as we drove north, calling up my most vivid childhood memory . . . the white flakes swirling against the black pines. The house was warm with welcome, the fire in the hearth fed with logs chopped on this hill, and I sat at dinner in my father's chair.

December 23. One of the pleasures of being here is that you don't feel bored with little to do. To walk down the road and speculate whether there will be more snow for Christmas can fill the bulk of an afternoon. Today had a high point, though. I gave Fray and Holly something not many children of this generation have. We all went out through the snowy woods and chose a fifty-foot balsam, which I felled, and cut the top ten feet for our Christmas tree, cut off our own land.

A tree grows from the top; those branches are much thicker and fuller, best for a Christmas tree. No, you don't waste the rest. You cut it up for fireplace logs.

December 24 (Sunday). The snow fell thick and quiet all day; the winter woods steadily whiter for Christmas. Walter called from California, back from London where I gather our unprepared and unexpected opening of WILL had disastrous results. This is depressing, of course, but not conclusive. I'll get into it when I get back . . . the hell with it meantime.

Paramount had a corporate upheaval that year, and the new management considered WILL PENNY an expendable film. (And may they burn in hell for it.) They dropped it into a London release unannounced, where it got the good notices the film encountered almost everywhere, but almost no business.

December 26. This was the day I'd planned to take Fray rabbit hunting, though I doubt he'd have slaughtered many of them. In any event, it was too cold to work the rabbit dog we'd planned on borrowing. So we went snow mobiling; snarling along the trails with far greater ease than you can travel them in any vehicle I know of. The cold was bitter, but a fire in the stable kept us warm enough to target-fire Fray's .22, dragged half across a continent for just such an exigency. It made a good day.

December 27, Los Angeles. No snow fell today, but there was time in the tangle of packing to go to Russ's grave, which I hadn't seen since he was buried, and brush the loose feathered snow off the copper plate. Fray stood with me in the bitter black cold, with the snow soaking through his tennis shoes, while we dropped some balsam twigs on the frozen earth.

December 31 (Sunday). It was a busy year, though the results are still in question. Of the three films finished, COUNTERPOINT looks now to be insignificant, WILL PENNY is beginning to dim a little (ahead of its openings, and perhaps only in terms of the London fiasco), PLANET OF THE APES is still an unknown quantity. I wouldn't say this has been the best year I've ever had professionally, but personally, it's been a happy, growing time.

1968

Tennis doings . . .

quarterbacking in *Number One* . . .

Planet of the Apes is a smash.

As an old pro quarterback in *Number One*
LYDIA HESTON

January 3, Los Angeles. The WILL PENNY tour's settled. I'll do London for four days, then home again; no other countries are ready anyway. Meantime, we've closed with Sandy Mackendrick to direct EAGLE AT ESCAMBRAY, with Waterhouse and Hall (sounds like an accounting firm) to do the script. I can meet with them when I'm over flacking for WILL.

January 10, London. The local Paramount people (one was a very junior publicity man when I came through on my first trip for GREATEST SHOW ON EARTH, some centuries ago) are determined to wring every hour of work from me they can. The press schedule was formidable; I never lifted my head till I finally reeled out of the last radio taping, after midnight. On rereading EAGLE [*we changed it to* BANANA MEN *about then*], some problems occur to me: Will it be feasible to shoot outside the U.S., considering the number of American actors needed? Also, what about the stern-wheeler? Also, there are some script problems (as usual).

January 13, London/Iceland. Dickensian snow swirled down Park Row when I looked out the window in the dawn dark to watch the Horse Guards leading the remounts down to the barracks. Then I had an hour of tennis indoors with Johnny McDonald [*an old friend from New Zealand, who plays far too well to put up with my game, but does, with unvarying good humor, whenever I'm in London. We drink on more even terms*]. My plane was an hour late departing, lost an engine over Scotland, and finally landed in Iceland, deep in its polar dark. I had a long drive over endless tundra to a decent hotel, first doing my duty by the press. But why am I not *home?* My teeth are grinding with frustration.

January 19, New York/Los Angeles. A long, useful day [*promoting* ELIZABETH AND ESSEX] starting at dawn. The sun over the United Nations building is worth getting up early for, though it was the *Today Show* that was actually responsible. At the end of the day I went up in the old brass elevator I remember from the *Studio One* days and played tennis at an indoor club they've opened on the television stages where I did all those scripts that boosted me up. I can remember that callow kid, and he was me. And he is me . . .

January 29, Los Angeles. I spent the morning happily in the desert with Fray, shooting empty bottles through the last morning of his semester layoff, then plunged into the afternoon, refreshed for the work. I wasn't enchanted with the first treatment of EAGLES. Much of it's OK, but the orientation is far too flip and funny. The SAG Board spent most of its time on the question of whether or not to join the protest over the closing of THE BEARD. I suspect they're seeking SAG support as a publicity tool.

I don't know whether THE BEARD *was obscene or not. I do know it wasn't any good.*

January 30. I seem to be facing an awful lot of TV cameras, damn few of them talking about acting, oddly enough.

This was my public figure period. Newsmen had gotten to the point where they'd ask anybody about anything. Congressmen, lady tennis players, actors, anybody. It's surprising how readily you can get people to display their areas of ignorance.

The APES running tonight was successful. The film comes off very well, including the black comment. I was a little disappointed in my own performance. There didn't seem to be enough *weight* to it, somehow. Some of it was cut, of course, but I still felt let down. All the talk afterward was good, but you can discount most of that.

This seems to have been my opinion when I first saw APES, though I'm very proud of the film now. I guess I expected a little more. You always expect a little more.

February 1. A full day working on two different films, neither of which is going to be ready very soon, it's clear. PRO has serious scheduling problems in terms of integrating with the Saints' schedule. It looks as though we'll shoot training camp in summer, the rest in the fall. At least I've made arrangements to learn quarterbacking from Bob Waterfield. I'd say he knows how to do it. We worked all afternoon with our English scriveners on the EAGLE treatment. They're very malleable; maybe *too* malleable.

February 5. The most outstanding event of the day was an offer from George Pal (not firm; I doubt his deal's that solid yet) to do a film of PEER GYNT. I remember musing once how ideal it would be to play the first part of the role when young, then wait twenty years and do the rest. I don't know if it can be written and directed up to what it should be, but you have to consider a role like that.

February 9. The best laid plans, again. As of yesterday's conference, it looks as though it'll cost about fifteen thousand dollars to repair the damage done on the north walkway by the earth slide in the fall rains. Doolittle's still anxious to do BECKETT at the Greek Theater, though casting the other part in balance is tough. Robert Shaw's the only likely possibility now (and probably the best, at that). Maybe Buzz Meredith to direct? I need to do this play, and I need to be good in it. In both parts.

February 13. The rain that's flirted in and out of the basin for nearly a week blotted through most of the day, killing both my run and my tennis, but we did get to go through the numbers on the football film. It looks like a negative cost of under a million, and some thirty-nine days of shooting, which seems incredible. I ran PEER GYNT for the kids tonight, so my son could see what I looked like, three years his senior.

February 15. The New York opening on APES seems to be better than good. If reports I've gotten prove out and are duplicated in other cities (several qualifications there, but I've learned to keep my jaundiced eye well polished for just such purposes), this will be the biggest hit I've had since EL CID. The notices we have so far are split, with the majority positive. A huge hit would be valuable just now. (I can use the money, too; both the BECKETT production and PRO will be almost for nothing.)

March 2. Lydia spent the whole day in the kitchen, I spent most of it on the court. I felt I'd earned every bounce of the ball after this past week on the road, flacking. The word from New York on APES continues to be astounding. If it holds like this through one more domestic city, and one foreign, we'll have a big, big hit.

March 5. The whole question of the degree to which actors can edge over into production and still serve SAG has blown up into a big item. I called a special meeting tonight to hear a committee from the membership at large on the subject. I think they're wrong, but I understand their anxiety. They're suspicious of me as an affluent, working actor who goes all over the world to act and spouts off all the time about why pictures aren't being made here. This is not the kind of comment unemployed actors relish hearing.

I always thought I did a better job for the guild because my own welfare was not involved.

March 5. I spent part of the morning mulling an offer to invest in the pro tennis circuit. It seems unlikely to be profitable, but the pro game needs all the friends it can find, till the dinosaurs that control the sport allow open play. I'll probably put in the few thousand I can afford to lose. In theory, I'll own a piece of Rod Laver and friends, if not their games.

It's hard to remember in the middle of the tennis explosion that there was a time when the best players in the world were barred from playing in the major tournaments because they were professionals. Open tennis was still a year away when I invested a small sum in the pro tour. I lost it, and considered it well spent.

March 14. I took my first crack at learning to quarterback. Bob Waterfield seems to have some domestic problems, so we decided to go with USC's backfield coach, Craig Fertig, along with Marv Goux, their line coach. They work very well, as far as I can tell. They know what they're doing and seem able to teach it . . . this is the whole thing, as I've learned with everything from conducting Beethoven to driving chariots, jousting, or painting the Sistine ceiling.

March 15. Well, we finally struck out on BECKETT. After going on and off and back and forth for three or four days, it finally became clear Anthony Quayle either didn't want, or was simply unable, to do it. I'm disappointed. Seeing THE MISER tonight for the first time at the Mark Taper whetted my hunger to get on that stage. Maybe next year.

March 18. We're getting down to business on the q-backing. I can tell from the extra strains that some muscles aren't fully stressed with either the running or the tennis. Each sport has its own set of stresses. I can learn to do this.

I've come to have total faith in this preparation period. It was never more severely tested than in this effort by Craig and Marv to coach me into some semblance of a world-class quarterback. As Craig said, "It's an interesting assignment. It really doesn't matter if you ever complete one pass. They can do that with the camera. What I have to do is teach you to step up to the center, read the defense, call the signals, take the snap, drop back in the pocket, and throw so it looks as though you'd been doing it for fifteen years."

March 20. Spring began appropriately enough with the kind of day all the old residents insist occurred without variation before the war. At least we appreciate it a little more now. I did, I know, working out on the football field this morning, with the smell of the grass warm in the sun. I'm getting perceptibly, if slowly, better at it. I'm confident it'll work. We're still waiting for Tom Gries's pages with the reworked scenes.

March 31 (Sunday), New York. Not a hard day, really. I woke up slowly over the Sunday *New York Times*, then to an easy rehearsal for the *Ed Sullivan Show*. I think I did the show well, later. The limo got me to my plane with no strain. I phoned Lydia from the VIP lounge at Kennedy and was shocked to hear that LBJ had announced his withdrawal from the presidential race. I think this is a mistake.

I'd stopped in New York to do the Sullivan show, en route to a quick European tour ahead of the PLANET OF THE APES openings there.

April 1, Rome. I slept well on the plane, waking as we tilted down through the clouds. The *campagna* was mostly green, white with blooming clover as we drove into Rome. The city's more crowded than before, but still beautiful, beneath all the Fiats. A proper dose of sleep and tennis put me in shape for the evening's press chores.

April 2. They insist Milan is worth a day, though I don't see it. [*I meant a day of publicity.*] We came up here primarily to do one TV show, which they insist is very important. I suppose it all counts. Meanwhile, a cable from L.A. said the first five days of the APES run broke the record for the *week* there.

Forgive me these fiscal gloatings. It's like presidents boasting about how many states they carried.

April 6, London. As I boarded the plane in Amsterdam, there was an emergency call from Lydia. It could only be one of the children, I thought, to call me while I was en route home. It was the Academy, asking me to wire the network to postpone the awards in deference to Dr. King's funeral. I did, then a press conference at the airport, and flew on home. I read a novel about the population explosion (MAKE ROOM, MAKE ROOM). Let's see if anyone likes it but me. [*We made it as* SOYLENT GREEN *a few years later.*]

April 10, Los Angeles/Hawaii. One of those tough, driven mornings I get when I'm leaving town. It's a shame packing's such a trauma for me, since I'm so frequently exposed to it, but there it is. As I signed my tax return, I decided I've earned a vacation. We arrived in a rain squall, but the hotel appears to be the place for it. (The vacation, not the rain.)

April 15, Hawaii. Citron called today: Kazan's interested in me for THE ARRANGEMENT. I've not read it, but I'm of course attracted by his reputation. It shoots this summer, which would mean a total rearrangement of the schedule on EAGLE. I really don't think any of this will work, but it's nice to be wanted.

April 18. We drove around the island to see the volcano at night, and the black beach, and various other tourist oddments. Fray chose to stay at the hotel and spear fish (a decision he regretted when we described the flowing river of lava, glowing red and black in the darkness, but it was important for him to make a choice for himself). A long drive back, with my legs cramped in the front seat, head lolled back, trying for sleep.

April 19. Our last day here was as pleasant as all the rest. I read Kazan's ARRANGEMENT today, since Citron had called again. I don't care for it. It's a loser's book, with a loser for protagonist. All these bloody stories are the same, and they're damn dreary. I don't think

I'll do this one, even to work with Kazan. I don't think there's a movie in it, for that matter, though God knows I may prove spectacularly wrong in that conviction. [*I was right, as it happens.*]

April 21 (Sunday), Los Angeles. After our Sunday tennis, Walter told me there are clouds on the CBS horizon [*as far as EAGLE was concerned*]. Their sales department feels this isn't the time to make a film about a U.S. president (it's not clear whether they think there would *ever* be a time, but it's not now, anyway). This puts us in a curious spot, though clearly we have a firm deal. I made a date with Citron to get a briefing on the situation.

April 22. Herman confirmed that our deal on EAGLE is firm, though it's now clear that CBS, for whatever reason, will not make the film, deal or no deal. OK, but I'll be damned if they don't pay for it. I'd rather make the picture. It's frustrating to have a part snatched out from under me, but you have to learn to roll with these things. The SAG meeting tonight went on interminably, sparked by another membership petition for "a mass meeting of the whole industry to discuss production decline." A theatrically attractive idea, but absolutely pointless. *I'm a little wise now. People need mass meetings when they're in trouble, not because they provide solutions, but because they provide comfort.*

May 2. On the very eve of his departure for Spain, Tom Gries delivered the scene with the old player he'd promised to write. I must say it's damn good. I feel very confident about this script now. To put it in perspective, if we had to have one project shot out from under us, I'm glad it wasn't PRO. The next imperative is to get the right actress for the wife. I have mixed feelings about Woodward and Saint. We may look at Suzanne Pleshette next week.

May 7. Things've been so crowded that today was my first football workout since before Easter. If my coaches are to be believed, I was better. I have noted there's a curious process of subliminal learning . . . in the nerve ends, maybe . . . during a layoff. Anyway, the football's a little easier in my hands, now.

It was about this time that Walter Seltzer dropped by one of our daily workouts. "How's Chuck doing?" he asked, as I took the snap from Marv Goux, dropped back, and completed a pass in the face of a simulated blitz from three friendly players. "Fine," said Craig. "I think he's getting to the point where he has delusions of adequacy."

May 8. I went down to USC today to watch football practice. I think it's vital for me to understand something of the pressure on these guys.

Even at the college level, they lean on them very hard, forcing them deep into their individual resources. This is part of excelling in anything, maybe: to find out just how hard you can push yourself.

May 16. Jean Simmons seems to be back in the picture on the PRO casting, through some agent's shenanigans of the kind that amaze me, and that Citron wouldn't dream of condoning, I'm sure. I think she'd be good for it, if it's at last to be actually submitted to her. Speaking of shenanigans, I'm getting a lot of pressure to do the Universal film about a giant computer [COLOSSOS]. I'd really rather do a play this summer. Christ knows I haven't acted since last October, in ELIZABETH AND ESSEX. That's too damn long.

May 21. We ran most of Glenville's THE COMEDIANS this morning, jumping reels frequently without losing the thread of the story, which tells you something about the piece. We were looking at the two black actors for PRO. Later, we dropped the script off at mimeo. That's a long pull from however many years ago it was that I read that article on the plane about the life of a quarterback.

May 23. We lunched with a candidate for the other woman in PRO. I don't think she's right, somehow; there's a feline quality that's wrong for this part. I don't know . . . we may not be able to do any better. The thing, always, is to get the best actress, but it's hard to do. At least, we got our scripts out of mimeo. A very handsome red cover . . . I hope it augurs well for us.

May 25. I got up at the traditional crack of, and tooled off up the coast through the darkling morning with Fray to meet the diving boat on which he was to journey out to Anacapa Island to do his test dive for his state scuba certification. When we anchored off the island, pitching in the sea raised by a stiff on-shore wind, the look of the thick knotted kelp rolling heavily in the waves was not reassuring, and I can't say I was sorry when the skipper decided it was too rough to dive.

May 26 (Sunday), Los Angeles/Washington, D.C. Since I was unemployed today (indeed, fired by CBS), I was glad to have an invitation for dinner at the White House. Not the kind of thing you can really become blasé about; I can't anyway. After the usual tennis, we took off to the airport, barely managing our planned stop at Holly's school picnic on the way. I don't like Washington much, and it was raining when we got there. Still . . .

May 29, Los Angeles. The quarterbacking is coming along, poco a poco. I keep pointing out to Craig that he has to drive me . . . I can't believe they treat their USC players so kindly on the practice field. We shot some movie film today, and Lydia covered more than she had the first time with her Leica. This should give us a much better idea of just where I stand. The young actor whose TV footage we liked so much seemed a little less impressive in the flesh, but of course he was nervous. What a torture chamber an audition is.

May 31. I did an interview today on the significance of male nudity in films. I don't know why I qualify as an expert on this vital subject; I've only been nude (and that fleetingly) in four films. Maybe it's because I'm so big . . . so *tall!* Our party tonight bon-voyaging the Guerins and the Matches off to England went well. Lydia's slide shows are becoming more and more expert. She chose the music for this one extremely well, and her English slides are brilliant. Her focus in-and-out technique could be useful for PRO, maybe. I threw in a reading of the John of Gaunt speech (not useful for PRO).

June 1. I'm supposed to be getting a script, which presupposes a firm offer, from Warner's for a thing called MARAUDERS, which Elliot Silverstein is to direct. Seems a little unlikely, but we'll see. I have never yet managed to get on a sound stage at that studio. [*I was clearly still smarting over* DARBY'S RANGERS *in '59.*] The RFK/McCarthy "debate" tonight merits the quote marks. It was a discussion, in which neither showed to enormous advantage, and each was elaborately friendly to the other. Speaking purely in theatrical terms (and never doubt this is important), neither seems to me ideal casting for president, though Kennedy is clearly the abler man.

June 5. Filling these two days in, sometime after the fact, I suddenly realized why it was so hard to recall any meaningful activity for them. They were covered by the black shock of still another political murder. No, I don't think Robert Kennedy's death reveals a hidden core of violence in the American spirit . . . simply that it runs like a red thread through the heart, or the reflexes, of the human animal. I do think it reveals that we've been wrong in letting our honorable fervor for the protection of dissent as one of the cornerstones of democracy blur the fact that dissent breeds disorder, and disorder breeds violence, and violence breeds murder. We must somehow break this chain of dark circumstance.

June 13, New York. National Council on the Arts meeting. I'm not an actor anymore, for God's sake . . . I'm an activist. Off on the plane again today for a quarterly session in support of the arts. My reputation as a hatchet man on the council must be formidable. Roger Stevens had a little heart-to-heart with me on the urgency of a grant to Lincoln Center, whose funding I've blocked since I've been there. Someone has to be the bad guy on this thing. [*I'm in favor of Lincoln Center; I'm against wasting money. A few years later, a lot of people were worrying about how New York City spent money.*]

June 15, Los Angeles. I fled back to L.A. a day early, having wound things up on the council a day ahead, much to everyone's surprise, I think. Before taking off, I spent some time this morning on this committee I somehow got involved in, supporting the administration position on gun control legislation. You've got to have the moderate opinions heard on this. Somehow, on any public issue, you hear only the wild-eyed screamers on both ends of the spectrum.

June 16. A good part of the day, between sets, on the phone with Hugh O'Brian (surely one of the most diligent workers I've ever encountered; why he hasn't been recruited for this kind of thing before I can't think), working over plans for the moves tomorrow on the gun law thing. We have Greg Peck, Jimmy Stewart, and hope for more. I suppose I'll end up making a pitch on TV. Well . . . I think this law is a good one. I'd rather stand to be counted on it than have some of my colleagues display their emotions on the subject.

For the record, what I regard as a moderate position on gun control does not include either registering or confiscating all the firearms in private hands. I grant I'm prejudiced; I've used guns all my life. Also, in my view, the Constitution establishes certain rights in this area not granted to citizens of other countries.

June 21, London. The usual rush to the airport . . . usual overweight on luggage . . . as life goes on, the same experiences seem to recur, experienced in the same way. Question: Is this the mark of growth? [*Answer: At least they don't weigh the luggage anymore.*] We arrived in London an hour late to find the suite not ready, so we bedded down in makeshift rooms for my obligatory nap, but I was plagued by calls from Berlin. I still got some sleep and to Queen's in time to see Sam Match win. The dinner tonight with the McDonalds was a proper return-to-London celebration.

Sam Match was playing in the Senior Doubles at Wimbledon with Gar Mulloy.

June 28, Ferndown. This was one of the most interesting days in the tour so far. We had a light enough schedule so we didn't have to leap into the car at first light and flog on toward the next stop; instead we loafed around Exeter and absorbed something of the cathedral. We crossed the Axe in flood and saw Maiden Castle, which is as fine a ruin of that period as I've seen. The feeling of the Second Augusta Legion slogging up those grass slopes against the flying stones still hangs in the air over the centuries, like the smell of blood. I'm always moved by the mark of the Romans in Britain, like the shadow of a long sentry duty.

June 29, Stratford. This was supposed to be the toughest day's drive, since we had to check into the hotel soon enough to dress for the play (AS YOU LIKE IT). It turned out to be no particular trick, even with brief stops at Salisbury, Stonehenge (for the third time), another earthen fort, and in Swindon, the town Muriel [*Ashby, who keeps our house*] comes from. We had tea with her family, saw the ruins of a country villa some Roman centurion built after serving his time in the legion, and got to our hotel in time to have a drink with the Guerins before we all left for the play (save Holly, who was through for the day). It was a good production of that most produceable of Shakespeare's comedies.

July 1, London. It was marvelous to be back in London again, luxuriating in the Dorchester, after kiting around the counties for a week. I touched base with British Equity, wearing my SAG hat, and then went out to Queen's to see how Sam was doing. His elbow is better, we had a bit of a hit (in the English phrase) before dinner. In the future, I'm determined to avoid the Indian restaurant we got trapped in, but the evening was fine, the week looks the same.

July 6. Through a kind of choke I never expected possible, Gar and Sam lost in straight sets in the Senior Finals. I suppose no one's immune to the steel elbow. Rod Laver won the Men's Singles handily. We had a pleasant time at the Wimbledon Ball tonight, though Sam and Dottie were understandably subdued, in the hour or so they spent there before taking off for their charter back home.

July 9, London/Los Angeles. Before we left for the plane, I took Holly to see them change the guard, or at least took her to the palace and sat in the car while our driver took her up to the gates, which I dared not go near, of course. I remember Fray on a cold winter day ten years ago, watching the same ceremony. The trip back was easy for me, very hard for Lydia. She had another headache and used all her strength to make it home. We did this, finally, driving in to the courtyard as the sun sank over the ridge.

July 12, Los Angeles. I fell back into harness on the quarterbacking today, with some lapses. It's interesting to observe the learning process at least, as it works for me in these things. I lost considerable ground while I was away from football, but it seems to be mostly in the area of concentration. If I put my mind on it, prodded by Fertig and Goux, I can get it back. I think we'll be all right. We've about decided to go with the black actor I talked to before London. I hate to have the deciding vote in these things; I'm frankly glad Walter and Tom feel strongly enough about it.

July 15. We've found our wife for the film. Jessica Walter, whose film looked good to us both, seemed straightforward and easy at lunch. She's old enough to be plausible as the wife, yet young enough to manage the flashbacks. I called Tom out of bed in Spain and got his sleep-groggy approval . . . if he knew what I was talking about.

July 19. I'm increasingly preoccupied with my weight. I can't seem to stay below 206, though the workout routine sweats me lower than that almost every day. This leaves me so dehydrated I absorb it all back in liquids, including beer, I'm afraid. I'm cutting down meals, since I still have a few weeks to work on it. It's harder each year to make the weight.

July 31. I had to go down to the USC campus and have a back treatment in the training room this afternoon. [*I'd put it out, quarterbacking.*] It really pisses me off that this should come back on me now. It's been more than two years since I last had a problem. I feel outraged, as I always do when I break down. I can keep up this kind of pressure on my body, but it has to be done very carefully, or the whole structure will collapse.

August 2. My daughter's seven years old today, and dancing with delight at the whole idea. She has an errant regret at the passing of her youth, I note ("I don't want to grow up *too* fast, Daddy . . ."), but she leaped into her birthday celebration, which Lydia had laid on most artfully, with unreserved ecstasy. My only contribution was getting a print of ALICE IN WONDERLAND to run for her guests, and driving up to the mountains to get Fray back for her party.

August 7. We still have no word from Tommy Gries on his reaction to our casting, save that he has second thoughts about Jessica Walter and would prefer Anne Jackson. He's wrong. It's too damn bad he's off in Spain on that two-bit Western . . . far too much of the preparation on this film has been done behind his back. This is bound to lead to uneasiness now and complications later.

August 9, Los Angeles/New Orleans. We launched off on another one, though the size of the unit was minuscule. We're trying to put this together as economically as possible, of course, and doing damn well. The below-the-line budget will be less than a million dollars. I haven't made a film at that budget since MAJOR BENSON. We flew to New Orleans with the second unit, me picking Craig Fertig's brain on quarterbacking on the way.

August 11 (Sunday), Los Angeles. I hadn't had a late night, but I
could've used more sleep than I got when Craig Fertig let some of his
old football buddies he found on the Saints get me up for breakfast at
eight. It was a gag, but the time we spent talking football till the
plane left was more learningful for me in many ways than any talk
I've had so far. It's a tough way to make a living, both on and off the
field. A big offensive lineman said to me over breakfast, "Playing one
game is just like going out in the alley and having three guys beat
the shit out of you."

August 13. My quarterbacking is creeping along, but we were
disappointed in the film we worked so hard to get in New Orleans.
The high camera covering the game with a 500mm lens simply lacked
enough light; it got nothing. As for the footage on the sidelines, I
was very unhappy with much of it. Not so much in acting terms,
though some of it was a little rushed. But it, too, was badly lit . . .
too much, in this case. It's all very disappointing. I'm tempted to push
for another trip back there, to start from scratch and shoot another
game.

August 20. A brief turmoil with Jessica Walter's agent, who submitted an
offer to her to play in a TV drama about pro football. We got her out
of it, but it made for some hurt feelings, maybe some residual
resentment that won't help us when we start shooting. I read that
script a month ago. It's appalling; a talky, cliché-ridden parody of an
old Jack Oakie football movie.

August 21. The quarterbacking seems to be progressing, though slowly.
Pain is a factor. I work each day till my arm starts to ache; the legs
knot with cramps as soon as they start to cool off. This is good . . .
it's what the script's about. Lunch with Geoff Shurlock [*of the
Ratings Board*] revealed an almost medieval (Victorian, I should say)
attitude toward the language in our script. How they can maintain
this view in a time when films with totally unrestrained dialogue are
playing I don't know.

By today's standards, the language that distressed them in PRO *was
not markedly raunchy . . . certainly it reflected the way men talk
in a locker room.*

August 22. The opening of Lydia's photo show seemed to me a smash.
Almost all the invited folk showed up and seemed impressed by her
work, as they should be. She has a firm and fertile creative eye.

August 27. We're still trying to cast the second woman in PRO. There's
harder work in the world, of course: When you compare heaving coal
in the engine room of a Glasgow tramp, or harvesting wheat at the

height of a Kansas summer, certainly looking at stills of pretty girls, having the likeliest in to talk to, and looking at movie footage of the best of all can't be called tough work. Nonetheless, I wish we'd get somewhere with it. We still haven't found anyone.

September 3. The roof finally fell in on our schedule. I spent an hour talking to Tommy in Spain this morning, then with his agent, trying to straighten it all out, but it's clear we won't be able to count on him for our original start date of October thirteenth. This creates all sorts of problems, not the least of them my own impatience. Still, a two-week postponement seems the only way out.

September 6. Our herculean efforts to reschedule PRO and give Tommy a little breathing space in which to cut his Fox film and shift gears before we start are going to work, I think. I'm itchy at the delay, of course, as always. The change will complicate my schedule, since it means I'll have to make a special trip back to be inaugurated again at SAG, but it's worth it. I read the best novel about war I have ever read. It's called ONCE AN EAGLE and would make an incredibly fine film, if anyone dared to afford it. [*Instead, much later, it made an incredibly ordinary TV series. I still look at it as my finest unmade film. I truly believe it could have been a great, great movie.*] Meanwhile, the Mirisches have offered me a sequel to HAWAII.

September 11. A not very satisfactory breakfast conference with Gordon Davidson [*director of the Mark Taper Forum*] this morning. Obviously, he wants me to play at his house, but he wants me to play his games only. I pointed out that the considerable commitment of time involved in my doing a play there can only be justified in terms of a really challenging part. He's not attracted by BECKETT or any of the other pieces I mentioned. This begins to look like a dead end for me, and it seemed such a ripe time for it, going in. Damn it to hell.

I'd still like to play the Taper; I think it's the most perfect small theater I've ever seen. I do a play in Los Angeles about every other season, almost invariably at the Ahmanson, which is the Taper's sister theater, and far from perfect. It does, however, seat twenty-two hundred people and can gross very large amounts for the Center Theater Group, which comprises the two houses. Gordon Davidson, who runs the Taper, does mostly experimental pieces, with superb success. When I do a play, I prefer to do a classic, testing part for an actor. So far, our aims have not coincided. I live in hope.

September 12. There's much pressure to have me choose one of three "commercial" projects now offered me for early next year. I'm really not overly attracted to any of them. An examination of the grosses of the films in release now seems to indicate that the "nonlinear" films (my new word, picked up from the academic types at the University of California Santa Barbara) are doing best anyway. Lydia's photos looked as good on a second visit as they had the first time. This was a valuable success for her. It makes me very proud, too.

September 17. Fray, well ensconced at the Harvard School for his second year, reports (on the basis of one day's experience) that all his masters are very superior; he finds it all very exciting. This is not what we were braced for as he turned into his teens. In the face of the alienation some parents find with their adolescent children, Fray seems to be still very much in sync with his family, and his life.

September 19. The damn quarterbacking is getting to be a problem in terms of staying in shape for it. Now that I've got the heel spur under control, I've picked up a pull in a rib muscle, on my right side. I've *got* to stay well to learn all this. Learning to speed-read will be a new experience, too. They promise to triple my speed, which would bring it up over two thousand words per minute—very useful for reading scripts. Lydia's all for it, enjoying it even, but I find it a little daunting. I may no longer have that kind of mental discipline.

September 30. Today, for the first time in several weeks, I was able to pass a football without pain in that side muscle. I still went down to USC for a session on the diathermy machine with their trainer, which made it a lot better. It'll be fine in a day or so, which means the PRO preparation hasn't been seriously held up. Fox is now willing to accept my proposal to do a brief transition bit for them in their new version of APES. I don't think it's a good idea, but of course I'll carry out my promise to them.

The overwhelming success of PLANET OF THE APES reasonably enough prompted Fox to undertake a sequel. I pointed out to Dick Zanuck that, while I sympathized with him from a corporate point of view, as an actor there was really no sequel possible. The only story you could tell had been told; anything further would just be adventures among the monkeys. While this might well be profitable (as indeed it was; I think they made five of them, plus a TV series), there was nothing new to act in it. Still, as Dick said, they couldn't really undertake a sequel if I weren't in it at all. Moved by this wistful observation, I offered to appear in the opening sequence, if they'd then kill me off. This proved agreeable, though they asked me to simply disappear in the opening sequence, and be killed off in the end. I agreed, thinking I could end the whole thing with a death that included the end of the world. I sold them on this, but they were cleverer than I; they still made several more sequels, though without me.

October 3. The one-hoss shay my body has become still holds together, though I've learned not to try my running and tennis on the same day we quarterback. The speed-reading class remains fascinating. I actually read a whole book . . . Steinbeck's *The Pearl* . . . in twelve minutes, with a more detailed level of comprehension than they expect at this point. If only I had the time (or the discipline to *make* the time) to do the home sessions adequately, I'm sure it would really work for me. At this point, nonetheless, I can read around eighteen hundred words a minute.

I can't anymore, because I lacked the discipline to continue with the class. Besides, as someone pointed out, there are some things you should really read very slowly, like poems . . . and the labels on medicine bottles.

October 10. A busy and valuable morning, though its only concrete result was eliminating two actresses from our shortening list of candidates for Ann. We now have left only one . . . Diana Muldaur, on whom we'll see film next week. It's amazing how hard it is to find the right girl. There should be more of them, or better ways to find them. [*We had found her. Diana was our choice, and excellent in her part.*]

October 13 (Sunday). I had time today for a good long think about Tommy Gries. His attitude toward this film . . . or, perhaps, his attitude at large . . . is very questionable. I talked to Walter about it. It seems to me it perhaps has to do with his recent achievements as a director in theatrical films. It's all come a bit late in the game for him, and he's finding the wine a bit heady, maybe. His attitudes are very arbitrary, his points of view on various creative elements very didactic (which is acceptable) and also very kaleidoscopic (which is not).

Tom's gone now. He died too young, without having done nearly all that he and his talent deserved. He was a gifted, mercurial, oddly unpredictable, and childlike man, but with the right material, he was a fine director. We made three pictures together, and the first, WILL PENNY, remains one of the best I've ever done.

October 27, St. Louis. Well . . . we're finally off and running. I think back five years to that day on the plane when I saw the photograph of Tittle on his hands and knees that started me into the musing that finally became this script. Now we begin. I had very little to do, actually. The sideline close-up of the young Catlin going into his first game running the team, and coming on the field with the Saints for the warm-up. It seemed to go all right, but it hardly could have failed to.

October 28, Los Angeles. I had my baptism of fire tonight with the team. I'd been a little nervous about the game contact, uncertain whether the players would be able to contain their standards of professional violence when tackling me, but it went surprisingly well. I was blitzed a total of sixteen times, each time by three Saints (defensive linesmen suited up as Cleveland Browns) with a combined weight of over 760 pounds, and only hit hard three times. This is important for me, to know I can handle the hitting, and important for the players, to know I'm willing to.

October 29. I wasn't supposed to get sacked in the shots today. I didn't either, dropping back coolly into the pocket to fire passes with what I thought was professional aplomb, until my offensive line playfully opened the gate on me just once, howling with laughter as I disappeared under the entire defense. This was good, too. I've got to get loose with these guys. I don't mix easily, but this is crucial. I actually completed several passes, though after the first one I tried, Monte Stickles said, "Chuck, next time it would be good if you could pass as far as the line of scrimmage!" I was supposed to throw a short pass to Abramowicz [*then the number-one receiver in the NFL*]. He said, "Look, man, I'll be right out there in the flat. You get the ball within three yards of me, I'll catch the sucker . . . just look for number forty-six." When he came back to the huddle after the play, he said, "Didn't you see my number?" "Number, hell!" I said. "I didn't even see any white jerseys!"

October 31. The work's going slowly. We've dropped about a day on the schedule so far, mostly on the football stuff and the night scenes. We had a meeting about it today, but it's a little difficult to approach Tom on this without great travail. Travail comes with the territory, of course. Certainly I don't want him fired (which will happen if we go too far over schedule) and have United Artists take over, because then I'll be the one left down here, shooting twenty pages a day for some hack.

The thing with Tommy and Frank is heating up more and more. We shot late again last night, on some tricky car stuff we don't really need. Tommy's shooting the frosting first and the meat and potatoes second. Something's got to give.

Tommy and Frank Baur (one of my oldest friends and one of the best production men in films) were like oil and water. Each rasped on the other's sore spots unceasingly.

November 2. Today I bought my ticket into the team. The shot of the tackle that ends Catlin's career just about ended mine in this film. Three big linebackers blitzed in on me, as they had rehearsed it, but the last time we did it I turned in midair after the second man hit me with a faked clothesline, so Doug Atkins (270 pounds) caught me a full-charge shot with his helmet in the ribs, cracking one. The pain was considerable, and the anger and frustration more than that. I ended the day taped and doped to the eyes, in the traditional bed of pain. Pain is the center of the game, of course, so it all counts as a plus, as long as it doesn't slow us . . .

These players are all superb athletes and were not clowning; they knew better than I how badly they could hurt me if they didn't control what they did. Nevertheless, their response to my injury was typical: Doug Atkins trotted over to where I lay writhing on the ground, leaned over to pat my cheek, and said, "Welcome to the NFL."

November 3 (Sunday), Tulane. This was a day I'd have normally expected to spend in bed, licking my wounds, but I spent it instead wrapped in tape and floating with medication, charging around the turf at Tulane while we filmed during the Dallas game. We shot all day long with the stands full of people, which should give us what we need for the end of the film. Under the circumstances, I literally felt no pain, so the day wasn't tough. It's just that I don't recall much of it.

November 6, Los Angeles. Tommy was tempting fate again this morning. He loves to cast nonactors, on the valid enough theory that you get some very unusual colors that way, especially casting within the individual's own experience. Using Vic Schwenk, the Saints general manager, as the Saints general manager was this sort of move, and it came off. He knows how to chew out a player very well, and that's what the scene was about. But the New York restauranteur crony of Tommy's who played a reporter was a bust. Our Dallas footage was extremely good, though. Almost exactly what we hoped to get.

November 7. I suppose I've known a few people as neurotic as Dick Elkins, but I've never known anyone who *enjoyed* his neurosis as much. He was late to work, which butts into *my* neurosis, of course, and then came in with the most bizarre interpretation of the scene I could imagine. Tommy pulled him down to earth a bit; the scene's OK, I think.

November 10 (Sunday). The first day off since we started in St. Louis, two weeks ago. Lydia looked lovely, I'm delighted to have her here, once we got over what we used to call our parking lot fight (which is where we used to have them, in the parking lot at the airport). It came a little later today, but the sun's lovely and warm when the storm has passed.

November 18, New Orleans. This was the longest and toughest of the football days, with fifteen hundred extras so we could shoot in the stands. I was choked a bit at first, just by the enormity of the whole masquerade. I mean, there I was, in the middle of Tulane stadium, running a pro team, and there was the Dallas team, waiting to eat me. They didn't, they were all infinitely helpful and patient. I eased as the day went on; absorbed the hard shots I had to take and completed the passes I had to complete.

November 22. This turned into quite a day. We started in the afternoon at the motel; shots of the team checking in the night before the game, mostly. I finished my part of this early and came in for my appearance at the opening of a local repertoire theater with the National Council on the Arts and Ladybird Johnson. I was only able to escort her down the aisle, and then race back out to Tulane, where we were shooting night football stuff. It must be the only time anyone ever went to the theater in a dinner jacket, jockstrap, and taped ankles.

November 26. We finished the location on schedule, straining a few tempers in the process. We had to press mightily on several things, but I don't think we sacrificed quality. Of course, we have some leeway in terms of moving scenes back to Hollywood that were set for New Orleans. Elkins was sent back to L.A. today, after making a spectacle of himself in the hotel lobby. We have only one more scene to do with him. I wish to God he hadn't turned out to be such a horse's ass.

November 29. My first day shooting on a Hollywood stage in about fifteen months; my first day ever on the Warner lot, though I still recall with relish that they paid me damages for one they pulled out from under me, some ten years ago. It's a roomy enough and solid lot, but the dressing rooms are sad and dingy, redolent of the thirties, somehow, and oddly depressing.

December 19. We finished the film on schedule, astounding the United Artists brass. This was possible only because of the driving pressure Frank Baur kept on at the cost of any sort of reasonable relationship with Tom. I don't really regret this, because I don't think it cost the picture anything meaningful, but it's too bad.

There's always a certain amount of tension between the production department, concerned with logistics and cost, and the director, concerned with quality. Ideally, it balances out. Many pictures have been spoiled because the production end was too stringent and cost-conscious, but pictures have also been spoiled because the director was too profligate and careless.

December 24. The day began sedately enough, but turned into one of the most complicated, emotion-fraught Christmas Eves I can remember. I finished my shopping in the nick, as usual, and looked forward to the carol-sing at the Manulises' with the family. What with one thing and another, lathered with storms of tears, we never made it. Not the least of our problems was the fact that our Michigan tree never showed up. I found myself driving the kids down Sunset at seven trying to remember where I'd seen trees for sale. We picked one of the last four; Holly said, "It looks like it needs a home."

December 25. Fraser was up before dawn, getting his orange minibike in operation, an undertaking that seemed to fascinate him endlessly. I think in his place I'd have finally lost interest in endlessly racing up and down the driveway, no matter how elegantly equipped I was, but then, it's been some time since I was thirteen years old. I'm going through the blue letdowns on the film. I can't get used to the idea that there's really nothing more I can do for the picture. Every time I see something in print about a quarterback, or the game, I gobble it up, forgetting I've done it all now.

December 27. I got up early to drive Fraser and Martin up to their first tennis tournament, but listened on the way to a far more historic event. We have finally sent men around the moon and brought them home again. It's such a staggering achievement there seems no way to mark it properly in a private journal, or the front page of *The New York Times,* for that matter. It somehow seems a group achievement . . . an American achievement. I guess the best comment is Borman's: "We did it."

December 31. This was a nothing sort of day to end the year on, though I passed a large part of it very pleasantly on a tennis court with Fray, whose game's progressing very well. We went to the Grieses' later to see the old year out, along with a mixed bag of Hollywood types. It was a pleasant evening, I guess, though this is not my favorite holiday. The year, though, is certainly one that counted. We had one film blown out from under us, but I finally made my football picture.

1969

A rising tide of
public service
appearances . . .

an *Apes* sequel . . .

Julius Caesar
in London and
Spain . . .

The Hawaiians . . .

an offer to run
for the Senate.

As Mark Antony in
Julius Caesar
JOHN BRYSON

As Whit Hoxworth in
The Hawaiians
LYDIA HESTON

January 9, Los Angeles. Walter and I talked a bit about mounting a trade press campaign for Academy nominations on WILL PENNY. We did get excellent notices on it, but I'm embarrassed at the idea of flacking for a nomination. I spent the evening presenting the awards at the College Theater Festival, which, in the time-honored fashion of awards banquets, took me two and a half hours.

January 12 (Sunday). There was very little in the day, aside from the usual pleasure of life on the ridge. I turned off the Super Bowl after I realized Namath's team was going to win. I have no great affection for the Colts, but the Jets' victory was, inevitably, a victory for the loudmouths of the world, and I hate to see them triumph. Now there will be a hundred small boys in the Pop Warner Leagues emulating Namath, and I think this is too bad. Really too bad.

January 15. I spoke with Tom Gries on the phone this morning about the HAWAIIANS script. He agrees it's wise to lose the whole political story line in the last third, as Walter Mirisch suggests. The main problem in films made from long novels is always that there's more story to tell, more character to develop than there is time to do it in. This has ruined several films for me (DUNDEE, PEKING) and flawed some others (GSET, CID).

The main problem with the HAWAIIANS script was that the story is really about Nyuk Tsin, the Chinese girl who becomes the matriarch of a prosperous clan in Hawaii. Though I was the top-lined actor in the film, my part was really less important than hers. In an effort to center the film on my role, the script took the story away from its real core.

January 22. I ran the first sequence I've seen assembled so far that really fell short. The flashback of Jessica and me in bed before the wedding just doesn't come off. For one thing, our underwear showed. Worse, the scene's flat. It was fine in the script, but not on the screen. I don't know what we can do about it, either, except cut it.

We did, but the scene was missed. Jessica Walter was excellent as my wife in NUMBER ONE; I think I failed, at least in this scene.

January 25. I awoke this morning to find that Bill Isaac's backyard had washed out my driveway. It also took out our waterline, and of course kept our cars marooned, but we're far better off than our neighbors below, who have a good bit of our ridge in their houses, leaving little room for them.

January 27, New York. A very full day, as I'm fond of observing in this journal. It was, though. Aside from the National Council on the Arts meeting that brought me here, I'd scheduled a SAG hearing with

John Cassavetes on his nonunion shooting of FACES. He proved oddly intransigent ("Fine me! I think you should."). My attempt to smooth it down in terms of arriving at some sort of compromise turned him off completely. I still think we could reach an equitable agreement, but he seems to have a need to discharge his guilt by accepting a fine.

I have great respect for John, the archetypical independent film maker. I'm not at all certain that he had "a need to discharge his guilt" at all. I think he felt perfectly justified, as an artist, in using union actors in a nonunion film. Frankly, I was inclined to sympathize with him, but the official SAG position required me to be unbending.

January 30, Los Angeles. We began to hack away at the horrendous mess that keeps us marooned on the ridge. I'd never used a chain saw before. It's a spectacular tool, but damned hard to use. It's heavy as sin, and as dangerous. We got the trees and heavy brush cut away, so a path can be made over the top of the mound of mud that cascades across the drive.

February 5. It rained again today; just as we were beginning to dig out from under, the drives are blocked again. One more day of good weather would have done it, but one more day is just what we're not likely to get. So there was no tennis, no work, and no repair on our slide damage. It's all covered with plastic, in the hope we lose nothing more.

February 13. Citron's upset with Fox over my appearance in the APES sequel. The part's longer than I want to do and the latest script's not good, but Fox insists I have to be in the film or they can't make it. Citron feels my relationship with Zanuck is such that I should make some compromise. I'm inclined to agree.

February 17, New York/Los Angeles. This was another one of those quick ones. The New York SAG meeting did what it was supposed to do . . . settle the Cassavetes thing and quell whatever stirrings of unease there was in the New York membership about it.

Happily, this was the end of it. I have no idea whether John has been careful to shoot his subsequent films under SAG rules. I hope so.

March 1, Los Angeles. I suppose it's some measure of my nature that I was more interested in talking to Tony Trabert on the tennis court today than to Edward Albee during Jennings Lang's party tonight. Albee has a febrile, coiled sort of nature that I found a little off-putting.

This seems a rather presumptive judgment. Albee may simply have been ill-adjusted to meeting strangers, as I am myself. Celebrity has its drawbacks for shy people.

March 17. I remember twenty-five years ago the way she looked, in violet, and how marvelous it seemed to me that she would marry me. That's still what I feel. There have been bad times, but I know I'm more because I married her than I would ever have been alone. I think we celebrated that tonight, and more, too.

March 21. The first day of spring offered inauspicious weather, raining the afternoon away. For that matter, it wasn't all that much of a day from any point of view. I went to MGM to discuss the makeup for HAWAIIANS with Bill Tuttle [*head of makeup there*]. It was very depressing to realize there wasn't a camera rolling on the entire lot. There may be a message in this for us all. If BEN-HUR turns a profit in its rerelease, it will all go to keeping the light bill paid in an empty studio.

March 23. I seem to be involved in a rising tide of public service appearances of one kind or another, though I've learned long since never to be available for the dinner that precedes all these performances. I read a poem (not a bad one) at a dinner for Helen Keller tonight, when I really would've liked to join the whole affair. I remember when she came to see ANTONY AND CLEOPATRA and sat with her hand on the apron of the stage, to feel the vibrations of the actors moving. Miss Cornell had her come back afterward to meet us all. She felt my armor and my face and said, "Strong. Roman." Tonight, though, we really did have an early dinner, with some old friends from Asheville, so we could only go to the Keller banquet in time for the program, in which I was glad to have a part.

March 25. I had a chance to talk a little with Tom Gries again about HAWAIIANS, but found little inspiration there. It may be this film is not his kind of thing. Nothing has yet ignited me on it, I'm ashamed to say. Meantime, Jim Franciscus called, frothing at what he feels are the inadequacies of the APES II script. I'm inclined to agree, but I don't know how much can be improved. As for putting my ridge back together, that's moving slowly too. (Just like doing a movie.)

March 26. I was dissatisfied with almost everything about the day, though I got a helluva lot done. I (or Citron, really) put the fear of God into the studio re the APES II script.

It was not only foolish, but wrong of me to expect to participate seriously in the script revisions on a project I was only peripherally involved in.

I did an acceptable job of supplying the introductions for a video-taped series of lectures by Alvina [*Krause, who taught me acting at Northwestern*]. I was a little annoyed at having to make still another speech before the ballet tonight, when the president of the bloody group is Joanne Woodward, whose husband [*Paul Newman*] is a perfectly serviceable public figure, suitable for occasions of this kind. Anyway, it was good ballet.

March 30–April 12. For the first time in the more than thirteen years I've been keeping this increasingly compulsive and no doubt finally trivial record, I lost two weeks of it. The net effect is merely to flaw the small virtue of its completeness, but it's a nagging error to have fallen into. The first days of the week of March 30 (to retrace my steps, however sketchily) were spent in the sort of desultory activity that had filled the week before: some conferences, a SAG meeting, a little work on projects ahead, and a little more on projects behind. And tennis. On April third, we flew to Mexico City as guests of the Mexican government (at last cashing in the trip they'd given me when I narrated their Sound and Light program at Teotihuacán some years ago). We were two days in Mexico City, seeing the Sound and Light, and doing various public relations chores. Then we went on to Yucatán and saw Merida, Uxmal, Chitzen Itza, and Cozumel, returning Saturday via PAA through Miami. It was a lovely week, full of sun, sea, and Mayan ruins.

April 14. After the mix-up yesterday, when I made my position clear on kiting off to the desert to spend three days there on these scenes [*for the APES sequel*] (not possible of course, with all I have to do), they flew me up on the crew's charter this morning and choppered me back home to the Mulholland fire station when I'd finished for the day. The script is still nothing much, the direction (by Ted Post of the old New York days) very brisk and permissive. This was all complicated by a terrible, tearing wind all day, plus the fact that the fall they made to match my long hair from the original APES is not good. I'm not hopeful of the result . . . but then, I won't be long in it.

April 15. The wind was blowing just as hard in the desert, the material's just as unappealing as before, but the day passed quickly, and I was whisked to and from location as briskly as I could've hoped for (tiny spring flowers spilling under us like yellow paint across the desert floor; from eight hundred feet in a chopper, it's breathtaking). The PRO screening tonight went well for me, but the United Artists types obviously didn't like the film. They did suggest a new, better title: NUMBER ONE. Otherwise, the evening was something like a disaster.

They were right: The film did not do particularly well domestically and has never had a full foreign release. Whether a more enthusiastic effort on the part of United Artists would've produced better results is hard to say. I like the film and feel my performance as the desperate quarterback facing the end of his career is some of the best contemporary work I've done, though I can see the character, a somewhat cold and self-centered man, is hard for audiences to empathize with. I'm nonetheless proud that every football player who's seen the film responded to the accuracy of its portrait of pro football. "Hey, man," they say, "that's what it's like!"

April 18, London. Our arrival in London was dented by the theft of Lydia's mink from the plane on landing. It's only a thing, of course, but she's very sad to lose it. I spent the day at the National Film Theatre, choosing and editing sequences from several films, on a very classy German Movieola of a type I've never seen in the U.S. With Lydia and Bea Sellmer, in from Madrid, I had steak at the Guinea, then we went to the National Film Theatre so I could introduce TOUCH OF EVIL. It would do better now than it did when it was made, like any innovative film.

The British Film Institute did a week-long retrospective of my films, screening seven or eight of them in toto, and running excerpts from several others in the seminars I gave. I enjoyed the whole thing thoroughly.

April 19. This was one of those days, of course. I finished picking the excerpts for the afternoon seminar only just in time to come back to the Dorchester and work on my opening for tonight. The lecture went very well; the audience was knowledgeable and enthusiastic. (Also large; they turned away twice the capacity of the hall.) Then a reception, a TV interview, and some time with the CAESAR group. Snell is young, bright, Canadian; Burge is older and very quiet. We might have done better there, but I know the play well myself, I can hope he does, too. The Gielgud play was good tonight, though over supper afterward Sir John raised some misgivings about Orson as Brutus.

John Gielgud is the most totally candid man I've ever met. We'd been considering Orson Welles as Brutus in the film of CAESAR we were planning. It was a part he'd played with distinction more than once. Sir John daunted us all, however, when he said abruptly, backstage in his dressing room, "Oh, but he's much too fat for it now." He was, I expect, but he could have acted it beautifully.

April 20 (Sunday). . . . and I *am* in England, now that April's there. It was too early to try the grass, but the clay courts at Wimbledon were perfect and the sun was warm . . . altogether the England the Lake poets eulogized. The afternoon came up to the morning, too . . . they turned away however many hundreds it was from the lecture, which I did damn well. I can't conceal my pleasure at this tribute (immodest though it is to call it that).

April 24, London/Wilmette. The usual pressure of a morning full of departure. As well as the welter of paper work that swirls in the air then (why is this such a burden? In earlier times, men seemed to *enjoy* their correspondence.), there was a conference with Peter Snell and Stuart Burge, back from Romania. No good locations there; we'll probably go to Spain for JULIUS CAESAR, though extras now cost twenty dollars a day there. (Tripled since the Bronston days.) I caught the plane on cue, worked on the CAESAR script all across the Atlantic, landed in Wilmette with the leaves coming out on the trees in a rich midwestern green. It's very good to be back here, now and again. In some sense, you *can* go home again. Indeed, in some sense, you can't leave.

April 28, Los Angeles. I'm still slaving away on my promised chore in the APES sequel. I'm beginning to regret it, for more than obvious reasons. This is the first film . . . first acting . . . I've ever done in my life for which I have no enthusiasm, which is a vital loss. To choose always the most expedient solution to a scene, to work without watching dailies . . . I can't adjust to this image of myself. I was comforted by the marvelously creative sport of redacting the CAESAR script to send back to Snell, indicating my proposed cuts. I think I've found valid and filmic solutions to several scenes.

April 30. It's very difficult to adjust to working on APES II. I thought there'd be nothing for me but a few simple physical scenes; instead, I find myself tangled in creative discussions in aid of a project in whose creative validity I have no confidence.

May 2. I was distressed to realize one scene of what we did in the cell (at *least* one scene) will not play. We also had to reshoot the stuff with the girl after she's shot, partly because she couldn't lie dead without blinking, but mainly because I simply failed to make it work at all. Maybe I played a fair death scene. The concept *was* good, in fact. At least I've done what I told Dick Zanuck I would do.

I did my best during the shooting of the few scenes I had in the APES sequel to keep my mouth shut and do my work, a salutary experience for me. Still, I detect in these entries an excess of self-pity, the worst of human failings.

May 3. They sneaked PRO (now officially NUMBER ONE) in San Diego tonight, but I felt a little spooked about going down and sweating in that dark womb while the great beast passed its judgment. I stayed home all day and tennised instead, as well as running Fray out to Port Hueneme in the middle of the bloody night for a diving expedition. When he got home, we profited to the extent of some abalone he'd gotten. APES II is finished, now I should concentrate on THE HAWAIIANS before I take off for CAESAR.

May 5. I trekked out to MGM again to let Bill Tuttle try to take fifteen years off my puss for the opening of HAWAIIANS. Good luck to him. They're at last pouring the curbings on our road, in black concrete. This week should see it back to where it was (only much better, and much, much more expensive).

May 6. I spent three weary hours fitting costumes for HAWAIIANS. They're very good (including some that are surprisingly back in style), but, Christ, I hate to stand there and be pinned and tucked at. Still, no one can fit costumes for you, no one can try makeups, no one can read scripts. I was glad to come home and spend the evening doing a map with Fray for his history assignment. I could've been a moderately happy and moderately good cartographer, I think.

May 12. I realized today that I've probably worn more false noses, cheeks, wigs, beards, sideburns, and moustaches than any actor since Lon Chaney. You could work up a helluva gallery of stills. I must do that sometime. For now, we arrived, by wearisome effort, at some good effects to create the aging of Whip Hoxworth. I wish I had as much confidence in the script as I do in the makeups and the wardrobe. Fray came home tonight from a date with a girl who had waited patiently for him in an empty house she no longer lived in, because she'd forgotten to tell him her new address. I didn't think girls did things like that anymore.

May 17, PAA for London. I don't know how many times I've climbed on PAA #120, but I feel as though I've worn a deep trail in the sky, like a boy driving the cows down through a muddy pasture. I got a scrap of time with the kids and time enough to pack, though not enough to do the paper work. There was certainly none to play tennis. When I kept my rackets out of the bag until the last minute, Muriel said to Lydia, "When he dies and knocks on the Pearly Gates, if the Devil taps him on the shoulder and says, 'How about a little tennis?' he'll go."

May 19, London. Of course I went to the wrong place first . . . to the grubby little hotel where we're rehearsing instead of to Nathan's for the costume fitting I was scheduled for. (Why is it that all . . . *all* . . . rehearsals are held in such depressing surroundings?) Also, the armor didn't fit, of course, and was obviously designed by a man who'd never worn the damn stuff, especially on horseback. I have.

May 20. I began the morning on the phone, buying an Andrew Wyeth for Lydia. Then I had the remarkable experience of rehearsing JULIUS CAESAR with John Gielgud. I vividly recall how much in awe of him I was when I was at Northwestern. I still am, for that matter. That incredible cello voice is still there, and he still reads verse as well as any man alive. Better. He and Jason Robards were to work on the murder scene, but Jason didn't show again. It gave us all the afternoon off; I spent it shopping for things I don't need, getting my stiff neck cracked (which I did need), and playing tennis. In the locker room at the All-England, Rod Laver told me he has a tennis elbow, too. It has to be the only thing our games have in common.

May 21, Cannes. I'd thought, with luck, I might get through an entire film career without going to the Cannes Festival, but it was not to be. Commonwealth United is anxious to show off our little Shakespeare production, so they're throwing a party here. It was a fine blowout, but I'd rather have the money it cost for an extra day or two of location shooting. As for the festival, I suspect the disheveled romp Cannes is reputed to be no longer exists. There are only a few actors here, fewer smashing girls, but a great number of press people, anxiously looking for something to write about.

May 22, Madrid. Having gone virtuously to bed at two in the morning, I got up earlier than most in this gathering, I suspect, and had my usual frustrating session on a clay court. At least I'm now at the point where I can beat a mediocre club player, even on clay. The flight to Madrid was odd, somehow. I haven't been here since PEKING. I settled into the same suite, in the same hotel. Then, we seemed doomed to disaster, as indeed we were. This time, the prospects are somewhat brighter.

May 24. Picking a horse for a film is always a good time, with just an edge of apprehension. (Will it work out again . . . have I enough seat and hands for the horse?) It did, I do; the horse is a baroque, dark bay with an actorish, flamboyant action, like a Delacroix painting of a lion hunt. Jason wanted no part of the undertaking, claiming riding's not his work. Fair enough. Little does he know how precarious my security in the saddle in fact is. I rediscovered this myself working on the mounted swordplay. [*It takes quite a while to get a twentieth-century horse to accept having a sword swung past his head, while other horses are running into him and men are screaming all around.*]

May 25 (Sunday). I spent my day off on an acrimonious armor fitting. Do they imagine a craft armorers took a lifetime to learn, spending a year at a time on one suit of plate, can be picked up by Cockney trade-school girls working from *measurements?* Of course the greaves will look like drainpipes! I threw out much of it and modified the rest. The result is wearable and looks reasonably OK, though the costume designer will no doubt be in tears. Never mind; I was wearing armor when he was still in art school, designing wedding gowns.

I sound very formidable in all this, and I was. Of all human apparel, armor is the most totally subjugated to function. If it doesn't work, it's not wearable. It's particularly hard to make it work on horseback.

May 26. The rehearsal went well today. We got Jason on a horse, where he discovered he will survive after all. Dick Chamberlain is serious and hardworking. What Stuart calls the picnic scene will work well . . . played on a broad flat rock where Antony lounges eating his shellfish lunch, all unbuttoned, contrasting Octavius's fully armored, mounted impatience for the conflict. ("Now, Antony, our hopes are answered . . .") It's a good concept for the scene; it should give us a chance to show the man. The confrontation with Brutus and Cassius is not so fully realized yet. Jason's still rattled a bit by the horses, but he'll improve, no doubt.

It's time I offered some sort of explanation for my scurrilous opinions of Jason Robard's performance as Brutus. Jason has proved himself to be one of the most distinguished actors in the American theater over the past generation and, more recently, in film. Nevertheless, I submit that Shakespeare is not the author that displays his talents to their best advantage.

May 28. We started off on JULIUS CAESAR somewhat limpingly, hampered by the bugs that always snag the first day on any film, as well as a sullen, cold drizzle that forced us out of the picnic scene. They started instead with Jason, who seemed somewhat tense and shaky on the words, but fitted well enough into Stuart's very good overall concept of the scene. The smaller roles were effective. When they got to it, I did the tag of the play pretty well, though I felt rushed a bit, fighting to get the scene before we lost the soft, last light.

June 1 (Sunday). They'd scheduled the Cassius suicide scene today, but we had solid overcast, so we shot the confrontation, a less crucial scene. It went all right. Richard Johnson's a very good, bitter Cassius. Jason seems to have no real sense of the language; it either comes out totally flat or totally verse. That's all the more reason to cut all we can from the play. Not every line has gold in it. If it has no treasure and doesn't advance the plot or character (and not every line does *that*, either), it should be cut.

This is sacrilege to people who read and write about Shakespeare. People who do *Shakespeare, cut him. I'd bet my soul that Shakespeare cut Shakespeare.*

June 3, London. It's nicer to be back in London, waiting to shoot, than still in Spain, waiting to shoot. The company, the tennis, and the hotel are all better. Also there was a huge packet of mail, including four letters from Lydia. Tennis and the evening with the McDonalds was pleasant, and the Guinea stood up to its usual standards. My choice of a play was only so-so . . . a bill of one acts, including a very ordinary Pinter. His gift consists largely of a clear ear for dialogue, it seems to me.

I realize this is a terribly unfashionable opinion, but I do not blush for it. Thirty or forty years more should suffice to determine Pinter's permanent value.

June 7. The rest of the location footage . . . several hours in all . . . looked OK. Joe Canutt's not happy with the battle cuts, but I think we have all we need for our film, the best that could be gotten in the time he had, using extras. A good rule to remember: Extras will not fight. You must use stunt men or soldiers.

We used local civilians as Brutus's legions, and our limited number of stunt men, led by me, as Antony's cavalry. Joe Canutt's best efforts could not persuade the locals to stand their ground to a cavalry charge. Take after take, they broke and bolted when we got within ten yards of them. You can't blame them, really; Napoleon's infantry did the same thing at Waterloo.

My work looks OK, but I wish I hadn't worn that damn lavender cloak. It's too Easter-eggy. I fear Robards's Brutus may be slightly boring. Chamberlain's good; so is Richard Johnson, his death scene especially.

June 9. They started in the studio today, and I couldn't resist going out there to brood over the proceedings, though there was nothing for me. I made some points about the set, including a fervent plea for black shadows. (My taste in camera work reduces itself to those specifications, which must be painful to theorists of the aesthetics of film. Just lots of black shadows.) I had a quiet solo evening, enjoying a steak tartare and a history of the Roman Imperial Army, which was better than the Axelrods' party afterward. (No reflection on George's party . . . just my mood.)

June 10. I was supposed to start today, but we got only as far as a
   lineup. We're not getting quick setups, I have to say. We *are* getting
   good-looking shots, but I hope this doesn't mean dropping a day a
   week. As I get on toward the mean old son of a bitch I'm planning to
   be as an elderly character actor, I realize I simply like to work at a
   brisk pace . . . especially on locations. Well, at least I got a chance to
   check out my costume and makeup. I had the BEN-HUR ring flown
   over to wear in these scenes. A good luck talisman?

June 15 (Sunday). I couldn't have had a better Father's Day gift than
   the arrival of the girl who made me a father in the first place. We
   spent the bulk of the day in bed, of course, but used up what looks
   like being the last of the perfect London weather by going out to
   lunch at a house in Chelsea. After dinner alone in the suite, we took a
   long walk in Hyde Park, through the dimming English summer
   twilight.

June 18. Lydia's in the grip of a bad migraine today and I had my
   problems, too. There are rumors of a palace revolution in the
   company, which is nonsense. Stuart is not the ideal director for us,
   but we have no other course at this point. You have to go home with
   the guy that brung you. We have too short a schedule, too slow a
   cameraman, and some performance problems. On the other hand, we
   have the play. I've seen nothing marvelous, but we haven't gotten to
   the central stuff yet. We must press ahead, and grip down harder.
   Harder.

June 27. Lydia's back from York [*where she'd gone with Mickey Seltzer*].
   She apparently had a marvelous time; the town lived up to her hopes.
   I worked hard, if wordlessly, escorting John Gielgud into the Senate.
   The shot was good; one of the most effective camera solutions to a
   scene Stuart's come up with so far. A good plastic movement,
   booming around and through the stairs, and the scene with
   Artemidorus [*Christopher Lee*] was effective. We shot on it all day,
   with great difficulty. (*Christ,* but it takes time to light a shot over here.)

June 29. A lazy morning, then a lovely drive down to Kent to pick up the
   Roman painting I'd commissioned. The forest there is surprisingly
   wild, in terms of my understanding of English forests, anyway. It
   included a peacock sitting on a fence for Lydia to photograph. Wood
   is a very direct, craftsmanlike kind of man. I like the painting he's
   done for me very much. It looks like the last legionary on Hadrian's
   Wall.

July 1. I started the biggest scene [*the funeral orations*] I have in the
   play (biggest scene *in* the play, for that matter). Typically, it's the
   last thing we do. At that, it's better than having it first. Jason stayed

home sick. (Poor Jason . . . you can't help being suspicious.) We were able to shoot around him readily, though we got only a long master on the first third of the speech. I felt good in it, my voice holding up well. I'm as well prepared on this speech as on anything I've ever done in film, and it's obviously the best scene I've ever had a chance at. (So don't blow it, dummy!)

July 3. The longest day was the last day, given my dawn commitment to do my run in Hyde Park early enough so Jim Murray could do a brief coffee interview about it before I left for the studio. (I also bet with him on Laver versus Ashe. I won.) I spent the rest of the day finishing on the oration scene, including Jason's part (he's back, and healthy). My voice barely lasted the distance, but it lasted. I'd been working fourteen hours when we did the last close-up on top of the steps with the will ("I must not read it!"), and I felt full of adrenaline and confidence. This is the best part I've ever played in film, and I'm happy with how it turned out. I can't tell about the film yet, but I'm damned sure I did well.

I was good in the part, but that's not a remarkable achievement. Marc Antony is the most actor-proof of the great Shakespearean parts. If you can't get by with that one, you'd better stay away from Shakespeare.

July 4, London/Los Angeles. The whole day was the trip home. London's the only foreign city I ever feel any pangs of regret at leaving, but I left with a high heart, eager for my ridge, not regretful to be missing the Wimbledon Final, or more of summer in England. Holly didn't come out to meet us, being "in charge of the decorations . . ." but Fray did, and we had a fine, family sort of evening, complete with fireworks, programmed by Fray, set off by all of us, with Holly and Lydia gingerly joining in on the sparklers.

July 10, Los Angeles. I spent a tough meeting exploring the latest ramifications of our long history on NUMBER ONE. Now it turns out United Artists doesn't want to make an overseas release at all, which is startling. We proposed they let us do it with another distributor, but they have second thoughts about that, naturally. It seems to me they're not in a position to argue too much, but they will. And argue . . . and argue.

The theory, I believe, was that foreign audiences don't understand football, but I don't think this is sound. The film wasn't about football anyway; it was about a man who played football for a living.

July 14. A damn full day, in which I had no time to do all the things I'd scheduled. I did my chores manfully at a cocktail do for Tina Chen, the Chinese actress playing Nyuk Tsin in *Hawaiians*. Being new to it, I imagine, she found it even more of a chore, but she held up beautifully.

Our best break in the making of this film was finding Tina for its major role. I'd pointed out to Walter Mirisch that my part was really secondary, and that the picture depended on finding somewhere an experienced and talented Oriental actress to play Nyuk Tsin. He found Tina.

July 17, to Honolulu. We got off on schedule, with remarkably few of the alarums and excursions that usually attend our departures, taking Muriel with us and leaving Helene Bean [*Lydia's secretary*] minding the store with Jolly in residence as surrogate household head till Lydia and the family get back. I'm depressed, and I don't really know why. I can't pull myself out of these doldrums and into a proper enthusiasm for the part.

THE HAWAIIANS is one of the few films in my career I've undertaken less than full-heartedly. I feel very guilty about this and can't really explain it. Perhaps my awareness of how far short we'd fallen with Caesar, and how hard it was proving to be to mount ANTONY AND CLEOPATRA, dampened my spirits. In any event, it was very nonconstructive on my part.

July 18. I started another one today. The ship is beautiful . . . somehow film never really captures the incredible beauty of full-rigged sailing ships. We're planning some chopper shots of the CARTHAGINIAN with zoom lenses. (How much the improved camera technology has changed film since I came into it.) The weather was calm and overcast much of the day, but we finally got a shot or two. It was an expensive day, especially since this is really just credit footage.

July 23. We finally wound up the sea sequences today finishing the scene with the dead Chinese. We were lucky, working in an almost flat calm. I'd painted lurid pictures to Tom of the seasickness problem with forty extras shut in the hold if any sort of sea was running. We've dropped about two and a half days on the sea stuff, but cutting the scene on the yacht reduces this in schedule terms to one day plus.

July 28. Lydia, to our mutual consternation, had to go to the hospital today. She slipped and strained her back in some way this morning, and was in spasm with it. The X rays indicate no spinal involvement, but she'll have to be there several nights. Sam Peckinpah called, we sat drinking awhile. He's bushy-tailed, fresh from the huge success of THE WILD BUNCH.

August 3 (Sunday). This was about as dreary a day off as you could have in an island paradise, I guess. I'd hoped to play tennis, but determined not to ask Fray to play, on the theory it's bad to press him, so the upshot was no tennis. I swam a bit, but came back to the beach to find a crowd of fans waiting at the water's edge with cameras. It reminded me of the scene we just shot of the lepers waiting on Molokai to plunder the new arrivals as they struggled in through the surf. I swam a quarter of a mile up the beach while two girls padded patiently along through the sand, waiting for my inevitable emergence. I felt like an idiot.

Celebrity is to a certain extent a paranoid condition. You have to be careful not to surrender to the feeling of being pursued. I take my responsibility to the people who buy the tickets very seriously, but my life has strengthened the reclusive strains in my nature.

August 6. Every morning I get up and go down and swim, then sit down for my makeup looking out at a sunrise that looks as though it were painted on a back cloth. But I lack heart for it . . . I lack heart. We're falling farther behind and, though I haven't seen a foot of film yet, I'm uneasy. I haven't spent enough time on the script to be sure what's wrong or to what degree my initial ennui about the project is coloring my reaction. But I worry.

August 9. We're into the waterfront scene saying good-bye to my son. The boy cast for the part doesn't look much like either me or John Philip Law (who plays him as a grown man). At my suggestion, they strengthened his nose and bleached his hair, which makes him a little closer to old Broken Beak. They spoke of having Fray do it, but this seemed an impossible idea to me, though not to Lydia, somewhat to my surprise.

Fray's performance as the infant Moses at the age of three months seems to have inoculated him against the acting bug. Perhaps one of the reasons for this is that he's had a clearer picture of the profession than most people, who know only famous actors. When Fray was ten years old, a reporter in the London airport said to him, "Don't you want to be a famous actor like your father?" "Most actors aren't famous," Fray replied stoutly. "My daddy knows a lot of good actors that don't even work."

August 19, En route to Los Angeles and New Orleans. We shot from eight to six today covering a one-page scene. Sixteen setups seemed too many. I'm glad it also seemed to be a good scene. I finished at six and plunged home to change for dinner with the kids, then to the airport with Lydia to undertake our argosy for NUMBER ONE.

We were flying to New Orleans for the premiere, and two days of work, over the weekend.

August 21, New Orleans. World premiere: NUMBER ONE. A very crowded day indeed. The usual press hoo-hoo was loaded with extra promotional gimmicks not really worth doing. Still, we were very lucky, all in all. If the premiere had been half an hour later, we would've been caught in a cloudburst. Instead, all went well. Except our hotel caught fire. The top three floors of the Roosevelt were burned out, including our suite, but I conned my way up and got our clothes out, slightly smoke-stunk, before they bedded us down in another hotel for the four hours' sleep we had coming before leaving for the airport. I must say it made for an unusual premiere.

August 22, Kauai, Hawaii. My day started at something like nine last night, Hawaiian time. I made one last trip to the sodden ruins of the Presidential Suite at the Roosevelt to pick up my shaving kit, forgotten in the rush when I rescued our clothes, then all day long on planes to get back here in time to climb into that damn juvenile makeup again for a scene in the empty house. Very late, we finally finished the sequence. The house will now be permitted to return to the jungle which had nearly digested it when our art director found it. Elliot Martin called; he now wants me to do not CAINE MUTINY but TIME OF YOUR LIFE, at the Music Center.

August 31 (Sunday), Kauai. The first day of a two-day holiday made me chafe a bit, but worked out pretty well. We idled up the river on a tourist trip (the same river where I'll be spending several days at the end of the schedule pretending I'm in French Guiana). We got Mother to her plane on time, happy from her visit, then settled into what's always the homestretch on a location . . . the time when all the guests have gone and there's only us.

September 6. The scene today was simple enough. Again, it needed rewriting, which we worked out on the set. It's largely a question of turning the obligatory exposition into real speech. Now that we need you, John O'Hara, where are you?

September 8. Peter Snell, on the phone from London, said he won't be ready with a print of CAESAR this week after all. Still, I'm happy with the way my editing of ANTONY AND CLEOPATRA is going. I've delved up ideas out of my subconscious stew where that play's been simmering for twenty years.

One of the most satisfying experiences in my career was extracting a screenplay from ANTONY AND CLEOPATRA. *In my mind, it's the most filmable of all Shakespeare's plays. He has been described as the first screenwriter. If so, this is his best screenplay.*

September 14, Los Angeles. The ANTONY cutting's progressing. I've no idea whether or not the film will ever be made, but I think my ideas for it are as valid as any thinking ever done on this play in screen terms. [*Not surprising, since no one had ever tried to adapt the play before.*] In effect, I'm writing a screenplay. A lot of men can write screenplays, but don't know much about Shakespeare. A lot of men know Shakespeare, but not screenplays. I know this play.

September 21 (Sunday). I didn't tell her I was coming home, and the look of her eyes, widening out of sleep as I stood by her bed, was worth flying all that way to see.

September 24, Kauai. United Artists persuaded me of the necessity of coming back before I'm needed for shooting so I could do a day of public relations (foreign press, a TV documentary, and film for the British Milk Board), so I boarded my commuter jet back to the Garden Isle. I was put to work on arrival with a press dinner I was just a little weary for. Besides, you have to work harder with the foreign press bunch.

September 26. We're moving slowly on the street. Scenes of disaster always seem to go that way: In real life, catastrophe takes seconds, on the screen, days. There's probably a profound observation in there somewhere. I did little today but dash up and down streets lined with elaborately blazing buildings. It all looked very brave, but it didn't bother me. *Heights* bother me; fire, animals, water, no. I also did my public service chore for the British Milk Board, which will garner us a little space on BBC for HAWAIIANS, come release time.

September 28 (Sunday). The drivers put on a luau; the first one I've ever been to that really worked the way they're supposed to. I still think poi is revolting, but the pig was as good as any I've ever tasted. Hawaiians must be the only people in history whose old people join so fully, so joyfully in any entertainment. It's truly lovely to watch these wrinkled septuagenarians writhing through a hula with surprisingly erotic effect.

September 30. At dinner with Walter Mirisch, I discovered he's decided to pull the plug Saturday, hot or cold. He can do this primarily by cutting the river sequence down. It's a good idea (aside from my pleasure at going home). No matter how well it's shot, that river stuff's the kind of thing Dennis O'Keefe used to do in the old Pine-Thomas pictures.

October 4, Return to Los Angeles. My birthday, and the best present I could've gotten was the finish of the location, which the gods, Walter Mirisch, and Tom (the last somewhat against his will) presented to me in slick order before the end of the afternoon. I had time for a swim after packing at the hotel. I walked along the beach, in the last light with a towel around my waist, suddenly moved (now that I was homebound?) by the beauty of the place. I stood ankle-deep in the soft surf watching the sun drop in the ocean. The sky was the blue they call cerulean when they're looking at Italian paintings, but the clouds were blue-ivory, like a baby's eyelids. The last sunlight was brilliant on the wave tops, but the foam on the sand was lavender, and the fine tracery of the palms on the point was black, like a Japanese drawing. The impression was still vivid in my mind four hours later, as I sat drinking in the VIP lounge in Oahu, waiting for the plane home.

October 14, Los Angeles. We're still bickering with United Artists about NUMBER ONE. The film's holding up well domestically . . . it's outgrossing IT MUST BE BELGIUM in some situations . . . but United Artists is still very leery of it overseas. They now want to try test engagements in England and *Japan,* which would skim off the cream, if we eventually acquired the film for foreign distribution. It's all very frustrating.

October 26 (Sunday), Anacapa Island. This was the long delayed diving trip Fray and I had planned. Since it wasn't a big charter boat full of people, my usual paranoia about strangers was no problem. My only real inadequacy was as a diver. Fray hovered round me like a protective mother hen the whole time we were on the bottom.

November 1. I'm going to London a week from Monday to see CAESAR and, I hope, plan for ANTONY. (If this is really possible. I want to do this so much, I can't believe it'll come off.) Walter Mirisch is also interested in proceeding (on a very limited budget, which no doubt also applies to my compensation) on I AM LEGEND. I'd like to work for him again. Would Sam Peckinpah be a possibility to direct?

November 5. Well, I finally finished the film. I recognized its value, coming sandwiched between two films of less than total appeal I wanted very much to make. Whether it'll work is, of course, a question; one I've learned long since not to try and answer at this stage. I can say it seems to me better than I thought it could be. Several performances are better than I hoped, including both the major Chinese roles. Tina and Mako are really very good, as are Geraldine and Alec. I think I'm OK, but I haven't seen enough yet to tell. I'll look at a rough cut in ten days.

November 11, London. London still has that "great city" quality, even on a wet November morning. I'd forgotten to inform the Dorchester of my arrival, but they scraped up a bedroom for the crucial nap essential to the Heston Plan for Polar Trips. I got two hours, then forced myself up (also essential) for lunch with Peter Snell (in the course of which Jolly West appeared, in town from an Oxford symposium). Later we ran Jack Gold's film, thinking of him for ANTONY. He did a good job on an ordinary script. Then we ran the rough cut on CAESAR; a fair job on a superb play. I'm very good, as is Dick Johnson, and Gielgud, of course. The rest are OK to good, except for Robards, who is barely adequate. The film moves well, after the opening scenes.

November 12. We ran Anne Bancroft's film, in which she's brilliant, but I'm not convinced she's right for Cleopatra. She has an American quality, also she seems somehow a *victim.* Vulnerability is one of her strongest colors. On the other hand, she's a hell of an actress. What about Irene Pappas? I think I'd like Jack Gold as director, if we can get him. Oddly enough, he also has an offer to direct MACBETH for Nicol Williamson. How many directors get two Shakespeare films in one season? Or two in one career? The Dorchester's moved me into the Harlequin Suite. They must think I'm Elizabeth Taylor.

November 14, London/Los Angeles. I didn't get quite as much done this morning as I should've, but managed a few letters and the rest of my SAG speech before Pan Aming for home. On balance, the trip was successful. I reassured myself of Peter's basic taste and intelligence and improved CAESAR. I'm sharply aware of the errors we made there (cameraman, director, Robards . . . Jesus . . . three major goofs). Still, the film is good. [*It's not really; it was OK. With Shakespeare, that's not good enough.*] Now we have to proceed on ANTONY, and I'm not sure how. Pappas is probably the best choice for Cleopatra, but I have to wait till we get a director. Is Gold best? I'll look at Dexter's film at home.

November 16 (Sunday), Los Angeles. This seemed the most important of the . . . what . . . five times I've run for this office. My opponent, a dual cardholder in SAG and SEG [*Screen Extras Guild*], polled very few votes, but his comments during the campaign required a response I could only make today at the meeting after the election. I'd worked hard on my speech (though not hard enough . . . I never work hard enough) and it came off. What had apparently been planned as a challenge from his supporters on the floor faded into a standing ovation. All in all, I have to say it worked out to a pretty good day.

November 20, Los Angeles/Washington, D.C.. I put in an appearance tonight at a dinner for Jack Warner, retiring (or being forced out) after however the hell many years it's been. He's one of the last of the giants, clearly. I didn't get to stay and weigh the rhetoric: I had to grab a limo early enough to catch the Red-Eye for Washington, changing out of my dinner jacket en route to the airport. I shucked out of my pants just as we stopped for a light at Sunset, to the high delight of a lady in the next lane.

November 21, Washington, D.C./Chicago. The only problem with flying American is that the arms don't come out from between the seats. Nonetheless, I got some sleep in the plane, an hour in the limo to D.C., one more in the hotel, and was fresh for the congressional hearing on communications. I've learned the prepared statement you always open with really means very little; how you handle the cross-questioning is what counts. I got my plane out to Chicago, where Mother waited, in good order. My family got in two or three hours later, all in good order as well, and we settled in for the night in that rambling old house, creaking with memories.

November 22. Two rivers. I had some time with Mother, then we drove up to Wisconsin for the dedication of the L. B. Clarke school. When I asked my father-in-law, "Well! How do you *feel*?", he replied "Ohhh, Chuck, I haven't been feeling at all well . . ." "*No!*, I said. "I mean about having a *school* named after you." Ohh, *that* . . . that's pretty nice." And it is. Pretty nice.

December 2, Los Angeles. I did another one of those long TV interviews, this time on "new film." It was one of those interviews where they supply you with the opinion they want when they frame the question —I was repelled, a bit. I don't believe in trends in art, or life, either, for that matter. I think people identify trends because they're lonely and want to join them. "New trends in film-making . . ." The dinner for Coretta King tonight went well, I think. Not my best speech ever, maybe, but not my worst, either, and I made my point about black racism. "Threats never got anything from decent men but their anger," I said . . . to applause.

December 3. The LEGEND project seems likelier to go to Warner's, who are very anxious to make a deal, than to Mirisch. Peter Snell writes me that Jack Gold wants to do MACBETH with Nicol Williamson before he comes to us for ANTONY. I'd rather he didn't, but I guess he'll come to us better equipped if he does MACBETH first.

December 5. A most unusual day. I was urged to run for the United States Senate by a group of Democratic politicians who obviously had their own interests in mind, but nonetheless seemed sincere. I'm pretty sure I don't want to do it, but it's the kind of thing you can't just brush off. They seem to feel I'm equipped for the job, or at least equipped to win (which is perhaps the rarer condition). I can't deny it's worth doing, but you can't do any job well unless you really *want* to do it. I want to act. I know it's trivial, but there it is.

December 6. I spent some part of the day mulling over the offer I had last night. I suppose from a politician's view, my qualifications to do the job aren't as important as my qualifications to *get* it, but that can't be the major factor for me. Lydia's against it, for several reasons, but the most important is the one I keep coming back to: I'd really rather act. I was tempted to discuss the problem with Paul at the Ziffrens tonight, but the party was too crowded with politicians (mostly Republican) for that.

December 7 (Sunday). Jolly West came over early this morning and delivered an eloquent analysis of why I *should* accept the Senate run. He pointed out the importance of a California senator's vote, coupled with a flattering version of how well I could exercise it. Even so, my home, my life, my work all weigh heavily against it. Even Rick Guerin's opinion, also positive, doesn't sway me, though he's from the opposition party, working with a Republican trying for the same job. I think I'm mulling this thing like a boy masturbating . . . you know it's pointless, but it *feels* so good.

December 11. Laver and Emerson were over for tennis, which was a good reason to devote the entire day to the game. We had a variety of matches, whose outstanding attribute was that they involved two of the best players in the world. They behaved as always, like champions. It was a marvelous day. Walter Seltzer called; Warner's willing to go on I AM LEGEND. Possibly Peckinpah to direct?

December 15. I took Lydia to the AFI, while I talked to George Stevens, Jr., and made myself available for his shop there. "Shop" is hardly the word; they've taken over the old Doheny mansion (for one dollar a year to the city of Beverly Hills). There they've set up a Center for Advanced Film Study. The splendor of what was old Los Angeles is now occupied by a number of very hairy young directors busy creating the Great American Film, equipped only with Bolexes and an absolute certainty they can do it.

This was while my public concerns were primarily the SAG and the National Council for the Arts. Since I later became intricately entangled with the AFI, I'm glad it impressed me initially.

December 19. After a desultory sort of day devoted largely to tennis and other self-indulgent activities, we had our Christmas party. Conspicuous consuption, no doubt, but very pleasant for all that.

Lydia laid on a group of harpsichordists and Renaissance singers, which turned out to be a great hit. The whole bash went well.

December 22. As usual, I'm enmeshed in the late-blooming responsibilities of my gift shopping, but I also had to dispose of my nonblooming political career. I talked to Paul Ziffren, who knows as much about it as anyone, and decided what I really felt all along: I don't want to do it enough to do it.

December 27, to Florida Keys. We got up very early, but got away in good time for our holiday in the Keys. [*With the kids, of course, and Fraser's good friend, Martin Shafer.*] The idea is tennis, fishing, diving, and photography, not in that order. The flight was uneventful, except that Fray won the navigation game and a bottle of domestic champagne. A long drive down the Keys; the hotel is new, the suite spacious, if a bit gimcracky.

December 31. On the last day of the year (of the decade, for that matter) I was towed by a porpoise . . . an experience I would have expected to go to my grave without, though I'm glad not to . . . and saw the old year out at one of those tin-horn-and-confetti hotel parties. I was struck by seeing my son across the table, looking as mature as anyone can in a paper hat. Lydia, on the other hand, looked lovely in hers. And when I took Holly's up to the suite and laid it on the pillow where she lay sleeping, she looked . . . cherished. She is. They all are.

1970

More work for
SAG and the National
Endowment for the
Arts . . .

The Omega Man . . .

testing for
Antony and Cleopatra.

Nearing the end of the line
in *The Omega Man*
THE MUSEUM OF MODERN ART/FILM
STILL ARCHIVE

January 1, Key West. We had maybe the best day of the trip today, on a chartered cruiser along the Keys. It was supposed to be primarily a diving trip, but we dove only once. Maybe conditions were as poor for diving as the skipper said, maybe he really prefers fishing. In any case, he found plenty for us. Fray caught a thirty-one-pound kingfish, Martin many smaller ones; even I got one. Holly pattered about the boat barefoot, delighting us all, Lydia took pictures, we basked in the sun. Yes.

January 2. We had a good diving day. Less than a fifth of a mile offshore, we went down on a newly discovered Spanish wreck, from which Fray got a genuine silver doubloon and some cannonballs. Lydia tried scuba, then we went on to lobster, where I felt as at home as I ever have, bubbling along twenty feet down. I didn't have gloves but I caught a couple, at the cost of slightly slashed hands (tricky little devils . . .). It was fine to have an experience we could all share. Holly had a fine time in the boat, applauding happily when I brought her up a sea urchin (which also speared me).

January 6, Los Angeles. Much back-and-forthing on I AM LEGEND. Should I take part in planning talks with Calley (the new Warner head), since I'm not officially tied to the film at this point? It seems silly to me not to, but Citron is determined to keep me clear till my deal is set, so I'll go along with him, of course. This means I must write an outline on what I feel the script should incorporate, and I hate writing.

January 9. You seldom get a chance to look at a film before you make it, but we did today, running a picture which was presumably based on I AM LEGEND. I don't know what we'd have done if it'd been good, but there was no worry on that score. I can't see how such a soporific film could've come from such a promising piece. It's incredibly botched; totally unfrightening, ill-acted, sloppily written and photographed. Let's see if we can do better.

January 19. The usual session with my mounting mail: complaints from out-of-work actors, letters from religious extravagants and academic pretenders; requests to speak at this, endorse that, narrate the other. Then I ran a good early Kurosawa/Mifune—the film Milton Sperling is convinced will translate gracefully into Mexico just after the Civil War.

January 24, Washington, D.C.. Winter meeting: National Council on the Arts. I scraped enough sleep out of the odd corners of the day to manage. The sessions are long and so filled with detail I don't concentrate well on all of it, especially the long sessions we had today on the arts I'm least involved in. Tonight we had an absolutely appalling film on (I think) architecture. I'm sorry to say we had financed it.

January 25 (Sunday). Another long day: At least this was on the arts I make my living in. Film came up; the American Film Institute got a grant, theater did well. It's clear, however, that all the arts are suffering from cost squeeze. Opera, symphony, dance are all on the verge of strangling on it. Simply increasing the grants when we have the money may not be the answer.

January 26. The agenda of the closing session was crowded with too many items. I performed my classic function as hatchet man by pointing out the disparity of paying Noguchi one hundred thousand dollars for his sculpture for Seattle when we give no individual in any other art any sum remotely like this. My rebuke went down a little hard with the staff people who'd engineered it all.

January 28, Los Angeles. I had intended to put off the exploration of etching until my declining days, when there were no more parts to act or tennis to play. Instead, since Lydia gave me a press this year, I'm undertaking it now. Dave Zeitlin's wife teaches a very small class in Brentwood; this seemed the ideal setup. It's technically complicated, but I managed to get a very ordinary sketch on zinc, bit it with acid, and then after printing a stage or two, added aquatint . . . just as I'd hoped it would work out.

January 29. I read a couple of stories by a Louisiana writer who might well have the talent we want on the LEGEND script. He's coming out here in a week; we can talk to him then. I've decided to go to Japan to promote CAESAR. If this seems to some an odd place to open this film, it does to me too. I'd like very much to see how it looks in final cut, with the score and dubbed tracks. From what Peter Snell tells me on the phone, this is unlikely before I have to leave for Japan.

February 6. Things are more or less on hold professionally. With the industry in the grip of a severe economic shutdown, it's remarkable even to have projects in the fire, I suppose. We still don't have a European release for NUMBER ONE. Meantime, there are abortive moves to reactivate KILLER KANE and MAKE ROOM, MAKE ROOM. Also, there are now some problems on the rights for LEGEND.

At some point while we were working on this film, the studio came up with the good idea of changing the title to THE OMEGA MAN. I don't know how many people understood the implication of that title, but it still rings well.

February 8 (Sunday). The tennis was good today, including Fray's. I'm now learning the classic tennis parent's lesson. When I complimented his play inordinately today, he said, "Dad, please don't compliment me on the court. You sound like a tennis mother."

February 9. The rain gave me a good excuse to work today, though the work was essentially ritualistic; the largest group I've ever seen in the big board room, with nameplates circling the edge of that vast table, agents of the technical unions crowding in chairs at the sides of the room. Walsh announced his concessions, which are much more far reaching than ours, we murmured applause, and that was really about it. I do think this can have a real effect on the production slowdown.

I was very proud of the part I played in this plan, which was designed to stimulate film production by setting somewhat lower wage scales for low-budget films using nonstar writers, directors, and performers. It would've provided opportunities for people in all aspects of film-making, and a healthy diversity in the films available in theaters. Unfortunately, it never really caught on. In recent years all film costs have increased drastically, resulting in fewer and fewer films being made, costing more and more and using, by and large, only the best-known artists to make them.

February 11. We talked to Bill Corrington, the writer we like so much for the LEGEND script. You never can really know, of course. I've never begun to understand what makes a writer good casting for a project in the sense you can tell whether an actor's good casting. Past performance . . . the genre of his work? By those counts, this man seems right. On the other hand, he's only done one other screenplay, which I've not read.

February 12. Fray's a little less than four inches taller than he was a year ago, a little more than a year older, I think. The day was hectic, even as birthdays go: the Isaacs' house was broken into by armed robbers who thought they were here. I think we'll have two dogs, not one. [*Now we have three.*] Meantime, Drago is home, with terminal leukemia, but perkier than he's been for three months.

Drago was our first, and best, shepherd. He's gone now, referred to always as "the sainted Drago."

March 1 (Sunday), Pan Am for Rome. The necessity of checking the Roman production facilities for ANTONY gave me a chance to try the 747. It's a lovely big airplane, no question, and the extra legroom is useful for me. We had a helluva rough ride, but that's God's fault, not the airplane's. I got some work done on ANTONY, but I remain doubtful whether Rome is the place for us to shoot it.

March 2, Rome. Rome no longer delights me. The glories of the Caesars are increasingly buried under the pasta and cheap plastic chairs. It would be conceivable for us to shoot here, but not easy, and very tricky. We saw what I suppose must be considered an important film tonight (SATYRICON). Fellini is something like a genius, it seems clear . . . the only man in films I've thought of calling that since Welles. His film is like a dream . . . a rather unpleasant one, but with a movingly dreamlike quality, both in geography and chronology, as well as the feel and tempo of the piece. The design and camera work are something to remember, too.

March 3, Rome/London. Peter Snell and Jack Gold spent part of the morning talking to Carlo Ponti, a pleasure I denied myself. Sophia is clearly (to me, at least) about as wrong for this film as an actress can be. Ponti's remark on the project was very revealing: "Dis is poem play, hah?" he asked. We got back to London later than I'd hoped, not enchanted by the results of the trip.

It seemed to me that a basic criterion for playing Cleopatra was some experience in Shakespeare, and English as a native tongue. This shortens the list of qualified actresses considerably, of course, and eliminates a lot of otherwise likely candidates.

March 5, London. A helluva full day, crammed with publicity on one film, plans for another, record albums, lunches, even some tennis viewing. It all worked out pleasantly enough: Plans for backing ANTONY seem to be proliferating. We now have Shaftel ready to go, Commonwealth is anxious, if they can find the dollars, Universal and Paramount are possibly interested. We feel we're better off with a major, shooting in England and Spain. We ran most of the D. H. Lawrence film (WOMEN IN LOVE) to see the work of the new girl, Jackson. She's good, but not right for Cleopatra, I think.

I was wrong. Glenda Jackson can play anything she puts her hand to.

March 6, Los Angeles. The days you fly west are the long ones, of course. I got in the better part of a full day's work, spent another day flying home, and then went to dinner when I got here. Before I left London, I decided I'd rather make ANTONY with Commonwealth United. I had a chance to go over with Peter some of the flaws of CAESAR, which may mean we can avoid some of the mistakes we made on that film. We progressed no further on the financing question, but I did work through the script with Jack.

March 11. I ran a TV special that completely reversed my opinion on Anne Bancroft's credentials for Cleopatra. She was excellent and looked marvelous. True, it was almost all light stuff, not tragedy, but she still persuaded me she would be our best choice, not only in terms of backing the film, but from a performance point of view, too: I worked with her in the old live TV days, but I don't know if she's ever done Shakespeare. Willy's film tonight was very well made (THE LIBERATION OF L. B. JONES), but it struck me as out of context with his previous film statements about the futility of violence. This one, as I told him, could start a war.

March 20. I found today that Commonwealth, after all the tumult and the shouting died, will not back ANTONY. They want to talk to Peter in London again next week, why, I don't know, since the nut of the whole thing is that they ain't gonna put up the money. This is a bitter draft to drink, but I guess no more bitter than for Larry Olivier when Rank pulled out of his MACBETH. I'm not discouraged. Downhearted, yes . . . but not discouraged.

March 29 (Sunday), Montego Bay, Jamaica. Today was Easter, but not a markedly peaceful day. I managed to get some eggs hard-boiled at breakfast, and decorated them with felt pens while I sat over my coffee among the jasmine blossoms. There is not enough for Lydia in this place, though. We might have done it better.

We'd gone, with the Isaacs and the Shafers, for a vacation in Jamaica, staying at a tennis club in which I'd made a token investment.

April 4, New York. A rather complicated travel plan: All the kids went back to Los Angeles with the Shafers for school Monday, while Clori came with us to New York to help us close the apartment. (God, what a task.) Before we left, I took Fray and Martin diving one last time. Martin has picked it up quickly, and Fray's slick as a seal underwater now.

April 6. Lydia is shaken by the stresses of giving up the apartment . . . which I can understand. We've been here eighteen *years,* for God's sake. A major defeat today: I got Mel Brooks on the phone and found Anne Bancroft [*Mrs. Brooks*] doesn't want to do Cleopatra. (Does she not *want* to, or is she afraid to, or both?) Whatever her reasons, I'm disappointed.

I still don't know her reasons, and I still think she was wrong. An actress of her gifts should not deny herself the great roles.

April 8, Los Angeles. We took a last look from the terrace, hurried our bags out through the denuded rooms, and closed the book on our New York identity. It was lovely to have, but I doubt we spent a total of one year there out of eighteen.

*Like many actors, I'd somehow felt a New York base was necessary
to a serious actor. The decentralization of the American theater
has made this less and less true. At the same time, New York has
become less and less attractive as a place to live, and more and
more expensive. Still, it was a fine apartment.*

April 10. A good day for brooding, reassessing the situation. It now
   seems likely I won't make a film this summer . . . any film. ANTONY's
   all but shot down for lack of financing and casting, the other projects
   are still iffy or unready. This is the tightest year for film financing
   since I came into the business. Still, it's important to keep active,
   unpressing. I'm tempted to break down and *beg* someone to make
   ANTONY ("Come on, fellas, *please* make it!"), but it's an impulse I've
   resisted so far. Walter Mirisch may be an avenue. (Could I beg Walter?)

April 13. We've struck out with MAKE ROOM, MAKE ROOM. [*We were to
   have better luck with this later, as* SOYLENT GREEN.] KILLER KANE is
   still alive, though I forget which bunch it is that's mulling it;
   INCIDENT AT 125TH STREET is moving between studios; and LEGEND is
   thriving at Warner's with Corrington out to the studio today to talk
   through his ideas with us. They're very sound, fleshed out since
   Saturday. Lederer and his assistant seemed impressed, anxious to
   press on with the project, which is refreshing. We have too many
   executives in this town who are more interested in making deals than
   making films.

April 14. I had too busy a day when I should've kept it free for Lydia.
   Birthdays aren't all that much fun for a woman after the first
   twenty-odd of them, I guess. We had a pleasant time with the gifts
   and cake, of course, and each of us had something for her to make
   her know we love her.

April 20. When the ANTONY project reached his desk, Dick Zanuck backed
   off like a cat stepping in wet cement, which is probably the way the
   proposal struck him, after their Burton/Taylor debacle. So now where
   are we? I ran APES II tonight, with many misgivings. It was a little
   better, actually, than I'd thought it could be. Aside from many
   careless errors in structure and detail, the main problem is that the
   leading character [*Jimmy Franciscus . . . a good actor*] really has
   nothing to play, as I predicted would be the case when I refused the
   role. I'm barely acceptable in a cameo reprise of the Taylor role from
   the first film.

May 1. ANTONY still hangs fire; we're still weighing how long we can
   afford to wait for a better deal than Shaftel offers. It's very
   frustrating. My daughter's May Day celebration was a far more
   sensible undertaking for the day. As it happens, this was the first

time I'd ever seen a Maypole dance; on the green ribbon, I thought she was sublime. We went to a sneak of HAWAIIANS tonight. It looked better than I thought it would. Given my limited experience of sneak previews, it seemed to play, too. The large house applauded (of course) at the end, and there were no walkouts. I liked what I did quite well, though I've played the same part before.

May 4. I put in my time as a witness (I'm beginning to think I should make this my profession, I get so many offers to do it) on the Dirty Committee (Congressional Committee on Pornography). I trod through a rather tricky course in the cross-questions, and felt I made my points.

Unlike some, I believe there are some things that should not be filmed . . . the rape of children, for an offhand example. The problem is definition, and it's a very difficult one.

May 6. We chose our new quarters at Warner's today. It all looks a little empty, as do most studios these days. At least they're not selling off the props and back lot, as at MGM. (I've not been able to bring myself to go out to Culver City and pick over the spoils, though I only made two films for them.) We're losing our offices at Cinema Center, at last. Warner's will be a little longer drive, somewhat less grand offices, but more room. This afternoon I served on the nominating committee for the Academy. Representing (I suppose) the Establishment, I nominated Greg Peck and a slate of four others. Everyone's putting great stress on "being with it" these days. With what, for God's sake?

May 15. I spent most of the working day on the statement for the congressional committee tomorrow on unemployment in the film industry. The hard statistics on this are enough to curl your hair. I got word from Peter Snell that Shaftel has gotten Peter Glenville as director, now that Jack Gold has pulled out in a difference with Shaftel over the time schedule. The whole thing seems strange, but God knows Glenville would be a respectable name in that spot. We must wait and see. It all may dissolve yet.

May 16. A lot of the day went to a parent's prime job: chauffeuring. I dropped Holly at her ballet class, where Fray watched her dance for the first time, to her delight. Then I dropped Fray off for a junket he's taking to equip himself for a mountain trek he plans with a friend after school is out. *Then* I attended the hearing on film unemployment. It went well, though I'm clearly annoying some of the craft unions with what I say. There hasn't been so severe a depression in production since I've been in films, certainly. This is true of the entire economy, perhaps, but it hits a business like film, where employment is by definition irregular, much harder.

May 18. It's clear that I'm going to have to make one of those red-eyed runs into D.C. at midnight and do my little dance, this time for Senator McClellan on the CATV copyright problems, before I go on back to St. Louis for the Council on the Arts. They can do without me for one day there well enough, God knows. I've got more work in these free jobs than I can do. I wish I could put something together in my own line, and get paid for it.

May 22, Washington, D.C. I got a reasonable amount of sleep on the plane slipping back into tourist after I'd eaten and taking the armrests out of a three-seat section. I grabbed another hour in the limo from the airport, and then another in the hotel waiting for the conference with Kuchel and Valenti. The meeting with McClellan went OK, considering his reputation as a crusty old son of a bitch. I slept a little more, played desultory doubles just to circulate the blood, then to a good dinner Jack gave to make some more Brownie points for us with various Hill and D.C. dignitaries. That's the way this game is played, of course, and worth staying over a half a day extra, missing the opening session of the council.

May 23, St. Louis. Meeting of the National Council on the Arts. Of all the extra pampering actors get, I do believe I like police escorts the best. Since I was already half a day late it didn't help much, but it gave me a helluvan entrance. The meeting kept falling further and further behind on the agenda, as I've found it tends to. Nancy Hanks runs that show with a very light gavel. I walked to dinner tonight through a street of leafing maples, with ripe mulberries dropping and staining the sidewalks. The broad midwestern lawns stretch back to the solid, cut-stone houses standing for the time they were built . . . when we would live and thrive forever.

June 8, Los Angeles. A startling development on ANTONY. A shadowy New York figure has turned up, one Kaufman, who apparently represents perfectly sound dollars and seems interested in financing the film. This is not quite the same as saying that Dick Zanuck is interested, but it's better than anything else in sight. It could be a creative approach to our problem. Holly had her own creative experience at her piano recital tonight and got through it "without *one* mistake . . . but I *thought* I would make one . . . !"

June 15. Corrington's work on the LEGEND rewrite is amazingly good. I suppose by that I mean partly that what he's written is what I wanted . . . but that's OK. There's abrasion in the scenes, as well as a sharp improvement in the dialogue. I'm happy about it. Now if only something would move on ANTONY.

June 17, New York. The usual trolley ride got me to New York with a little time to relax in the suite before starting on the evening chores for HAWAIIANS. I've never done so many days of public relations work in one city on a film before . . . but maybe it's been a while since the success of one film could be so important to me. If this one goes, I don't need to worry . . . for another few years.

June 22, Los Angeles. I'm still unable to pin down Kaufman (or even determine his whereabouts), to find out how the ANTONY deal is progressing, if it is at all, which I doubt more with each passing day. I did get a lot of work done with Bill Corrington on our LEGEND script. He's certainly one of the fastest and more responsive writers I've ever worked with, though I'm well aware this wouldn't seem an asset to the Writers Guild. He's picked up the things which seem important to us and changed them.

June 24. The curious farce on ANTONY continues . . . I'm beginning to be so bored by the constant backing and filling of the shifting cast of characters who want, or think they want, or perhaps might be willing to consider, or on the other hand don't find it feasible, to back the project that I wish the whole damn thing would go away. No, I don't. I have to make this picture . . . I think it can be the best film I ever made . . . and I hope, desperately, someone with a million and a half dollars thinks so too.

June 26. Instead of starting on the column I promised to do for Victor Reisel, I lunched with George Stevens, Jr., at the American Film Institute. I was able to give him some encouragement on SAG letting our people work under scale in their films.

We arrived at an agreement whereby SAG members work without any compensation at all in AFI films. This arrangement is without either precedent or parallel, and is one of the most popular of all SAG programs.

When I got home, Fray was there, magnificently filthy, back from his first two-man trip into the high and lonely. They hiked the Sierra successfully, though his friend couldn't cut it with a full pack. Fray handled it well enough, I gather; he comforted his buddy, got the camps set up, and carried both packs in stages part of the time. He'll do.

June 29. Lederer called to say he was very much impressed with the LEGEND script. This is only one down, of course . . . Calley's the man who must yea or nay on the whole project. In the light of the staggering cost problems shaking most studios, this is a tougher year than at any time since I've come to this odd town. Still, I think they'll get a "Go." We'll see.

July 4. A hot, hot Fourth, as so often this day is. I remember it hot when I was a boy and blew coffee cans end over sailing end with cherry bombs, and the summer when we had our first married Fourth after I got back from the war, and sat in the backyard and watched the fireworks at Dyche Stadium, and the party we gave for the PEKING company in Madrid, and Bill Blowitz's birthday parties, with Walter swimming a cake down the pool. It went well, and Fray's old enough now to barbecue the steaks and set off the fireworks.

July 6. Julian Blaustein is back from London, full of stories and plans, though his determination to do OFFICER FACTORY is still unrealized. This is a dry summer for film projects, it would appear. Mike Nichols has done some interesting things with CATCH-22, but it's a long way from a successful film. Naturally, it pisses me off a little, as it undoubtedly did everyone who was in airplanes in World War II. His contention that the war was fought for profit and the air corps run by Fascists is adolescent, and 1935 adolescent, at that. If they hadn't fought the war a little better than Nichols suggests, he'd be a bar of soap now; he spent most of the war in a German concentration camp.

July 7. I investigated the sobering truth that we're out of money today. True, much of what I made this year went to repay the loan, more for tax, and more for commissions. True, my net worth increased. All this is fine, but one of the things I pay my accountant for is to see I don't get nasty surprises like this. There's no reason this couldn't have been predicted, and avoided. We should be able to get some money from Fox, out of what they owe me on APES, but I really don't like this.

July 9. Everything this week . . . this *month,* and it sometimes seems to me this *year* . . . is hanging in some damn limbo, like an egg drifting in warm oil, waiting to happen. Still nothing from any of the various groups on ANTONY. (I'd prefer a flat turndown, then at least we'd know where we are . . . or aren't.) I took some comfort driving my daughter to school . . . my sunny, lovely girl. I read something the other day that's surely true of her: ". . . that purity of spirit, as pure as sunlight, which suffuses little girls just before they enter adolescence."

July 17. My day began with an endless conversation with Peter Snell in London. (He uses the overseas phone like an intercom to the kitchen.) The ramifications of money people moving in and out of the ANTONY financing stagger the imagination. First the Chicago people are willing to back the film, then they want a distribution guarantee. I can't begin to keep track of who's in and who's out, and what their current positions are. The film's still ripe, but we are running out of time for this year. I went over to Bel Air to talk to Tony Quinn about the Four Star deal. He has three or four things, all for me, all "great," all hard for me to believe in.

I have great respect for Tony and liked several of the projects he had in mind for me. Four Star was basically a TV company, though, and by this time I had stopped doing television.

July 20. A good day, though I had to postpone the reservations I made to fly to London tomorrow. Westcourt and his people are very mysterious, though they finally put Peter in touch with their Chicago money man, name of Cohen. He apparently is willing to go without a distributor. Meantime, for the first time since Bancroft, I saw another actress I think could cut it with Cleopatra. Susannah York is very good in THEY SHOOT HORSES DON'T THEY?, and though a hair young, I think could do the part. Now if only we can find someone to pay for it.

July 21. I really think we've played out the string on ANTONY, for this year anyway. Westcourt and his partner were simply conning, hoping something would work out. Cohen never had any intention of going without a distribution deal. This leaves us still with a faint hope of ABC, but this is very remote. God . . . when I think of the effort this year, and the hope and the bloody damn sweat. Well, I have LEGEND, at least. I'd probably cut my damn wrists but for that. Corrington's new pages seem very good, and as before, incredibly quick.

July 24. We seem to be where we want to be with Warner's on LEGEND. They're not at the point of making a firm offer to me yet, but they like the script, they'll budget it, and we'll go from there. I ran a dull film tonight (THE VIRGIN AND THE GYPSY), looking for a director. This is not the man. I also wasted some time realizing once again how much time I waste because I find it hard to say no. (This time to Tony Quinn.)

August 13. The meeting with Calley at Warner's was strange. He seems curiously young, behind his black beard, and perhaps a little uncertain, though easy enough. He reiterated what seems clear: They want to go ahead on LEGEND, but want a polish on the dialogue. So do we. It's time now to get a director on it and make a deal with Citron for me.

August 18. We decided, with Warner's, to hire Bill Blatty, who wrote KILLER KANE [*and a couple of years later,* THE EXORCIST], to do a dialogue polish on LEGEND. It's a good idea, though it'll delay the start. Meanwhile, ANTONY still throws new frustrations, new seeds of hope at me. At least I've relaxed into the realization it can't go this year.

August 19. I spent most of the morning at SAG, meeting with the boy who used to play in the LASSIE series, now grown into an actor who can't support his family and has set up a nonunion actors' agency. He actually doesn't seem to see the threat to his fellow actors in what he's doing. We're going to have to do something, but it's sad that desperate performers are driven to such ends to make a living.

August 26. A damn crowded day today. I had to pick up Fray at Burbank, found his luggage has been checked to LAX, cleared *that* up, got him home for his tennis tournament, then out to the studio to look at some contact lenses they used in CAMELOT and a luminous makeup base from MY FAIR LADY, for our creature makeup in OMEGA MAN, as well as a girl I rather liked from LANDLORD. Then I hurried in to SAG for a real hair-raiser with the Chicano committee. It's the closest I've ever come to losing control of a meeting. I found myself standing up, white with anger. I kept my voice down (don't yell, talk *under* them) and kept it in hand. Oddly enough, it shook down into some kind of communication at the end. It was worth it: We may have reached them.

August 30 (Sunday), San Francisco. I'd promised SAG I'd go up to San Francisco for the state AFL-CIO convention today, primarily to have dinner with George Meany tonight and host a reception tomorrow. That more or less ruined my Sunday, which was OK, I guess. My departure was somewhat harried: I felt guilty having to go, Lydia felt guilty because I did . . . and so on. It straightened out.

September 1, Sun Valley, Idaho. We're off for a week in the mountains, short-funded this time, which is one reason we picked a place so close. It's spectacularly beautiful country . . . as good as any I've ever seen, I think. The Lodge, where we are staying, is reminiscent of the thirties, when it was opened by the Union Pacific, but comfortable and clean. We seem to be between seasons, which should mean less crowd. That's fine.

September 3. I got Lydia to come photographing while Fray and I went fly-fishing. There are few sports we can undertake together, and a camera integrates very well with a fly rod. The Wood River's a beautiful stream. Lydia got more pictures than we did trout, but that's not the point of fly-fishing, of course. You can catch fish better with worms, and superbly with hand grenades. Holly, meantime, is having English riding lessons, to her pleasure and my pride.

September 7. The last day of our vacation was the best. We rafted down the white water of the Salmon, the kind of thing you should do for a much longer trip. Maybe next year, with kayaks, and some friends, as in Greece. Today was fine, though. We went in a surplus navy assault raft: half a mile of really exciting rapids, then smaller ones here and there. There was fishing, a lovely stop on a pebbled bar for lunch, and an easy drive back up to watch the salmon spawn.

September 18, Los Angeles. I played out one scene of an Oedipal confrontation this afternoon. I'd carelessly gotten myself into a bet with Fray that he couldn't beat me two out of three sets of singles; if he did, I'd buy him a car. I was perfectly confident this wouldn't come to pass for a year or two, but he won the first set today when I got careless, then had me down 1–4 in the third, fighting off two match points before I escaped. It was exhausting for us both, physically and emotionally, and now I have a bear by the tail. I wish I hadn't gotten into this, but I don't know how to get out of it. Fathers and sons . . .

September 23, En route to London. Not a pleasant leave-taking. I hate to go on these trips . . . not least because Lydia so hates to have me go that she sails under a black flag the last few hours I'm with her. I know she's seized by a compulsion she cannot challenge . . . but it's tough. At least as tough for her, of course.

September 24, London/Amsterdam. My responsibility to SAG (which is paying my way here) made me skip my usual sleep-on-arrival remedy for jet lag and go right to work. I checked into the Amsterdam Hilton (I overlook one of the canals), then straight to the FIA Congress [*Federation of International Actors Unions*] and gave the SAG report. An international congress seems to produce even more tendentious nonsense than a domestic one . . . I can see why the UN is in such trouble. Then to lunch with the Soviet delegation, the largest here, since they have the largest union. Small catch, of course: It's not a union.

September 25, KLM to London. I finished my chores here: a press conference on SAG's role in the labor scene, as well as a briefing on the future of video cassettes.

SAG, of course, has negotiated the best wages and working conditions available to actors anywhere in the world, and our contracts are models for other performers' unions (in the countries that have unions). We also briefed them on negotiating tactics.

I caught my plane: a short flight to London where Peter waited for further conferences on ANTONY. I couldn't get into the Dorchester. The Hilton's OK, but it's not the same.

September 26, London. I ran three films today . . . well . . . not all of ULYSSES, but enough to see that Barbara Jefford's a fine actress, with perhaps not quite enough sexual charisma (classy syntax for "not sexy enough") to play Cleopatra. On film, anyway. On the other hand, from the Maugham film we saw with Hildegarde Neil, I couldn't tell whether she's quite up to acting Cleopatra, but she seems to have the requisite erotic X. Orson's CHIMES AT MIDNIGHT is remarkable. Peter and I were both knocked out by it; not only as a film, but by Orson's Falstaff . . . perhaps his best since KANE. He's done an impressive job, making one film out of four of Shakespeare's plays. The battle, grinding down almost to slow motion, is especially good. I think he should direct ANTONY, if he will.

October 1, Los Angeles. Back home, I made a fruitless attempt to reach Orson today. This is the kind of game you have to play with him. He's working, and maybe really couldn't call back; God knows, often I can't. The difference is that with Orson, you always assume his telephone neurosis is responsible, simply because you know it exists.

October 2. I got the ANTONY script to Peter Bogdanovitch to give to Orson, since he's likely to see him before I can. The SAG awards committee chose Cantinflas for the SAG Award, which seemed appropriate to me, but the board rejected the recommendation. Dick Fleischer's film tonight (TORA! TORA! TORA!) had less content than PATTON, but it worked on another level. Fox must have spent as much money pretending to attack Pearl Harbor as the Japanese did really doing it in 1941.

October 5. While casting for LEGEND, we saw a number of actresses, one or two actors for Richie and Dutch, and looked at film on others. This is always a hard time for me. I hate to be involved in these readings and interviews. No one remarkable came up today, though one girl is possible. Orson called to say that he liked the ANTONY script. I'm pleased, but not surprised. (Surprised that he *called*, of course.)

October 6. I had word that CAESAR's doing very well in its first week in Los Angeles. This is very meager evidence, but augurs well. [*In the end, it did only moderately.*] Our casting on LEGEND proceeds very slowly. Warner's are reluctant to move on Tony Zerbe. I hate to use muscle, but I'm convinced he's the best actor for the part. He is enormously flexible and hasn't been used up in TV. The UCLA seminar on CAESAR went well. Students are easy to talk to, perhaps because they're so used to having it done to them.

October 8. We're not getting very far in our search for the girl in LEGEND. It should be an easy part, requiring only a certain swinging, pert quality, coupled with as much physical attractiveness as possible.

So far, we've only come up with two girls that seem close. It's tough, of course. For years, most black actresses have been conditioned to register as ladies. We want a girl for this role. I hope we can find one.

October 10. Orson called again this morning, and I went over to discuss ANTONY with him. He seems most interested in directing it, as indeed he should be. Still, with Orson you never know. He said to me, "Do you have a *great* Cleopatra?" "We don't have any, yet," I replied. "You direct it and we'll pick an actress and you make her great." "Not with that part, dear boy," Orson rumbled. "Believe me, if you don't find a great Cleopatra, you can't do this play." If he comes to London to test actresses, then I'll believe he wants to do it. I hope he does. He could make it the kind of picture it deserves to be.

October 13, Boston. This Red-Eye Special thing really only works if you get to sleep on arrival. I didn't. We had the usual routine. (I seem to have been coming to Boston longer than to most towns.) Nearly a whole generation of critics has died off or retired. Dear old Marjorie Adams is still thriving, though; she came to the critics' lunch and got swashed. Elliot Norton, on the other hand, said I was the best Antony he'd ever seen, and he's seen a lot. The students were fine . . . an ideal audience.

October 15, Washington, D.C. Down to D.C., and another round of interviews. The D.C. critics *hated* the film (unlike the Boston lot, who loved it), but I can get some mileage out of the town all the same. (Of the three film critics I recall from my first tours here, one's dead, one's retired, and one's on theater.) Still the advance is good. So much for critics.

October 19, Los Angeles. Still nothing from Orson. We read an actress for LEGEND (Judy Pace) today who seemed very good; the first one to come on with the flip kind of thing we want for the part, and the first one with anything like a string of professional credits behind her. We'll look at film on her tomorrow, but this seems the best bet we've had so far. I've screwed myself up next week on my trips. I'm committed to go to Chicago for SAG on November 1, and there may be no time to do that between New York and London. If I could contact Orson, I'd know a little better what the hell is going to work there.

October 20. Judy Pace looks very good in her film COTTON COMES TO HARLEM. I'd like to use her. Now it develops she may be stuck in a sinking TV series, and thus unavailable. Damn. Orson finally called, he won't be free for ANTONY. This is either true, or he doesn't want to do it. In any case, we won't have him. I've now come to feel the best course is to direct it myself. None of the two or three men who could really do it can (or will). If there is a film in the world I can direct, it's this one.

There aren't a lot of Shakespearean directors who know film, nor many film directors who know Shakespeare. Indeed, the list essentially consists of two names: Welles and Olivier. Given their unavailability, I still think I was wise to do it myself. As it happens, almost all the films made from Shakespeare's plays have been directed by the actors playing in them.

October 21. We read a good actress (Rosalind Cash) today . . . leading us in a different direction for the role. She's not as flip and swingy as Pace, but she's a very good actress and perhaps a more textured person. I think we'll go with her.

October 29, To New York. Much talk at Warner's about using Diahann Carroll in LEGEND. I'm still not sure the gains warrant the cost override (to lapse into Pentagonese). Rosalind Cash's test looked good to me. We're still keeping the thing open, but I think this is the choice to make. Tonight, the eastbound Red-Eye.

October 30, Tarrytown, New York. National Council on the Arts meeting. Arrived a little red-eyed (naturally, off that plane), but on time. We drove up the Hudson through the smolder (they aren't quite blazing this year, for some reason) of fall color on the trees, checked in and settled into a day of work listening as carefully as I could make myself, and speaking as seldom and usefully as my judgment allowed. We spent the money for the day, pretty well, I think.

November 1, Chicago. We barely got through most of the theater program before I had to leave on the shuttle-schedule events have forced on me. I *can't* get to London from Chicago tonight. I failed to plan SAG/Chicago ahead of New York (or after London). So here I am, as usual, sleeping on jet planes and in the backs of limousines. I saw Mother, briefly, which was supportive as well as pleasant, and the speech for the Chicago branch went down well.

November 2, En route to London. This week is going to be full of a great many things, but sleep is not among them. I got a little in Chicago, a little more in the first plane, and a little on Pan Am to London, as well as some in the motel. London was waiting, as she is wont to do. Now, let's see about this directing business.

November 3, London. We got right into it. Nathan's had a loose, properly decadent Oriental robe for Antony in the first scene ("If it be love indeed, tell me how much . . .") and a Roman tunic for the other sequence was no problem. The rehearsal with Hildegarde Neil went well. She can read verse, she can act, she's strong . . . and she wants to work hard. The scenes blocked out well. It was odd, having the *responsibility* of telling her the things I've always kept myself from saying to other actors all these years.

November 4. We shot tests for ANTONY today. It was a little hairy, but I think it came off all right. She was tense, so was I, but I knew what I was doing more than I thought I would. The hardest part is acting in the shots and not being able to *see* what you're doing. I must get a good actor to stand in for me when I'm setting up shots. The camera crew wasn't fast, but we did well enough. I got the first scene fully covered and rehearsed the master for the second, longer scene. It's exciting, absorbing, and gratifying work.

I knew the play better than any other script I'd ever worked on, and I felt at ease handling the actors. I was green and anxious with the camera, though I'd prepared as carefully as I could, discussing the lenses with Frank Schaffner, who was in London editing at the time. I also had a very good cameraman. I outlined the first shot to him in precise detail, and when he had it lit, asked for the finder off the camera to check the setup for myself. I was irritated not to be able to see through it, whereupon the cameraman said to me gently, "Guv'nor, you're lookin' through the wrong end."

November 5. The second day was more valuable, and more revealing . . . I was better; so was the makeup, wardrobe, camera, and Hildegarde. She worked very well all day long and persuaded me she's the best we can get for the role, and, what's more, very close to being damn good. Tonight I worked with Jefford. She's clearly not as right physically, but she's done the part three times, and I thought she might show us something incredible in acting terms. I don't think she did. Neil is the best, and I'd like to use her.

November 6. The day began early, and well . . . yesterday's dailies and the one retake looked fine. Hildegarde was better photographed, though the dress is lousy. Peter agreed with me she's the girl for the part. I had the pleasure of telling her so at lunch, then spent the afternoon picking stills. (I have to find the best to take back with me.) I also edited both scenes. This is fascinating work, and I fell into it eagerly. Peter and I had a long session on the sets (what to shoot in Pinewood, what in Spain), then, after a late dinner with the McDonalds, I was happy to fall into bed at last. It's going . . . it's really going.

November 7, To Chicago. I had a good night's sleep, the work behind me, and woke feeling wonderful. The flight to Chicago was easy, and filled with stimulating ideas about ANTONY. That project's enormously stimulating for me. Everywhere you stick a spade in the script, green comes up.

November 8 (Sunday), Chicago/Los Angeles. The week behind made me a little ragged this morning for the breakfast meeting, with Cohen's group, but I did the best I could. I don't know how to promote money, really. "The best collateral I can post for ANTONY is my own deep conviction about its viability, and my record in films for the past twenty years," I said. This seemed to make a point with them, though I lack, among other skills in this area, any special capacity to read these people as individuals.

I stopped off in Chicago overnight, though I was exhausted, because a group of potential investors had surfaced there and were anxious to talk to me about backing ANTONY. All they really wanted was a lion for their party the night I got there. The meeting over money was utterly without substance.

November 9, Los Angeles. I worked at clearing my unclearable desk (I should really dispense with finished desk tops . . . I never get to see them anyway). I'm considering undertaking a low-carbohydrate diet; I'm now at 212, which is much too high.

November 12. I picked the shots from WOODSTOCK which will best help make our wry point in the movie sequence in OMEGA MAN. I also looked at some more makeup tests. Our zombie's eyes are still not right . . . they'll have to try the lenses over again.

We used opaque lenses for these characters, not very successfully. We failed badly with the whole concept of this part of the film.

November 15 (Sunday). I began OMEGA MAN today. We started with a small crew (no sound) and me in the Sunday-silent downtown streets. At that, we drew a larger crowd than I suspect paid to get into the Pantages today. I think the shots will work. They're well conceived, and I like the way they felt.

November 24. The scene went well today; perhaps one of the best we've done yet. This was the first time we've used the Family makeup (on Richie, in the secondary stage of the disease), and it seemed to look OK; I can't tell till we see the dailies. The eyes are still not right, but they're only revealed in one short cut in this scene; matching's no problem if we manage to improve the lenses. I finally saw the test I shot with Hildegarde for ANTONY. [*It had been delayed in the lab in England.*] I liked her, I liked me; I even liked my direction. I can improve it all, of course. Now if only, for God's dear sake, if *only* someone can be persuaded to put up the last half million so we can do it. *Do it!*

November 25. An early start today, in an effort to pick up a little of the time we've dropped on our schedule. We didn't, partly because I was unable to drive a car through a window with quite the dispatch Joe Canutt brought to it. Herman saw the ANTONY test. He said he liked it, but Warner's has backed off the idea of doing the film. Apparently, because CAESAR has petered off a bit, everyone is leery of ANTONY. Damn it to hell.

December 4. Russ Metty and Boris [*Sagal, our director*] don't quite hit it off. Boris is a somewhat volatile personality; I can see where he'd rub Russ the wrong way. Still, he seems to be getting good footage. The stuff we're shooting now is the kind you can't judge at all till it's cut, so there's not much I can react to from this week's work.

December 8. We offered Boris a chance to replace Russ Metty as cameraman. He backed off. It would've seemed to me a madly inept move, but one we were willing to countenance, in terms of preserving directorial authority. I'm uneasy about directors who have to fire people to control a company.

December 10. I died this morning, blood staining the water in the fountain, in what may or may not be a Christ analogy. It's hard to tell whether a thing like that'll work or not, but I feel very good about this part of the film. Lydia's party tonight for the benefit of the Oriental Institute cost us a pretty penny, and may not have netted them anything, but it went well.

December 14. Walter Mirisch saw the ANTONY test today. He liked it . . . or said he did . . . but I don't think he was bowled over. He accepted my direction as a plus in the film, from his point of view, but clearly had reservations about Hildegarde as Cleopatra. I recognize this, but still feel she's the only girl around who can come close to playing it. I remember Orson: "If you don't have a perfect Cleopatra, you have nothing." Maybe so, but I can't wait for the perfect Cleopatra. Now is the time for me to play Antony. This may be the only chance I'll have.

December 15. We did a sequence I've always thought had as much cinematic potential as anything in the script. It explores the universal last-man-on-earth fantasy: shopping in an empty world. It went well. The mannequins in the empty store made chilling images.

December 20 (Sunday). A nice day, if a trifle aimless. We'd planned to rehearse this afternoon, but Boris begged off (not the first time this has happened, come to think of it . . .), leaving my afternoon free. I spent part of it helping Fray repair the error he'd made at the party last night by feeding his girl a marguerita. I took him to visit her parents' house to apologize, etc., etc. It was a tough experience for him but maybe valuable: traumatic enough to remember, yet there was no permanent damage done to the girl. I did observe she seemed to have one helluva hangover.

December 27 (Sunday). A desultory hour or so on the courts . . . then to Warner's to rehearse with Rosalind in the Sunday quiet. She seems to have some insecurity as a performer (who doesn't?), and she hasn't worked enough yet to develop a very sound sense of timing. The main scene we worked on . . . the dinner scene with her expository speech outlining her background . . . is tricky. She carries almost the full burden of it, and she'll have to make it interesting. The rehearsal time was useful.

December 28. A number of piddling little scenes today, including one of the two we tested the girls on. It took several takes to get the master shot. Rosalind was a little uncertain about her marks, and was distressed at the number of times this made me repeat my stumble and fall on the floor. "Never mind, honey," I said. "Willy Wyler made me do twenty-six takes of a fight scene in BEN-HUR where I got knocked down a flight of steps with a chain in the kisser." The rest of the day was inconsequential stuff. I wonder if anyone's done a rundown on a film to determine what proportion of a shooting schedule is actually concerned with acting? Very small, I think.

I really think, all things considered, I could've done without 1970. Personally, it had many complications, with the onset of adolescence for Fraser, and little-girlhood for Holly, both events being harder for Lydia, perhaps, than for me.

Professionally, the worst year films have seen in a long time was more or less reflected in my career. The two films I had released in 1970 were both disappointments, creatively and commercially, though my personal notices were good in both. It would've done my record a lot of good, though, if HAWAIIANS could've succeeded at the box office (though it did fairly in a year when damn little succeeded), and of course it would've meant everything to me to have had CAESAR come off. It's a bitter dose not only to have it fail, but to know that it's not very good. At least it hardened my resolve, if I do ANTONY, to direct it myself.

1971

Directing *Antony and Cleopatra* in Spain . . .

a seminar at Cambridge . . .

elected chairman of The American Film Institute.

Bemused by the Alexandrian queen (Hildegarde Neil) in *Antony and Cleopatra*
PETER SNELL PRODUCTIONS

January 1, Los Angeles. The year, which God knows had better turn out to be higher quality than 1970, didn't start out too well. Dinner and the film we saw were fine, but things got a little tense afterward. There's a lot of pressure on Lydia, most of it from me, I guess.

January 5. I've never seen a ball game in Dodger Stadium, but it would have to be more fun than shooting a picture there. They were picking up the rest of the escape (much racing around on motorcycles, etc). I worked very little, and would've finished before dinner, save for a generator breakdown just before my last shot. It turns out I'll have to work Sunday, which will kill the second day of the La Quinta tourney.

January 7. A damn full day. I shot intensively on very difficult scenes with Roz and Richie. I ran John Ford's film on Vietnam at lunch . . . I was impressed; I'll be glad to narrate it for USIA. [*This* was *a good film . . . Ford's last . . . but it was never released.*] I "hosted" a party to call attention to Melvyn Douglas's performance in I NEVER SANG FOR MY FATHER for Academy consideration, which it deserves. We had a good turnout. I also had a chance to talk to Walter Mirisch. He's uncertain about our Cleopatra, also about Turkey. I disagree on the first point, but I'm with him on the last. The thought of shooting in Turkey scares me to death.

January 14. Save for next Sunday's work, we wound up LEGEND today, by lunchtime. This brings us, I think, a total of two days over, which is not bad. The logistics of production are preoccupying me, of course, reassessing everything I learn against my plans and possibilities for ANTONY, which goes on being likely but uncertain, as it has for a year. Walter Mirisch reinforced my conviction that Turkey's impossible for us; Spain is the only answer. He's going to London next week and will convey this to Peter Snell.

January 18. I read an ordinary script, based on Jack London's extraordinary CALL OF THE WILD, that they want me to do in Norway this winter. I'm surprised you could get such a flat script out of a novel as good, and as cinematic, as London's. I was considering the project because it would provide some hard dollars this year, when I'll need it.

January 24 (Sunday). I'm still struggling to decide whether I'm justified in making the sacrifice that must be made to film ANTONY. God knows the theater's always been a high-risk enterprise. I'm risking money and reputation. I should welcome the chance to risk reputation in a part like this, and what else can I buy that I want so much?

Nothing, obviously. The banks were requiring my personal
guarantee for the part of the production cost of ANTONY *they were*
to provide. Shakespeare is a high-risk enterprise.

January 25. I spent part of the morning discussing the problems and
future of the AFI with Jim Silke. The main problem, of course, is that
they're training film makers for an industry that's almost ceased to
exist. There are more and more film schools producing more and more
film makers, but all this avails nothing if there are no films for them
to make. What the answer to this may be, I'm not sure, but I know
it's rooted in the basic, the primary definitive characteristic of film . . .
the cost of the raw materials.

This was a somewhat gloomy estimate of the state of the profession.
Also, the AFI's film school was then still in the shadow of the
pugnacious sixties student generation, whose attitude tended to be,
"Give me a camera and step back while I make the Great
American Film." Since then, things have changed and a gratifying
number of AFI Fellows are making a considerable mark in the
film world.

January 26. I'm still eating at the ANTONY problem, or it's eating at me.
For myself, I have no qualms. Still, I have to risk not only money to
which my family has a basic right, but also my time, of which they'll
be grievously deprived. In a sense this is silly; I've made more money
than most men dream of and can still make more. My time's more my
own and my family's than that of most men. I want desperately to do
this. I think I *need* desperately to do it.

January 27. Another factor in this decision about ANTONY is the amount
of energy, both physical and mental, I have on tap for the project.
Things will get very thin in a second-rate Spanish hotel along about
the fifth week of shooting. I'm in good shape; my body'll hold up. But
I must be alert for any slackness. I tend to get slapdash about things,
and that won't do. Not for this, not for what it'll cost me.

January 30. I talked at some length to Lydia today about my dilemma.
She's committed to the project, willing to sacrifice for it, but, having
at last seen the Neil test, she was not overwhelmed. You could even
say she was underwhelmed. It's not a smashing test, of course, but
it's difficult to say how much her work can be improved, not to
mention mine. The point everyone seems to have missed is that there
is simply no one else equipped to do the part.

February 5. This is the first time I've ever been involved in a banking
meeting; it was much more offhand than I'd imagined. "Well, that's
OK, then." So now I have the dollars for ANTONY . . . at last. (Of

course there's still the discounting of the European contracts with distributors, but that's not too tough, and not my end anyway.)

February 6. I was back again, all morning, at the AFI. I was invited on the board, which failed to surprise me, though I confess I was flattered. Greg Peck said my seminar there was considered the best one they've ever held, which covers a lot of ground. Warner Brothers sent over the script of DELIVERANCE, which I probably won't have time to do, but it's nice to know they consider me employable. *I'm still sorry to have missed it. It was a good film.*

February 21 (Sunday), London. My metabolic transitional plan worked flawlessly. I got two hours' sleep in the morning, long afternoon of work, early dinner and dead unconscious for the night. We got a lot done on ANTONY, but the whole casting question on Cleopatra is reopened, in terms of Irene Pappas. Peter's now inclining that way, partly due to Hildegarde Neil's appalling notices in MACBETH, here in London. Reluctantly, I'll consider it. Pappas would make a contribution, though she might be difficult to handle, in a project where I'll have no time for difficulty.

February, later. I somehow lost some pages of this damn journal when I was in Almería checking locations. I flew from London to Madrid with Peter Snell to meet with the Izaro Film people. It looks as though Spanish nationality is a definite possibility. There will be complications, but if I can accept a Spanish cameraman and cast some of the parts with Spanish actors, it may work.

February 23, Almería. This was the second day lost. In my journal, I mean, in life, it was a damn good day. We took the late (the only) plane down to Almería, after a difficult negotiation with the Spanish government. We arrived in Almería in time to see the Alcazaba, which could provide us excellent sets for Caesar's palace. There we could photograph something of the grandeur that was Rome.

February 24. The famous Almería dunes, the only desert left on the European continent, are not really very extensive. Frank Schaffner, who shot his North African sequences for PATTON there, described them to me as "peanut dunes." They are, but they are still indubitably *dunes*, highly photogenic and classic in all standard characteristics but size. They'll work, barely. I'm a little dubious about the helicopter shot fitting in, at that. We also found some really excellent places for all the seacoast scenes. Better than I'd hoped to find . . . seven or eight locations in one day.

February 25. Back to Alcazaba (which has also the virtue of minimal travel time, being right in the center of town) to go over the sets we found yesterday, and stumbled, in the back of the castle, on a fine gate for the Antony/Caesar farewell. We went on from there to a port which will work surprisingly well for Alexandria. Mediterranean architecture, it occurs to me, has altered only very slowly. The red tile roofs are still properly Roman, the squat white buildings equally right for Rome and Egypt. I also found exactly . . . *exactly* . . . the hill I'd imagined for my land battle.

Location hunting can be very boring and very frustrating. This was a piece of cake, and thus very satisfying. I'd been imagining the sets, both interior and exterior, for this film for so long that they'd come to seem real to me. Fortunately, I found them.

February 26. Again my treasure chest of sets, the Alcazaba, produced a perfect arena for the gladiators to struggle in during the Triumvirate scene. Also another, and better, set for the stable. We were far less fortunate in finding housing, but at least we go back to Madrid lacking only a location for the front of Cleopatra's palace. It was lovely to see Frank Schaffner tonight, deep in NICHOLAS AND ALEXANDRA. "Frank," I said rather diffidently over Scotch, "I think I'm going to direct this as well." "Why not?" he replied, grinning. "Nothing to it."

February 27, Madrid/London. The morning was crowded with meetings, including an endless session on contracts. I kept going out to the washroom, since I had no contribution to make to it. I saw Frank again and got some recommendations on Spanish crewpeople, of whom he thinks very highly. I saw some footage by an excellent cameraman, Luis Alejandro, whom I'll be glad to use. We must move on this; he's much in demand. [*We didn't move fast enough. We lost him.*] I finally left Peter behind to sort through the contracts one more time (to his frustration) and came back to London with a good week's work behind me. It was tough, and I'm tired, but the Dorchester's worth coming back to.

March 6. I ran ten reels of Fox's CLEOPATRA this morning and saw Hildegarde Neil's MACBETH tonight. Her Lady Macbeth is better than Taylor's Cleopatra. Fox would've done better with their film if they'd had less money; most of the flaws are those of excess. Too many sets, too richly dressed, too many costume changes . . . all this is like a whole meal of marzipan. Taylor seems somehow modern in the part; besides, Mankiewicz is not Shakespeare. Him, we have. Neil's a good Lady Macbeth, which relieved and surprised me, since the notices are bad.

March 8, Los Angeles. The flu had slowed things down around the house, with Fray still in bed, Holly and Muriel just up. I refocused on my last picture again, ran the rough cut with Boris and Walter Seltzer. The bizarre quality of the story works, I think. It's under two hours now, but still long, which means we won't have any length problems in the end. I'm determined this'll be true with ANTONY, too. I don't intend to cut a scene merely because it's too long overall.

March 9. Well, today we had the big meeting I suppose Peter's trip here was all about. It was sticky, for me almost unbearable. I hate negotiation; I hate the idea of having to persuade, to urge people into doing something. For me, it always should be something you leap to, or don't do at all. Surely for this project it should be that. Clearly, though, it won't be. Bank of America is prepared to discount the European contracts, but they expect to be amply secured in doing so, and to get a profit as well. Bankers . . .

March 11. I'm content with the script. Peter will have it mimeoed again when he gets back to London (in black covers, this time . . . appropriate for classic tragedy, I guess). It looks like I'll go back to Spain for a week to check the sets, then spend a week rehearsing with Hildegarde in London on her scenes, then a week with the English cast, also in London, then a week rehearsing on location in Almería, starting May 31. It also now seems a possibility to cut the film here, in my own projection room, bringing Eric [*Boyd-Perkins, the editor*] over for the several weeks it'll take. This would be ideal for me.

March 12. I went to Warner's for a somewhat stormy running of OMEGA MAN. Boris had a tantrum about the way it was to be shown to the Warner brass, which seems bloody childish. The film's getting better; they put back the scene with the little girl I suggested. [*Later, they took it out again.*] We're close to it now, I think. We went to the Screen Directors Guild Ball; I was delighted when Frank Schaffner won for PATTON. I had the pleasure of phoning Madrid and waking him up with the news.

March 14 (Sunday). Peter left for London, with the usual obligatory hectic departure. I felt faintly guilty delivering him to the airport in tennis clothes (me, not him), but he caught the plane. En route, we discussed the possibility of Bob Shaw playing Pompey. He'd be excellent, of course, though it's too small for his current eminence.

March 16. I had a constructive morning, tennis serving my profession more directly than it usually does. I played singles with Bob Shaw, trying not to beat him badly, since I still entertain a faint hope he might play Pompey. When I asked him, over beer after the match, he accepted. I'm well aware this may all fall through when it reaches his agent and his cooler second thoughts, but it's a casting coup at this point. He also gave me a lovely idea for Pompey's party for the Triumvirate on his galley: have him do a drunken impersonation of Antony. It betters my idea . . . [*Unhappily, Bob didn't play the part in the end, but I used his idea.*]

March 24. We got OMEGA MAN down to where we want it (though Walter's still playing with it a little). I think the cut's good now. It works on the levels where it needs to work, and the element of dread runs well through the whole piece. This is another of a not very long list of films I have more or less personally conceived, and this may turn out to be the best of them. My performance is good . . . there is a chance for a kind of lightness, or at least a wryness, that I don't often have a place for in the men I play. It'll be interesting to see how it works with audiences.

This picture doesn't please me that much now, and neither does my performance in it. You sometimes imagine you see things you planned in a performance that in fact hardly exist in it, or only flicker faintly through the film.

March 26. For some damn reason, ANTONY won't stay buttoned up. You get one end nailed down and a board curls up at the other corner. Now both Leo and Citron have misgivings about moving with the City National money till the Bank of America makes up its mind about all the European contracts it's discounting for the other half. I had a long transatlantic talk with Peter Snell again, all very painful. He feels this was established when he was over here. It'll be straightened out, but it makes for some sticky interludes meantime.

April 3. MGM has refused me access to the BEN-HUR stock. As owner of the company, Kirk Kerkorian can of course overrule this edict, but I hesitate to ask him.

There are always thousands of feet of unused footage from a major location sequence, such as the galleys in BEN-HUR. I wanted to buy some of this for long shots we couldn't afford to make for ANTONY. This is a common practice, but MGM considered their film unique and was reluctant to sell any of the footage.

April 15. I thought MGM was only in the business of selling old props; it seems they still want to make movies. They want me to do a novel called HIJACKED Walter's given them. Maybe I can use this as leverage to persuade them to let me buy some BEN-HUR stock for ANTONY.

April 29, London. I can finally see the end of the casting. It's a hard part of the work for me, because it's so painful for the actors. I've tried to do it well, though, and avoid crony-casting. Tennis provided its usual respite. I'm tempted by an invitation to attend the Iranian Open with Lydia as guests of the Shah.

April 30. I saw all of the actors I'll have time to see, and found the ones I want. I think I'll end up with only three I've ever worked with before, which is OK. John Castle seemed very keen at lunch. I liked his ideas on Caesar, he seemed to like mine. I decided the Iranian trip is just not feasible. The film needs the time. I began at last on the good part of the work, reading through all Cleopatra's scenes with Hildegarde. There's a way to go with her, but I think I can use this time to map out the road, at least. She seems responsive to direction, listens, thinks. One of my problems is that I know so well what I want in the scenes. I must be careful not to rush her.

May 2 (Sunday), London. Rehearsal proceeded. It's hard to say how well, at this point; what I want is so far beyond what it's fair to ask Hildegarde to reach yet. This sounds terribly snobbish, and I don't mean it that way, but I've been thinking about this part for twenty years . . . she for six months. After tennis, I had a pleasant dinner at Peter's house, then taped all the Spanish bit parts to send to the respective actors, so they can work on their English readings.

May 3. I went out to look at the cinebuses we'll be using on location. They're quite impressive: huge and maybe not quite as mobile as they should be, but God knows the facilities they incorporate are needed, and usually lacking on location. I hope they're ready on time. Rehearsal proceeded. We've worked through all of Cleopatra's scenes in some detail now, except for the last half of the monument scene, which we'll get into tomorrow. I'm finding out some new and valuable things about the part, and the play . . . I think she is too.

May 4, Los Angeles. The best part of the day was the last part, getting home to my ridge and my family. I had a very intricate morning scheduled before that, though, in which everything fell into place precisely. I got the shopping I needed done, saw the people I'd promised to see, worked through to the end of the play, as I was determined to do, packed and caught my plane. The time away has been long, but valuable. Now I'm home . . . and happy.

May 6. I spent the morning looping OMEGA MAN, which shouldn't have taken as much time as it did. I always find myself in a contest to see how quickly I can do the damn things, which is a bad fault. Of course there are always breakdowns which hold you up, but this is hardly the proper frame of mind to approach any area of work, anyway. I don't think I really care to have as my epitaph "He was the fastest looper in films."

May 7. MGM surprised me by deciding to sell us the BEN-HUR shots we need. I went out to look at the outtakes from the galley stuff. Though most of it was done with models in the back-lot tank, it's really remarkable footage, surely better than what Fox did on CLEOPATRA. Among all the films, we can find cuts for a helluva sequence. I ordered prints of several angles to be sent to Eric [*Boyd-Perkins*] in London, to cut into what we already have. I'm damn grateful MGM had a change of heart on this.

May 23 (Sunday), London. This was far from my favorite ride on that familiar PAA polar flight; after a late departure we had to land for two hours in Gander to fix an oil leak. Joe Canutt [*who was to direct my second unit*] thus missed his connection to Madrid, but it gave us time to plan some changes in the second unit schedule. Joe'll shoot the whole land battle before the first unit schedule starts. We've lost our cameraman to another film and our armorer fell suddenly and violently ill. I replaced him, not yet the cameraman. Possibly Berenger?

May 25. I began it. I drove to the little rehearsal hall near Covent Garden in a cab and as I came through Leicester Square, I swear the statue of Shakespeare there lifted his head from his books and said, "Don't fuck it up." We read through. I pointed out to them this was the only time the play will exist as a whole for us until I finish cutting it. Then we began working on it in detail. It begins to move. Tonight I went to see MERCHANT at the National. Olivier is a remarkable Shylock, though it's not my favorite of his performances. Afterward in his dressing room, he gave me some good whiskey and better advice, about both ANTONY and directing.

May 27. Messenger scenes went very well indeed. Joe Melia is dead on in the part. Cleopatra has further to go, of course. She must reach the rage, but bring the audience back to pity at the end. John Castle will be excellent as Caesar . . . very cold, very flat. He's not playing any of the easy colors with it. I gave him a touch or two of red, which he took readily, but overall it will be cool. Cleopatra's suicide is a monster. She must come farther up, of course, but I must be careful not to drive her. She must continue to be sure she can do it.

June 3, Madrid. Phase one finished, we moved to Spain. I could hardly wait to get out to Moro Studios where I had time only to begin to weigh some of the decisions I must make in the next few days. I find direction is primarily a problem of making choices, largely logistic. The first of these is also of enormous creative importance: which cameraman to use. I'm inclined to Berenger, principally because he's shot second unit on so many important international films [*EL CID for one*], but also because of Frank Schaffner's recommendation. Esteban, of Izaro Films [*our Spanish backers*], has another candidate.

June 4. I have a secretary here, a legacy from Frank Schaffner, who seems very efficient, very British. She settled me in my office, helped me work through a good bit of paper work before they were ready for me to shoot the tests with Esteban's cameraman, Pacheco. These were hard to judge. How can you tell what kind of camerawork a man can do by watching him work on the floor? [*"On the floor" means seeing it shot. The footage often looks very different in projection.*] Makeup, I can judge. I'm very pleased with Cristobal; he makes Hildegarde look very good, solves her not inconsiderable makeup problems with great subtlety. The Greek wig (Wendy Dickson's idea) works very well. [*Cleopatra was not an Egyptian, but an Alexandrian Greek. The Greek hairstyle and costumes helped make this point.*] On the floor, the test looks several times better than the one we shot in November.

June 5. Berenger shot today. He seemed to me much more professional, but there's of course no way to tell till we see the footage. I'm more or less privately committed, though. Of greater concern is the problem at Sevilla Studios: The roof fell in on their large stage, leaving us with no stage in Spain big enough for our palace interior. Many alternatives were proposed, ranging from three small stages at Sevilla to renting an airplane hangar. All have drawbacks, all will cost money. Cost factors I can't control are creeping up on me. I'm still convinced I can do this within the budget.

June 7, Madrid/Almería. This turned out to be a damn full day. I found a fine exterior garden for Antony's house in Athens, which saves us a very expensive set. I also found a decent apartment to live in when the family joins me. It's not as grand as the first villa in Italy, but we're not on the budget BEN-HUR had. We had a long go-round on which cameraman to use. Pacheco's stuff looked better than I thought. I had to leave for Almería before I could see Berenger's footage. By phone, Peter persuaded me Pacheco's was better, so we go with him. I saw the galley down here . . . it's coming. My apartment here reminds me of the cold-water flat we had in Hell's Kitchen, when we were first in New York.

June 9, Almería. I clambered around on the rocks at Cabo del Gato and found good spots for the shots of Enobarbus's death. I also found time to rearrange the family's flight from the U.S. They'd been coming into Almería at my suggestion, which was a lousy idea; it's much simpler to fly to Madrid, then down here tomorrow night. All else seems to be going well. I have a little more time than I need this week, which has to be the last time I'll say this for the next two months. My actors arrived tonight. I welcomed them with pathetic gratitude . . . I need somebody to work with.

June 11. I needed my cameraman desperately today, but didn't get him till the late plane (the only plane) from Madrid, along with Peter Snell, who finally left Madrid when he was assured that his mobile units had finally escaped from customs in Bilbao, thanks to a temporary bond posted (inevitably) by me. I had a chance to rehearse the mounted scenes with the cast on horses, where none of them was really very easy (few English actors have a chance to learn to be). Later, I had my family back with me, as comforting as a bowl of good soup in your belly.

June 13 (Sunday). I felt like a general the day before an amphibious landing, racing around checking all possible contingencies. The cinebuses arrived from Bilbao at the last possible moment, but now they can't get into position at the Alcazaba because of overhead wires. I don't know yet how we'll handle that, but we will. The wardrobe's OK, a little last-minute work required. Set's OK, actors are all in order. I can hardly believe it's coming to pass at last. Now "the day, my friends, and all things wait for me."

June 14. We began shooting. It's a difficult scene, with reverses back and forth across the arena, bad wind conditions ruining the sound, but we did well, I think. I got the setups I needed and I think the performances were good. The key to it, of course, is the rehearsal period. Without it, we'd be lost . . . or I would be. As it is, we're coasting loose and easy. Well . . . not loose, maybe, but we're getting it done. Now I have a small problem: My Octavia is in Argentina.

June 15. I'm a full day ahead of schedule, as I took some pleasure in cabling to Citron. The scene is good, too, I think, though damn hard to shoot. We had to hold a long time tonight to get the stable lit, but it should make a good sequence . . . it's one of my favorites in the script, perhaps because I patched it together out of three different scenes in the play. The crew worked well through a bloody long day. Now I may run out of work here, since I still don't have Carmen Sevilla [*Octavia*], and she works day after tomorrow, in the garden.

June 18. I had to shoot Octavia's return without Octavia. Carmen's just back from a film in Argentina and felt unable to get down from Madrid in shape to shoot today, a fact I wasn't told till midmorning. I shot anyway, around her, minimizing her coverage in the scene. There are a number of complications to directing a film that never occur to *Cahiers du cinéma.*

June 21. A series of disasters today. The galley was unfinished, or unofficially immovable or *something.* Anyway, I wasn't able to get it to Roquetas, so I had to switch to a scene with Antony there instead. Tonight we got a very late start on Pompey's galley scene in Almería Harbor, then a heavy swell came up, making the ship roll badly. It was impossible to get anything but static shots. We still got a good way into the scene before dawn. We did *not* finish in the two nights scheduled. I'm only now beginning to realize one of the problems: The summer light is so long in these latitudes, we don't get more than seven hours of darkness. This scene's bloody difficult to shoot, too. I still haven't been able to get the camera off the boat . . . hard to show that it *is* a boat, in real damn water. The second unit shot on the felucca during the day with a not very competent pilot, I think. Three hours late there, and missing some equipment. We got some shots, at last, and I raced back for dinner with my family on the pier before going back to work for the night.

June 24. We finally finished on that damn galley just as gray morning killed our darkness. It went much better . . . the boat didn't roll in calm waters, so we could take the camera on the pier and shoot the boat. The nude dancer diving into the water looked good, I got the coverage I need for the dance (but barely), and failed to get Lepidus falling out of the rowboat properly. I'll have to get other shots for that, somehow. I'm reasonably satisfied I have the scene, though. I slept, then did a second unit runby on a horse for the battle scene. ("My heart makes only wars on thee.") Tonight, we went out to the dunes for the death of Eros. We began late and high winds made a problem for the shooting, but a plus for the scene.

June 26. A helicopter is the most fascinating film toy since the Chapman boom, but our pilot was so minimal, I was too worried whether we were getting the shots at all to enjoy the camera capacity the chopper gave me. The monument works well for this scene, but it'll give me hell to shoot from the ground tomorrow. The scene in the desert with Antony's bloody sword played exactly as I imagined it when I cut the play two years ago. I was really pleased with the setups, the way the actors played it, everything. We got our day in good shape for once. Even the weather in the dunes was on our side . . . not too hot. The day wouldn't have been either so long or so hard if that monument had been designed in terms of my specifications in the script. The business of getting Antony in and Proculeius capturing it successfully is always a major staging problem, as I well knew from doing the play with Cornell in '47, which is why I worked it out so carefully. Now Pelling's edifice complex has presented me with a set on which I can't shoot either of these scenes honestly. I think we can get by with them nevertheless, but I have damn few shootable angles. I think I played well in the scene, and Julian Glover was excellent in his daring dash up the shield stairway.

Julian, a fine English actor, was not only excellent as Proculeius (the part I'd played with Cornell in 1947), but did an absolutely superb job of performing Antony while I was lining up the shots. What's more, he played it not as he would play it (and did, in London a year or two later), but as I was playing it, an act of taste hard to come by.

June 28. A brute of a day. Preparing to shoot two simple riding cuts I wanted, an absentminded costume man took my armor to the other set, losing us half an hour. Thus we failed to finish the third scene in Caesar's camp, which was not easy to shoot anyway, thanks to Pelling's design problems. (The whole set was only just barely ready to shoot, as it was.) We still got good stuff, including a sunset scene. Taking a deep breath, I then began a night on Antony's suicide scene, with Lydia and Bea watching. (Bea's just down from Madrid for a few days.) I think I acted it well, but it may have been only exhaustion. We worked till three in the morning, then slept three hours and gave the first unit the day off, then went out and did the battle stuff all day with Joe's unit. This was a piece of cake for me . . . exactly the kind of thing I've been doing with one Canutt or another for fifteen years.

July 4 (Sunday). I felt a long way from home today, facing the fact that our logistic failures will prevent me from finishing the location on schedule. I must stay over at least tomorrow to shoot with the second unit, so we wrapped the first unit last night and sent them back to Madrid. It was rushed; I didn't have time to do what I would've liked with the actors, nor get the coverage the scene should've had. This is the first time I've really felt I sacrificed quality for the schedule.

July 6, Madrid. I goofed in picking the apartment. It won't do for all of us. During the day Lydia moved us out and got us checked into the Monte Real. It's more expensive, but it'll be a more comfortable arrangement. Meanwhile in *my* day, I found the set construction on schedule, though the walls are wastefully higher than can be shot usefully. The Octavia/Antony scene in Athens was easy; we got well into Enobarbus's classic description of Cleopatra. Eric Porter's excellent in this; it's going to be hard to find cutaways.

Cutaways are moments when you cut away from the actor doing a long speech to some other angle.

July 8. We fell a little behind today. Pacheco shoots more slowly on a stage than he did on location. The set's difficult and complicated to light, I well understand, but he *must* do his work in reasonable time if I'm to have any chance of doing mine within the time schedule. I sacrifice shots I want every day because he fails in this. We went to a late and dull dinner with a gaggle of international types; I wasn't up to them tonight.

July 9, Madrid/Almería. I got a good chunk of the pardon scene today, though I failed to finish because I had to catch my flight back to the second unit, waiting to immortalize my contribution to the battle of Actium. It seemed best to close down the first unit and shift to Almería, where they've been having more than a few problems with the boat and weather. Lydia and Holly saw me off to Almería; Fray, still slaving for Joe Canutt, met me there. There's so much to do, and not enough time or money to do it right.

July 10, Almería. We found a new anchorage for the galley closer to shore, though we had new problems with an offshore breeze that blew all day, hampering operations for any number of more or less valid reasons, primary among them being the faint-heartedness of the sailors responsible for moving the galley. As Joe Canutt said, "Without 'no puedo' and 'imposible,' they'd be tongue-tied." I understand Joe's perfectionism (I'm married to one), but we're getting good stuff.

July 12, Madrid. I felt sadly plagued by the gods (playing Shakespeare, you tend to fall into classic theology). We lost an hour to rain during the day, and thus didn't finish either the day or the night work. Cleopatra's little boat, a rather handsome papyrus craft, sank during supper. It also rained again later, but we got some excellent stuff in the rowboat, anyway. It may have been one of my best acting scenes so far.

July 13. After a reasonable night's sleep, up and to the studio to see more assembled footage than I've had yet. It looks very impressive, an opinion apparently also held by the Rank men who turned us down when we were trying to raise money a year ago. Now they want to distribute the film. It rained again on location, but we only lost half an hour. The day, including Alexas's swim, was very good. So was the night, though I was desperately pressed by a crew unanxious to work late. I don't blame them, but I had to have the shots. I got them, by compromising the coverage I'd planned. That's happening too often.

July 17. Another bitch of a day . . . I'm afraid they're all getting to be that. I think it might almost be fun to make this picture on a ten-week schedule, but all the fun's leached out of it in eight weeks. Every day's a desperate effort to achieve the scene without surrendering its quality, or my own dream of it. The messenger scene had such simple blocking it was a piece of cake, but there hasn't been a scene like that in a while.

July 22. I almost broke my career-long record of never having missed an hour of work time today. I woke in reasonable energy, but collapsed with giddiness while shaving, stomach churning. Lydia turned to and got me dressed and into the studio, I stumbled through makeup and wardrobe in a sick daze and survived the morning, when I fortunately only had to work behind the camera. Directors at least get to sit down. Having slept through the lunch break, I felt in better shape by the time I had to perform. I managed (I think) a good close-up for "Where hast thou been, my heart . . ." I have no idea what caused it, but it didn't sink me.

July 26. Since we'd scheduled both day and night interiors in the throne room, I planned the day carefully for Pacheco's benefit. I laid out all the shots beforehand, so he could prelight the different areas of the hall and not have to switch from day to night. We did pretty well, too, till we got to the shot of Antony running his horse into the hall to confront the fleeing Cleopatra. I'd told Pelling exactly what we needed as long ago as last March. The floor had to be built to bear the weight of a rearing horse. It did, all right, but it was far too slick to run him on, let alone rear him. We had a good hot rearing horse, too, which I'd tried out on the back lot before breakfast. All for nothing. *Damn!* That killed the end of the day, so I took my family and Mother (she's here for a visit, and I've hardly seen her) to the Prado the last twenty minutes it was open, so we could check out the Velázquezes one more time. That amounts to a helluva rich twenty minutes.

July 30. I worked on through the death of Antony, going not as fast as I'd hoped, but nearly as well as I'd hoped . . . I think. Peter's seen the rough-cut scenes I saw two days ago and doesn't feel happy about Hildegarde. He also has misgivings about today's daily, on the banquet scene. I liked it, he didn't. Perhaps we'll not have a great Cleopatra. Whether we can have a great film anyway is a question. I ran OMEGA MAN for the company tonight. That's certainly not a great film, but it looks like a successful one. They've cut it deeply since I last saw it. I'm more annoyed that they didn't tell me than I am that they made the cuts.

August 4. I got my actress snakebit and laid out, not without problems . . . but not the ones I figured. I'd anticipated pure hell getting the snake shots and was prepared to double her for them, but she did very well, though terrified. Our main problem was keeping her from breathing after her death. The poor lady smokes so much she has little lung capacity. It was really very tough for her. All of it has been, I guess.

August 7. I worked very hard, very long through the night in Antony's garden, getting not quite all the coverage I'd hoped for before the sun came up. I think we got the scene, though. I went somewhat wearily back to the studio to do the retake on the close-up of Hildegarde's death. You could see her breathing in the close angle. Then I did the close-up on John Castle's tag speech, and . . . finished . . . *the* . . . *film.* I poured drinks for the company, trying to absorb the end of it. I've been looking forward to this for so long, and now it's over. I have no way of telling if it's any good at this point. I only know I've done it, and survived.

August 9. I spent a frustrating day at the studio in conferences on how the damn film could possibly have gone $194,000 over budget. They apparently simply failed to keep Peter up to date on the money that was being spent. He's had them prepare detailed breakdowns on exactly how this happened in each area, but it doesn't help much really. It was spent. Where it'll come from, I don't know.

I think the distributor was indulging in what is known as "creative bookkeeping." It is not unknown among American studios, as perhaps everyone knows by now.

August 10. One last sort of housekeeping day at the studio, one further attempt to solve the frightening mysteries of our huge overage. [*It wasn't huge by normal studio standards, but it was to us.*] I looked at the last dailies, which were just structural shots, gluing sequences together. I walked down on the stage where they were already tearing down the monument set and stood alone in the center of the tomb where the play and the shooting had ended. I can't tell whether my dream of doing it ended there or not. I only know I'm tired . . . as tired as I've ever been. I want to go home.

August 11, For New York. We made it out of Spain. I often get this feeling of being trapped in a country when I find myself making a film there over a long period. God knows this was no exception. Lydia, of course, was not as happy to leave as I. The departure was smooth enough, though the accumulation of luggage was monumental. We still managed to get it across the ocean and settled in the suite in reasonable order. Lydia and Holly collapsed, I went on doing what brought me here: taping TV interviews for OMEGA MAN. Apparently the early openings are very strong; the film may do well.

August 14, Chicago/Los Angeles. I finally made it back to my ridge, almost exactly three months from when I left it on my crippling odyssey after windmills. The Chicago routine was familiar: the same hotel, the same limo going to the same studios for the same shows. Some of the cast is changing, though, I notice. I've been at this trade long enough to outlast most of the press, as well as a number of my colleagues. Tony Weitzel, Sam Lesner, Ann Marsters . . . all gone now. Only Kup remains, bearish and warm as always.

August 19, Los Angeles. I can't seem to get going back here. Lydia's migraines are driving her ever more deeply into the depression that destroyed her summer. No one seems to have any answers as to what causes them, or how to cure them. I only know I must hang on. Meantime, I have to prod myself into some kind of an active state. MGM's apparently ready to make a deal on HIJACKED.

Lydia's headaches were increasing in frequency, intensity, and duration by this time. They were an indescribable pain for her, and pressure for all of us.

August 26. Walter Mirisch seems interested in getting me into a film, which is encouraging, since he's willing to pay Citron's price, something MGM so far refuses to do. He gave me a script called DANGERFIELD (a good spy piece, with an unacceptable philosophy) and also wants to make a film on the battle of Midway, and possibly MAKE ROOM, MAKE ROOM. I saw Fray off on his trip backpacking in the mountains. I envy him, but I can't go with him on those long trips.

September 1. Personally, it's still black weather for me. I go through the motions of the days, but I can't hook into them with any enthusiasm. It will pass . . . it will pass. Once the film gets here and I can begin editing, life will look up.

September 6. Today was better . . . infinitely better. I got Dennis [*Whitehouse, the assistant editor*] squared away with a car and an apartment. Eric gets in tomorrow. Lydia, free of migraine today, came with me to tape a CBS interview with Merv Griffin, to my delight and surprise (and to hers, I think). We came home to find Fray back, stinking well of three days in the outback. We sat all evening and talked happily (if oddly) of the history of World War II.

Eric Boyd-Perkins and Dennis did a fine job of correcting my errors as a director (and actor, too, for that matter). We rented the editing equipment and set them up in our projection room, at the other end of the tennis court. It really worked very well.

September 8. Well, I finally saw my rough assembly . . . and Frank Schaffner was right. It's *terrible*.

Frank had warned me before I began ANTONY, *"I'll tell you one thing: The first time you see your film all assembled, you will* hate *it. Don't be discouraged."*

I was braced for this response to my first look at a rough assembly, but it's disheartening, nonetheless. It's amazing how nothing seems to *play,* even scenes that you know perfectly well *did* play. There are exceptions. The last part of the film is much the best. Most of the excess forty minutes (running time now, three hours) will come out of the first part.

September 9, Washington, D.C. We were up early and got off to Washington for the NEA Arts Council meeting. Lydia was in good spirits, no migraine. I got an AFI briefing on the chore I'm to do for them Saturday. (I'm not entirely happy about the film clips they've chosen, but they'll do, I suppose.) Kennedy Center [*we were there for its opening*] is a very impressive example of the edifice complex. The interiors are more successful to my eye than the rather boxlike whole. Still, they need a theater in Washington.

September 12 (Sunday). A long meeting today: We didn't accomplish our agenda. I'm deeply concerned over the degree to which an increasing proportion of the funds we vote are granted to programs primarily social in purpose. This is totally against the theory of the legislation as I understand it, and certainly beyond the scope of our funding. A long debate about this, then a hurried departure from Dulles. Home at last.

I was coming to feel that the limited funds the NEA had were going to projects and programs that, while basically admirable (street dancing, finger painting, and so forth), were primarily designed to meet social needs, not creative ones. It seemed to me, and still does, that the Department of Health, Education, and Welfare, which has the largest share of the federal budget, should assume these responsibilities, and leave the NEA to fry other fish.

September 14, Los Angeles. The ideal way to make a film would be to shoot it, sit down and edit it, *and then go back and shoot what you really need.* I guess this is what Thalberg used to do, but cost makes it a dream now. I know I ache for about a hundred feet of intercut, scattered through the footage we have now. It would make all the difference.

September 15. Lydia's still plagued beyond bearing with migraine. I'm trying to persuade her to let Jolly get her an appointment with a good headache man . . . this apparently being a separate specialty of medicine. She looks like agreeing, which I devoutly hope she does. Meantime, both kids are reasonably settled back in school.

September 21. This is the first day of autumn . . . and I still have a mountain of work to do on ANTONY. Indeed, at this point, it hardly seems like my film, it's so far from what I want. We cut away, though, and shape and knead it into some semblance of the dream. Maybe this is what every director does at this point. We're up to the intermission now, which will be on the return from Actium. This scene (the pardon) plays well, though we've found ways to shorten it.

September 23. The cutting progresses, slowly. I must check with Frank or Willy Wyler to find out if there's a way for the director to work more of the day during the editing of a film. I'd estimate, at this point, I only work about ten percent of the editing day. I wonder if this is typical?

I never got an answer to that question, but if I ever direct another film I will. While cutting, a director examines and discusses a sequence with the editor, they come to conclusions about how to handle it, then the director waits all day for this to be accomplished. I found this frustrating.

September 25. A crowded kind of day, not the way weekends run in Coldwater. We're still hacking our way through the jungle of film out there in the projection room . . . sixty-eight cans, sitting implacably in racks against the wall, with my picture in there somewhere. I've gotta find it.

October 1. I ran the picture for the first time in my version. It's still a rough cut, only half an hour shorter. My coverage is less than I wanted, so there can't be all that many ways to approach a scene in editing. In what we have now, I can see my vision of the film, compromised by what I failed to shoot and what I shot that won't work. It's beginning to look like a film, though I can't call it great yet. If it never is, I'll have failed; the play is great.

October 6. It seems clear we'll finish the fine-cut by next week. Maybe there'll be time for Joe Canutt to work on the battle footage with Eric. I decided to take out the armoring scene today . . . reluctantly. I also got my interview with the *Times*, though I had to run down the hill for it, half-dressed in dinner clothes for a later banquet for Princess Alexandra. This distressed Lydia, but she's very much on a thin edge just now. Her headaches are excruciating, for both of us. More for her, I know, more for her.

October 13. I ran the fine-cut this morning. It's now down to two hours and twenty-four minutes, with the battles still only rough-cut. It looks very much like the picture I want, though maybe not all I could've hoped for. Now I must send it back to England, leaving it to the sound editor for a month. While we were running, Walter Seltzer called from MGM: They've backed off their determination not to pay any actor a percentage of gross from the first dollar. They're ready to make a deal with Citron, on his terms.

October 18. We have John Guillermin to direct HIJACKED (which needs a different title). Having seen two of his films, I think that he can make the film move within the restricted confines of a 707. He also seems to have a good eye for casting. I'm pleased. My last SAG meeting was complicated by emotion. An extravagant speech from Vic Jory, and others. I confess to being touched.

October 19. MGM made a deal with John Guillermin today, whereupon I met with him for the usual drink to seal the bargain. He seems a quiet type . . . perhaps rather like Guy Green. Lydia doesn't like the script, but I think it's just what I need to follow ANTONY.

October 21. I have one last congressional committee hearing to do before retiring from the SAG. Dent's committee, which has never done a particle of good in all the years I've been appearing before it, is still in business, and still anxious to reap what publicity benefits can be wrought from dealing with people like me. I'll play the game out. I thought of a good motto to put on the gavel I'm presenting for my successors at SAG: "Use this with all the patience you possess, all the courage you can muster, and all the common sense you can call on." I spent an hour with Leo, answering questions about our mud slide, over which I'm being sued by our neighbor below. Why doesn't he sue God?

October 26. We lost a good friend today. It seems a sad cliché to describe a dog as "faithful," but he was. Drago was a noble animal and we loved him. Unable to move his hindquarters, he lay uncomplaining for two days, his eyes dimming a little, but still bearing as well as he could the indignity of his last hours. When the vet came to inject in him the relief he surely wouldn't have refused had he been able to choose, he rested his head in my lap, breathed once, and was quiet. Fray and I buried him out on the point, cutting deep into the rocky soil with a harsh effort we both needed to mark the loss we all feel.

October 27. Our writer came out to discuss changes in the HIJACKED script. They're not many, but they're essential. We must sharpen the character of the hijacker, make it utterly clear he deserves no sympathy, that his end is inevitable and just. I see this as social, not merely dramatic, responsibility. There was some discussion about this, but not much. Script approval is a useful tool.

I've always felt, given the enormous power film has to shape the way we feel and think about things, that the film maker has a very serious social responsibility, sometimes overriding his creative independence, in the way he treats subjects like terrorism, racism, and a surprising number of other public issues.

October 31 (Sunday). Fray and I had a great day, hunting boar with Joe Canutt above Santa Barbara. We covered a lot of country, some of it on hands and knees, not the ideal position for meeting a wild pig. I killed a fair-sized boar. The shot wasn't difficult, but you had to be careful of the dogs. I was pleased, but I wish Fray had gotten him. Still, we took the whole day as a success, which it was. The hills up north are like fat yellow cows lying in the fall sun.

November 3. Last night the SAG election returns became clear . . . the good guys won, every seat and every office by a two-to-one margin. I can't help but take it as evidence of the success of my time in office, but I'm very glad on other grounds as well. Much cheerful phoning around this morning, exchanging congratulations.

November 5. I was embarrassed to be late for the special SAG session they set to give me things, but I still made my little speech, and gratefully accepted my gold lifetime membership card, and some Steuben crystal from the branches.

November 7 (Sunday). This was the last time I'll speak to the SAG membership, I expect. I took Lydia and Fray along, to watch me turn it over. I spoke as well as I could, and the response seemed genuine, even heartfelt. It was worth the eleven years. I meant what I said . . . you get more than you give. I'm a better man than I was when I went on the board. I passed the rest of the day in the pleasant glow of family warmth, then let them run me out to the plane for the usual red-eyed argosy east.

November 8, Washington, D.C./New York. This was a wasted day. I worked as hard as I could, spoke as resourcefully as I was able, using all Greg Peck said to me yesterday, on a subject I feel very strongly about: the gradual dilution of the arts program away from quality to a politically diluted program, oriented to the kind of thing HEW should handle. The staff's instincts for a *big* agency and the political choices necessary to sustain it, combined with the councillors' knee-jerk impulse to approve any program labeled socially good, defeated my best effort. There's not much chance of getting Columbia to give money to the AFI, either, but I trundled off to New York to try.

November 9, London. It's certainly an easier shot going to London from New York than from Los Angeles. That four hours closer makes all the difference. I arrived in the evening, in good shape, and had time for a dinner conference with Peter before checking into the Dorchester, ready for a full night's sleep, instead of the nap I usually get after a morning arrival.

November 11. Richard Johnson very kindly contributed his considerable talents absolutely free of charge (or credit) to revoice Lepidus, Alexas, and Ventidius. [*Replacing the accented English of our Spanish actors.*] It's a pleasure to hear those lines read properly at last. On balance, the Spanish arrangement was probably a mistake. Of course we couldn't have undertaken the film there without it, but in the end it cost us (given the overage) as much as the film would've cost in England, and of course we lost many creative advantages that would've been ours here. Hindsight . . .

November 12. I'm learning a lot I never knew about sound with this work; things I may never have a use for in my own acting, but certainly will prove useful if I ever direct another picture. It continued to be fascinating . . . far more interesting to direct another performer in looping than to do it yourself, which is certainly not true of any other part of acting. The posters Rank has roughed out aren't bad; one or two of the ideas are right (all you need is one that's right).

November 14 (Sunday). Cambridge University [*where I'd been invited to give a seminar on the play*] gave me a marvelous day. The students involved in the seminar were world class, of course, though they couldn't resist the tendency almost everyone shares to interpret ANTONY (or any work of art) in terms of their own values and prejudices, instead of Shakespeare's. It still made for a most involved, and involving, session. Cambridge itself was lovely . . . flawlessly what you expected it would be. The most beautiful thing I saw was the Wren Library at King's College, with late light streaming through the windows. The most impressive was the crooked stairway at Jesus College, where students have climbed to their cramped rooms to study for four centuries.

November 17. I'd never have believed it could be so interesting, even creative, guiding six actors through the fragments of offscreen dialogue and odd grunts and groans that constituted our work load today. Even a dying scream has varying possibilities. ("Each man give me three deaths . . . two long, one short, please.")

November 19. No need to go to the studio today; I got a basket of paper work going in the suite with an agency secretary, then over to Warwick to look at the film one more time. There are always little things you can do, bits and pieces you see, every time. Still, I'm at the point now where I find it very difficult to concentrate on the film. I know it so well. Eric and Peter have tightened it a bit, and well. We decided against the Fellinian cut-aheads in the arena sequence; too splashy for a conventionally structured film. We had a long conference on the posters. The Rank people think they should say "Charlton Heston's film of . . ." I vetoed this. I'll be damned if I take a possessive credit on a film Shakespeare wrote every word of.

This was prudent of me. Hollywood will never forget the writer who insisted that the credits for one of the versions of ROMEO AND JULIET *read "Additional dialogue by Samuel Taylor."*

November 20, London/Los Angeles. I wound everything up on schedule, had time to pop over to the Burlington Arcade and buy some oddments for the family, then a final conference with Peter on various details. It's now clear we'll have to get an English composer for the film . . . there's simply no time to do it any other way.

Our Spanish composer had fallen ill and furnished an incomplete and unsatisfying score. Peter found a very talented Englishman, John Scott, who did a brilliant score for us. It remains one of the strengths of the picture.

Then out to Heathrow and over the Pole home. A long flight, but a happy return.

November 22, Los Angeles. Things are moving slowly on SKYJACKED . . . or perhaps it's just that I can't control them so readily. I'm unused to that now. It's damn near a decade since Yvette Mimieux and I worked in DIAMOND HEAD, but she's still a startling-looking lady. I think she'd be right for the stewardess, if we can get her.

December 1. I have to learn to be a pilot for this film, which is not the same as learning how to fly. I conferred with the pilot who'll be our technical adviser and made plans to spend several days in a jet simulator, so I'll at least know where I'm at when we do the flying sequences. I also realized shooting those sequences in January will preclude my getting the time off I'd planned to finish my Antony dubbing. I'll be lucky to get a week off, which is not enough. Hildegarde's loops will have to be supervised by Peter and Eric. Another compromise. At least the day ended well. I went back up into the canyons shooting with Fray, waiting through the winter twilight for the doves to come down to water, which they did at last, in the last of the fading light. Fray shot well; I didn't.

December 11. Halfway through an AFI Board meeting, I went to the men's room and came back to find I'd been elected chairman. There is a really serious fund-raising problem, which is not something I'm good at. Well, what the hell . . . it'll be interesting.

December 13. Another windy winter day, but I spent the bulk of it indoors, in Western Airlines' jet simulator, a very convincing duplication of the flight deck of a 707. All controls respond, in terms of sound and feel, to what they would do in an actual aircraft. If I knew how to fly, it'd be an even better experience, but I can achieve here just about what I've done before on NUMBER ONE and COUNTERPOINT. Not learn how to do it, learn how to look as if I can do it.

December 15. I heard from Peter today that Hildegarde has finished all her looping and improved enormously in the process. It's hard to gauge his enthusiasm, save that it seemed considerable. Seeing that he's been very dour about much of her Cleopatra, this is good news. You have to put it in perspective, of course. There's only so much you *can* do with a performance in looping.

December 24. It poured rain again all day, allowing me no excuse not to get at my paper work and the last of my gift shopping. I had a desperate rush at the end of the afternoon, when I discovered that Holly had still gotten nothing for her mother and was counting on me, reasonably enough, to help her do it. We went down to Ventura, pelting through the rain from shop to shop, fruitlessly searching antique shops, dress shops, finally settling on a little gold and pearl ring. Holly was very firm in her opinions as to just what would and would not do. My sweet Munchkin. Then dinner and a pleasant time finishing the tree.

December 26 (Sunday), Chicago. You'd think it would be very hard to get up the day after Christmas and climb on an airplane. As a matter of fact, it was smooth and easy, with the bags ready when the limo arrived, and the drive to the airport without friction. The flight was tranquil . . . a lovely interlude in the 747 upper lounge playing cards with Holly . . . the arrival in Wilmette as wet as Los Angeles had been. Still, we had a pleasant evening in the old frame house on Maple.

December 27. As usual, our plans had to be reworked today. I'd expected to stay here till Wednesday, but Walter phoned to say they needed me early in Albuquerque for the day I have in the 707. So today was my only day here. I spent a good part of it downtown spending a remarkable sum of money on snow clothes for Yellowstone. My Scottish soul enhanced the memory of shopping in those same stores thirty years ago, taking two days to spend fifteen dollars.

December 29, Albuquerque, New Mexico. I had a good break on the flight
from Chicago: The captain granted me the now-rare privilege of riding
on the flight deck during the whole trip. (Highly useful for this part,
of course.) We arrived slightly late, with my bag left behind in
Denver. I got a little sleep and barely caught the 707 we were
working in at the end of the runway, boarding through the belly
hatch. We spent the day in aerial shots, most with me flying. This
aircraft is remarkably easy to control in simple situations, giving a
heady feeling of power. It was also exciting watching the F100s
(painted as Soviet MIG's) coming in on near-miss courses. It was
worth interrupting my vacation for.

December 31, Yellowstone Park. A good way to end the year . . . skiing
through the looming pines, thickened with snow, past the clouds of
vapor rising from the geysers and thermal pools. It was a bit cold for
Holly, poor baby, so Lydia took her back at last, but we all had it
together, and it was fine. New Year's Eve, as I've long since
discovered, is not a remarkable celebration. The mood is almost
always halfhearted, the joy laced with melancholy. The feeling of the
year passing, inadequately used, is inescapable for everyone, I guess.

1972

The Call of the Wild in Norway . . .

Skyjacked does well, *Antony* poorly . . .

on to *Soylent Green* . . .

The Crucible at the Ahmanson Theater.

Under great duress in *Skyjacked* and *Soylent Green*
THE MUSEUM OF MODERN ART/FILM
STILL ARCHIVE

January 1, Yellowstone Park. We skied again along the drifted roads, stopping to look at the thermal pools steaming in the winter air, watching the bison and elk placidly munching in the drifts, clots of snow thick on their hides, geese swinging over the river, ducks paddling through the steam rising off the water, ending at the Grand Canyon of the Yellowstone, chunked with ice.

January 3, Los Angeles. You forget how hard it is to fly out of a remote place, when you're used to traveling from metropoli. We had to drive two hours, wait nearly three for our puddle jumper, then wait another hour in the VIP lounge in Boise before we finally got on a 707 for home. It was worth it, though. Even the long drive to Bozeman, careful over the icy roads, was pleasant. We saw a pair of bighorns within half a mile of the highway, where they'd never come in season.

January 4. This picture [SKYJACKED] started off appropriately enough for me . . . standing on the sidelines watching. I've never done a film with so many scenes I wasn't in. Still, there was the 707, all becrewed and passengered. I did get a chance to try my uniform on. I look OK; the equipment's holding up. With careful attention, it should last a few more films.

January 5. I began again today, if you don't count those few shots at thirty thousand feet over New Mexico. It's odd how much time can go by when I'm totally immersed in my identity as an actor without acting at all. Of course there's been the odd narration here and there, several interviews and whatnot, but I've not acted since early August, and the last several days of that consisted of lying dead, diligently not breathing. My first scene today consisted of walking out of the cockpit and into the can. Very demanding bit of emoting there.

January 11. No call today, from MGM, that is. Peter called to say that Rank's preempted our February date at the Odeon, since they're holding over the Bond film. This means we have a choice of waiting till May for a London date (not good for several reasons) or taking the Astoria March 2. That seems best. I'll have time to finish SKYJACKED and get over well in advance for publicity on ANTONY, then go to Japan for the opening there. If CALL OF THE WILD comes through, I can then go straight on to that.

January 20, Oakland. At last I had a full day's work. The opening shots went well, John Guillermin utilizing his talent for richly textured full shots, most with a moving camera. He provided a good introductory scene for me. I'm beginning to realize this is not a rich role, of course. Nonetheless, if the film comes off, it'll help me. I'm beginning to think it will, too.

January 25. Today I finished everything I have in the cabin of the plane. Indeed, except for one flashback scene, I finished everything I have in the film except for scenes in the flight deck. Also I confirmed that the longest I can hope to stay in London is Monday, since they can find almost no work to do around me here past then.

January 26, To London. As seems now to be my invariable habit, I rose early enough on departure day to get a large slice of paper work done before leaving for the airport. It was pleasant to fly that long, familiar route with Lydia for a change.

January 28. The trailer and the credits looked fine when I checked them this morning, save for the fact that Shakespeare's name needs some enlarging. It seems incredible that his name of all in the world should need defense. They now want me to write two pieces for the program: on my experience as a director and on the background of history between the two plays. I don't see how I can do it in the time I have. We also have a problem with Rank on the ads . . . they're getting very 1950s-MGM in their concept.

January 31, To Los Angeles. Lydia spent most of the night working on my piece for the program on the history of Rome between the death of Caesar and the opening scene of ANTONY AND CLEOPATRA, which I'd had no time to work on. I woke to find she'd written the whole thing. It's very good, but I can't let it go over my signature, however loving an act it is (and it is). I spent most of the trip home writing the other piece they want. The printers in London are screaming for both of them yesterday.

February 3. They touched the raw nerve I have about late actors this morning. I don't like to be summoned to rehearsal before my scheduled call for the first scene of the day. If they want me early, call me early. They did this morning, and then all the other actors were late, but my point was made. This flight deck is an incredibly cramped set, not only to act in, but to shoot as well. John G.'s proving very resourceful with it. He has all his shots laid out in advance, with the lens picked for each.

February 12. Fray was seventeen today. The time back to his birth seems impossibly long, and at the same time, no more than the flicker of a bird's wing. He's tall now, and lean, with a quiet, cool quality stemming from some closed place within himself that he's never opened. I'm proud of him, and I love him very much. The party we had tonight was pleasant, though Lydia wasn't able to be there for all of it, having fought her headache to complete its preparations.

February 15. Another long day on the flight deck, followed by a dinner date we were already late for when I got home from the studio. I was also faced with a despondent son who'd blown a tennis match, playing for his school, and was realizing he really hated the idea of tournament play. It'll be a disappointment to me if he gives it up, but I can see he well may do so.

February 19. Now there's the pleasant expansion of spirit that sometimes comes with the end of a role. This has been a curiously detached kind of picture for me. There was very little part for me to play, something I didn't quite realize when we were preparing. There are, in fact, no strong acting scenes for anyone. It's an exploration of an event . . . the hijacking. Let's see how well it turns out.

February 27, Land at Orly, then to London. This has to have been my worst commercial flight ever. Even being overnighted in Iceland when Pan Am lost an engine was better than that ugly VIP lounge at Orly, all colored neon tubes. We got back to London at last to find Peter had finished the dub, *today*, fighting the power cuts.

March 2, London. Astoria, world premiere: ANTONY AND CLEOPATRA. Our first notices were not encouraging . . . in fact they were bad. I'm dashed a little, of course, though you learn to be toughened for it. The premiere itself seemed to go well. Very few coughs, especially for a premiere audience. The voice track was sometimes lost in the effects and the music tracks; I wish I'd been able to follow through on the whole dub. I wish, I wish . . .

March 3, Los Angeles. On the basis of the notices so far, we have a critical disaster. It's easy (indeed, mandatory) to comfort yourself in such moments of trauma by finding all the examples of pictures that have failed with excellent notices (MACBETH) and that have succeeded with terrible ones (ROMEO AND JULIET). Nonetheless, we didn't get good ones. Of course I disagree, of course I'm outraged, but it still sticks a little. I guess it might be true to say that, by and large, Shakespeare *never* gets great notices. They expect so much. (And I thought I gave it to them.)

March 4, JAL for Tokyo via Moscow. I took along a huge pile of scripts, including two firm offers (one already rejected, for a thin sort of "Get Carter" piece). On the way to the airport, Peter pressed for some cuts in the Nile scene and the interior of the monument with Proculeius and Caesar, on the ground that Hildegarde is obviously the prime target of the critics' anger. I'm not sure this is a good move.

March 5 (Sunday), Land Tokyo. The trip to Japan over Russia was longer than my familiar run over the Pole from Los Angeles. The brief look we had at Moscow was grim: surly guards with Bren guns in the airport, shrill propaganda all over the transit lounge. Siberia looked bleak and endless, living up to its notices. We arrived on time, to the usual cheery circus of Japanese welcome. I've now stayed in three versions of the Imperial Hotel. In some ways, old Frank Lloyd Wright's was the best.

March 6. The Japanese know how to get coverage. Either that or I have one helluva draw in this country. Possibly a little of both. We had a press turnout that staggered me: rows and rows of eyeglasses and notebooks, a platoon of photographers. It's always difficult to get any clear idea of how we communicate through an interpreter. Do they have any idea what I'm saying?

March 9, Kyoto. Peter called, somewhat encouraged. Business is good for the first week, considering the notices, and we had good reviews from *Variety,* and the *Sunday Telegraph* (obviously very perceptive fellows; I take back all I ever said against them when they didn't like me). The day went well, although I'm wrung out with the same interviews, over and over. The Japanese are tireless gift-givers; I collected maybe twenty pounds or more of various items.

March 10, To Los Angeles. The last day in Tokyo seemed to go very well; we had a last spate of interviews, and then the royal do, at which I had to read my Japanese speech, with no time to memorize it. Then we swam back home through the time zones, stuffing two days into one. The plane was late; we took off at midnight, slept and indulged through the long night gaining on the sun, had a fragrant hour in the moist blossom smell of Honolulu, and then the last long leg back to California.

March 13. SKYJACKED looks surprisingly good, I was relieved to see. The first assembly fell into place very quickly, at 103 minutes. It seems very tight. A pleasure for a change to be in a film that runs under two hours . . . it's been some time. It's still simply a story of an event, with very little room for character, but it works. I won't get any kudos for this job, but I'll earn some money. That's necessary too.

March 14. A full day, beginning with a stint for deaf children; crippled in the worst way of all: language. Your heart moves seeing how hard it is for them to speak. After a good singles session, I raced out to go over the situation with Herman. Aside from ANTONY, which he's of course no better able than I to evaluate at this point, all seems to be going well. We have four or five projects in the oven, all ripening well, several ready to pop. At the same time, I was able to postpone my departure for Norway so I could celebrate our anniversary here at home. Joe Mankiewicz's son seems a likely candidate to script the OSTERMAN WEEKEND novel.

March 18, To London. After much back and forthing with Citron, we decided I'd fly as far as London today, even though Towers hasn't yet deposited my total guarantee in escrow in the U.S. [*In deals with foreign companies, Herman has always required this before I leave the country. It's saved us a lot of the grief other actors encounter.*] I have work to do on ANTONY, and it'll also be useful rest to break the trip for a day in London. I have many reservations about the CALL OF THE WILD script still, but most of them can be resolved by judicious cutting. The ending, with anachronistically hostile Indians in '98, can be changed by substituting the heavy we've disposed of earlier in the story. [*But we didn't.*]

March 19 (Sunday). I'm having bad luck with my planes lately. An hour in Prestwick isn't as bad as five in Paris, but it was irritating to be held up again, especially with my cold shifting into high gear. I ran the proposed cuts Peter wants to make in ANTONY. I found ways to shorten several scenes (the farewell, river, monument) without eliminating them entirely. It'll take out about ten minutes, I think.

March 21, Oslo. The spring equinox found me leaving London with some reluctance, though I have nothing more to do there. Norway looks about as I expected (film has taken away all our capacities for geographic surprise). I was disturbed to note that the last big snow, two weeks old, is steadily melting under what I assume is the spring thaw. My cold still looms sullenly between me and the world.

Colds seem to be the only illness I suffer from. I'm absolutely convinced they are invented by the inner me to annoy the outer me (who is my favorite of the two).

March 22. So another one began. What is it? My fortieth, I think. Can I really have been standing in front of different cameras all that time, pretending to be somebody else while film sprockets passed the gate? Perhaps art has only rarely occurred in the course of all this, but it's been great to try. I've seen a lot of the world and done some remarkable things. I've ridden into captured cities, and won chariot races, and conducted symphony orchestras, and painted the Sistine, and now I've driven a dog sled.

March 23. The second day seemed to go well, though the Norwegian crew works very slowly. They seem to have little experience of the way a professional company works. Sort of like a good amateur theater group. But the set's good (though the snow's going fast), and Ken

Annakin seems to know what he's about. He's another of those directors who works it all out and then has you step into the shot. I don't mind . . . I can do it that way, too.

March 24. I'd expected to stand by all day, dropping us a day further behind, with the snow melting every hour. At last I was called out, driven around the intricate edge of a frozen fjord, and accomplished exactly one shot with the dog team, after having been run over by them in the first attempt. It turns out dog teams are really much more interested in fighting with one another than they are in dragging the sled.

March 25. My family arrived today, late by several hours, having missed their connection in London and lost one bag. Still, they were all in good spirits and welcome, God knows, welcome. I'd spent the large part of the day on standby, seizing the chance to look at some second unit daily of the snow trek stuff, which looked very impressive. Then of course my work call came just as I was going to the airport to meet them. We did the scene shooting across the lake at the wolves; incredibly, they had no blanks for the carbine. I had to use live rounds, putting the slugs well over the animals' heads. What if I hadn't known how to shoot?

March 26 (Sunday). My first full day off here; I happily spent it with my family. I had a reasonable hit with Fray in the late morning, on an indoor clay court, though the visibility's not good against the canvas bubble. Then we did the museums; they have some marvelous Viking dragon ships. Half my ancestors leaped over the sides of those ships when they grounded on the English beaches a thousand years ago, the other half waited for them in the shallows with axes.

March 30. Another easy day, though increasingly springlike temperatures provide a new problem: trying not to sweat visibly in my sealskin anorak. There are others, less trivial. The dogs are not working well. They're not really trained for this. The film will stand or fall on the performance of the lead dog, Buck; his role, not mine, is the central one. So far, Ken's been sluffing past the weaknesses in the dog's work, but this won't do.

The film, of course, should've been shot in the Yukon, where the story is laid, and where there are still good dog teams available. We also then could've cast a dog in the leading role that had been properly trained for film work, something that is really only done in Hollywood.

April 3. We spent an interesting, if somewhat slushy, morning examining the detritus of Norway's past. Beautifully shaped flint spearheads (how curious that, all over the world, early man found flint for this, and knew how to shape it, and now no man alive can do it). There are good iron Viking swords, remarkably preserved twelfth-century houses that are almost carvings. We saw a fine stone church, its pagan carving oddly congruous with the Christian motifs. We switched over to night shooting on a set with snow slightly augmented by today's weather. The usual fumble and confusion of night shooting . . . just like home.

April 4. Oslo finally creaked open, its indulgent Easter over at last. The town literally shut down for five days. Bars, tennis courts, TV, movies, and most restaurants were all closed tight. I wonder what happened to the spirit that drove the Vikings to the edge of the world? Word from Peter Snell indicates no improvement in the London business, though Tokyo's apparently excellent. He's still getting the cut version ready for the U.S. Here, we're faced with the endless problems of organization, personnel, dogs, publicity (we still have no one on location). I fear I've fallen in with amateurs and con men.

This had not been a picture, really, but a production deal, patched together with incredible adroitness and negotiating skill, and no film-making talent whatever. It ended up as a joint British, French, German, Italian, Norwegian, Spanish production, which meant that actors and technicians from all those countries had to be employed. It's a shame that the resulting hodgepodge undertook a work so valuable as London's novel.

April 5. An April snowstorm, thick, wet, and day-long, slushed production almost to a halt today. We needed chains on the cars to get into the location, which looked ideal. The Oslo slaughterhouse contributed enough horse carcasses to lend reality to Dead Horse Pass, so the footage, however hard come by, was valuable. We had a dinner at a restaurant Ibsen frequented, with a director I'm supposed to remember from Bermuda twenty years ago, but don't, then put Fray, loaded with climbing gear, on a train to his adventure snow-climbing in the north.

April 6. Yesterday's heavy snow improved the location in camera terms, but did nothing for its comfort. Nevertheless, we got some good shots, as well as some improvements in dialogue. The day, however, centered for me around my incredibly beautiful daughter . . . my all-the-way-through beautiful daughter. With her mother in Bergen and her brother in the Arctic, I took her on location with me. Waiting for shots on location, we made her first snowman (and possibly my best). I remember the look of her snuggled inside my sealskin anorak in the icy trailer after lunch, sleeping like a chilly angel, her feet warming in my lap.

April 10. We bogged down today, literally as well as figuratively. The dogs were good in some scenes, maddeningly uncooperative in others. [*We were using various dogs and various trainers, with various results.*] The continuing thaw, compounded with a fine rain, made shooting difficult and damned uncomfortable. We were working along a mountain road where you didn't have room to scratch, let alone maneuver a film company. It's like what Wellington writes about operating in the Pyrenees against Napoleon. This can be a complicated way to make a living. Lydia took off on her trip to research the path of Juana the Mad in the Low Countries, for her play.

Juana was the daughter of Isabella, and the last Spanish queen of Spain. She was quite a lady. Of the play, more later.

April 11. Lydia is busy and safe in Holland, but the cathedral she wanted to look at burned down yesterday, after waiting there for her since 1320. I worked, but very little. Annakin's method of shooting—having the shot all lined up and lit before calling the actor—plus the noncentral nature of my part, puts a light work load on me, considering what they're paying me. On the other hand, the dog has the star part, and he gets paid in dog food.

April 15. Today was tough. I spent a large part of it falling down the mountainside, then being buried in snow, and dug out by a surprisingly cooperative new dog we found. The day was shockingly marked, though, by the total nervous collapse of Juan Luis Galliardo, whose increasing insecurity over the past few days came to a climax today when he proved unable to either comprehend anything said to him in any language or perform on any level whatever. God, what pressure can do to actors.

It was heartbreaking to see someone crumble under the anxieties of this insane profession. Juan Luis had been an assured and sunny-natured young leading man when he played in ANTONY. *The last day he worked in Norway, he could not respond to a cue as well as the dog in the scene, God help him.*

April 19. Lydia flew off over the Pole for home this morning, with barely time for me to see her through the plane gate and make my shooting call on time. The day went well enough, but Oslo seems a bleaker place now, even though I'm close to the end. This hasn't been a very enjoyable film, which may be the film's fault, or mine. Mine, I'm afraid.

I don't know whether I had enough leverage to insist on the film being made in terms that could have resulted in a good picture. I could've turned it down. I'm not proud of it.

April 20. Our French lady, Michele Mercier, is beginning to prove a little fractious and, like most of our colleagues in this flick, is really underqualified to act in English. I know, I couldn't act in French, but then, I wouldn't try. Even with the speech on an idiot board she was a little at sea (actually, it was the first time in forty films I've seen that classic expedient used). We at last made a decision to replace Galliardo; I visited him in the hospital; he's still only semicoherent, even in Spanish. We'll use Sancho Gracia (my Canidius in ANTONY) to replace him, splitting the role into two characters, which is luckily barely possible at the point where Juan Luis collapsed. A sorry end, as it almost certainly is, to Galliardo's career.

It was, I'm afraid. Like athletes and politicians, a serious physical failing usually renders an actor unemployable. Moral failings are dealt with more generously.

I took Leo, the dog who plays Buck, to the press party tonight, as our star and the only Norwegian performer since Sonja Henie to head the cast of an international film. He comported himself with great dignity. Better than some actors I know.

April 26. Things are beginning to move with some pace, though still with limited assistance from the local contigent in the crew. It would be interesting to see what could've been done with this piece if a real script had been written, instead of carpentering each scene into some semblance of reality as we came to shoot it.

May 2. We finally wound up shooting, on schedule, for which Ken Annakin deserves credit, given the problems of the script, the production company, and our multinational confusions. It's hard to assess the film now; there're such serious weaknesses in the structure and the character relationships. It's better than it looked going in; it may be all right. [*It wasn't. For the record, it's probably the worst film I ever made. I'm embarrassed to have screwed up Jack London.*]

May 3, Los Angeles. It was a long, long day, and a long, long flight, but I sustained it with high spirits, plus my usual dose of airborne sleep. This time of the year, combining maximum weather plus a still small number of tourists makes for the best chance of arriving on schedule, which we did. Los Angeles looked fine as we slid down through the late afternoon light; Lydia and Fray looked even better waving behind the barrier as I went by the gate on my way to customs. I had a huge load of baggage, some of it Lydia's. I'm bloody glad to get it and me home.

May 4. I was sorry to have to rush into a crisis meeting at the AFI my first morning back, but things are building to a head there. I'm not sorry I'm not going to Wilmington for the NCA meeting this weekend. We're really in a confrontation with them, and I'm clearly one of the running dogs of Hollywood in their eyes. Obviously, the current bunch at NCA doesn't view the AFI warmly. To the bureaucrats, we're a bunch of dirty elitists. (Since when did a commitment to quality mark you as a bad guy?)

May 5. Exactly four months from our first day of shooting in New Mexico we screened an answer print on SKYJACKED, which is some sort of a record for an A film. It plays very well indeed. It's in no way profound; what the critics like to call (I *hope* they'll like to) a movie movie. It does have a socially responsible statement to make (hijacking is bad for you), but other than that there's little but a tight suspense story. My part's not difficult; I do what can be done with it. I think it may do well.

May 9. Not a vital day for me, either professionally or personally. This journal is concerned primarily with the former, only glancingly with the latter. On the state of the world, it touches not at all. Nations fall and are not noted here. I do mark now and again, though, the fading fortunes of our own nation. They announced the blockade of North Vietnam two days ago; a little late, I'm afraid.

Along with most Americans, I agree this country erred seriously in Southeast Asia. The most serious error would seem to have been not blockading the North at once, a move that would've ended the war very soon, with little loss of life on either side. It was not taken, I understand, because of fear of Russian or Chinese response, which proved nonexistent when the action was finally taken, far too late.

May 16, New York. We had a real issue in our press conference on violence today, regrettably. The attempt to shoot Governor Wallace yesterday, while he was campaigning in Maryland, focused attention once again on the degree to which violence is chosen as a solution for the problems of modern life. I'm convinced the media bear a deep responsibility here. I said so as eloquently as I could. "We're becoming a nation of violent people," they like to say. That's utter crap. We risk violence in this country because our system tolerates dissent, as it must. When the media report violence, they can seem to encourage it. Man is a carnivorous, highly territorial animal; the capacity for violence is as endemic to him as the patella reflex. One of the functions of society is to control these impulses. Dictatorships can do this more easily than democracies.

May 20, Los Angeles. Fray's off pig hunting, but Lydia was without migraine, so the day was pleasant, except for my lousy tennis in the Braemar tourney. We're still mulling the problems of MAKE ROOM. One of the toughest is how to suggest a city of eighty million people without huge numbers of extras, which are impossible at Extras Guild rates. If there's no solution to this, it seems to me almost impossible to make the film at all. I made this point over the phone to Walter Seltzer, still busy flacking in Canada.

It's now impossibly expensive to use more than a few hundred extras at union rates, which means that pictures that require them are either not made or made outside the jurisdiction of the Extras Guild. In this case, MGM agreed to employ a few hundred union extras and hire the rest freely outside the union. Even so, of course, we had to make do with far fewer people than we needed.

May 22. A long discussion with the MGM fellas about the MAKE ROOM script. There's still a lack in the last scene. The whole payoff on the cannibalism element lacks impact. It's kind of talked around and never really functions in the structure of the piece, let alone in the characters. Nevertheless, the script's better than it was. I'm beginning to have a very good feel for this one. I wish I weren't going right back into a film for the same studio again, but this is irrational; actors used to spend their entire film careers at one studio.

May 25. Reports on the first day's business on SKYJACKED are not too encouraging, but that's not always conclusive. You can torment yourself to distraction trying to follow too closely the fortunes of something you can't control anyway. If we have a good opening weekend on the film it'll be valuable for me, not only in terms of money, but in demonstrating my viability one more time. (You have to keep demonstrating it till it no longer exists, of course.)

May 29. We mark our dead today, though many seem to mock them. It's very easy to find echoes of Gibbon in the querulous cacaphony that passes for the voice of the Republic this year. I saw the JFK documentary I narrated for him a decade ago. How unacceptable his voice and his views would be to the party that has deified him.

May 30. We're moving well at MGM on MAKE ROOM, which title they propose changing to SOYLENT GREEN. I like it. Harry Alan Towers wants me to make another film for him. OLD FISH HAWK still trembles on the verge of being put together, we have a development deal on OSTERMAN WEEKEND at Universal, and the first week of SKYJACKED grossed over two and a half million. But there is still no U.S. distributor for ANTONY.

June 4 (Sunday). Having had a rather disastrous Saturday evening quarrel, involving one of my rare losses of temper ("Why can't a woman be more like a man?"), I undertook to cool off with a run along Mulholland in the dark, brooding on my injustices. I came back and found my daughter circling the drive on her bicycle, sadly singing in her silver, true voice, "When the dog bites, when the bee stings/When I'm feeling sad/I try to remember my favorite things/And then I don't feel so bad," waiting to comfort me. A lovely and loving girl. I hope she finds a man who deserves her. Is there one?

June 7. I think we have a director. Dick Fleischer's LAST RUN is a damn good film, even though I saw it sitting soaked from a downpour (rain in Los Angeles in *June?*) that caught us walking to the projection room. I talked to Dick later over a drink; he seems a quiet, contained kind of man. This counts with me . . . the good captain theory. I hope we get him.

June 11 (Sunday). Since Fray's off backpacking somewhere above Lake Edison (X's marked on a map in case he's late back) and Lydia's still off in Honolulu doing whatever it is she is doing there (both writing her play and being away from me, or something very close to that), Holly and I tend to rattle around here a little bit. I've decided to go pick my wife up and bring her home.

June 13, Honolulu. The day was spent en route to Hawaii. Traveling with my daughter is an increasingly delightful experience. She looks prettier every day and is a more enchanting companion than I could've imagined a ten-year-old girl could be. The lovely thing about little girls is their demureness, somehow. We missed Lydia, who'd come to meet us, in the terminal, but we got together at the hotel. Fray joined our rump vacation, too, having come home early from his backpacking trip into the High Sierra, blocked by snow from the deepest country he was after, and somewhat daunted by a broken finger. All's well. The Royal Hawaiian is now surrounded by the tall towers of other, newer hotels. I don't like it as much, but the Hawaiian sunset is still the same. So is my wife.

June 17, Los Angeles. It's good to be back home, all put together again. Life's a complicated tightrope to walk, much of the time, but it's fun. *My* life is fun, anyway, and worth the effort put into it. Besides, what else could you do with your time?

June 21. I touched base with Walter Mirisch today. United Artists [*with whom Walter was then associated*] have had very bad luck with me, come to think of it. What with KHARTOUM, THE HAWAIIANS, and NUMBER ONE, I'm surprised they have any appetite left for hiring me, but they seem determined. Walter gave me the script he's finally finished on the battle of Midway. It might be an interesting thing to do. It's at least reassuring to contemplate so many potential employers. The consensus of the Center Theater Group Board was they'd much rather I did THE CRUCIBLE than BECKETT. I was also interested to see how much improvement they've made in the acoustics at the Ahmanson.

The Ahmanson is a fine theater, but really too large for plays. At this time few actors would risk their voice or their reputation in the house. Under Bob Fryer, who had just taken over as managing director, the sound system had been dramatically (and expensively) revised in an attempt to deal with this. As a member of the board, I was about to try the water.

June 22. I read THE CRUCIBLE, struck with its quality and power. Obviously, it offers as good a part for me as there is in contemporary theater, with the possible exception of Thomas More. MAN FOR ALL SEASONS may be a better play, too . . . but not much. I had a working meeting with Dick Fleischer, now that he's officially directing SOYLENT GREEN. That's always a little delicate, till you know each other. I think this one went well. Walter Seltzer had a few sketches from the art director; very good concepts.

June 27, Northwestern University, Chicago. It's odd to come back to the campus where so much began for me. Perhaps because the setting puts me back thirty years, to the callow anxieties and callow certainties. I feel a certain number of doubts about this job, but not that it's worth doing. They needed a new theater when I tried to learn to act here in 1941.

I had, somewhat reluctantly, accepted the chairmanship of a campaign to raise the money for the theater. They are at last breaking ground.

July 5, New York/Madrid. The event of the day . . . one of the events of the year, or any year . . . was Lydia's delivery to me of the manuscript of her play on Juana la Loca, as we boarded the jet for Madrid; I read it over the Atlantic. I'm impressed beyond telling that she should actually have finished such a labor, and beyond measuring that it's so good. It's well-structured, moving, even funny, and I'm very proud of her for it.

Even though there's no part for me, it's a marvelous play, with the best woman's part I've read since HEDDA GABLER.

July 6, Madrid. The plane was two hours late into Madrid [*where I'd gone to loop CALL OF THE WILD*], which meant I had only an hour to sleep before I was due at the studio. I ran the film then (an undubbed fine-cut). It's not much. I'm not very much. I got enough loops done to be sure I could finish tomorrow, and went to dinner.

July 8, London. My Spanish plan worked as I'd determined it would, getting me to London in time for the last day of Wimbledon, if only just. The kids were waiting for us in the suite at the Dorchester, but we were so rushed, I wasn't really sorry for the rain-out, canceling the finals for today. We had a lazy, good evening enjoying the luxury of the Harlequin Suite, watching the earlier matches run on the BBC.

The next day I had the pleasure of seeing Stan Smith beat Nastase in five sets, in what is now considered one of the best Wimbledon finals ever played.

July 12, Inverlochy Castle, Scotland. We got away in good order, though I had to muscle BEA a little to allow us to check in and get the bags aboard, with fifteen minutes to go before departure. The Highlands lived up to their billing, though the Loch Ness monster failed to show. Inverlochy is exactly what you imagine a Scottish castle to be like. We picked the right place.

July 17, Isle of Iona. This was a long day—thirteen and a half hours by sea and land, to see the spot Johnson describes as the holiest in Britain. It's that, even for a modern agnostic. There's a clean, sea-wind quality about the place that's very moving. The graveyard where forty Scottish kings are buried is the only such place I've seen where I could want to lie.

July 19, Beauly. We left the manor-house luxuries of Inverlochy for the very different delights of the Fraser country. Having been invited to join a clan gathering, we of course accepted, staying at one of the Lovat houses and joining in the group activities . . . and that's not the kind of thing I do readily. I was moved by the field of Culloden, where several hundred Frasers died in a last desperate effort to put Bonnie Prince Charlie on the English throne.

July 20. A very full Fraser day. We hiked across the moors to the yew tree, supposed to be the oldest in Britain, where the clan gathered for some centuries. Not too tough a trek, though no stroll. Marvelous to do it in a kilt . . . it made all the difference, somehow. That's a fine garment, as suited to its time as the toga. We continue to fit happily into the clan here, to my surprise. At the last minute, Fray canceled his return to the U.S., where he had a dive trip scheduled, and drove back from the airport with us for more time as a Scot. I understand.

July 21, To London. Simon, Lord Lovat, MacShimi of the Frasers is a breathing refutation of the concept that breeding cannot produce a superior man. He proved this adequately at Dieppe and Sword Beach where he led the commandos ashore, but it remains evident watching him standing in hip boots and a torn sweater, directing the netting of salmon in his stream. You can pick him out of the crowd at fifty yards, instantly. The day was full of unique and valuable experiences, not the least of which was the last: the American contingent of the clan racing us madly, in a truck and three cars, to catch the train at Aviemore that we'd just missed at Inverness, all crowding onto the platform at last to say good-bye. A fine bunch, and a fine time. I'm prouder than ever of my Fraser blood.

July 22, To Los Angeles. A train journey has much to recommend it. Though I didn't sleep marvelously, I certainly did better than I could on a 747, later. We had an easy breakfast at the Dorchester, then an enriching stroll through the Turners at the Tate, and back in time for my conference with Peter Snell, en route to the airport. He didn't have much to report on ANTONY, though it seems we're progressing in terms of finding a single small house for the film in New York. (At least we've determined that's the way to go there.) Peter now heads British Lion films, which gives him a good executive base.

July 24. The mail stands in toppling heaps on my desk, but I sank back on my ridge like an old dog settling, sighing down by the fire. We have a small dilemma at MGM. Rendered greedy by the success of SKYJACKED (which has grossed almost as much in seven weeks of domestic release as OMEGA MAN has done in a year), they're eager to have SOYLENT GREEN in time for Christmas. This is of course simply not possible, but if they don't *know* that, it's difficult to tell them. If you don't know how long it takes to make a film, how can you *be* in that job? Never mind; they'll find out.

August 2. My daughter . . . my lovely Munchkin . . . is eleven and shimmering on the edge of adolescence. Lydia laid on a fine party, of course, in which I played a somewhat larger part than usual . . . blowing up balloons and pool toys. I also got what I thought would be a marvelous film for them: the Marx Brothers' DAY AT THE RACES, which they found totally incomprehensible.

I have no explanation for this, but it's worth noting. The Marx Brothers depended a great deal on puns and topical references that were meaningless to an audience of seventies eleven-year-olds.

August 3. I made a significant change today. After a lifetime of voting for Democratic candidates for president (though often Republican for other offices), I felt impelled to endorse Richard Milhous Nixon for this fall. Not only his record, contrasted with McGovern's potential, but his basically affirmative posture persuades me. I recognize he's a political animal, but I question whether any man can be anything else in a political job. Given this, I want the man who can be successfully political, and Nixon's demonstrated he can. Also, I reject McGovern. As I said in the press conference, America is not spelled with a *k*.

In the aftermath of Watergate, I'm often asked what I think of my virgin Republican vote. I feel the way Chevalier said he felt on reaching the age of eighty. "When you consider the alternative, I feel fine."

August 4. We don't seem to be making a helluva lot of progress on our casting for SOYLENT, which surprises me. It shouldn't really be that hard, but no girl we've read has impressed me very much. MGM's offer to Eddie Robinson of twenty-five thousand, plus twenty-five thousand deferred, elicited his unarguable response: "At seventy-nine, I'm not much interested in deferrals." I hope they'll pay whatever it takes to get him.

August 7. I had the curious experience of being invited to Hillcrest to play tennis with the vice-president. Politics also makes strange tennis partners. For one thing, I gathered a win was imperative. Though I was the best player on the court (which was saying very little), he was by far the worst; we were hard put to hold his serve. We managed, however, predictably. Certainly I've never felt so safe from marauders as on a court surrounded by the Secret Service.

August 11, Washington, D.C. I don't know that it was of any particular value to the planners of the Bicentennial, but at least we responded to their request for some brainstorming on the celebration. My only real contribution was a caution to the chairman that our report to the commission and the president be couched in language that did not include the word "relevant." The laughter was muted. Many people think that's the most important word in the language, I'm afraid.

August 14, Los Angeles. We're really just winding up our casting now. We have Eddie Robinson, Joe Cotten, Leigh Taylor Young, Chuck Connors (whom I haven't worked with since BIG COUNTRY—his first film, in which he was damn good), also probably Brock Peters, maybe Leslie Uggams. This is a pretty formidable group, better than I usually have for company, as far as name value goes, anyway. I'm impressed.

August 21. Lydia's coming with me on this Eastern trip, to my convenience as well as my pleasure. Otherwise, I'd have had to come back here for a day, then Red-Eye east again. I think she'll enjoy the trip; surely it will at least distract her from the pressure of her migraines.

August 23, Miami. Opening session of the GOP convention. I woke in a flamboyantly Floridian whorehouse of an apartment and tennised the morning away in steamy weather. I made a spectacular water transfer with Lydia to a yacht full of governors on parade. A waterborne parade's superior to the kind I've done so often in the back of convertibles. Tonight I had the moving experience of facing an audience of fifteen thousand and reading a prayer for the POW's. It meant something to me.

August 24, New York. We left later than we should've, cutting our arrival in New York awfully close. There was a limo waiting to whip me to the studio where Cavett was already on the air. The other guest Ramsey Clark, fresh from his visit to Hanoi. I was there to plug the Kennedy tennis tournament Saturday, but I seized the chance to debate the POW thing with Clark. It was snotty of me, no doubt, considering our relative trades (an idle mountebank, talking world affairs with a former Cabinet officer?), but I couldn't pass it up. I said what needs to be said, often. Hanoi is treating our POW's with unspeakable barbarism. What's more, Ramsey Clark *knows* it.

August 26, Forest Hills, New York. The Robert Kennedy pro-celeb tournament . . . I thought I played OK, but Denny Ralston (off the circuit now with a bad knee) wasn't able to take the requisite twenty percent off his shots and still avoid errors, which is the crucial responsibility of the good player in what is really mixed doubles. We lost, on center court in front of cheering thousands, after being a break up. Ah well . . . had we won we would've had to take a later plane home, so this was not without consolation.

August 27 (Sunday), San Clemente/Los Angeles. The Democrats yesterday, Republicans today. The Western White House is a good example of Spanish Colonial architecture, on a bluff over the sea. The party was as nicely laid on as Ethel Kennedy's in New York, though here you had more Secret Service men, of course.

August 29. The climate around the ridge blossomed into spring again, with the good news about Lydia's thyroid. Even her compulsion to take the worst possible interpretation of any situation melted under Solomon's diagnosis.

Dr. Solomon had decided an operation was not necessary at that point, since no malignancy existed.

Now she's plunging ahead with renewed energy into the final (?) revisions of the first draft on her play. I don't really understand why she insists on a perfectly clean copy before she lets me read it again, but she does. I'm itching to get another look at it.

August 30. I undertook to evaluate some films made by applicants for AFI fellowships. Three were terrible, one surprisingly good. All show some technical skill, all but one displayed total ignorance of how to deal with actors . . . or acting.

September 4. Last Labor Day I was cutting my picture, this Labor Day I've failed to sell it in my own country. I can't say this preoccupies me, though. For one thing, there is faint progress being made on the problem, through Herman's mysterious ways. Besides, mourning it won't improve it. Anyway, everything else seems to be going very well. SKYJACKED is now over five million in domestic film rentals, and we picked up extra money on both AGONY and HAWAIIANS this week. But I mourn my film.

September 5. The first day of shooting on SOYLENT GREEN. We began today, though I had no call. I guess I've done one or two films in which I didn't work the first day, but it always makes me itch. I went in and inspected the set. Fleischer seems to be moving surely and easily. We're off on another one; the sixth I've done with Walter.

September 11. Dick's father died this morning at the Motion Picture Home, so we canceled, for the day at least. Walter Seltzer wants me to direct for a few days if Dick's unable to return tomorrow, but this seems unlikely. Max Fleischer was, of course, one of the pioneers in animated cartoons. Dick's deeply shaken by his death, understandably.

September 18. We were back to work early this morning, with Leigh Taylor Young, on the last love scene, if this is still what you call them. As written, it was slightly more explicit than we shot it; we're determined on a PG rating. Besides, I'm convinced there's no creative gain in playing these scenes nude. I've yet to see a film love scene that gained in erotic content by stripping the actors. At worst, it's funny, at best, distracting. We got what we were after, I think. At least bed scenes are usually comfortable. This was.

October 4. The major preoccupation of a man as close to fifty as the day brings me should be his adjustment to that watershed date; but I don't find it difficult, somehow. I'm in better shape than I was, my tennis is better, I run two miles in fifteen minutes, and still seem eminently employable, in a time when fewer and fewer of my colleagues are. No . . . I can't complain.

October 7. Having gained a full day on the sports arena scenes (doubling for the exterior of "home"), we moved into the last stuff in the apartment (which has been a fine set, incidentally). Eddie Robinson's a lovely actor to work with. The chemistry between us is good. I finished in time to get gussied up for dinner at Gene Wyman's party for Democratic congressmen. I promised Gene I'd attend in return for his joining my theater board at Northwestern. Most of the men there seemed busy dissociating themselves from McGovern. It's a curious spectacle in a presidential year. All in all, not a bad party, though the Democratic Whip was falling down drunk.

October 16. We got into one of the major physical scenes today . . . where we prove with the camera the press of people in New York City in the year 2022. Accordingly, we had five hundred extras; with the matte shots, that's meant to suggest forty million. Shot carefully, I think it will.

November 3. We finished shooting exactly on schedule today, including retakes. Jim Aubrey asked for one of my last big speech, on the grounds it was too low-keyed photographically. I was dubious about the possibility of reaching the pitch of the scene, out of context and all alone, but it went well. I did it better, in fact. The film is good.

The film is very good, not least because of Eddie Robinson's superb performance. He knew while we were shooting, though we did not, that he was terminally ill. He never missed an hour of work, nor was late to a call. He never was less than the consummate professional he had been all his life. I'm still haunted, though, by the knowledge that the very last scene he played in the picture, which he knew was the last day's acting he would ever do, was his death scene. I know now why I was so overwhelmingly moved playing it with him.

November 6. The first day of rehearsal for THE CRUCIBLE. I got back to it today. It's close to six years since I last stepped on a stage . . . that's the longest I've been off one in my life. The stage we're using for the rehearsal for the moment is a rambling old theater, properly redolent of grime and tattered grandeur. The company seems very good indeed, with a surprisingly high incidence of Northwestern alumni. Joe Hardy has a rather flip manner, but he seems to know what he's doing, blocks very swiftly, with much movement. We moved with assurance through a difficult scene to stage. The set, from the model, looks very promising.

November 7. I voted, with some misgivings but a wholer heart than I'd thought I'd have, for RMN. So, apparently, did almost everyone else. The returns were clear before the polls closed, the concession speech made by eight-thirty in the evening. I rehearsed all day, of course, and blocked out the longest scene in the play, one where I'm never off. After dinner I made a ritual appearance at the Reagan suite, which was jammed with happy GOP's, then dropped by the little office where Fray has been laboring for Proposition Twenty (which won). They were having a lot more fun.

Fray had his first exposure to public service working on the campaign to pass legislation protecting the California coastline from unrestricted development.

November 8. I ran CALL OF THE WILD, which Paramount now refuses to distribute. I don't blame them. The revoicing of the foreign actors simply doesn't work. This was a blunder, even if I sort of backed into it unawares. It's my responsibility to watch for that. Ironic . . . of my last five films, two are almost unreleasable, two are hits, one looks as though it will be.

November 16. The problem with THE CRUCIBLE, I begin to perceive, will be to keep John Proctor the simple man Miller's written, when he must speak with Miller's rich eloquence. Quite different from Thomas More, with whom he seems to have much in common. More was in fact at least as eloquent as his playwright. An interesting problem.

November 22. We very nearly have the whole play in hand now, at least to the point where we are off the book. This is always a terrible floundering time. I'm finding my way through the part, but there's much that's not easy for me in it. I can't yet bring off the confession as I want to . . . nor the end of the trial.

November 27. We had our last run-through on the rehearsal stage today, really having learned all we could there a day ago. I wish we could've had our sets there. At least we got to look at them being lit tonight. I also had the ineffable pleasure of moving into a theater dressing room again. They're different from a film studio suite.

November 30. Well, I finally got back where I belong tonight . . . or at least where I must come back from time to time. It felt good . . . it surely felt good. I'd been too long away. To stand in the wings and feel the chill stab that always comes the first time before an audience was a feeling I need. Every actor does.

December 5. We opened THE CRUCIBLE. The day was properly paced. I had an easy morning, and a late call for rehearsal . . . which gave me time between to sleep in the dressing room. The house was good, and so were we. The play worked, and I think they liked it. We had a good party afterward, and I'm back in actor's country. The stage, after all, is it.

That's a little overstated. I'd be sorry to have to give up either medium. Film is the performing medium of this century, and no actor in our time has made an international reputation without it.

December 9. Holly's seen me in dozens of films, but she saw me act on the stage for the first time today. Before the matinee she said, "Now, Daddy, will you really *be* there?" I think she liked it.

December 25. The day was lovely, though I note that Holly revels especially in the spirit of Christmas getting. The presents, and the tree, were successes. It wasn't really hard to go to work at night, though we played our first less-than-sold-out house. THE CRUCIBLE is not precisely Christmas fare, I guess.

1973

Richelieu for
Lester's *The Three
Musketeers* . . .

a run down the
river . . .

Washington doings.

Two pictures for the price
of one: As Richelieu in
The Three Musketeers and
The Four Musketeers
LYDIA HESTON

January 2, Los Angeles. It's interesting to chart the performance problems in this (or any) part. After you get the shape of it set and a certain amount of sandpapering done, it becomes a question of deepening . . . and keeping it fresh. By now, mostly the latter, which is concentration.

January 7 (Sunday). My day off was full, as I find it tends to be. This evening I went to an industry banquet and made a speech; normally not the kind of thing I take any relish in. This was a little special, though. It was Adolph Zukor's one hundredth birthday. You don't get invited to all that many hundredth birthday parties, especially for the man who started the town. He looked well, and did his speech, and I think everyone was more than ordinarily glad to be a part of it. As Hope said, "If the roof fell in here, Troy Donahue would have a whole new career." I wondered if, back there in a quiet corner of his mind, the old man was laughing at it all?

I was standing at the head table when Hope came over to greet the guest of honor. "It's Bob, Mr. Zukor," he said, "Bob Hope." "Bob Hope?!" the old man said slowly. "Why, I thought you were dead."

January 13. So I finished it tonight, and cleaned out the dressing room. Nowhere in my life is there so sharp a sense of the swift, inexorable rush of passing time as when you're doing the last performance of a play you've liked. You go down and dress, and now comes the first entrance for the last time, then the first act's over, and the costume changed, and now you're into the court scene, and it's done, and I've finished the beard and the blood, and then the applause wells, and I've made the curtain speech . . . and it's over. It was a rich, rich experience. I'm glad it went so well, glad I was good in it. I think I became a better actor. I know I became a happier one.

January 18, Washington, D.C. As with so many of my decisions, the one to attend the inaugural was tardily come by and fraught with problems. (To take Holly? What to do with Mother? What about Fray?) Mother was willing (though not exactly overwhelmed, I think) to stay here with Holly, who's really a bit young for the pleasures of the event, if there prove to be any. The rest of us whipped off for D.C., crammed with hundreds of others (thousands, I guess, really) on the same errand. We managed to check in tonight to a hotel absolutely alive with people.

January 19. A very crowded day. I did a publicity sort of luncheon, which I spent largely talking with Billy Graham. Then I went over to the Kennedy Center to check on the music, the lectern height, mike, etc., for the concert. I'm not too happy about the music, and the concert itself is too long (though that's not my problem). I think I should have insisted that Jefferson's words stand alone, without music, but then how do you justify including them in a concert?

January 20, Inauguration Day. It's the kind of thing you only do once, I guess, but it's worth the fuss and discomfort. The weather was cold, with a light wind cutting sharply. The crowds were enormous; we were seated near the platform where Richard Nixon swore to uphold the Constitution for four more years. His speech was not eloquent, but had some truth in it, I think. The parade, like the concert last night, was too long, but impressive. The service academy contingents make all the other marching units look sloppy. Even the prettier drum majorettes were blue with cold. The inaugural balls tonight were jammed too, but they're supposed to be.

January 24, Los Angeles. Mother finished her visit here, a happy one, I think, this time. I had only my looping session for SOYLENT to do today and it was a brief one. There've been useful changes in looping techniques since I began doing it. Even the term's inaccurate now: There are no loops made; you work with a black-and-white dupe of the work print, reel by reel, threaded up on a rock and roll projector [*which means forward and reverse*]. There are no inked lines as visual cues; they use a triple bleep instead, which isn't laid on ahead of time but synced on the spot as each line is set to be looped.

February 3, Guadalajara. A quiet, easy day; we drove to Lake Chapala. Lydia was interested because it's the setting of a book she's always liked. I'm not quite as passionately interested in this place as she, nor quite so taken with Miller [*a historian Lydia had come to Mexico to consult about her play*]. I think she knows as much about medieval Spain as he does. Never mind; she got some valuable work done on her play. She seems very happy here. She always plunges readily into a new milieu, quite secure.

February 4 (Sunday), Los Angeles. We came home today on short notice, with some difficulty getting space, so we'd have time to prepare for the trip to D.C. for the White House dinner with King Hussein. We got up at bloody dawn, then couldn't find Lydia's tourist card. After much heart-in-mouth planning about talking our way past the Mexican immigration people, we found it just before landing, tucked into her passport. When we got home, having accepted the invitation, I found I had already committed to do a Shakespearean panel discussion on Tuesday, so the trip was all off. Anyway, we're home.

February 7. It turns out some outfit in the East wants to buy some of my pen-and-ink sketches to lithograph and market on a large scale. They'll function only as glorified autographs, but it's flattering anyway. They're paying more than a grand apiece for them, which seems vastly overpriced to me. On the strength of this largess, I ordered a new dinner jacket and had a good tennis lesson from Alex Olmedo. I diddled away the evening in white tie and tailcoat being photographed for the cover of *TV Guide*, for God's sake. It's been a long time since I've gotten so gussied up for so thin a purpose.

February 10. It bloody poured rain all day long, filling me with a high quotient of unspent nervous energy. I finally drove aimlessly off to catch three or four reels of DEEP THROAT, the current porno hit. As erotic stimulation, it failed totally for me, possibly because it's so incredibly badly acted and ill-produced in every way. You can argue whether it's obscene; there's absolutely no question it's lousy. I came home even more bored and read the latest MGM submission, a sort of sketch of a large World War II film, without any character and really no production possibilities either. No on this.

February 13. Not much doing professionally, but I had a chance to confer with John Brademas, one of the most active men on the Hill. He chairs the committee responsible for arts legislation and I wanted to get to know him. I outlined my view that it might eventually be best to separate the AFI from the National Council on the Arts, since they seem to make uneasy bedfellows. I think Nancy Hanks resents that the AFI was created before her chairmanship and would like to see it sink (though I doubt she'd pull the plug). This is not a healthy situation. We have to set up separate channels with the federal government, I'm convinced.

February 24. The rain ruled out tennis, which gave me a good reason to get at a new version of THREE MUSKETEERS I've been offered. It's a good script, very funny, but not a parody. Why do they want to spend as much as they have to pay me to play Athos? It's not that good a part; nothing like the brilliant kind of key cameo role actors look for, as with Olivier in KHARTOUM. I also found time to read THE OUTFIT again, which I'd turned down after a skim. Maybe I made a mistake. It's a good script and should make a good film.

February 26. The AFI Board meeting went much better today. Planning paid off. I got through the agenda with reasonable debate on each item. I tried to run with a relatively firm gavel, though you have to be careful about that with so many company presidents on the board. Jack Warner's not one of them, but he did give us a cool quarter of a mil for a film theater in Kennedy Center. Nevertheless, after the dinner we gave at Greystone tonight, he failed to be impressed by two films we made by AFI Fellows. "Jesus *Christ*, but those are lousy," he said. "What the hell ya gonna *do* with that crap!?" "Jack," I said, "please don't take your money back."

February 27. This was the second day of the AFI Board meeting. I spent all of it in conference on our dinner for John Ford where we'll give him our Life Achievement Award. Apparently the president will attend and give him the Medal of Freedom. Jack deserves it. It's valuable to the industry as a whole, since it'll be the first time any U.S. president has involved himself in anything in film . . . even attending a premiere. It also should raise some money for the AFI.

March 1. Nixon announced his attendance at the Ford dinner, nailing it down for us nicely. There's a lot of work to be done, but not much of it by me. I do have to go to D.C. for the AFI, and now probably for SAG as well, God help me. Meantime, I've still made no decision on my next film. American International doesn't want me to direct the vampire thing; they'll submit a list of directors. MGM doesn't know what the hell they want to do; I'm still thinking on MUSKETEERS, though it seems unlikely.

March 2. Dick Lester called from London to tell me why he wanted me to play Athos in his MUSKETEERS film. If they plan to cast the whole film at this level, their above-the-line costs will reach astronomical heights. I still don't see playing Athos, standing around in Spain all summer with nothing to do. I suggested to Lester the possibility of my doing a bit, for fun, but it all looks a little unlikely.

I admired George McDonald Fraser's script and liked the idea of working for Richard Lester so much that I just wanted to be in the film. It was Dick who suggested that I play Richelieu, instead, a part so far outside my usual range that it hadn't even occurred to me. When he further stipulated that he would shoot all my scenes (for what later turned out to be two films) in ten days, I couldn't resist. Indeed, I didn't try to.

March 5. I lost my boy today. Not my son; he'll be that, still. But the boy drove off in the cool early light, and when he comes back he'll be a man, surely, and only a visitor here. It was more painful than I would've thought, though of course I didn't let him know that. For Lydia, it was worse: There were things like coat hangers and so on she wanted him to take, and motels she wanted him to stay in, instead of sleeping in his car. For him, of course, it was life, waiting for him. [*Fray was taking advantage of an opportunity to earn his final semester of high school credit working in a marine biology laboratory on the Gulf of Mexico.*]

March 12. Somewhat to my surprise, I found myself back on the SAG Board again, where I never thought I'd be. It's strange to climb the stairs to that same boardroom, where my picture now hangs among the past presidents, and sit in the same chair at the end of the room where I began, thirteen years ago. After announcing that I planned to keep a very low profile, I got deeply involved in a debate on the Writers Guild strike, and the threat it poses to SAG jurisdiction. I finally made a long complicated motion of censure to be transmitted to them, whereupon Walter Pidgeon said from the other end of the table, "Well, there goes the low profile . . ."

March 13. I discussed with Ziggy [*Geike, one of the best make-up men alive*] this morning the problems of the Richelieu makeup. I have no clear recollection of his looks . . . Vandyke beard, long hair, piercing eyes, strong, sharply beaked nose. (I don't think I've ever before played a historical figure with a nose bigger than mine.) I must get some good biographies and some prints of the major portraits.

March 16, Washington. Tennis is played in the early morning in this town, to allow for proper work schedules for the public servants that populate it. The quality of senatorial tennis is slightly higher than I'd thought. Ted Kennedy's not overwhelming, but his partner, a tennis pro, was. [*Senator Tunney and I had been blown away by Senator Kennedy and his partner.*] Having coffee in the house afterward, my spirits darkened, seeing several pictures of the three brothers together. That sad, doomed family. My testimony later before John Brademas's committee went well. I think we strengthened our position. My last chore was a TV interview with Jack Valenti and Pauline Kael. She's an interesting lady, but she doesn't know nearly as much about film as she thinks she does. Even less about acting. As Larry Olivier has observed, "They none of them know fuck-all, laddie."

March 27, Academy telecast: Dorothy Chandler Pavilion. It really was one of the outstanding humiliations of my life. To run along the sidewalk by the Music Center, my car abandoned, and hear over the loudspeakers carrying the telecast audio "Charlton Heston is supposed to be emceeing this part of the show, but . . ." Clint Eastwood was doing his best with my cue cards, but as he said, "Why pick on a fella who hasn't said eight lines in his last three pictures?" I've never been late to work in my life, and I have to do it in front of eight million viewers. For me, it overshadowed Brando's nonappearance to pick up his Oscar.

March 30. We now have another problem with the AFI. George Stevens canceled the showing of STATE OF SIEGE at the D.C. theater. I agree. The film details and implicitly supports the abduction and murder of a U.S. diplomat. This is not the film to show in our theater this year . . . not in a center named after an assassinated president.

George had simply decided not to show the film for a single screening that had been announced at the AFI theater. He was quite right. The film is or is not a good film, depending on your opinion. It's unquestionably an endorsement of terrorism.

March 31, AFI Life Achievement Award dinner for John Ford. This has been a helluva week. There turned out to be not quite enough time to prepare for the show, in terms of nailing down what should be said, and who should say it, still the whole thing seemed to be something of a smash. It seemed to me better than the Academy show. (At least I wasn't late.) It was well and enthusiastically attended. My job consisted largely of introducing the president of the United States, which tends to hold your attention. Ford seemed pleased with the tribute paid him, though he is now very old, very sick. This will be his last appearance, I think. I'm glad we brought it off.

April 2, Boston. The schedules on these tours aren't as tough as I recall they used to be. Fewer papers, fewer schlocky things to do (opening dime stores, judging beauty contests). Maybe they think I'm just too grand for all that now. By now almost all the faces have changed. The graying, bibulous Boston movie press has been largely replaced by sharp, shaggy New Journalists. Never mind . . . I can play it with them, too.

April 3, Washington, D.C. Open AFI theater, reception after. After clearing up my last press chores in Boston, I arrived early in D.C., but hardly did enough for MGM today to justify their picking up my tab. The AFI absorbed me from the minute I stepped off the plane. I had to edit my comments on the Griffith footage, of course, and do the opening of the theater. But there is also a large (and somewhat media-hyped, I think) clamor about George's canceling the Costa-Gavras STATE OF SIEGE. The film hasn't been censored; it's playing both here and in New York, to improved business because of all this. (In France, Costa-Gavras's country, they *do* censor films.)

April 5, Philadelphia/Milwaukee. I suppose it's the narrow old eighteenth-century streets, but Philadelphia strikes me now as having the worst traffic of any U.S. city. Nevertheless, we managed to get a full press schedule in, touting not only SOYLENT GREEN, but doing my chores on the Costa-Gavras flap. That's my main value to any public service group. I can get on more talk shows and do them better. In Milwaukee, I stayed with the Nashes, prior to going to Two Rivers to arrange affairs with Lydia's father, now probably terminally ill, no longer able to live in his own house. Even with ample funds, which he has, the final indignity of having to surrender your autonomy like this is demeaning.

April 7, Two Rivers. Death is the common experience . . . the only common experience . . . and all men meet it differently. Most fear it, fight it, some seek it. Lydia's father seems only to be waiting for it, with the irritable temper of a man pacing a cold and drafty platform for a long-overdue train. It's painful to see her efforts to reach him, to touch somehow the father she fears has forgotten her. I have only a small supportive function here, which I'm trying to fulfill as unobtrusively as possible. This must be a heavy time for her. I only hope she doesn't remember it as horrible.

April 17, New York. [After a solid week of interviews in Chicago, Detroit, and Houston, I'd had two days with my family in Galveston, where Fray was still working in the marine biology station.] An early rising, racing against the sun across the continent, arriving in New York in time for a full schedule after checking into the Pierre. (After Lydia's wallet was stolen last year, she's not easy in the Sherry anymore . . . how MGM knew this is a mystery, but here we are.) The Cavett show was OK. He always pushes you just enough to make the interview a hair bristly, without turning it into a slugfest. I got into the STATE OF SIEGE thing, which makes for a very tricky path to walk, but I think I brought it off.

April 18. For some reason, I choked a little on the *Today Show.* Maybe because I'm so tired, maybe because Barbara Walters strikes me as such a ball-cutting lady. Not that I klutzed it entirely . . . it's just that I didn't have the kind of control I've learned to have over TV interviews.

April 19, Los Angeles. This was the end of it, and a long two and a half weeks it's been. I've learned how to do these tours a lot better than I could twenty-three years ago, and they're scheduled much more comfortably now. I suppose I do them as well as anyone (after all, not many of my bunch will do them at *all*). Still, it was good to slump down in the 707 for the slide downhill to the barn. Lydia looked lovely and happy to have me back home. My Munchkin was delightful, of course, and my ridge still stands. My son does well in Galveston . . . I guess I can't ask for more.

April 21. This was really not a good day. I don't have any particular insights as to why Lydia's headaches have become so chronic, to what degree I give them to her. It's perhaps fairer to say that the agony of the headaches makes the me she perceives difficult to bear. Naturally, this is not my version of me. She'll perhaps feel better after a few days of rest in the neutral milieu of the hospital. She couldn't feel worse, surely.

By this time, Lydia's migraine problem was beginning to color her whole attitude toward her life and ours.

April 26. We kicked around a deal for ANTONY with Leo, all far too complicated for my simple brain. It's also beyond my comprehension how I could make so much last year and have so little of it left, even counting taxes and commissions. That will be looked into, they promise. The bottom of the American International deal is that I'm not going to do their film. I had Herman come to a meeting today and we told them so. They really have another picture in mind, and the pressure of a thirty-six-day schedule is too great. This is the last possible time to pull out of it with no one hurt.

I'd agreed two days before to do a vampire film for them, and then had sudden, and late, misgivings.

I still feel bad about this, though I'm convinced the decision was correct. It's the only time I've ever withdrawn from a film I said I would do.

April 27. This turned out to be one of the very worst days of my life. Everything was wrenched out of joint. For the first time in my life, I believed Lydia would leave me. I spent some bleak hours trying to find some adjustment to it. She didn't in the end and I don't think she will, but it isn't yet over, and may not be for some time. I can't live without her, as I well know, and it seems she can't live without me. We must begin with that . . . and end with it, too, I guess.

April 28. Things painfully lurched back into some semblance of normality, though I have no clear idea at this point of what constitutes normality. Lydia's home, in command of herself, if not her headaches, and thus our life is in balance. I don't mean to put this on her. Obviously, if she's not happy it's largely my fault. Anyway, here we are. I don't know of any other place I could bear to be.

May 1. The weather is breaking into summer now on the ridge; when I run in the mornings, the sweat really rolls and I don't have to wear gloves, as sometimes in the winter. Still, this is sort of a fallow period, my having dropped out of one film, not yet ready for another. I'm still not even certain of my start date on THREE MUSKETEERS. Laziness is setting in, meanwhile.

May 4. I'm much preoccupied with plans for THREE MUSKETEERS (well, that's a lot of crap, really . . . I'm not *much* preoccupied, by any means). I had a designer over to discuss the costumes. I had no idea a cardinal had that much opportunity to change his pants. The costumes are good, though they'll necessitate my going to London for a fitting, which will complicate our schedule. I haven't yet locked into preparation for the part, though I've gone through some necessary steps. I seem to need the shadow of the sword over me to function.

May 9. It's now clear that Lydia will have to have that thyroid operation after all. Since I must go overseas on the eighteenth, the best plan seems to be to have this done Monday, so I can be here during her hospitalization. She's a little anxious, and I don't blame her, but I'm confident all will be well.

May 14. I think Lydia may have solved a great deal with this operation. To wait, as she has for ten months, was bound to create enormous pressure. It was a long, bleak day sitting beside her in the recovery room, able to offer only the small comfort of my being there, though she was only barely aware of this.

May 15. Lydia moved into her room today, recovering quickly, better almost each time I saw her. Richelieu's nose is another story. I sculpted on it a little in Ziggy's shop today, but I'm not certain my harsh-boned, Scots face can be readily transformed into that ascetic French cleric. There are parts for which a more neutral face would be useful.

May 18, To London. I took my daughter to a school we feel she belongs in now, for an entrance exam that will determine her acceptance. Taking Lydia home from the hospital was not a success, though all friction was avoided. It has to do, I fear, with her anxiety at my departures. They're often marked with really tearing scenes of trauma. I drove off fairly shattered and phoned from the airport to find her recovered. I flew overseas calm, though somewhat shaken.

May 19, London. My time-tested plan for surmounting the transatlantic jet lag worked again. I checked in, slept, and worked in reasonable comfort through my first fitting on the Richelieu wardrobe. The costumes are OK, though badly fit, first time around. This'll be an interesting fella to play. I find myself very much filled when I'm in London now with an awareness of time past. I've been coming here so long now, since the first sweet flush of youth, riches, fame. I'm no longer young, God knows, though still rich and famous. (Not bad, after all; you can't keep the first, I'm lucky to still have the last.)

May 20 (Sunday), Washington. It seemed bloody soon to be trailing out to Heathrow and climbing on a transatlantic jet again. I arrived only moderately wrung out, and plunged into a policy meeting. The AFI has certain serious budget problems, an intensified hostility from the Endowment, and a very full agenda tomorrow. I was glad we had time to go into as much as we did today.

May 21. This is really only the third meeting of the AFI I've chaired (and only about the tenth I've attended), but I'm beginning to get on top of it. Shirley MacLaine did *not* attend, just a little bit to my disappointment, being still very busy in China, interviewing Mme. Mao. Her beef about the AFI's stand on the pending obscenity law received full discussion and no action, for the same reasons that seemed to me sound when I turned her down before the John Ford dinner (when her point was even less valid). The rest of the meeting went well, given that we have too much agenda for a one-day meeting. We also have to have a head-to-head with the NEA, soon.

May 22, London. The pressure put on my metabolic clock by all this racing around in jets threw me a little askew, but a hit on the wood counts at Queen's made me tired enough to get my arrival nap. I accomplished very little more, but had a most pleasant time later with the McDonalds . . . watching the English summer twilight fall over their lush English lawn.

May 24, Madrid. I checked out of the Dorchester, as I always do, with some regret. MGM wants me to do a bit of work for them in early July, when SOYLENT GREEN goes into secondaries. I hope I can work it out so I can be here for Wimbledon. I was met in Madrid, as I have been since 1960, by a gaggle of producer's people and swept into the familiar front suite at the Castellana where Tony Mann first showed me the EL CID designs. I had a drink in the bar, which developed into several drinks at the bar, with Oliver Reed (who's playing Athos) and his entourage. Clearly, he subscribes to the ancient tradition of the drinking actor common among the English. When I finally got back to the suite, I never got down to dinner. [*Obviously, I don't hold my whiskey as well as Oliver.*]

May 25. The long sleep I clearly needed lasted thirteen hours. I can't remember having slept that long in years . . . ever, maybe. Anyway, I feel much the better for it. I sort of settled into my cave today: buying oddments, getting a proper desk light and a big bar of soap . . . all the things you never bother with when you're only in a hotel for a few days. The wardrobe's not here yet, but I tried a run at the makeup with moderate success. Cristobal [*the makeup man I work with in Spain*] needs practice with it, and we'll never make me look startlingly like Richelieu. [*Actually, we did pretty well.*] I had dinner and a long talk with Lester, who impresses me very much.

"Dick," I said, "I haven't done as many comedies as you have. How much of a comic adjustment do you want me to make to Richelieu?" "None, for God's sake!" he said. "You're the villain in this piece, and you have to be absolutely credible, and genuinely threatening. Otherwise it won't work."

May 28. Once more unto the breach. I eased into it gently today with two simple sequences, made easier by Dick Lester's use of multiple cameras (makes a lot of sense, especially with comic stuff; then you're sure to have the good accident on all angles). He works very easily and chaffingly, and has wit enough to do it well. When we moved to a new set, I said ruefully, "God, I've really been in this trade too long. I recognize this location. We shot here on EL CID." "Really?" Dick said. "Now, if you could just remember where you put the cameras . . . ?"

May 31. We've been going so fast, picking up time so readily, that they gave us a day off in accordance with one of the omnipresent Spanish religious holidays. This was ideal for me, since I could thus meet my family, minus only the Tiger, arriving at Barajas. His place was taken by Lydia's niece, Cookie, who will be pleasant to have and also extra help for Lydia, still precarious from her operation. Her strength is spread thin just now. Still, I'm sure she's happy to be here. We passed a quiet day in the suite, ate there tonight, and to bed early.

June 1. We shot at Aranjuez today, within a mile of the river set I used in ANTONY. This was Richelieu's first appearance in the film; I'm glad we decided to use cardinal's robes for this. My physical effect, plus the shadow of most of the parts I've done, needs as much counterforce as possible for this part, especially in setting the audience's first impressions. I found the designer had been mistaken in an old engraving plate she used as authority for designing lay costumes instead of cardinal's robes for Richelieu in two scenes, just as I told her in England. The figure she thought was Richelieu in the engraving was someone else. We've shot one of them already, but we can change the other. Eternal vigilance is the price of quality.

June 6, Segovia. We're cutting driving and makeup time down a bit. The makeup now takes thirty minutes, plus fifteen for wardrobe and a safety margin.

It's crucial to determine exactly how long a complicated makeup actually takes if you're to make your calls on time. Otherwise the production department simply protects itself and gives you an extra-early call. You'd be surprised how many actors haven't figured this out.

The scene today was with Spike Mulligan, a very talented English comic with the undercurrent of pain you often find in such men, all the way back to Shakespeare's fools, who laughed to keep from crying. The scene should be good; Spike is funny without lapsing into slapstick; for Richelieu, I can rely on the edged irony that seems to serve me for this part.

June 7. We managed a crash makeup in fifteen minutes, since the set was ready ahead of schedule. I finished the scene with Spike in good time. (Good scene, too, though I failed to get Dick to let me use still another genuine Richelieu quote, as I've done twice so far.)

For almost every historical part I've played I have discovered in the biographies several actual quotations of the man involved that fit the script and are superior to anything invented for the film.

Lester worked very quickly. He's very sure of his setups and blocking; so far he hasn't used a moving camera once on the film. In fact, we don't even carry a crab dolly with the company. His ultimate simplification of film technique illustrates the technical ignorance of the critical community, since they laud Lester in terms of the brilliance of his camera work. What they mean, of course, is his cutting. I'm enormously impressed with his talent and find his method very easy to respond to, as well.

June 16. In theory, I was to finish the film today, and did complete the cardinal's part of the ball sequence. It was effective stuff, too, I thought. It turns out, though, that Dick wants some extra coverage from the scene in the king's tent; I'm to be picked up in the studio Monday. This means altering our plans to fly to Stuttgart, where we'll be met by Lydia's brother.

Bob, a career army officer, was by this time a full colonel. We were to visit his family in Germany.

June 18, Madrid. I had a long, easy day, waiting to pick up two shots. It gave me the chance for an hour with Velázquez and friends at the Prado. The shots, when we finally got to them, were simple enough, only complicated by the fact that Jean-Pierre Cassel, the French actor playing the king, had gone off on another film; thus Dick Lester had to suit up in armor, wig, and moustache to do the over-the-shoulder shot in his place. It worked well enough, and Dick was good-natured under the obvious ribs. On sum, finishing this, I'll be damn surprised if it doesn't turn out. The script is very good, the cast at least that, and Lester's a lot more. I have a good feeling about this one.

June 19, Arrive Stuttgart. The usual hassle of packing and getaway, ending up with fifteen bags, plus hand luggage. We sent two back to California, which entailed some extra racing around at the airport. When I retire as an actor, I think I'll never fly again. I've become so spoiled by having everything done for me by the studio when I'm working. When I'm traveling privately, I feel very put upon having to handle it myself, like everybody else. It was nice to see Bob and his family again . . . the last time we visited them on post was the summer of '57, in Puerto Rico, when Bob was a lieutenant and Willy Wyler was wooing me to do BIG COUNTRY.

June 20. A peaceful garrison-post kind of day, which pleased me very well. I had a chance to catch up on some of my overdue paper work, sleep a bit, and even get in some not very good and ill-matched tennis. The unwinding process is crucial after a film. I'd like to run back to my ridge to do it, but this is proving very pleasant. We've decided we'll go to Nuremberg tomorrow, stay overnight, and try and cover as much as possible in two days there.

June 24 (Sunday). The weather cleared slightly today, enough for Lydia to go into a museum in Stuttgart and for me to get in some good tennis with an ex-fighter-jockey general as a partner. I'm enjoying life here on the post. As I observed to Bob, I have an idea I could've been content with a military career, in another life.

June 25. Word came in the middle of the night that Belle Clarke, Lydia's father's sister, had died during surgery for a broken hip. There was much talk about who should go back to the States, if anyone. Lydia's Aunt Ruth may now go back with Lydia from London, to see her father. As for me, I found that SOYLENT GREEN has opened to "smash business in London and Tokyo." This is a common sort of public relations quote, subject to a wide latitude of interpretation, but it certainly means we aren't a flop.

June 30, To Vienna. We got away reasonably close to our target time, and the tension of departure dissipated when we broke for coffee in Berchtesgaden, which really is more beautiful than Garmisch. I can see why Hitler chose it for his Eagle's Nest. The spot for lunch was even more lovely; Holly could hardly bear to leave, and I can't blame her. Poor Munchkin, she's had about all of this kind of tightly packed, high-culture tour she can digest at one time; she'd really have much preferred to stay on the lake at Fuschl and ride paddle boats for a day or so. Vienna is very big, rather like Chicago in the gathering dusk (that can't be right). The hotel is a Belle Époque confection, doubtless very expensive, with the value of the dollar dropping each day.

July 2, Vienna. All morning in the Albertina with the Durers made the day special, but we also had time for a look at a Roman camp, and the diligent scars left in the earth by that incredible people. The fall of Rome was bad luck for the world, no matter what the church says. Conversely, walking home from a concert this evening, we passed a huge, incredibly vulgar statue of a Russian soldier the Russians insisted be erected as part of the price of their departure after World War II.

July 3, For London. I've really had enough of continental capitals. It was with a real sense of homecoming I climbed on the BEA flight to London and checked into the Dorchester. The weather's lovely, my chores are light . . . if only there was a full draw at Wimbledon, it would be a good week. Unhappily, there isn't. [*This was the year most of the pros boycotted Wimbledon for what seemed to me good reason.*]

July 4, Wimbledon/London. The day was clouded by a Force Ten migraine that hit Lydia late last night, after the theater. The British National Health made a doctor readily available; he administered a strong sedative, which knocked her out completely and made me feel it would be possible to take advantage of John McDonald's kind provision of Wimbledon tickets. The women were playing and Holly and Elizabeth were anxious to see Goolagong. The matches were actually not bad, and they enjoyed having entrée to the players' lounge, and so forth. We came back to the hotel to find Lydia still sleeping. So we ate here, then had an easy kind of film evening at POSEIDON ADVENTURE.

July 9, Los Angeles. I haven't really slipped back into my routine here, but it's creeping back up on me. Fray sounded marvelous on the phone . . . sure of himself, with his life in his hands. I envied him, and was proud of him. My own situation seems more mundane. I have two or three film possibilities . . . some debt to pay off from the ANTONY loan . . . other than that, all is in order. I more or less agreed to accept the office of vice-president on the SAG Board, though the meeting tonight was shot through with the kind of factionalism I never saw when I was there before.

July 13. I'm still more or less cruising along, trying to pick a script. I have a firm offer from United Artists on HIGH RISE, which doesn't appeal to me. Herb Jaffe (also the producer of HIGH RISE) has bought VANDENBERG, which United Artists doesn't want to do. He does, with Walter Seltzer. My idea of the POW film seems more or less dead, but there's still some sort of action on OLD FISH HAWK, believe it or not. MACBETH's still alive, but I'm backing off from the Washington, D.C. engagement. I'd better pick *something.*

July 19. After tennis, Herb Jaffe told me he's reconsidered his previous willingness to coproduce VANDENBERG with Walter. This apparently has to do with the terms of his separation contract as the head of United Artists, and I suppose is plausible. It poses an awkward moral dilemma for me though; should I still go forward with Jaffe? On consideration, I think I will, since it was I who first read the novel and gave it to Walter, rather than the reverse. It's a damned annoying situation, all the same.

July 24. Our day was made . . . our week was made, if you like . . . by the unheralded and unexpected appearance of our son as we were dressing to go out for dinner. He looked lean, rangy, dirty as an old boot, and glad to be home. God knows we were glad to have him. Lydia's heart lifted like a kite in the breeze to see him, grinning under his mop of hair and my old WILL PENNY hat.

July 30. Not much stirring today. Walter Seltzer was off to South America on what is doubtless a fruitless errand, scouting locations for a film he doubts MGM really wants to make. We at last made a deal for the U.S. release of ANTONY, at least in Washington, at the same theater where JULIUS CAESAR played. I recall touring there for that film and being impressed with the arrangements its owner [*Marvin Goldman*] had made. I've put all I can into promoting this release; so much hinges on it.

July 31. I did a breakfast this morning with the various company presidents to discuss the AFI. We had a thin turnout, but an attentive bunch. I'm not marvelous in this part of the job . . . I'm reluctant to press people to do things. I don't like to be *beholden* to them, I expect.

August 2. It's Holly's twelfth birthday. She's very much a young girl now, as opposed to being a little girl. She still likes me to call her Munchkin, but I have to be careful about patting her bottom (an irresistible urge), and snuggles are hard to come by. She's lovely and I'm proud of her. She had a happy day with her five friends celebrating rather more sedately than they did two or three years ago.

August 4. I had to skip my chance to open the deer season upstate with Fray, since we had to go to a party here tonight. This is a problem for me. I'm missing a crucial time with my son by passing these chances by. On the other hand, I'm reluctant to put any further pressure on Lydia by skipping off to the boondocks. I don't know . . . there doesn't seem to be any right way to do it. Still, we're surviving, all of us.

I combined my urge to get out in the high and lonely with my equally pressing urge to have a family vacation by devising a raft trip on the white water of the Salmon, in Idaho.

August 11, Elkhorn, Idaho. Our great adventure on the River of No Return began with some complications. Lydia woke with her migraine still raging, fought it through packing, but had to give up at last. We sent Fray off on the first leg of the trip, with us to follow tomorrow. Holly and I adjusted our day while Lydia slept, sedated. It was traumatic for us all, of course, but I think we've salvaged the trip. Meantime, I had a hilarious hour sailing on the pond with my daughter in a plastic dingy. "Look out, Daddy! You'll tip us *over!*"

August 12 (Sunday), River of No Return. We got it all together today, flying over the wild country of the River of No Return, five days' float time upriver, landing on a sandbar where we picked up the rafts, full of Texans, and Fray, one day into the trip. The day was marvelous, the river indescribable and endlessly changing. It makes you proud to be on it . . . you seem to own it then.

August 15, Camp at Ship Island. The day included perhaps the richest and most unique experience of the run down the river so far: To see the fall of water from that cliff arching high above us, shivering into vaporous drops before it struck the little amphitheater we stood in, was worth not only the climb, and the day, but perhaps the whole trip. Later we had a tough climb up the creek; an hour to go half a mile over rocks and tearing water . . . but to see Lydia and Holly sporting in the falls at the top was worth it. The sauna tent we built by the river tonight was special, too.

August 16, Idaho/Los Angeles. It was our last day on the river, and a little rushed. Our charter out of the bush was late and fighting head winds, leaving us no time to change clothes before checking on our United Airlines flight in Boise. We finally fell on the plane, still in river-rat rags, but made it home at last.

August 20. A full day. I had to run my daughter down to start off her summer school project, catching her up on the hard sciences (syntax, spelling, arithmetic) that her old school failed to ground her in. Then I had a long session in which Mrs. Chandler, a very tough lady, finally wore down the last of my defenses about accepting the chairmanship of the Center Theater Group. I suppose a man can sit in more than one chair at the same time, but how much weight can he put in each?

August 21. Peter came over tonight, and I made, with many misgivings, the cuts I'd agreed to in ANTONY, to get it down from the two-and-a-half-hour length we're at now. I did it reel by reel and found I could lose the entire party on Pompey's barge, which never amounted to anything anyway. I'll also examine where and how much to cut from the first scene with Cleopatra. ("If it be love indeed, tell me how much.") It's her least good scene: She perhaps will be better served not to be seen till later. I hope I can save the last half of the scene, though: "Let Rome in Tiber melt . . ."

August 26 (Sunday). I turned down the offer from whomever it is to do that film in Germany this fall. WHO? it's called. It's not bad:

essentially a man-in-the-iron-mask story. There's really not a helluva lot to act, though, and there seems no reason to do it other than the money they offered and the startling fact that they were willing (for the first time in my experience, or anyone's that I know of) to pay a percentage of the gross *plus*, not against, a guarantee. The point, I suppose, is Walter's observation: "There are fewer and fewer actors they want . . . they're willing to pay them more and more."

August 30. I got up at dawn to have breakfast with my son, still lean, but hardening formidably with muscle now. He's off again for the river, intent on soaking himself in the kayak thing. Lydia found the phrase for him, in a book she bought him: He's imbued with the Ulysses factor. He likes to test himself under stress. Not programmed stress, like tennis matches, but individual stress, like climbing mountains or learning to turn a kayak over. If I can learn it too, it would be a fine kind of vacation to spend next summer, on the same river.

September 1, Las Vegas. This is going to be a tough weekend. When I went back up to the suite after tennis I found Lydia had thrown her back out of joint again . . . a thing that hasn't happened since we were in Hawaii on the Mirisch film. About an hour after this development, news came from Wisconsin that her father had died. This was neither unexpected nor really other than what he himself wanted, I'm sure, but it was nonetheless a shock for Lydia, worse because she's trapped in a hotel here. I don't know how soon we can move her.

September 3, Los Angeles. Another early breakfast with Bill and the two little girls, followed by a reasonably easy departure for the airport (Lydia in a wheelchair). Deplaning in Los Angeles was horrendous, though, following a rough flight. It took half an hour and a stretcher to get her off the plane. This next week will not be easy.

September 6. Lydia's back's beginning to respond. I'm confident she'll make the funeral, as she is determined to do. She also found the perfect piece for me to read at the services: Cicero's essay on old age. I spent some time redacting it; it's a remarkable piece. It told me more than I ever knew about Cicero, a figure I'd never liked (taking Mark Antony's view of him, I suppose), and also made me understand why Lydia's father admired him so much. He was *like* him.

September 7, Two Rivers. We made it, accomplishing an intricate schedule of meeting Fray in Chicago, who changed planes three times to get out of the Idaho boonies. As we drove north through Wisconsin, Lydia's spirits sank to darkness. This is a strain for her, of course, but there's something that happens to her, going back home.

September 8. We buried Lydia's father today. My girl bore up well, not in great physical pain, certainly vastly supported by having both children beside her (and me, I suppose). I thought the services were well and decently arranged, with some thought to their proper length. The Cicero was the right choice.

September 9, Two Rivers/Los Angeles. Holly was heart-touching as we prepared to leave for home today. "Will we ever come back here now?" she said. When I explained this was unlikely, since there was now no one in the family left in Two Rivers, she then wanted to be taken through the house where her mother had been a child, and the room where she'd slept, and down by the river where she'd played. It was a flawless midwestern day on which to look at this town, if it was indeed for the last time.

September 10, Los Angeles. Entering my daughter in Westlake School reminded me overwhelmingly of entering my son at Harvard School. It still seems only yesterday I took Fray down the hill in the other direction and watched him line up at the short end of the seventh-grade platoon. Now Holly, in her gray pleated skirt and 1940s saddle shoes, her shining face faintly clouded with apprehension, goes her way to adolescence.

September 19. Fray went off to La Jolla to register at UCSD. It was traumatic for Lydia, coming hard upon her father's death. Nevertheless, he seems enormously sanguine. "Cool," in the current jargon. I remember feeling much the same as I began Northwestern. I think I remember.

September 26, Washington, D.C. The day started with a frustrating singles with John Tunney, who I'm about to concede can beat me on clay, where his speed gets him to too many balls that would be winners on concrete (so I tell myself). The rest of the day was a full, if routine, kind of schedule, though Maury Povich got me into a more political kind of interview than I would've preferred to undertake this trip. On the other hand, I managed to blunt the edge of a hostile young lady reporter, secure in the certainty that all actors are egocentric idiots. I think we'll get a favorable story from her. I've spent a long time learning to do that. ANTONY played very well at the AFI theater tonight, perhaps as well as it ever has.

October 7 (Sunday), Los Angeles. The word from D.C. on ANTONY is gloomy, like the production prospects around Los Angeles. There are two or three projects surfacing that will probably come by me; meantime, there's tennis. I like playing with Tunney, though it's a tough match for me. I don't feel easy with the kind of Hollywood crowd around Jerry Weintraub's pool, though he himself seems a decent sort of guy. (As the producer of all those late Tarzans, I gather he was a hard-nose.) Anyway, his guests seem to run to people like Warren Beatty and girls of various ages.

October 10. I'm still shaken by Agnew's resignation. Not because I supported him (I didn't) or because I voted for him (I did), but because it seems a black mark on the system that so clear a crook could rise so high. David Lean was effective at his AFI seminar, although, like many directors who come to do that stint, he was a little apprehensive about the Fellows' reaction. He needn't have been, of course: He knocked 'em over.

"I must seem terribly old hat to this lot," he said to me gloomily before we began. "David," I replied, "they have all seen every film you've ever made and probably remember them shot-for-shot better than you do." They did, too.

November 5, Washington, D.C.. The TWA strike forced me into an earlier departure, which did me out of the pleasure of driving Holly to school. On the flight east, I rebriefed myself on subscription and cable TV. Once we got in, we were able to plan what each of us could say about it. We're an artfully chosen delegation: Greg Morris (minority member), Bob Stack (TV series actor), Bob Wise (director), Howard Koch (producer), as well as a couple of pretty actresses. It's a long way to fly for all this, but the stakes are high, and it's the kind of thing I've gotten used to doing.

If all this strikes you as an exercise in public relations, I agree with you. It occurs to me that a great deal of what passes for open government is just that.

November 6, FCC hearings. One of those long, densely scheduled days that somehow gains from being taken as a challenge. Even tennis isn't loafing if you have to fit it into a schedule as adroitly as I did today. The hearings went well, I thought; my testimony was OK. The feeling is we may get a relaxation on the prohibitive rules governing cable TV now. This could be very valuable for a film industry really struggling for a survival foothold. It could provide another generation of revenue for films between theaters and network TV.

November 8, Los Angeles. It turns out Dennis Weaver won the SAG election handily, carrying a whole slate of independently nominated officers into office with him. I was almost the only board candidate elected from the regular nominating committee slate. (Conversely, I also had the largest plurality in the election.) This is not surprising. The members really vote for the best-known candidates . . . as happens in any election, I suppose. I think Dennis will be a good president. I called him on location in Hawaii to tell him so, and assured him of my support.

November 28, Los Angeles. Our house, even our life, is becoming more and more affected by the oil shortage the Arab boycott has created. The pool is cold, the house not much warmer. We'll survive, but I'm glad tennis requires no gas.

December 4, Washington. White House dinner for the Romanian president. The best-laid plans, etc. . . . we got to the airport in good time, boarded in leisured, self-assured fashion, only to find the toilets wouldn't flush, thus, apparently making it impossible to fly the airplane. By the time the plumbing was fixed, we were an hour late. This made for a very nervous time at the other end. Lydia had no chance to rest or even to change her makeup. I must say she looked fine, as did the Romanian president and the beleaguered RMN, who seemed intent on putting his best face forward (and foot too, no doubt). It all seemed somewhat remote, in the insulated atmosphere of federal festivity prevailing. They serve a good meal, though the Romanian president spoke twenty minutes . . . in Romanian.

December 7, Los Angeles. There're various professional possibilities being juggled assiduously: Warner's is backing and filling on OLD FISH HAWK, Universal is horrified at the stiffness of the firm offer required to get Herman to have me read a script they want me to do. There's also some TV thing hovering in the background, linked to a network play for ANTONY. All this is now involved with my increasing determination to do Warwick in ST. JOAN at the Ahmanson if I'm free the next six weeks or so. In the face of all of this, I turned down Walter Mirisch's offer to produce the Academy Awards in April. It's very flattering, considering my limited experience in that field, but I can't fit it in. I don't think I know how to *do* it, either.

December 11, Paris. World premiere of THREE MUSKETEERS. We arrived in fairly decent time for a trip so long, checking into a hotel I recall from our first visit here . . . in '52? Paris seemed unaffected by the energy crisis that preoccupies the rest of the West, save that Parisians are perhaps a little nicer to Americans than they were under de Gaulle. Tonight I was made, apparently authentically, a Musketeer. An odd thing to happen to Richelieu.

December 13. The picture's damned good. They did a startling thing: The film is now two films, the second not to be released till next year. The first covers the plot of all the other versions of the Three Musketeers . . . the story with the queen's diamonds. Lester's done an excellent job. All the performances are OK to excellent, and the camera and production are first rate. He's brought the comedy as far as he can without threatening the plausibility of the plot. My role as Richelieu functions as expected . . . to provide a serious and formidable antagonist. I'm content with what I did in the part.

The other actors were very exercised at having worked four months to make one film that turned out to be two films . . . for the price of one, as it were. I don't blame them, but I had only worked a short time, been very well compensated, and had an absolutely marvelous part. Understandably, I took a more tolerant view.

December 14, Paris/London. How ironic that France, a country I've never felt comfortable in, and that seems to me more hostile to mine than any other country in the West, should give me a medal. It was a rigged award, of course, but I've learned that a lot of them are, up to the Nobel Prize. This was presented in a most solemn ceremony in a beautiful old building where Richelieu, as it happened, functioned as minister of France. We had a lovely lunch at Maxim's afterward (you can be damn sure you'll get a good meal out of the French), then caught our plane to London rather precariously.

December 17, En route to Los Angeles. We left in reasonable order . . . you learn to accept delays up to an hour over the Pole as unexceptional. The next eight hours were exceptional, though, all stemming from the fuel shortage. Heathrow wouldn't give us more than just enough gas to reach Gander. When we landed there, Canada wouldn't give us *any*, only grudgingly gave up enough to get us to Detroit after some firm pressure from Washington on the phone. I fell asleep while we were refueling in Detroit, so I'm a little uncertain *how* long that stop took, but we weren't on our way to California again till after midnight. Life is coming closer to SOYLENT GREEN every month.

December 19, Los Angeles. Universal bettered their offer for their film, but they still haven't satisfied Citron. They clearly long for me, though, which is some sort of comfort for giving up G. B. Shaw.

I'd hoped to play the Duke of Warwick in the production of ST. JOAN they were mounting for the Ahmanson. It's a lovely short part, with one marvelous scene. It didn't work, though.

I was vigorously seduced about doing a TV special, which I won't. I'd damn well better do *something*, though.

December 20. Ironically enough, I half-crippled myself setting an example for the country on physical fitness. With the European trip, I haven't been running regularly. I did a lot of it today for a government film, with much back and forth, stop and starting, and ended up with a strained tendon. I did whirlpool therapy and massage, but it's not much better. It did give me a chance to read the giant catastrophe script which Universal feels they need me in as some sort of insurance or talisman or something. The part's not much, which I expected, given a story of this sort. In addition, however, the character seems unscathed by his relationships. I'm not overjoyed at the prospect of spending my next commitment on it.

December 22. Lydia's locked into the rat race of Christmas preparations, Fray's still off cross-country skiing in Idaho, and Holly was completely preoccupied with two ballet performances today, *plus* a lesson in the morning ("Yes, I *do* want to take it today, I'm badly out of shape"). I'm brooding over possible solutions to the thin character development of the EARTHQUAKE script for Universal, though I'm still very uneasy about it in creative terms.

December 24. Christmas Eve worked out about as it always has. I like to reinforce the traditions, especially the ones I've established, like buying most of my presents on the last day. (Today, as last year, I took some of Ray Bradbury's first editions down to his office for him to autograph to Fray.) We were delighted to find Katie Manulis is well enough now to do their carol party again. It's very Waspishly unfashionable in this non-Christian era, but there's a special pleasure in the children singing and reading the Nativity. We saw our Michigan tree rise again, too, with our friends to help.

December 28. I sat up dozing in my big red chair, over a biography of Will Rogers Fray'd been given for Christmas, until Holly got back from her last performance of NUTCRACKER. Poor Munchkin . . . she was cross-eyed with fatigue, but full of pride at a good show. "It's really harder than acting, Daddy," she said. "*You* just have to remember your lines and get on a horse sometimes." Our day was very quiet, with the kind of special quality I still find in the holiday season, with the tree looming large and mysterious in the front room. Lydia and I enjoyed Ted Ashley's party tonight. He has the old Selznick place, where I went for those early rehearsals on RUBY GENTRY, more than twenty years ago. I usually don't like parties that big . . . you can never sit down.

1974

Earthquake,
reluctantly . . .

then *Airport '75* . . .

Macbeth at the
Ahmanson, with
Vanessa Redgrave as
Lady Macbeth.

Saving Ava Gardner in *Earthquake*
THE MUSEUM OF MODERN ART/FILM
STILL ARCHIVE

Raising a bloody fist
as Macbeth at the Ahmanson
LYDIA HESTON

January 7, Los Angeles. Something like eight inches of rain have fallen on the basin in the last three weeks; I doubt there's any area in the country with worse weather. It gave me a good chance to talk through the rewrite I asked for on my character in EARTHQUAKE, which they seem to've done some good digging on. They've complicated his relationship with his wife, put some texture into his back story, and given him anxieties and misgivings about the girl.

It's terribly difficult to find room on the crowded canvas of physical events in a film like EARTHQUAKE for any character texture. We managed to get some into the script on this, but not a lot of it reached the screen, I'm afraid.

January 29. This was not a productive day. At Universal, Mark Robson's still deep in his preparation on EARTHQUAKE. The casting's still up in the air as far as the two women I work with, though, as God is my judge, Universal's high on Ava Gardner.

This is a bit harsh, but my memories of 55 DAYS AT PEKING were bitter ones.

February 6. Nothing important in the day; just scraps here and there. I talked with Walter Seltzer on the Indian film, and also asked for his ideas on "1066."

The Indian piece was a fine story about an old drunken Indian in Ohio in 1905, called OLD FISH HAWK. I haven't made it yet, nor "1066," for that matter. Maybe someday. I haven't given up.

I moved back on the Universal lot, where I've not worked since COUNTERPOINT some . . . what . . . five years ago? They put me in Rock Hudson's dressing room, which means, I suppose, that his TV series is kaput. [*It wasn't, just on hiatus.*] I think it's also the dressing room I had when we made WAR LORD, but that's so long ago I can't be sure. Nothing is permanent . . . actors learn that more quickly than real people.

February 12. Fray's nineteen today. He's bursting through into manhood, just as I'm grumbling and sulking about accepting middle age. He seems . . . more *graceful,* somehow, than is usual in late adolescence. He may switch to UCLA and literature, but he's a boy I can be proud of, as I was when Lydia bore him, almost two decades ago. We flew down to La Jolla to celebrate the day with him.

He did switch from his study of marine biology at UCSD to a literature major at UCLA. I told him at the time it was an even tougher way to make a living than acting, but at this writing, he's sold a few pieces.

February 23, Los Angeles. I ran Wyler's THE WESTERNER. Sam Goldwyn's estate is interested in having me do a remake. Coop's very good in it. *Very* good. It could work . . . I'd love to do it. I also learned Universal's signed Ava Gardner. In annoyance and despair at my dissatisfaction with the script, I said last week they could sign whom they liked. So, of course, they did.

February 26. I began another one today, EARTHQUAKE, with far less enthusiasm than I should have. This one, I guess, is done at least partly for the money . . . a lousy reason to do a film. On the other hand, if I hadn't undertaken some parts whose prime potential is popular success, how much choice of better parts would I have? It's really not as simple as it seems.

March 4. The work wasn't difficult, save that Ava was fighting it. She's still tense and tends only to approximate the exact text (which is not deathless prose, God knows, but you make what changes you can as well as you can, and then stick with them). We did fourteen takes on one fairly simple setup. I'm not too happy with the results, but [*director Mark*] Robson seemed content. "You have to recognize when you've got all there is," he said. True.

March 11. A good chunk of work today. Genevieve Bujold will be an interesting color in this role; she's a very loose, live actress; there should be an original chemistry between us. The scene's not bad now, including an unusual acting problem. In my character as an engineer, I help Denise rehearse a scene. It's not easy to read lines the way a man who doesn't know how to read lines would.

March 13. AFI Life Achievement Award to James Cagney, Century Plaza Hotel. The Cagney dinner was the major part of the day, of course. I had time to go over what I was going to say and had it more or less learned, which is far better for me than trying to read it off those damn cue cards, like Sinatra, or ad-libbing, like Lemmon. (It got both of them into trouble.) But the dinner was honestly the best of that kind I've ever seen, an opinion shared by all 'round. Fray looked fine in his new dinner jacket, Lydia was marvelous. She had to rush off at the end to catch her plane for Washington for her cousin's funeral, but it still made a magnificent evening. For Cagney, too, I think.

March 18. Good news on the dollar front . . . from several quarters, as a matter of fact. It turns out the IRS approved our deduction on the ANTONY loss (God knows it was real). Also, the current releases of SOYLENT GREEN and SKYJACKED in foreign venues are doing well. All in all, I'm not in immediate danger of starving.

March 22. I welcomed the chance to earn my salary today. I worked hard and long on a key scene in Lorne Greene's office. He's an easy actor to work with . . . professional, with a slightly florid quality that's good for the part. The chemistry with me seemed good, too, though you can't tell till you see some film.

March 24. On a quiet Sunday, it's perhaps good to note in passing the remarkable events in the world at large I usually ignore in this odd journal. The past six months have seen the almost total erosion of Nixon's popular base, if not indeed his capacity to govern, as they keep putting it. The Arab successes in the Yom Kippur war, coupled with their subsequent oil embargo, have transformed the West's economy of abundance. Standing in the gas lines to fill our tanks, we've realized there's a bottom to the cup.

April 2. A full day, though there was again no shooting in it for me. I found out MUSKETEERS is doing fantastically well, which is gratifying. My diet, vitamin, and workout regime seems to be paying off, too. I'm under 205 and looked good, therefore, in a brief appearance at the Academy Awards, giving the little gold man to Glenda Jackson's surrogate. I felt oddly alienated, somehow, and left immediately after my chore was done.

April 9. We're beginning to work on the stair scene, which involves several matte-shot angles and an elaborate set of the twenty-third to twenty-ninth floors of a high-rise building. We did a lot of stuff up and down ropes, lowering cringing extras, etc. I'm not too great at this kind of thing, even though our set is only twenty feet up, not twenty stories . . . horses, fights, and fire, yes. Heights, no. Still, I did mysmall chores (Joe Canutt is doing the scary stuff for this sequence).

April 10. Universal must be happy about the film, or what I'm doing in it. They've offered me another one. It's the logical extension of AIRPORT's success, coupled with the current trend toward large "movie movies." This isn't really a sequel, but another airplane-in-distress story. I wouldn't be so uncertain about it perhaps, if I hadn't done SKYJACKED recently. Also, my last two films have been large, physical pieces. Well . . . they'll wait a bit.

April 11. We finished in the interior of the building. It should make a good scene, after the matte shots are cut in. I had time to read Universal's big airplane thing. It's well enough done, but not an acting role. Nor is it a long one . . . I doubt there're two weeks of work in the part.

April 12. I told Jennings Lang, met by chance driving on the lot, that I'd decided to accept his offer to do their airplane picture. I have misgivings about doing another large film, with a nonacting part. Still, Citron's point is valid . . . these are the parts that earn me the time and the choices to do what I want to. That's oversimplified, of course . . . but what isn't?

April 25. The friction that's been building with the studio for some time came to a head today. I never approved the original ending where my character survived the earthquake. They agreed to a change to accommodate my death in a futile, doomed effort to save my bitchy wife, which seems to me to lend some credibility to a basically implausible story. (An earthquake destroys the whole *city*, this guy with the mean wife and the neat girl friend escapes scot-free, wife killed, neat girl left alive for him while he rebuilds Los Angeles?) Anyway, they kept edging up on me about shooting an alternate ending. I've been at this trade too long not to know better than that. Script approval doesn't help you if you've shot it. We had it out today; we won't shoot two versions.

Against great pressure, I succeeded in dying in the film. I think it's one of the most important changes I've ever managed to make in a script.

April 26. There was very little significant shooting, though of course these geographic shots are as important in the structure of a film as anything else. They just aren't very interesting to make. I did a few public relations chores, then a reception for the foreign press, who had just come from seeing our demo reel of earthquake effects, complete with a low range of fifty-cycle sound played loud enough, though below the range of human hearing, to vibrate the seats. It's scary as hell.

It scared the audiences, too. When the picture opened at Grauman's Chinese, the Sensurround system shook some plaster out of the ceiling.

May 2. I've been offered a film version of Ibsen's ENEMY OF THE PEOPLE, adapted by Arthur Miller. This is for American Film Theater, a subscription service that's had some success this year. The part's right for me, and it would be a good balance (for the critical fraternity, if no one else) for the commercial choices I've made in the last few months. On the other hand . . . is it a good part?

Not necessarily. Most translations of Ibsen are very stiff, and almost unplayable.

May 3. I finally got Orson Welles on the phone (always an achievement). He was full of charm, as ever, quite delightful to talk to, but I doubt he'll direct MACBETH, though he was most warm about it.

I'd decided to take another crack at that man-killer part the following winter for Bob Fryer at the Ahmanson.

My death scene (which I had to fight to keep in the film in the first place) was wet and uncomfortable, and shot about seven times, each one requiring emptying and refilling the storm drain. I must say their decision to build it below as ground out by the WAR LORD lake on the back lot was a good one. We moved late to the New York street to pick up one shot I now won't have to do Monday night.

May 6. The usual sort of wrap day. I'm always filled with energy for paper work that's been sitting for days, and get vast chunks of it torn away. The shooting left to do was minimal: a long shot and two close-ups that wrapped me up in the film. I've made a very small creative contribution to it, I'm afraid, though I suppose a somewhat larger chemical one. The SAG meeting tonight was interesting and instructive. Dennis Weaver reversed himself publicly on his plan to use members at large for contract negotiations. His openness earned him the approval of the whole board. Nixon could've done the same thing any time in the last eighteen months with the same results, had it occurred to him. I wonder why it didn't?

May 7, Washington, D.C. Begin principal photography on AIRPORT *'75.* I slept on the airplane, having read the Ibsen/Miller ENEMY OF THE PEOPLE. I'd discussed it with Orson on the phone. He said, "Miller is really the Ibsen of our time: talented, socially concerned, and absolutely humorless." I like the part better than I thought I would. I think I may do it, if only as a creative balance to these nonacting roles. Fifteen hours after I finished my last shot in EARTHQUAKE in Los Angeles, I was in the passenger terminal at Dulles in Washington, doing my first shot for AIRPORT. It was the first scene with Karen Black; just about my only acting scene in the whole piece. It was OK, though the two of us didn't strike the sparks I thought we would. Photographically the shot was interesting. I'm not certain the scene will be.

May 8. This was my Washington day, and very artfully scheduled it was. I touched all the bases, got into our problems at AFI, though failing to solve them, and uncovered some exciting possibilities for the Bicentennial. There's a good possibility for a series of fifty great American films, toured as a package.

May 9, Dallas. Another bloody long day, but it all worked smoothly. I flew to Dallas to spend time on the 747 simulator American Airlines has there. It's a more sophisticated machine than the 707 simulator I worked with in SKYJACKED. I tried an experiment. They put a succession of nonflying stewardesses at the controls, and over the intercom I managed to talk them through some simple maneuvers, which proves to my satisfaction that the basic premise of the script is OK. That's what I have to do in the film with Karen.

May 15, Los Angeles. I have more or less concluded a deal to do ENEMY OF THE PEOPLE for practically nothing. That's OK; the deals Citron makes for films like AIRPORT '75 let me do Ibsen and Shakespeare from time to time.

May 28, Salt Lake City, Utah. My usual fever of paper work before a departure, leaving sheaves of IBM belts for Carol behind me. I suspected they'd called for me before they needed me and I was right. Never mind; the hotel's OK, and I found a decent steak tonight. Lydia reports she's going down to San Diego to bail Fray out of his apartment, a chore she looks forward to; delighting in his cry for motherly help. One inevitable result of my going on location is how it organizes . . . even galvanizes . . . her life. There is a paradox there I don't understand. She hates to have me gone, but she's never healthier than when I *am*.

May 29. I had a miserable night's sleep, having wakened early thrashing with an itch, which gradually spread over my body in angry red welts. I never get this kind of thing, or any kind of thing, but it kept me awake till dawn, then disappeared while I did two hours of interesting work flying in a small jet. On returning to the hotel and lying down for a nap, it developed again. We decided it was the fake fur coverlet on the bed (or possibly the large portraits of Robert Redford on the walls of the suite). Anyway, we changed the bed and I rushed to get some doctoring before I was due back to shoot a short scene at the airport before coming in for dinner with a local TV interviewer.

June 1. I'd planned to go home in the Lear with the film at the end of shooting today, but they've gotten permission for me to actually fly the 747 tomorrow morning for the second unit. On instinct, I went out after dinner to see that the night shooting moved well, since we can't start on time tomorrow unless they finish the boarding shots with the 747 tonight. There was the usual gefuffle that's so likely on a big company, especially at night. I realized the reason the shot was going wrong was that the driver running a loading ramp was absolutely smashed. I pointed this out to the first assistant, who replaced him, and we finished in time, huzzah. As Walter Mirisch told me, I have the soul of a production manager.

June 5. This was a marking-time kind of day . . . I finally figured out that the company really didn't want to finish up here today, which is why they were reluctant to finish me. They will, though. We couldn't get into the control tower till late at night, when the air traffic quits, so we started in the evening, and of course ripped off the requisite shots very readily, as I knew we would. I saw my first batch of dailies, which included very little to examine in acting terms. What was there, I accomplished. They want me in the film so they'll have someone they can bill over the 747, I suppose.

June 15. Fray called to tell us we almost lost him yesterday. On his first raft trip as an apprentice river guide, his boss at the sweeps, the raft flipped over in the highest water the river has seen in years, trapping everyone underneath. Fray somehow fought his way clear, swam ashore, and hailed an army convoy. They finally rescued the raft, along with most of the passengers, but two drowned. Fray was shaken, Lydia desolate. I can't help but feel there may be some profit for a nineteen-year-old to learn he is mortal. His future this summer is now uncertain. The Forest Service has closed the river till it goes down. Fray will stay there, at least for now. I'm certain this is right, though Lydia yearns for her bunny to come home.

June 17. They're having trouble with a special effect shot for a midair collision on the film: The rerigging delayed shooting significantly. This is crucial. Along with the midair transfer into the 747, it's the key shot in the picture. If they don't work, the picture doesn't work. Joe Canutt feels they should do the collision with stunt men, not dummies, but it's too late to rig for that. A shining example of poor preplanning. At least they'll use a stunt man to double the pilot, since this will fit into the shot as it's now rigged.

Far too often, film makers hire stunt men like Joe Canutt, but plan the shots themselves, thinking to hire only his courage instead of his brains.

June 19. A very crowded but effective day, mostly on the AFI. George Stevens's idea about forming a fund-raising group seems plausible, and we have two other pieces of good news: Martin Manulis will join us as West Coast director, and we've been commissioned by the Bicentennial people to make a montage film from the great American films. This can be our major success to date. After running a terrible feature at home tonight, I ran a really effective sixteen-minute film made by an AFI Fellow named Marvin Kupfer. Jack Lemmon gave his services with a fine performance as a disc jockey. We're just beginning to make this all work . . . if only we don't run out of money first.

June 28. The shooting's going very sludgily, now we're into the process shots. I waited all evening to do one shot, then left to rejoin the SAG negotiations. After some dicey moments when it might've all collapsed, we finally reached formal agreement on a contract, around midnight. The main gain for actors is in the area of TV rerun payments, thus helping our journeymen players, who need it. To me, we have a deal that responds to the major needs of our membership and to the needs of the industry as well. I think the SAG has again demonstrated its responsibility as well as its muscle.

July 3. I finished my stuff on the flight deck . . . on the whole film, really, save for the interior of the helicopter, which can't be shot till next week, for various complicated reasons too boring to list. This will require readjusting our plans for the float trip (which the Seltzers won't come on now, anyway. I think Mickey was put off the white water by Fray's accident.). Still, we'll be able to make the trip, and the delay won't be significant, except that I'll be even more hard put to try and learn enough about kayaking to do it.

July 8. I finished work on the film with another short day. This has to have been the easiest film I ever did . . . which makes it the least interesting. There're no real acting scenes in it for me . . . the whole role is really structural, requiring only that I be plausible as a pilot. Oddly, I think the film will work.

It did work, perhaps partly because I made a plausible pilot. Parting the Red Sea will do that for you, I guess.

July 10, Salmon River, Idaho. Of course we were late starting . . . the usual hassle of leaving complicated further by a steady, cold rain that fell most of the trip. The river is higher now, and much wilder. It really is almost too dangerous to run. We lost a kayak, and I got clipped on the head trying to rescue it while we were running a rapid. (I will undoubtedly live.) A different experience from last year . . . but memorable.

This turned out to be a marvelous trip, with Jolly and Kay West, Bill and Clori Isaac, two of their children, and ours.

July 18, Los Angeles. The meeting with Bill Friedkin went well, though it was fairly superficial in terms of any real examination of the play or the production. I think we see more or less in the same direction on it, though. I'm pleased.

William Friedkin wanted to direct a play, and the MACBETH we were planning seemed a provocative challenge to him. At the time it was an idea I responded to.

July 26. I spent most of the day on cutting the MACBETH text. I'm amazed at how much can come out of it still, when I've been working on it to this end through all the other times I've done the play. Bobby Fryer called in some anxiety as to whether or not Bill Friedkin should have "artistic control" over the production. I have no misgivings. A play's not like a film, and I know more about this one than he does.

August 2. Holly, my lovely sprite, became a teen-ager today. I bought her a most extravagant grown-up bracelet, whose significance was instantly clear to her. She clouded with womanly tears.

August 8. I decided it was necessary to write a detailed exposition of the Daniel affair to all of the board that have not been directly involved.

Frank Daniel was dean of the Center for Advanced Film Studies the AFI maintains in Beverly Hills. His resignation became an issue enlarged out of all proportion to its significance, it seems to me.

A tough letter, but I took pains with it. I then enjoyed doubles with George Plimpton, whose writing I admire. All this nonsense, while, for the first time in the history of the country, a president resigned from office. Since Agnew had already done so, his successor, Gerald Ford, will be the first president not chosen by the vote of the people.

August 19. Our usual Monday dose of trade paper comment on the AFI/Daniel hassle today. Another call from Billy Friedkin, who seems more interested in this than MACBETH, moved me to invite Daniel to the Thursday meeting in New York, paying his way. I want to demonstrate that nothing was left undone to open this completely. There will doubtless be some still unconvinced, but the record will stand. Whatever the screaming, it's clear trustee support for the original decision is overwhelming, and growing.

August 22, New York. The late, one-stop Red-Eye got me in midmorning, but a Universal car met me, took me to Bo Polk's really smashing duplex where I had time for only a bath in his huge tub before off to view a first-rate film (THE APPRENTICESHIP OF DUDDY KRAVITZ). We should get this director. The AFI meeting on Daniel ran on incredibly . . . over seven hours, nonstop. I was determined every question must be answered, though. The executive committee was finally affirmed, with one dissent, just before midnight. A long time without food, but it was managed rightly, I think.

August 24, Forest Hills. Robert Kennedy pro-celeb. I had any number of good excuses: (1) We were in the toughest group. (2) The grass courts were strange, in poor condition, and wet to boot. (3) The four-game-match format made luck a large factor. (4) The chokey quality of my match play in any tournament situation that has any unusual conditions. I suppose the best excuse of all is the old standby, "I can't understand it." That's what I'm using, anyway. I felt bad about losing, dragging Roy Emerson all the way east for that, but they raised a lot of money for a good cause. What the hell . . . the Scotch on the flight back was good.

August 27, Los Angeles. I was pleased to get the computerized (how impressed we all are at any results that are certified by computer) results of my physical exam of a fortnight ago. It seems I'm healthier than all but two point ninety-two percent of the men in my age group. Christ, I'd better be. Bill Ball is out as director for MACBETH. There was much talk of how much he'd like to do it, to work with me and Vanessa, but he still has another show to do.

By this time Billy Friedkin had, I think, had second thoughts about trying his hand as a stage director with a project like MACBETH and in any event found himself committed to a film, which precluded his involvement.

August 28. Not much today, though I enjoyed it all. We are still nowhere on a director for either ADDER or MACBETH. ACROSS THE RIVER is still hanging fire, though a deal looks likely there. I did hear from Herman Citron that the sneak on AIRPORT '75 in Detroit produced the best preview reaction *ever* for a Universal film: ninety-four percent excellent. If we have a flop, which we still could, that's one helluvan atypical movie audience they found there. Also, the advance on EARTHQUAKE is apparently phenomenal.

September 6. Peter Snell arrived a day late, to determine whether the AIP film has been so altered as to make it not worth doing. We decided to go ahead, with some reluctance. ("I am in blood stepp'd in so far . . .") I approved Mickey Anderson as director. He's English, professional, talented, and I've done a film with him before. [*We were considering PROGENY OF THE ADDER, which I'd almost made a year or two earlier with AIP, but without Peter.*]

September 11. It was a very awkward morning indeed. I had to pull out of the PROGENY OF THE ADDER. My own misgivings about it, combined with Lydia's, seemed too heavy to ignore. There are many things wrong with the new script, primarily that, at best, it will now be simply a police story. I said this, and they all accepted it with good grace, though some shock. A sticky business, but at least it's still possible to pull out without chaos. Oddly, this is the second time I've pulled out of a deal for this project.

I really don't know what attracted me a second time, except my interest in working with Peter again.

September 12. Somewhat to my surprise, Universal called and offered me a special screening of AIRPORT for any guests I want, with dinner afterward. It's really very generous of them. We'll do it next week. I did my public chores like a good boy all day (two board meetings, with a spot of doubles thrown in). Now that I'm out of ADDER, I'll be available for a public relations tour on AIRPORT '75. It begins to look as this one will put, if not stars to my crown, at least money in my purse. There is still the firm offer from Columbia for their horror flick EMBRYO. I don't like it, but it's interesting in terms of precedent. The percentage of the gross they offer is *plus* the guarantee, not against. If this is the new trend, the market's getting damn rich, especially for an old dog like me.

September 17. Seeing AIRPORT '75 I understand Universal's conviction the film will be a huge hit. I'm convinced it will, too. [*So it was.*] It works very well, it's quite gripping, and the airplane footage is incomparably superior to the first film Seaton made. On the other hand, there are neither characters nor performances equal to what Stapleton and Hayes did in his film. On still another hand, I'm a more plausible pilot than Dean Martin was. That's not saying much.

September 26. It'll obviously be necessary to go to London to discuss the MACBETH text, casting, design, and overall production with Peter Wood. I feel some misgivings about the difficulty of selling him on my cutting of the play. Of course it must be cut, and I believe I've done it well, but he may cavil at some of the transpositions, straight-lining, and melding of roles, though they seem to me eminently desirable. As for the few word substitutions ("mask" for "vizard," for example), I think this is required by the evolution of the language since Shakespeare's time.

Looking at the formidable reputation he had earned at the British National Theatre, I'd endorsed Bob Fryer's suggestion that Peter Wood direct our MACBETH.

September 27. I ran EARTHQUAKE. I'm afraid I'm not too keen on it. Of course it works as a film; the quake effect is genuinely frightening. It's probably true that Sensurround is the first new film effect since CinemaScope, more or less guaranteeing the success of the film. The story's so-so, much of what character interplay there was is cut out now. I'm principally unhappy with my own performance. Ava's no better than I thought she would be (I was *right,* damn it), but I would've thought I could've performed more professionally in the scenes with her. I'm really quite unbelievable. I do well with Bujold, but the total performance is not much.

Commercially, this turned out to be one of my most successful films, but I'm very disappointed with what I did in it.

September 29 (Sunday). With some distaste, I handled the difficult phone calls to Mickey and Peter, on closing out ADDER. Mickey took it with cheerful humor, Peter asked me to delay one more day in the hope this will somehow change things. It won't. The script is *not* remarkable. At best it would be a more or less well-done suspense story, but the bottom line is that there is no overwhelming reason to *do* it. I should've figured this out long ago.

October 9, New York. I started damn early (one drawback to this sort of tour . . . some of the best TV talk shows get you up at bloody dawn to do them). I spent much of the day feeling stabs of déjà vu. There are so many places in this town where I've done so many things . . . and I go through the day remembering them.

October 12, London. This is still my favorite city. Whenever I come back to it after some time away, I'm struck again, as I was the first time, with the simple fact of *being in London.* No matter who's here that I have to see or who's absent that I wish were with me, I'm still in London, and glad of it.

October 13 (Sunday). Peter Wood seems intelligent, relaxed, witty, a somewhat detached personality of the kind that's familiar both in Englishmen and good directors. I was favorably impressed. I dined tonight with Peter Snell, still totally committed to "1066" of course. He's coming over to read the weather on financing it in a few weeks when the success of AIRPORT '75 will have registered.

October 14. I stopped by to replenish my tennis wardrobe from the Fred Perry free list, then had a decent hit on the wood at Queen's before lunch with Bobby, Peter Wood, and Vanessa Redgrave. It was what you'd call an exploratory meal, I guess. (Each of us equally anxious to explore the other, no doubt.) She seemed to've taken some pains for the meeting . . . neatly dressed, hair, makeup, rather nontypical of her Trotskyite image, one would think (although one might be quite wrong, of course). There was little of substance accomplished, predictably. This was just a formal step in a ritual pavane.

October 16. I checked out with the usual feeling of faint regret I have at leaving this city. It's changed a great deal in the years I've been coming here, and now seems to be trembling on the brink of final collapse, with the Labor government in again for what looks like a bleak and brutal dismantling of the whole structure of English society. Nevertheless, the city of London is still beautiful, and I flew out of it sadly. Of course I'm always eager to get home and snug into my ridge again. I did, and found all waiting for me.

October 21, Los Angeles. AFI fall meeting, Board of Trustees. This was another long one. Either the meetings are getting tougher or my stamina's diminishing: I came home from this one really exhausted and slumped off early to bed with a broken blood vessel in my eye (I interpret this as a result of suppressing my annoyance with Billy Friedkin during the meeting). He's really an odd man. I'm beginning to doubt his value on the board, and now have no doubt whatever of his value as a director of MACBETH. Whatever happens with the play, we're better off with Peter Wood.

October 23. I had another of my spasmodic meetings to try and understand my financial situation. I'm not being stolen from, and I don't think I live all that extravagantly, but I do know I make a helluva lot of money every year and I never seem to have much of it left at the end. I know, there was ANTONY and all that, but *Christ!* Leo Ziffren says we should have an independent audit, just on general principles.

I'm not good with figures, I'm of Scottish descent, and I was raised in the depression. I get these hot flashes every so often. At this point, my affairs could not be in better hands.

October 28. I spent most of the day thrashing through the thickets of footnotes that make up the bulk of the Variorum edition of MACBETH. It has useful suggestions of substitutes for the misprints in the original Folio test. When one of these makes it clearer, I'll pick it every time. Purity, yes. Obscurity, no.

November 2. I got a little more time with Peter Wood today, though we still haven't turned up anyone remarkable in the auditions. (I suppose that's not really surprising; we've only interviewed some forty actors.) We haven't had a chance to go over much of the text yet, but we will before he goes back to London. I feel I have it right now; it'll be difficult to compromise with what are bound to be his differing views. It'll be a stimulating week.

November 6. Peter and I worked through the play, line by line. He's more of a purist on text than I, but we compromised amicably enough, retaining some of my redactions, most importantly in that endless, opaque London scene, which I've cut by two thirds. [*In rehearsal Peter put most of that scene back and disguised its opacity with very resourceful staging.*]

November 7, Anchorage, Alaska. We rose at dawn . . . striving mightily to get our bags packed with everything from Arctic gear for the first stage of our trip to tennis and Shakespearean gear for the second. It was strange to fly back to the country I haven't seen since I climbed on that plane after the war to go back and begin the life that's carried me around the world, and now back here. Lydia and the kids have never seen it, of course. It lived up to its promise of a strange and far place, though I could no longer see in this modern city the rackety boomtown of dirt streets, bars, and whorehouses I remember. There is, in fact, nothing here I remember . . . except the mountains. They stay the same.

November 9, Anchorage. Premiere of AIRPORT *'75, reception after.* A very full day, in which we did everything we'd planned . . . barely. We had only one free hour for cross-country skiing, but it was worth doing all the same. This country is overwhelming. We had snow today, and it turned cold tonight. The openings nevertheless went very well (nationally, it's gotten a distributor's gross of seven million in two weeks).

November 10, Chicago/Washington, D.C. We took off at an ungodly hour, but it's a helluva long shot down across the continent. Indeed, it took the whole day, including holding over O'Hare for forty-five minutes. The day was clear, all across Alaska, and it all looked absolutely spectacular. This is surely as beautiful as any part of the continent.

November 11, Washington, D.C. I spent most of the day working on the readings for tonight. [*I'd been invited by the Folger Library to do some readings from Shakespeare for a benefit there.*] Over the last week, I've managed to free myself from the text, at least to the extent you need for a reading performance. This was my first experience on an Elizabethan stage (the Folger has a replica of the Globe). It works well . . . so did I, I think. The audience held dead quiet and responded fully. The dinner afterward was great fun. It was a Scottish banquet duplicating one that was given in 1605 for James I. Several of the guests, including me, wore highland dress. I may be the first actor ever to play Othello in a kilt.

November 13, Los Angeles. We more or less agreed on actors for Macduff, Malcolm, Lennox, Seyton, Banquo. Peter feels he can't find a good enough Malcolm of eighteen, so he's reluctantly abandoned that concept. We still have a problem on the designer. George Stevens's concept on the Bicentennial film received somewhat muted endorsement from the committee I'd appointed to review the plans.

November 18. I got to hit a tennis ball or two, and think of something besides SAG affairs. [*We'd just concluded several days of national meetings.*] I worked some time with Ziggy on the Macbeth makeup. We agreed on red hair and beard, though there's an old tradition against that for tragedy. I was rather drawn to the idea of just a Saxon moustache, but Peter felt a beard is requisite for the role (as did Lydia, for that matter). Citron moved to close a deal with Walter

Mirsch for his film on the battle of Midway, which will require a crew cut, I would think.

November 20. I did the ABC *Morning Show,* speaking another of my little pieces on behalf of another of my constituencies. I hardly know which hat I'm putting on these days, but none of them's an acting hat. That'll come to a halt soon, when we swing into MACBETH. Meantime, I find some of the problems diverting . . . well, not diverting, challenging, I guess, and you come to worry about getting it done right. Like who should handle the Bicentennial film for the AFI? Is Kathy Nolan to be supported in her play for the SAG presidency?

December 3. We have a deal on MIDWAY. Herman gave them the usual bargain in my up-front guarantee, but upped my piece of the gross. Now to find a director, plus a writer who can make the dialogue work a little. The script we have is little more than an effective structure laying out the battle. I had a long, amicable talk with Walter [*Mirisch*] on all this, then went to do another chore for the AFI. I'm going to have to turn all this off when we start digging into the bloody Scot, so I might as well give it a good shot while I have some time.

December 5. I spent a long time going over the whole money picture with the Ziffrens. I suddenly realized very tardily that they've been outrageously undercompensated for all they accomplish for me. I'll correct that. Several new scripts are coming in, though nothing that seems very good. I don't really want to think too hard about anything beyond MACBETH.

December 10. Peter Wood gets in tomorrow night, but Vanessa's now not arriving until the day before formal rehearsals begin, though she promised she'd get here in time for some early work on our scenes before things really start. If she won't come, she won't come, but I'm disappointed. I'll know more about it when I see Peter. A full day of paper work, plus another firm offer from AIP. The joint success of the two current pictures is getting me a flood of scripts.

December 11, Washington, D.C. Senate hearing, Pell subcommittee on arts: give deposition on the AFI funding legislation. This was another one . . . the last, till I finish MACBETH in March. Our side did well in the hearings, especially in view of Pell's reluctance to back the bill. He did make clear, however, that he's determined to protect the AFI's interests and publicly chastised NEA for their "niggardly attitude" to the institute. George doubts Nancy Hanks will really change her spots, I doubt this legislation will pass. Still, as I testified, what I want is the growth of the AFI, under the NEA or independently.

December 12, Los Angeles. Today was MACBETH, end to end. Peter reports Vanessa doesn't like any of my redactions in her role. I wasn't such a fool as to cut any of her lines, of course, but she wants them arranged as the Old Gentleman wrote them. She's mistaken, but it's certainly her privilege. Peter, who's directed her before, soothed me. "It will take her time," he said, "to realize you have not suggested these changes to improve your part." The rest of the day was constructive, though we've still not found a Malcolm. Peter has an excellent idea on Seyton . . . giving him the Porter scene and most of the Messenger bits, and playing him as a classic court fool, as in LEAR. [*This worked superbly.*]

December 14. The set's going to be good . . . possibly fantastically good. I'm worried about the costumes. They have too much stylistic unity about them, like a set of chessmen. It's also very hard to judge from the renderings because Kirkpatrick, like most costume designers, can't draw worth a damn. The discussion stopped just this side of being heated, but I'm really not happy with the clothes. They are more Tudor than anything else, and seem wrong to me. The crown, for example, is a great heavy pastry. I've worn more crowns than most living actors, and I know damn well that most of them look downright hilarious. The thing to do with a crown is minimize it.

December 19. Start rehearsal: MACBETH. When you're nineteen, you can face the prospect of a great role with utter equanimity; the older you get, the more they tower like ice-shrouded Everests, unreachable in the mists. Today, before we began the simple read-through that was the whole of the workday, I had a moment of near-panic, just at the thought of reading through the role. We did it, and it had some sort of rough sound to it, which I suppose gave Peter a chart to steer by, but it didn't tell me anything, except how much work there is ahead.

December 21. We moved on very well today, though Vanessa is proving a strange lady to work with. She is not bitchy, or late, or any of the boring things I've found actresses can be, but she's a balky kind of performer to work with. For one thing, she's *very* reluctant to accept any deviation from the published text. This will lose us many things I'm convinced are good, but the net will still be, I'm sure, a better Lady Macbeth than I've ever played with (or than most anyone else has, for that matter). You have to give up something to get something. (Talking to Peter about Lady V, he said, "Well, at least you don't get any of the standard great-actress behavior." "My experience with great actresses is quite limited," I said. "What do they do?" "Ohhh . . ." he mused, "they rehearse with their hats on.")

December 23. Holly having received, to her surprise, permission from her mother to get her ears pierced now instead of when she's eighteen, I had an easy answer to the gift problem and bought her tiny diamonds to decorate her pierced lobes. (A somewhat barbaric custom, but current.) Peter and I had another round on the costumes. "You really would've been happier with a much more primitive getup, wouldn't you, Chuck?" said Peter. "I'd have been happier with anything that made me look less like the King of Hearts," I replied.

December 25. The day went very well . . . our massive present-opening task accomplished just in time to deal with the unusually large gaggle of guests. I'd invited Vanessa and her children, impelled alike by Christmas feeling and self-interest. She remained silent, largely, but seemed to enjoy the day. Certainly her children did, as well as Franco Nero, who came, too. It was a very nice lunch, actually. We got a bit of rest, then on to the Seltzers' thing, which is always fun. Lydia seemed taken by her pendant, Holly overwhelmed by her earrings. Fray was quite happy with a plane ticket to Idaho and back. I got more than I needed from them all, including love I need very much.

December 30. We finished the blocking, then started detailing from the top of the play. Peter does this resourcefully, arriving often at new ideas from those we pointed toward in the blocking. He's very stimulating. I did a TV talk show with Vanessa (she's unwilling to do interviews alone, no doubt nervous lest they get onto politics, her private life, etc.). She doesn't really do a very good interview; I begin to apprehend she's in fact almost painfully shy.

This was a complicated year, both from the very narrow focus I reflect in these work jottings and the broader view I share with everyone breathing the world's air at the same time I am. I try not to be a latter-day Pepys; I lack the talent. But you have to at least note that the Republic was shaken this year. A president resigned, the economy tottered as it hasn't since I was a boy . . . but we're still here. As for my work, I didn't do anything remarkable creatively (though I'm launched on a part that *should* be, God knows). I did make two enormously successful films, which means I can still feed my family doing work I still love.

1975

A trip to
South Africa . . .

Earthquake,
a successful
disaster . . .

aboard the
U.S.S. *Lexington* for
Midway . . .

then,
The Last Hard Man.

In *Midway* and in
The Last Hard Man

January 3, Los Angeles. We began again at the top. For one thing, we're still maneuvering on the text. We kid about it, but Peter's instinct, really, is to get it back to what was printed in the First Folio (which is no guarantee, mind you, that that's what Shakespeare wrote, much less what was played in his theater). Anyway, Peter's found a good solution for the witches' scene. I really think this'll be the best version of it I've ever seen. We also arrived at good ideas for some of the later scenes and finished in time for a leisured drive with Lydia and the kids down to La Quinta, for something like the fifteenth time, for our annual tennis bash.

January 6. I'm beginning to get into serious work on the combat scenes. It's bloody tiring; more than the other times I've done the part. The fight will be up to higher standards, and I'm getting a little long in the tooth for a broadsword fight after four acts of MACBETH. Still, we'll make it. I continue to be impressed with Peter's resources as we dig deeper and deeper into the play. He's stressing the mordantly comic aspects of the role, playing the scene with the murders as black comedy, for example.

January 9. The work today was somewhat shortened by Vanessa's political activism. She just joined Equity, though not required to be a member to do this one play. This afternoon she called a company meeting so she could submit a resolution in the West Coast Membership meeting tomorrow asking for the "immediate amalgamation of all entertainment unions and confiscation, without compensation, of all theaters and television stations in the U.S." I'd thought most Communists were a little more expert politically than that. I suspect she doesn't know a lot about the world, really.

January 11. We're beginning to fall into a routine with the rehearsals now. We have the broad shape of the thing, I'd say, though much is changed every time we work on it. I think we've shifted across the crucial point where most of it's wrong to where more and more of it's right. Peter's leading me more and more toward the center of the character. "Your problem with the part, Chuck," he says, "is that you feel any man must be in agony to have done what Macbeth has done. You must learn not only to accept it, but to *embrace* it." That's bloody good. He's right, about me, and about Macbeth.

January 12 (Sunday). The stage work-week makes for a damn short day off, and the intensity we're pouring into this play makes a tennis court almost a strange environment . . . I've spent more time there this last week working on the combat than I have playing tennis. I've discovered that the Isaacs' Jacuzzi pool is one of the best places to rehearse I've ever found . . . I really got at some useful things there this afternoon, rolling about like a great whale, spouting iambics. I still see miles ahead, though, and know I've never come within shouting distance of this part before. Maybe now . . .

January 16. Today was a brute, but rehearsals are supposed to be. The great problem with this one, aside from those the sets present, is the necessity of getting enough time to rehearse the combat. We'll do it . . . *just.* The sets aren't lit yet, of course, but they're beginning to look very striking, even under work lights. Any serious work on the acting has stopped dead for me during these technical rehearsals, though you do stumble across the odd point or two, even backing away from the part. I also picked up a blister from the costume boots, though I've been wearing them in rehearsals for three weeks.

January 17. I seized the opportunity provided by doing a public relations chore at Universal to use the studio dispensary to get my blister properly insulated. I didn't wear the boots tonight. Technical rehearsal still continues very slowly, but they allowed for this; Peter says we're still on schedule. The set's ideal for this house . . . that great tilting oval seems to present the play to the audience like an outstretched hand. Some of the scenes, like the end of the banquet and the apparitions, are enormously enhanced by this . . . still, I wish I had another week to work on the man.

January 22. MACBETH lived up to its reputation as a hard-luck play. I remember when I was run over by a motorcycle the afternoon of opening in it in Bermuda; this afternoon Richard Jordan [*our Macduff*] tripped over a cable (*not* rehearsing the combat) and sprained his ankle. After much debate, the listed understudy went on in the part for the preview audience, reading much of it. Of course he didn't know the combat and couldn't possibly do it. Tony de Longis [*who'd helped Joe Canutt stage the combats and played Young Siward*] got up after I'd killed him, and killed me as Macduff, carrying through the rest of the scene. It worked well enough, and the audience, as they usually do in emergencies, rose to the occasion. I was fairly good in some scenes, not up to it yet in others. My energy level is rising, though. It's going to get better.

January 28. Tonight's opening was certainly the best performance I've ever given as Macbeth, and I think probably the best I've ever given in anything. My energy was high, I'd worked up to the right night, and it came together for me. A lot of people sensed it, including Peter and Vanessa, also Lydia, but I knew it myself, which is the main thing. It's a delicious thing to have that part in your hand and feel it rise. The audience was good for an opening, and they stayed with us, I think. The party after was pleasant, mildly drunk and mildly late.

January 29. The big thing was the notices. They shouldn't be, but you can't help focusing on them. They were pans. Bad ones, with one or two exceptions. There's no remedy for it, and no recourse. You just breathe deep and go on. Peter said, "You have to remember that most critics don't really *like* classics to be popular. For a masterpiece, they prefer to beat a solitary drum." It may be true. In any case, our ticket sales continue enormous, and I'm still convinced I'm a goddamn good Macbeth.

February 5. This was another rather frantic day in a week not designed for leisure. Mother came along while I did the *Johnny Carson Show* to promote the AFI Welles dinner. We had time for a rather hurried meal across the street from NBC in Beautiful Downtown Burbank, then I raced off to my nightly encounter with the Bard. I can't pretend to've come even, but I'm gaining on him as we round the far turn. The houses continue to be all but sold out, which is very gratifying. After the critical slings and arrows, I need it.

February 9 (Sunday). Really rather a crowded day. In the midst of getting Mother ready for her plane, I found that one of the staff people at SAG had become dangerously psychotic and was threatening Chet Migden's life. This meant getting Jolly into it, insuring that proper measures be taken. Then at the rehearsal for the Welles dinner I couldn't read the damn cue cards *(of course)*, so I had to memorize the material at home. Also, Orson had endless demands about using footage of his current film . . . very difficult. But the [*AFI Life Achievement Award*] dinner for him went well, though there were some stupid stage waits. The sound in the room was bad, but the film clips will go well for the later telecast. Orson's speech was just first class . . . a celebration of the maverick.

February 15. Vanessa's still out of the play [*with the flu*], I'm still in it. I think I'm learning new things about the part every day, and we aren't hurt that badly by Vanessa's absence. She's a much better actress than her understudy, but on the other hand, you learn new things, about your own performance and the play, acting with someone else. Still, I'll be glad when my Red Lady is back.

February 18. At lunch, Citron recapped the general state of the industry and my career, both of which seem in pretty good shape. It's something of a mystery to me why I'm all but the sole survivor of my generation of stars, when I never seemed to quite top the list in anything but the overall grosses of my films. I suppose this is part of it. Citron's somewhat reluctant to have me proceed with Peter Snell on "1066." I suspect he's uneasy about Peter, after our bad luck with ANTONY.

February 24. I took a somewhat detached part in the Academy nominations this time. I hadn't seen many of the films this year, and the deadline for voting snuck up on me. For the first time since I've been a member, I couldn't fill in my ballot. Meanwhile, I'm honest-to-God getting better in MACBETH. It's not clear to me why this is happening (or why it didn't happen sooner, if you like), but there are a lot more shadings in the part now. I'm pleased to grow.

February 26. The Italian offer came through. Unfortunately it's another disaster epic. I doubt I want to risk becoming so firmly identified with this type of film. This one's called CASSANDRA CROSSING: It's about a train full of people who've been exposed to bubonic plague, or something like it. It's not that good a script and will be made in Europe, with a Greek director. They're engaged in a rewrite, but I'm really not excited.

March 4. The classic MACBETH luck continues to dog us, into the final week, though my personal luck didn't fail me. Into the last phase of the combat with Macduff, my sword blade snapped at the hilt, probably from metal fatigue. I was holding a head parry at the time; how Jordan's blade didn't slice my face open, I don't know. Perhaps he pulled his stroke, perhaps I was quick enough to duck back a bit. It only nicked the mended bone in my nose. Very little blood, but it scared hell out of me. I lay dead under the stairs through Richard's last speech, panting and wet with sweat, tasting the blood on my face in the dark, trying to tell which was real and which was prop.

March 6. I blew my breakfast date with Walter Mirisch. I must be getting senile. He plans to replace Guillermin [*as director on* MIDWAY]. John's a thorny and truculent man; I think this was a factor. Jack Smight seems the likely replacement. Walter also discussed the possibility of making a nonexclusive deal for one or two pictures. It seems to have some advantages; I'd have a viable channel to develop properties for me. I think Herman will be opposed to it. He likes to keep all options open.

March 8, Closing night of MACBETH. Well, I've done the play again. I've climbed the bloody mountain, I've seen the goddamn elephant. Every one of these mother-loving parts is a man-killer, and I've only barely escaped alive from this one each time. But I've come back each time, and done the part better each time (yes, I have), and this was the best time of all. I learned more and got deeper into it.

March 9 (Sunday). Today was unremarkable, save as the first day of my freedom. I marked it by taking my children to see Marcel Marceau, who is remarkable. But all day, I was still full of MACBETH. It goes so fast, like life. The whole production, the last performance: You're in the dressing room, with the smell of spirit gum in the familiar ritual of the makeup, then standing offstage right, waiting through the first scene, breathing in the feeling of the cue speech, striding across the black painted floor, leaping up into the light and the entrance hand . . . and then, in a breath, you lie under the stairs heaving with sweat after the combat, and it's over . . . all the work, all the glory, all the lovely bloody trying.

March 14. Today ended a week almost exclusively devoted to public service projects. I've never seen one quite like this somehow . . . everybody and his brother wanted me to make a speech for this or that. I did them all, or almost all of them, but ended feeling very put-upon, I confess. [*Not good. If you don't want to do 'em, don't. But don't bitch.*] EARTHQUAKE set a Hollywood record at the Chinese, before moving across the street, on a literal red carpet with all the old Hollywood public relations trimmings, to the Paramount. Presumably, it'll make a bundle there, too.

March 19. I turned down the large film Ponti's been trying to lure me into. Even the prospect of Sophia Loren's not quite enough to get me on that train full of plague victims being sent to their doom by an unscrupulous American colonel, while a scrupulous American doctor . . . well, it's all very complicated, and the thought of twelve weeks in Italy and Switzerland does not excite me. Herman's not pleased, but he never argues these things. As Walter Mirisch points out, not in jest, movies about disease almost never work for audiences.

March 25, Madrid. Back again to Spain [*where we'd gone to play, for once, not to work*]; how many times have I checked into this same hotel since EL CID? Since then, how many triumphs, how many disasters began here? This time is for fun; nothing's at stake.

March 28, Sevilla. This was as late as I recall staying up for some years; indeed I'd lost my taste for it by three in the morning. Lydia was flying, however, and I had to fly with her. Thus we ended with the traditional (I *think* traditional) churros and hot chocolate in the street, then slept most of the day away, leaving time only for a walk along the river before dinner. Back at the hotel, I got a phone call from Richard Lester. He's launched on DEATH OF ROBIN HOOD and has another smashing cameo for me. I may take it, because I like working for him, but I wish he'd offered me the main part instead. As it stands, I'm merely insurance for his English actors. I'll read the script, of course.

March 30 (Easter Sunday). How far we've tracked the Romans across Europe. North to Scotland, south to the Sudan, east to Austria, and now nearly to the Atlantic. What a people they were, from plumbing and central heating to theaters and libraries . . . and the Roman peace, as well. What happened? How did they lose it? I have the growing conviction that, sifting through the ashes of New York some centuries hence, the same puzzled question will be posed. I was hard put to make clear to room service why I wanted hard-boiled eggs, but we managed, and my watercolor set served to decorate them, so the Munchkin could have her egg hunt, as always.

April 3. My Munchkin went home today [*back to school, after her Easter vacation*]. I can remember so clearly those first halting solos from the nest when Fraser took them, and now Holly's fluttering off, too. We had her checked at each stop, but she floated up the steps to the plane knowing as deeply as we did that it was a step into her life. We went on with our tour, a little dashed, but happy to have some time together, which we both need. I'd not been aware of Ronda, but it turned out to be one of the most spectacular places I've seen in Spain . . . or anywhere, for that matter. The old hotel where Rilke lived is perched on the edge of a throat-catching gorge.

April 5, Cádiz/Sevilla. We managed our departure well enough, leaving time for an interview in Spanish for the local press. Touring a sherry bodega, I saw a cask of sherry laid down for the Duke of Wellington when he was in Spain whipping Napoleon. When we finally got back to Sevilla, the hotel seemed like home. Lydia fell into bed, I went off to an evening with the American matador/painter, John Fulton, photographer Bob Vavra, and assorted friends. A most interesting evening, including bull meat for dinner, and a turn or two with the muleta and sword after. It takes a certain kind of man to be an expatriate. I'm not one of them.

April 12, London to Johannesburg. This was one of those days that disappears into itinerary. We got up earlier than we needed . . . for the first time in memory we were ready ahead of departure time, which was set too early anyway. (Why do travel agencies always want you at the airport an hour ahead of flight time?) The flight to London was easy . . . we got some rest at the airport motel, then boarded the 747, glad of the extra room, and started the long, long jump down the spine of Africa.

We were going to a charity premiere of FOUR MUSKETEERS.

April 13 (Sunday), Johannesburg. I slept badly, thwarted by the permanent armrests they've put in the upstairs lounge, designed to keep canny passengers like me from sleeping there during the movie. I woke to the endless bulk of Africa flowing below, had a glimpse of Nairobi, then the modern metropolis of Jo'burg. There were masses of people to greet us at the airport, also at both press parties later. It looks like I'll be able to attract some attention, both to the WCT tournament and the FOUR MUSKETEERS opening as well. It should be an interesting week.

April 15, Johannesburg. I got a bit of paper work done and a reasonable hit with Johnny McDonald, in preparation for the exhibition match, which was thereupon rained out, so the whole afternoon was sort of a bust, aside from a spate of interviews I managed. TOWERING INFERNO tonight was curiously disappointing. I'd expected it to be better than EARTHQUAKE, but it's not. It has the same flaws, and is also fifteen minutes longer. Oddly, it got better notices, though EARTHQUAKE is attracting more people. Are earthquakes more popular than burning buildings?

April 19. The final day of the tourney was the best weather . . . really flawless. Mottram played well to win, Ashe was a tiger in dominating the doubles (as he was not in singles). The opening tonight was a great success in monetary terms, generating a good sum for the Black Tennis Foundation, and making a significant landmark in that it was the first major opening in Johannesburg history that was totally integrated. This is worth having done. I wasn't impressed with the film, on second viewing, somehow. It seemed to me a little long and lacking in spine, and I think it seemed that way to the audience, too. Still, I've done worse work.

I attended the premiere in Johannesburg and played in an exhibition match in the tennis tournament held concurrently, for the same reason Arthur Ashe played in the tournament: Both events were totally integrated and raised money for valuable causes. This seemed to me, and I think to Arthur, far more constructive acts than picketing the South African Davis Cup team.

April 21, For Los Angeles. I believe this was about the longest day of all the long days I've spent on airplanes. We arrived late in London and had some minor problem with the baggage (whether the camera case, for which we had no check, was or wasn't on the plane). This cut short our rest period in the layover, and we had the usual polar run to get through as well. Finally, we let down in Los Angeles and got through customs, and there was Fray, waiting with the car.

April 23, Los Angeles. I'm fitting gradually back into harness again. The casting on MIDWAY's proceeding apace, in the classic phrase. We have Fonda for Nimitz, Mitchum for Halsey, Glenn Ford for Spruance, plus Hal Holbrook and a couple of other highly identifiable actors. I got my World War II haircut from Ziggy, and a bit of doubles as well. I'll need more than tennis. I'm fat beyond belief. Really disgusting.

May 1. Today I finally decided to leave the SAG Board. I was faintly
surprised when Chet Migden didn't fall down and weep about this,
but he's wise enough to have seen it coming. I should never have
come back, of course; I probably did it out of ego. ("They *need* me!")
They don't now. The board's changed radically recently, and I've
become a surly curmudgeon, bitching about policies they go ahead
and vote through anyway. I'll miss it, but I can no longer serve
effectively enough to be worth the irritation and time it takes.

May 6. Billy Blatty, rich and confident from THE EXORCIST, wants to direct
the EIGHTH CONFIGURATION himself. [*This was* KILLER KANE, *which I'd
been involved in for some years.*] It's not as unique as it was when I
first read it, but it's still a helluva part for me. It's an attractive idea.

May 8. This day was not bad, on balance. MGM offered me a film in which
a homicidal maniac is the hero, the U.S. government is the heavy, and
I have no part. Turning it down gave me a high moral feeling of
achievement, if only negative.

May 14, Pensacola, Florida. So one more black limousine pulled up to my
door at dawn and I started off on another one. I can't remember much
about the start of DARK CITY [*my first film*], but I remember we
started shooting on location. This was the same, exchanging shop talk
on the plane going down with Walter [*Mirisch*] on the possibilities of
VANDENBERG. I also read two new scripts he has. The motel we
checked into was like all the motels I've locationed out of. This
location will be unique in that the cast includes a really good tennis
player, Dabney Coleman, who is also a good actor. The public
relations man has taken the pains to arrange some courts and
opponents for us. I'm looking forward to the *Lexington*, too.

May 15, First day of shooting on MIDWAY. We began today and got a
great deal done. Harry Stradling (SKYJACKED) is the cameraman and
ideally suited to this kind of film. We're using the little Panaflex—a
very handy piece of gear for working in tight places. The CIC room's
jammed with communications equipment; add one film company and
you really get crowded. The content of the scenes is not much, but
it's possible to improve each of them by turning the dialogue into
talk. This is hard to manage with the technical language required, but
it can be done.

May 16. An interesting conflict has come up on the film. We've found,
partly through talking to some of Admiral Fletcher's old shipmates,
that he was really not up to command at Midway. This makes possible
some very interesting colors in the scenes I have with Bob Webber as
Fletcher. But the retired admiral who is our technical adviser on the
film is a bit edgy about portraying anything other than an ideal

staff/command relationship. It can be handled, but it tells you something about people . . . navy people, and other people. The shooting continues good; I'm beginning to revise my estimate of the possibility of getting a good film.

May 17. Glenn Ford started work today, as Spruance. I saw only a bit of his scene; he seemed a little nervous, so I left. He's an extremely likable man. Actually, I think Fletcher is the more interesting role of the two. Bob Webber's doing a good job with it. I worked well in a short scene with Eddie Albert, Jr., in the surgery. It was very easy for me to call on the father/son reaction the scene needed. I had only to think of Fray in the river last summer in his rafting accident and change one line, calling Albert "Tiger," and I was as full as I needed to be. It's a tricky sort of thing; you can go over the edge in a shot like that very easily.

May 19, On board the Lexington. We're at sea. The *Lex* is a lovely lady, middle-aged though she is. She slid down the channel and out into the Gulf like a fast youngster. Her size is overwhelming, as is the wandering maze below decks. I have more room than I'd expected to bunk in . . . a tiny room to myself, over the inward curve of the port bow and alongside the piston of the steam catapult. [*When it went off at six the next morning as they began launching aircraft, I thought a torpedo had hit by my head.*] We spent a great deal of time rescuing my son from a crashed plane, a scene to which I made only a tiny contribution. Still, we're away and the stuff should look remarkable. The ocean does, and the ship does. The rest, I suppose, is up to us.

May 20, At sea. We're moving well. Jack Smight [*the director*] had time for some extra pickup stuff of Garth [*my character*] moving through the ship after the bomb hits. We have an incredible opportunity here to shoot on the only World War II carrier still afloat, and the shots aren't anything you could get anywhere else. I watched the night operations from control after work. It's incredible to see those jets come in after dark. The catapult shots are something to watch, too.

The making of MIDWAY *depended on two factors over which we had no control. One was the fact that the U.S. Navy in World War II shot all its combat footage in color. This footage was crucial to the film and impossible to duplicate. We also needed a carrier from the period, to shoot the sequences at sea. The navy has one still in commission, the* Lexington. *We were lucky to get her.*

May 22. The *Lex* finished its training mission today and gave us the flight deck, which we've had to avoid almost all the voyage so far, because of jet operations. The banshee agony of A-3s landing was replaced by a forty-knot wind, though, which made it almost impossible to shoot there. We'll be cutting it awfully close to finish by the time we make port tomorrow. A Soviet group came aboard on inspection today. (I was happy to note the navy picked the oldest carrier we have in commission to show them.) Dinner with the captain was very good, the conversation not bad, though largely devoted to drinking, of which we're doing not one drop, of course, on a navy vessel.

May 23, Pensacola. We barely got the stuff we had to shoot at sea before we landed, with white sand beaches visible off the port bow while we were shooting the last scene on the flight deck over the starboard quarter. I picked up a trace of a cold, probably from working in the wind yesterday. Walter Seltzer phoned to say Fox wants to proceed on WILL ADAMS . . . a good script that's been kicking around two or three years about a Puritan sea captain and a Japanese mikado. We had a good evening tonight with Hank Fonda, who seems most amiable, and looks marvelous at seventy. Henry Fonda, *seventy?*

May 24. A very easy day today, winding up my location work here. I had a short scene to play with Fonda, my contribution consisting entirely of "Aye, aye, sir." Nevertheless, I was impressed to be in a shot with him, recalling things I've liked all the way back to DRUMS ALONG THE MOHAWK. He looks amazingly like Nimitz and is very good in the role, too, not surprisingly. I did OK in a scene with my son as he checks aboard the *Yorktown.* Eddie Albert will be OK, though he was distracted by the watching civilians. This is a tough thing for an actor to get used to. I then checked out, took a private jet to Miami, and did a nontaxing, potentially valuable party for one of the AFI's friends on the Hill. To bed in plenty of time for a decent night's sleep.

May 27, Los Angeles. I'm back at work on a sound stage again . . . just short of a year since I've set foot on one for pay. The scene was a fairly good one; I was able to make it better by cutting out the beginning and the end (a good rule, always . . . start the scene after it's begun, finish before it's over), and reworking my two major speeches.

June 1 (Sunday). The conference on WILL ADAMS seemed productive. I'm not clear how the director, an Englishman I've never heard of, seems so irrevocably locked into the project; I'm also uneasy that the project can't start before September, and will shoot in Spain and London, but we'll proceed with a step deal, I think.

June 2. It's clear this film will follow the pattern of my last two in one respect, at least: I'll work less than twenty days on the whole thing. It also looks more and more promising as a film, perhaps even as a part. Garth is beginning to take shape as some kind of coherent character, I think, partly because of the whittling I've been doing on the edges. There's damn little room inside the frame of the crowded story we're telling to construct *any* kind of character, but I believe we're getting a hint on film here and there.

June 4. The scenes today, shot against the foggy background of the Terminal Island Navy Base (doubling for Pearl Harbor) really went smooth as milk, largely because we were working with professionals. Fonda, Holbrook, and I went through several pages of dialogue (all nuts and bolts, overlapping stuff), all in movement, in and out of boats, jeeps, without anyone ever blowing a take for any reason. This pressed the crew to keep their standards up, too, as always happens. Professionalism will not necessarily create art, but in film, it's almost impossible to have art, or even a film, without it.

June 5. The professional standards I prated about yesterday broke down this morning. The studio car picked me up half an hour late. We had such a light day no harm was really done, except for putting me in the vile temper this kind of thing always engenders. Actually, my irritation worked well for the scene; Garth is supposed to be curt and pressured. I let this tone carry over from the scene with the repair officer into the scene with my son, as often happens in life. You use as much experience in acting as you do emotion . . . you remember how and why things happen as often as you summon past emotion.

June 13. Except for one day of process in the cockpit of the torpedo plane, I finished in the film today. Friday the thirteenth is not an auspicious day for this, but the work seemed good, nevertheless. We did two retakes . . . one for performance (Walter Mirisch felt the scene with the son on the pier required more sparks, so we supplied them in close-up). I ran the scene in the opening of the film where my son arrives in Pearl and we meet. I'd used my memories both as a father and as a son for it. It worked.

June 14. The day was fine . . . a little tennis in the morning with Fray, who's putting together his gear for the odyssey to Alaska. (A trek that's driving his mother up the wall, I may add.) Whether or not he actually has a job waiting for him at the end of the Alcan is another matter, but he's right in wanting to take off from the nest.

July 8, Chicago.

My mother had at last sold the house where she'd lived for so long, moving with my sister to a newer and smaller house in the same suburb. We'd gone to visit them, as well as spend a few days in Michigan.

This is the last time I'll ever be in this house. The new one will do Mother and Lilla very well, but I'll miss this rambling, slightly ramshackle repository of so many memories. So much of what I am began here. My work, my wife. This last visit, then, for the last memory here.

July 14, St. Helen. The scenes of my childhood, through a light, misting rain, deepening the dark landscape of pines crowding in on the highway. The house where I remember taking what? tea? as a boy from my grandmother is changed, as is the village . . . as is the boy. But it is the same still, too, as is the boy.

July 16, Picnic at Norway Point. Some of the best memories I have of the postwar time up here are the picnics on Norway Point . . . one of not many places up here that still looks the same as it was. The shallows as you jump out of the boat, the look of the virgin trees, tall as the sun goes down. I wish Fray were with us, too.

July 20 (Sunday), Los Angeles. Yesterday Fox made a firm offer (though they are reportedly a bit daunted by some details of the deal) for ANTICHRIST. The story derives both from THE EXORCIST and ROSEMARY'S BABY. Not bad . . . maybe? I saw JAWS later; it works very well. It also has some first-class performances.

July 27. I decided finally not to do ANTICHRIST, after discussing the project with Lydia. You have to be skeptical . . . I do, anyway . . . of accepting an offer just to reassure yourself you're employable. I've only just finished MIDWAY, but there are always the old doubts rising almost at once. This Fox film could have been effective, if perfectly done, but it could have come off very cheaply, too. On top of which, it would've put me overseas throughout the fall.

It was made very effectively as THE OMEN, competing with MIDWAY as the most successful film of 1976.

July 30. George Stevens and I made a major effort to alter Universal's opposition to the AFI at the source, by proposing to Lew Wasserman that he take over as chairman, and I step down. He refused . . . more or less . . . Lew is a compex and private man, and he would have no reason to reveal either himself or his motives to me.

August 12. I mulled through a little on Peter Snell's outlandish proposal to reshoot the role of Cleopatra. It seems utterly bizarre; certainly it's never been undertaken before with any released film, as far as I know. Still, there is the nagging possibility of saving my lovely project. The thing is, it's hard for me to accept what everyone else insists is the case . . . that Hildegarde Neil is not adequate to the role. I don't know if it's possible, let alone if I want to do it.

I still don't know if it would've been possible or even if it would've been wise. But we almost persuaded one of the two or three conceivable actresses for the role to try it. It would've been a fascinating experiment.

August 13. It seems I'm back at work again. Herman worked out a very complicated deal for THE LAST HARD MAN. The problem will be to get a costar . . . this script demands one . . . and a good director. We're beginning with Sean Connery or Robert Shaw. Jack Smight seems right as director, but that's a safe choice. Now that I can control so much, it's wrong to always go in the direction of safety. Let's try and take some chances.

August 14. We're not having a lot of luck on the director for this piece. I think it's a good script and can be a good film (especially if we get Connery for the other part). Stu Rosenberg's working on another film, which is something we should've known before. I had a breakfast meeting with Bob Haggiag on ACROSS THE RIVER AND INTO THE TREES (again!). They say I'm the only actor right for the part (correct), and that the script they showed me last winter is no good. (Also correct.) Whether it's possible to work out something, I don't know.

September 9. Apparently Andy McLaglen has closed enthusiastically for the directing slot. He's done his best work in Westerns; it may work out very well. We also looked at James Coburn for the principal antagonist. Walter and the studio people are very high on him, but Citron is dubious, on the grounds that he doesn't constitute the "major costar" we insisted, going in, was necessary for the project. This may be true, but he's involved in several important films at this point. He's also very good in one (HARD TIMES) we ran tonight. He's a good actor.

September 20. Walter called to say that he had a stroke of luck on the writing assignment for HARD MAN. He called John Gay, just on his way to accept a similar patch job on another project, but he took ours instead. This may turn out very well; he's very good. I must learn to be more hard-nosed about things; instead I'm too often soft-nosed (or softheaded). I would've made the worst studio head in history. Fray came home tonight, in good shape. How he can sustain those thirteen-hour drives, I don't know.

September 26. We began the academic year at Greystone again; I performed the not-unpleasant chore of welcoming the new Fellows. Simsie Field [*Joe and Maggie's daughter*] was one of them. The new

AFI magazine *(American Film)* came out, and I'm very impressed with it. Fox made an offer for Barbara Hershey for the role of the daughter in HARD MAN. I think it's the right choice.

October 3. I spent a little time doing a totally inept interview for the cable TV release of AIRPORT. It was worth doing, I thought, because it's a new and important area of distribution. But the lady was a bit green and didn't have a clue as to what she was about. I've been doing interviews for so long, I forget you have to learn how. I then spent some more time discussing another MACBETH in London next spring. One question: Will Peter Wood be available to direct?

October 8. Emperors are surely an endangered species; lunch with one at the Music Center is worth noting. I think Emperor Hirohito may be the only one left in the world, come to think of it. Anyway, Mayor Bradley threw a large lunch to welcome him to the city, and there we were. Duke Wayne seemed to be the only other actor present. I wonder why the mayor invited two of the tallest actors in town to a lunch for a short emperor? Anyway, it was fun.

October 16. The AFI meeting went well . . . perhaps as constructive a meeting as I remember chairing there. We got through the agenda on schedule . . . in itself an achievement . . . and got board support for all the positions that needed it. I was most happy that Willy Wyler won the Life Achievement Award. He deserves it, if any living film maker does. I phoned him in San Francisco and he seemed really touched and delighted.

October 22. The rough assembly on the first two sections of our AFI Bicentennial film really knocked me out. You forget how many marvelous films have been made, and how scenes from them can be cut together and interrelated, as Jim Silke and George have done, so that the total is more than the sum of the parts. The prologue, using footage of the *Mayflower* from PLYMOUTH ADVENTURE, GODFATHER II, AMERICA, AMERICA, says some moving things about the immigrant surge to the New World. This can be the best thing that's happened to the AFI. Also to the Bicentennial.

October 23. Universal's pressing for an answer on TWO-MINUTE WARNING, since they need a reply before I leave on location. This is reasonable, but I want to brood about it a bit. It's a good script, but another multiple-jeopardy film. Damn! Lunch today was interesting, as public relations dates go. The secretary of the navy was very informative about the Soviet navy's capabilities and intentions. A bit scary, too. I believe him . . . not certain whether the power base (is it those fine fellas in the media, or Congress?) does, too. Holly's current favorites, two young actors whose chemistry makes their show work well, were very nice to her on the location of *Starsky and Hutch*. We watched a routine setup, but she enjoyed it . . . so I did, too.

October 24. A very fine film-oriented day: I saw two of them, and decided to do another (TWO-MINUTE WARNING), and finalized plans for the location on my current one. After depositing my daughter en route to her weekend in the mountains, I had a meeting with the producer and the director of what it appears will be my next film. A good story; I play a cop. I think this may turn out well (or is it that it's an easy job?). MIDWAY will work, I think, though I saw it without dubbing, color, balance, or score. My performance is not much . . . only adequate, especially since we've cut some of the telling personal textures. This is the risk of a part in a piece of this kind. Still, I think it'll work overall very well.

October 26 (Sunday), Tucson. For some reason, I can always remember with sharp clarity the departures for the locations. Over all the years and all the films, some of the details of the shooting fade, but I can remember enplaning for the first location, in Las Vegas . . . to Sarasota, and Cairo, and Rome, and Madrid, and Phoenix, and Rapid City . . . and all the others. The flurry of packing, and the pressure on Lydia, who came happily with me to the plane today. The city's OK and my quarters are first class. They gave me the private hiding place I seem to need on location.

October 27. So I began . . . what is it? The forty-eighth? Something like that. I now never do a film in the U.S. without finding some crew members I've worked with before. Oddly, though, I know few of the actors in this one. Andy [*McLaglen, the director*] seems to know what he's doing. It's too soon to tell about the cameraman, but sound and the other major departments will be OK, I think. The wardrobe man left my pants in L.A., but recovered them in time for the shooting.

October 28. This was the first day we really had a scene to play. I was able to make what I'm convinced are crucial improvements in the dialogue in the manner I've come to depend on . . . selling them on the set, after working them out there, too. It's curious, but I really can do this best walking around the set in wardrobe and makeup. Now the man sounds righter for Tucson in 1910 than he did before. We had to do a retake of me reading a telegram because I forgot I'd planned to play him, as a retired gunfighter, farsighted enough to need glasses for reading and did the take without them. I find myself comfortable with Andy.

November 3. We started a little late today, to turn the company around from day interiors into night for night exteriors. [*Day for night is what you see on television shows. To actually shoot at night is very time-consuming.*] I was glad to shoot on a sound stage again. It's a very small one, but a handy adjunct to this location setup; it allows you full cover. [*Shooting on location, you always try to have an interior set to which you can retreat in case of bad weather. A "cover set."*] I found myself using my father's silent laugh in a scene, for the first time I can recall. I'm beginning to get some kind of dimension to this guy, though I have curiously ambiguous feelings about the script. Apparently the studio is ecstatic . . . the kind of report I've learned to be skeptical about.

November 5. I was delighted to discover they'd shifted the schedule so I could finish tonight, then have next week off, barring bad weather, when I'd have to go back for the cover stuff we have indoors. Shooting was easy today . . . the first scene with Barbara Hershey went OK. She seems an intelligent, able actress, and looks dead right for the part. As has often happened before, I barely finished my last shot in time to leap out of my clothes and spirit gum, into the car for the dash to the airport, then home to the bosom of my family.

November 26, Los Angeles. Lydia's Aunt Ruth is with us. I admire enormously the resolute good will, at eighty-four, with which she deals with the problems of age and loneliness. Oddly enough, she seems in far better spirits now than I recall her twenty years ago. There are lessons in her example. I'm trying to set up meetings on the London MACBETH, which is rather daunting, the more I think about it . . . I will be the first American actor to do Shakespeare in the West End since John Barrymore did it. Still, there it is, waiting like Everest for Mallory. (Now, *there's* an inspiring simile.)

I've since remembered Orson Welles played Lear in London, but the list of Americans playing Shakespeare in the seat of his glory is a dauntingly short one.

November 28. MACBETH looks more and more likely for summer, somewhat to my surprise. Peter Wood called from London; he's willing and probably available to direct. I seem to be falling into a pattern of getting not very challenging parts in huge commercial successes in films, thus allowing me the freedom to do the real giants on the stage. It could be worse.

November 29. Lydia's unimpressed with TWO-MINUTE WARNING, for which I can't blame her. Again, they're meeting Herman's very tough deal for me to play a relatively small part in a film in which I'm regarded as an insurance policy. There's more talk at Universal of MACARTHUR, but I'm dubious of this coming through.

December 2, Rio Rico. We're slowing down a bit. I really had very little to do tonight and had to wait some time to do it. Jimmy Coburn is not a fast actor, which is OK; fast acting is no great virtue. On the other hand, slow acting isn't either. He likes to discuss, to have things explained and argued through. This is fine, too, but it can be an indulgence. To want to change and improve the scenes is, God knows, something I understand, but you have to know what you want. If you don't, and often Jimmy doesn't, then you have to *do* it. His questions are better than his answers. Still, he's very good in the part. He's made a brave choice to use none of the smiling charm he's used so effectively in other roles.

December 3. With Joe [*Canutt*]'s help, I beat Grant to death very effectively tonight and got back to the hotel in time for a decent meal. Later, when the company came in, I asked Morgan Paul (who plays the vilest of my daughter's despoilers) if they'd dilled him off yet. "Oh, no," he said, "When you rape Chuck Heston's daughter, you don't die easy!"

December 9. Though all Joe's planning on the special effects and the choreography of the fight worked well, we didn't finish the tag scene. I'm afraid this was primarily because Barbara had arrived at a curious idea for playing it. She somehow felt her line of action in the scene should be rage (at all the killing, thus telling us something about violence?). In any event, you cannot play this while simultaneously comforting your desperately wounded father, which is what she had to do. We fiddled about with this endlessly, with little success. I'm afraid we would've blown the scene completely, except that it can probably be cut around her. It's all very strange. She's really very good in the rest of the part and has been totally professional in the film so far.

December 11. We finished the film before lunch, shooting some four pages of five different scenes in four different locations. It was all good stuff, too. There's a lot to be said for mosaic-polishing away at a scene as Wyler does . . . if you're Wyler. Most of the time, though, after a certain point you don't really get it better, only slower, no matter how much you're enjoying masturbating through the thing. All in all, I think we turned out very well with this one. My estimate of the cast rose throughout the shooting, and I think I did quite well, too. I'll have to wait for the rough cut before I can make a clearer judgment.

December 12, Los Angeles. I took Walter's script out of my battered green leather binder (how many of those binders have I gone through now, I wonder . . . four . . . five?) and put in Ed Feldman's for the next one. I went in for a conference with them and found that for clarity the agreement to have Joe handle the action scenes as a second unit has somehow dissolved. I really consider that a little tricky on their part, though I'm partly at fault for getting into it late, too. It can be a rotten business, sometimes.

December 17. I spent breakfast trying to communicate to John West [*Jolly and Kay's son*] some of the problems of making a living as an actor, a profession he seems intent on. I hope I made some sense. The Wyler seminar for the Fellows at the AFI this evening went well. Willy doesn't communicate verbally as well as he does with a camera, but what he has to say is worth listening to. His summing up was great: "Don't be boring."

December 22. For what must be something like the twenty or thirtieth time, old Doc Gourson checked my blood pressure for the huge insurance policy the studio takes out on me. How they determine that's all he needs to do, I don't know. Perhaps my never having had a claim or missed an hour of work has something to do with it. [*Boasting again!*] It really took much longer to pick my wardrobe, and God knows *that* couldn't be simpler, consisting of one cheap suit off the rack.

December 25. One of the advantages of having your children growing up is that they sleep in a bit on Christmas. I remember when they were small, they'd be shrieking with eager delight by six in the morning. We had a later and leisured start this year, and a fine day, with too many presents, as always. Nevertheless, it was a happy time.

1976

Henry VIII in
London . . .

a Far East tour
for *Midway* . . .

submarining in
Gray Lady Down . . .

the Ahmanson again
for *Long Day's
Journey into Night.*

As James Tyrone in
Long Day's Journey into Night
at the Ahmanson
LYDIA HESTON

January 8, London. My over-the-Pole technique gave me three hours of sleep, then I lunched with the producers on the projected MACBETH. I'm filled with ill-formed anxieties on this thing. Partly it's just the thought of being gone from home so long, partly the recognition that I may come out of it with little credit, certainly with no money. Nevertheless . . . *those are the parts.* If you don't play them, what are you doing? The theater is a perfect size . . . 1066 seats, though the stage is small for Shakespeare.

January 10. I thought all fashionable stage directors, especially the English, were bearded, disheveled types. Michael Blakemore isn't. He's a short-haired Australian with a tie, but he's done an impressive number of plays at the National. I also like what he said and what he seemed to think about the play. For the first time my mood, which has verged on black despair (panic?) all during this trip, lightened.

January 11 (Sunday), To Los Angeles. I've closed my bag so many times in the Dorchester suites, sliding it off the slick taffeta spreads, pressing the button for the porter . . . meeting the car down below at the sweep of the drive. They've taken out the statue of St. George and put in new phones, but it's still really the same place, and if I do the play here in London, it will surely be my main comfort . . . the closest thing I know to home away from home. Now Pan Am doesn't even have the polar route I rode so many times . . . but the Pole below is the same and the vast seas of cloud, coming home, coming home.

January 14, Los Angeles. Rough cuts are always difficult to judge, and allowances must be made. On the other hand, you have to keep a harsh eye honed to look at your own work. It's hard to strike a balance between the two. HARD MAN, on first look, seems OK, but not fantastic. I like what I do pretty much and what Coburn does very much. It needs a lot of looping, some sharpening.

January 15. I began work in TWO-MINUTE WARNING. It must be about my fiftieth film and should be successful, but not memorable. [*It was neither.*] I played a forgettable scene on the roof of the Los Angeles Coliseum with Marty Balsam, not a forgettable actor. I just wish I could find a better piece to do. (MACBETH, I guess, is a better piece.)

January 19. Early this morning (the classic time for overseas calls) Elliot phoned to say Blakemore's not free to direct MACBETH. The news was ironic, just as I'd conquered my misgivings about the project. Now I'm uncertain what to do. I put in calls to both Peter Snell and Bobby Fryer to have them do some research on another director the producers now like. I must be sure we're not barrel-scraping here.

January 20. Both Bobby Fryer and Peter Snell called back with negative reports on the director I'd asked them about. Later, on the Paramount back lot where he's shooting MARATHON MAN, Larry Olivier confirmed their judgment. Wandering around the studio's New York street waiting for Larry, I found myself standing in the false-front store entrance where I made my first setup in my first film, twenty-six years ago. Christ, but I've exposed a good many miles of raw stock since then . . .

January 21. Elliot and Jay are frantic at the thought of my not doing the London MACBETH. I discussed with Herman my growing conviction this won't work now. To do MACBETH in London would be fine, but not unless it can be the best I can do. As this stands, I can't feel it would be.

January 25. It's a highly instructive experience, playing tennis for a lot of money. Somewhat to my surprise, certainly to my relief, I played fairly well. We won, as it turned out, handily, though we lost the first three games. Martin, as he often does, began very tight. Fortunately, I managed to be steady till he loosened and began to hit winners. By the second set, he was flying. It was a good sign that, even in poor lighting, when neither of us could return that well, we could still break serve. I gave him my share of the two thousand dollars, of course. My reward, a rich one, was functioning well in a competitive situation.

This was the first match of a round robin pro-celebrity tennis circuit organized to raise money for the Muscular Dystrophy Fund, with prize money contributed by Hiram Walker. My partner was Martin Shafer, who'd played doubles with Fray in high school. He was by this time a law student and a formidable player.

January 26. I shot on TWO MINUTE WARNING again . . . when I'd all but decided they'd recast the part, it's been so long since they called me. I had little to do, but find myself a good bit more comfortable with Larry Peerce than I thought I would be. He has an extravagant manner, but he's very bright.

January 27. We hacked away at a series of tiny scenes. There are over five hundred scene numbers in the script . . . most of them one eighth of a page. Larry likes to improvise. I usually improvise about fifteen percent of my lines . . . but I do it walking around waiting for the camera . . . trying it till it comes right, then setting it. I think you have to get it right first, then get it good. True improvisation works just the reverse of that.

January 29. I accepted a firm offer today from Walter Mirisch for his
submarine film, which precludes my doing the MACBETH. I'm sorry not
to be doing it, but there'll be one more chance, sometime.

February 5. I felt good about the work today, though they finished me
early in order to get me out to the studio for lunch with some
overseas executives, who professed the most extravagant admiration
for MIDWAY. It may do more than EARTHQUAKE, they claim. I then
talked with Walter Mirisch about casting on GRAY LADY DOWN. He
had been entertaining ideas about Sidney Poitier, which he's now
backing away from, though I'm not clear why, save the cost of
having us both in the film. We'll see where we go with it.

February 12. My son is twenty-one today. At the same time, he's vividly
newborn, serene in his mother's arms, waving as a three-year-old
from the train coming into the year in Rome, leaping off the furniture
to my arms at five, grimly intent at twelve with a racket and no
backhand, shooting a wild pig at fifteen, and rafting us down the
Salmon at nineteen. He is also a whole and decent man, I think. The
day he was born I was acting with Sal Mineo, who was stabbed to
death today in a random street assault . . . poor soul.

February 18. This was a very busy day, largely doing unpaid acting and
practicing for paid tennis. (Things have surely gotten confused here,
somehow.) Citron and I decided I was doing too many films. In his
opinion, this is why I didn't get MACARTHUR, despite his expert
pressure. I don't quite buy this. Still, greater selectivity, thus even
fewer films than I do now, would be the answer, if it's true.

February 19. I spent almost the entire morning on what should've been a
one-hour chore, shooting TV promos for the Academy show. The crew
and the producer were all very green. (It's downright scary, as I
move through my third decade in this profession, to realize how
really green a crew can be.) They began by neglecting to tell me not
to wear a black jacket, since they were using a black backdrop, then
fussed and fidgeted through eight takes for every setup (none
chargeable to me, by my fierce, Calvinist standards). It all worked
out, of course, in the end.

February 23. This film's a very curious experience for me; my work in it
is so fragmented and spasmodic that I don't really feel that I'm doing
a movie . . . I don't feel the kind of *commitment* you need for a film.
I like Peerce, but I keep feeling his film is intruding on my days,
which is an absolutely appalling attitude.

February 26. Visiting Walter Seltzer fits in very well with my early
morning schedule, and it seems to cheer him. I suspect you don't get

many early morning visitors in hospitals. [*Walter had gone in to repair a retina detached while we were in Arizona shooting* LAST HARD MAN.] I then went to the Mirisch office to discuss the MIDWAY publicity tour (a very fat, very demanding schedule) and GRAY LADY DOWN. There's still not much progress on the script. He wants to postpone it a little, which may be OK. Casting still goes slow, but we'll have time to mull on all this. The director is another question.

March 2. The main thing I did today was read O'Neill's lacerating masterpiece LONG DAY'S JOURNEY INTO NIGHT. I'd seen it more than once, including the world premiere performance, but had never read it. It's a major piece, of course, arguably the best American play. What does that mean? I guess it means it's one of those plays you *have* to do. It doesn't matter if you're any good, or if anyone likes it . . . you *have* to do it, once you're faced with it. As I said to Peter Wood, when he suggested it at lunch yesterday, "You . . . son . . . of . . . a . . . bitch!" Actually, there's a great deal in this part I can empathize with. Perhaps this partly defines great art, but it gives me a handle on the role I need, as I need my size and physicality for MACBETH. I understand James Tyrone and his problems on a far more specific level than I can Macbeth.

March 3. Curious irony: A day after I agreed to do LONG DAY, I get another offer for an O'Neill play, A TOUCH OF THE POET, in New York. I was polite, of course, because I was flattered, but I can't do two plays. Besides, I know POET and find it a smaller work. LONG DAY is his masterpiece, I think.

March 9. The AFI Wyler dinner, which should've been a triumph, was something like a disaster. The taped version for TV will work, of course, but in trying to serve the TV show, we failed Willy and all the friends who came to honor him. Mostly it was just technical fuck-ups. (Frank Schaffner said to me, "Remember when we used to do these things live?") I don't know who screwed up on the seating, the room amplification, or the film clips, but I know the producer is ultimately on the spot. This time, it's not the catbird seat. *God,* I'd like this to have gone perfectly!

March 22. I surely shot a full day today, mostly the geographics of getting up into the tower. We didn't do the interior, since it wasn't finished to Peerce's satisfaction, but skipped ahead to do the death of the sniper. This may have given me a character resolution the script didn't. Now my character moves in the end to the icy contempt for the sniper that is the SWAT leader's position through the rest of the script. We arrived at an exchange with the dying sniper that I think works well, based on the standard police procedure of trying to get a dying declaration. LAST HARD MAN, on the other hand, is now being recut a little. The second sneak was not as successful as the first.

March 24. The set we're working in now is one of the most interesting I've shot on: a set with twenty-four TV monitors flickering with shots of the game supposedly taking place while the scene played; blimp shots, players, Howard Cosell and Don Meredith. Peerce is using real TV game crews for the personnel in the truck. This creates a useful core of reality . . . they can ad-lib in the background with total verisimilitude. It should be good stuff.

March 29, Washington. I seem to have completed acting in my fiftieth film, God save the mark. This not only counts both the 16mm for David Bradley, but fifteen or twenty that I shouldn't have done, or at least should've done better, across the last quarter century.

April 2, Los Angeles. I read the script for THE PRINCE AND THE PAUPER, in which David Salkind (and director Richard Fleischer) wants me to do Henry VIII as a two-week cameo in late May. The script, by George McDonald Fraser, is really quite good, but I don't know if I should do another film now.

April 5. I spent all day recording Hemingway's THE OLD MAN AND THE SEA for Caedmon. It was worth skipping lunch for, it's reasonable to say. It wasn't an easy choice . . . its structure is highly subjective, hard to render in dramatic terms. It's such a helluva good book, though; a very challenging thing to work on. It was also rewarding to hear that Mary Hemingway would only allow Caedmon the rights to record the piece at all if I were stipulated as the reader. I'm proud to have done it, hope very much that it turns out. [*It did, even managing a Grammy nomination.*]

April 6. Herman's just about nailed up the deal to do Henry VIII in PRINCE AND THE PAUPER [*released as* CROSSED SWORDS]. It could be very interesting . . . and a good switch from recent roles. The makeup will be the great problem.

April 9. I've been working on the Henry makeup with Ziggy. He says it would be a mistake to try for a total likeness. Henry's round fleshy face is something I can only reach with makeup so heavy it becomes a mask . . . and that's death to a performance. I agree. We had an invitational screening of LAST HARD MAN tonight. It seemed good to me, even with some cuts I'd opposed, but I thought the (invited) audience response was muted, and courteous.

April 14. Birthdays have not always been happy days for Lydia, but this one was valuable . . . the first day I can remember in weeks when she was entirely free of migraine. This as much as the necklace I had Marie Shafer design for her gave us both a happy birthday.

April 19. Bobby Fryer called. We're now on the point of offering Deborah Kerr the role of Mary Tyrone in LONG DAY'S JOURNEY. I think she'd be close to ideal for the part, and good casting in marquee terms too.

April 24, Dallas. A new technique for covering an area for a public relations tour, which I first remember a couple of years ago touring for SOYLENT GREEN, has now been refined. Aside from the usual schedule for the metropolitan dailies, I accomplished thirty-one filmed interviews today, with TV reporters from as far away as Tulsa and Corpus Christi. This is really using your time. It's not really all that exhausting; you waste no time at all bounding around town in the back of a limo, or waiting for some cookery show to finish taping so you can get on and sing your piece. It's the best way to do it, no question.

April 28. This was much more a traditional kind of public relations day . . . even down to the visit to the film exchange that used to be mandatory in every city you stopped in. The offices are small now, and all the companies are concentrated in one modern building instead of each in its own art deco four-story building on Film Row, with the manager's office and the booker's cubicles and the old ladies with white gloves inspecting film in the basement. My back was a bit stiff today, so I skipped tennis and took a massage instead. I want to be in shape for the King of the Hill matches in Detroit.

This was another stop on the pro-celebrity circuit I spoke of. We lost this one, not because my back was bad, because my play was.

May 3, London. It seems a much shorter trip, flying from Detroit, but it's all relative, of course. In fact, arriving later in the morning in London means you don't have a chance to sleep at all before lunch, which is absolutely vital to the success of the whole Heston Polar Plan. Never mind, it all worked OK. The suite's beautiful, so is London. Plans for the film seem to be proceeding apace, and Dick Fleischer is in good spirits. We were unable to do tests today, but tomorrow will be fine.

May 4. All morning at Berman's [*the theatrical costume house*] on Henry's clothes, then much of the evening trying to work out the makeup. I really could hardly look less like Henry, save for my height and big frame. It's certainly possible to pad up for the flesh he carried in his last months, but it wouldn't match with my face.

Besides, if you load on too much, both for face and figure, we'll have a makeup, not a performance. I think we got close to what we want today. The Spanish makeup man was on THREE MUSKETEERS. He seems to know what he's doing, though he's altered some elements of Ziggy's original concept of the makeup. You have to let a man express his own creative instincts.

I've hidden behind a startling number of complex makeups, but this was surely one of the trickiest.

May 5. Much of the day was spent doing public relations, which is OK. The interviews can be held for later use, and we had time to get some of them out of the way on this trip. Yesterday's tests looked OK too. I'm quite content; we were able to get the makeup away from my own image, which is really our aim, I think. We shaved off my eyebrows and padded my nostrils, also experimented with appliances to pad my cheeks, but discarded these; they alter my voice. I think we have it, really. The part should be fun, which is a lot more than can be said for the play tonight. This Pinter, let me go on record, is bloody dull, even with two Sirs, Gielgud and Richardson, acting their brilliant best. I also walked into a glass door and cut my nose, but that was going out, not coming in.

May 13, Los Angeles. My last day here for some time, and glad to have it go so well. I crowded in all the last-minute responsibilities waiting for me this week, and felt I'd buttoned things up for my time away. Lydia's pleased to be going to London, as who would not be? *I* am.

May 17, England. I've started off on the fifty-first. A long commute, to a very impressive great house we're using for Henry's palace. The makeup is onerous and takes almost two hours . . . the longest I can recall since the older Moses makeups. I'm able to sleep through some of it, though [*I'm boasting, but it's true*] the result is spectacular; I'm as physically changed as I've ever been. It's not far off old Hal, either. As for my characterization, I'm searching for it a bit still, which is OK, since we shot only on my back all day. Penshurst helps, in the way a good location always does. Henry was actually a guest here . . . he seems to have left a shadow or two.

As often happens, the setting gave me a great deal for this role. To play Henry in a house where he had stayed somehow worked very usefully for me.

May 20, London. We shot the scene with the boy again: It's good now. Dick [*Fleischer*] and I have planned the blocking well to show Henry's physical decline through these scenes preceding Hal's death: limping in the first, then reclining on a couch, then in bed. Tonight

Lydia and I had dinner with Bobby and Peter, with much talk about LONG DAY'S JOURNEY. That will be a mountain.

May 21. Hal's death went very well. Actors love to play death scenes, of course, and I've played more than my share, surely, but this fearsome old tyrant's demise seemed a better than ordinary opportunity . . . gasping away in that great bed like a beached whale. We used Henry's real last words: "Monks . . . monks . . . monks."

May 24. We started again at Pinewood, which remains one of my very favorite studios in the world . . . perhaps in part because it's near London. They've gone to self-service in the restaurant (which was the best of any studio anywhere), a sign of sinking Britain, I suppose. I like the British crews, too. They now even lack that touchiness about work rules that used to be a complication of shooting here. The collapse of the English film industry has changed all that; now everyone's full of eagerness to show how well it can be done. Once again, happily, the shots were all over my shoulder today, giving me time to play with the scene before I'm committed to my shots.

May 25. They got around to me today. The whole scene's only five and a half pages, but it *is* complex, with entrances, exits, intercuts across the hall, three dances . . . and old Hal sitting there with his sore foot in a girl's lap, alternating between vindictive gloom and roaring jollity. In a way, he's an easy character to play, because he's full of high-colored extremes. Also, the spectacle of power is always fascinating. The old actors' adage about the foolproof nature of drunks and madmen as roles should maybe be extended to include tyrants . . . especially fat ones. Also, as in Shakespeare, kings always get to sit down.

May 31. Our last day in London was spent at a shrine to England's greatness. Coventry Cathedral is magnificent in its ruined defiance, from a time when Englishmen viewed themselves differently. They've built a new cathedral there, too, decorated with the fruits of English genius, which is still green.

June 1, Washington, D.C. I'd toyed with the thought of flying to D.C. on the Concorde, just beginning supersonic service on a trial basis, but a British Airways captain at a party advised against it. "You're too tall, I'm afraid. The Concorde's a lovely aircraft, but it discriminates against two classes of people: the poor and the tall." So we flew on the 747; comfortable, if subsonic. D.C. was steamy, but the suite's cool. We settled in, some hours ahead of our cohorts from Los Angeles. Lydia slept, I flushed my blood around with a good hit indoors.

June 2. MIDWAY press tour . . . the day was very full, as it was designed to be. A little blurred around the edges in terms of planning the filming of interviews . . . as compared with the Fox schedule in Dallas . . . but all went *reasonably* well. Hank Fonda seems not entirely well yet, but is obviously determined to keep his commitments. It's like him.

June 3. I went to the Pentagon for a navy briefing on carriers . . . then lunch with the secretary of the navy, the secretary of defense, and assorted admirals. The day was crammed with schedule, of course, but quite a lot of it was interesting, all of it worth doing. I found the Pentagon briefing fascinating and a little reassuring. Odd to note that Rumsfeld, secretary of defense, is a fellow New Trier High alumnus, in my kid brother's class. An easy trip to New York (by limo, for the last leg) and was shocked to find Danny's closed. That was the best steak in New York. [*It's reopened, thank God.*]

June 4, New York/Nashville. The Regency is a nicer hotel than the Sherry, but the city's deteriorated badly in the year or so since I was here last. Now they regard the hotels as armed camps, more or less, instructing you as to what must be locked in the safe (money, air tickets, jewelry, passports). The schedule was full, but with no surprises. We should be getting some good exposure here. Lydia held up well on the trip to Nashville, which is still as pretty a city as I remember when we were here for THE PRESIDENT'S LADY twenty-five years ago. Coming here from New York you get the feeling that you're out of the trenches, back in what is increasingly valued as Middle America. [*I took a day out of the tour to go to Nashville for another King of the Hill match. We won this one.*]

June 8, New York. The day began very early, very rushed, but I managed well enough, considering the pressures of the schedule. Still, the rest of the day wasn't too demanding, assuming my capacity for sleep in airplanes. The filmed interviews went predictably, and one assumes the value to the film will be well worth the energy invested. Maybe that's why I'm still around when so many of my peers are doing TV commercials . . . or nothing. Still, I'm as much of a salesman as Willy Loman ever was. It's just that the life is considerably easier . . . and I know the territory.

June 9, Chicago. After a night in Wilmette, where it became clear that Mother's new house, though much smaller than the old place on Maple, actually has more useful space for them, I checked into the hotel the studios are now using (the Ambassador having sunk slowly into neglect). It's hard to imagine the Pump Room closed, nevertheless. Eating in the Pump Room was one part of the celebrity life that seemed all it was supposed to be. I noted again how very effective Donahue is on TV, relying almost totally on his studio audience of Middle American women. I'm surprised that his format is not copied more . . . or at all.

June 21, Tokyo.

Where I'd gone on the first leg of an extensive tour of the Far East, promoting MIDWAY.

The family went off touring while I settled into what is not really a very formidable public relations schedule here. All of it is in the hotel; a pleasant improvement over the days I well remember when you had to slop about from studio to studio. The video tape recorder's a great blessing for actors doing public relations tours. I did all the things I've learned so well, their value never clearer than here in Japan. Mifune turned up as well (which was kind of him). We got a formidable chunk of space, plus TV time. Happy news from the U.S.: Walter reports that the first three days of the film are tremendous. "Ahead of EARTHQUAKE." It may not hold, but it's heartening word. This one has the feel of it, somehow. I went to a geisha dinner tonight; surely one of the last holdouts of male chauvinism.

June 22. There are special problems in giving interviews in a language you neither speak nor understand. It takes longer, so your patience is strained (and impatience is fatal in interviews); also you're not sure what's really being communicated. In the end, both the questions and the answers get very simplified, which means you tend to become bored about the seventh time a journalist begins by having the interpreter say, "Perhaps you have heard some of these questions before, but . . ." Still, this is a major audience for me . . . I must hang in. I *am* hanging in. The family seems to be enjoying Kyoto and Nara.

June 23, Manila. It's been a helluva time since I was last here, in '60 for BEN-HUR. The country seems more clearly independent of the U.S. now and somewhat more prosperous under martial law, distressing though both these observations may seem to different groups, for opposite reasons. The hotel suite is one of the most luxurious I've ever been in, which covers a good bit, when you think of it. No further word from the U.S. on the MIDWAY business (how greedy we become for news of success), but Walter Seltzer cables that Fox had a good opening of LAST HARD MAN in London and is now considering a new U.S. effort in August. Lydia had the usual problems on the flight, but rested in the evening while Holly and Fray shopped, then was fine tonight. We were treated to a spectacular sunset, just off the end of our terrace, followed by an equally spectacular cloudburst.

June 25, Hong Kong. This day was really something of a bitch. We took off late . . . our plane was delayed out of San Francisco, or some such . . . just squeaking out ahead of a tropical storm, after racing to the airport in dramatic style with a motorcycle escort. (Manila must be one of the few cities in the free world where this is still possible.) We stayed in Hong Kong just long enough for me to do the interviews, then we worked our way through a full-drill Chinese dinner (I'd always thought bird's nest soup really had little black twigged nests in it, somehow), then on the plane and off for Sydney. It was a helluva pressure on Lydia, but she didn't want to miss Hong Kong. They had time to visit the floating bazaars.

June 26, Sydney, Australia. I slept quite well flying down over the China Sea, then went up front for the spectacular approach to the city, which I remembered. If you're going to ride on the flight deck, coming down over Sydney Harbor is the place to do it. The Aussie press met me with a cold can of Foster's, which was welcome. Lydia and Holly napped; Fray and I went out for tennis at Cary Packer's. (I remember his father entertaining me there when I was first out here, in '60.) We had a fine day: plenty of tennis with the likes of Adrian Quist, who still plays well, and David Frost, who still doesn't. Fray was able to make some connections through Cary Packer for his blue water sailing.

June 28. The schedule (eight interviews and a cocktail reception) speaks for itself. I can manage a day like this without too much strain, but it's really taxing. I'm amused at how often an interviewer, usually a young one, will say confidently . . . "Now, I know how tired you must be of answering the same questions over and over. We'll just talk in a very offhand, *informal* way, of all *kinds* of things, and get a *different* interview." They then proceed to ask exactly the same questions everyone else has asked, of course. We all ate in the suite, then Lydia and Holly went early to bed against their trip to the Outback. [*They were determined to see the Australian desert most tourists miss.*]

July 2, Sydney/Los Angeles. Fray and I were to play doubles with Rosewall before taking off for the States, but we were rained out of that. I'd gotten up at four in the morning to meet Lydia and Holly, who were stranded in the Outback by a hostess strike: They had to struggle back to Sydney in a chartered light plane. They really had a horrible ride, but managed a gallant recovery by the time we got on the 747. The flight was compressed by the dateline; we eventually arrived back in Los Angeles only an hour and a half after taking off from Sydney. Once you've done three or four thousand miles, you don't feel any more tired, no matter how far you go. Still, I was damn glad to put my head down on my own pillow tonight.

July 3, Philadelphia. Both Fray and Holly fell by the wayside at home, but my girl pressed on regardless, to share tomorrow with me. (We've decided not to stay on for the dinner with the queen of England, though.) When we checked into the hotel in Philadelphia, I was so tired that I accepted with weary docility Mayor Rizzo's decision to take over my introduction of the president tomorrow. I don't like controversies where my ego might seem involved. Lydia pointed out how foolish this was, and I saw she was right. I called them back and said I really preferred to either do what they had invited me to fly from Australia for, or go home. I will introduce the president.

July 4, Philadelphia/Los Angeles. As master of ceremonies for the Bicentennial proceedings, and to introduce President Ford. It really was a glorious Fourth . . . not only in Philadelphia, but, as nearly as TV could convey it, all over the country. This was a proper two hundredth birthday party. I did what I was supposed to do, and I was proud to be there, as a performer and as a citizen. It was fine to walk with Lydia through the easy, happy crowds afterward, savoring the city.

July 5, Los Angeles. Today I was home, with no trip hanging over me. In the last seven weeks, I've visited eighteen cities in five countries . . . six, if you count Hong Kong. I've made part of one picture, sold the hell out of another one; played in two tennis tournaments, raising considerable money for the Muscular Dystrophy Fund; and introduced a president. So much for a quiet summer.

July 29. Bobby called from London in distress: Deborah Kerr wants first billing for LONG DAY'S JOURNEY INTO NIGHT. That hasn't happened to me since NAKED JUNGLE, with Eleanor Parker. I find it irritating, but it's nonsense, really. We want her in the part, we'll give her the billing. (I remember what Spencer Tracy said, though, to a similar proposal made by Katharine Hepburn. "What about ladies first?" she said. "This is a movie, not a lifeboat," he snorted.)

July 30. Tony's problem turned out to be a malignant tumor, against all expectations. It's hard to lose a good dog . . . even if he's a long step below Drago. Their deaths and the graves I dug were the same. The grass waits for all of us. The AFI film tonight played well for an audience. But in all honesty, it's not great [*though I'd originally thought it was*].

August 1. A quiet Sunday on the ridge, with Fray away on the white water. Tony's in his grave where the children's slide molders into the brush. Lydia is fighting a migraine, but Holly is sanguine, as always. That's a colorless word. She bubbles, really, but she's a long, long way from bubble-headed. At fifteen, she knows where she is, where the world is, and has a clear idea of the pressures that surround her. At the same time, she has a basic optimism and a warm kind of *charity* about things that supports her strongly. My best moments today were spent with her improving Tony's grave.

August 7, Seattle, Washington. I was filled with a strange malaise all day, which conceivably was a factor in our startling straight-set loss to the easiest team on the King of the Hill circuit. Also, the fact that the lights were bad (Martin and I are the only players who wear glasses). But the major element was overconfidence, I think, plus the fact that the other team played very well. I was able to accept the defeat, but Bill Cosby, whom I'd always thought the coolest of performers, was completely unable to handle his loss in the other match. He decided in the first game that his professional partner was not strong enough, and thereupon proceeded to tank the match in the most flagrant fashion possible. It was appallingly embarrassing to watch . . . he was actually booed. Actors can be horrible people.

August 9, Under the Pacific off San Diego. I spent the day on a nuclear submarine, soaking in some atmosphere for GRAY LADY DOWN. They're incredible craft. It was much like the *Lexington* its display of a high level of a vast array of disparate and complex skills by every man of the crew. It was a very strange feeling to spend hours charging about under the ocean running mock torpedo attacks on a formation of surface vessels, which had no success whatever at avoiding us. I also got a lot of useful little stuff about the look and sound of submarine officers at work . . . the kind of thing nobody could tell you.

August 10, Los Angeles. Back to O'Neill today, after too long doing other things. The sons are not easy to cast. Bruce Dern would be ideal for Jamie, but we still don't know about him. None of the actors we read was remarkable in either part. Peter Wood has a marvelous way with actors reading for roles, easing them into it, giving them some insight on the play. I learned from the day, but we didn't find anyone.

August 13. The best news of the day . . . of the week . . . was a call from Bruce Dern committing himself to Jamie in LONG DAY'S JOURNEY. He has his misgivings and professional anxieties, all of which I understand. Still, in the end you come down to the part . . . and it's a great part. He will be world class in it, I think. Black, mordant charm. That's Jamie, and that's Bruce's color.

August 20. The usual rush agenda for the last day. Walter Mirisch has still not made a deal with Stacy Keach for GRAY LADY DOWN. On the plus side, I played reasonable tennis, my son came home, my weight is 208, and MIDWAY now looks like it'll do over forty million dollars in

the world. I've not yet worked through all of the Peter Wood cuts for
LONG DAY'S JOURNEY, but they seem right. The piece must be
shortened, clearly.

August 21, Madrid.

> *We were en route for another sailing vacation in the Greek
> Islands. As before, the Isaacs and the Seltzers were with us, this
> time the Wests as well. I'd stopped in Spain for some publicity
> chores.*

One of those endless airplane days. You feel cocooned, cut off from
the world and time, floating on Scotch at thirty-eight thousand feet.
Lydia's not in great shape, but she's aboard, and eager. If she can get
through this trip and get some of the pleasure from Greece she needs
and dreams of, then we can get her well again.

August 22. Madrid seems little changed since Franco, though much
changed since EL CID. Even the Hilton's run down now. They have us
in a fine new hotel, the Villa Magna. Lydia was badly jet-lagged and
went at once to bed. I followed my usual routine: slept two hours,
then tennised, and had a good meal with the public relations people
and my daughter.

August 23. A full day of interviews, complicated by the necessity of doing
them in Spanish. This requires intense concentration for me, but I
was surprised to find my Spanish has slightly improved, somehow.
Dinner tonight was in a restaurant I remember from the EL CID days.

August 24. This was a slightly lighter day, especially since we had a
no-show. One of the journalists was a thorny, truculent type . . . I
finally daunted him by offering to write his piece for him. I did, too, in
the veiled, adversary terms he obviously had in mind. I took Bea and
Luis to dinner (Horcher's is still good), but Lydia was unable to stay
the course. This is one of the roughest migraines she's had, poor
baby.

August 25, Rome. The plane to Rome was late, and I was saddened to
find the city deteriorated visibly in ten years. The modern city, I
mean; the ancient stones remain the same, but the Hilton looks
terrible. Lydia rested. The rest of us went out to dinner and then
drove around checking the major sites. I wanted Holly to see them
since she can't recall them from when she was here the summer we
did AGONY AND THE ECSTASY.

August 27, Messina. On board the Occita *to begin our voyage to the
Ionian Sea.* Lydia was very ill, but she was determined not to hold
up the sailing. I got her on board, then, while she slept, we cast off

and sailed down the Straits of Messina past the classic Scylla and Charybdis, and around the toe of the Italian boot. The boat is not quite so racy as *Lisa* was, but is slightly roomier. Oddly, it doesn't seem so. Perhaps, as we grow older, we become less tolerant, and expect more luxury. I'm also slightly gloomy: concerned about my girl.

August 28. At sea all day, bearing northeast for Corfu. We were under sail most of the time, in a very light breeze. Lydia's better; I think she'll come around. The weather is clear, the sea is like a lake. Fray and Mark swung out from the mast on a line, diving. I came to realize again that I have surrendered my physical dominance. In other words, I don't compete there anymore.

August 31. Corfu's had a busy history for so quiet an island. It's been occupied in turn by Romans, Turks, Venetians, French, English, Germans, and finally Greeks. Our party is not quite so homogeneous as on the last voyage . . . the children are now more independent. The rest of us are older, more crotchety, and I'm subject to moods of bloody-mindedness. I ended the evening alone on the foredeck with a Scotch, looking into the dark water.

September 3, Levkás. The run down to Levkás was bright and brisk. The heart-lifting sight of three dolphins racing under our bow brought Lydia on deck for a bit, but it was a tough crossing for her. Loss of our generator means we must stay a day here. We put the women ashore to sleep in a hotel.

September 4. While the captain worked on the generator, the rest of us took the chance to visit the place where Actium was fought, two thousand years ago, and Mark Antony was destroyed. In the brush on the headlands over the bay, the ruins are still there. Cut in the broken marble stumps of the monument Octavius built to commemorate his victory, you can see the holes where the prows of Antony's galleys were set as trophies.

September 5. We eased south in quiet waters, stopping for lunch in a quiet bay. We passed Onassis's island where his huge yacht lies, still shiny, six months after his death. "I had rather be a slave under the sun than a king in this place," said the ghost of Achilles from Hades. We had an interesting time winching off a mischarted sandbar, using an apparently derelict tramp, which later sailed off, nearly running us down in the dark.

September 6, Ithaca. Under full sail, we ran before a freshening wind southwest to Ulysses's island. It's a high and rocky place, with a deep sheltered harbor . . . fit for a sailor. Tacking in, I had the helm for an hour while Jolly and my daughter sang songs for me, in sweet harmony.

September 10, Corfu/London. This was a very full day. We docked at Corfu, shopped for a gift for the captain, had a farewell lunch, then off to the airport whence we flew to London and checked into the Dorchester. Aside from the sense of crowded days and distance traveled, there was an inner distance covered, too. It's farther than you would imagine from the *Occitan,* anchored in a silent bay in Greece, to the wide beds and long tubs at the Dorchester. At this point, I welcome the latter.

September 11, London/Los Angeles. I put in a useful and pleasant couple of hours before leaving the Dorchester. The Arabs have bought it, but it's still the same hotel it was. The flight west to Los Angeles always seems long . . . as indeed the whole trip does, somehow. Still, I'm glad we went. It was often sad, but there were happy times, too. Almost all of it was happy for the kids . . . much of it for my girl.

September 21, San Diego. First day of shooting GRAY LADY DOWN. And away we go again. I had little to do, which was just as well, breaking in on a new film. The ship is most interesting: I had a full briefing on her, then I played my only scene with Stacy Keach. It was the tag of the picture, and a key scene, but it seemed to go all right. David Greene is a most meticulous director. Fine. I can use some of that. Willy Wyler was meticulous, too.

September 25, London. I wonder how many times I've climbed on the plane to London? For me, it's still the most attractive city on the star circuit. When I'm here, I often eat and drink too much, and exercise too little. I'm still invariably stirred just to be in this city.

September 30, Hamburg. Today tested my capacity to answer the same questions, yet make it all seem fresh and interested as well as interesting. It's the same problem as in a film or a performance each night on stage. You must focus your energy. A man's a fool to let himself be bored. (Do you decide you're bored when you may be only tired?) The last interview actually *was* interesting, with a man who knew film.

October 1, Frankfurt/Hanover. To bed somewhat late, but the day wasn't too hairy. We've gotten so much space that we canceled two interviews today. I did do one with an interesting hostile young journalist: an absolutely archetypical Baader-Meinhoff radical. It was fun to bait him a bit, but Marxists are not really good debaters.

*He challenged me for making a film glorifying a meaningless
battle in a war fought to exploit the workingman. "The battle of
Midway," I said, "was one of the crucial events of the twentieth
century." "I'm a Communist," he said. "I care nothing for the
survival of the imperialist countries." "If the United States had
lost Midway," I pointed out, "we would have been tied up in the
Pacific for ten years, and unable to play a part in the European
war. Britain could hardly have defeated Hitler alone. Where would
you be then?"*

October 4, Los Angeles. I enjoyed my birthday, even though I can't help
wincing when I count them. The day was full, with pleasant news
from Walter Mirisch that the Spanish MIDWAY grosses are still
enormous. I had some good tennis, a relaxed interview, and
champagne with my birthday cake. This hasn't been my worst year.

October 8, Philadelphia. Off again on another leg of the King of the Hill
circuit, which Lydia views with muted enthusiasm. I think it's
something I badly need. I recognize that sports can be (are?) a
middle-aged male yearning for youth; they are also an expression of
the competitive instinct that's part of an actor's equipment. However
that may be, we lost in Philadelphia.

October 13, Los Angeles. Walter Mirisch called; he's anxious to cast
Ronnie Cox as Samuelson. He was good in DELIVERANCE . . . and will
be in GRAY LADY DOWN, I think. I got an award tonight [from the
theater owners], largely for showing up . . . and for making fifty
films, which they claim have grossed a billion dollars. I'm not certain
this is true, but it's nice to hear, anyway.

October 15. I finished reading a submission from Warners: THE PACK. I
think not. It could work very well, but there's no part really. It's
about time I found a film that will offer me something besides
success, though I'm well aware that if you can't offer *them* success,
they won't offer you a film . . . *any* film. TWO-MINUTE WARNING
(another entry in my recent list of almost sure hits) played very well
for a houseful of friends. (If it won't work for your friends, you're in
trouble.) You can tell, though, by just counting the coughs and toilet
traffic. In this case, none of either. I still feel Larry Peerce did a
first-class job of getting some texture into the characters, when none
of us had more than ten minutes' screen time.

October 16. Tonight I saw a film I turned down a year ago, largely out of
laziness . . . THE OMEN. I had liked the script, and the part was
obviously right, but the exploitive potential of the film was off-putting,
and I disliked the idea of working alone through a European winter.
It was called THE ANTICHRIST then, and I first accepted it, then turned
it down. Greg Peck did it, and it's now the only film this year doing

better than MIDWAY. It's a better film, too. Greg is just right, at least as good as I would've been. On balance, I suppose I should have done it. On the other hand, it would be downright obscene to be in the two biggest hits of the year.

October 20. I like working for David Greene . . . he gives the actors a great deal, and I find myself stimulated by almost all the suggestions he makes. But he runs a rather loose ship. You find yourself hung always between these two extremes, it seems . . . whether to take the firm captain or the free-souled artist. Both are needed for a good film, and they seldom live in the same man. Of course, they are not mutually exclusive either. Look at Willy, Frank Schaffner, George Stevens. But it's rough to make it work in those terms.

October 28. We are shooting with some better success, since the crew is working faster, following the rocket Walter Mirisch shot off yesterday.

October 29. The day went very well . . . revealed to me more clearly than I have ever seen what one of my prime creative problems is: I become preoccupied with giving an *efficient* performance rather than a creative one. The pressures I feel (or the standards I set myself) to be a consummate professional make me focus on getting it right, which is not quite the same as getting it good. Greene, to his great credit, perceived this, actually reshot two important shots, putting in offstage actors I'd said I could dispense with, and much improved them.

November 10. Up until BEN-HUR, I had made almost all of my films at Paramount, so it was a very nostalgic experience going back today, where I've not been since WILL PENNY. We shot on the stage where de Mille wrecked the circus train in THE GREATEST SHOW ON EARTH, where Fray floated in the bulrushes in THE TEN COMMANDMENTS (and where I made bricks for the pharaoh, entered his palace in triumph, and was led out in chains). It's also the stage where I stood over the writhing orgiasts in the Golden Calf sequence, where a weary extra girl said one day to the first assistant director, "Tell me, Eddie, who do you have to fuck to get off this picture?"

November 11. I write this in the morning, standing by at home while they wrestle with the front of the projection setup over at Paramount. We got one shot yesterday . . . demonstrating what seems to me to be a monumental incompetence in the process work. An old Paramount crewman came up to me while we were waiting and said cheerily, "Just like the old times with de Mille, eh, Chuck?" "No, sir," I gritted. "de Mille would've had five guys' heads on stakes by now." He would've too. Aside from my neurosis about sloppy work, the fact is that this slop has added some thirty thousand dollars to the negative cost. Multiply the negative by three, add overhead, and distribution cost, and you have the money I'm expected to earn back. If the film fails, it's my failure, not some sloppy crewman who can't do his job right.

November 12. A slightly more efficient production would've gotten me out earlier today, I guess, but I'm supposed to serve the film, not vice versa. (Nevertheless, to paraphrase Galileo, it *should move!*) It moves very slowly indeed at this point. The rear projection stuff is better than the front projection we had planned, but we're still going like glue. I lose my momentum in a situation like this; the creative fervor has no chance to build. You need this. Lew Wasserman has bought the outstanding seats for Sunday's Ram's game, thus forcing it on TV locally. In gratitude, the team owner is arranging for me to do a TV interview on TWO-MINUTE WARNING at half time. Lew is no fool, as I've observed before now.

November 15. Somewhat to my surprise, the initial word on TWO-MINUTE WARNING is not impressive. I've been spoiled, I guess . . . of my last twelve pictures, all but three have been hits (and none of the failing three had a full release). That's an unusual record, but I've come to expect it. Not with this one, I guess.

December 1. I didn't know Roz Russell very well, but I went to her funeral. The church was jammed: a full high Catholic mass. It was a very long service, but she deserved to have her passing marked.

December 6. My interview with the accountants reveals that I seem to have managed to make a fortune acting for pay. I can't resist recording the boast here, but I also feel apologetic. Why? Is it unfair to make that much? I don't think I believe that. It's appropriate on the same day to discuss, however fruitlessly, the possible reasons for the failure of TWO-MINUTE WARNING. Sid Sheinberg had no answers, but he agreed that all at Universal had expected another huge hit. I think the answer lies somewhere in the fact that I had no meaningful part, and no sympathy was created, indeed, for any of the characters. Also, an R rating is not a plus.

December 10. My working routine for Tyrone is beginning to bear fruit, I think. I've found, in fact, that almost *any* routine will be productive if only it firmly establishes some kind of regular working discipline. *Work* on whatever it is, that's the main thing. If you work, you'll get better. I chewed over possibilities for next season at the Ahmanson . . . a lot of likely bets. We may get Jack Lemmon to do COUNTRY GIRL, for one.

December 15. This preholiday week is kind of slack. I did a little gift buying, though Lydia really has all that in hand. I talked to Bob

Easton about drilling me on some voice work, getting it in shape for the play. I've been neglecting this kind of training when I do a play, and that's stupid.

December 17. A fairly full day, arranged to point my energy to take the crucial work on that horrendous role that looms ahead of me in '77. Dick Shepherd, who's now head of production at MGM, called and asked me to read, unofficially, a project he wants me for, but can't submit yet. This is always tricky. It's hard to turn down a request like that from anyone you know at all, yet it runs directly against the grain of Citron's whole position: If they want me to read a script, they have to make a firm offer. Of course I said I'd read it.

December 18. I read the MGM script, which is a variation on ONE FLEW OVER THE CUCKOO'S NEST (and a lot of other similar pieces, for that matter). It works well enough and it's a fashionable kind of counterculture piece, to examine an element of society and say, "The world's an asylum, but the inmates are sane, the keepers are mad." In this case, the asylum is the U.S. Army. In this time in the twentieth century, given the realities of the world, I don't care to make that point. I don't believe it, and besides, the part's not that good.

December 22. Up betimes, as Pepys was wont to say, and off to the hills after quail and a bit of the kind of camaraderie you can have with a son different from that you find on the tennis court. We put up a covey toward the end of the morning, but put down no birds.

December 24. With Carol away on vacation, I got up a part-time secretary to help me shovel out here. I have to thin down this mountain of paper before I take off on the European promotion tour for MIDWAY. I didn't really feel like working on Christmas Eve, but I did my chores on LONG DAY'S JOURNEY with Bob Easton, too, trying to get Tyrone's accent right. The tree got in from Michigan just in time for our decorating party tonight. With our friends, we got it up, tall and thick as the dark, deep woods of my boyhood. This party is our own tradition, and I love it. This year, Lydia was migrained and couldn't take part.

December 26 (Sunday). There is a tacit ban on Christmas tennis (as Martin said, "Only us Jews played yesterday"), but we got in some practice for our next King of the Hill match today. I like the day after Christmas, really. The frantic pace and hubbub of the holiday can spoil it. At sunset, I sat alone by our huge, blue spruce, its lights reflecting in the darkening pool outside, thinking of the man-killing part that waits for me next year, and the trip to England I have to take next week, and my sweet, sad girl I have to leave behind.

The end of 1976 seemed a good place to stop, though I still continue this random record of my mountebank life. I did the tour for MIDWAY, which repeated in the rest of the world its enormous success in this country. I did, but did not conquer LONG DAY'S JOURNEY INTO NIGHT. (I'll do it better next time, but we broke a house record at the Ahmanson.) Martin and I even won the King of the Hill tournament, six months later, though my forehand volley remains suspect to this day. But the best of all is that, miraculously, Lydia has had no migraines now for more than a year. Her photographic career is burgeoning with jobs and exhibitions; she is again the girl she always was, beneath the pain. We have, all of us, life to live and work to do. I'm a lucky man.

Coldwater Canyon, March 1, 1978